The Postal Service Guide to U.S. Stamps

UPDATED STAMP VALUES
33RD EDITION

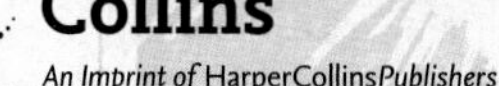

The U.S. Postal Service thanks DC Comics for its generous contributions to the design theme of *The Postal Service Guide to U.S. Stamps*.

HarperCollins books may be purchased for educational, business, or sales promotional use. For information please write: Special Markets Department, HarperCollins Publishers Inc., 10 East 53rd Street, New York, NY 10022.

Printed in the United States of America.

Library of Congress Cataloging-in-Publication Data has been applied for.

ISBN-10: 0-06-114551-3
ISBN-13: 978-0-06-114551-3

06 07 08 09 10 ❖/QWT 10 9 8 7 6 5 4 3 2 1

Table of Contents

2006 Discovering America

NEW 2006 U.S. POSTAGE STAMPS AND POSTAL STATIONERY

Each year the U.S. Postal Service commemorates a broad range of subjects and people in its stamp program. From movie screens to the open road and everywhere in between, our colorful, far-flung country has been miraculously shrunk to the size of a breathtaking array of postage stamps.

This year is no different, and indeed its theme, Discovering America, calls attention to the variety of subjects found on the 2006 stamps. Here is a preview of these exciting new issues with more information found on page 9 and also stories about each stamp throughout the book.

Love: True Blue

Lady Liberty and U.S. Flag

Pikes Peak Stamped Card

Benjamin Franklin Stamped Envelope

Favorite Children's Book Animals

2006 Olympic Winter Games

Black Heritage: Hattie McDaniel

Yosemite National Park, California

Bryce Canyon, Utah

Great Smoky Mountains, North Carolina/Tennessee

Our Wedding 63¢

Our Wedding 39¢

Distinguished Americans: Dr. Jonas Salk

Distinguished Americans: Dr. Albert Sabin

Common Buckeye

X-Planes: $4.05 Priority Mail

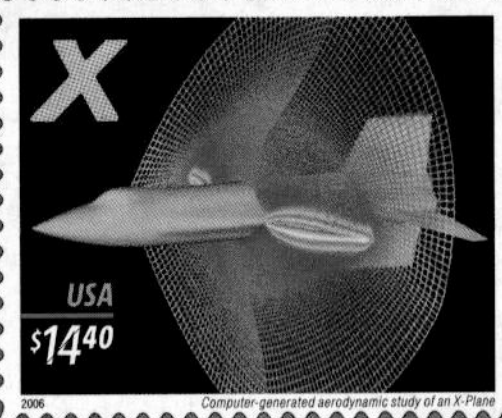

X-Planes: $14.40 Express Mail

Benjamin Fr

Sugar Ray Robinson

Crops of the Americas

The Art of Disney: Romance

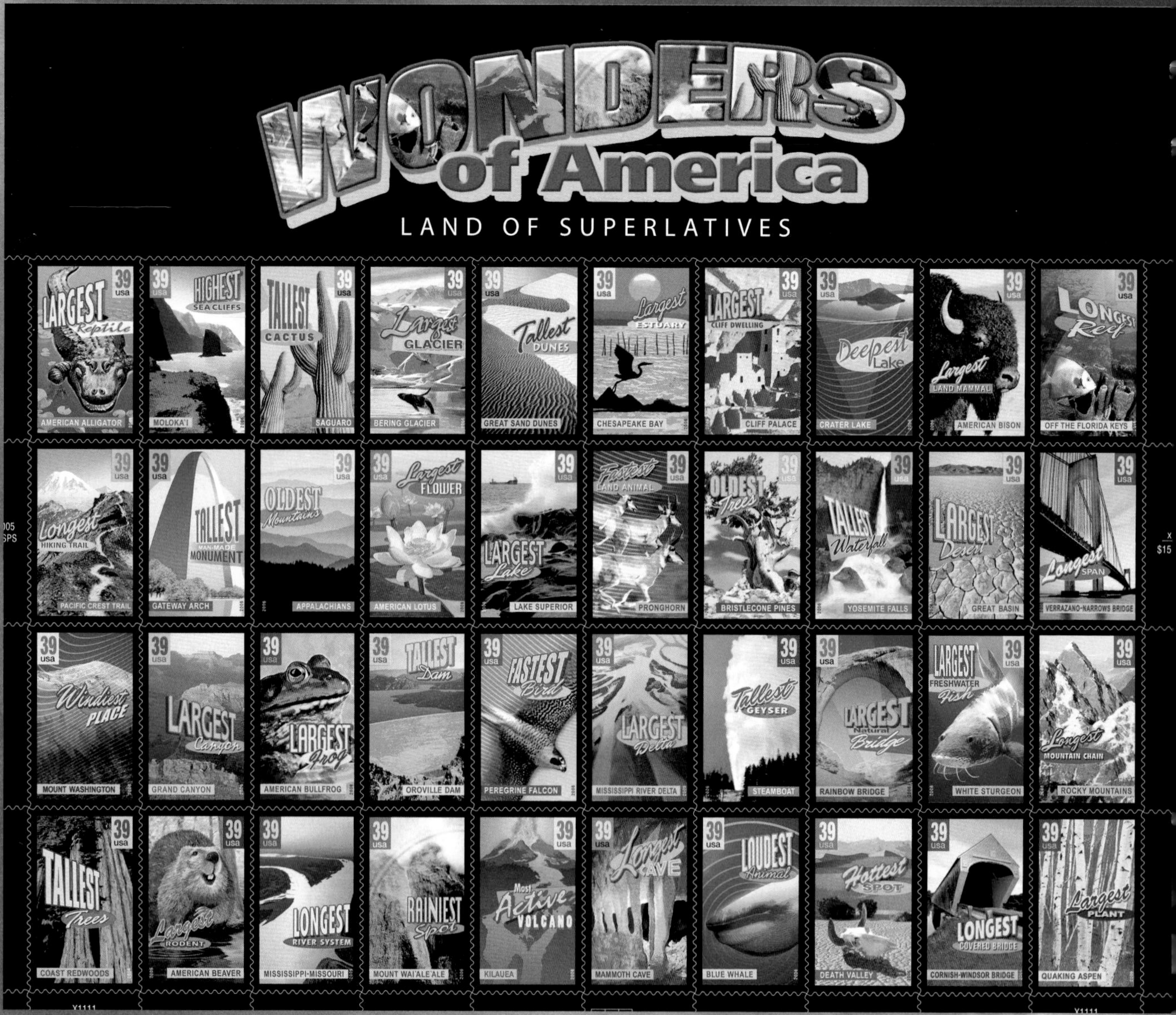

Wonders of America: Land of Superlatives

Literary Arts:
Katherine Anne Porter

AMBER Alert

The 1606 voyage of Samuel de Champlain

Le voyage de 1606 de Samuel de Champlain

A skilled cartographer, Samuel de Champlain played a key role in French exploration of North America. In 1606, he served with a coastal expedition that began in what is now Nova Scotia and sailed as far south as modern-day Massachusetts.

Habile cartographe, Samuel de Champlain a joué un rôle clé dans l'exploration de l'Amérique du Nord au nom de la France. En 1606, il a participé à une expédition côtière, prenant la mer dans la région qu'on appelle aujourd'hui la Nouvelle-Écosse et naviguant loin au sud, jusque dans l'actuel Massachusetts.

The 1606 Voyage of Samuel de Champlain

Washington 2006 World Philatelic Exhibition

Distinguished American Diplomats

Legends of Hollywood: Judy Garland

DC Comics Super Heroes

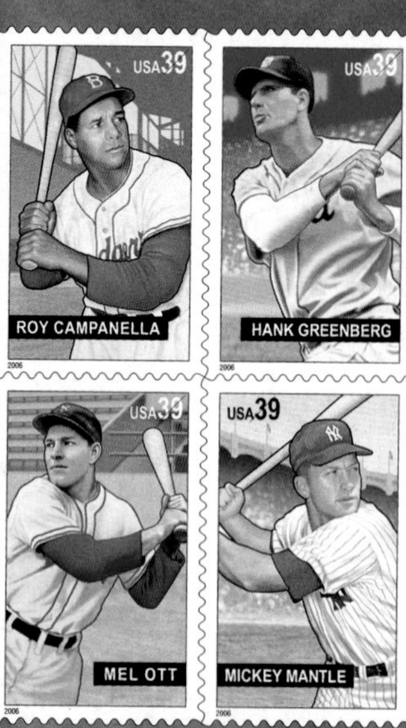

Baseball Sluggers

American Motorcycles

Christmas: Chacón *Madonna and Child with Bird*

Holiday Snowflakes

American Treasures: Quilts of Gee's Bend

Nature of America: Southern Florida Wetland

2006 *Stamp Issue Dates & Locations*

To learn more about these exciting new stamps, turn to the page listed under each title for details.

Love: True Blue
January 3, 2006
Washington, DC
See page 165.

Lady Liberty and U.S. Flag
January 9, 2006
Washington, DC
See page 181.

Pikes Peak Stamped Card
January 9, 2006
Washington, DC
See page 137.

Benjamin Franklin Stamped Envelope
January 9, 2006
Washington, DC
See page 209.

Favorite Children's Book Animals
January 10, 2006
Findlay, OH and
London, England
See page 242.

2006 Olympic Winter Games
January 11, 2006
Colorado Springs, CO
See page 241.

Black Heritage: Hattie McDaniel
January 25, 2006
Beverly Hills, CA
See page 161.

Yosemite National Park, California
February 24, 2006
St. Louis, MO
See page 258.

Bryce Canyon, Utah
February 24, 2006
St. Louis, MO
See page 177.

Great Smoky Mountains, North Carolina/Tennessee
February 24, 2006
St. Louis, MO
See page 61.

Our Wedding
March 1, 2006
New York, NY
See page 190.

Distinguished Americans: Dr. Jonas Salk
March 8, 2006
Washington, DC
See page 77.

Distinguished Americans: Dr. Albert Sabin
March 8, 2006
Washington, DC
See page 141.

Common Buckeye
March 8, 2006
Washington, DC
See page 154.

Crops of the Americas
March 16, 2006
New York, NY
See page 142.

X-Planes: Priority Mail & Express Mail
March 17, 2006
New York, NY
See page 57.

Sugar Ray Robinson
April 7, 2006
New York, NY
See page 245.

Benjamin Franklin
April 7, 2006
Philadelphia, PA
See page 114.

The Art of Disney: Romance
April 21, 2006
Lake Buena Vista, FL
See page 266.

Literary Arts: Katherine Anne Porter
May 15, 2006
Kyle, TX
See page 117.

AMBER Alert
May 25, 2006
Washington, DC and
Arlington, TX
See page 213.

Wonders of America: Land of Superlatives
May 27, 2006
Washington, DC
See page 246.

The 1606 Voyage of Samuel de Champlain
May 28, 2006
Washington, DC and
Ticonderoga, NY
See page 238.

Washington 2006 World Philatelic Exhibition
May 29, 2006
Washington, DC
See page 189.

Distinguished American Diplomats
May 30, 2006
Washington, DC
See page 210.

Legends of Hollywood: Judy Garland
June 10, 2006
New York, NY
See page 121.

DC Comics Super Heroes
July 20, 2006
San Diego, CA
See page 198.

Baseball Sluggers
July 15, 2006
Bronx, NY
See page 58.

American Motorcycles
August 7, 2006
Sturgis, SD
See page 157.

American Treasures: Quilts of Gee's Bend
August 24, 2006
Rosemont, IL
See page 186.

Nature of America: Southern Florida Wetland
October 4, 2006
Naples, FL
See page 94.

Holiday Celebrations: Holiday Snowflakes
October 5, 2006
New York, NY
See page 169.

Holiday Celebrations: Christmas: Chacón *Madonna and Child with Bird*
October 6, 2006
Denver, CO
See page 122.

Explanation of Catalog Prices

The United States Postal Service sells only the commemoratives and special issues released during the past few years. Current postal stationery and regular issues remain on sale for longer periods of time. Prices in this book are called "catalog prices" by stamp collectors. Collectors use catalog prices as guidelines when buying or trading stamps. ***It is important to remember the prices are simply guidelines to the stamp values. Stamp condition is very important in determining the actual value of a stamp.***

Prices are Estimated

Listed prices are estimates of how much you can expect to pay for a stamp from a dealer. ***A 20-cent minimum valuation has been established that represents a fair-market price to have a dealer locate and provide a single stamp to a customer. Dealers may charge less per stamp to provide a group of such stamps, and may charge less for such a single stamp. Similarly, a $1.00 minimum has been established for First Day Covers (FDCs).*** If you sell a stamp to a dealer, he or she may offer you much less than the catalog price. Dealers pay based on their interest in owning a particular stamp. If they already have a full supply, they may only buy additional stamps at a low price.

Condition Affects Value

The catalog prices are given for unused (mint) stamps and used (canceled) stamps that have been hinged and are in "very fine" condition. Stamps in "superb" condition that have never been hinged may cost more than the listed price. Stamps in less than "fine" condition may cost less.

The prices for used stamps are based on a light cancellation; a heavy cancellation lessens a stamp's value. Canceled stamps may be worth more than uncanceled stamps. This happens if the cancellation is of a special type or for a significant date. Therefore, it is important to study an envelope before removing a stamp and discarding its "cover."

Understanding the Listings

- Prices in ***regular type*** for single unused and used stamps are taken from the *Scott 2006 Specialized Catalogue of U.S. Stamps & Covers,* whose editors have based these prices on ***actual retail values*** as they found them in the marketplace. The Scott numbering system for stamps is used in this book. Prices quoted for unused and used stamps are for "very fine" condition, except where "very fine" is not available.

- Stamp values in ***italic*** type generally refer to items difficult to value accurately.

- A dash (—) in a value column means the item is known to exist but information is insufficient for establishing a value.

- The stamp listings contain a number of additions designated "*a*," "*b*," "*c*," etc. These represent recognized variations of stamps as well as errors. These listings are as complete as space permits.

Occasionally, a new stamp or major variation may be inserted by the catalog editors into a series or sequence where it was not originally anticipated. These additions are identified by capital letters "*A*," "*B*" and so forth. For example, a new stamp which logically belonged between 1044 and 1045 is designated 1044A, even though it is entirely different from 1044. The insertion was preferable to a complete renumbering of the series.

- Prices for Plate Blocks, First Day Covers, American Commemorative Panels and Souvenir Pages are taken from the *Scott 2006 Specialized Catalogue of U.S. Stamps & Covers.*

Sample Listing

Issue	Date	Un	U	PB/LP/PNC	#	FDC	Q(M)
3069 32¢ Georgia O'Keefe	05/23/96	.85	.20	5.00	(4)	1.25	156

Scott Catalog Number (bold type indicates stamp is pictured)

Denomination

Description

Date of Issue

Unused Catalog Price

Used Catalog Price

Plate Block Price, Line Pair Price or **Plate Number Coil Price**

Number of stamps in Plate Block, Line Pair or Plate Number Coil

First Day Cover Price

Quantity Issued in **Millions** (where known)

3069

Sample Variation Listing

Issue		Date	Un	U	PB/LP/PNC	#	FDC	Q(M)
2281	25¢ Honeybee	09/02/88	.45	.20	3.75	(3)	1.25	
a	Imperf. pair		50.00					
b	Black omitted		*60.00*	—				
d	Pair, imperf. between		*750.00*					

2281

Stamp collecting can be a lifetime hobby. It's fun and educational for all ages and it's easy to start without a big investment.

The study of stamps and postal materials is called *philately* and collectors are sometimes called *philatelists*.

How do I start collecting stamps? You can start by saving stamps from letters, packages, and postcards. Many beginning collectors choose a favorite subject like art, history, sports, transportation, or animals as the theme of their collection. You can have a great time on a limited budget with just a few inexpensive accessories such as an album and stamp hinges.

What kinds of stamps are there? There are many types of stamps—for example, commemorative, definitive, and special—and formats such as sheets, booklets, or coils. Stamps may be conventional adhesive ("lick-and-stick") or self-adhesive ("no-lick, peel-and-stick"). *Definitive stamps* are the most common. Generally less than an inch square, they are printed in large quantities, and often more than once. *Commemorative stamps,* larger and more colorful than definitives, are printed in smaller quantities and typically only once. They honor people, events, or subjects of importance to American life and culture. *Special stamps*—Christmas and Love, Holiday Celebration, international rate, Priority Mail, and Express Mail—usually are on sale for a limited time.

How do I remove stamps from an envelope? *Soaking* is the best way to remove stamps from envelopes. Tear the envelope around the stamp, leaving a small margin. With the stamp facing down, place into a pan of warm, not hot, water. After a few minutes (self-adhesive gum may take longer), the stamp should sink to the bottom. When all adhesive is dislodged, remove the stamp preferably using stamp tongs. Place the stamp between two paper towels and put a heavy object, such as a book, on top to keep the stamp from curling as it dries. Leave overnight.

How can I store my stamps? The best way to store stamps is in a *stamp album* or on loose-leaf paper in a binder. Affix your stamps by using *stamp hinges,* glassine strips with gum on one side, or *stamp mounts,* clear plastic sleeves that offer better protection for unused stamps.

Is there anything else I need? Collectors use a variety of other materials and accessories. Transparent *glassine envelopes* protect stamps from grease and air. A *stamp catalog* is a reference book (like this one) with illustrations and stamp values. A *magnifying glass* is useful when examining stamps; *tongs* are used to pick up and move stamps. A *perforation gauge* measures perforations along the edges of stamps. *Watermark fluid* will enhance a watermark, a design or pattern that is pressed into some stamp paper during manufacturing.

How can I tell what a stamp is worth? When figuring the value of a stamp, ask yourself two questions: "How rare is it?" and "What condition is it in?" Stamp catalog prices will give you an idea of the stamp's rarity. However, the stamp may sell at more or less than the catalog price, depending on its condition. Stamp dealers categorize stamps according to their condition. A stamp in *mint condition* is the same as when purchased from the Post Office. Hinge marks on mint stamps can reduce value, which is why stamp mounts are recommended for mint stamps.

How should I judge the condition of a stamp? To evaluate the condition of a stamp, first look at the front. Are the colors bright or faded? Is the stamp clean, dirty, or stained? Is it torn or creased? Torn stamps are not considered "collectible," but they can be used as space fillers until you get better ones. Are the perforations intact? Has the stamp been canceled? A stamp with a light cancellation is in better condition than one with heavy marks across it. Is the stamp design centered, crooked, or off to one side? Centering can range from "superb" (perfectly centered on the stamp) to "good" (the design on at least one side is marred somewhat by the perfs). Anything less would be graded "fair" or "poor" and, like torn copies, should be saved only as space fillers. Centering varies widely on older stamps. An examination of the back of the stamp will reveal whether it has been carelessly treated and thus is less valuable.

The values listed in this book are for used and unused stamps in "very fine" condition.

What other stamp materials can I collect? Many philatelists collect postal stationery—products with a printed or embossed stamp design—such as *Stamped Envelopes*, *Stamped Cards* (or postal cards), and *Aerogrammes.* Other philatelic collectibles include: *Plate numbers* (including *plate blocks*) appear on or adjacent to stamps. Found most often on sheet stamps, plate blocks are the stamps—usually a group of 4—that have the printing plate numbers in the adjoining selvage, or margin. *Booklet panes* are panes of stamps affixed in, or as part of, a thin folder to form a booklet. Collectors of booklet panes usually save the entire pane or booklet. *Marginal blocks* (including *copyright blocks)* feature marginal inscriptions other than plate numbers. The most common is the copyright block, which features the copyright symbol ©, copyright date, and U.S. Postal Service. All U.S. stamp designs since 1978 are copyrighted. *First Day Covers* (FDCs) are envelopes bearing new stamps postmarked on the first day of sale. For each new issuance, the U.S. Postal Service generally selects one location, usually related to the stamp subject, as the place for the first day dedication ceremony and the first day postmark. *First Day Ceremony Programs* are given to those who attend first day ceremonies. They contain a list of participants, information on the stamp subject, and the actual stamp attached and postmarked.

Are there any stamp groups I can join? Stamp clubs are a great source for new stamps and stamp collecting advice. Ask your local postmaster or librarian about stamp clubs in your area and contact information including Internet sites.

Superb

Very Fine

Fine

Good

Light Cancel–Very Fine

Medium Cancel–Fine

Heavy Cancel

1847-1875

1

2

3

4

5

11

12

14

17

30

37

38

39

40

62B

Postmasters' Provisionals

1845-1847

9X1

	Issue	Date	Un	U
	Imperf., Typeset			
1X1	5¢ black, *buff,* type I	1846		—
1X2	5¢ black, *blue,* type I	1846		—
2XU1	5¢ carmine red, *white*	1846		*225,000.00*
	Engraved, Imperf.			
3X1	5¢ black	1845		*5,500.00*
3X2	10¢ black, on cover	1845		*50,000.00*
3X3	5¢ black, *bluish*	1845	*65,000.00*	*5,500.00*
3X4	10¢ black, *bluish*	1845		*60,000.00*
	Various Papers, Handstamped			
3XU1	5¢ blue	1845		*6,500.00*
3XU2	5¢ red	1845		*9,000.00*
3XU3	10¢ blue	1845		*16,000.00*
3XU4	10¢ blue	1845		*19,000.00*
	Imperf., Typeset			
4X1	5¢ dull blue, *yellowish,* on cover	1846(?)		*225,000.00*
	Imperf., Thick Soft Wove Paper, Color Coming Through			
5X1	5¢ black, *buff*	1846		*10,000.00*
	Imperf., Handstamped			
6X1	5¢ red, *buff,* on cover	1846		*225,000.00*

	Issue	Date	Un	U
	Imperf.			
7X1	5¢ black, *bluish*	1846	*130,000.00*	*20,000.00*
8XU1	5¢ red (Bl or M)	1845		*80,000.00*
8XU2	5¢ red, *light bluish* (Bk)	1845		*110,000.00*
8XU3	5¢ dull blue, *buff* (Bl)	1845		*110,000.00*
8XU4	5¢ dull blue, (Bl)	1845		*110,000.00*
	Engraved, Imperf., Bluish Wove Paper			
9X1	5¢ black	1846	1,400.00	525.00
9X2	5¢ black	1847	*6,500.00*	3,500.00
	Engraved, Imperf., Gray Wove Paper			
9X3	5¢ black	1847	5,250.00	2,100.00
	Engraved, Imperf., Yellowish White Paper			
10X1	5¢ gray black	1846	350.00	*1,750.00*
10X2	10¢ gray black	1846	1,100.00	*15,000.00*
	Imperf., Wove Paper Colored Through			
11X1	5¢ black, *greenish*	1845-46	*10,000.00*	*6,000.00*
11X2	10¢ black, *greenish*	1845-46	*10,000.00*	*6,000.00*
11X3	20¢ black, *greenish*	1845-46		*85,000.00*
11X4	5¢ black, *gray lilac*	1846	—	*25,000.00*
11X5	10¢ black, *gray lilac*	1846	*10,000.00*	*5,500.00*
11X6	20¢ black, *gray lilac*	1846	*82,500.00*	*25,000.00*
	Pelure Paper			
11X7	5¢ black, *bluish*	1846	—	*7,500.00*
11X8	10¢ black, *bluish*	1846		*7,500.00*

Issues of 1847-1875		Un	U
	Thin, Bluish Wove Paper, Imperf., Unwmkd.		
1	5¢ Benjamin Franklin	6,500.00	550.00
a	5¢ dark brown	7,750.00	625.00
b	5¢ orange brown	8,250.00	850.00
c	5¢ red orange	*17,500.00*	*5,500.00*
	Pen cancel		275.00
	Double transfer of top and bottom frame lines		700.00
	Double transfer of top, bottom and left frame lines and numerals		3,250.00
2	10¢ George Washington	*30,000.00*	1,350.00
	Pen cancel		750.00
	Vertical line through second "F" of "OFFICE"	—	1,900.00
	With "stick pin" in tie, or with "harelip"	—	1,900.00
	Double transfer in lower right "X," or of left and bottom frame lines	—	2,000.00
	Double transfer in "POST OFFICE"	—	2,750.00
	Issues of 1875, Reproductions of 1 and 2, Bluish Paper, Without Gum		
3	5¢ red brown Franklin	750.00	
4	10¢ black Washington	925.00	

5¢. On the originals, the left side of the white shirt frill touches the oval on a level with the top of the "F" of "Five." On the reproductions, it touches the oval about on a level with the top of the figure "5."

10¢. On the originals, line of coat points to "T" of TEN and right line of coat points between "T" and "S" of CENTS.

On the reproductions left, line of coat points to right tip of "X" and right line of coat points to center of "S" of CENTS.

On the reproductions, the eyes have a sleepy look, the line of the mouth is straighter, and in the curl of hair near the left cheek is a strong black dot, while the originals have only a faint one.

	Issues of 1851-1852, Imperf.		
5	1¢ Franklin, type I	*225,000.00*	*55,000.00*
5A	1¢ blue, type Ib	*17,500.00*	*7,500.00*
	#6-9: Franklin (5), *1851*		
6	1¢ blue, type Ia	*40,000.00*	*12,000.00*
7	1¢ blue, type II	1,200.00	160.00
	Cracked plate	1,450.00	375.00
8	1¢ blue, type III	*16,000.00*	3,250.00
8A	1¢ blue, type IIIa	4,750.00	1,050.00
9	1¢ blue, type IV, *1852*	850.00	130.00
	Triple transfer, one inverted	1,000.00	180.00

Issues of 1851-1861		Un	U
	#10-11, 25-26a all had plates on which at least four outer frame lines (and usually much more) were recut, adding to their value.		
10	3¢ orange brown Washington, type I (11)	3,500.00	130.00
	Copper brown	4,000.00	400.00
	On part-India paper	—	*1,100.00*
11	3¢ deep claret	375.00	21.00
	Double transfer, "GENTS" for "CENTS"	440.00	52.50
12	5¢ Jefferson, type I	*20,000.00*	900.00
13	10¢ green Washington, type I (14)	*18,000.00*	900.00
14	10¢ green, type II	5,500.00	200.00
15	10¢ green, type III	5,000.00	200.00
16	10¢ green, type IV (14)	*35,000.00*	1,600.00
17	12¢ black	5,500.00	325.00
	Issues of 1857-1861, Perf. 15.5		
	(Issued in 1857 except #18, 27, 28A, 29, 30, 30A, 35, 36b, 37, 38, 39)		
	#18-24: Franklin (5)		
18	1¢ blue, type I	2,250.00	650.00
19	1¢ blue, type Ia	*35,000.00*	*9,000.00*
20	1¢ blue, type II	1,250.00	275.00
21	1¢ blue, type III	*16,500.00*	2,750.00
22	1¢ blue, type IIIa	2,500.00	550.00
23	1¢ blue, type IV	9,000.00	800.00
24	1¢ blue, type V	180.00	45.00
	"Curl" on shoulder	240.00	72.50
	"Earring" below ear	600.00	100.00
	Long double "curl" in hair	300.00	85.00
b	Laid paper		*1,750.00*
	#25-26a: Washington (11)		
25	3¢ rose, type I	3,000.00	125.00
	Major cracked plate	*4,500.00*	600.00
26	3¢ dull red, type II	75.00	8.00
	Brownish carmine	150.00	19.00
	Claret	170.00	25.00
	Left or right frame line double	110.00	19.00
	Cracked plate	*750.00*	*250.00*
26a	3¢ dull red, type IIa	300.00	75.00
	Double transfer	400.00	150.00
	Left frame line double	—	170.00
	Perf. 15.5		
	#27-29: Jefferson (12)		
27	5¢ brick red, type I	*30,000.00*	1,700.00
28	5¢ red brown, type I	6,250.00	1,150.00
b	Bright red brown	6,750.00	1,300.00
28A	5¢ Indian red, type I	*75,000.00*	3,500.00
29	5¢ brown, type I	3,000.00	425.00
	Defective transfer	—	—
30	5¢ orange brown, type II	1,250.00	1,300.00
30A	5¢ brown, type II (30)	2,250.00	325.00
b	Printed on both sides		*40,000.00*
	#31-35: Washington (15)		
31	10¢ green, type I	*20,000.00*	1,200.00

Issues of 1857-1875		Un	U
	Perf. 15.5		
32	10¢ green, type II	6,000.00	300.00
33	10¢ green, type III	6,000.00	300.00
	"Curl" on forehead or in left "X"		375.00
34	10¢ green, type IV	*37,500.00*	2,250.00
35	10¢ green, type V	275.00	65.00
	Small "curl" on forehead	325.00	77.50
	"Curl" in "e" or "t" of "Cents"	350.00	90.00
	Plate I Outer frame lines complete		
36	12¢ blk. Washington (17), plate I	1,500.00	350.00
	Triple transfer	1,800.00	—
36b	12¢ black, plate III	800.00	225.00
	Vertical line through rosette	975.00	300.00
37	24¢ gray lilac	1,700.00	400.00
a	24¢ gray	1,700.00	400.00
38	30¢ orange Franklin	2,250.00	500.00
	Recut at bottom	2,700.00	625.00
39	90¢ blue Washington	3,500.00	*8,000.00*
	Double transfer at top or bottom	3,750.00	—
	Pen cancel		2,750.00
	Note: Beware of forged cancellations of #39. Genuine cancellations are rare		
	Issues of 1875, Government Reprints, White Paper Without Gum, Perf. 12		
40	1¢ bright blue Franklin (5)	*625.00*	
41	3¢ scarlet Wash. (11)	*3,250.00*	
42	5¢ orange brown Jefferson (30)	*1,400.00*	
43	10¢ blue green Washington (14)	*3,000.00*	—
44	12¢ greenish black Washington (17)	*3,250.00*	
45	24¢ blackish violet Washington (37)	*3,250.00*	
46	30¢ yellow orange Franklin (38)	*3,250.00*	
47	90¢ deep blue Washington (39)	*4,500.00*	
48-54	Not assigned		
	Issue of 1861, Thin, Perf. 12 Semi-Transparent Paper		
	#55-62 are no longer considered postage stamps. Many experts consider them to be essays and/or trial color proofs.		
62B	10¢ dark green Washington (58)	*7,500.00*	1,300.00

Details

5

Bust of Benjamin Franklin.

Detail of **#5a** Type Ib

Lower scrollwork is incomplete, the little balls are not so clear.

Detail of **#5, 18, 40** Type I

Has curved, unbroken lines outside labels. Scrollwork is substantially complete at top, forms little balls at bottom.

Detail of **#6, 19** Type Ia

Same as Type I at bottom but top ornaments and outer line partly cut away. Lower scrollwork is complete.

Detail of **#5a** Type Ib

Lower scrollwork is incomplete, the little balls are not so clear.

Detail of **#7, 20** Type II

Lower scrollwork incomplete (lacks little balls and lower plume ornaments). Side ornaments are complete.

Detail of **#8, 21** Type III

Outer lines broken in the middle. Side ornaments are substantially complete.

Detail of **#8A, 22** Type IIIa

Outer lines broken top or bottom but not both.

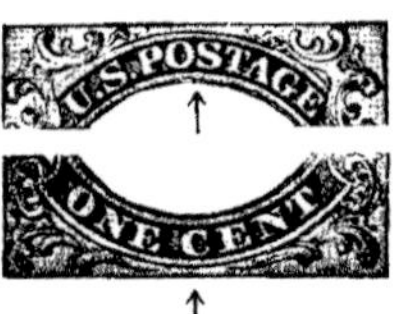

Detail of **#9, 23** Type IV

Similar to Type II, but outer lines recut top, bottom or both.

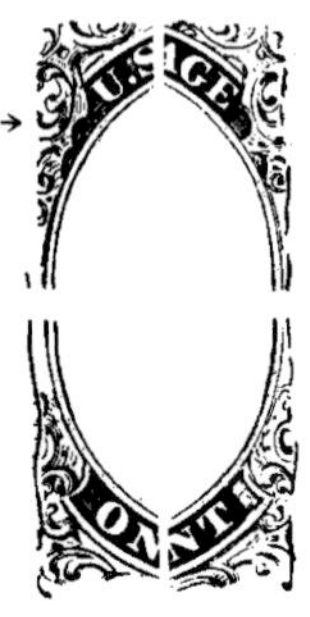

Detail of **#24** Type V

Similar to Type III of 1851-1857 but with side ornaments partly cut away.

3¢ Washington Types I-IIa, Series 1851-1857, 1857-1861, 1875

10
Bust of George Washington

Detail of **#10, 11, 25, 41**
Type I

There is an outer frame line at top and bottom.

Detail of **#26**
Type II

The outer frame line has been removed at top and bottom. The side frame lines were recut so as to be continuous from the top to the bottom of the plate.

Detail of **#26a**
Type IIa

The side frame lines extended only to the bottom of the stamp design.

5¢ Jefferson Types I-II, Series 1851-1857, 1857-1861

12
Portrait of Thomas Jefferson

Detail of **#12, 27-29**
Type I

There are projections on all four sides.

Detail of **#30-30a**
Type II

The projections at top and bottom are partly cut away.

10¢ Washington Types I-IV, Series 1851-1857, 1857-1861, 1875

15
Portrait of George Washington

Detail of **#13, 31, 43**
Type I

The "shells" at the lower corners are practically complete. The outer line below the label is very nearly complete. The outer lines are broken above the middle of the top label and the "X" in each upper corner.

Detail of **#14, 32**
Type II

The design is complete at the top. The outer line at the bottom is broken in the middle. The shells are partly cut away.

Detail of **#15, 33**
Type III

The outer lines are broken above the top label and the "X" numerals. The outer line at the bottom and the shells are partly cut away, as in Type II.

Detail of **#16, 34**
Type IV

The outer lines have been recut at top or bottom or both. Types I, II, III and IV have complete ornaments at the sides of the stamps and three pearls at each outer edge of the bottom panel.

Detail of **#35**
Type V
(Two typical examples.)

Ornaments slightly cut away. Outer lines complete at top except over right "X." Outer lines complete at bottom and shells nearly so.

	Issues of 1861-1863	Un	U
	Perf. 12		
63	1¢ blue Franklin	350.00	40.00
	Double transfer	—	52.50
	Dot in "U"	375.00	45.00
a	1¢ ultramarine	*2,200.00*	*600.00*
b	1¢ dark blue	750.00	150.00
c	Laid paper	—	*4,000*
d	Vert. pair, imperf. horizontally		—
e	Printed on both sides	—	*4,000.00*
64	3¢ pink Washington	*9,500.00*	850.00
a	3¢ pigeon blood pink	*20,000.00*	*3,750.00*
b	3¢ rose pink	600.00	150.00
65	3¢ rose Washington	150.00	3.00
	Cracked plate	—	—
	Double transfer	175.00	6.00
b	Laid paper	—	500.00
d	Vertical pair, imperf. horizontally	*6,000.00*	*750.00*
e	Printed on both sides	*22,500.00*	*5,000.00*
f	Double impression		*7,500.00*
66	3¢ lake Washington is considered a Trial Color Proof		*2,000.00*
67	5¢ buff Jefferson	*21,000.00*	950.00
68	10¢ yellow green Washington	1,100.00	55.00
	Deep yellow green on thin paper	1,250.00	65.00
	Double transfer	1,200.00	60.00
a	10¢ dark green	1,200.00	65.00
b	Vert. pair, imperf. horizontally		*3,500.00*
69	12¢ blk. Washington	2,000.00	110.00
	Intense black	2,100.00	125.00
	Double transfer of top or bottom frame line	2,100.00	140.00
	Double transfer of top and bottom frame lines	2,200.00	145.00
70	24¢ red lilac Washington	2,750.00	250.00
	Scratch under "A" of "POSTAGE"		—
a	24¢ brown lilac	2,500.00	225.00
b	24¢ steel blue	*10,000.00*	900.00
c	24¢ violet	*12,000.00*	1,700.00
d	24¢ grayish lilac	7,500.00	2,000.00

	Issues of 1861-1867	Un	U
	Perf. 12		
71	30¢ orange Franklin	2,000.00	175.00
a	Printed on both sides		—
72	90¢ bl. Washington	3,250.00	475.00
a	90¢ pale blue	3,250.00	475.00
b	90¢ dark blue	4,000.00	650.00
73	2¢ blk. Andrew Jackson	375.00	65.00
	Double transfer	425.00	70.00
	Major double transfer of top left corner and "POSTAGE"		*12,500.00*
	Cracked plate	—	—
	#74 3¢ scarlet Washington was not regularly issued and is considered a Trial Color Proof.		
75	5¢ red brown Jefferson (67)	5,000.00	525.00
76	5¢ brown Jefferson (67)	1,600.00	150.00
a	5¢ black brown	1,900.00	275.00
	Double transfer of top or bottom frame line	1,700.00	160.00
77	15¢ blk. Lincoln	3,500.00	175.00
	Double transfer	3,750.00	190.00
78	24¢ lilac Washington (70)	2,500.00	200.00
a	24¢ grayish lilac	2,500.00	250.00
b	24¢ gray	2,500.00	250.00
c	24¢ blackish violet	*60,000.00*	*7,500.00*
d	Printed on both sides		*25,000.00*
	Grills on U.S. Stamps		
	Between 1867 and 1870, postage stamps were embossed with pyramid-shaped grills that absorbed cancellation ink to prevent reuse of canceled stamps.		
	Issues of 1867, With Grills, Perf. 12		
	Grills A, B and with C: Points Up		
	A. Grill Covers Entire Stamp		
79	3¢ rose Washington (56)	8,500.00	1,350.00
b	Printed on both sides		—
80	5¢ brown Jefferson (57)	—	*130,000.00*
a	5¢ dark brown		*130,000.00*
81	30¢ orange Franklin (61)		*80,000.00*
	B. Grill about 18 x 15mm		
82	3¢ rose Washington (56)		*190,000.00*
	C. Grill about 13 x 16mm		
83	3¢ rose Washington (56)	6,500.00	1,100.00
	Double grill	*7,750.00*	2,400.00

	Issues of 1867	Un	U
	With Grills, Perf. 12		
	Grills, D, Z, E, F with Points Down		
	D. Grill about 12 x 14mm		
84	2¢ black Jackson (73)	*15,000.00*	3,750.00
85	3¢ rose Washington (56)	6,750.00	1,050.00
	Split grill		1,150.00
	Z. Grill about 11 x 14mm		
85A	1¢ blue Franklin (55)		*935,000.00*
85B	2¢ black Jackson (73)	8,500.00	1,300.00
	Double transfer	*9,000.00*	1,350.00
85C	3¢ rose Washington (56)	*17,500.00*	3,500.00
	Double grill	*19,000.00*	
85D	10¢ grn. Washington (58)		*100,000.00*
85E	12¢ blk. Washington (59)	*14,000.00*	2,200.00
	Double transfer of top frame line		2,300.00
85F	15¢ black Lincoln (77)		*260,000.00*
	E. Grill about 11 x 13mm		
86	1¢ blue Franklin (55)	3,500.00	525.00
a	1¢ dull blue	3,500.00	500.00
	Double grill	—	650.00
	Split grill	3,700.00	575.00
87	2¢ black Jackson (73)	1,750.00	190.00
	Intense black	1,700.00	225.00
	Double grill	—	—
	Double transfer	1,750.00	190.00
88	3¢ rose Washington (65)	1,000.00	25.00
	Double grill	—	—
	Very thin paper	1,050.00	30.00
a	3¢ lake red	1,100.00	45.00
89	10¢ grn. Washington (68)	5,500.00	325.00
	Double grill	7,000.00	525.00
90	12¢ blk. Washington (69)	5,000.00	400.00
	Double transfer of top or bottom frame line	5,250.00	425.00
91	15¢ black Lincoln (77)	11,000.00	675.00
	Double grill	—	975.00
	F. Grill about 9 x 13mm		
92	1¢ blue Franklin (63)	3,000.00	525.00
a	1¢ pale blue	2,500.00	425.00
	Double transfer	3,250.00	575.00
	Double grill	—	900.00

63

64

65

67

68

70

71

72

73

77

Details

Issues of 1861-1862, 1861-1866, 1867 and 1875

Detail of #63, 86, 92

There is a dash in 63, 86 and 92 added under the tip of the ornament at the right of the numeral in upper left corner.

Detail of #67, 75, 80, 95

There is a leaf in 67, 75, 80 and 95 added to the foliated ornaments at each corner.

Detail of #69, 85E, 90, 97

In 69, 85E, 90 and 97, ovals and scrolls have been added at the corners.

Detail of #64-66, 74, 79, 82-83, 85, 85C, 88, 94

In 64-66, 74, 79, 82-83, 85, 85C, 88 and 94, ornaments at corners have been enlarged and end in a small ball.

Detail of #68, 85D, 89, 96

There is an outer line in 68, 85D, 89 and 96 cut below the stars and an outer line added to the ornaments above them.

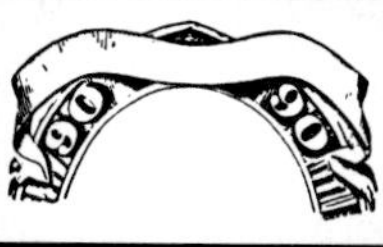

Detail of #72, 101

In 72 and 101, parallel lines form an angle above the ribbon containing "U.S Postage"; between these lines a row of dashes has been added, along with a point of color to the apex of the lower line.

16

117

118

120

121

122

Details

5¢ Landing of Columbus, Types I-III, Series 1869-1875

Detail of #118 Type I

Picture unframed.

Detail of #119 Type II

Picture framed.

#129 Type III

Same as Type I but without fringe of brown shading lines around central vignette.

Lewis & Clark Prestige Booklet The Corps of Discovery

Item #882600 $8.95

Lewis & Clark: The Corps a 32-page booklet comme anniversary of the Lewis a The booklet includes two individual portraits of Mer William Clark painted in a

To order these items and other related philatelic products call 1 800 STAMP-24 or visit us online at www.usps.com

	Issues of 1867	Un	U
	Issues of 1867, With Grills, Perf. 12		
	F. Grill about 9 x 13mm		
93	2¢ black Jackson (73)	500.00	55.00
	Double grill	—	180.00
	Very thin paper	550.00	62.50
94	3¢ red Washington (65)	425.00	10.00
a	3¢ rose	425.00	10.00
	Double grill		—
	End roller grill		350.00
	Quadruple split grill	750.00	130.00
c	Vertical pair, imperf. horizontally	*1,500.00*	
d	Printed on both sides	*7,500.00*	
95	5¢ brown Jefferson (67)	3,500.00	850.00
a	5¢ black brown	4,000.00	1,200.00
96	10¢ yellow green Washington (68)	3,500.00	250.00
a	10¢ dark green	3,500.00	350.00
	Double transfer	—	—
	Quadruple split grill		700.00
97	12¢ blk. Washington (69)	3,500.00	275.00
	Double transfer of top or bottom frame line	3,900.00	300.00
	Triple grill		—
98	15¢ black Lincoln (77)	4,500.00	300.00
	Double transfer of upper right corner	—	—
	Double grill	—	450.00
	Quadruple split grill	5,250.00	625.00
99	24¢ gray lilac Washington (70)	8,000.00	1,200.00
100	30¢ orange Franklin (71)	8,000.00	850.00
	Double grill	10,500.00	1,750.00
101	90¢ bl. Washington (72)	13,000.00	1,750.00
	Double grill	*17,500.00*	

	Issues of 1869-1875	Un	U
	Issues of 1875		
	Reissue of 1861-1866 Issues		
	Without Grill, Perf. 12		
102	1¢ blue Franklin (63)	*950.00*	*1,200.00*
103	2¢ black Jackson (73)	*4,000.00*	*5,500.00*
104	3¢ brown red Washington (65)	*4,000.00*	*6,750.00*
105	5¢ brown Jefferson (67)	*3,000.00*	*2,900.00*
106	10¢ grn. Washington (68)	*3,750.00*	*12,500.00*
107	12¢ blk. Washington (69)	*4,500.00*	*6,750.00*
108	15¢ black Lincoln (77)	*5,000.00*	*9,000.00*
109	24¢ deep violet Washington (70)	*6,000.00*	*10,000.00*
110	30¢ brownish orange Franklin (71)	*6,500.00*	*13,500.00*
111	90¢ bl. Washington (72)	*7,000.00*	*55,000.00*
	Issues of 1869		
	With Grill, Perf. 12, Hard Wove Paper,		
	G. Grill about 9.5 x 9mm		
112	1¢ buff Franklin	850.00	175.00
	Double grill	1,250.00	350.00
b	Without grill	*6,000.00*	
113	2¢ brown Post Horse and Rider	775.00	90.00
	Split grill	925.00	115.00
	Double transfer		110.00
114	3¢ ultra. Locomotive	350.00	20.00
	Triple grill	—	—
	Sextuple grill	—	*6,500.00*
	Gray paper	—	97.50
a	Without grill	*1,500.00*	
115	6¢ ultra. Washington	3,250.00	240.00
	Quadruple split grill	—	850.00

	Issues of 1869-1880	Un	U
	Issues of 1869		
	With Grill, Perf. 12, Hard Wove Paper,		
	G. Grill about 9.5 x 9mm		
116	10¢ yel. Shield and Eagle	2,500.00	150.00
	End roller grill	—	—
117	12¢ green *S.S. Adriatic*	2,600.00	160.00
	Split grill	3,100.00	190.00
118	15¢ brown & blue Landing of Columbus, type I	9,000.00	750.00
119	15¢ brown & blue type II (118)	4,000.00	275.00
b	Center inverted	*415,000.00*	*15,000.00*
c	Center double, one inverted		*80,000.00*
120	24¢ grn. & violet Declaration of Independence	9,000.00	775.00
b	Center inverted	*285,000.00*	*17,500.00*
121	30¢ Shield, Eagle and Flags	8,000.00	550.00
	Double grill	—	1,100.00
b	Flags inverted	*275,000.00*	*75,000.00*
122	90¢ Lincoln	12,000.00	2,250.00
	Split grill	—	—
	Issues of 1875		
	Reissue of 1869 Issue		
	Without Grill, Perf. 12, Hard White Paper		
123	1¢ buff (112)	675.00	400.00
124	2¢ brown (113)	800.00	600.00
125	3¢ blue (114)	*5,500.00*	*22,500.00*
126	6¢ blue (115)	2,250.00	*2,100.00*
127	10¢ yellow (116)	2,250.00	1,750.00
128	12¢ green (117)	3,000.00	3,000.00
129	15¢ brown and blue, type III (118)	1,900.00	1,150.00
a	Imperf. horizontally	*6,000.00*	*7,000*
130	24¢ grn. & violet (120)	2,750.00	1,600.00
131	30¢ ultra. & carmine (121)	3,250.00	2,500.00
132	90¢ car. & black (122)	4,750.00	*5,500.00*
	Issue of 1880		
	Reissue of 1869		
	Without Grill, Soft Porous Paper		
133	1¢ buff (112)	375.00	225.00
a	1¢ brown orange, issued without gum	250.00	225.00

	Issues of 1870-1871	Un	U
	With Grill, Perf. 12, White Wove Paper, No Secret Marks		
	H. Grill about 10 x 12mm		
134	1¢ Franklin	2,500.00	175.00
	End roller grill		700.00
135	2¢ red brown Jackson	1,200.00	80.00
136	3¢ Washington	750.00	25.00
	Cracked plate	—	95.00
137	6¢ Lincoln	5,000.00	525.00
	Double grill	—	900.00
138	7¢ Edwin M. Stanton	4,000.00	475.00
139	10¢ Jefferson	5,500.00	725.00
140	12¢ Henry Clay	*25,000.00*	3,000.00
141	15¢ Daniel Webster	7,500.00	1,200.00
142	24¢ Gen. Winfield Scott	—	*6,500.00*
143	30¢ Alexander Hamilton	17,000.00	3,250.00
144	90¢ Commodore Perry	15,000.00	2,200.00
	Split grill		2,300.00
	Without Grill, Perf. 12, White Wove Paper, No Secret Marks		
145	1¢ ultra. Franklin (134)	650.00	20.00
146	2¢ red brown Jackson (135)	350.00	15.00
147	3¢ green Washington (136)	325.00	1.75
148	6¢ carmine Lincoln (137)	1,000.00	35.00
	Brown carmine	1,050.00	65.00
	Violet carmine	1,200.00	90.00
149	7¢ vermilion Stanton (138)	1,200.00	95.00
150	10¢ brown Jefferson (139)	1,600.00	30.00
151	12¢ dull violet Clay (140)	2,750.00	200.00
152	15¢ bright orange Webster (141)	2,750.00	200.00
153	24¢ purple Scott (142)	2,000.00	160.00
154	30¢ black Hamilton (143)	6,750.00	250.00
155	90¢ carmine Perry (144)	4,750.00	350.00

	Issues of 1873-1875	Un	U
	Issues of 1873, Without Grill, Perf. 12, White Wove Paper, Thin to Thick, Secret Marks		
156	1¢ ultramarine Franklin	300.00	5.00
	Paper with silk fibers	—	27.50
e	With grill	*2,000.00*	
f	Imperf. pair	—	*1,500.00*
157	2¢ brown Jackson	400.00	22.50
	Double paper	1,000.00	105.00
c	With grill	*1,850.00*	*750.00*
158	3¢ green Washington	130.00	1.00
	olive green	*375.00*	15.00
	Cracked plate	—	32.50
	Without Grill, White Wove Paper, Thin to Thick, Secret Marks		
159	6¢ dull pink Lincoln	450.00	20.00
b	With grill	*1,800.00*	
160	7¢ orange vermilion Stanton	1,500.00	90.00
	Ribbed paper	—	105.00
161	10¢ brown Jefferson	1,200.00	25.00
162	12¢ blackish violet Clay	2,750.00	125.00
163	15¢ yellow orange Webster	2,750.00	140.00
a	With grill	*5,500.00*	
164	24¢ purple Scott		*357,500*
165	30¢ gray black Hamilton	3,250.00	130.00
166	90¢ rose carmine Perry	2,750.00	275.00
	Issues of 1875, Special Printing, Perf. 12, Hard, White Wove Paper, Without Gum, Secret Marks, Perf. 12		
	Although perforated, these stamps were usually cut apart with scissors. As a result, the perforations are often much mutilated and the design is frequently damaged.		
167	1¢ ultramarine Franklin (156)	*14,000.00*	
168	2¢ dark brown Jackson (157)	*6,500.00*	

	Issues of 1875-1879	Un	U
169	3¢ blue green Washington (158)	*17,500.00*	—
170	6¢ dull rose Lincoln (159)	*17,500.00*	
171	7¢ reddish vermilion Stanton (160)	*4,000.00*	
172	10¢ pale brown Jefferson (161)	*16,000.00*	
173	12¢ dark violet Clay (162)	*5,500.00*	
174	15¢ bright orange Webster (163)	*17,000.00*	
175	24¢ dull purple Scott (142)	*4,000.00*	*5,000.00*
176	30¢ greenish black Hamilton (143)	*13,500.00*	
177	90¢ violet carmine Perry (144)	*16,000.00*	
	Regular Issue, Yellowish Wove Paper, Perf. 12		
178	2¢ vermilion Jackson (157)	450.00	12.50
b	Half used as 1¢ on cover		*750.00*
c	With grill	800.00	*2,750.00*
179	5¢ blue Zachary Taylor	750.00	25.00
	Cracked plate	—	*170.00*
	Double paper	*900.00*	
	Paper with silk fibers	—	37.50
c	With grill	4,500.00	
	Special Printing, Hard, White Wove Paper, Without Gum		
180	2¢ carmine vermilion Jackson (157)	*60,000.00*	
181	5¢ bright blue Taylor (179)	*115,000.00*	
	Issues of 1879, Soft, Porous Paper, Thin to Thick, Perf. 12		
182	1¢ dark ultramarine Franklin (156)	350.00	4.50
183	2¢ vermilion Jackson (157)	150.00	3.25
a	Double impression	—	*5,500.00*

Details

Detail of **#134, 145**

Detail of **#135, 146**

Detail of **#136, 147**

Detail of **#137, 148**

Detail of **#138, 149**

Detail of **#156, 167, 182, 192**

1¢. In the pearl at the left of the numeral "1" there is a small crescent.

Detail of **#157, 168, 178, 180, 183, 193**

2¢. Under the scroll at the left of "U.S." there is a small diagonal line. This mark seldom shows clearly.

Detail of **#158, 169, 184, 194**

3¢. The under part of the upper tail of the left ribbon is heavily shaded.

Detail of **#159, 170, 186, 195**

6¢. The first four vertical lines of the shading in the lower part of the left ribbon have been strengthened.

Detail of **#190**

30¢. In the "S" of "CENTS," the vertical spike across the middle section of the letter has been broadened.

134

135

136

137

138

139

140

141

142

143

144

156

157

158

159

160

161

162

163

179

Details

Detail of #139,150,187, 151

Detail of #140, 151

Detail of #141, 152

Detail of #143, 154, 165, 176

Detail of #161, 172, 188, 197

10¢. There is a small semicircle in the scroll at the right end of the upper label.

Detail of #162, 173, 198

12¢. The balls of the figure "2" are crescent-shaped.

Detail of #163, 174, 189, 199

15¢. In the lower part of the triangle in the upper left corner two lines have been made heavier, forming a "V." This mark can be found on some of the Continental and American (1879) printings, but not all stamps show it.

Detail of #190

30¢. In the "S" of "CENTS," the vertical spike across the middle section of the letter has been broadened.

205

206

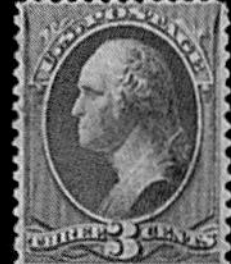
207

208

209

210

211

212

219

220

221

222

223

225

226

227

228

229

Details

Issues of 1881-1882, Re-engravings of 1873 Designs

Detail of #206

1¢. Upper vertical lines have been deepened, creating a solid effect in parts of background. Upper arabesques shaded.

Detail of #207

3¢. Shading at sides of central oval is half its previous width. A short horizontal dash has been cut below the "TS" of "CENTS."

Detail of #208

6¢. Has three vertical lines instead of four between the edge of the panel and the outside of the stamp.

Detail of #209

10¢. Has four vertical lines instead of five between left side of oval and edge of the shield. Horizontal lines in lower part of background strengthened.

	Issues of 1879-1880	Un	U
	Issues of 1879, Soft, Porous Paper, Thin to Thick, Perf. 12		
184	3¢ grn. Washington (158)	120.00	.80
	Double transfer	—	—
	Short transfer	—	6.25
185	5¢ blue Taylor (179)	550.00	15.00
186	6¢ pink Lincoln (159)	1,100.00	27.50
187	10¢ brown Jefferson (139) (no secret mark)	3,500.00	27.50
188	10¢ brown Jefferson (161) (with secret mark)	2,500.00	27.50
	Black brown	2,750.00	40.00
	Double transfer		47.50
189	15¢ red orange Webster (163)	350.00	25.00
190	30¢ full black Hamilton (143)	1,100.00	80.00
191	90¢ carmine Perry (144)	2,500.00	325.00
	Issues of 1880, Special Printing, Soft Porous Paper, Without Gum, Perf. 12		
192	1¢ dark ultramarine Franklin (156)	*50,000.00*	
193	2¢ black brown Jackson (157)	*17,500.00*	
194	3¢ blue green Washington (158)	*65,000.00*	
195	6¢ dull rose Lincoln (159)	*40,000.00*	
196	7¢ scarlet vermilion Stanton (160)	*6,500.00*	
197	10¢ deep brown Jefferson (161)	*40,000.00*	
198	12¢ black purple Clay (162)	*8,500.00*	
199	15¢ orange Webster (163)	*32,500.00*	
200	24¢ dark violet Scott (142)	*8,500.00*	
201	30¢ greenish black Hamilton (143)	*22,500.00*	
202	90¢ dull carmine Perry (144)	*32,500.00*	
203	2¢ scarlet vermilion Jackson (157)	*70,000.00*	
204	5¢ deep blue Taylor (179)	*100,000.00*	

	Issues of 1881-1887	Un	U
	Perf. 12		
205	5¢ Garfield, 04/10	325.00	10.00
	Special Printing, Soft Porous Paper, Without Gum, Perf. 12		
205C	5¢ gray brown Garfield (205)	*65,000.00*	
	Issues of 1881-1882, Designs of 1873 Re-engraved		
206	1¢ Franklin, 08/81	85.00	1.00
	Double transfer	110.00	6.00
207	3¢ Washington, 07/16/81	90.00	.55
	Double transfer	—	12.00
	Cracked plate	—	
208	6¢ Lincoln, 06/82	675.00	100.00
a	6¢ deep brown red	625.00	160.00
209	10¢ Jefferson, 04/82	190.00	6.00
b	10¢ black brown	2,250.00	240.00
	Issues of 1883, Perf. 12		
210	2¢ Washington, 01/01/83	50.00	.60
	Double transfer	55.00	2.25
211	4¢ Jackson, 01/01/83	350.00	22.50
	Cracked plate	—	
	Special Printing, Soft Porous Paper, Perf. 12		
211B	2¢ pale red brown Washington (210)	450.00	—
c	Horizontal pair, imperf. between	*2,000.00*	
211D	4¢ deep blue green Jackson (211) no gum	*45,000.00*	
	Issues of 1887, Perf. 12		
212	1¢ Franklin, 06/87	120.00	2.25
	Double transfer		—
213	2¢ green Washington (210), 09/10/87	50.00	.50
	Double transfer	—	3.25
b	Printed on both sides		—
214	3¢ vermilion Washington (207), 09/03/87	80.00	62.50

	Issues of 1888-1893	Un	U
	Issues of 1888, Perf. 12		
215	4¢ carmine Jackson (211), 11/88	250.00	22.50
216	5¢ indigo Garfield (205), 02/88	275.00	15.00
217	30¢ orange brown Hamilton (165), 01/88	475.00	120.00
218	90¢ pur. Perry (166), 02/88	1,200.00	260.00
	Issues of 1890-1893, Perf. 12		
219	1¢ Franklin, 02/22/90	30.00	.60
	Double transfer	—	—
219D	2¢ lake Washington (220), 02/22/90	250.00	1.75
	Double transfer	—	—
220	2¢ Washington, 1890	25.00	.55
	Double transfer	—	3.25
a	Cap on left "2"	150.00	10.00
c	Cap on both "2s"	700.00	30.00
221	3¢ Jackson, 02/22/90	85.00	7.50
222	4¢ Lincoln, 06/02/90	110.00	4.00
	Double transfer	125.00	—
223	5¢ Grant, 06/02/90	95.00	4.00
	Double transfer	110.00	3.75
224	6¢ Garfield, 06/02/90	85.00	20.00
225	8¢ Sherman, 06/02/90	65.00	14.00
226	10¢ Webster, 06/22/90	200.00	3.75
	Double transfer	—	—
227	15¢ Clay, 02/22/90	275.00	25.00
	Double transfer	—	—
	Triple transfer		—
228	30¢ Jefferson, 02/22/90	425.00	35.00
	Double transfer	—	—
229	90¢ Perry, 02/22/90	650.00	140.00
	Short transfer at bottom	—	—

	Issues of 1893	Date	Un	U	PB	#	FDC	Q(M)
	Columbian Exposition, Printed by The American Bank Note Co., Perf. 12							
230	1¢ Columbus in Sight of Land	01/02/93	22.50	.40	400.00	(6)	*9,000.00*	449
	Double transfer		27.50	.75				
	Cracked plate		90.00					
231	2¢ Landing of Columbus	01/02/93	21.00	.30	375.00	(6)	*12,500.00*	1,464
	Double transfer		26.00	.35				
	Triple transfer		62.50	—				
	Quadruple transfer		95.00					
	Broken hat on third figure left of Columbus		65.00	.45				
	Broken frame line		22.50	.35				
	Recut frame lines		22.50	—				
	Cracked plate		87.50	—				
232	3¢ *Santa Maria,* Flagship	01/02/93	60.00	15.00	725.00	(6)	*11,000.00*	12
	Double transfer		80.00	—				
233	4¢ ultramarine, Fleet	01/02/93	87.50	7.50	1,050.00	(6)	*16,500.00*	19
a	Blue (error)		*18,500.00*	*16,500.00*	*145,000.00*	(4)		
	Double transfer		125.00	—				
234	5¢ Columbus Soliciting Aid from Queen Isabella	01/02/93	95.00	8.00	1,400.00	(6)	*27,500.00*	35
	Double transfer		145.00	—				
235	6¢ Columbus Welcomed at Barcelona	01/02/93	85.00	22.50			*22,500.00*	5
a	Red violet		85.00	22.50	1,175.00	(6)		
	Double transfer		110.00	30.00				
236	8¢ Columbus Restored to Favor	03/93	80.00	11.00	825.00	(6)		11
	Double transfer		90.00	—				
237	10¢ Columbus Presenting Natives	01/02/93	140.00	8.00	3,350.00	(6)	*32,500.00*	17
	Double transfer		180.00	12.50				
	Triple transfer		—					
238	15¢ Columbus Announcing His Discovery	01/02/93	240.00	70.00	*3,750.00*	(6)		2
	Double transfer		—	—				
239	30¢ Columbus at La Rábida	01/02/93	300.00	90.00	*8,500.00*	(6)		0.6
240	50¢ Recall of Columbus	01/02/93	600.00	180.00	*14,000.00*	(6)		0.2
	Double transfer		—	—				
	Triple transfer		—	—				
241	$1 Queen Isabella Pledging Her Jewels	01/02/93	1,200.00	625.00	*47,500.00*	(6)		0.05
	Double transfer		—	—				
242	$2 Columbus in Chains	01/02/93	1,250.00	600.00	*67,500.00*	(6)	*65,000.00*	0.05
243	$3 Columbus Describing His Third Voyage	01/02/93	1,900.00	1,000.00				0.03
a	Olive green		1,900.00	1,000.00	*85,000.00*	(6)		

	Issues of 1893-1894	Date	Un	U	PB	#	FDC	Q(M)
	Columbian Exposition, Printed by The American Bank Note Co., Perf. 12							
244	$4 Queen Isabella and Columbus	01/02/93	2,600.00	1,300.00				0.03
a	Rose carmine		2,600.00	1,300.00	*250,000.00*	(6)		
245	$5 Portrait of Columbus	01/02/93	3,000.00	1,500.00	*190,000.00*	(6)		0.03

Unwmkd., Perf. 12

Bureau Issues Starting in 1894 and continuing until 1979, the Bureau of Engraving and Printing in Washington produced all U.S. postage stamps except #909-21, 1335, 1355, 1410-18 and 1789. Beginning in 1979, security printers in addition to the Bureau of Engraving and Printing started producing postage stamps under contract with the U.S. Postal Service.

	Issues of 1893-1894	Date	Un	U	PB	#	FDC	Q(M)
246	1¢ Franklin	10/94	32.50	5.00	450.00	(6)		
	Double transfer		40.00	6.00				
247	1¢ blue Franklin (246)	11/94	75.00	3.00	900.00	(6)		
	Double transfer		—	4.50				
248	2¢ pink Washington type I	10/94	30.00	7.50	300.00	(6)		
	Double transfer		—	—				
249	2¢ carmine lake type I (248)	10/94	175.00	5.50	2,500.00	(6)		
	Double transfer		—	6.50				
250	2¢ carmine type I (248)		30.00	2.50				
a	Rose		30.00	4.50				
b	Scarlet		30.00	1.00	375.00	(6)		
	Double transfer		—	5.00				
d	Horizontal pair, imperf. between		*2,000.00*					
251	2¢ carmine type II (248)		350.00	11.00	3,250.00	(6)		
252	2¢ carmine type III (248)		130.00	11.00				
a	Scarlet		130.00	11.00	1,900.00	(6)		
b	Horizontal pair, imperf. vertically		*1,500.00*					
c	Horizontal pair, imperf. between		*1,750.00*					
253	3¢ Jackson	09/94	125.00	10.00	1,500.00	(6)		
254	4¢ Lincoln	09/94	160.00	7.50	2,000.00	(6)		
255	5¢ Grant	09/94	115.00	7.00	1,250.00	(6)		
	Worn plate diagonal lines missing in oval background		115.00	5.00				
	Double transfer		140.00	6.50				
c	Vertical pair, imperf. horiz.		*4,000.00*					
256	6¢ Garfield	07/94	175.00	25.00	2,750.00	(6)		
a	Vertical pair, imperf. horizontally		*1,750.00*		*14,000.00*	(6)		
257	8¢ Sherman	03/94	160.00	18.50	2,100.00	(6)		
258	10¢ Webster	09/94	300.00	15.00	3,350.00	(6)		
	Double transfer		350.00	15.00				
259	15¢ Clay	10/94	325.00	60.00	5,000.00	(6)		

1 232 233 234 235

238 239 240 241

242 243 244 245

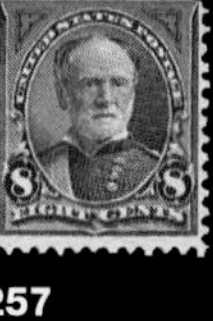

253 254 255 256 257 258 259

Details

2¢ Washington Types I-III, Series 1894-1898

Triangle of #248-50, 265 Type I

Horizontal lines of uniform thickness run across the triangle.

Triangle of #251, 266, Type II

Horizontal lines cross the triangle, but are thinner within than without.

Triangle of #252, 267, 279B-279Be Type III

The horizontal lines do not cross the double frame lines of the triangle.

260

261

262

263

277

282C

285

286

287

288

289

290

291

292

293

Details

10¢ Webster Types I-II, Series 1898

USPS

Watermark 191
Double-line
"USPS" in
capital letters;
detail at right.

Detail of #282C
Type I

The tips of the foliate ornaments do not impinge on the white curved line below "TEN CENTS."

Detail of #283
Type II

The tips of the ornaments break the curved line below the "E" of "TEN" and the "T" of "CENTS."

$1 Perry, Types I-II, Series 1894

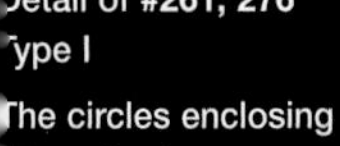

Detail of #261, 276
Type I

The circles enclosing $1 are broken.

Detail of #261A, 276A
Type I

The circles enclosing $1 are complete.

	Issues of 1894-1900	Date	Un	U	PB	#	FDC	Q(M)
	Unwmkd., Perf. 12							
260	50¢ Jefferson	11/94	575.00	135.00	10,500.00	(6)		
261	$1 Perry, type I	11/94	1,100.00	350.00	*18,000.00*	(6)		
261A	$1 black Perry type II (261)	11/94	2,300.00	750.00	*27,500.00*	(6)		
262	$2 James Madison	12/94	3,250.00	1,250.00	*42,500.00*	(6)		
263	$5 John Marshall	12/94	5,000.00	2,600.00	*23,500.00*	(3)		
	Wmkd. 191, Horizontally or Vertically, Perf. 12							
264	1¢ Franklin (246)	04/95	6.50	.50	250.00	(6)		
265	2¢ Washington, type I (248)	05/95	30.00	3.00	400.00	(6)		
	Double transfer		45.00	6.75				
266	2¢ Washington, type II (248)	05/95	35.00	5.00	500.00	(6)		
267	2¢ Washington, type III (248)	05/95	5.50	.40	190.00	(6)		
268	3¢ purple Jackson (253)	10/95	37.50	2.00	725.00	(6)		
	Double transfer		45.00	4.50				
269	4¢ Lincoln (254)	06/95	50.00	3.00	750.00	(6)		
	Double transfer		55.00	5.00				
270	5¢ Grant (255)	06/11/95	37.50	3.00	700.00	(6)		
	Double transfer		45.00	4.50				
	Worn plate, diagonal lines missing in oval background			40.00	3.25			
271	6¢ Garfield (256)	08/95	125.00	7.50	3,000.00	(6)		
	Very thin paper		140.00	7.50				
a	Wmkd. USIR		*12,500.00*	*8,000.00*				
272	8¢ Sherman (257)	07/95	70.00	2.50	975.00	(6)		
	Double transfer		85.00	4.00				
a	Wmkd. USIR		*5,000.00*	850.00	*20,000.00*	(3)		
273	10¢ Webster (258)	06/95	100.00	2.00	1,750.00	(6)		
	Double transfer		125.00	4.50				
274	15¢ Clay (259)	09/95	240.00	15.00	3,750.00	(6)		
275	50¢ orange Jefferson (260)	11/95	300.00	35.00	6,000.00	(6)		
a	Red orange		350.00	42.50	6,500.00	(6)		
276	$1 Perry type I (261)	08/95	675.00	95.00	*14,000.00*	(6)		
276A	$1 Perry type II (261)	08/95	1,500.00	225.00	*25,000.00*	(6)		
277	$2 bright blue Madison (262)	08/95	1,100.00	450.00				
a	Dark blue		1,100.00	450.00	*21,000.00*	(6)		
278	$5 Marshall (263)	08/95	2,300.00	650.00	*75,000.00*	(6)		
279	1¢ Franklin (246)	01/98	9.00	.50	185.00	(6)		
	Double transfer		12.00	1.10				
279B	2¢ red Washington type III (248)	01/98	9.00	.40	200.00	(6)		
c	Rose carmine type III	03/99	250.00	100.00	2,900.00	(6)		
d	Orange red, type IV	06/1900	11.50	.55	220.00	(6)		
e	Booklet pane of 6	04/16/1900	425.00	*1,250.00*				
f	Carmine, type IV	11/1897	10.00	.50	220.00	(6)		
g	Pink, type IV	11/1897	15.00	1.75	250.00	(6)		
h	Vermillion, type IV	11/1898	11.00	.55	235.00	(6)		
i	Brown orange, type IV	01/1899	*100.00*	*10.00*	*450.00*	(3)		

	Issues of 1898	Date	Un	U	PB	#	FDC	Q(M)
	Wmkd. 191, Horizontally or Vertically, Perf. 12							
280	4¢ rose brn. Lincoln (254)	10/98	30.00	3.00				
a	Lilac brown		30.00	3.00				
b	Orange brown		30.00	3.00	700.00	(6)		
	Extra frame line at top		50.00	9.00				
281	5¢ Grant (255)	03/98	35.00	2.00	650.00	(6)		
	Double transfer		45.00	4.00				
	Worn plate, diagonal lines missing in oval background			40.00	2.25			
282	6¢ lake Garfield (256)	12/98	47.50	6.00	900.00	(6)		
	Double transfer		60.00	8.50				
a	Purple lake		75.00	12.50	1,250.00	(6)		
282C	10¢ Webster (258), type I	11/98	200.00	6.00	2,600.00	(6)		
	Double transfer		225.00	10.00				
283	10¢ orange brown Webster (258), type II		150.00	5.00	1,900.00	(6)		
284	15¢ Clay (259)	11/98	160.00	10.00	2,100.00	(6)		
	Trans-Mississippi Exposition, Wmkd. 191, Perf. 12							
285	1¢ Jacques Marquette on the Mississippi	06/17/98	30.00	6.50	350.00	(6)	*15,000.00*	71
	Double transfer		40.00	7.50				
286	2¢ Farming in the West	06/17/98	27.50	2.50	350.00	(6)	*17,500.00*	160
	Double transfer		42.50	3.75				
	Worn plate		30.00	3.00				
287	4¢ Indian Hunting Buffalo	06/17/98	140.00	24.00	1,500.00	(6)	*27,500.00*	5
288	5¢ John Charles Frémont on the Rocky Mountains	06/17/98	140.00	21.00	1,400.00	(6)	*17,500.00*	8
289	8¢ Troops Guarding Wagon Train	06/17/98	200.00	42.50	2,900.00	(6)	*22,500*	3
a	Vertical pair, imperf. horizontally		*25,000.00*		*80,000.00*	(4)		
290	10¢ Hardships of Emigration	06/17/98	180.00	30.00	3,250.00	(6)	*27,500.00*	5
291	50¢ Western Mining Prospector	06/17/98	700.00	190.00	*26,000.00*	(6)	*50,000.00*	0.5
292	$1 Western Cattle in Storm	06/17/98	1,250.00	600.00	*50,000.00*	(6)	—	0.06
293	$2 Mississippi River Bridge	06/17/98	2,100.00	1,000.00	*150,000.00*	(6)		0.06

	Issue	Date	Un	U	PB/LP #	FDC	Q(M)
	Pan-American Exposition, Wmkd. 191, Perf. 12						
294	1¢ Fast Lake Navigation	05/01/01	20.00	3.00	275.00 (6)	5,500.00	91
a	Center inverted		11,000.00	12,000.00	85,000.00 (4)		
295	2¢ Empire State Express	05/01/01	17.50	1.00	275.00 (6)	3,000.00	210
a	Center inverted		45,000.00	55,000.00	425,000.00 (4)		
296	4¢ Electric Automobile	05/01/01	85.00	15.00	2,100.00 (6)		6
a	Center inverted		35,000.00		175,000.00 (4)		
297	5¢ Bridge at Niagara Falls	05/01/01	95.00	14.00	2,250.00 (6)	35,000.00	7
298	8¢ Canal Locks at Sault Ste. Marie	05/01/01	120.00	50.00	4,000.00 (6)		5
299	10¢ Fast Ocean Navigation	05/01/01	160.00	25.00	6,750.00 (6)		5
	Wmkd. 191, Perf. 12						
300	1¢ Franklin	02/03	12.00	.25	210.00 (6)		
	Double transfer		17.50	1.00			
	Worn plate		13.00	.35			
	Cracked plate		14.00	.30			
b	Booklet pane of 6	03/06/07	600.00	12,500.00			
301	2¢ Washington	01/17/03	16.00	.40	250.00 (6)		
	Double transfer		27.50	1.25			
	Cracked plate		—	1.25			
c	Booklet pane of 6	01/24/03	500.00	2,250.00			
302	3¢ Jackson	02/03	55.00	3.50	800.00 (6)		
	Double transfer		77.50	4.75			
303	4¢ Grant	02/03	60.00	2.30	825.00 (6)		
	Double transfer		77.50	2.75			
304	5¢ Lincoln	01/03	60.00	2.00	825.00 (6)		
305	6¢ Garfield	02/03	72.50	5.00	925.00 (6)		
	Brownish lake		72.50	5.00			
	Double transfer		77.50	4.50			
306	8¢ Martha Washington	12/02	45.00	3.00	750.00 (6)		
	Lavender		55.00	3.75			
307	10¢ Daniel Webster	02/03	70.00	2.80	1,100.00 (6)		
308	13¢ Benjamin Harrison	11/18/02	50.00	9.00	700.00 (6)		
309	15¢ Henry Clay	05/27/03	190.00	12.00	3,400.00 (6)		
	Double transfer		230.00	14.00			
310	50¢ Jefferson	03/23/03	475.00	27.50	7,500.00 (6)		
311	$1 David G. Farragut	06/05/03	750.00	75.00	20,000.00 (6)		
312	$2 Madison	06/05/03	1,200.00	200.00	32,500.00 (6)		
313	$5 Marshall	06/05/03	2,900.00	750.00	110,000.00 (6)		
	For listings of #312 and 313 with perf. 10, see #479 and 480.						
	Imperf.						
314	1¢ blue green Franklin (300)	10/02/06	16.00	15.00	200.00 (6)		
314A	4¢ brown Grant (303)	04/08	75,000.00	45,000.00			
	#314A was issued imperforated, but all copies were privately perforated at the sides.						
315	5¢ blue Lincoln (304)	05/12/08	240.00	900.00	2,750.00 (6)		
	Coil, Perf. 12 Horizontally						
316	1¢ Franklin (300)	02/18/08	55,000.00		225,000.00 (2)		
	Coil, Perf. 12 Horizontally						
317	5¢ Lincoln (304)	02/24/08	6,000.00		55,000.00 (2)		
	Coil, Perf. 12 Vertically						
318	1¢ Franklin (300)	07/31/08	6,000.00		32,500.00 (2)		
	Wmkd. 191, Perf. 12						
319	2¢ Washington	11/12/03	6.00	.25	160.00 (6)		
a	Lake, type I		—	—			
b	Carmine rose, type I		8.50	.40	225.00 (6)		
c	Scarlet, type I		7.00	.30	150.00 (6)		
d	Vertical pair, imperf. horiz.		7,500.00				
e	Vertical pair, imperf. between		2,500.00				
f	Lake, type II		10.00	.30	325.00 (6)		
g	Booklet pane of 6, carmine, type I	12/03/03	125.00	550.00			
h	Booklet pane of 6, carmine, type II		500.00				
i	Carmine, type II		75.00	50.00			
j	Carmine rose, type II		50.00	1.75	1,000.00 (6)		
k	Scarlet, type II		50.00	.65	1,000.00 (6)		
n	Booklet pane of 6, carmine rose		225.00	650.00			
p	Booklet pane of 6, scarlet		185.00	575.00			
q	Booklet pane of 6, lake		300.00	750.00			
	Washington 319, Imperf.						
320	2¢ carmine	10/02/06	16.00	17.50	200.00 (6)		
	Double transfer		24.00	21.50			
a	Lake, type II		45.00	45.00	725.00 (6)		
b	Scarlet		18.50	12.50	225.00 (6)		
c	Carmine rose, type I		50.00	40.00			
d	Carmine, type II		100.00	250.00			
	Coil, Perf. 12 Horizontally						
321	2¢ carmine pair, type I	02/18/08	375,000.00		—		
	Coil, Perf. 12 Vertically						
322	2¢ carmine pair, type II	07/31/08	6,000.00	—	15,000.00 (2)		
	Louisiana Purchase Exposition, Wmkd. 191, Perf. 12						
323	1¢ Robert R. Livingston	04/30/04	30.00	5.00	300.00 (6)	7,500.00	80
	Diagonal line through left "1"			50.00	12.50		
324	2¢ Thomas Jefferson	04/30/04	27.50	2.00	300.00 (6)	5,000.00	193
325	3¢ James Monroe	04/30/04	90.00	30.00	950.00 (6)	20,000.00	5
326	5¢ William McKinley	04/30/04	95.00	25.00	1,000.00 (6)	22,500.00	7
327	10¢ Map of Louisiana Purchase	04/30/04	175.00	30.00	2,250.00 (6)	24,000.00	4
	Jamestown Exposition, Wmkd. 191, Perf. 12						
328	1¢ Captain John Smith	04/26/07	30.00	5.00	300.00 (6)	10,000.00	78
	Double transfer		35.00	6.00			
329	2¢ Founding of Jamestown, 1607	04/26/07	35.00	4.50	400.00 (6)	15,000.00	149
330	5¢ Pocahontas	04/26/07	150.00	30.00	2,750.00 (6)		

294

295

296

297

298

299

300

301

302

303

304

305

306

307

308

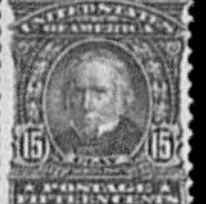

309

310

311

312

313

319

323

324

325

326

327

328

329

330

Details

2¢ Washington Die I-II, Series 1903

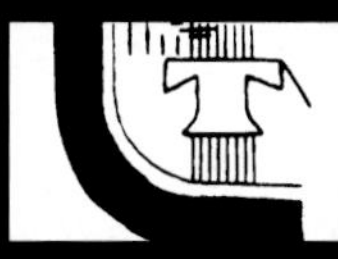

Detail of #319a, 319b, 319g Die I.

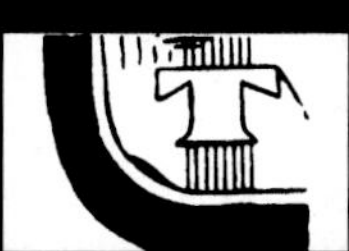

Detail of #319c, 319f, 319h, 319i Die II.

331

332

333

334

335

336

337

338

339

340

341

342

Details

3¢ Washington Types I-IV, Series 1908-1919

Detail of #333, 345, 359, 376, 389, 394, 426, 445, 456, 464, 483, 493, 501-501b
Type I

Top line of toga rope is weak and rope shading lines are thin. Fifth line from left is missing. Line between lips is thin.

Detail of #484, 494, 502, 541 Type II

Top line of toga rope is strong and rope shading lines are heavy and complete. Line between lips is heavy.

Detail of #529
Type I

Top row of toga rope is strong but fifth shading line is missing as in Type I. Toga button center shading line consists of two dashes, central dot. "P," "O" of "POSTAGE" are separated by line of color.

Detail of #530, 535
Type IV

Top rope shading lines are complete. Second, fourth toga button shading lines are broken in middle, third line is continuous with dot in center. "P," "O" of "POSTAGE" are joined.

367

370

372

USPS

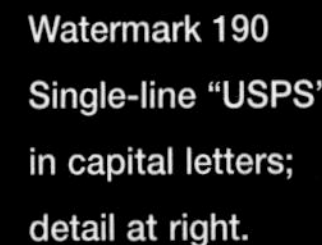

Watermark 190
Single-line "USPS" in capital letters; detail at right.

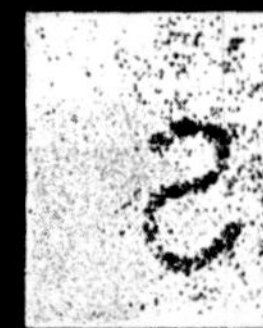

	Issue	Date	Un	U	PB/LP	#	FDC	Q(M)
	Wmkd. 191, Perf. 12							
331	1¢ Franklin	12/08	7.25	.40	77.50	(6)		
	Double transfer		9.50	.75				
a	Booklet pane of 6	12/02/08	160.00	*450.00*				
b	"China Clay" paper		*1,000.00*					
332	2¢ Washington	11/08	6.75	.35	70.00	(6)		
	Double transfer		12.50	—				
a	Booklet pane of 6	11/16/08	135.00	*400.00*				
333	3¢ Washington, type I	12/08	35.00	3.00	350.00	(6)		
a	"China Clay" paper		*1,000.00*		*7,500.00*	(6)		
334	4¢ Washington	12/08	42.50	1.50	425.00	(6)		
	Double transfer		55.00	—				
a	"China Clay" paper		*1,300.00*					
335	5¢ Washington	12/08	55.00	2.50	525.00	(6)		
a	"China Clay" paper		*1,000.00*					
336	6¢ Washington	01/09	65.00	6.50	750.00	(6)		
a	"China Clay" paper		*1,000.00*					
337	8¢ Washington	12/08	50.00	3.00	525.00	(6)		
	Double transfer		57.50	—				
a	"China Clay" paper		*1,000.00*					
338	10¢ Washington	01/09	70.00	2.00	800.00	(6)		
a	"China Clay" paper		*1,000.00*					
339	13¢ Washington	01/09	42.50	19.00	500.00	(6)		
	Line through "TAG" of "POSTAGE"		70.00	—				
a	"China Clay" paper		*1,000.00*		*7,500.00*	(6)		
340	15¢ Washington	01/09	70.00	6.50	650.00	(6)		
a	"China Clay" paper		*1,000.00*		*9,000.00*	(6)		
341	50¢ Washington	01/13/09	350.00	20.00	*7,000.00*	(6)		
342	$1 Washington	01/29/09	525.00	100.00	*17,500.00*	(6)		
	Imperf.							
343	1¢ green Franklin (331)	12/08	4.50	4.50	47.50	(6)		
	Double transfer		11.00	7.00				
344	2¢ carmine Washington (332)	12/10/08	5.50	3.00	77.50	(6)		
	Double transfer		12.50	4.00				
	Foreign entry, design of 1¢		*1,250.00*	—				
	#345-347: Washington (Designs of 333-335)							
345	3¢ deep violet, type I	1909	10.50	*20.00*	155.00	(6)		
	Double transfer		22.50	—				
346	4¢ orange brown	02/25/09	17.50	*22.50*	175.00	(6)		
	Double transfer		37.50	—				
347	5¢ blue	02/25/09	32.50	35.00	275.00	(6)		
	Coil, Perf. 12 Horizontally							
	#350-351, 354-356: Washington (Designs of 334-335, 338)							
348	1¢ green Franklin (331)	12/29/08	37.50	25.00	290.00	(2)		
349	2¢ carmine Washington (332)	01/09	80.00	20.00	550.00	(2)		
	Foreign entry, design of 1¢		—	*1,750.00*				
350	4¢ orange brown	08/15/10	160.00	140.00	1,250.00	(2)		
351	5¢ blue	01/09	175.00	175.00	1,250.00	(2)		
	Coil, Perf. 12 Vertically							
352	1¢ green Franklin (331)	01/09	95.00	75.00	750.00	(2)		
	Coil, Perf. 12 Vertically							
353	2¢ carmine Washington (332)	01/12/09	95.00	20.00	750.00	(2)		
354	4¢ orange brown	02/23/09	220.00	150.00	1,500.00	(2)		
355	5¢ blue	02/23/09	230.00	130.00	1,500.00	(2)		
356	10¢ yellow	01/07/09	2,850.00	*3,000.00*	*13,000.00*	(2)		
	Bluish Paper, Perf. 12, #359-366: Washington (Designs of 333-340)							
357	1¢ green Franklin (331)	02/16/09	100.00	*100.00*	1,000.00	(6)		
358	2¢ carmine Washington (332)	02/16/09	90.00	*100.00*	1,000.00	(6)		
359	3¢ deep violet, type I	1909	2,000.00	*5,000.00*	*22,500.00*	(6)		
360	4¢ orange brown	1909	*24,000.00*		*110,000.00*	(4)		
361	5¢ blue	1909	5,000.00	*15,000.00*	*85,000.00*	(6)		
362	6¢ red orange	1909	1,500.00	*5,000.00*	*16,000.00*	(6)		
363	8¢ olive green	1909	*27,500.00*		*125,000.00*	(3)		
364	10¢ yellow	1909	1,850.00	*5,500.00*	*32,500.00*	(6)		
365	13¢ blue green	1909	3,000.00	*2,250.00*	*30,000.00*	(6)		
366	15¢ pale ultramarine	1909	1,450.00	*11,000.00*	*11,000.00*	(6)		
	Lincoln Memorial, Wmkd. 191, Perf. 12							
367	2¢ Bust of Abraham Lincoln	02/12/09	5.50	2.00	175.00	(6)	*500.00*	148
	Double transfer		7.50	2.75				
	Imperf.							
368	2¢ carmine (367)	02/12/09	20.00	22.50	190.00	(6)	*13,000.00*	1
	Double transfer		45.00	30.00				
	Bluish Paper, Perf. 12							
369	2¢ carmine (367)	02/09	225.00	*275.00*	*3,000.00*	(6)		0.6
	Alaska-Yukon-Pacific Exposition, Wmkd. 191, Perf. 12							
370	2¢ Willam H. Seward	06/01/09	8.75	2.25	200.00	(6)	*3,000.00*	153
	Double transfer		10.50	5.00				
	Imperf.							
371	2¢ carmine (370)	06/09	22.50	25.00	225.00	(6)		0.5
	Double transfer		37.50	30.00				
	Hudson-Fulton Celebration, Wmkd. 191, Perf. 12							
372	2¢ *Half Moon & Clermont*	09/25/09	12.00	4.75	280.00	(6)	*900.00*	73
	Double transfer		16.00	5.00				
	Imperf.							
373	2¢ carmine (372)	09/25/09	25.00	27.50	240.00	(6)	*7,000.00*	0.2
	Double transfer		45.00	32.50				
	Wmkd. 190, #376-382: Washington (Designs of 333-338, 340,) **Perf. 12**							
374	1¢ green Franklin (331)	11/23/10	7.00	.25	100.00	(6)		
	Double transfer		14.00	—				
a	Booklet pane of 6	10/07/10	200.00	*300.00*				
375	2¢ carmine Washington (332)	11/23/10	7.00	.25	100.00	(6)		
	Double transfer		12.00	—				
	Foreign entry, design of 1¢		—	*1,450.00*				
a	Booklet pane of 6	11/30/10	125.00	*200.00*				
b	2¢ lake		*900.00*					
376	3¢ deep violet, type I	01/16/11	21.50	2.00	220.00	(6)		

	Issue	Date	Un	U	PB/LP	#	FDC	Q(M)
	Wmkd. 190, Perf. 12							
377	4¢ Washington	01/20/11	32.50	1.00	260.00	(6)		
378	5¢ Washington	01/25/11	32.50	.75	350.00	(6)		
379	6¢ Washington	01/25/11	37.50	1.00	500.00	(6)		
380	8¢ Washington	02/08/11	115.00	15.00	1,100.00	(6)		
381	10¢ Washington	01/24/11	105.00	6.00	1,125.00	(6)		
382	15¢ Washington	03/01/11	275.00	17.50	2,500.00	(6)		
	Imperf.							
383	1¢ Franklin (331)	12/10	2.25	2.00	45.00	(6)		
	Double transfer		6.50	—				
384	2¢ Washington (332)	12/10	3.75	2.50	130.00	(6)		
	Double transfer		7.50	—				
	Rosette plate, crack on head		*150.00*	—				
	Coil, Perf. 12 Horizontally							
385	1¢ Franklin (331)	11/01/10	40.00	25.00	450.00	(2)		
386	2¢ Washington (332)	11/01/10	85.00	30.00	1,400.00	(2)		
	Coil, Perf. 12 Vertically							
387	1¢ Franklin (331)	11/01/10	200.00	85.00	900.00	(2)		
388	2¢ Washington (332)	11/01/10	1,250.00	*550.00*	*8,500.00*	(2)		
389	3¢ Washington, type I (333)	01/24/11	*65,000.00*	*10,000.00*	*140,000.00*	(2)		
	Coil, Perf. 8.5 Horizontally							
390	1¢ Franklin (331)	12/12/10	5.00	*7.00*	37.50	(2)		
391	2¢ Washington (332)	12/23/10	40.00	17.50	260.00	(2)		
	Coil, Perf. 8.5 Vertically #394-396: Washington (Designs of 333-335)							
392	1¢ Franklin (331)	12/12/10	30.00	27.50	200.00	(2)		
393	2¢ Washington (332)	12/16/10	47.50	12.50	125.00	(2)		
394	3¢ Washington, type I	09/18/11	60.00	55.00	425.00	(2)		
395	4¢ Washington	04/15/12	62.00	55.00	475.00	(2)		
396	5¢ Washington	03/13	60.00	52.50	425.00	(2)		
	Panama Pacific Exposition, Wmkd. 190, Perf. 12							
397	1¢ Vasco Nunez de Balboa	01/01/13	20.00	2.00	250.00	(6)	*5,000.00*	335*
	Double transfer		24.00	3.25				
398	2¢ Pedro Miguel Locks, Panama Canal	01/13	20.00	1.00	325.00	(6)		504*
	Double transfer		40.00	3.50				
a	Carmine lake		*1,500.00*					
b	Lake		*2,500.00*					
399	5¢ Golden Gate	01/01/13	80.00	10.00	1,900.00	(6)	*21,000.00*	29*
400	10¢ Discovery of San Francisco Bay	01/01/13	135.00	22.50	2,350.00	(6)	10,000.00	17*
400A	10¢ orange (400)	08/13	210.00	17.50	*12,000.00*	(6)		
	*Includes perf. 10 printing quantities.							
	Wmkd. 190, Perf. 10							
401	1¢ green (397)	12/14	27.50	7.00	340.00	(6)		335
402	2¢ carmine (398)	01/15	75.00	2.75	1,950.00	(6)		504

	Issue	Date	Un	U	PB/LP	#	FDC	Q(M)
	Wmkd. 190, Perf. 10							
403	5¢ blue (399)	02/15	175.00	19.00	4,000.00	(6)		29
404	10¢ orange (400)	07/15	875.00	70.00	*12,500.00*	(6)		17
	Wmkd. 190, Perf. 12							
405	1¢ Washington	02/12	7.00	.25	95.00	(6)		
	Cracked plate		14.50	—				
	Double transfer		8.50	—				
a	Vertical pair, imperf. horizontally		*1,750.00*	—				
b	Booklet pane of 6	02/08/12	65.00	*75.00*				
406	2¢ Washington, type I	02/12	7.00	.25	105.00	(6)		
	Double transfer		9.00	—				
a	Booklet pane of 6	02/08/12	65.00	*90.00*				
b	Double impression		—					
c	Lake		*1,750.00*	*2,750.00*				
407	7¢ Washington	04/14	80.00	14.00	1,200.00	(6)		
	Imperf. #408-413: Washington (Designs of 405-406)							
408	1¢ Washington	03/12	1.00	.65	18.00	(6)		
	Double transfer		2.40	1.00				
409	2¢ Washington, type I	02/12	1.20	.65	35.00	(6)		
	Cracked plate		14.00	—				
	Coil, Perf. 8.5 Horizontally							
410	1¢ Washington	03/12	6.00	5.50	30.00	(2)		
411	2¢ Washington, type I	03/12	10.00	5.00	55.00	(2)		
	Double transfer		12.50	—				
	Coil, Perf. 8.5 Vertically							
412	1¢ Washington	03/18/12	25.00	6.50	120.00	(2)		
413	2¢ Washington, type I	03/12	55.00	2.25	300.00	(2)		
	Double transfer		52.50	—				
	Wmkd. 190, Perf. 12							
414	8¢ Franklin	02/12	45.00	2.00	475.00	(6)		
415	9¢ Franklin	04/14	55.00	13.50	650.00	(6)		
416	10¢ Franklin	01/12	45.00	.75	500.00	(6)		
417	12¢ Franklin	04/14	50.00	5.00	625.00	(6)		
	Double transfer		55.00	—				
	Triple transfer		72.50	—				
418	15¢ Franklin	02/12	85.00	4.50	850.00	(6)		
	Double transfer		—	—				
419	20¢ Franklin	04/14	200.00	18.50	2,000.00	(6)		
420	30¢ Franklin	04/14	125.00	17.50	1,450.00	(6)		
421	50¢ Franklin	08/14	425.00	30.00	*10,00.00*	(6)		
	Wmkd. 191							
422	50¢ Franklin (421)	02/12/12	250.00	22.00	*4,750.00*	(6)		
423	$1 Franklin	02/12/12	525.00	75.00	*12,000.00*	(6)		
	Double transfer		550.00	—				
	Wmkd. 190, Perf. 12 x 10							
423A	1¢ Washington	1914	*7,500.00*	*6,000.00*	*12,500.00*	(2)		
	Wmkd. 190, Perf. 10 #424-430: Wash. (Designs of 405-406, 333-336, 407)							
424	1¢ Washington	09/05/14	2.50	.20	42.50	(6)		
	Double transfer		4.75	—				
c	Vertical pair, imperf. horiz.		*2,800.00*	*2,500.00*				
d	Booklet pane of 6		5.25	*7.50*				
e	As "d", imperf.		*1,600.00*					
425	2¢ Washington, type I	09/05/14	2.30	.20	27.50	(6)		
	Cracked plate		9.50	—				
e	Booklet pane of 6	01/06/14	17.50	*25.00*				

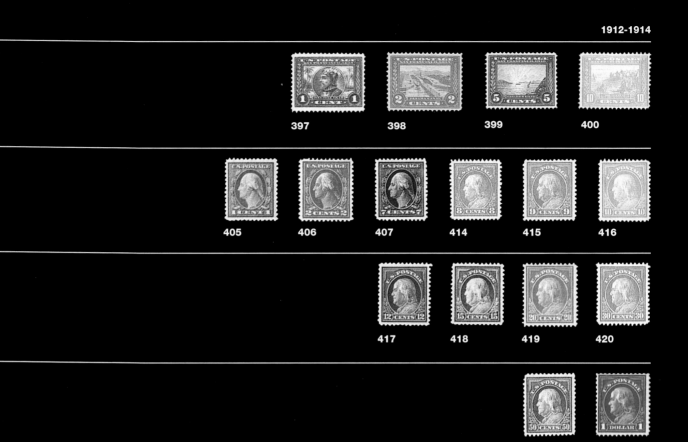

397  398  399  400

405  406  407  414  415  416

417  418  419  420

421  423

The Art of Disney: Friendship Stamped Stationery

Add more character to your mail with this pre-stamped stationery!

All you have to do is write a message, an address, then just fold, seal and mail. Each pad comes with 12 sheets featuring four different designs. It's fun and easy especially for kids!

Item #566794 $14.95

For more information call 1 800 STAMP-24

434

After 1915 (from 1916 to date), all postage stamps, except #519 and 832b, are on unwatermarked paper.

Details

2¢ Washington, Types I-VII, Series 1912-1921

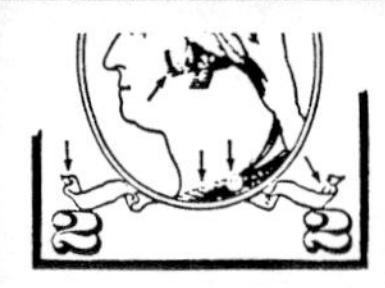

Detail of #406-406a, 411, 413, 425-425e, 442, 444, 449, 453, 461, 463-463a, 482, 499-499f Type I

One shading line in first curve of ribbon above left "2" and one in second curve of ribbon above right "2." Toga button has only a faint outline. Top line of toga rope, from button to front of the throat, is very faint. Shading lines of face end in the front of the ear, with little or no joining, to form lock of hair.

Detail of #482a, 500
Type Ia

Similar to Type I but all lines are shorter.

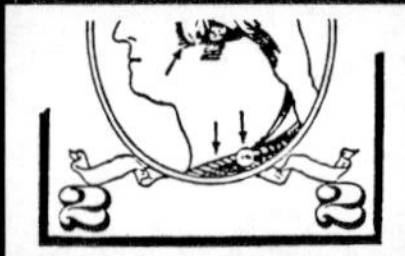

Detail of #454, 487, 491, 539
Type II

Shading lines in ribbons as in Type I. Toga button, rope and rope shading lines are heavy. Shading lines of face at lock of hair end in strong vertical curved line.

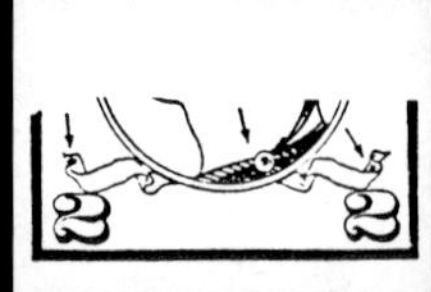

Detail of #450, 455, 488, 492, 540, 546
Type III

Two lines of shading in curves of ribbons.

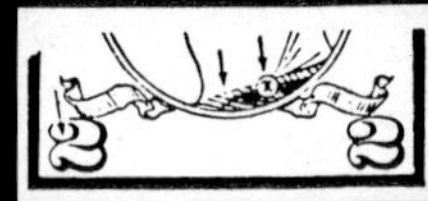

Detail of #526, 532
Type IV

Top line of toga rope is broken. Toga button shading lines form "DID." Line of color in left "2" is very thin and usually broken.

Detail of #527, 533
Type V

Top line of toga rope is complete. Toga button has five verticle shading lines. Line of color in left "2" is very thin and usually broken. Nose shading dots are as shown.

Detail of #528, 534
Type Va

Same as Type V except third row from bottom of nose shading dots has four dots instead of six. Overall height of design is 1⁄3mm shorter than Type V.

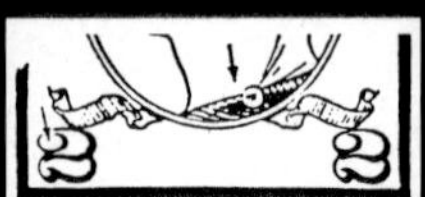

Detail of #528A, 534A
Type VI

Generally same as Type V except line of color in left "2" is very heavy.

Detail of #528B, 534B
Type VII

Line of color in left "2" is continuous, clearly defined and heavier than in Type V or Va but not as heavy as Type VI. An additional vertical row of dots has been added to upper lip. Numerous additional dots appear in hair at top of head.

Issue		Date	Un	U	PB/LP #	FDC Q(M)
	Wmkd. 190, Perf. 10					
426	3¢ deep violet, type I	09/18/14	15.00	1.50	210.00 (6)	
427	4¢ brown	09/07/14	35.00	1.00	475.00 (6)	
	Double transfer		45.00	—		
428	5¢ blue	09/14/14	35.00	1.00	390.00 (6)	
429	6¢ red orange	09/28/14	50.00	2.00	525.00 (6)	
430	7¢ black	09/10/14	90.00	5.00	950.00 (6)	
	#431-433, 435, 437-440: Franklin (Designs of 414-421, 423)					
431	8¢ pale olive green	09/26/14	37.50	3.00	550.00 (6)	
432	9¢ salmon red	10/06/14	50.00	9.00	725.00 (6)	
433	10¢ orange yellow	09/09/14	47.50	1.00	825.00 (6)	
434	11¢ Franklin	08/11/15	25.00	8.50	275.00 (6)	
435	12¢ claret brown	09/10/14	27.50	6.00	325.00 (6)	
	Double transfer		35.00	—		
	Triple transfer		40.00	—		
a	Copper red		32.50	7.00	325.00 (6)	
436	Not assigned					
437	15¢ gray	09/16/14	135.00	7.25	1,125.00 (6)	
438	20¢ ultramarine	09/19/14	220.00	6.00	3,250.00 (6)	
439	30¢ orange red	09/19/14	260.00	16.00	*4,100.00* (6)	
440	50¢ violet	12/10/15	575.00	16.00	*15,000.00* (6)	
	Coil, Perf. 10 Horizontally					
	#441-459: Washington (Designs of 405-406, 333-435; Flat Press, 18.5-19 x 22mm)					
441	1¢ green	11/14/14	1.00	1.00	8.00 (2)	
442	2¢ carmine, type I	07/22/14	10.00	6.00	60.00 (2)	
	Coil, Perf. 10 Vertically					
443	1¢ green	05/29/14	25.00	7.50	155.00 (2)	
444	2¢ carmine, type I	04/25/14	40.00	3.00	300.00 (2)	
445	3¢ violet, type I	12/18/14	225.00	150.00	1,300.00 (2)	
446	4¢ brown	10/02/14	125.00	65.00	750.00 (2)	
447	5¢ blue	07/30/14	47.50	32.50	260.00 (2)	
	Coil, Perf. 10 Horizontally (Rotary Press, Designs 18.5-19 x 22.5mm)					
448	1¢ green	12/12/15	6.00	4.00	45.00 (2)	
449	2¢ red, type I	12/05/15	2,800.00	600.00	*15,000.00* (2)	
450	2¢ carmine, type III	02/16	10.00	5.00	100.00 (2)	
451	Not assigned					
	Coil, Perf. 10 Vertically (Rotary Press, Designs 19.5 20 x 22mm)					
452	1¢ green	11/11/14	10.00	4.00	75.00 (2)	
453	2¢ carmine rose, type I	07/03/14	150.00	7.50	725.00 (2)	
454	2¢ red, type II	06/15	82.50	10.00	425.00 (2)	
455	2¢ carmine, type III	12/15	8.50	1.40	50.00 (2)	
456	3¢ violet, type I	02/02/16	240.00	110.00	1,250.00 (2)	
457	4¢ brown	02/18/16	25.00	22.50	150.00 (2)	
	Cracked plate		35.00	—		
458	5¢ blue	03/09/16	30.00	22.50	180.00 (2)	
	Horizontal Coil, Imperf.					
459	2¢ carmine, type I	06/30/14	230.00	*1,100.00*	1,000.00 (2)	
	Wmkd. 191, Perf. 10					
460	$1 Franklin (423)	02/08/15	850.00	140.00	*12,500.00* (6)	
	Double transfer		900.00	—		
	Wmkd. 190, Perf. 11					
461	2¢ Washington (406), type I	06/17/15	150.00	*325.00*	*1,500.00* (6)	
	Privately perforated copies of #409 have been made to resemble 461.					

Issue		Date	Un	U	PB/LP #	FDC Q(M)
	Unwmkd., Perf. 10 #462-469: Washington (Designs of 405-406, 333-336, 407)					
462	1¢ green	09/27/16	7.00	.35	160.00 (6)	
	Experimental precancel, Springfield, MA, or New Orleans, LA			10.00		
a	Booklet pane of 6	10/15/16	9.50	*12.50*		
463	2¢ carmine, type I	09/25/16	4.50	.40	130.00 (6)	
	Experimental precancel, Springfield, MA			22.50		
	Double transfer		6.50	—		
a	Booklet pane of 6	10/08/16	110.00	*110.00*		
464	3¢ violet, type I	11/11/16	75.00	17.50	1,350.00 (6)	
	Double transfer in "CENTS"		*90.00*	—		
465	4¢ orange brown	10/07/16	45.00	2.50	650.00 (6)	
466	5¢ blue	10/17/16	75.00	2.50	950.00 (6)	
	Experimental precancel, Springfield, MA			175.00		
467	5¢ carmine (error in plate of 2¢)		550.00	*800.00*		
468	6¢ red orange	10/10/16	95.00	9.00	1,350.00 (6)	
	Experimental precancel, Springfield, MA			175.00		
469	7¢ black	10/10/16	130.00	15.00	1,350.00 (6)	
	Experimental precancel, Springfield, MA			175.00		
	#470-478: Franklin (Designs of 414-416, 434, 417-421, 423)					
470	8¢ olive green	11/13/16	60.00	8.00	600.00 (6)	
	Experimental precancel, Springfield, MA			165.00		
471	9¢ salmon red	11/16/16	60.00	18.50	750.00 (6)	
472	10¢ orange yellow	10/17/16	110.00	2.50	1,350.00 (6)	
473	11¢ dark green	11/16/16	40.00	18.50	360.00 (6)	
	Experimental precancel, Springfield, MA			*575.00*		
474	12¢ claret brown	10/10/16	55.00	7.50	625.00 (6)	
	Double transfer		65.00	8.50		
	Triple transfer		77.50	11.00		
475	15¢ gray	11/16/16	200.00	16.00	3,000.00 (6)	
476	20¢ light ultramarine	12/05/16	250.00	17.50	3,600.00 (6)	
476A	30¢ orange red		*4,500.00*		*75,000* (6)	
477	50¢ light violet	03/02/17	1,100.00	80.00	*57,500.00* (6)	
478	$1 violet black	12/22/16	800.00	25.00	*13,000.00* (6)	
	Double transfer		825.00	32.50		
	Unwmkd., Perf. 10					
479	$2 Madison (312)	03/22/17	260.00	42.50	*4,000.00* (6)	
480	$5 Marshall (313)	03/22/17	220.00	40.00	3,100.00 (6)	
	Imperf. #481-496: Washington (Designs of 405-406, 333-335)					
481	1¢ green	11/16	.95	.65	15.00 (6)	
	Double transfer		2.50	1.50		
482	2¢ carmine, type I	12/08/16	1.30	1.25	25.00 (6)	
482A	2¢ deep rose, type Ia			*50,000.00*		
483	3¢ violet, type I	10/13/17	11.50	7.50	115.00 (6)	
	Double transfer		17.50	—		
484	3¢ violet, type II		9.00	5.00	87.50 (6)	
	Double transfer		12.50	—		
485	5¢ carmine (error in plate of 2¢)	03/17	*12,000.00*		130.00 (6)	

	Issue	Date	Un	U	PB/LP #	FDC Q(M)
	Coil, Perf. 10 Horizontally					
	#481-496: Washington (Designs of 405-406, 333-335)					
486	1¢ green	01/18	.85	.80	4.50 (2)	
	Double transfer		2.25	—		
487	2¢ carmine, type II	11/15/16	12.50	5.00	100.00 (2)	
488	2¢ carmine, type III	1919	2.40	2.25	20.00 (2)	
	Cracked plate		12.00	8.00		
489	3¢ violet, type I	10/10/17	4.75	2.00	32.50 (2)	
	Coil, Perf. 10 Vertically (Designs 19.5 x 20 x 22mm)					
	#481-496: Washington (Designs of 405-406, 333-335)					
490	1¢ green	11/17/16	.50	.50	3.25 (2)	
	Cracked plate (horizontal)		7.50	—		
	Cracked plate (vertical) retouched		9.00	—		
	Rosette crack		*60.00*	—		
491	2¢ carmine, type II	11/17/16	2,200.00	750.00	*12,000.00* (2)	
492	2¢ carmine, type III		9.00	.90	55.00 (2)	
493	3¢ violet, type I	07/23/17	14.00	3.50	110.00 (2)	
494	3¢ violet, type II	02/04/18	10.00	1.75	75.00 (2)	
495	4¢ orange brown	04/15/17	10.00	5.00	75.00 (2)	
	Cracked plate		25.00	—		
496	5¢ blue	01/15/19	3.25	1.40	30.00 (2)	
497	10¢ Franklin (416)	01/31/22	19.00	11.00	130.00 (2)	*5,000.00*
	Unwmk., Perf. 11, #498-507: Washington (Designs of 405-406, 333-336, 407)					
498	1¢ green	03/17	.35	.25	16.50 (6)	
	Cracked plate		7.50	—		
a	Vertical pair, imperf. horizontally			650.00		
b	Horizontal pair, imperf. between			375.00		
c	Vertical pair, imperf. between			*450.00*	—	
d	Double impression		250.00	*2,500.00*		
e	Booklet pane of 6	04/06/17	2.50	*2.00*		
f	Booklet pane of 30	09/17	*1,150.00*			
g	Perf. 10 top or bottom		*5,000.00*	*12,500*		
499	2¢ rose, type I	03/17	.35	.25	16.50 (6)	
	Double transfer		6.00	—		
a	Vertical pair, imperf. horizontally		175.00			
b	Horizontal pair, imperf. vertically		*300.00*	*225.00*		
c	Vertical pair, imperf. between		*850.00*	*250.00*		
e	Booklet pane of 6	03/31/17	4.00	*2.50*		
f	Booklet pane of 30	09/17	*28,000.00*	—		
g	Double impression		175.00	—		

	Issue	Date	Un	U	PB/LP #	FDC Q(M)
	Unwmk., Perf. 11					
	#498-507: Washington (Designs of 405-406, 333-336, 407)					
500	2¢ deep rose, type Ia		275.00	240.00	2,100.00 (6)	
	Pair, types I and Ia		*1,275.00*			
501	3¢ light violet, type I	03/17	11.00	.40	125.00 (6)	
b	Booklet pane of 6	10/17/17	75.00	*60.00*		
c	Vertical pair, imperf. horizontally, type I		*1,500.00*			
d	Double impression		*2,750.00*	*2,750.00*		
502	3¢ dark violet, type II		14.00	.75	140.00 (6)	
b	Booklet pane of 6	02/28/18	60.00	*55.00*		
c	Vertical pair, imperf. horizontally		*550.00*	*300.00*		
d	Double impression		625.00	300.00		
e	Perf. 10, top or bottom		*9,500.00*	*6,000.00*		
503	4¢ brown	03/17	10.00	.40	130.00 (6)	
504	5¢ blue	03/17	9.00	.35	125.00 (6)	
	Double transfer		11.00	—		
505	5¢ rose (error in plate of 2¢)		350.00	*550.00*		
506	6¢ red orange	03/17	12.00	.40	170.00 (6)	
507	7¢ black	03/17	27.50	1.25	250.00 (6)	
	#508-518: Franklin (Designs of 414-416, 434, 417-421, 423)					
508	8¢ olive bister	03/17	12.00	.65	170.00 (6)	
b	Vertical pair, imperf. between		—	—		
c	Perf. 10 top or bottom			*5,250.00*		
509	9¢ salmon red	03/17	13.00	1.75	140.00 (6)	
510	10¢ orange yellow	03/17	17.50	.25	180.00 (6)	
511	11¢ light green	05/17	9.00	2.50	125.00 (6)	
	Double transfer		12.50	3.25		
512	12¢ claret brown	05/17	9.00	.40	125.00 (6)	
a	Brown carmine		10.00	.50		
b	Perf. 10, top or bottom		—	*4,250.00*		
513	13¢ apple green	01/10/19	11.00	6.00	125.00 (6)	
	Deep apple green		12.50	6.50		
514	15¢ gray	05/17	37.50	1.50	550.00 (6)	
515	20¢ light ultramarine	05/17	45.00	.45	600.00 (6)	
	Deep ultramarine		50.00	.55		
b	Vertical pair, imperf. between		*2,000.00*	*1,750.00*		
c	Double impression		*1,250.00*			
d	Perf. 10 at top or bottom		—	*12,000.00*		
516	30¢ orange red	05/17	37.50	1.50	600.00 (6)	
a	Perf. 10 top or bottom		*5,000.00*	*5,500.00*		

498  499  500  501  502  503

504  505  506  507

508  509  510  511  512

512a  513  514  515  516

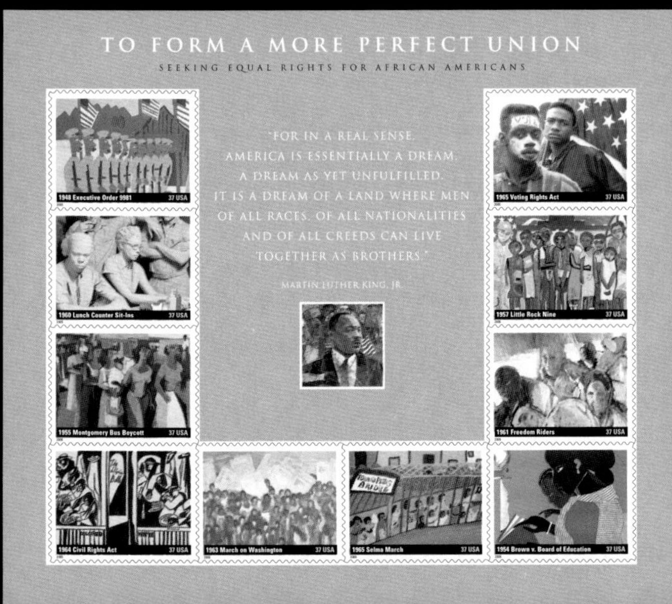

To Form a More Perfect Union Souvenir Sheet

This Souvenir Sheet commemorates the courage and achievement of the men and women who struggled during the civil rights movement. Our nation's founders created the Constitution "in order to form a more perfect union," and the civil rights movement helped to correct the misconception that great numbers of people were considered second-class citizens.

Item #457340 $3.70

517 523 524 537 547 548

549 550 551 552 553

554 555 556

Issue		Date	Un	U	PB #	FDC	Q(M)
	Unwmkd., Perf. 11						
517	50¢ Franklin	05/17	65.00	.75	1,600.00 (6)		
b	Vertical pair, imperf. between and at bottom		*6,000.00*	*6,000.00*			
c	Perf. 10, top or bottom			*10,000.00*			
518	$1 Franklin	05/17	50.00	1.50	1,300.00 (6)		
b	Deep brown		*1,800.00*	*1,050.00*			
	Wmkd. 191, Perf. 11						
519	2¢ carm. Washington (332)	10/10/17	450.00	*1,200.00*	3,500.00 (6)		
	Privately perforated copies of #344 have been made to resemble #519.						
520-522	Not assigned						
	Unwmkd., Perf. 11						
523	$2 Franklin	08/19/18	625.00	240.00	*12,000.00* (8)		
524	$5 Franklin	08/19/18	200.00	35.00	4,500.00 (8)		
	#525-535: Washington (Designs of 405-406, 333)						
525	1¢ gray green	12/18	2.50	.90	22.50 (6)		
	Emerald		3.50	1.25			
a	Dark green		6.00	1.75			
c	Horizontal pair, imperf. between		100.00				
d	Double impression		40.00	—			
526	2¢ carmine, type IV	03/06/20	27.50	4.00	240.00 (6)	*850.00*	
	Gash on forehead		40.00	—			
	Malformed "2" at left		37.50	6.00			
527	2¢ carmine, type V	03/20/20	20.00	1.25	165.00 (6)		
	Line through "2" and "EN"		30.00	—			
a	Double impression		65.00	—			
b	Vertical pair, imperf. horizontally		*850.00*				
c	Horizontal pair, imperf. vertically		*1,000.00*	—			
528	2¢ carmine, type Va	05/04/20	9.50	.40	82.50 (6)		
c	Double impression		27.50				
g	Vertical pair, imperf. between		*2,500.00*				
528A	2¢ carmine, type VI	06/24/20	52.50	2.00	425.00 (6)		
d	Double impression		160.00	—			
f	Vertical pair, imperf. horizontally		—				
h	Vertical pair, imperf. between		*1,000.00*				
528B	2¢ carmine, type VII	11/03/20	22.50	.75	175.00 (6)		
	Retouched on cheek		400.00	—			
e	Double impression		70.00				
529	3¢ violet, type III	03/18	3.60	.50	75.00 (6)		
a	Double impression		40.00	—			
b	Printed on both sides		*2,500.00*				
530	3¢ purple, type IV		1.80	.30	24.00 (6)		
	"Blister" under "U.S."		4.75	—			
	Recut under "U.S."		4.75	—			
a	Double impression		30.00	—			
b	Printed on both sides		*350.00*				
	Imperf.						
531	1¢ green	01/19	12.00	12.00	110.00 (6)		
532	2¢ carmine rose, type IV	03/20	40.00	35.00	370.00 (6)		
533	2¢ carmine, type V	05/04/20	110.00	95.00	1,100.00 (6)		
534	2¢ carmine, type Va	05/25/20	14.00	9.00	130.00 (6)		
534A	2¢ carmine, type VI	07/26/20	47.00	32.50	400.00 (6)		
534B	2¢ carmine, type VII	12/02/20	2,100.00	1,250.00	*17,000.00* (6)		
535	3¢ violet, type IV	1918	10.00	5.00	80.00 (6)		
a	Double impression		95.00	—			
	Perf. 12.5						
536	1¢ Washington (405)	08/15/19	21.00	20.00	200.00 (6)		
a	Horizontal pair, imperf. vertically			*900.00*			

Issue		Date	Un	U	PB #	FDC	Q(M)
	Unwmk., Perf. 11						
537	3¢ Allied Victory	03/03/19	10.00	3.25	175.00 (6)	*800.00*	100
a	deep red violet		*1,250.00*	*2,000.00*	9,000.00 (6)		
b	light reddish violet		75.00	10.00	650.00 (6)		
c	red violet		90.00	20.00			
	Unwmkd., Perf. 11 x 10						
	#538-546: Washington						
538	1¢ green	06/19	11.00	8.50	110.00 (4)		
	Double transfer		17.50	—			
a	Vertical pair, imperf. horizontally		50.00	*100.00*	900.00 (4)		
539	2¢ carmine rose, type II		2,750.00	*5,250.00*	*17,500.00* (4)		
540	2¢ carmine rose, type III	06/14/19	13.00	9.50	55.00 (4)		
	Double transfer		22.50	—			
a	Vertical pair, imperf. horizontally		50.00	*100.00*	1,000.00 (4)		
b	Horizontal pair, imperf. vertically		*1,000.00*				
541	3¢ violet, type II	06/19	45.00	30.00	360.00 (4)	—	
	Perf. 10 x 11 (Design 19 x 22.5-22.75mm)						
542	1¢ green	05/26/20	14.00	1.50	165.00 (6)	*1,750.00*	
	Perf. 10						
543	1¢ green	05/21	.60	.30	14.00 (4)		
a	Horizontal pair, imperf. between		*2,750.00*				
	Perf. 11						
544	1¢ green		*20,000.00*	*3,250.00*			
545	1¢ green	05/21	200.00	210.00	1,150.00 (4)		
546	2¢ carmine rose, type III	05/21	125.00	*160.00*	775.00 (4)		
	Recut in hair		140.00	*185.00*			
a	Perf. 10 at left		*7,500.00*	*10,000.00*			
547	$2 Franklin	11/01/20	160.00	40.00	4,500.00 (8)		
	Pilgrim Tercentenary, Unwmk., Perf. 11						
548	1¢ The *Mayflower*	12/21/20	4.75	2.25	60.00 (6)	*1,000.00*	138
549	2¢ Landing of the Pilgrims	12/21/20	6.50	1.60	75.00 (6)	*750.00*	196
550	5¢ Signing of the Compact	12/21/20	45.00	14.00	475.00 (6)	—	11
	America, Unwmk., Perf. 11						
551	½¢ Nathan Hale	04/04/25	.25	.20	8.00 (6)	17.50(4)	
	"Cap" on fraction bar		.75	.20			
552	1¢ Franklin	01/17/23	1.30	.20	25.00 (6)	25.00(2)	
	Double transfer		3.50	—			
a	Booklet pane of 6	08/11/23	7.50	*4.00*			
553	1½¢ Warren G. Harding	03/19/25	2.30	.20	50.00 (6)	30.00(2)	
554	2¢ Washington	01/15/23	1.20	.20	30.00 (6)	37.50	
	Double transfer		2.50	.80			
a	Horizontal pair, imperf. vert.		*250.00*				
b	Vertical pair, imperf. horiz.		*4,000.00*				
c	Booklet pane of 6	02/10/23	7.00	*3.00*			
d	Perf. 10 at top or bottom		*7,000.00*	*5,000.00*			
555	3¢ Lincoln	02/12/23	17.50	1.25	225.00 (6)	35.00	
556	4¢ Martha Washington	01/15/23	20.00	.50	225.00 (6)	60.00	
a	Vertical pair, imperf. horiz.		*10,500.00*				
b	Perf. 10, top or bottom		*3,000.00*	*15,000.00*			

Issue		Date	Un	U	PB	#	FDC	Q(M)
	America, Unwmk., Perf. 11							
557	5¢ Theodore Roosevelt	10/27/22	20.00	.30	250.00	(6)	*125.00*	
a	Imperf., pair		*1,500.00*					
b	Horizontal pair, imperf. vertically		—					
c	Perf. 10, top or bottom		—	*9,500.00*				
558	6¢ Garfield	11/20/22	35.00	1.00	400.00	(6)	225.00	
	Double transfer		55.00	2.00				
	Same, recut		55.00	2.00				
559	7¢ McKinley	05/01/23	8.50	.75	100.00	(6)	175.00	
560	8¢ Grant	05/01/23	50.00	1.00	575.00	(6)	175.00	
561	9¢ Jefferson	01/15/23	14.00	1.25	225.00	(6)	175.00	
562	10¢ Monroe	01/15/23	17.50	.35	275.00	(6)	175.00	
a	Vertical pair, imperf. horizontally			*2,250.00*				
b	Imperf., pair		*1,500.00*					
c	Perf. 10 at top or bottom			*5,500.00*				
563	11¢ Rutherford B. Hayes	10/04/22	1.40	.60	40.00	(6)	600.00	
a	Light bluish green		1.40	.60				
d	Imperf., pair			*20,000.00*				
564	12¢ Grover Cleveland	03/20/23	6.00	.35	90.00	(6)	175.00	
a	Horizontal pair, imperf. vertically			*1,750.00*				
565	14¢ American Indian	05/01/23	4.00	.90	60.00	(6)	400.00	
566	15¢ Statue of Liberty	11/11/22	20.00	.30	275.00	(6)	550.00	
567	20¢ Golden Gate	05/01/23	20.00	.30	275.00	(6)	*500.00*	
a	Horizontal pair, imperf. vertically			*2,000.00*				
568	25¢ Niagara Falls	11/11/22	18.00	.75	300.00	(6)	*650.00*	
b	Vertical pair, imperf. horizontally			*2,000.00*				
c	Perf. 10 at one side		*5,000.00*	*11,000.00*				
569	30¢ Buffalo	03/20/23	30.00	.60	275.00	(6)	*800.00*	
	Double transfer		55.00	—				
570	50¢ Arlington Amphitheater	11/11/22	47.50	.40	575.00	(6)	*1,250.00*	
571	$1 Lincoln Memorial	02/12/23	45.00	.65	325.00	(6)	*7,000.00*	
	Double transfer		95.00	1.60				
572	$2 U.S. Capitol	03/20/23	80.00	9.00	750.00	(6)	*17,500.00*	
573	$5 Head of Freedom, Capitol Dome	03/20/23	110.00	15.00	2,100.00	(8)	*32,500.00*	
a	Carmine lake and dark blue		200.00	20.00	2,750.00	(8)		
574	Not assigned							
	Imperf. (Design 19.25 x 22.25mm)							
575	1¢ Franklin (552)	03/20/23	5.25	5.00	70.00	(6)		
576	1½¢ Harding (553)	04/04/25	1.30	1.50	20.00	(6)	40.00	
577	2¢ Washington (554)		1.40	1.25	25.00	(6)		
	Perf. 11 x 10							
578	1¢ Franklin (552)	1923	85.00	*160.00*	800.00	(4)		
579	2¢ Washington (554)	1923	80.00	*140.00*	600.00	(4)		
	Recut in eye		*110.00*	*150.00*				

Issue		Date	Un	U	PB/LP	#	FDC	Q(M)
	Perf. 10							
580	Not assigned							
581	1¢ Franklin (552)	04/21/23	11.00	.75	150.00	(4)	*6,000.00*	
582	1½¢ Harding (553)	03/19/25	5.50	.65	65.00	(4)	40.00	
	Pair with full horiz. gutter between			*160.00*				
583	2¢ Washington (554)	04/14/24	2.75	.30	50.00	(4)		
a	Booklet pane of 6	08/27/26	95.00	*85.00*			*1,500.00*	
584	3¢ Lincoln (555)	08/01/25	30.00	3.00	275.00	(4)	50.00	
585	4¢ Martha Washington (556)	03/25	18.00	.65	275.00	(4)	50.00	
586	5¢ T. Roosevelt (557)	12/24	18.00	.40	275.00	(4)	57.50	
587	6¢ Garfield (558)	03/25	9.25	.60	175.00	(4)	60.00	
588	7¢ McKinley (559)	05/29/26	12.50	6.25	175.00	(4)	60.00	
589	8¢ Grant (560)	05/29/26	27.50	4.50	300.00	(4)	65.00	
590	9¢ Jefferson (561)	05/29/26	6.00	2.50	100.00	(4)	77.50	
591	10¢ Monroe (562)	06/08/25	60.00	.50	475.00	(4)	95.00	
592-593	Not assigned							
	Perf. 11							
594	1¢ Franklin (552), design 19.75 x 22.25mm	1923	*16,000.00*	6,750.00				
595	2¢ Washington (554), design 19.75 x 22.25mm	1923	275.00	*350.00*	2,150.00	(4)		
596	1¢ Franklin (552), design 19.25 x 22.5mm	1923		*120,000.00*				
	Coil, Perf. 10 Vertically							
597	1¢ Franklin (552)	07/18/23	.25	.20	2.00	(2)	*600.00*	
	Gripper cracks or double transfer		2.60	1.00				
598	1½¢ Harding (553)	03/19/25	.90	.20	4.50	(2)	60.00	
599	2¢ Washington (554) type I	01/23	.35	.20	2.25	(2)	*1,750.00*	
	Double transfer		1.90	1.00				
	Gripper cracks		2.30	2.00				
599A	2¢ Washington (554) type II	03/29	120.00	11.00	650.00	(2)		
600	3¢ Lincoln (555)	05/10/24	6.25	.20	22.50	(2)	80.00	
601	4¢ M. Washington (556)	08/05/23	3.75	.35	27.50	(2)		
602	5¢ T. Roosevelt (557)	03/05/24	1.50	.20	9.50	(2)	85.00	
603	10¢ Monroe (562)	12/01/24	3.50	.20	25.00	(2)	100.00	
	Coil, Perf. 10 Horizontally							
604	1¢ yellow green Franklin (552)	07/19/24	.30	.20	3.50	(2)	90.00	
605	1½¢ yellow brown Harding (553)	05/09/25	.30	.20	3.00	(2)	70.00	
606	2¢ carmine Washington (554)	12/31/23	.30	.20	2.25	(2)	125.00	
607-609	Not assigned							

557

558

559

560

561

562

563

564

565

566

567

568

569

570

571

572

573

599

Details

2¢ Washington, Types I-II, Series 1923-1929

Detail of #599, 634
Type I

No heavy hair lines at top center of head.

Detail of #599A, 634A
Type II

Three heavy hair lines at top center of head.

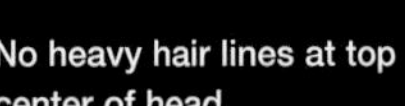

610 614 615 616 617 618

619 620 621 622 623 627 628

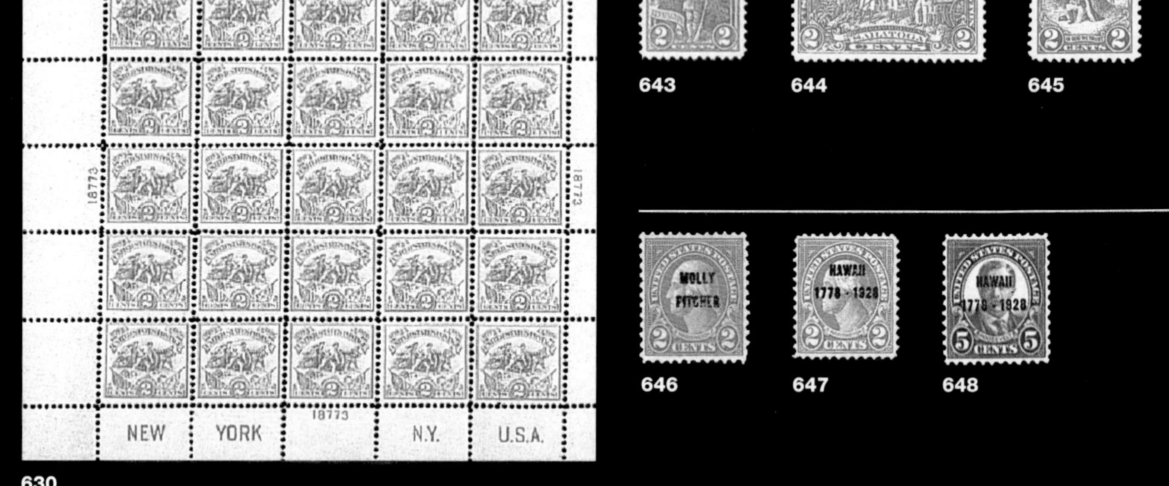

629 630 643 644 645

646 647 648

649 650 651 654 657

	Issue	Date	Un	U	PB	#	FDC	Q(M)
	Harding Memorial, Perf. 11							
610	2¢ Warren Gamaliel Harding	09/01/23	.55	.25	20.00	(6)	30.00	1,459
	Double transfer		1.75	.50				
a	Horizontal pair, imperf. vertically		*1,750.00*					
	Imperf.							
611	2¢ Harding (610)	11/15/23	5.25	4.00	70.00	(6)	90.00	0.8
	Perf. 10							
612	2¢ Harding (610)	09/12/23	15.00	1.75	300.00	(4)	100.00	100
	Perf. 11							
613	2¢ Harding (610)	1923		*42,500.00*				
	Huguenot-Walloon Tercentary, May 1, Perf. 11							
614	1¢ Ship *Nieu Nederland*	05/01/24	2.50	3.25	40.00	(6)	35.00	51
615	2¢ Walloons' Landing at Fort Orange (Albany)	01/05/24	4.75	2.25	55.00	(6)	50.00	78
	Double transfer		12.00	3.50				
616	5¢ Huguenot Monument to Jan Ribault at Duval County, Florida	01/05/24	20.00	13.00	225.00	(6)	75.00	6
	American Revolution Sesquitennial, Lexington-Concord, Perf. 11							
617	1¢ Washington at Cambridge	04/04/25	2.25	2.50	40.00	(6)	30.00	16
618	2¢ "The Birth of Liberty," by Henry Sandham	04/04/25	4.75	4.00	55.00	(6)	35.00	27
619	5¢ "The Minute Man," by Daniel Chester French	04/04/25	18.00	13.00	200.00	(6)	75.00	5
	Line over head		42.50	19.00				
	Norse-American, Perf. 11							
620	2¢ Sloop *Restaurationen*	05/18/25	4.00	3.00	200.00	(8)	20.00	9
621	5¢ Viking Ship	05/18/25	12.50	11.00	500.00	(8)	32.50	2
	Perf. 11							
622	13¢ Benjamin Harrison	01/11/26	12.50	.75	175.00	(6)	22.50	
623	17¢ Woodrow Wilson	12/28/25	14.00	.30	200.00	(6)	27.50	
624-626	Not assigned							
	American Revolution Sesquitennial, Perf. 11							
627	2¢ Independence Sesquicentennial Exposition	05/10/26	2.75	.50	37.50	(6)	10.00	308
	Perf. 11							
628	5¢ John Ericsson Memorial	05/29/26	6.25	3.25	75.00	(6)	30.00	20
	American Revolution Sesquitennial, Perf. 11							
629	2¢ Alexander Hamilton's Battery	10/18/26	2.10	1.70	35.00	(6)	6.25	41
	International Philatelic Exhibition Souvenir Sheet, Perf. 11							
630	2¢ Battle of White Plains, sheet of 25 with selvage inscription (629)	10/18/26	375.00	450.00			1,500.00	0.1
	Dot over first "S" of "States"		400.00	475.00				
631	1½¢ Harding (553)	08/27/26	1.90	1.70	57.50	(4)	35.00	
	Perf. 11 x 10.5							
632	1¢ Franklin (552)	06/10/27	.20	.20	2.00	(4)	45.00	
	Pair with full vertical gutter between		150.00	—				
a	Booklet pane of 6	11/02/27	5.00	*4.00*			*3,250.00*	
b	Vertical pair, imperf. between		*3,500.00*	*125.00*				
c	Horizontal pair, imperf. between		*5,000.00*					
633	1½¢ Harding (553)	05/17/27	1.70	.20	62.50	(4)	45.00	

	Issue	Date	Un	U	PB/LP	#	FDC	Q(M)
	Perf. 11 x 10.5							
634	2¢ Washington (554), type I	12/10/26	.20	.20	3.25	(4)	47.50	
	Pair with full vertical gutter between		200.00					
b	Carmine lake, type I		*900.00*	—				
c	Horizontal pair, imperf. between		*7,000.00*					
d	Booklet pane of 6	02/25/27	1.50	*1.50*				
634A	2¢ Washington (554), type II	12/28/27	350.00	13.50	2,000.00	(4)		
	Pair with full vertical or horizontal gutter between		700.00	—				
635	3¢ Lincoln (555)	02/03/27	.45	.20	17.50	(4)	47.50	
a	Bright violet Lincoln	02/07/34	.20	.20	11.00	(4)	25.00	
	Gripper cracks		3.25	2.00				
636	4¢ Martha Washington (556)	05/17/27	2.00	.20	75.00	(4)	50.00	
	Pair with full vertical gutter between		*200.00*					
637	5¢ T. Roosevelt (557)	03/24/27	2.00	.20	17.50	(4)	50.00	
	Pair with full vertical gutter between		*275.00*					
638	6¢ Garfield (558)	07/27/27	2.00	.20	15.00	(4)	57.50	
	Pair with full vert. gutter between		*200.00*					
639	7¢ black McKinley (559)	03/24/27	2.00	.20	15.00	(4)	57.50	
a	Vertical pair, imperf. between		*325.00*	*250.00*				
640	8¢ olive green Grant (560)	06/10/27	2.00	.20	14.00	(4)	67.50	
641	9¢ orange red Jefferson (561)	1931	2.00	.20	13.00	(4)	72.50	
642	10¢ orange Monroe (562)	02/03/27	3.25	.20	22.50	(4)	90.00	
	Perf. 11							
643	2¢ Vermont Sesquicentennial	08/03/27	1.30	.80	37.50	(6)	6.00	40
	American Revolution Sesquitennial, Perf. 11							
644	2¢ Burgoyne at Saratoga	08/03/27	3.75	2.10	32.50	(6)	12.50	26
645	2¢ Valley Forge	05/26/28	1.00	.50	25.00	(6)	4.00	101
	Perf. 11 x 10.5							
646	2¢ Battle of Monmouth/ Molly Pitcher	10/20/28	1.10	1.10	37.50	(4)	15.00	10
	Wide spacing, vertical pair		50.00	—				
	Hawaii Sesquicentennial, Perf. 11 x 10.5							
647	2¢ Washington (554)	08/13/28	4.50	4.50	150.00	(4)	15.00	6
	Wide spacing, vertical pair		125.00					
	Perf. 11 x 10.5							
648	5¢ T. Roosevelt (557)	08/13/28	12.50	13.50	275.00	(4)	22.50	1
	Aeronautics Conference, Perf. 11							
649	2¢ Wright Airplane	12/12/28	1.10	.80	10.00	(6)	7.00	51
650	5¢ Globe and Airplane	12/12/28	4.75	3.25	47.50	(6)	10.00	10
	Plate flaw "prairie dog"		27.50	12.50				
	American Revolution Sesquitennial, Perf. 11							
651	2¢ George Rogers Clark	02/25/29	.75	.50	10.50	(6)	6.00	17
	Double transfer		4.25	2.25				
652	Not assigned							
	Perf. 11 x 10.5							
653	½¢ Nathan Hale (551)	5/25/29	.20	.20	1.60	(4)	27.50	
	Electric Light's Golden Jubilee, Perf. 11							
654	2¢ Thomas Edison's First Lamp	06/05/29	.65	.70	22.50	(6)	10.00	32
	Perf. 11 x 10.5							
655	2¢ carmine rose (654)	06/11/29	.60	.20	35.00	(4)	80.00	210
	Coil, Perf. 10 Vertically							
656	2¢ carmine rose (654)	06/11/29	14.00	1.75	65.00	(2)	90.00	133
	American Revolution Sesquitennial, Perf. 11							
657	2¢ Sullivan Expedition	06/17/29	.65	.60	22.50	(6)	4.00	51
a	Lake		360.00		*2,750.00*	(6)		

	Issue	Date	Un	U	PB/LP	#	FDC	Q(M)
	Perf. 11 x 10.5 (#658-668 overprinted "Kans.,")							
658	1¢ Franklin	05/01/29	2.25	2.00	35.00	(4)	50.00	13
a	Vertical pair, one without overprint		*375.00*					
659	1½¢ Harding (553)	05/01/29	3.75	2.90	50.00	(4)	57.50	8
	Wide spacing, pair		70.00					
660	2¢ Washington (554)	05/01/29	4.25	1.00	45.00	(4)	57.50	87
661	3¢ Lincoln (555)	05/01/29	20.00	15.00	210.00	(4)	65.00	3
662	4¢ Martha Washington (556)	05/01/29	20.00	9.00	200.00	(4)	65.00	2
663	5¢ T. Roosevelt (557)	05/01/29	12.50	9.75	150.00	(4)	90.00	3
664	6¢ Garfield (558)	05/01/29	30.00	18.00	450.00	(4)	100.00	1
665	7¢ McKinley (559)	05/01/29	30.00	27.50	500.00	(4)	100.00	1
666	8¢ Grant (560)	05/01/29	95.00	70.00	775.00	(4)	125.00	2
667	9¢ Jefferson (561)	05/01/29	14.00	11.25	240.00	(4)	150.00	1
668	10¢ Monroe (562)	05/01/29	26.00	12.00	350.00	(4)	200.00	3
	#669-679 overprinted "Nebr."							
669	1¢ Franklin	05/01/29	3.75	2.25	50.00	(4)	50.00	8
a	Vertical pair, one without overprint		—					
670	1½¢ Harding (553)	05/01/29	3.50	2.50	52.50	(4)	52.50	9
671	2¢ Washington (554)	05/01/29	3.50	1.30	42.50	(4)	57.50	73
672	3¢ Lincoln (555)	05/01/29	13.50	12.00	175.00	(4)	70.00	2
673	4¢ Martha Washington (556)	05/01/29	20.00	15.00	250.00	(4)	75.00	2
	Wide spacing, pair		120.00					
674	5¢ T. Roosevelt (557)	05/01/29	18.00	15.00	275.00	(4)	75.00	2
675	6¢ Garfield (558)	05/01/29	42.50	24.00	525.00	(4)	100.00	1
676	7¢ McKinley (559)	05/01/29	22.50	18.00	300.00	(4)	100.00	0.8
677	8¢ Grant (560)	05/01/29	35.00	25.00	400.00	(4)	125.00	1
678	9¢ Jefferson (561)	05/01/29	40.00	27.50	525.00	(4)	150.00	0.5
679	10¢ Monroe (562)	05/01/29	120.00	22.50	925.00	(4)	200.00	2
	Warning: Excellent forgeries of the Kansas and Nebraska overprints exist.							
	American Revolution Sesquitennial, Perf. 11							
680	2¢ Battle of Fallen Timbers	09/14/29	.80	.80	22.50	(6)	3.50	29
681	2¢ Ohio River Canalization	10/19/29	.70	.65	15.00	(6)	3.50	33
682	2¢ Mass. Bay Colony	04/08/30	.60	.50	22.50	(6)	3.50	74
683	2¢ Gov. Joseph West and Chief Shadoo, a Kiowa	04/10/30	1.20	1.20	40.00	(6)	3.50	25
	Perf. 11 x 10.5							
684	1½¢ Warren G. Harding	12/01/30	.35	.20	2.10	(4)	4.50	
	Pair with full horizontal gutter between			*175.00*				
	Pair with full vertical gutter between			—				
685	4¢ William H. Taft	06/04/30	.90	.25	15.00	(4)	6.00	
	Gouge on right "4"		2.10	.60				
	Recut right "4"		2.10	.65				
	Pair with full horizontal gutter between		—					
	Coil, Perf. 10 Vertically							
686	1½¢ brn. Harding (684)	12/01/30	1.75	.20	6.50	(2)	5.00	
687	4¢ brown Taft (685)	09/18/30	3.25	.45	13.00	(2)	20.00	
	American Revolution Sesquitennial, Perf. 11							
688	2¢ Battle of Braddock's Field	07/09/30	1.00	.85	32.50	(6)	4.00	26
689	2¢ Gen. von Steuben	09/17/30	.55	.55	20.00	(6)	4.00	66
a	Imperf., pair		*2,750.00*		*12,500.00*	(6)		

	Issue	Date	Un	U	PB	#	FDC	Q(M)
	American Revolution Sesquitennial, Perf. 11							
690	2¢ General Pulaski	01/16/31	.30	.25	10.00	(6)	4.00	97
691	Not assigned							
	Perf. 11 x 10.5							
692	11¢ Hayes (563)	09/04/31	2.60	.25	14.00	(4)	100.00	
	Retouched forehead		20.00	1.00				
693	12¢ Cleveland (564)	08/25/31	5.25	.20	25.00	(4)	100.00	
694	13¢ Harrison (622)	09/04/31	2.00	.25	15.00	(4)	100.00	
695	14¢ American Indian (565)	09/08/31	3.75	.45	26.00	(4)	100.00	
696	15¢ Statue of Liberty (566)	08/27/31	8.00	.25	37.50	(4)	120.00	
	Perf. 10.5 x 11							
697	17¢ Wilson (623)	07/25/31	4.25	.25	37.50	(4)	*2,750.00*	
698	20¢ Golden Gate (567)	09/08/31	8.00	.25	37.50	(4)	300.00	
	Double transfer		20.00	—				
699	25¢ Niagara Falls (568)	07/25/31	8.50	.25	47.50	(4)	*2,000.00*	
700	30¢ Buffalo (569)	09/08/31	15.00	.25	75.00	(4)	300.00	
	Cracked plate		26.00	.85				
701	50¢ Arlington Amphitheater (570)	09/04/31	35.00	.25	180.00	(4)	400.00	
	Perf. 11							
702	2¢ "The Greatest Mother"	05/21/31	.25	.20	1.90	(4)	3.00	99
a	Red cross omitted		*40,000.00*					
	American Revolution Sesquitennial, Perf. 11							
703	2¢ Yorktown	10/19/31	.40	.25	2.30	(4)	3.50	25
a	Lake and black		4.50	.75				
b	Dark lake and black		*450.00*		*2,250.00*	(4)		
c	Pair, imperf. vertically		*5,000.00*					
	Washington Bicentennial, Perf. 11 x 10.5							
704	½¢ Portrait by Charles W. Peale	01/01/32	.20	.20	6.00	(4)	5.00 (4)	88
	Broken circle		.75	.20				
705	1¢ Bust by Jean Antoine Houdon	01/01/32	.20	.20	4.50	(4)	4.00 (2)	1,266
706	1½¢ Portrait by Charles W. Peale	01/01/32	.40	.20	17.50	(4)	4.00 (2)	305
707	2¢ Portrait by Gilbert Stuart	01/01/32	.20	.20	1.50	(4)	4.00	4,222
	Gripper cracks		1.75	.65				
708	3¢ Portrait by Charles W. Peale	01/01/32	.55	.20	17.50	(4)	4.00	456
709	4¢ Portrait by Charles P. Polk	01/01/32	.25	.20	5.50	(4)	4.00	151
	Broken bottom frame line		1.50	.50				
710	5¢ Portrait by Charles W. Peale	01/01/32	1.60	.20	16.50	(4)	4.00	171
	Cracked plate		5.25	1.10				
711	6¢ Portrait by John Trumbull	01/01/32	3.25	.20	52.50	(4)	4.00	112
712	7¢ Portrait by John Trumbull	01/01/32	.25	.20	9.00	(4)	4.00	83
713	8¢ Portrait by Charles B.J.F. Saint Memin	01/01/32	2.75	.50	50.00	(4)	4.50	97
714	9¢ Portrait by W. Williams	01/01/32	2.40	.20	35.00	(4)	4.50	76
715	10¢ Portrait by Gilbert Stuart	01/01/32	10.00	.20	90.00	(4)	4.50	147

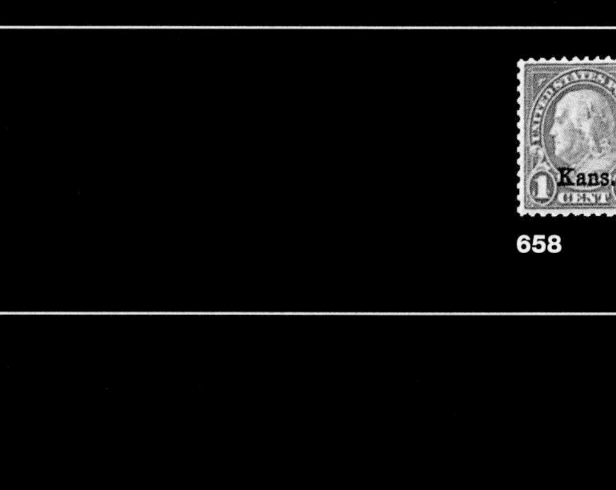

658 669 680 681 682 683

684 685 688 689 690

702 703 704 705 706

707 708 709 710 711

712 713 714 715

716

717

718

719

720

724

725

726

727

728

729

730

731

732

733

734

735

736

737

739

740

741

742

743

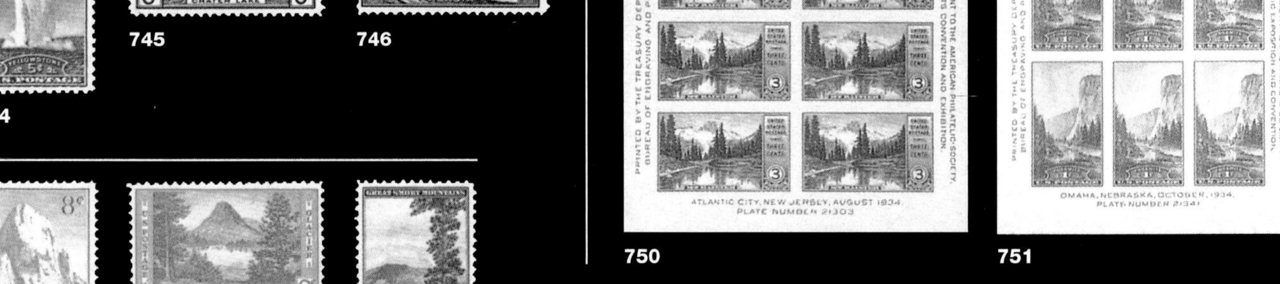

744

745

746

750

751

747

748

749

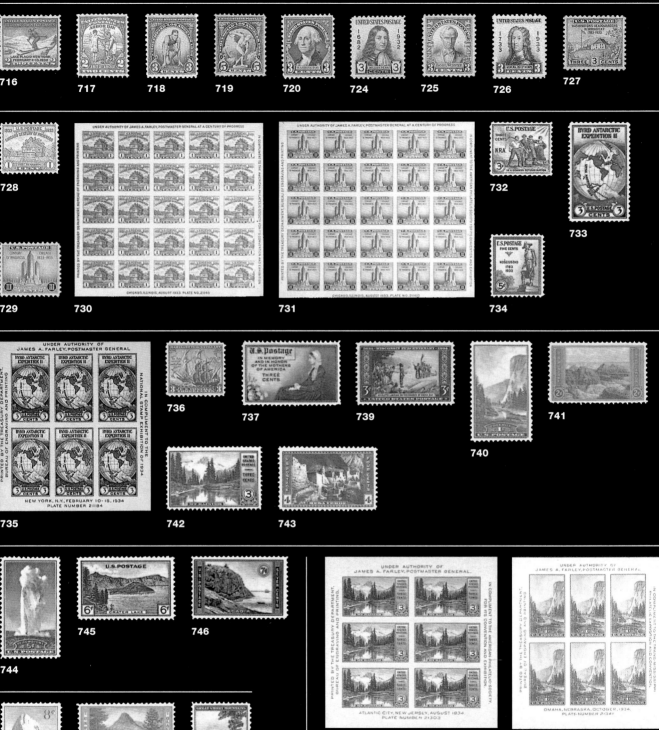

	Issue	Date	Un	U	PB/LP #	FDC	Q(M)
	Olympic Games, Perf. 11						
716	2¢ Ski Jumper	01/25/32	.40	.20	10.00 (6)	6.00	51
	Recut		3.50	1.50			
	Colored "snowball"		25.00	5.00			
	Perf. 11 x 10.5						
717	2¢ Arbor Day	04/22/32	.20	.20	6.00 (4)	4.00	100
	Olympic Games, Perf. 11 x 10.5						
718	3¢ Runner at Starting Mark	06/15/32	1.40	.20	12.00 (4)	6.00	169
	Gripper cracks		4.25	.75			
719	5¢ Myron's Discobolus	06/15/32	2.20	.20	20.00 (4)	8.00	52
	Gripper cracks		4.25	1.00			
	Perf. 11 x 10.5						
720	3¢ Washington	06/16/32	.20	.20	1.30 (4)	7.50	
	Pair with full vertical or horizontal gutter between		*200.00*				
	Recut lines on face		2.00	.75			
b	Booklet pane of 6	07/25/32	35.00	*12.50*		100.00	
c	Vertical pair, imperf. between		*700.00*	*1,350.00*			
	Coil, Perf. 10 Vertically						
721	3¢ Washington (720)	06/24/32	2.75	.20	10.00 (2)	15.00	
	Coil, Perf. 10 Horizontally						
722	3¢ Washington (720)	10/12/32	1.50	.35	6.25 (2)	15.00	
	Coil, Perf. 10 Vertically						
723	6¢ Garfield (558)	08/18/32	11.00	.30	60.00 (2)	15.00	
	Perf. 11						
724	3¢ William Penn	10/24/32	.35	.20	8.00 (6)	3.25	50
725	3¢ Daniel Webster	10/24/32	.35	.25	16.50 (6)	3.25	50
726	3¢ Georgia Settlement	02/12/33	.35	.20	10.00 (6)	3.25	62
	American Revolution Sesquitennial, Perf. 10.5 x 11						
727	3¢ Peace of 1783	04/19/33	.20	.20	3.75 (4)	3.50	73
	Century of Progress, Perf. 10.5 x 11						
728	1¢ Restoration of Fort Dearborn	05/25/33	.20	.20	1.90 (4)	3.00 (3)	348
	Gripper cracks		2.00	—			
729	3¢ Federal Building at Chicago	05/25/33	.25	.20	2.40 (4)	3.00	480
	American Philatelic Society Souvenir Sheets, Without Gum, Imperf.						
730	1¢ sheet of 25 (728)	08/25/33	27.50	27.50		100.00	0.4
a	Single stamp		.75	.50	3.25 (3)		11
731	3¢ sheet of 25 (729)	08/25/33	25.00	25.00		100.00	0.4
a	Single stamp from sheet		.65	.50		3.25	11
	Perf. 10.5 x 11						
732	3¢ National Recovery Act	08/15/33	.20	.20	1.50 (4)	3.25	1,978
	Gripper cracks		1.50	—			
	Recut at right		2.00				
	Perf. 11						
733	3¢ Byrd Antarctic Expedition II	10/09/33	.50	.50	12.00 (6)	10.00	6
	Double transfer		2.75	1.00			
	American Revolution Sesquitennial, Perf. 11						
734	5¢ General Tadeusz Kosciuszko	10/13/33	.55	.25	27.50 (6)	4.50	45
a	Horizontal pair, imperf. vertically		*2,250.00*		*25,000.00* (8)		

	Issue	Date	Un	U	PB #	FDC	Q(M)
	National Stamp Exhibition Souvenir Sheet, Without Gum, Imperf.						
735	3¢ Byrd sheet of 6 (733)	02/10/34	12.00	10.00		40.00	0.8
a	Single stamp from sheet		1.90	1.65		5.00	5
	Perf. 11						
736	3¢ Maryland Tercentenary	03/23/34	.20	.20	6.00 (6)	1.60	46
	Perf. 11 x 10.5						
737	3¢ Portrait of his Mother, by James A. McNeill Whistler	05/02/34	.20	.20	1.00 (4)	1.60	193
	Perf. 11						
738	3¢ Portrait of his Mother, by James A. McNeill Whistler (737)	05/02/34	.20	.20	4.25 (6)	1.60	15
739	3¢ Wisconsin Tercentenary	07/07/34	.20	.20	2.90 (6)	1.10	64
a	Vert. pair, imperf. horizontally		*350.00*				
b	Horiz. pair, imperf. vertically		*500.00*		*2,000.00* (6)		
	National Parks, Unwmkd., Perf. 11						
740	1¢ El Capitan, Yosemite (California)	07/16/34	.20	.20	1.00 (6)	2.25	85
	Recut		1.50	.50			
a	Vertical pair, imperf. horizontally, with gum		*1,300.00*				
741	2¢ Grand Canyon (Arizona)	07/24/34	.20	.20	1.25 (6)	2.25	74
	Double transfer		1.25	—			
a	Vertical pair, imperf. horizontally, with gum		*475.00*				
b	Horizontal pair, imperf. vertically, with gum		*575.00*				
742	3¢ Mt. Rainier, and Mirror Lake, (Washington)	08/03/34	.20	.20	1.75 (6)	2.50	95
a	Vertical pair, imperf. horizontally, with gum		*700.00*				
743	4¢ Cliff Palace, Mesa Verde (Colorado)	09/25/34	.35	.40	7.00 (6)	2.25	19
a	Vertical pair, imperf. horizontally, with gum		*1,000.00*				
744	5¢ Old Faithful, Yellowstone (Wyoming)	07/30/34	.70	.65	8.75 (6)	2.25	31
a	Horizontal pair, imperf. vertically, with gum		*600.00*				
745	6¢ Crater Lake (Oregon)	09/05/34	1.10	.85	15.00 (6)	3.00	17
746	7¢ Great Head, Acadia Park (Maine)	10/02/34	.60	.75	10.00 (6)	3.00	16
a	Horizontal pair, imperf. vertically, with gum		*600.00*				
747	8¢ Great White Throne, Zion Park (Utah)	09/18/34	1.60	1.50	15.00 (6)	3.25	15
748	9¢ Glacier National Park (Montana)	08/27/34	1.50	.65	14.00 (6)	3.50	17
749	10¢ Great Smoky Mountains (North Carolina)	10/08/34	3.00	1.25	22.50 (6)	6.00	19
	American Philatelic Society Souvenir Sheet, Imperf.						
750	3¢ sheet of 6 (742)	08/28/34	30.00	27.50		40.00	0.5
a	Single stamp		3.50	3.25		3.25	3
	Trans-Mississippi Philatelic Exposition Souvenir Sheet						
751	1¢ sheet of 6 (740)	10/10/34	12.50	12.50		35.00	0.8
a	Single stamp		1.40	1.60	3.25 (3)		5

	Issue	Date	Un	U	PB #	FDC	Q(M)
	American Revolution Sesquitennial, Special Printing (#752-771), **Without Gum, Unwmk., Perf. 10.5 x 11**						
752	3¢ Peace of 1783 (727)	03/15/35	.20	.20	27.50 (4)	5.00	3
	Perf. 11						
753	3¢ Byrd Expedition II (733)	03/15/35	.50	.45	20.00 (6)	6.00	2
	Imperf.						
754	3¢ Whistler's Mother (737)	03/15/35	.60	.60	14.00 (6)	6.00	2
755	3¢ Wisconsin (739)	03/15/35	.60	.60	14.00 (6)	6.00	2
	National Parks, Imperf.						
756	1¢ Yosemite (740)	03/15/35	.20	.20	4.00 (6)	6.00	3
757	2¢ Grand Canyon (741)	03/15/35	.25	.25	5.75 (6)	6.00	3
758	3¢ Mt. Rainier (742)	03/15/35	.50	.45	14.00 (6)	6.00	2
759	4¢ Mesa Verde (743)	03/15/35	.95	.95	20.00 (6)	6.50	2
760	5¢ Yellowstone (744)	03/15/35	1.50	1.40	25.00 (6)	6.50	2
761	6¢ Crater Lake (745)	03/15/35	2.40	2.25	37.50 (6)	6.50	2
762	7¢ Acadia (746)	03/15/35	1.50	1.40	30.00 (6)	6.50	2
763	8¢ Zion (747)	03/15/35	1.60	1.50	37.50 (6)	7.50	2
764	9¢ Glacier (748)	03/15/35	1.90	1.75	42.50 (6)	7.50	2
765	10¢ Smoky Mts. (749)	03/15/35	3.75	3.50	50.00 (6)	7.50	2
	Imperf.						
766	1¢ Restoration of Fort Dearborn (728), pane of 25	03/15/35	25.00	25.00		*250.00*	0.1
a	Single stamp		.70	.50		5.50 (3)	2
767	3¢ Federal Building, Chicago (729), pane of 25	03/15/35	23.50	23.50		*250.00*	0.1
a	Single stamp		.60	.50		5.50	2
768	3¢ Byrd Antarctic Expedition II (733), pane of 6	03/15/35	20.00	15.00		*250.00*	0.3
a	Single stamp		2.80	2.40		6.50	2
769	1¢ El Capitan, Yosemite (California) (740), pane of 6	03/15/35	12.50	11.00		*250.00*	0.3
a	Single stamp		1.85	1.80		4.00	2
770	3¢ Cliff Palace, Mesa Verde (Colorado) (742), pane of 6	03/15/35	30.00	24.00		*250.00*	0.2
a	Single stamp from pane		3.25	3.10		5.00	1
771	6¢ Great Seal of U.S.	03/15/35	2.40	2.40	50.00 (6)	12.50	1

	Issue	Date	Un	U	PB #	FDC	Q(M)
	Unwmk., Perf. 11 x 10.5						
	Beginning with #772, unused values are for never-hinged stamps.						
772	3¢ Connecticut Tercentenary	04/26/35	.25	.20	1.75 (4)	10.00	71
	Defect in cent design		1.00	.25			
773	3¢ California Pacific International Expo	05/29/35	.25	.20	1.10 (4)	10.00	101
	Unwmk., Perf. 11						
774	3¢ Boulder Dam	09/30/35	.20	.20	1.65 (6)	10.00	74
	Unwmk., Perf. 11 x 10.5						
775	3¢ Michigan Centenary	11/01/35	.25	.20	1.25 (4)	10.00	76
776	3¢ Texas Centennial	03/02/36	.25	.20	1.25 (4)	17.50	124
	Unwmk., Perf. 10.5 x 11						
777	3¢ Rhode Island Tercentenary	05/04/36	.35	.20	1.50 (4)	9.00	67
	Pair with full gutter between		*200.00*				
	Third International Philatelic Exhibition Souvenir Sheet, Unwmk., Imperf.						
778	Sheet of 4 different stamps (#772, 773, 775 and 776)	05/09/36	1.75	1.75		13.00	3
a-d	Single stamp from sheet		.40	.35			3
	779-781 Not assigned						
	Unwmk., Perf. 11 x 10.5						
782	3¢ Arkansas Statehood	06/15/36	.30	.20	1.30 (4)	12.00	73
783	3¢ Oregon Territory	07/14/36	.20	.20	1.10 (4)	8.50	74
	Double transfer		1.00	.50			
784	3¢ Susan B. Anthony	08/26/36	.20	.20	.75 (4)	12.00	270
	Period missing after "B"		.75	.25			

A number of position pieces can be collected from the panes or sheets of the 1935 Special Printing issues, including horizontal and vertical gutter (#752, 766-770) or line (#753-765, 771) blocks of four (HG/L and VG/L), arrow-and-guideline blocks of four (AGL) and crossed-gutter or centerline blocks of four (CG/L). Pairs sell for half the price of blocks of four. Arrow-and-guideline blocks are top or bottom only.

	HG/L	VG/L	AGL	CG/L
752	5.75	9.50		50.00
753	2.25	25.00	52.50	67.50
754	1.75	1.40	3.00	7.25
755	1.75	1.40	3.00	7.25
756	.45	.55	1.25	3.00
757	.70	.55	1.25	3.50
758	1.40	1.25	2.75	5.25
759	2.75	2.25	4.75	8.50
760	3.50	4.25	9.00	15.00
761	6.50	5.50	12.50	20.00
762	4.25	3.75	8.25	14.00
763	3.75	4.75	11.00	17.50
764	5.00	4.50	10.50	22.50
765	9.00	10.50	24.00	30.00
766	5.50	7.00		15.00
767	5.25	6.75		15.00
768	7.50	9.00		20.00
769	6.00	9.00		15.00
770	12.50	11.00		30.00
771	6.50	5.50	12.50	60.00

Gutter Block 752

Centerline Block 754

Cross-Gutter Block 768

Line Block 756

Arrow Block 763

772

773

774

775

776

777

778

782

783

784

785 786 787 788 789

790 791 792 793 794

795  796  798  799  800 801

802 803 804 805 806 807 808 809

810 811 812 813 814 815 816 817 818

819 820 821 822 823 824 825 826 827

828 829 830 831 832 833 834

	Issue	Date	Un	U	PB #	FDC	Q(M)
	Army, Unwmk., Perf. 11 x 10.5						
785	1¢ George Washington, Nathanael Greene and Mount Vernon	12/15/36	.20	.20	.85 (4)	6.00	105
786	2¢ Andrew Jackson, Winfield Scott and The Hermitage	01/15/37	.20	.20	.85 (4)	6.00	94
787	3¢ Generals Sherman, Grant and Sheridan	02/18/37	.20	.20	1.50 (4)	6.00	88
788	4¢ Generals Robert E. Lee and "Stonewall" Jackson and Stratford Hall	03/23/37	.30	.20	8.00 (4)	6.00	36
789	5¢ U.S. Military Academy at West Point	05/26/37	.60	.25	8.50 (4)	6.00	37
	Navy, Unwmk., Perf. 11 x 10.5						
790	1¢ John Paul Jones, John Barry, *Bon Homme Richard* and *Lexington*	12/15/36	.20	.20	.85 (4)	6.00	105
791	2¢ Stephen Decatur, Thomas MacDonough and *Saratoga*	01/15/37	.20	.20	.75 (4)	6.00	92
792	3¢ David G. Farragut and David D. Porter, *Hartford* and *Powhatan*	02/18/37	.20	.20	1.00 (4)	6.00	93
793	4¢ Admirals William T. Sampson, George Dewey and Winfield S. Schley	03/23/37	.30	.20	9.00 (4)	6.00	35
794	5¢ Seal of U.S. Naval Academy and Naval Cadets	05/26/37	.60	.25	9.00 (4)	6.00	37
	Perf. 11 x 10.5						
795	3¢ Northwest Territory Ordinance	07/13/37	.25	.20	1.10 (4)	9.00	85
	Unwmk., Perf. 11						
796	5¢ Virginia Dare and Parents	08/18/37	.20	.20	6.50 (6)	11.00	25
	Society of Philatelic Americans Souvenir Sheet, Unwmk., Imperf.						
797	10¢ blue green (749)	08/26/37	.60	.40		10.00	5
	Perf. 11 x 10.5						
798	3¢ Constitution Sesquicentennial	09/17/37	.35	.20	1.50 (4)	9.00	100
	Territorial, Unwmk., Perf. 10.5 x 11						
799	3¢ Hawaii	10/18/37	.25	.20	1.25 (4)	10.00	78
	Territorial, Perf. 11 x 10.5						
800	3¢ Alaska	11/12/37	.25	.20	1.25 (4)	10.00	77
801	3¢ Puerto Rico	11/25/37	.25	.20	1.25 (4)	10.00	81
802	3¢ Virgin Islands	12/15/37	.25	.20	1.25 (4)	10.00	76
	Pair with full vertical gutter between		*275.00*				
	Presidential, Unwmk., Perf. 11 x 10.5						
	(#804b, 806b, 807a issued in 1939, 832b in 1951, 832c in 1954, rest in 1938)						
803	½¢ Benjamin Franklin	05/19/38	.20	.20	.40 (4)	3.00	
804	1¢ George Washington	04/25/38	.20	.20	.30 (4)	3.00	
	Pair with full vertical gutter between		*160.00*	—			
b	Booklet pane of 6	01/27/39	2.00	*.50*			

	Issue	Date	Un	U	PB #	FDC	Q(M)
	Presidential continued, **Unwmk., Perf. 11 x 10.5**						
805	1½¢ Martha Washington	05/05/38	.20	.20	.30 (4)	3.00	
	Pair with full horizontal gutter between		*175.00*				
b	Horizontal pair, imperf. between		160.00	20.00			
806	2¢ John Adams	06/03/38	.20	.20	.30 (4)	3.00	
	Recut at top of head		3.00	1.50			
b	Booklet pane of 6	01/27/39	4.75	*.85*		15.00	
807	3¢ Thomas Jefferson	06/16/38	.20	.20	.30 (4)	3.00	
a	Booklet pane of 6	01/27/39	8.50	*2.00*		17.50	
b	Horizontal pair, imperf. between		*1,500.00*	—			
c	Imperf., pair		*2,750.00*				
808	4¢ James Madison	07/01/38	.75	.20	2.50 (4)	3.00	
809	4½¢ The White House	07/11/38	.20	.20	1.50 (4)	3.00	
810	5¢ James Monroe	07/21/38	.20	.20	1.00 (4)	3.00	
811	6¢ John Quincy Adams	07/28/38	.20	.20	1.00 (4)	3.00	
812	7¢ Andrew Jackson	08/04/38	.35	.20	1.50 (4)	3.00	
813	8¢ Martin Van Buren	08/11/38	.30	.20	1.40 (4)	3.00	
814	9¢ William H. Harrison	08/18/38	.30	.20	1.40 (4)	3.00	
	Pair with full vertical gutter between		—				
815	10¢ John Tyler	09/02/38	.25	.20	1.25 (4)	3.00	
816	11¢ James K. Polk	09/08/38	.65	.20	3.00 (4)	5.00	
817	12¢ Zachary Taylor	09/14/38	.90	.20	4.00 (4)	5.00	
818	13¢ Millard Fillmore	09/22/38	1.25	.20	7.00 (4)	5.00	
819	14¢ Franklin Pierce	10/06/38	.90	.20	4.50 (4)	5.00	
820	15¢ James Buchanan	10/13/38	.40	.20	1.90 (4)	5.00	
821	16¢ Abraham Lincoln	10/20/38	.90	.25	6.00 (4)	7.00	
822	17¢ Andrew Johnson	10/27/38	.90	.20	4.50 (4)	6.00	
823	18¢ Ulysses S. Grant	11/03/38	1.75	.20	8.75 (4)	6.00	
824	19¢ Rutherford B. Hayes	11/10/38	1.25	.35	6.25 (4)	6.00	
825	20¢ James A. Garfield	11/10/38	.70	.20	3.50 (4)	7.00	
826	21¢ Chester A. Arthur	11/22/38	1.25	.20	7.50 (4)	7.00	
827	22¢ Grover Cleveland	11/22/38	1.00	.40	9.00 (4)	8.00	
828	24¢ Benjamin Harrison	12/02/38	3.50	.20	15.00 (4)	8.00	
829	25¢ William McKinley	12/02/38	.75	.20	3.25 (4)	8.00	
830	30¢ Theodore Roosevelt	12/08/38	3.50	.20	15.00 (4)	9.00	
a	Blue		15.00	—			
831	50¢ William Howard Taft	12/08/38	5.00	.20	22.50 (4)	12.50	
	Perf. 11						
832	$1 Woodrow Wilson	08/29/38	6.50	.20	31.50 (4)	50.00	
a	Vertical pair, imperf. horizontally		*1,500.00*				
b	Watermarked "USIR"	1951	175.00	65.00	*1,650* (4)		
c	$1 red violet and black	08/31/54	6.00	.20	30.00 (4)	25.00	
d	As "c," vert. pair, imperf. horiz.		*1,500.00*				
e	Vertical pair, imperf. between		*2,750.00*				
f	As "c," vert. pair, imperf. between		*8,500.00*				
833	$2 Warren G. Harding	09/29/38	18.00	3.75	95.00 (4)	100.00	
834	$5 Calvin Coolidge	11/17/38	85.00	3.00	375.00 (4)	175.00	
a	$5 red, brown and black		*3,000.00*	*7,000.00*			

	Issue	Date	Un	U	PB/LP #	FDC	Q(M)
	Perf. 11 x 10.5						
835	3¢ Constitution Ratification	06/21/38	.45	.20	3.50 (4)	15.00	73
	Perf. 11						
836	3¢ Swedish-Finnish Tercentenary	06/27/38	.30	.20	2.25 (6)	15.00	59
	Perf. 11 x 10.5						
837	3¢ Northwest Territory Sesquicentennial	07/15/38	.30	.20	6.00 (4)	15.00	66
838	3¢ Iowa Territorial Centennial	08/24/38	.25	.20	6.00 (4)	15.00	47
	Coil, Perf. 10 Vertically						
839	1¢ Washington (804)	01/20/39	.30	.20	1.40 (2)	4.75	
840	1½¢ Martha Washington (805)	01/20/39	.30	.20	1.50 (2)	4.75	
841	2¢ John Adams (806)	01/20/39	.40	.20	1.75 (2)	4.75	
842	3¢ Jefferson (807)	01/20/39	.50	.20	2.00 (2)	4.75	
	Thin, translucent paper		2.50	—			
843	4¢ Madison (808)	01/20/39	7.50	.40	27.50 (2)	5.00	
844	4½¢ White House (809)	01/20/38	.70	.40	5.00 (2)	5.00	
845	5¢ James Monroe 810)	01/20/39	5.00	.35	27.50 (2)	5.00	
846	6¢ John Quincy Adams (811)	01/20/39	1.10	.20	7.50 (2)	6.50	
847	10¢ John Tyler (815)	01/20/39	11.00	.50	42.50 (2)	9.00	
	Coil, Perf. 10 Horizontally						
848	1¢ Washington (804)	01/27/39	.85	.20	2.75 (2)	5.00	
849	1½¢ Martha Washington (805)	01/27/39	1.25	.30	4.50 (2)	5.00	
850	2¢ John Adams (806)	01/27/39	2.50	.40	6.50 (2)	5.00	
851	3¢ Thomas Jefferson (807)	01/27/39	2.50	.40	7.25 (2)	5.50	
	Perf. 10.5 x 11						
852	3¢ Golden Gate Exposition	02/18/39	.25	.20	1.25 (4)	15.00	114
853	3¢ New York World's Fair	04/01/39	.30	.20	1.75 (4)	15.00	102
	Perf. 11						
854	3¢ Washington's Inauguration	04/30/39	.55	.20	3.50 (6)	15.00	73
	Perf. 11 x 10.5						
855	3¢ Baseball Centennial	06/12/39	1.75	.20	7.50 (4)	35.00	81
	Perf. 11						
856	3¢ Panama Canal	08/15/39	.30	.20	3.25 (6)	17.50	68
	Perf. 10.5 x 11						
857	3¢ Printing	09/25/39	.20	.20	.90 (4)	14.00	71
	Perf. 11 x 10.5						
858	3¢ 50th Anniversary of Statehood (Montana, North Dakota, South Dakota, Washington)	11/02/39	.20	.20	1.10 (4)	12.50	67

	Issue	Date	Un	U	PB/LP #	FDC	Q(M)
	Famous Americans, Perf. 10.5 x 11						
	Authors						
859	1¢ Washington Irving	01/29/40	.20	.20	.95 (4)	3.00	56
860	2¢ James Fenimore Cooper	01/29/40	.20	.20	.95 (4)	3.00	53
861	3¢ Ralph Waldo Emerson	02/05/40	.20	.20	1.25 (4)	3.00	53
862	5¢ Louisa May Alcott	02/05/40	.30	.20	8.25 (4)	4.00	22
863	10¢ Samuel L. Clemens (Mark Twain)	02/13/40	1.65	1.20	32.50 (4)	8.00	13
	Poets						
864	1¢ Henry W. Longfellow	02/16/40	.20	.20	1.75 (4)	3.00	52
865	2¢ John Greenleaf Whittier	02/16/40	.20	.20	1.75 (4)	3.00	52
866	3¢ James Russell Lowell	02/20/40	.20	.20	2.25 (4)	3.00	52
867	5¢ Walt Whitman	02/20/40	.35	.20	9.50 (4)	4.00	22
868	10¢ James Whitcomb Riley	02/24/40	1.75	1.25	30.00 (4)	6.00	12
	Educators						
869	1¢ Horace Mann	03/14/40	.20	.20	1.90 (4)	3.00	52
870	2¢ Mark Hopkins	03/14/40	.20	.20	1.50 (4)	3.00	52
871	3¢ Charles W. Eliot	03/28/40	.20	.20	1.75 (4)	3.00	52
872	5¢ Frances E. Willard	03/28/40	.40	.20	9.00 (4)	4.00	21
873	10¢ Booker T. Washington	04/07/40	1.50	1.10	27.50 (4)	10.00	14
	Scientists						
874	1¢ John James Audubon	04/08/40	.20	.20	.85 (4)	3.00	59
875	2¢ Dr. Crawford W. Long	04/08/40	.20	.20	.95 (4)	3.00	58
876	3¢ Luther Burbank	04/17/40	.20	.20	1.10 (4)	3.00	58
877	5¢ Dr. Walter Reed	04/17/40	.25	.20	5.00 (4)	4.00	24
878	10¢ Jane Addams	04/26/40	1.10	.85	16.00 (4)	6.00	15
	Composers						
879	1¢ Stephen Collins Foster	05/03/40	.20	.20	.95 (4)	3.00	57
880	2¢ John Philip Sousa	05/03/40	.20	.20	1.00 (4)	4.00	58
881	3¢ Victor Herbert	05/13/40	.20	.20	1.10 (4)	3.00	56
882	5¢ Edward A. MacDowell	05/13/40	.40	.20	9.25 (4)	4.00	21
883	10¢ Ethelbert Nevin	06/10/40	3.75	1.35	32.50 (4)	6.00	13
	Artists						
884	1¢ Gilbert Charles Stuart	09/05/40	.20	.20	1.00 (4)	3.00	54
885	2¢ James A. McNeill Whistler	09/05/40	.20	.20	.95 (4)	3.00	54
886	3¢ Augustus Saint-Gaudens	09/16/40	.20	.20	1.00 (4)	3.00	55
887	5¢ Daniel Chester French	09/16/40	.50	.20	8.00 (4)	4.00	22
888	10¢ Frederic Remington	09/30/40	1.75	1.25	20.00 (4)	7.00	14
	Inventors						
889	1¢ Eli Whitney	10/07/40	.20	.20	2.10 (4)	3.00	48
890	2¢ Samuel F.B. Morse	10/07/40	.20	.20	1.25 (4)	3.00	53
891	3¢ Cyrus Hall McCormick	10/14/40	.25	.20	1.75 (4)	3.00	54
892	5¢ Elias Howe	10/14/40	1.10	.30	12.50 (4)	4.00	20
893	10¢ Alexander Graham Bell	10/28/40	11.00	2.00	57.50 (4)	10.00	14

835 836 837 838 852 853 854

855 856 857 858 859 860 861

862 863 864 865 866 867 868 869

870 871 872 873 874 875 876 877

878 879 880 881 882 883 884 885

886 887 888 889 890 891 892 893

894

895

896

897

898

899

900

901

902

903

904

905

906

907

908

909

910

911

912

913

914

915

916

917

918

919

920

921

922

923

924

925

926

	Issue	Date	Un	U	PB	#	FDC	Q(M)
	Perf. 11 x 10.5							
894	3¢ Pony Express	04/03/40	.40	.20	2.75	(4)	10.00	46
	Perf. 10.5 x 11							
895	3¢ Pan American Union	04/14/40	.30	.20	2.75	(4)	7.00	48
	Perf. 11 x 10.5							
896	3¢ Idaho Statehood	07/03/40	.20	.20	1.75	(4)	7.00	51
	Perf. 10.5 x 11							
897	3¢ Wyoming Statehood	07/10/40	.25	.20	1.50	(4)	7.00	50
	Perf. 11 x 10.5							
898	3¢ Coronado Expedition	09/07/40	.25	.20	1.50	(4)	7.00	61
	Win the War, Perf. 11 x 10.5							
899	1¢ Statue of Liberty	10/16/40	.20	.20	.45	(4)	5.00	
	Cracked plate		3.00					
	Gripper cracks		3.00					
a	Vertical pair, imperf. between		*650.00*	—				
b	Horizontal pair, imperf. between		35.00	—				
900	2¢ 90mm Anti-aircraft Gun	10/16/40	.20	.20	.45	(4)	5.00	
a	Horizontal pair, imperf. between		40.00	—				
	Pair with full vertical gutter between		*275.00*					
901	3¢ Torch of Enlightenment	10/16/40	.20	.20	.60	(4)	5.00	
a	Horizontal pair, imperf. between		25.00	—				
	Win the War, Perf. 10.5 x 11							
902	3¢ Thirteenth Amendment	10/20/40	.25	.20	3.00	(4)	10.00	44
	Win the War, Perf. 11 x 10.5							
903	3¢ Vermont Statehood	03/04/41	.35	.20	1.75	(4)	10.00	55
904	3¢ Kentucky Statehood	06/01/42	.25	.20	1.25	(4)	6.50	64
905	3¢ Win the War	07/04/42	.20	.20	.40	(4)	6.50	
	Pair with full vertical or horizontal gutter between		*175.00*					
b	3¢ purple			*500.00*				

	Issue	Date	Un	U	PB	#	FDC	Q(M)
	Win the War, Perf. 11 x 10.5							
906	5¢ Chinese Resistance	07/07/42	.85	.20	9.00	(4)	12.00	21
907	2¢ Allied Nations	01/14/43	.20	.20	.30	(4)	5.50	1,700
	Pair with full vertical or horizontal gutter between		*225.00*					
908	1¢ Four Freedoms	02/12/43	.20	.20	.60	(4)	5.50	1,200
	Overrun Countries, Perf. 12							
909	5¢ Poland	06/22/43	.20	.20	3.50*	(4)	5.00	20
910	5¢ Czechoslovakia	07/12/43	.20	.20	2.75*	(4)	4.00	20
911	5¢ Norway	07/27/43	.20	.20	1.30*	(4)	4.00	20
912	5¢ Luxembourg	08/10/43	.20	.20	1.20*	(4)	4.00	20
913	5¢ Netherlands	08/24/43	.20	.20	1.20*	(4)	4.00	20
914	5¢ Belgium	09/14/43	.20	.20	1.10*	(4)	4.00	20
915	5¢ France	09/28/43	.20	.20	1.25*	(4)	4.00	20
916	5¢ Greece	10/12/43	.35	.25	10.00*	(4)	4.00	15
917	5¢ Yugoslavia	10/26/43	.25	.20	4.25*	(4)	4.00	15
918	5¢ Albania	11/09/43	.20	.20	4.25*	(4)	4.00	15
919	5¢ Austria	11/23/43	.20	.20	3.50*	(4)	4.00	15
920	5¢ Denmark	12/07/43	.20	.20	5.25*	(4)	4.00	15
921	5¢ Korea	11/02/44	.20	.20	4.50*	(4)	5.00	15
	"KORPA" plate flaw		17.50	12.50				
	*Instead of plate numbers, the selvage is inscribed with the name of the country.							
	Perf. 11 x 10.5							
922	3¢ Transcontinental Railroad	05/10/44	.20	.20	1.40	(4)	9.00	61
923	3¢ Steamship	05/22/44	.20	.20	1.25	(4)	7.50	61
924	3¢ Telegraph	05/24/44	.20	.20	.90	(4)	7.50	61
	Win the War, Perf. 11 x 10.5							
925	3¢ Philippine	09/27/44	.20	.20	1.10	(4)	7.50	50
	Perf. 11 x 10.5							
926	3¢ Motion Pictures	10/31/44	.20	.20	.90	(4)	8.00	53

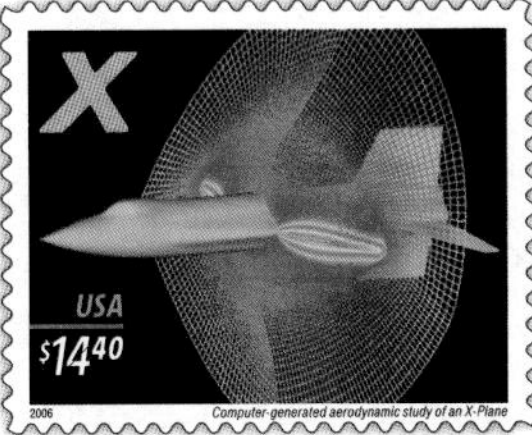

X-PLANES

In 2006, the U.S. Postal Service issued new Priority Mail and Express Mail stamps commemorating X-Planes, a series of experimental vehicles that have helped to extend the nation's leadership in cutting-edge aerospace technologies. Since 1946, these vehicles—first built by companies such as Bell, Douglas, Northrop, and North American Aviation—have involved the U.S. military and the National Aeronautics and Space Administration (NASA). The term "X-plane" is derived from the U.S. military designation for experimental aircraft. These highly specialized aircraft are built in very small numbers. Each X-plane is created with specific research objectives in mind. Some are intended for speeds and altitudes otherwise unreachable by conventional aircraft; others are created to evaluate new vehicle shapes or to serve as test beds for unproven technologies. One of the best known—and the fastest and highest-flying, winged vehicle—was the X-15. By the late 1960s, it had flown at speeds exceeding 4,500 miles per hour and reached an altitude of more than 60 miles. Eight X-15 pilots earned astronaut wings for achieving an altitude of 50 miles or more as a result of their flights in this plane. The stamps feature computer-generated images of the X-15 from NASA studies conducted in the 1990s. The images were reproduced with permission of the National Aeronautics and Space Administration.

	Issue	Date	Un	U	PB	#	FDC	Q(M)
	Perf. 11 x 10.5							
927	3¢ Florida Statehood Centenary	03/03/45	.20	.20	.50	(4)	7.50	62
	Win the War, Perf. 11 x 10.5							
928	5¢ United Nations Conference	04/25/45	.20	.20	.45	(4)	7.50	76
	Win the War, Perf. 10.5 x 11							
929	3¢ Iwo Jima (Marines)	07/11/45	.25	.20	2.00	(4)	15.00	137
	Win the War, Perf. 11 x 10.5							
930	1¢ Franklin D. Roosevelt and Hyde Park Residence	07/26/45	.20	.20	.25	(4)	4.00	128
931	2¢ Franklin D. Roosevelt and "The Little White House" at Warm Springs, Ga.	08/24/45	.20	.20	.45	(4)	4.00	67
932	3¢ Roosevelt and White House	06/27/45	.20	.20	.45	(4)	4.00	134
933	5¢ Roosevelt, Map of Western Hemisphere and Four Freedoms	01/30/46	.20	.20	.45	(4)	4.00	76
934	3¢ Army	09/28/45	.20	.20	.45	(4)	9.00	128
935	3¢ Navy	10/27/45	.20	.20	.55	(4)	9.00	139
936	3¢ Coast Guard	11/10/45	.20	.20	.45	(4)	9.00	112
937	3¢ Alfred E. Smith	11/26/45	.20	.20	.40	(4)	3.00	309
938	3¢ Texas Statehood	12/29/45	.20	.20	.40	(4)	8.00	171
939	3¢ Merchant Marine	02/26/46	.20	.20	.45	(4)	8.00	136
940	3¢ Veterans of World War II	05/09/46	.20	.20	.40	(4)	9.00	260
	Perf. 11 x 10.5							
941	3¢ Tennessee Statehood	06/01/46	.20	.20	.45	(4)	3.50	132
942	3¢ Iowa Statehood	08/03/46	.20	.20	.40	(4)	3.50	132
943	3¢ Smithsonian Institution	08/10/46	.20	.20	.35	(4)	3.50	139
944	3¢ Kearny Expedition	10/16/46	.20	.20	.30	(4)	3.50	115

	Issue	Date	Un	U	PB	#	FDC	Q(M)
	Perf. 10.5 x 11							
945	3¢ Thomas A. Edison	02/11/47	.20	.20	.35	(4)	4.00	157
	Perf. 11 x 10.5							
946	3¢ Joseph Pulitzer	04/10/47	.20	.20	.35	(4)	3.50	120
947	3¢ Postage Stamps Centenary	05/17/47	.20	.20	.30	(4)	3.50	127
	Centenary International Philatelic Exhibition Souvenir Sheet, Imperf.							
948	Souvenir sheet of 2 stamps (#1-2)	05/19/47	.55	.45			3.50	10
a	5¢ single stamp from sheet		.20	.20				
b	10¢ single stamp from sheet		.25	.25				
	Perf. 11 x 10.5							
949	3¢ Doctors	06/09/47	.20	.20	.30	(4)	8.00	133
950	3¢ Utah Settlement	07/24/47	.20	.20	.30	(4)	2.00	132
951	3¢ U.S. Frigate *Constitution*	10/21/47	.20	.20	.35	(4)	6.50	131
	Perf. 10.5 x 11							
952	3¢ Everglades National Park	12/05/47	.20	.20	.35	(4)	3.00	122
953	3¢ Dr. G.W. Carver	01/05/48	.20	.20	.45	(4)	3.00	122
	Perf. 11 x 10.5							
954	3¢ California Gold	01/24/48	.20	.20	.30	(4)	2.50	131
955	3¢ Mississippi Territory	04/07/48	.20	.20	.50	(4)	2.00	123
956	3¢ Four Chaplains	05/28/48	.20	.20	.50	(4)	6.00	122
957	3¢ Wisconsin Statehood	05/29/48	.20	.20	.35	(4)	1.50	115
958	5¢ Swedish Pioneer	06/04/48	.20	.20	.45	(4)	1.50	64
959	3¢ Progress of Women	07/19/48	.20	.20	.30	(4)	1.50	118
	Perf. 10.5 x 11							
960	3¢ William Allen White	07/31/48	.20	.20	.40	(4)	1.50	78

BASEBALL SLUGGERS

The Sluggers stamps recognize the accomplishments of four baseball greats: Mickey Mantle, Mel Ott, Roy Campanella, and Hank Greenberg. Remembered as powerful hitters who wowed fans with awesome and often record-breaking home runs, these four men were also versatile players who helped to lead their teams to victory and set impressive standards for subsequent generations. Nicknamed "Campy," Roy Campanella (1921-1993) hit 242 home runs during his ten-year career with the Brooklyn Dodgers, the famous "Boys of Summer." A three-time National League MVP, he was also the first black catcher in the history of Major League Baseball. Hank Greenberg (1911-1986) is remembered as one of the all-time greatest right-handed batters. During his time with the Detroit Tigers, "Hammerin' Hank" led the American League in home runs and in RBI four times each, and he was twice named Most Valuable Player. Synonymous with the New York Yankees for nearly two decades, switch-hitter Mickey Mantle (1931-1995) hit 536 homers, including a record 18 home runs in World Series play. A three-time American League MVP, he won the Triple Crown in 1956. Known for his unusual powerful high-leg-kick batting stance, Mel Ott (1909-1958) distinguished himself with the New York Giants for 22 seasons. Ott was the first National League player to hit 500 home runs, and he led the league in homers six times.

927

928

929

930

931

932

933

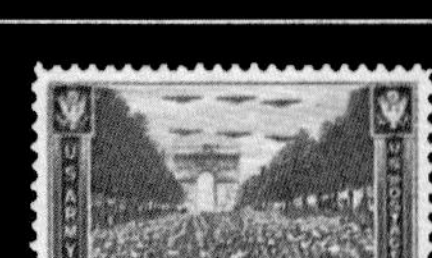

934

935

936

937

938

939

940

941

942

943

944

945

946

947

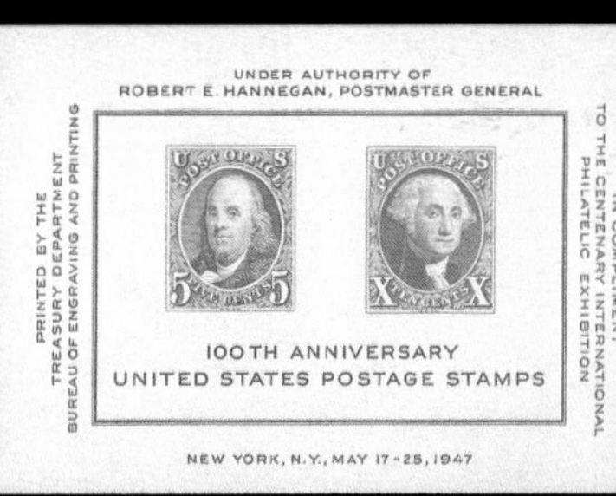

948

949

950

951

952

953

954

955

956

957

958

959

960

961 962 963 964 965 966

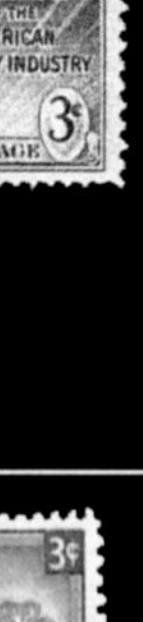

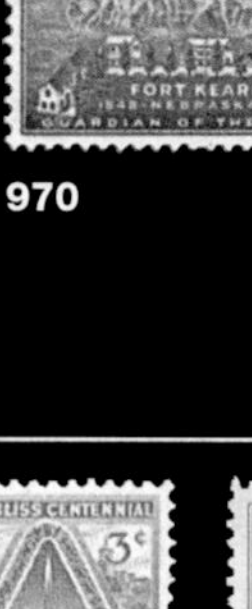

967 968 969 970 971 972

973 974 975 976 977 978 979

980 981 982 983 984 985

986 987 988 989 990 991

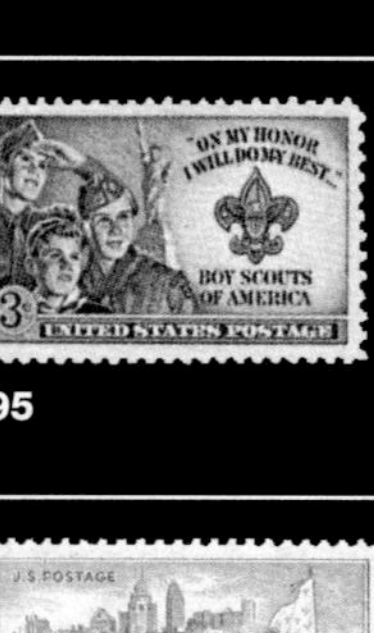

992 993 994 995 996

997 998 999 1000 1001

No.	Issue	Date	Un	U	PB	#	FDC	Q(M)
	Perf. 11 x 10.5							
961	3¢ U.S.-Canada Friendship	08/02/48	.20	.20	.30	(4)	1.50	113
962	3¢ Francis Scott Key	08/09/48	.20	.20	.40	(4)	1.50	121
963	3¢ Salute to Youth	08/11/48	.20	.20	.30	(4)	1.50	78
964	3¢ Oregon Territory	08/14/48	.20	.20	.35	(4)	1.50	52
	Perf. 10.5 x 11							
965	3¢ Harlan F. Stone	08/25/48	.20	.20	.60	(4)	1.50	54
966	3¢ Palomar Observatory	08/30/48	.20	.20	.95	(4)	4.00	61
a	Vertical pair, imperf. between		*425.00*					
	Perf. 11 x 10.5							
967	3¢ Clara Barton	09/07/48	.20	.20	.30	(4)	3.00	58
968	3¢ Poultry Industry	09/09/48	.20	.20	.50	(4)	3.00	53
	Perf. 10.5 x 11							
969	3¢ Gold Star Mothers	09/21/48	.20	.20	.40	(4)	2.00	77
	Perf. 11 x 10.5							
970	3¢ Fort Kearny	09/22/48	.20	.20	.40	(4)	2.00	58
971	3¢ Volunteer Firemen	10/04/48	.20	.20	.50	(4)	7.50	56
972	3¢ Indian Centennial	10/15/48	.20	.20	.45	(4)	1.50	58
973	3¢ Rough Riders	10/27/48	.20	.20	.45	(4)	1.50	54
974	3¢ Juliette Gordon Low	10/29/48	.20	.20	.40	(4)	7.00	64
	Perf. 10.5 x 11							
975	3¢ Will Rogers	11/04/48	.20	.20	.45	(4)	1.50	67
976	3¢ Fort Bliss	11/05/48	.20	.20	1.00	(4)	2.50	65
	Perf. 11 x 10.5							
977	3¢ Moina Michael	11/09/48	.20	.20	.45	(4)	1.50	64
978	3¢ Gettysburg Address	11/19/48	.20	.20	.50	(4)	1.75	63
	Perf. 10.5 x 11							
979	3¢ American Turners	11/20/48	.20	.20	.30	(4)	1.25	62
980	3¢ Joel Chandler Harris	12/09/48	.20	.20	.55	(4)	1.50	57
	Perf. 11 x 10.5							
981	3¢ Minnesota Territory	03/03/49	.20	.20	.35	(4)	2.00	99
982	3¢ Washington and Lee University	04/12/49	.20	.20	.30	(4)	2.00	105
	Perf. 11 x 10.5							
983	3¢ Puerto Rico Election	04/27/49	.20	.20	.30	(4)	2.00	109
984	3¢ Annapolis Tercentenary	05/23/49	.20	.20	.30	(4)	2.00	107
985	3¢ Grand Army of the Republic (GAR)	08/29/49	.20	.20	.40	(4)	2.00	117
	Perf. 10.5 x 11							
986	3¢ Edgar Allan Poe	10/07/49	.20	.20	.45	(4)	2.50	123
	Thin outer frame line at top, inner frame line missing		6.00					
	Perf. 11 x 10.5							
987	3¢ American Bankers	01/03/50	.20	.20	.40	(4)	2.00	131
	Perf. 10.5 x 11							
988	3¢ Samuel Gompers	01/27/50	.20	.20	.30	(4)	1.00	128
	National Capital Sesquicentennial, Perf. 10.5 x 11, 11 x 10.5							
989	3¢ Statue of Freedom on Capitol Dome	04/20/50	.20	.20	.30	(4)	1.00	132
990	3¢ Executive Mansion	06/12/50	.20	.20	.40	(4)	1.00	130
991	3¢ Supreme Court Bluilding	08/02/50	.20	.20	.30	(4)	1.00	131
992	3¢ U.S. Capitol	11/22/50	.20	.20	.40	(4)	1.00	130
	Gripper cracks		1.00	.50				
	Perf. 11 x 10.5							
993	3¢ Railroad Engineers	04/29/50	.20	.20	.40	(4)	3.00	122
994	3¢ Kansas City, MO	06/03/50	.20	.20	.40	(4)	1.00	122
995	3¢ Boy Scouts	06/30/50	.20	.20	.50	(4)	7.50	132
996	3¢ Indiana Territory	07/04/50	.20	.20	.50	(4)	1.00	122
997	3¢ California Statehood	09/09/50	.20	.20	.30	(4)	2.00	121
	United Confederate Veterans Final Reunion, Perf. 11 x 10.5							
998	3¢ United Confederate Veterans (UCV)	05/30/51	.20	.20	.35	(4)	2.00	119
	Perf. 11 x 10.5							
999	3¢ Nevada Settlement	07/14/51	.20	.20	.30	(4)	1.00	112
1000	3¢ Landing of Cadillac	07/24/51	.20	.20	.30	(4)	1.00	114
1001	3¢ Colorado Statehood	08/01/51	.20	.20	.30	(4)	1.00	114

GREAT SMOKY MOUNTAINS NORTH CAROLINA/ TENNESSEE

This international rate stamp in the Scenic American Landscapes series features a photograph of the Great Smoky Mountains, which stretch along the border of eastern Tennessee and western North Carolina. The photograph, which was taken by David Muench of Santa Barbara, California, features the view from Clingmans Dome and includes portions of both North Carolina and Tennessee. Encompassing approximately 800 square miles of mountainous terrain in both North Carolina and Tennessee, Great Smoky Mountains National Park is renowned for the diversity of the plant and animal life found along some 800 miles of hiking trails. Also found in the park are structures that represent the Southern Appalachian mountain culture of the settlers who once lived in the area. Established by Congress in 1934 and dedicated by President Franklin D. Roosevelt in 1940, the park receives some 10 million visitors annually.

	Issue	Date	Un	U	PB	#	FDC	Q(M)
	Perf. 11 x 10.5							
1002	3¢ American Chemical Society	09/04/51	.20	.20	.40	(4)	1.50	117
1003	3¢ Battle of Brooklyn	12/10/51	.20	.20	.30	(4)	1.00	116
1004	3¢ Betsy Ross	01/02/52	.20	.20	.35	(4)	1.00	116
1005	3¢ 4-H Club	01/15/52	.20	.20	.50	(4)	3.00	116
1006	3¢ B&O Railroad	02/28/52	.20	.20	.45	(4)	2.00	113
1007	3¢ American Automobile Association	03/04/52	.20	.20	.40	(4)	1.50	117
1008	3¢ NATO	04/04/52	.20	.20	.30	(4)	1.00	2,900
1009	3¢ Grand Coulee Dam	05/15/52	.20	.20	.30	(4)	1.00	115
1010	3¢ Arrival of Lafayette	06/13/52	.20	.20	.45	(4)	1.00	113
	Perf. 10.5 x 11							
1011	3¢ Mt. Rushmore Memorial	08/11/52	.20	.20	.40	(4)	1.00	116
	Perf. 11 x 10.5							
1012	3¢ Engineering	09/06/52	.20	.20	.45	(4)	1.00	114
1013	3¢ Service Women	09/11/52	.20	.20	.30	(4)	1.50	124
1014	3¢ Gutenberg Bible	09/30/52	.20	.20	.30	(4)	1.00	116
1015	3¢ Newspaper Boys	10/04/52	.20	.20	.30	(4)	1.00	115
1016	3¢ International Red Cross	11/21/52	.20	.20	.30	(4)	1.50	136
1017	3¢ National Guard	02/23/53	.20	.20	.30	(4)	1.00	115
1018	3¢ Ohio Statehood	03/02/53	.20	.20	.45	(4)	1.00	119
1019	3¢ Washington Territory	03/02/53	.20	.20	.30	(4)	1.00	114
1020	3¢ Louisiana Purchase	04/30/53	.20	.20	.50	(4)	1.00	114
1021	5¢ Opening of Japan	07/14/53	.20	.20	.65	(4)	1.25	89
1022	3¢ American Bar Association	08/24/53	.20	.20	.30	(4)	5.50	115
1023	3¢ Sagamore Hill	09/14/53	.20	.20	.35	(4)	1.00	116
1024	3¢ Future Farmers	10/13/53	.20	.20	.30	(4)	1.00	115
1025	3¢ Trucking Industry	10/27/53	.20	.20	.30	(4)	1.25	124
1026	3¢ General George S. Patton, Jr.	11/11/53	.20	.20	.40	(4)	3.00	115
1027	3¢ New York City	11/20/53	.20	.20	.35	(4)	1.00	116
1028	3¢ Gadsden Purchase	12/30/53	.20	.20	.30	(4)	1.00	116
1029	3¢ Columbia University	01/04/54	.20	.20	.30	(4)	1.00	119
	Liberty, Perf. 11 x 10.5 (Designs of 1030-1059)							
1030	½¢ Benjamin Franklin	10/20/55	.20	.20	.25	(4)	1.00	
a	Wet printing		.20	.20	.35	(4)		
1031	1¢ George Washington	03/56	.20	.20	.25	(4)		
	Pair with full vertical or horizontal gutter between		*150.00*					
b	Wet printing		.20	.20	.25	(4)	1.00	
	Liberty, Perf. 10.5 x 11							
1031A	1¼¢ Palace of the Governors	06/17/60	.20	.20	.45	(4)	1.50	
1032	1½¢ Mt. Vernon	02/22/56	.20	.20	1.75	(4)	1.00	

	Issue	Date	Un	U	PB	#	FDC	Q(M)
	Liberty, Perf. 11 x 10.5 (Designs of 1030-1059)							
1033	2¢ Thomas Jefferson	09/15/54	.20	.20	.25	(4)	1.00	
1034	2½¢ Bunker Hill Monument and Massachusetts Flag	06/17/59	.20	.20	.50	(4)	1.00	
1035	3¢ Statue of Liberty	06/24/54	.20	.20	.25	(4)		
a	Booklet pane of 6	06/30/54	4.00	*1.25*			3.50	
b	Tagged	07/06/66	.30	.25	5.50	(4)	40.00	
c	Imperf., pair		*2,000.00*					
d	Horizontal pair, imperf. between		—					
e	Wet printing	06/24/54	.20	.20	.35	(4)	1.00	
f	As "a," untagged		5.00	*1.50*				
g	As "a," vertical imperf. between		*5,000.00*					
1036	4¢ Abraham Lincoln	11/19/54	.20	.20	.35	(4)		
a	Booklet pane of 6	07/31/58	2.75	*1.25*			4.00	
b	Tagged	11/02/63	.60	.40	8.50	(4)	50.00	
	Liberty, Perf. 10.5 x 11							
1037	4½¢ The Hermitage	03/16/59	.20	.20	.65	(4)	1.00	
	Liberty, Perf. 11 x 10.5							
1038	5¢ James Monroe	12/02/54	.20	.20	.45	(4)	1.00	
	Pair with full vertical gutter between		*200.00*					
1039	6¢ Theodore Roosevelt	11/18/55	.25	.20	1.25	(4)		
a	Wet printing	11/18/55	.40	.20	2.00	(4)	1.00	
1040	7¢ Woodrow Wilson	01/10/56	.20	.20	1.00	(4)	1.00	
	Liberty, Perf. 11							
1041	8¢ Statue of Liberty	04/09/54	.25	.20	2.00	(4)	1.00	
a	Carmine double impression		*575.00*					
1042	8¢ Statue of Liberty, redrawn	03/22/58	.20	.20	.90	(4)	1.00	
	Liberty, Perf. 11 x 10.5							
1042A	8¢ Gen. John J. Pershing	11/17/61	.20	.20	.90	(4)	1.25	
	Liberty, Perf. 10.5 x 11							
1043	9¢ The Alamo	06/14/56	.30	.20	1.30	(4)	1.25	
1044	10¢ Independence Hall	07/04/56	.30	.20	1.40	(4)	1.00	
b	Tagged	07/06/66	.25	.20	1.10	(4)	40.00	
d	Tagged	07/06/66	2.00	1.00	*35.00*	(4)		
	Liberty, Perf. 11							
1044A	11¢ Statue of Liberty	06/15/61	.30	.20	1.50	(4)	1.25	
c	Tagged	01/11/67	2.00	1.60	*35.00*	(4)	40.00	
	Liberty, Perf. 11 x 10.5							
1045	12¢ Benjamin Harrison	06/06/59	.35	.20	1.50	(4)	1.25	
a	Tagged	1968	.35	.20	4.00	(4)	40.00	
1046	15¢ John Jay	12/12/58	.60	.20	3.00	(4)	1.25	
a	Tagged	07/06/66	1.10	.50	13.00	(4)	40.00	
	Liberty, Perf. 10.5 x 11							
1047	20¢ Monticello	04/13/56	.40	.20	1.75	(4)	1.25	

1002 1003 1004 1005 1006 1007

1008 1009 1010 1011 1012 1013

1014 1015 1016 1017 1018 1019

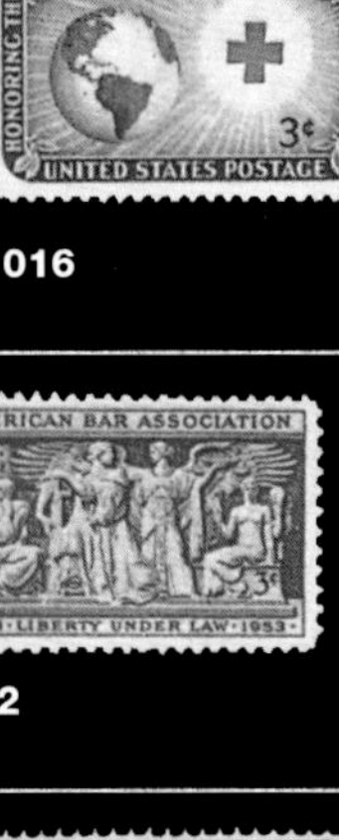

1020 1021 1022 1023 1024 1025

1026 1027 1028 1029 1030 1031 1031A

1032 1033 1034 1035 1036 1037 1038 1039 1040

1041 1042 1042A 1043 1044 1044A 1045 1046 1047

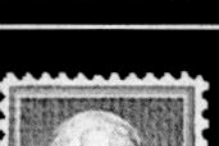

1048

1049

1050

1051

1052

1053

1060

1061

1062

1063

1064

1065

1066

1067

1068

1069

1070

1071

1072

1073

1074

5TH INTERNATIONAL PHILATELIC EXHIBITION, 1956
IN COMPLIMENT TO
U.S. POSTAGE 3¢ IN GOD WE TRUST LIBERTY
U.S. POSTAGE 8¢ IN GOD WE TRUST LIBERTY
Arthur E. Summerfield
POSTMASTER GENERAL OF THE UNITED STATES
NEW YORK, N.Y., APR. 28 - MAY 6

1075

1076

1077

1078

1079

1080

1081

1082

1083

1084

1085

1086

1087

1088

1089

	Issue	Date	Un	U	PB	#	FDC	Q(M)
	Liberty, Perf. 11 x 10.5 (Designs of 1030-1059)							
1048	25¢ Paul Revere	04/18/58	1.10	.75	4.75	(4)	1.25	
1049	30¢ Robert E. Lee	09/21/55	.70	.20	4.00	(4)		
a	Wet printing	09/21/55	1.10	.75	5.00	(4)	2.00	
1050	40¢ John Marshall	04/58	1.50	.20	7.50	(4)		
a	Wet printing	09/24/55	2.25	.25	12.50	(4)	2.00	
1051	50¢ Susan B. Anthony	04/58	1.50	.20	7.00	(4)		
a	Wet printing	08/25/55	1.75	.20	11.00	(4)	6.00	
1052	$1 Patrick Henry	10/58	4.50	.20	19.00	(4)		
a	Wet printing	10/07/55	5.25	1.00	22.50	(4)	15.00	
	Liberty, Perf. 11							
1053	$5 Alexander Hamilton	03/19/56	60.00	6.75	275.00	(4)	50.00	
	Liberty, Coil, Perf. 10 Vertically							
1054	1¢ dark Washington (1031)	08/57	.20	.20	1.00	(2)		
b	Imperf., pair		*2,500.00*	—				
c	Wet printing	10/08/54	.35	.20	1.75	(2)	1.00	
	Liberty, Coil, Perf. 10 Horizontally							
1054A	1¼¢ Palace of the Governors (1031A)	06/17/60	.20	.20	2.25	(2)	1.00	
	Liberty, Coil, Perf. 10 Vertically							
1055	2¢ Jefferson (1033)	05/57	.35	.20	1.50	(2)		
a	Tagged	05/06/68	.20	.20	.75	(2)	32.50	
b	Imperf., pair (Bureau precanceled)			*475.00*				
c	As "a," imperf., pair		*550.00*					
1056	2½¢ Bunker Hill (1034)	09/09/59	.30	.25	3.50	(2)	2.00	
1057	3¢ Statue of Liberty (1035)	10/56	.35	.20	2.75	(2)		
a	Imperf., pair		*1,500.00*	*850.00*	*2,750.00*	(2)		
b	Tagged	06/26/67	1.00	.50	25.00	(2)		
c	Wet printing	07/20/54	.35	.20	2.75	(2)	1.00	
1058	4¢ Lincoln (1036)	07/31/58	.50	.20	2.50	(2)	1.00	
a	Imperf., pair		90.00	75.00	200.00	(2)		
	Liberty, Coil, Perf. 10 Horizontally							
1059	4½¢ The Hermitage (1037)	05/01/59	1.50	1.20	14.00	(2)	1.75	
	Liberty, Coil, Perf. 10 Vertically							
1059A	25¢ Revere (1048)	02/25/65	.50	.30	2.00	(2)	1.25	
b	Tagged, shiney gum	04/03/73	.80	.20	3.25	(2)	40.00	
	Tagged, dull gum	1980	1.25		5.00	(2)		
c	Imperf., pair		40.00		80.00	(2)		
	Perf. 11 x 10.5							
1060	3¢ Nebraska Territory	05/07/54	.20	.20	.30	(4)	1.00	116
1061	3¢ Kansas Territory	05/31/54	.20	.20	.30	(4)	1.00	114
	Perf. 10.5 x 11							
1062	3¢ George Eastman	07/12/54	.20	.20	.30	(4)	1.00	128
	Perf. 11 x 10.5							
1063	3¢ Lewis and Clark Expedition	07/28/54	.20	.20	.60	(4)	1.50	116
	Perf. 10.5 x 11							
1064	3¢ Pennsylvania Academy of the Fine Arts	01/15/55	.20	.20	.45	(4)	1.00	116

	Issue	Date	Un	U	PB	#	FDC	Q(M)
	Perf. 11 x 10.5							
1065	3¢ Land-Grant Colleges	02/12/55	.20	.20	.30	4)	1.25	120
1066	8¢ Rotary International	02/23/55	.25	.20	1.25	(4)	2.25	54
1067	3¢ Armed Forces Reserve	05/21/55	.20	.20	.30	(4)	1.00	176
	Perf. 10.5 x 11							
1068	3¢ New Hampshire	06/21/55	.20	.20	.50	(4)	2.00	126
	Perf. 11 x 10.5							
1069	3¢ Soo Locks	06/28/55	.20	.20	.30	(4)	1.00	122
1070	3¢ Atoms for Peace	07/28/55	.20	.20	.35	(4)	1.00	134
1071	3¢ Fort Ticonderoga	09/18/55	.20	.20	.30	(4)	1.00	119
	Perf. 10.5 x 11							
1072	3¢ Andrew W. Mellon	12/20/55	.20	.20	.35	(4)	1.00	112
1073	3¢ Benjamin Franklin	01/17/56	.20	.20	.40	(4)	1.00	129
	Perf. 11 x 10.5							
1074	3¢ Booker T. Washington	04/05/56	.20	.20	.40	(4)	2.00	121
	Fifth International Philatelic Exhibition Souvenir Sheet, Imperf.							
1075	Statue of Liberty Sheet of 2 stamps (1035, 1041)	04/28/56	2.00	2.00			5.00	3
a	3¢ (1035), single stamp from sheet		.80	.80				
b	8¢ (1041), single stamp from sheet		1.00	1.00				
	Perf. 11 x 10.5							
1076	3¢ New York Coliseum and Columbus Monument	04/30/56	.20	.20	.30	(4)	1.00	120
	Wildlife Conservation, Perf. 11 x 10.5							
1077	3¢ Wild Turkey	05/05/56	.20	.20	.35	(4)	1.75	123
1078	3¢ Pronghorn Antelope	06/22/56	.20	.20	.35	(4)	1.75	123
1079	3¢ King Salmon	11/09/56	.20	.20	.35	(4)	1.75	109
	Perf. 10.5 x 11							
1080	3¢ Pure Food and Drug Laws	06/27/56	.20	.20	.50	(4)	1.00	113
	Perf. 11 x 10.5							
1081	3¢ Wheatland	08/05/56	.20	.20	.30	(4)	1.00	125
	Perf. 10.5 x 11							
1082	3¢ Labor Day	09/03/56	.20	.20	.30	(4)	1.00	118
	Perf. 11 x 10.5							
1083	3¢ Nassau Hall	09/22/56	.20	.20	.50	(4)	1.00	122
	Perf. 10.5 x 11							
1084	3¢ Devils Tower	09/24/56	.20	.20	.30	(4)	1.00	118
	Perf. 11 x 10.5							
1085	3¢ Children's Stamp	12/15/56	.20	.20	.30	(4)	1.00	101
1086	3¢ Alexander Hamilton	01/11/57	.20	.20	.30	(4)	1.00	115
	Perf. 10.5 x 11							
1087	3¢ Polio	01/15/57	.20	.20	.30	(4)	1.50	187
	Perf. 11 x 10.5							
1088	3¢ Coast and Geodetic Survey	02/11/57	.20	.20	.30	(4)	1.00	115
1089	3¢ American Institute of Architects	02/23/57	.20	.20	.30	(4)	1.25	107

	Issue	Date	Un	U	PB	#	FDC	Q(M)
	Perf. 10.5 x 11							
1090	3¢ Steel Industry	05/22/57	.20	.20	.30	(4)	1.00	112
	Perf. 11 x 10.5							
1091	3¢ International Naval Review-Jamestown Festival	06/10/57	.20	.20	.30	(4)	1.00	118
1092	3¢ Oklahoma Statehood	06/14/57	.20	.20	.35	(4)	1.00	102
1093	3¢ School Teachers	07/01/57	.20	.20	.35	(4)	2.00	102
	Perf. 11							
1094	4¢ Flag	07/04/57	.20	.20	.35	(4)	1.00	84
	Perf. 10.5 x 11							
1095	3¢ Shipbuilding	08/15/57	.20	.20	.45	(4)	1.00	126
	Champion of Liberty, Perf. 11							
1096	8¢ Bust of Ramon Magsaysay on Medal	08/31/57	.20	.20	.85	(4)	1.25	39
	Perf. 10.5 x 11							
1097	3¢ Marquis de Lafayette	09/06/57	.20	.20	.30	(4)	1.00	123
	Wildlife Conservation, Perf. 11							
1098	3¢ Whooping Cranes	11/22/57	.20	.20	.35	(4)	1.25	174
	Perf. 10.5 x 11							
1099	3¢ Religious Freedom	12/27/57	.20	.20	.30	(4)	1.00	114
1100	3¢ Gardening-Horticulture	03/15/58	.20	.20	.30	(4)	1.00	123
1101-1103		Not assigned						
	Perf. 11 x 10.5							
1104	3¢ Brussels Universal and International Exhibition	04/17/58	.20	.20	.30	(4)	1.00	114
1105	3¢ James Monroe	04/28/58	.20	.20	.30	(4)	1.00	120
1106	3¢ Minnesota Statehood	05/11/58	.20	.20	.35	(4)	1.00	121
	Perf. 11							
1107	3¢ International Geophysical Year	05/31/58	.20	.20	.35	(4)	1.00	126
	Perf. 11 x 10.5							
1108	3¢ Gunston Hall	06/12/58	.20	.20	.30	(4)	1.00	108
	Perf. 10.5 x 11							
1109	3¢ Mackinac Bridge	06/25/58	.20	.20	.30	(4)	1.00	107
	Champion of Liberty, Perf. 10.5 x 11							
1110	4¢ Bust of Simon Bolivar on Medal	07/24/58	.20	.20	.35	(4)	1.25	116
	Champion of Liberty, Perf. 11							
1111	8¢ Bust of Bolivar on Medal	07/24/58	.20	.20	1.25	(4)	1.25	40
	Plate block of four, ocher # only		—					
	Perf. 11 x 10.5							
1112	4¢ Atlantic Cable	08/15/58	.20	.20	.35	(4)	1.00	115

	Issue	Date	Un	U	PB	#	FDC	Q(M)
	Abraham Lincoln Sesquicentennial, Perf. 10.5 x 11 (Designs of 1113-1116)							
1113	1¢ Portrait by George Healy	02/12/59	.20	.20	.25	(4)	1.50	120
1114	3¢ Sculptured Head by Gutzon Borglum	02/27/59	.20	.20	.40	(4)	1.50	91
	Perf. 11 x 10.5							
1115	4¢ Lincoln and Stephen Douglas Debating, by Joseph Boggs Beale	08/27/58	.20	.20	.60	(4)	1.50	115
1116	4¢ Statue in Lincoln Memorial by Daniel Chester French	05/30/59	.20	.20	.40	(4)	1.50	126
	Champion of Liberty, Perf. 10.5 x 11							
1117	4¢ Bust of Lajos Kossuth on Medal	09/19/58	.20	.20	.30	(4)	1.25	121
	Champion of Liberty, Perf. 11							
1118	8¢ Bust of Kossuth on Medal	09/19/58	.20	.20	1.10	(4)	1.25	44
	Perf. 10.5 x 11							
1119	4¢ Freedom of the Press	09/22/58	.20	.20	.30	(4)	1.00	118
	Perf. 11 x 10.5							
1120	4¢ Overland Mail	10/10/58	.20	.20	.30	(4)	1.00	126
	Perf. 10.5 x 11							
1121	4¢ Noah Webster	10/16/58	.20	.20	.40	(4)	1.00	114
	Perf. 11							
1122	4¢ Forest Conservation	10/27/58	.20	.20	.30	(4)	1.00	157
	Perf. 11 x 10.5							
1123	4¢ Fort Duquesne	11/25/58	.20	.20	.35	(4)	1.00	124
1124	4¢ Oregon Statehood	02/14/59	.20	.20	.30	(4)	1.00	121
	Champion of Liberty, Perf. 10.5 x 11							
1125	4¢ Bust of José de San Martin on Medal	02/25/59	.20	.20	.30	(4)	1.25	134
a	Horizontal pair, imperf. between		*1,250.00*					
	Champion of Liberty, Perf. 11							
1126	8¢ Bust of San Martin on Medal	02/25/59	.20	.20	.90	(4)	1.25	46
	Perf. 10.5 x 11							
1127	4¢ NATO	04/01/59	.20	.20	.30	(4)	1.00	122
	Perf. 11 x 10.5							
1128	4¢ Arctic Explorations	04/06/59	.20	.20	.40	(4)	1.00	131
1129	8¢ World Peace Through World Trade	04/20/59	.20	.20	.85	(4)	1.00	47
1130	4¢ Silver Centennial	06/08/59	.20	.20	.30	(4)	1.00	123
	Perf. 11							
1131	4¢ St. Lawrence Seaway	06/26/59	.20	.20	.35	(4)	1.25	126

1090

1091

1092

1093

1094

1095

1096

1097

1098

1099

1100

1104

1105

1106

1107

1108

1109

1110

1111

1112

1113

1114

1115

1116

1117

1118

1119

1120

1121

1122

1123

1124

1125

1126

1127

1128

1129

1130

1131

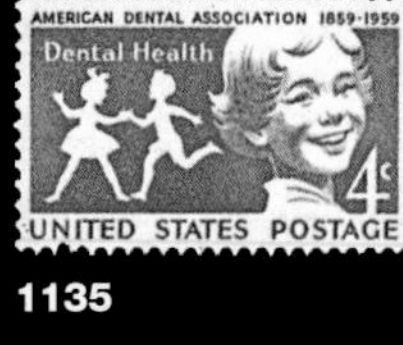

1132 1133 1134 1135 1136 1137 1138

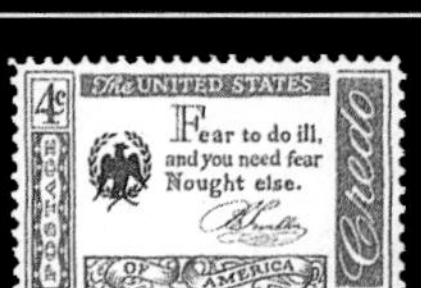

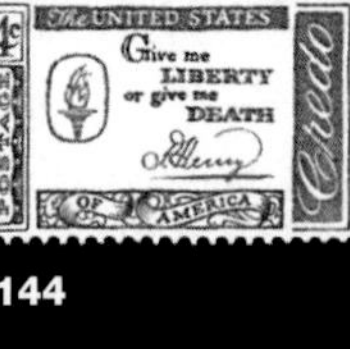

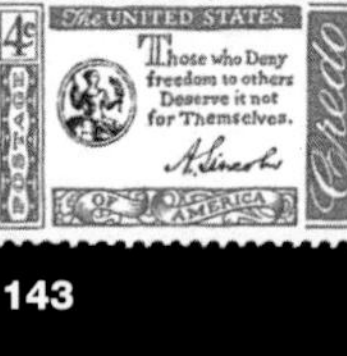

1139 1140 1141 1142 1143 1144

1145 1146 1147 1148 1149 1150 1151

1152 1153 1154 1155 1156 1157 1158 1159

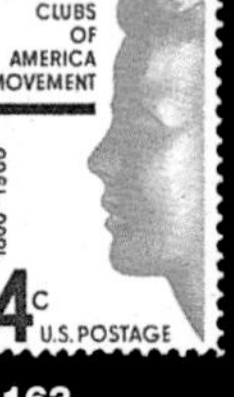

1160 1161 1162 1163 1164 1165 1166

1167 1168 1169 1170 1171 1172 1173

Issue		Date	Un	U	PB	#	FDC	Q(M)
	Perf. 11							
1132	4¢ 49-Star Flag	07/04/59	.20	.20	.40	(4)	1.00	209
1133	4¢ Soil Conservation	08/26/59	.20	.20	.35	(4)	1.00	121
	Perf. 10.5 x 11							
1134	4¢ Petroleum Industry	08/27/59	.20	.20	.40	(4)	1.50	116
	Perf. 11 x 10.5							
1135	4¢ Dental Health	09/14/59	.20	.20	.40	(4)	3.50	118
	Champion of Liberty, Perf. 10.5 x 11							
1136	4¢ Bust of Ernst Reuter on Medal	09/29/59	.20	.20	.30	(4)	1.25	112
	Champion of Liberty, Perf. 11							
1137	8¢ Bust of Reuter on Medal	09/29/59	.20	.20	.90	(4)	1.25	43
a	Ocher missing	*4,250.00*						
b	Ultramarine missing	*4,250.00*						
c	Ocher & ultramarine missing	*4,500.00*						
d	All colors missing	*2,500.00*						
	Perf. 10.5 x 11							
1138	4¢ Dr. Ephraim McDowell	12/03/59	.20	.20	.40	(4)	1.25	115
a	Vertical pair, imperf. between	*450.00*						
b	Vertical pair, imperf. horizontally	*300.00*						
	American Credo, Perf. 11							
1139	4¢ Quotation from Washington's Farewell Address	01/20/60	.20	.20	.40	(4)	1.00	126
1140	4¢ Benjamin Franklin Quotation	03/31/60	.20	.20	.40	(4)	1.00	125
1141	4¢ Thomas Jefferson Quotation	05/18/60	.20	.20	.45	(4)	1.00	115
1142	4¢ Francis Scott Key Quotation	09/14/60	.20	.20	.50	(4)	1.00	122
1143	4¢ Abraham Lincoln Quotation	11/19/60	.20	.20	.50	(4)	1.00	121
1144	4¢ Patrick Henry Quotation	01/11/61	.20	.20	.50	(4)	1.00	113
	Perf. 11							
1145	4¢ Boy Scouts	02/08/60	.20	.20	.45	(4)	4.00	139
	Olympic Games, Perf. 10.5 x 11							
1146	4¢ Olympic Rings and Snowflake	02/18/60	.20	.20	.40	(4)	1.00	124
	Champion of Liberty, Perf. 10.5 x 11							
1147	4¢ Bust of Thomas Masaryk on Medal	03/07/60	.20	.20	.30	(4)	1.25	114
a	Vertical pair, imperf. between	*2,750.00*						
	Champion of Liberty, Perf. 11							
1148	8¢ Bust of Masaryk on Medal	03/07/60	.20	.20	.95	(4)	1.25	44
	Perf. 11 x 10.5							
1149	4¢ World Refugee Year	04/07/60	.20	.20	.30	(4)	1.00	113
	Perf. 11							
1150	4¢ Water Conservation	04/18/60	.20	.20	.35	(4)	1.00	122
a	Brown orange missing	*2,400.00*						
	Perf. 10.5 x 11							
1151	4¢ SEATO	05/31/60	.20	.20	.35	(4)	1.00	115
a	Vertical pair, imperf. between	*140.00*						

Issue		Date	Un	U	PB	#	FDC	Q(M)
	Perf. 11 x 10.5							
1152	4¢ American Woman	06/02/60	.20	.20	.30	(4)	1.25	111
	Perf. 11							
1153	4¢ 50-Star Flag	07/04/60	.20	.20	.30	(4)	1.00	153
	Perf. 11 x 10.5							
1154	4¢ Pony Express	07/19/60	.20	.20	.55	(4)	1.75	120
	Perf. 10.5 x 11							
1155	4¢ Employ the Handicapped	08/28/60	.20	.20	.30	(4)	1.50	118
1156	4¢ 5th World Forestry Congress	08/29/60	.20	.20	.30	(4)	1.00	118
	Perf. 11							
1157	4¢ Mexican Independence	09/16/60	.20	.20	.30	(4)	1.00	112
1158	4¢ U.S.-Japan Treaty	09/28/60	.20	.20	.35	(4)	1.00	125
	Champion of Liberty, Perf. 10.5 x 11							
1159	4¢ Bust of Ignacy Jan Paderewski on Medal	10/08/60	.20	.20	.30	(4)	1.25	120
	Champion of Liberty, Perf. 11							
1160	8¢ Bust of Paderewski on Medal	10/08/60	.20	.20	.90	(4)	1.25	43
	Perf. 10.5 x 11							
1161	4¢ Sen. Robert A. Taft Memorial	10/10/60	.20	.20	.45	(4)	1.00	107
	Perf. 11 x 10.5							
1162	4¢ Wheels of Freedom	10/15/60	.20	.20	.30	(4)	1.00	110
	Perf. 11							
1163	4¢ Boys' Clubs of America	10/18/60	.20	.20	.30	(4)	1.00	124
1164	4¢ First Automated Post Office	10/20/60	.20	.20	.30	(4)	1.00	124
	Champion of Liberty, Perf. 10.5 x 11							
1165	4¢ Bust of Gustaf Mannerheim on Medal	10/26/60	.20	.20	.30	(4)	1.25	125
	Champion of Liberty, Perf. 11							
1166	8¢ Bust of Mannerheim on Medal	10/26/60	.20	.20	.80	(4)	1.25	42
	Perf. 11							
1167	4¢ Camp Fire Girls	11/01/60	.20	.20	.55	(4)	2.50	116
	Champion of Liberty, Perf. 10.5 x 11							
1168	4¢ Bust of Giuseppe Garibaldi on Medal	11/02/60	.20	.20	.30	(4)	1.25	126
	Champion of Liberty, Perf. 11							
1169	8¢ Bust of Garibaldi on Medal	11/02/60	.20	.20	.85	(4)	1.25	43
	Perf. 10.5 x 11							
1170	4¢ Sen. Walter F. George Memorial	11/05/60	.20	.20	.45	(4)	1.00	124
1171	4¢ Andrew Carnegie	11/25/60	.20	.20	.35	(4)	1.00	120
1172	4¢ John Foster Dulles Memorial	12/06/60	.20	.20	.35	(4)	1.00	117
	Perf. 11 x 10.5							
1173	4¢ Echo I-Communications for Peace	12/15/60	.20	.20	.65	(4)	2.50	124

	Issue	Date	Un	U	PB/LP	#	FDC	Q(M)
	Champion of Liberty, Perf. 10.5 x 11							
1174	4¢ Bust of Gandhi on Medal	01/26/61	.20	.20	.30	(4)	1.25	113
	Champion of Liberty, Perf. 11							
1175	8¢ Bust of Gandhi on Medal	01/26/61	.20	.20	1.00	(4)	1.25	42
	Perf. 11							
1176	4¢ Range Conservation	02/02/61	.20	.20	.40	(4)	1.00	111
	Perf. 10.5 x 11							
1177	4¢ Horace Greeley	02/03/61	.20	.20	.45	(4)	1.00	99
	Civil War Centennial, Perf. 11 x 10.5							
1178	4¢ Fort Sumter	04/12/61	.25	.20	1.10	(4)	4.00	101
1179	4¢ Shiloh	04/07/62	.20	.20	.85	(4)	4.00	125
	Civil War Centennial, Perf. 11							
1180	5¢ Gettysburg	07/01/63	.20	.20	.85	(4)	4.00	80
1181	5¢ The Wilderness	05/05/64	.20	.20	.60	(4)	4.00	125
1182	5¢ Appomattox	04/09/65	.30	.20	1.40	(4)	4.00	113
a	Horizontal pair, imperf. vertically		*4,500.00*					
	Perf. 11							
1183	4¢ Kansas Statehood	05/10/61	.20	.20	.35	(4)	1.00	106
	Perf. 11 x 10.5							
1184	4¢ Sen. George W. Norris	07/11/61	.20	.20	.40	(4)	1.00	111
1185	4¢ Naval Aviation	08/20/61	.20	.20	.35	(4)	1.50	117
	Pair with full vertical gutter between		*150.00*					
	Perf. 10.5 x 11							
1186	4¢ Workmen's Compensation	09/04/61	.20	.20	.35	(4)	1.00	121
	With plate # inverted				.60	(4)		
	Perf. 11							
1187	4¢ Frederic Remington	10/04/61	.20	.20	.40	(4)	1.25	112
	Perf. 10.5 x 11							
1188	4¢ Republic of China	10/10/61	.20	.20	.45	(4)	5.50	111
1189	4¢ Naismith-Basketball	11/06/61	.20	.20	.50	(4)	6.50	109
	Perf. 11							
1190	4¢ Nursing	12/28/61	.20	.20	.50	(4)	10.00	145
1191	4¢ New Mexico Statehood	01/06/62	.20	.20	.30	(4)	1.50	113
1192	4¢ Arizona Statehood	02/14/62	.20	.20	.30	(4)	1.50	122
	Space, Perf. 11							
1193	4¢ Project Mercury	02/20/62	.20	.20	.35	(4)	3.00	289
	Perf. 11							
1194	4¢ Malaria Eradication	03/30/62	.20	.20	.30	(4)	1.00	120
	Perf. 10.5 x 11							
1195	4¢ Charles Evans Hughes	04/11/62	.20	.20	.30	(4)	1.00	125
	Perf. 11							
1196	4¢ Seattle World's Fair	04/25/62	.20	.20	.30	(4)	1.00	147
1197	4¢ Louisiana Statehood	04/30/62	.20	.20	.50	(4)	1.00	119
	Perf. 11 x 10.5							
1198	4¢ Homestead Act	05/20/62	.20	.20	.30	(4)	1.00	123
1199	4¢ Girl Scout Jubilee	07/24/62	.20	.20	.30	(4)	5.00	127
	Pair with full vertical gutter between		*250.00*					
1200	4¢ Sen. Brien McMahon	07/28/62	.20	.20	.40	(4)	1.00	131
1201	4¢ Apprenticeship	08/31/62	.20	.20	.30	(4)	1.00	120
	Perf. 11							
1202	4¢ Sam Rayburn	09/16/62	.20	.20	.30	(4)	1.50	121
1203	4¢ Dag Hammarskjold	10/23/62	.20	.20	.30	(4)	1.00	121
1204	4¢ Dag Hammarskjold, black, brown and yellow (yellow inverted), special printing	11/16/62	.20	.20	1.00	(4)	5.00	40
	Holiday Celebrations: Holiday, Perf. 11							
1205	4¢ Wreath and Candles	11/01/62	.20	.20	.30	(4)	1.10	862
	Perf. 11							
1206	4¢ Higher Education	11/14/62	.20	.20	.35	(4)	1.25	120
1207	4¢ Winslow Homer	12/15/62	.20	.20	.45	(4)	1.25	118
a	Horizontal pair, imperf. between		*6,750.00*					
1208	5¢ Flag over White House	01/09/63	.20	.20	.40	(4)	1.00	
a	Tagged	08/25/66	.20	.20	*2.00*	(4)	30.00	
b	Horizontal pair, imperf. between		*1,500.00*					
	Perf. 11 x 10.5							
1209	1¢ Andrew Jackson	03/22/63	.20	.20	.20	(4)	1.00	
a	Tagged	07/06/66	.20	.20	.40	(4)	30.00	
1210-1212	Not assigned							
1213	5¢ George Washington	11/23/62	.20	.20	.40	(4)	1.00	
a	Booklet pane of 5 + label		3.00	*2.00*			4.00	
b	Tagged	10/28/63	.50	.20	4.50	(4)	30.00	
c	As "a," tagged	10/28/63	2.00	*1.50*			100.00	
1214-1224	Not assigned							
	Coil, Perf. 10 Vertically							
1225	1¢ green Jackson (1209)	05/31/63	.20	.20	2.00	(2)	1.00	
a	Tagged	07/06/66	.20	.20	.75	(2)	30.00	
1226-1228	Not assigned							
1229	5¢ dark blue gray Washington (1213)	11/23/62	1.10	.20	3.50	(2)	1.00	
a	Tagged	10/28/63	1.40	.20	6.50	(2)	30.00	
b	Imperf., pair		*375.00*		*1,000.00*	(2)		
	Perf. 11							
1230	5¢ Carolina Charter	04/06/63	.20	.20	.40	(4)	1.00	130
1231	5¢ Food for Peace-Freedom from Hunger	06/04/63	.20	.20	.40	(4)	1.00	136
1232	5¢ West Virginia Statehood	06/20/63	.20	.20	.40	(4)	1.00	138

1174

1175

1176

1177

1178

1179

1180

1181

1182

1183

1184

1185

1186

1187

1188

1189

1190

1191

1192

1193

1194

1195

1196

1197

1198

1199

1200

1201

1202

1203

1204

1205

1206

1207

1208

1209

1213

1230

1231

1232

1233

1234

1235

1236

1237

1238

1239

1240

1241

1242

1243

1244

1245

1246

1247

1248

1249

1250

1251

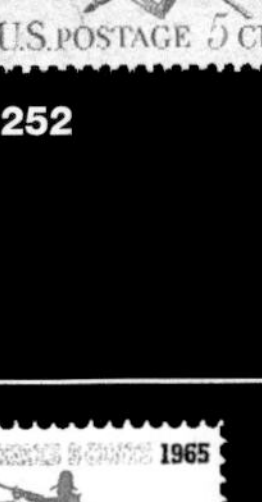

1252

1253

1254 1255

1256 1257 1257b

1258

1259

1260

1261

1262

1263

1264

1265

1266

1267

1268

1269

Issue		Date	Un	U	PB	#	FDC	Q(M)
	Perf. 11							
1233	5¢ Emancipation Proclamation	08/16/63	.20	.20	.50	(4)	1.75	132
1234	5¢ Alliance for Progress	08/17/63	.20	.20	.40	(4)	1.00	136
	Perf. 10.5 x 11							
1235	5¢ Cordell Hull	10/05/63	.20	.20	.50	(4)	1.00	131
	Perf. 11 x 10.5							
1236	5¢ Eleanor Roosevelt	10/11/63	.20	.20	.45	(4)	1.00	133
	Perf. 11							
1237	5¢ The Sciences	10/14/63	.20	.20	.40	(4)	1.25	130
	Tagged, Perf. 11							
1238	5¢ City Mail Delivery	10/26/63	.20	.20	.50	(4)	1.25	128
a	Tagged omitted		7.50					
1239	5¢ International Red Cross	10/29/63	.20	.20	.50	(4)	1.50	119
	Holiday Celebrations: Holiday, Perf. 11							
1240	5¢ National Christmas Tree and White House	11/01/63	.20	.20	.50	(4)	1.25	1,300
a	Tagged	11/02/63	.65	.50	5.00	(4)	60.00	
	Perf. 11							
1241	5¢ John James Audubon (See also #C71)	12/07/63	.20	.20	.45	(4)	1.25	175
	Perf. 10.5 x 11							
1242	5¢ Sam Houston	01/10/64	.20	.20	.45	(4)	1.75	126
	Perf. 11							
1243	5¢ Charles M. Russell	03/19/64	.20	.20	.40	(4)	1.25	128
	Perf. 11 x 10.5							
1244	5¢ New York World's Fair	04/22/64	.20	.20	.45	(4)	1.75	146
	Perf. 11							
1245	5¢ John Muir	04/29/64	.20	.20	.45	(4)	1.50	120
	Perf. 11 x 10.5							
1246	5¢ President John Fitzgerald Kennedy Memorial	05/29/64	.20	.20	.60	(4)	2.50	512
	Perf. 10.5 x 11							
1247	5¢ New Jersey Tercentenary	06/15/64	.20	.20	.50	(4)	1.00	124
	Perf. 11							
1248	5¢ Nevada Statehood	07/22/64	.20	.20	.40	(4)	1.00	123
1249	5¢ Register and Vote	08/01/64	.20	.20	.45	(4)	1.25	453
	Perf. 10.5 x 11							
1250	5¢ Shakespeare	08/14/64	.20	.20	.40	(4)	1.50	123
1251	5¢ Doctors William and Charles Mayo	09/11/64	.20	.20	.60	(4)	3.00	123

Issue		Date	Un	U	PB	#	FDC	Q(M)
	Perf. 11							
1252	5¢ American Music	10/15/64	.20	.20	.40	(4)	1.50	127
a	Blue omitted		*900.00*					
1253	5¢ Homemakers	10/26/64	.20	.20	.40	(4)	1.00	121
	Holiday Celebrations: Holiday, Perf. 11							
1254	5¢ Holly	11/09/64	.25	.20				352
a	Tagged, Nov. 10		.60	.50				
1255	5¢ Mistletoe	11/09/64	.25	.20				352
a	Tagged, Nov. 10		.60	.50				
1256	5¢ Poinsettia	11/09/64	.25	.20				352
a	Tagged, Nov. 10		.60	.50				
1257	5¢ Sprig of Conifer	11/09/64	.25	.20				352
a	Tagged, Nov. 10		.60	.50				
b	Block of four, #1254-1257		1.00	1.00	1.10	(4)	3.00	
c	As "b," tagged		2.50	2.25	5.50	(4)	57.50	
	Perf. 10.5 x 11							
1258	5¢ Verrazano-Narrows Bridge	11/21/64	.20	.20	.45	(4)	1.00	120
	Perf. 11							
1259	5¢ Fine Arts	12/02/64	.20	.20	.40	(4)	1.00	126
	Perf. 10.5 x 11							
1260	5¢ Amateur Radio	12/15/64	.20	.20	.60	(4)	5.00	122
	Perf. 11							
1261	5¢ Battle of New Orleans	01/08/65	.20	.20	.60	(4)	1.00	116
1262	5¢ Physical Fitness-Sokol	02/15/65	.20	.20	.50	(4)	1.25	115
1263	5¢ Crusade Against Cancer	04/01/65	.20	.20	.40	(4)	2.50	120
	Perf. 10.5 x 11							
1264	5¢ Winston Churchill Memorial	05/13/65	.20	.20	.40	(4)	1.50	125
	Perf. 11							
1265	5¢ Magna Carta	06/15/65	.20	.20	.40	(4)	1.00	120
1266	5¢ International Cooperation Year-United Nations	06/26/65	.20	.20	.40	(4)	1.00	115
1267	5¢ Salvation Army	07/02/65	.20	.20	.40	(4)	3.00	116
	Perf. 10.5 x 11							
1268	5¢ Dante Alighieri	07/17/65	.20	.20	.40	(4)	1.00	115
1269	5¢ President Herbert Hoover Memorial	08/10/65	.20	.20	.45	(4)	1.00	115

	Issue	Date	Un	U	PB	#	FDC	Q(M)
	Perf. 11							
1270	5¢ Robert Fulton	08/19/65	.20	.20	.40	(4)	1.00	116
1271	5¢ Florida Settlement	08/28/65	.20	.20	.45	(4)	1.00	117
a	Yellow omitted		*350.00*					
1272	5¢ Traffic Safety	09/03/65	.20	.20	.45	(4)	1.00	114
1273	5¢ John Singleton Copley	09/17/65	.20	.20	.50	(4)	1.00	115
1274	11¢ International Telecommunication Union	10/06/65	.35	.20	2.25	(4)	1.10	27
1275	5¢ Adlai E. Stevenson Memorial	10/23/65	.20	.20	.40	(4)	1.00	128
	Holiday Celebrations: Holiday, Perf. 11							
1276	5¢ Angel with Trumpet (1840 Weather Vane)	11/02/65	.20	.20	.40	(4)	1.00	1,140
a	Tagged	11/15/65	.75	.25	5.50	(4)	42.50	
1277	Not assigned							
	Prominent Americans, Perf. 11 x 10.5, 10.5 x 11							
1278	1¢ Thomas Jefferson	01/12/68	.20	.20	.20	(4)	1.00	
a	Booklet pane of 8	01/12/68	1.00	*.75*			2.50	
b	Bklt. pane of 4 + 2 labels	05/10/71	.80	*.60*			11.50	
c	Untagged (Bureau precanceled)		6.25	1.25				
d	Tagging omitted		3.50	—				
1279	1¼¢ Albert Gallatin	01/30/67	.20	.20	6.00	(4)	1.00	
1280	2¢ Frank Lloyd Wright	06/08/66	.20	.20	.25	(4)	1.00	
a	Booklet pane of 5 + label	01/08/68	1.25	*.80*			3.50	
b	Untagged (Bureau precanceled)		1.35	.40				
c	Booklet pane of 6	05/07/71	1.00	*.75*			15.00	
d	Tagging omitted		3.50	—				
1281	3¢ Francis Parkman	09/16/67	.20	.20	.25	(4)	1.00	
a	Untagged (Bureau precanceled)		3.00	.75				
b	Tagging omitted		4.50	—				
1282	4¢ Abraham Lincoln	11/19/65	.20	.20	.40	(4)	1.00	
a	Tagged	12/01/65	.20	.20	.55	(4)	30.00	
	Pair with full horizontal gutter between		*500.00*					
1283	5¢ George Washington	02/22/66	.20	.20	.50	(4)	1.00	
a	Tagged	02/23/66	.20	.20	.60	(4)	30.00	
1283B	5¢ George Washington	11/17/67	.20	.20	.50	(4)	1.00	
	Tagged, shiney gum		.20	.20				
	Dull gum		.20	.20	1.40	(4)		
d	Untagged (Bureau precanceled)		13.25	1.00				
1284	6¢ Franklin D. Roosevelt	01/29/66	.20	.20	.60	(4)	1.00	
a	Tagged	12/29/66	.20	.20	.80	(4)	40.00	
b	Booklet pane of 8	12/28/67	1.50	*1.00*			2.75	
c	Booklet pane of 5 + label	01/09/68	1.50	*1.00*			100.00	
1285	8¢ Albert Einstein	03/14/66	.20	.20	.85	(4)	2.50	
a	Tagged	07/06/66	.20	.20	.85	(4)	40.00	
1286	10¢ Andrew Jackson	03/15/67	.20	.20	1.00	(4)	1.00	
b	Untagged (Bureau precanceled)		57.50	1.75				
1286A	12¢ Henry Ford	07/30/68	.25	.20	1.00	(4)	1.50	
c	Untagged (Bureau precanceled)		4.75	1.00	145.00	(4)		
1287	13¢ John F. Kennedy	05/29/67	.30	.20	1.50	(4)	1.75	
a	Untagged (Bureau precanceled)		5.95	1.00	100.00	(4)		
b	Tagging omitted		*15.00*	—				
1288	15¢ Oliver Wendell Holmes	03/08/68	.30	.20	1.25	(4)	1.00	
a	Untagged (Bureau precanceled)		.75	.75	29.50	(4)		
d	Type II		.55	.20	8.00	(4)		
f	As "d", tagging omitted		7.50	—				

	Issue	Date	Un	U	PB/LP	#	FDC	Q(M)
	Booklet, Perf. 10							
1288B	15¢ magenta, tagged (1288), Single from booklet		.35	.20			1.00	
c	Booklet pane of 8	06/14/78	2.80	*1.75*			3.00	
e	As "c," vert. imperf. between		*1,750.00*					
	Prominent Americans, Perf. 11 x 10.5, 10.5 x 11							
1289	20¢ George C. Marshall	10/24/67	.40	.20	1.75	(4)	1.10	
a	Tagged	04/03/73	.40	.20	1.75	(4)	40.00	
1290	25¢ Frederick Douglass	02/14/67	.55	.20	2.25	(4)	2.50	
a	Tagged	04/03/73	.45	.20	2.00	(4)	45.00	
b	Magenta		*25.00*	—	*150.00*			
1291	30¢ John Dewey	10/21/68	.65	.20	2.90	(4)	1.75	
a	Tagged	04/03/73	.50	.20	2.25	(4)	45.00	
1292	40¢ Thomas Paine	01/29/68	.80	.20	3.25	(4)	1.75	
a	Tagged	04/03/73	.65	.20	2.75	(4)	45.00	
1293	50¢ Lucy Stone	08/13/68	1.00	.20	4.25	(4)	2.50	
a	Tagged	04/03/73	.80	.20	3.50	(4)	45.00	
1294	$1 Eugene O'Neill	10/16/67	2.25	.20	10.00	(4)	6.00	
a	Tagged	04/03/73	1.65	.20	6.75	(4)	60.00	
1295	$5 John Bassett Moore	12/03/66	10.00	2.25	42.50	(4)	40.00	
a	Tagged	04/03/73	8.50	2.00	35.00	(4)	120.00	
1296	Not assigned							
	Prominent Americans, Coil, Tagged, Perf. 10 Horizontally							
1297	3¢ Parkman (1281)	11/04/75	.20	.20	.45	(2)	1.00	
a	Imperf., pair		*22.50*		*45.00*	(2)		
b	Untagged (Bureau precanceled)		.25	.25	62.50	(2)		
c	As "b," imperf., pair		*6.00*	—	22.50	(2)		
1298	6¢ Franklin D. Roosevelt (1284)	12/28/67	.20	.20	1.10	(2)	1.00	
a	Imperf., pair		*2,000.00*					
b	Tagging omitted		6.00					
	Prominent Americans, Coil, Tagged, Perf. 10 Vertically							
1299	1¢ Jefferson (1278)	01/12/68	.20	.20	.25	(2)	1.00	
a	Untagged (Bureau precanceled)		8.00	1.75	*295.00*	(2)		
b	Imperf., pair		*25.00*	—	*55.00*	(2)		
1300-1302	Not assigned							
1303	4¢ Lincoln (1282)	05/28/66	.20	.20	.75	(2)	1.00	
a	Untagged (Bureau precanceled)		8.75	.75	*250.00*	(2)		
b	Imperf., pair		*750.00*		*1,750.00*	(2)		
1304	5¢ Washington (1283)	09/08/66	.20	.20	.40	(2)	1.00	
a	Untagged (Bureau precanceled)		6.50	.65	*195.00*	(2)		
b	Imperf., pair		*150.00*		*275.00*	(2)		
e	As "a," imperf. pair			*300.00*	*900.00*	(2)		
1304C	5¢ redrawn (1283B)	1981	.20	.20	1.25	(2)		
d	Imperf., pair		*600.00*					
1305	6¢ Franklin D. Roosevelt	02/28/68	.20	.20	.55	(2)	1.00	
a	Imperf., pair		*65.00*		*125.00*	(2)		
b	Untagged (Bureau precanceled)		20.00	1.00	*675.00*	(2)		
1305C	$1 Eugene O'Neill (1294)	01/12/73	2.00	.40	5.50	(2)	4.00	
d	Imperf., pair		*2,000.00*		*4,250.00*	(2)		
1305E	15¢ Oliver Wendell Holmes, type I, (1288)	06/14/78	.25	.20	1.10	(2)	1.00	
	Dull finish gum		.60		3.50	(2)		

1270

1271

U.S.POSTAGE 5¢
Stop traffic accidents
enforcement·education·engineering

1272

1273

INTERNATIONAL TELECOMMUNICATION UNION
1865 1965
11 CENTS UNITED STATES POSTAGE

1274

STEVENSON
U.S. 5 CENTS

1275

1276

1278

1279

1280

1281

1282

1283

1283B

1284

1285

1286

1286A

1287

1288

1289

1290

1291

1292

1293

1294

1295

1305

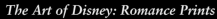

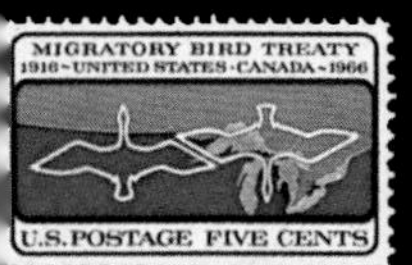

306

1307

SESQUICENTENNIAL
INDIANA
1816 1966
5¢
U.S. POSTAGE

1308

1309

1310

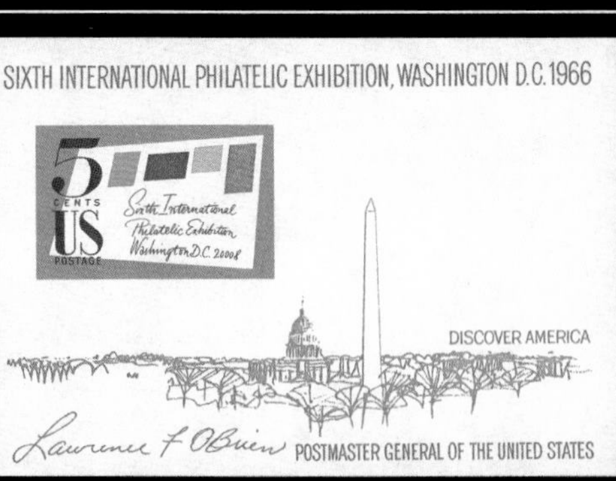

311

1312

1313

1314

1315

316

1317

1318

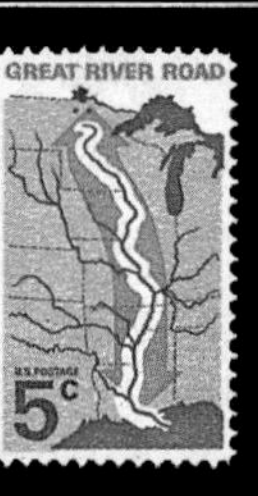

1319

1320

1321

1322

1867-1967
NATIONAL
GRANGE
U.S. 5 CENTS

323

1324

1325

1326

1327

1328

VOICE
OF
AMERICA
5¢ U.S. POSTAGE

1329

1330

1331 1332 1332b

1333

1334

Issue		Date	Un	U	PB	#	FDC	Q(M)
	Perf. 11							
1306	5¢ Migratory Bird Treaty	03/16/66	.20	.20	.40	(4)	1.75	117
1307	5¢ Humane Treatment of Animals	04/09/66	.20	.20	.40	(4)	1.25	117
1308	5¢ Indiana Statehood	04/16/66	.20	.20	.50	(4)	1.00	124
1309	5¢ American Circus	05/02/66	.20	.20	.50	(4)	2.00	131
	Sixth International Philatelic Exhibition, Perf. 11							
1310	5¢ Stamped Cover	05/21/66	.20	.20	.40	(4)	1.00	122
	Souvenir Sheet, Imperf.							
1311	5¢ Stamped Cover (1310) and Washington, D.C., Scene	05/23/66	.20	.20			1.10	15
	Perf. 11							
1312	5¢ The Bill of Rights	07/01/66	.20	.20	.45	(4)	1.75	114
	Perf. 10.5 x 11							
1313	5¢ Poland's Millennium	07/30/66	.20	.20	.45	(4)	1.50	128
	Perf. 11							
1314	5¢ National Park Service	08/25/66	.20	.20	.45	(4)	1.00	120
a	Tagged	08/26/66	.30	.25	2.00	(4)	35.00	
1315	5¢ Marine Corps Reserve	08/29/66	.20	.20	.45	(4)	1.50	125
a	Tagged		.30	.20	2.00	(4)	35.00	
b	Black and bister omitted		*16,000.00*					
1316	5¢ General Federation of Women's Clubs	09/12/66	.20	.20	.45	(4)	1.25	115
a	Tagged	09/13/66	.30	.20	2.00	(4)	35.00	
	American Folklore, Perf. 11							
1317	5¢ Johnny Appleseed and Apple	09/24/66	.20	.20	.45	(4)	1.00	124
a	Tagged	09/26/66	.30	.20	2.00	(4)	35.00	
	Perf. 11							
1318	5¢ Beautification of America	10/05/66	.20	.20	.45	(4)	1.00	128
a	Tagged		.30	.20	2.00	(4)	35.00	
1319	5¢ Great River Road	10/21/66	.20	.20	.60	(4)	1.00	128
a	Tagged	10/22/66	.30	.20	2.00	(4)	35.00	
1320	5¢ Savings Bond-Servicemen	10/26/66	.20	.20	.45	(4)	1.00	116
a	Tagged	10/27/66	.30	.20	1.75	(4)	35.00	
b	Red, dark bl. and blk. omitted		*4,250.00*					
c	Dark blue omitted		*5,500.00*					
	Holiday Celebrations: Christmas, Perf. 11							
1321	5¢ Madonna and Child, by Hans Memling	11/01/66	.20	.20	.40	(4)	1.00	1,174
a	Tagged	11/02/66	.30	.20	1.50	(4)	35.00	
	Perf. 11							
1322	5¢ Mary Cassatt	11/17/66	.20	.20	.60	(4)	1.00	114
a	Tagged		.30	.25	1.75	(4)	35.00	
	Tagged, Perf. 11							
1323	5¢ National Grange	04/17/67	.20	.20	.40	(4)	1.00	121
a	Tagging omitted		*6.00*	—				
1324	5¢ Canada Centenary	05/25/67	.20	.20	.40	(4)	1.00	132
a	Tagging omitted		*6.00*	—				
1325	5¢ Erie Canal	07/04/67	.20	.20	.40	(4)	1.00	119
a	Tagging omitted		*11.00*	—				
1326	5¢ Search for Peace	07/05/67	.20	.20	.40	(4)	1.00	122
a	Tagging omitted		*7.50*	—				
1327	5¢ Henry David Thoreau	07/12/67	.20	.20	.50	(4)	1.00	112
1328	5¢ Nebraska Statehood	07/29/67	.20	.20	.40	(4)	1.00	117
a	Tagging omitted		*7.50*	—				
1329	5¢ Voice of America	08/01/67	.20	.20	.40	(4)	2.00	112
a	Tagging omitted		*15.00*	—				
	American Folklore, Tagged, Perf. 11							
1330	5¢ Davy Crockett	08/17/67	.20	.20	.60	(4)	1.25	114
a	Vertical pair, imperf. between		*7,000.00*					
b	Green omitted		—					
c	Black and green omitted		—					
e	Tagging omitted		*8.00*	—				
	Space, Tagged, Perf. 11							
1331	5¢ Space-Walking Astronaut	09/29/67	.50	.20			3.00	60
b	Tagging omitted		*25.00*	—				
1332	5¢ Gemini 4 Capsule and Earth	09/29/67	.50	.20	2.50	(4)	3.00	60
a	Tagging omitted		*25.00*	—				
b	Pair, #1331-1332		1.10	*1.25*				
c	As "b", Tagging omitted		*60.00*	—				
	Tagged, Perf. 11							
1333	5¢ Urban Planning	10/02/67	.20	.20	.50	(4)	1.00	111
a	Tagging omitted		*30.00*					
1334	5¢ Finland Independence	10/06/67	.20	.20	.50	(4)	1.00	111

DR. JONAS SALK

In 2006 the Distinguished Americans series continues with a stamp honoring Dr. Jonas Salk (1914-1995), who was awarded the Presidential Medal of Freedom in 1977 for developing the first safe and effective vaccine against paralytic poliomyelitis. Periodic outbreaks of this worldwide viral disease—also called infantile paralysis or simply "polio"—paralyzed or killed thousands of people annually in the United States alone before the Salk vaccine became available in 1955. In the mid-1940s, Dr. Salk's research helped to develop the first effective influenza vaccine—still the basis of all "flu shots" given today. In 1947, at the University of Pittsburgh's Virus Research Laboratory, Dr. Salk began studies funded by the National Foundation for Infantile Paralysis to develop a successful vaccine for polio. The resulting injectable, killed-virus vaccine was tested and licensed for general use on April 12, 1955, the tenth anniversary of the death of President Franklin D. Roosevelt, who had been stricken by polio in 1921. The world hailed Dr. Salk as a hero. President Dwight D. Eisenhower called him a "benefactor of mankind," and the U.S. Congress gave him the Congressional Gold Medal. In the years following the polio vaccine success, Dr. Salk pursued studies of multiple sclerosis and cancer, helped develop a killed poliovirus vaccine that is effective in a single dose, and worked to develop an AIDS vaccine.

March of Dimes Birth Defects Foundation

No.	Issue	Date	Un	U	PB	#	FDC	Q(M)
	Tagged, Perf. 12							
1335	5¢ Thomas Eakins	11/02/67	.20	.20	.50	(4)	1.40	114
a	Tagging omitted		*35.00*	—				
	Holiday Celebrations: Christmas, Tagged, Perf. 11							
1336	5¢ Madonna and Child, by Hans Memling	11/06/67	.20	.20	.40	(4)	1.25	1,209
a	Tagging omitted		*5.00*	—				
	Tagged, Perf. 11							
1337	5¢ Mississippi Statehood	12/11/67	.20	.20	.60	(4)	1.00	113
a	Tagging omitted		*10.00*	—				
	Tagged, Perf. 11							
1338	6¢ Flag over White House design 19 x 22mm	01/24/68	.20	.20	.45	(4)	1.00	
k	Vertical pair, imperf. between		*450.00*					
m	Tagging omitted		*4.00*	—				
	Coil, Perf. 10 Vertically							
1338A	6¢ dk bl, rd and grn (1338), design 18.25 x 21mm	05/30/69	.20	.20	.30	(2)	1.00	
b	Imperf., pair		*500.00*					
q	Tagging omitted		*8.50*	—				
	Tagged, Perf. 11 x 10.5							
1338D	6¢ dark blue, red and green (1338), design 18.25 x 21mm	08/07/70	.20	.20	2.60	(20)	1.00	
e	Horizontal pair, imperf. between		*150.00*					
n	Tagging omitted		*5.00*	—				
1338F	8¢ dk bl, rd and slt grn (1338)	05/10/71	.20	.20	3.00	(20)	1.00	
i	Imperf., vertical pair		40.00					
j	Horizontal pair, imperf. between		50.00					
o	Tagging omitted		*5.00*	—				
	Coil, Tagged, Perf. 10 Vertically							
1338G	8¢ dk bl, rd and slt grn (1338), design 18.25 x 21mm	05/10/71	.20	.20	.40	(2)	1.00	
h	Imperf., pair		*50.00*					
r	Tagging omitted		*6.00*	—				
	Tagged, Perf. 11							
1339	6¢ Illinois Statehood	02/12/68	.20	.20	.60	(4)	1.00	141
1340	6¢ HemisFair '68	03/30/68	.20	.20	.50	(4)	1.00	144
a	White omitted		*1,200.00*					
	Untagged, Perf. 11							
1341	$1 Airlift	04/04/68	2.00	1.25	8.50	(4)	7.00	
	Pair with full horizontal gutter between				—			
	Tagged, Perf. 11							
1342	6¢ Support Our Youth-Elks	05/01/68	.20	.20	.50	(4)	1.00	147
a	Tagging omitted		*7.50*	—				
1343	6¢ Law and Order	05/17/68	.20	.20	.50	(4)	2.00	130
1344	6¢ Register and Vote	06/27/68	.20	.20	.50	(4)	1.00	159
	Historic Flags, Tagged, Perf. 11							
1345	6¢ Ft. Moultrie Flag, 1776	07/04/68	.40	.25				23
1346	6¢ Ft. McHenry (U.S.) Flag, 1795-1818	07/04/68	.30	.25				23
1347	6¢ Washington's Cruisers Flag, 1775	07/04/68	.25	.25			3.00	23
1348	6¢ Bennington Flag, 1777	07/04/68	.25	.25			3.00	23
1349	6¢ Rhode Island Flag, 1775	07/04/68	.25	.25			3.00	23
1350	6¢ First Stars and Stripes, 1777	07/04/68	.25	.25			3.00	23
1351	6¢ Bunker Hill Flag, 1775	07/04/68	.25	.25			3.00	23
1352	6¢ Grand Union Flag, 1776	07/04/68	.25	.25			3.00	23
	Historic Flags continued, **Tagged, Perf. 11**							
1353	6¢ Philadelphia Light Horse Flag, 1775	07/04/68	.25	.25			3.00	2
1354	6¢ First Navy Jack, 1775	07/04/68	.25	.25			3.00	2
a	Strip of 10, #1345-1354		2.75	*3.25*	6.00	(20)	15.00	
	Tagged, Perf. 12							
1355	6¢ Walt Disney	09/11/68	.40	.20	1.75	(4)	25.00	15
a	Ocher omitted		*500.00*	—				
b	Vertical pair, imperf. horizontally		*650.00*					
c	Imperf., pair		*550.00*					
d	Black omitted		*2,000.00*					
e	Horizontal pair, imperf. between		*4,750.00*					
f	Blue omitted		*2,000.00*					
g	Tagging omitted		*15.00*	—				
	Tagged, Perf. 11							
1356	6¢ Father Marquette	09/20/68	.20	.20	.60	(4)	1.00	13
a	Tagging omitted		*6.00*	—				
	American Folklore, Tagged, Perf. 11							
1357	6¢ Pennsylvania Rifle, Powder Horn, Tomahawk, Pipe and Knife	09/26/68	.20	.20	.50	(4)	1.25	13
	Tagged, Perf. 11							
1358	6¢ Arkansas River Navigation	10/01/68	.20	.20	.50	(4)	1.00	13
1359	6¢ Leif Erikson	10/09/68	.20	.20	.50	(4)	1.00	12
	Tagged, Perf. 11 x 10.5							
1360	6¢ Cherokee Strip	10/15/68	.20	.20	.60	(4)	1.00	12
a	Tagging omitted		*7.50*	—				
	Tagged, Perf. 11							
1361	6¢ John Trumbull	10/18/68	.20	.20	.60	(4)	2.00	12
1362	6¢ Waterfowl Conservation	10/24/68	.20	.20	.65	(4)	1.25	14
a	Vertical pair, imperf. between		*450.00*	—				
b	Red and dark blue omitted		*800.00*					
	Holiday Celebrations: Christmas, Tagged, Perf. 11							
1363	6¢ Angel Gabriel, from "The Annunciation," by Jan Van Eyck	11/01/68	.20	.20	2.00	(10)	1.25	1,41
a	Untagged	11/02/68	.20	.20	2.00	(10)	10.00	
b	Imperf., pair (tagged)		*200.00*					
c	Light yellow omitted		*55.00*					
d	Imperf., pair (untagged)		*275.00*					
	Tagged, Perf. 11							
1364	6¢ American Indian	11/04/68	.20	.20	.70	(4)	1.25	125
	Beautification of America, Tagged, Perf. 11							
1365	6¢ Capitol, Azaleas and Tulips	01/16/69	.25	.20			1.00	48
1366	6¢ Washington Monument, Potomac River and Daffodils	01/16/69	.25	.20			1.00	48
1367	6¢ Poppies and Lupines along Highway	01/16/69	.25	.20			1.00	48
1368	6¢ Blooming Crabapple Trees Lining Avenue	01/16/69	.25	.20			1.00	48
a	Block of 4, #1365-1368		1.00	*1.75*	1.25	(4)	4.00	
1369	6¢ American Legion	03/15/69	.20	.20	.45	(4)	1.00	14
	American Folklore, Tagged, Perf. 11							
1370	6¢ "July Fourth" by Grandma Moses	05/01/69	.20	.20	.50	(4)	1.50	13
a	Horizontal pair, imperf. between		*200.00*	—				
b	Black and Prussian blue omitted		*750.00*					
c	Tagging omitted		7.50	—				
	Space, Tagged, Perf. 11							
1371	6¢ Apollo 8	05/05/69	.20	.20	.65	(4)	2.25	187

1335

1336

1337

1338

1339

1340

1341

1342

1343

1344

1345

1346

1347

1348

1349

1350

1351

1352

1353

1354

1354

1355

1356

1357

1358

1359

1360

1361

1362

1363

1364

1365 1366 1367 1368 1368a

1369

1370

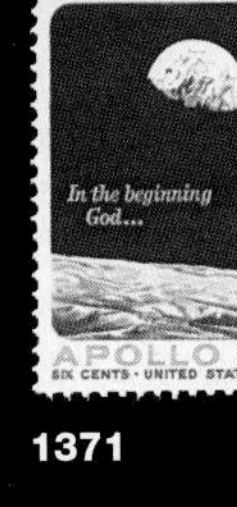
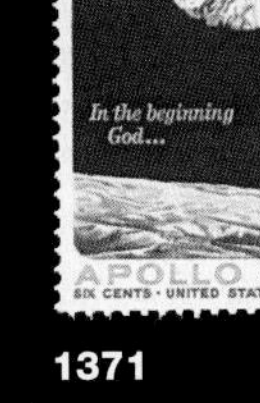

1371

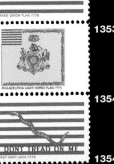

1372 · 1373 · 1374 · 1375 · 1376 · 1377 · 1378 · 1379 · 1379a

1380 · 1381 · 1382 · 1383 · 1384 · 1384 Precancel

1385 · 1386 · 1387 · 1388 · 1389 · 1390 · 1390a · 1391 · 1392 · 1393 · 1393D · 1394

1396 · 1397 · 1398 · 1399 · 1400 · 1405 · 1406 · 1407

1408 · 1409 · 1410 · 1411 · 1412 · 1413

	Issue	Date	Un	U	PB	#	FDC	Q(M)
	Tagged, Perf. 11							
1372	6¢ W.C. Handy	05/17/69	.20	.20	.65	(4)	2.25	126
a	Tagging omitted		7.50	—				
1373	6¢ California Settlement	07/16/69	.20	.20	.45	(4)	1.00	144
1374	6¢ John Wesley Powell	08/01/69	.20	.20	.60	(4)	1.00	136
a	Tagging omitted		9.00	—				
1375	6¢ Alabama Statehood	08/02/69	.20	.20	.60	(4)	1.00	151
	Botanical Congress, Tagged, Perf. 11							
1376	6¢ Douglas Fir (Northwest)	08/23/69	.35	.20			1.50	40
1377	6¢ Lady's Slipper (Northeast)	08/23/69	.35	.20			1.50	40
1378	6¢ Ocotillo (Southwest)	08/23/69	.35	.20			1.50	40
1379	6¢ Franklinia (Southeast)	08/23/69	.35	.20			1.50	40
a	Block of 4, #1376-1379		1.50	*2.50*	1.75	(4)	5.00	
	Tagged, Perf. 10.5 x 11							
1380	6¢ Dartmouth College Case	09/22/69	.20	.20	.50	(4)	1.00	130
	Tagged, Perf. 11							
1381	6¢ Professional Baseball	09/24/69	.55	.20	2.50	(4)	12.00	131
a	Black omitted		*850.00*					
1382	6¢ Intercollegiate Football	09/26/69	.20	.20	1.00	(4)	6.50	139
1383	6¢ Dwight D. Eisenhower	10/14/69	.20	.20	.50	(4)	1.00	151
	Holiday Celebrations: Holiday, Tagged, Perf. 11 x 10.5							
1384	6¢ Winter Sunday in Norway, Maine	11/03/69	.20	.20	1.40	(10)	1.25	1,710
	Precanceled		.50	.20				
b	Imperf., pair		*900.00*					
c	Light green omitted		*25.00*					
d	Light green and yellow omitted		*750.00*	—				
e	Yellow omitted		*2,250.00*					
f	Tagging omitted		*5.00*	—				
	Precanceled versions issued on an experimental basis in four cities whose names appear on the stamps: Atlanta, GA; Baltimore, MD; Memphis, TN; and New Haven, CT.							
	Tagged, Perf. 11							
1385	6¢ Hope for the Crippled	11/20/69	.20	.20	.50	(4)	1.25	128
1386	6¢ William M. Harnett	12/03/69	.20	.20	.55	(4)	1.00	146
	Natural History, Tagged, Perf. 11							
1387	6¢ American Bald Eagle	05/06/70	.20	.20				50
1388	6¢ African Elephant Herd	05/06/70	.20	.20				50
1389	6¢ Tlingit Chief in Haida Ceremonial Canoe	05/06/70	.20	.20				50
1390	6¢ Brontosaurus, Stegosaurus and Allosaurus from Jurassic Period	05/06/70	.20	.20				50
a	Block of 4, #1387-1390		.55	*.80*	.70	(4)	4.00	
	Tagged, Perf. 11							
1391	6¢ Maine Statehood	07/09/70	.20	.20	.60	(4)	2.50	172
	Tagged, Perf. 11 x 10.5							
1392	6¢ Wildlife Conservation	07/20/70	.20	.20	.50	(4)	1.00	142
	Prominent Americans, Tagged, Perf. 11 x 10.5							
1393	6¢ Dwight D. Eisenhower	08/06/70	.20	.20	.50	(4)	1.00	
a	Booklet pane of 8		1.50	*.75*			3.00	
b	Booklet pane of 5 + label		1.50	*.75*			1.50	
c	Untagged (Bureau precanceled)		12.75	3.00	*175.00*	(4)		

	Issue	Date	Un	U	PB/LP	#	FDC	Q(M)
	Prominent Americans, Perf. 10.5 x 11							
1393D	7¢ Benjamin Franklin	10/20/72	.20	.20	.60	(4)	1.00	
e	Untagged (Bureau precanceled)		4.25	1.00	52.50	(4)		
f	Tagging omitted		4.00	—				
	Prominent Americans, Perf. 11							
1394	8¢ Eisenhower	05/10/71	.20	.20	.60	(4)	1.00	
a	Tagging omitted		4.50	—				
	Perf. 11 x 10.5 on 2 or 3 sides							
1395	8¢ deep claret Eisenhower (1394), Single from booklet		.20	.20			1.00	
a	Booklet pane of 8	05/10/71	1.80	*1.25*			2.50	
b	Booklet pane of 6	05/10/71	1.25	*1.10*			2.50	
c	Booklet pane of 4 + 2 labels	01/28/72	1.65	*1.00*			2.25	
d	Booklet pane of 7 + label	01/28/72	1.90	*1.10*			2.25	
	Prominent Americans, Perf. 11 x 10.5							
1396	8¢ U.S. Postal Service	07/01/71	.20	.20	2.00	(12)	1.00	
1397	14¢ Fiorello H. LaGuardia	04/24/72	.25	.20	1.15	(4)	1.00	
a	Untagged (Bureau precanceled)		*145.00*	17.50				
1398	16¢ Ernie Pyle	05/07/71	.35	.20	1.50	(4)	1.50	
a	Untagged (Bureau precanceled)		22.50	5.00	95.00	(4)		
1399	18¢ Dr. Elizabeth Blackwell	01/23/74	.35	.20	1.50	(4)	1.25	
1400	21¢ Amadeo P. Giannini	06/27/73	.40	.20	1.65	(4)	1.50	
	Coil, Tagged, Perf. 10 Vertically							
1401	6¢ dark blue gray Eisenhower (1393)	08/06/70	.20	.20	.50	(2)	1.00	
a	Untagged (Bureau precanceled)		19.50	3.00	*525.00*	(2)		
b	Imperf., pair		*2,000.00*		—	(2)		
1402	8¢ deep claret Eisenhower (1394)	05/10/71	.20	.20	.60	(2)	1.00	
a	Imperf., pair		40.00		70.00	(2)		
b	Untagged (Bureau precanceled)		6.75	.75	*185.00*	(2)		
c	Pair, imperf. between		*6,250.00*					
1403-1404	Not assigned							
	Tagged, Perf. 11							
1405	6¢ Edgar Lee Masters	08/22/70	.20	.20	.50	(4)	1.00	138
a	Tagging omitted		—	—				
1406	6¢ Woman Suffrage	08/26/70	.20	.20	.50	(4)	1.00	135
1407	6¢ South Carolina Settlement	09/12/70	.20	.20	.55	(4)	1.00	136
1408	6¢ Stone Mountain Memorial	09/19/70	.20	.20	.50	(4)	1.00	133
1409	6¢ Ft. Snelling	10/17/70	.20	.20	.50	(4)	1.00	135
	Anti-Pollution, Tagged, Perf. 11 x 10.5							
1410	6¢ Save Our Soil Globe and Wheat Field	10/28/70	.25	.20			1.25	40
1411	6¢ Save Our Cities Globe and City Playground	10/28/70	.25	.20			1.25	40
1412	6¢ Save Our Water Globe and Bluegill Fish	10/28/70	.25	.20			1.25	40
1413	6¢ Save Our Air Globe and Seagull	10/28/70	.25	.20			1.25	40
a	Block of 4, #1410-1413		1.10	*1.50*	2.25	(10)	4.00	

	Issue	Date	Un	U	PB	#	FDC	Q(M)
	Holiday Celebrations: Christmas, Tagged, Perf. 10.5 x 11							
1414	6¢ Nativity, by Lorenzo Lotto	11/05/70	.20	.20	1.10	(8)	1.25	684*
a	Precanceled		.20	.20	1.90	(8)	7.50	
b	Black omitted		475.00					
c	As "a," blue omitted		1,500.00					
d	Type II		.20	.20	2.75	(8)		
e	Type II, precanceled		.25	.20	4.00	(8)		
	#1414a-1418a were furnished to 68 cities. Unused prices are for copies with gum and used prices are for copies with or without gum but with an additional cancellation. *Includes #1414a.							
	Holiday Celebrations: Holiday, Tagged, Perf. 11 x 10.5							
1415	6¢ Tin and Cast-iron Locomotive	11/05/70	.30	.20			1.50	122
a	Precanceled		.75	.20				110
b	Black omitted		2,500.00					
1416	6¢ Toy Horse on Wheels	11/05/70	.30	.20			1.50	122
a	Precanceled		.75	.20				110
b	Black omitted		2,500.00					
c	Imperf., pair			4,000.00				
1417	6¢ Mechanical Tricycle	11/05/70	.30	.20			1.50	122
a	Precanceled		.75	.20				110
b	Black omitted		2,500.00					
1418	6¢ Doll Carriage	11/05/70	.30	.20			1.50	122
a	Precanceled		.75	.20				110
b	Block of 4, #1415-1418		1.25	1.75	3.00	(8)	5.50	
c	Block of 4, #1415a-1418a		3.25	3.75	6.25	(8)	15.00	
d	Black omitted		2,500.00					
	Tagged, Perf. 11							
1419	6¢ United Nations	11/20/70	.20	.20	.50	(4)	1.00	128
a	Tagging omitted		25.00					
1420	6¢ Landing of the Pilgrims	11/21/70	.20	.20	.50	(4)	1.00	130
a	Orange and yellow omitted		750.00					
1421	6¢ Disabled American Veterans Emblem	11/24/70	.20	.20			2.00	67
1422	6¢ U.S. Servicemen	11/24/70	.20	.20			2.00	67
a	Attached pair, #1421-1422		.30	.40	1.00	(4)	3.00	
	Tagged, Perf. 11							
1423	6¢ American Wool Industry	01/19/71	.20	.20	.50	(4)	1.00	136
a	Tagging omitted		11.00	—				
1424	6¢ Gen. Douglas MacArthur	01/26/71	.20	.20	.60	(4)	1.50	135
1425	6¢ Blood Donor	03/12/71	.20	.20	.50	(4)	1.00	131
a	Tagging omitted		11.00	—				
	Tagged, Perf. 11 x 10.5							
1426	8¢ Missouri Statehood	05/08/71	.20	.20	2.00	(12)	1.00	161
	Wildlife Conservation, Tagged, Perf. 11							
1427	8¢ Trout	06/12/71	.20	.20			1.25	44
b	Red omitted		1,250.00					
1428	8¢ Alligator	06/12/71	.20	.20			1.25	44
1429	8¢ Polar Bear and Cubs	06/12/71	.20	.20			1.25	44
1430	8¢ California Condor	06/12/71	.20	.20			1.25	44
a	Block of 4, #1427-1430		.80	1.00	.90	(4)	3.00	
b	As "a," light green and dark green omitted from #1427-1428		4,500.00					
c	As "a," red omitted from #1427, 1429-1430		7,000.00					
	Tagged, Perf. 11							
1431	8¢ Antarctic Treaty	06/23/71	.20	.20	.65	(4)	1.00	139
a	Tagging omitted		10.00					
b	Both colors omitted		500.00					
	Prominent Americans, Tagged, Perf. 11							
1432	8¢ Bicentennial Commission Emblem	07/04/71	.20	.20	.85	(4)	1.00	138
a	Gray and black omitted		600.00					
b	Gray omitted		1,000.00					
	Tagged, Perf. 11							
1433	8¢ John Sloan	08/02/71	.20	.20	.70	(4)	1.00	152
a	Tagging omitted		—					
	Space, Tagged, Perf. 11							
1434	8¢ Earth, Sun and Landing Craft on Moon	08/02/71	.20	.20				88
a	Tagging omitted		30.00				2.00	
1435	8¢ Lunar Rover and Astronauts	08/02/71	.20	.20	.65	(4)		88
a	Tagging omitted		30.00					
b	Pair #1434-1435		.40	.45				
c	As "b", tagging omitted		80.00					
d	As "b", blue & red omitted		1,350.00					
	Tagged, Perf. 11							
1436	8¢ Emily Dickinson	08/28/71	.20	.20	.65	(4)	1.00	143
a	Black and olive omitted		650.00					
b	Pale rose omitted		6,500.00					
1437	8¢ San Juan, Puerto Rico	09/12/71	.20	.20	.65	(4)	1.00	149
a	Tagging omitted		9.00					
	Tagged, Perf. 10.5 x 11							
1438	8¢ Prevent Drug Abuse	10/04/71	.20	.20	1.00	(6)	1.00	139
1439	8¢ CARE	10/27/71	.20	.20	1.25	(8)	1.00	131
a	Black omitted		2,750.00					
b	Tagging omitted		5.00					
	Historic Preservation, Tagged, Perf. 11							
1440	8¢ Decatur House, Washington, D.C.	10/29/71	.20	.20			1.25	43
1441	8¢ Whaling Ship *Charles W. Morgan*, Mystic, Connecticut	10/29/71	.20	.20			1.25	43
1442	8¢ Cable Car, San Francisco	10/29/71	.20	.20			1.25	43
1443	8¢ San Xavier del Bac Mission, Tucson, Arizona	10/29/71	.20	.20			1.25	43
a	Block of 4, #1440-1443		.75	1.00	.90	(4)	3.00	
b	As "a," black brown omitted		1,800.00					
c	As "a," ocher omitted		—					
d	As "a," tagging omitted		75.00					
	Holiday Celebrations: Christmas, Tagged, Perf. 10.5 x 11							
1444	8¢ Adoration of the Shepherds, by Giorgione	11/10/71	.20	.20	1.80	(12)	1.25	1,074
a	Gold omitted		425.00					
	Holiday Celebrations: Holiday, Tagged, Perf. 10.5 x 11							
1445	8¢ Partridge in a Pear Tree	11/10/71	.20	.20	1.80	(12)	1.25	980

1414

1414a

1415 1416

1417 1418 1418b

1419

1420

1421 1422 1422a

1423

1424

1425

1426

1427 1428

1429 1430 1430a

1431

1432

1433

1434 1435 1435b

1436

1437

1438

1439

1440 1441

1442 1443 1443a

1444

1445

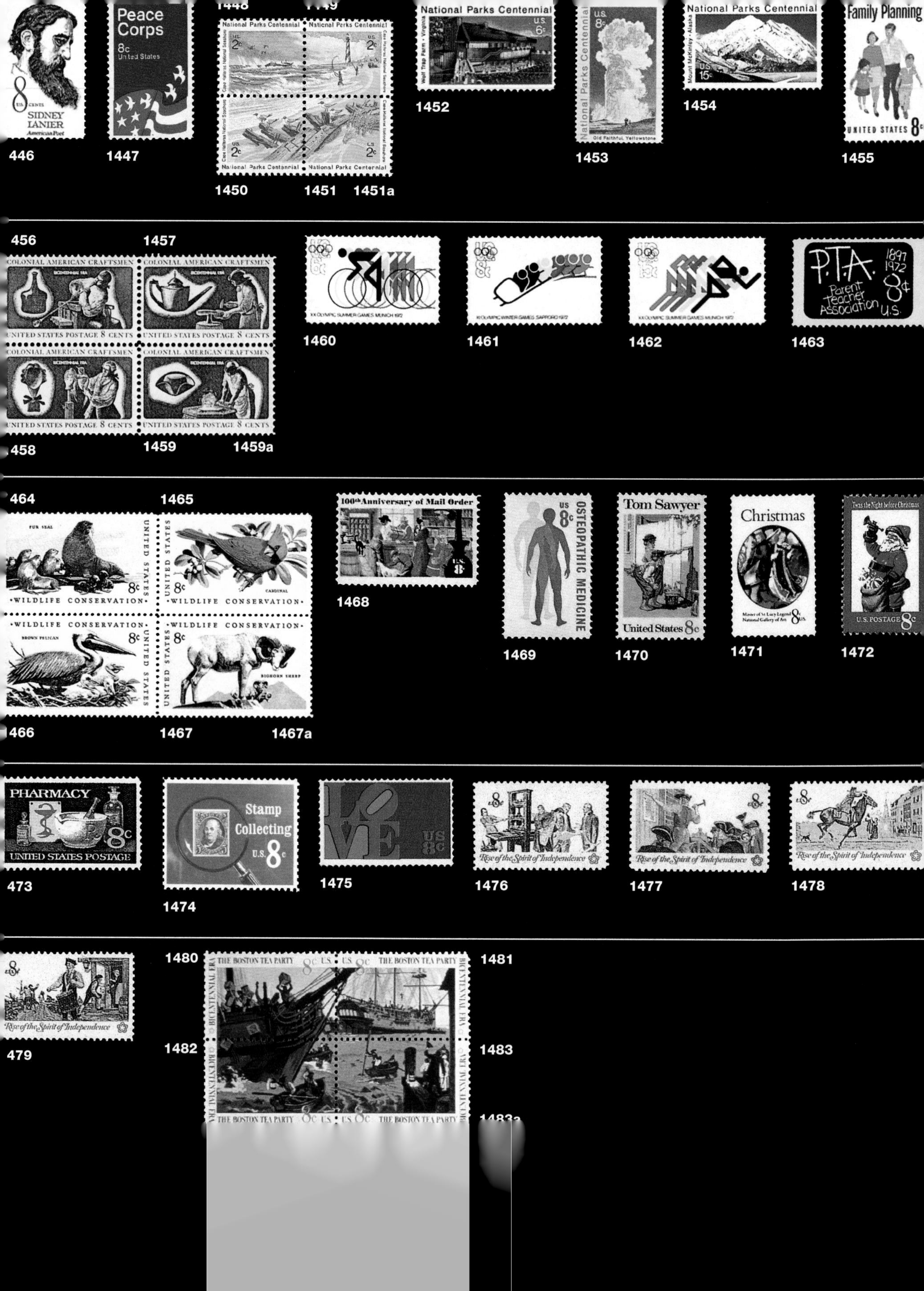

SIDNEY LANIER
American Poet
Peace Corps
8c United States
National Parks Centennial
National Parks Centennial
Wolf Trap Farm • Virginia
National Parks Centennial
Old Faithful, Yellowstone
National Parks Centennial
Mount McKinley • Alaska
Family Planning
UNITED STATES 8c
COLONIAL AMERICAN CRAFTSMEN
UNITED STATES POSTAGE 8 CENTS
XX OLYMPIC SUMMER GAMES MUNICH 1972
XI OLYMPIC WINTER GAMES SAPPORO 1972
P.T.A. 1897 1972 Parent Teacher Association 8¢ U.S.
WILDLIFE CONSERVATION
UNITED STATES
FUR SEAL
CARDINAL
BROWN PELICAN
BIGHORN SHEEP
100th Anniversary of Mail Order
OSTEOPATHIC MEDICINE
Tom Sawyer
United States 8c
Christmas
'Twas the Night before Christmas
U.S. POSTAGE 8c
PHARMACY
UNITED STATES POSTAGE
Stamp Collecting
LOVE
Rise of the Spirit of Independence
THE BOSTON TEA PARTY
BICENTENNIAL ERA

1446 1447 1448 1449 1450 1451 1451a 1452 1453 1454 1455

1456 1457 1458 1459 1459a 1460 1461 1462 1463

1464 1465 1466 1467 1467a 1468 1469 1470 1471 1472

1473 1474 1475 1476 1477 1478

1479 1480 1481 1482 1483 1483a

Issue		Date	Un	U	PB	#	FDC	Q(M)
	Tagged, Perf. 11							
446	8¢ Sidney Lanier	02/03/72	.20	.20	.65	(4)	1.00	137
a	Tagging omitted		—					
	Tagged, Perf. 10.5 x 11							
447	8¢ Peace Corps	02/11/72	.20	.20	1.00	(6)	1.00	150
a	Tagging omitted		5.00					
	National Parks Centennial, Tagged, Perf. 11							
448	2¢ Ship at Sea	04/05/72	.20	.20				43
449	2¢ Cape Hatteras Lighthouse	04/05/72	.20	.20				43
450	2¢ Laughing Gulls on Driftwood	04/05/72	.20	.20				43
451	2¢ Laughing Gulls and Dune	04/05/72	.20	.20				43
a	Block of 4, #1448-1451		.25	*.45*	.50	(4)	3.00	
b	As "a," black omitted		*1,500.00*					
452	6¢ Performance at Wolf Trap Farm, Shouse Pavilion	06/26/72	.20	.20	.55	(4)	1.00	104
a	Tagging omitted		*11.00*					
453	8¢ Old Faithful, Yellowstone	03/01/72	.20	.20	.70	(4)	1.00	164
a	Tagging omitted		—					
454	15¢ View of Mount McKinley in Alaska	07/28/72	.30	.20	1.30	(4)	1.00	54

Note: Beginning with this National Parks Centennial issue, the USPS began to offer stamp collectors first day cancellations affixed to 8" x 10½" souvenir pages. The pages are similar to the stamp announcements that have appeared on Post Office bulletin boards beginning with Scott #1132. See "American Commemorative Panels" listed in the Table of Contents.

Issue		Date	Un	U	PB	#	FDC	Q(M)
	Tagged, Perf. 11							
455	8¢ Family Planning	03/18/72	.20	.20	.65	(4)	1.00	153
a	Yellow omitted		*425.00*					
c	Dark brown missing		*9,000.00*					
d	Tagging omitted		—					
	American Bicentennial, Tagged, Perf. 11 x 10.5							
456	8¢ Glass Blower	07/04/72	.20	.20			1.00	50
457	8¢ Silversmith	07/04/72	.20	.20			1.00	50
458	8¢ Wigmaker	07/04/72	.20	.20			1.00	50
459	8¢ Hatter	07/04/72	.20	.20			1.00	50
a	Block of 4, #1456-1459		.65	*.90*	.80	(4)	2.50	
b	As "a," tagging omitted		*150.00*					
	Olympic Games, Tagged, Perf. 11 x 10.5							
460	6¢ Bicycling and Olympic Rings	08/17/72	.20	.20	1.25	(10)	1.00	67
	Cylinder flaw (broken red ring)		10.00					
461	8¢ Bobsledding and Olympic Rings	08/17/72	.20	.20	1.60	(10)	1.00	180
a	Tagging omitted		7.50					
462	15¢ Running and Olympic Rings	08/17/72	.30	.20	3.00	(10)	1.00	46
	Tagged, Perf. 11 x 10.5							
463	8¢ Parent Teachers Association	09/15/72	.20	.20	.65	(4)	1.00	180
	Wildlife Conservation, Tagged, Perf. 11							
464	8¢ Fur Seals	09/20/72	.20	.20			1.50	50
465	8¢ Cardinal	09/20/72	.20	.20			1.50	50
466	8¢ Brown Pelican	09/20/72	.20	.20			1.50	50

Issue		Date	Un	U	PB	#	FDC	Q(M)
	Wildlife Conservation continued, **Tagged, Perf. 11**							
1467	8¢ Bighorn Sheep	09/20/72	.20	.20			1.50	50
a	Block of 4, #1464-1467		.65	*.90*	.75	(4)	3.00	
b	As "a," brown omitted		*4,000.00*					
c	As "a," green and blue omitted		*4,000.00*					
d	As "a," red & brown omitted		*4,000.00*					

Note: With this Wildlife Conservation issue the USPS introduced the "American Commemorative Panels". Each panel contains a block of four or more mint stamps with text and background illustrations. See these pages in the Table of Contents.

Issue		Date	Un	U	PB	#	FDC	Q(M)
	Tagged, Perf. 11 x 10.5							
1468	8¢ Mail Order Business	09/27/72	.20	.20	1.75	(12)	1.00	185
	Tagged, Perf. 10.5 x 11							
1469	8¢ Osteopathic Medicine	10/09/72	.20	.20	1.00	(6)	1.50	162
	American Folklore, Tagged, Perf. 11							
1470	8¢ Tom Sawyer Whitewashing a Fence, by Norman Rockwell	10/13/72	.20	.20	.65	(4)	1.50	163
a	Horizontal pair, imperf. between		*4,500.00*					
b	Red and black omitted		*1,500.00*					
c	Yellow and tan omitted		*2,250.00*					
	Holiday Celebrations: Christmas, Tagged, Perf. 10.5 x 11							
1471	8¢ Angels from "Mary, Queen of Heaven" by the Master of the St. Lucy Legend	11/09/72	.20	.20	1.75	(12)	1.00	1,003
a	Pink omitted		*125.00*					
b	Black omitted		*3,500.00*					
1472	8¢ Santa Claus	11/09/72	.20	.20	1.75	(12)	1.00	1,017
	Tagged, Perf. 11							
1473	8¢ Pharmacy	11/10/72	.20	.20	.65	(4)	8.00	166
a	Blue and orange omitted		*750.00*					
b	Blue omitted		*1,900.00*					
c	Orange omitted		*1,900.00*					
1474	8¢ Stamp Collecting	11/17/72	.20	.20	.65	(4)	1.25	167
a	Black omitted		*550.00*					
	Love, Tagged, Perf. 11 x 10.5							
1475	8¢ Love	01/26/73	.20	.20	1.00	(6)	2.00	320
	American Bicentennial, Tagged, Perf. 11							
1476	8¢ Printer and Patriots Examining Pamphlet	02/16/73	.20	.20	.65	(4)	1.00	166
1477	8¢ Posting a Broadside	04/13/73	.20	.20	.65	(4)	1.00	163
	Pair with full horizontal gutter between		—					
1478	8¢ Postrider	06/22/73	.20	.20	.65	(4)	1.00	159
1479	8¢ Drummer	09/28/73	.20	.20	.65	(4)	1.00	147
	American Bicentennial, Boston Tea Party, Tagged, Perf. 11							
1480	8¢ British Merchantman	07/04/73	.20	.20			1.00	49
1481	8¢ British Three-Master	07/04/73	.20	.20			1.00	49
1482	8¢ Boats and Ship's Hull	07/04/73	.20	.20			1.00	49
1483	8¢ Boat and Dock	07/04/73	.20	.20			1.00	49
a	Block of 4, #1480-1483		.65	*.90*	.75	(4)	3.00	
b	As "a," blk. (engraved) omitted		*1,250.00*					
c	As "a," blk. (lithograph) omitted		*1,250.00*					

	Issue	Date	Un	U	PB	#	FDC	Q(M)
	American Arts, Tagged, Perf. 11							
1484	8¢ George Gershwin and Scene from "Porgy and Bess"	02/28/73	.20	.20	1.75	(12)	1.00	139
a	Vertical pair, imperf. horizontally		200.00					
1485	8¢ Robinson Jeffers, Man and Children of Carmel with Burro	08/13/73	.20	.20	1.75	(12)	1.00	128
a	Vertical pair, imperf. horizontally		250.00					
1486	8¢ Henry Ossawa Tanner, Palette and Rainbow	09/10/73	.20	.20	1.75	(12)	2.50	146
1487	8¢ Willa Cather, Pioneer Family and Covered Wagon	09/20/73	.20	.20	1.75	(12)	1.00	140
a	Vertical pair, imperf. horizontally		250.00					
	Tagged, Perf. 11							
1488	8¢ Nicolaus Copernicus	04/23/73	.20	.20	.65	(4)	1.25	159
a	Orange omitted		875.00					
b	Black omitted		900.00					
	Postal Service Employees, Tagged, Perf. 10.5 x 11							
1489	8¢ Stamp Counter	04/30/73	.20	.20			1.00	49
1490	8¢ Mail Collection	04/30/73	.20	.20			1.00	49
1491	8¢ Letter Facing on Conveyor	04/30/73	.20	.20			1.00	49
1492	8¢ Parcel Post Sorting	04/30/73	.20	.20			1.00	49
1493	8¢ Mail Canceling	04/30/73	.20	.20			1.00	49
1494	8¢ Manual Letter Routing	04/30/73	.20	.20			1.00	49
1495	8¢ Electronic Letter Routing	04/30/73	.20	.20			1.00	49
1496	8¢ Loading Mail on Truck	04/30/73	.20	.20			1.00	49
1497	8¢ Mail Carrier	04/30/73	.20	.20			1.00	49
1498	8¢ Rural Mail Delivery	04/30/73	.20	.20			1.00	49
a	Strip of 10, #1489-1498		1.75	2.00	3.75	(20)	5.00	
b	As "a," tagging omitted		175.00	—				
	#1489-1498 were the first United States postage stamps to have printing on the back. (See also 1559-1562.)							
	Tagged, Perf. 11							
1499	8¢ Harry S. Truman	05/08/73	.20	.20	.75	(4)	1.25	157
a	Tagging omitted		11.00					
	Progress in Electronics, Tagged, Perf. 11							
1500	6¢ Marconi's Spark Coil and Gap	07/10/73	.20	.20	.55	(4)	1.00	53
1501	8¢ Transistors and Printed Circuit Board	07/10/73	.20	.20	.70	(4)	1.00	160
a	Black inscriptions omitted		400.00					
b	Tan and lilac omitted		1,100.00					
1502	15¢ Microphone, Speaker, Vacuum Tube, TV Camera Tube	07/10/73	.30	.20	1.30	(4)	1.00	39
a	Black inscriptions omitted		1,350.00					
	Tagged, Perf. 11							
1503	8¢ Lyndon B. Johnson	08/27/73	.20	.20	2.20	(12)	1.00	153
a	Horizontal pair, imperf. vertically		300.00					

	Issue	Date	Un	U	PB/LP	#	FDC	Q(M)
	Rural America, Tagged, Perf. 11							
1504	8¢ Angus and Longhorn Cattle, by F.C. Murphy	10/05/73	.20	.20	.65	(4)	1.00	146
a	Green and red brown omitted		850.00					
b	Vertical pair, imperf. between		5,000.00					
1505	10¢ Chautauqua Tent and Buggies	08/06/74	.20	.20	.85	(4)	1.00	151
b	Black (litho) omitted		2,000.00					
1506	10¢ Wheat Fields and Train	08/16/74	.20	.20	.85	(4)	1.00	141
a	Black and blue omitted		700.00					
	Holiday Celebrations: Christmas, Tagged, Perf. 10.5 x 11							
1507	8¢ Small Cowper Madonna, by Raphael	11/07/73	.20	.20	1.75	(12)	1.00	885
	Holiday Celebrations: Holiday, Tagged, Perf. 10.5 x 11							
1508	8¢ Christmas Tree in Needlepoint	11/07/73	.20	.20	1.75	(12)	1.00	940
a	Vertical pair, imperf. between		275.00					
	Tagged, Perf. 11 x 10.5							
1509	10¢ 50-Star and 13-Star Flags	12/08/73	.20	.20	4.25	(20)	1.00	
a	Horizontal pair, imperf. between		50.00	—				
b	Blue omitted		175.00	—				
c	Imperf., pair		900.00					
d	Horizontal pair, imperf. vertically		1,000.00					
e	Tagging omitted		9.00					
1510	10¢ Jefferson Memorial	12/14/73	.20	.20	.85	(4)	1.00	
a	Untagged (Bureau precanceled)		4.00	1.00	50.00	(4)		
b	Booklet pane of 5 + label		1.65	.90			2.25	
c	Booklet pane of 8		1.65	1.00			2.50	
d	Booklet pane of 6	08/05/74	5.25	1.75			3.00	
e	Vertical pair, imperf. horizontally		450.00					
f	Vertical pair, imperf. between		500.00					
g	Tagging omitted		5.00					
1511	10¢ ZIP Code	01/04/74	.20	.20	1.75	(8)	1.00	
a	Yellow omitted		50.00					
1512-1517	Not assigned							
	Coil, Tagged, Perf. 10 Vertically							
1518	6.3¢ Liberty Bell	10/01/74	.20	.20	.80	(2)	1.00	
a	Untagged (Bureau precanceled)		.35	.20	1.65	(2)		
b	Imperf., pair		175.00		475.00	(2)		
c	As "a," imperf., pair		90.00		200.00	(2)		
1519	10¢ 15-star and 13-star Flags (1509)	12/08/73	.20	.20			1.00	
a	Imperf., pair		35.00					
b	Tagging omitted		12.50					
1520	10¢ blue Jefferson Memorial (1510)	12/14/73	.25	.20	.75	(2)	1.00	
a	Untagged (Bureau precanceled)		5.50	1.25	185.00	(2)		
b	Imperf., pair		35.00		65.00	(2)		
1521-1524	Not assigned							
	Tagged, Perf. 11							
1525	10¢ Veterans of Foreign Wars	03/11/74	.20	.20	.85	(4)	1.50	144
a	Tagging omitted		15.00					

US 8 CENTS
AMERICAN COMPOSER
GEORGE GERSHWIN

1484

US 8 CENTS
AMERICAN POET
ROBINSON JEFFERS

1485

1486

WILLA CATHER

1487

Copernicus
1473 - 1973
8¢ US

1488

U.S. POSTAL SERVICE 8¢
U.S. POSTAL SERVICE 8¢
U.S. POSTAL SERVICE 8¢
U.S. POSTAL SERVICE 8¢
U.S. POSTAL SERVICE 8¢

1489 1490 1491 1492 1493

U.S. POSTAL SERVICE 8¢
U.S. POSTAL SERVICE 8¢
U.S. POSTAL SERVICE 8¢
U.S. POSTAL SERVICE 8¢
U.S. POSTAL SERVICE 8¢

1494 1495 1496 1497 1498

Nearly 27 billion U.S. stamps are sold yearly to carry your letters to every corner of the world.
People Serving You
Mail is picked up from nearly a third of a million local collection boxes, as well as your mailbox.
People Serving You
More than 87 billion letters and packages are handled yearly—almost 300 million every delivery day.
People Serving You
The People in your Postal Service handle and deliver more than 500 million packages yearly.
People Serving You
Thousands of machines, buildings, and vehicles must be operated and maintained to keep your mail moving.
People Serving You

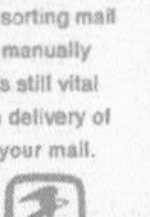
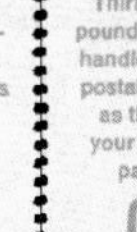
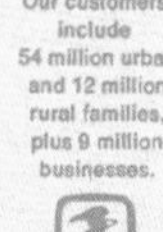

The skill of sorting mail manually is still vital to delivery of your mail.
People Serving You
Employees use modern, high-speed equipment to sort and process huge volumes of mail in central locations.
People Serving You
Thirteen billion pounds of mail are handled yearly by postal employees as they speed your letters and packages.
People Serving You
Our customers include 54 million urban and 12 million rural families, plus 9 million businesses.
People Serving You
Employees cover 4 million miles each delivery day to bring mail to your home or business.
People Serving You

Harry S. Truman

U.S. Postage 8 cents

1499

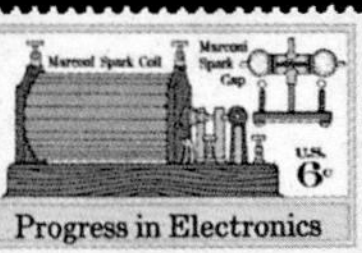

Progress in Electronics
U.S. 6¢

1500

Progress in Electronics
U.S. 8¢

1501

Progress in Electronics
U.S. 15¢

1502

Lyndon B. Johnson
United States 8 cents

1503

RURAL AMERICA
U.S. 8¢

1504

RURAL AMERICA
US 10¢

1505

RURAL AMERICA
US 10¢

1506

Christmas
Raphael National Gallery of Art
8¢ U.S.

1507

US 8¢
CHRISTMAS

1508

1509

UNITED STATES 10¢

1510

IT ALL DEPENDS ON
ZIP CODE
US 10¢

1511

6.3¢
U.S. Postage

1518

VFW
75th Anniversary
VETERANS of SPANISH-AMERICAN and OTHER FOREIGN WARS • US 10¢

1525

1526 1527

1528

US10c Skylab

1529

1530 1531 1532 1533

1534 1535 1536 1537 1537a

1538

1539

1540

1541 1541a

1542

1543 1544

1545 1546 1546a

1547

1548

1549

1550

1551

1552

1553

1554

1555

1556

1557

1558

Issue		Date	Un	U	PB	#	FDC	Q(M)
	Tagged, Perf. 10.5 x 11							
1526	10¢ Robert Frost	03/26/74	.20	.20	.85	(4)	1.00	145
	Tagged, Perf. 11							
1527	10¢ Expo '74 World's Fair	04/18/74	.20	.20	2.50	(12)	1.00	135
	Tagged, Perf. 11 x 10.5							
1528	10¢ Horse Racing	05/04/74	.25	.20	3.50	(12)	3.00	157
a	Blue omitted		*825.00*					
b	Red omitted		—					
	Space, Tagged, Perf. 11							
1529	10¢ Skylab	05/14/74	.20	.20	.85	(4)	1.50	165
b	Tagging omitted		*10.00*					
	Universal Postal Union, Tagged, Perf. 11							
1530	10¢ Michelangelo, from "School of Athens," by Raphael	06/06/74	.20	.20			1.00	25
1531	10¢ "Five Feminine Virtues," by Hokusai	06/06/74	.20	.20			1.00	25
1532	10¢ "Old Scraps," by John Fredrick Peto	06/06/74	.20	.20			1.00	25
1533	10¢ "The Lovely Reader," by Jean Etienne Liotard	06/06/74	.20	.20			1.00	25
1534	10¢ "Lady Writing Letter," by Gerard Terborch	06/06/74	.20	.20			1.00	25
1535	10¢ Inkwell and Quill, from "Boy with a Top," by Jean-Baptiste Simeon Chardin	06/06/74	.20	.20			1.00	25
1536	10¢ Mrs. John Douglas, by Thomas Gainsborough	06/06/74	.20	.20			1.00	25
1537	10¢ Don Antonio Noriega, by Francisco de Goya	06/06/74	.20	.20			1.00	25
a	Block of 8, #1530-1537		1.75	1.60	2.25	(10)	4.00	
b	As "a," imperf. vertically		*7,000.00*					
	Mineral Heritage, Tagged, Perf. 11							
1538	10¢ Petrified Wood	06/13/74	.20	.20			1.00	42
a	Light blue and yellow omitted		—					
1539	10¢ Tourmaline	06/13/74	.20	.20			1.00	42
a	Light blue omitted		—					
b	Black and purple omitted		—					
1540	10¢ Amethyst	06/13/74	.20	.20			1.00	42
a	Light blue and yellow omitted		—					
1541	10¢ Rhodochrosite	06/13/74	.20	.20			1.00	42
a	Block of 4, #1538-1541		.80	.90	.90	(4)	2.75	
b	As "a," light blue and yellow omitted		*1,750.00*					
c	Light blue omitted		—					
d	Black and red omitted		—					
	Tagged, Perf. 11							
1542	10¢ First Kentucky Settlement - Ft. Harrod	06/15/74	.20	.20	.85	(4)	1.00	156
a	Dull black omitted		*700.00*					
b	Green, black and blue omitted		*3,000.00*					
c	Green omitted		*3,750.00*					
d	Green and black omitted		—					
e	Tagging omitted		—					

Issue		Date	Un	U	PB	#	FDC	Q(M)
	American Bicentennial: First Continental Congress, Tagged, Perf. 11							
1543	10¢ Carpenters' Hall	07/04/74	.20	.20			1.00	49
1544	10¢ "We Ask but for Peace, Liberty and Safety"	07/04/74	.20	.20			1.00	49
1545	10¢ "Deriving Their Just Powers from the Consent of the Governed"	07/04/74	.20	.20			1.00	49
1546	10¢ Independence Hall	07/04/74	.20	.20			1.00	49
a	Block of 4, #1543-1546		.80	.90	.90	(4)	2.75	
b	Tagging omitted		*60.00*					
	Tagged, Perf. 11							
1547	10¢ Energy Conservation	09/23/74	.20	.20	.85	(4)	1.00	149
a	Blue and orange omitted		*825.00*					
b	Orange and green omitted		*550.00*					
c	Green omitted		*825.00*					
d	Tagging omitted		*7.50*					
	American Folklore, Tagged, Perf. 11							
1548	10¢ Headless Horseman and Ichabod Crane	10/10/74	.20	.20	.85	(4)	2.50	157
	Tagged, Perf. 11							
1549	10¢ Retarded Children	10/12/74	.20	.20	.85	(4)	1.00	150
a	Tagging omitted		7.50					
	Holiday Celebrations: Christmas, Tagged, Perf. 10.5 x 11							
1550	10¢ Angel from Perussis Altarpiece	10/23/74	.20	.20	2.10	(10)	1.00	835
	Holiday Celebrations: Holiday, Perf. 11 x 10.5							
1551	10¢ "The Road-Winter," by Currier and Ives	10/23/74	.20	.20	2.50	(12)	1.00	883
a	Buff omitted		10.00					
	Untagged, Self-Adhesive, Die-Cut, (Inscribed "precanceled")							
1552	10¢ Dove Weather Vane atop Mount Vernon	11/15/74	.20	.20	4.25	(20)	1.50	213
	American Arts, Tagged, Perf. 10.5 x 11							
1553	10¢ Benjamin West, Self-Portrait	02/10/75	.20	.20	2.10	(10)	1.00	157
	American Arts, Perf. 11							
1554	10¢ Paul Laurence Dunbar and Lamp	05/01/75	.20	.20	2.10	(10)	1.50	146
a	Imperf., pair		*1,250.00*					
1555	10¢ D.W. Griffith and Motion-Picture Camera	05/27/75	.20	.20	.85	(4)	1.00	149
a	Brown omitted		*625.00*					
	Space, Tagged, Perf. 11							
1556	10¢ Pioneer 10 Passing Jupiter	02/28/75	.20	.20	.85	(4)	1.25	174
a	Red and yellow omitted		*1,200.00*					
b	Blue omitted		*800.00*					
c	Tagging omitted		*11.00*					
1557	10¢ Mariner 10, Venus and Mercury	04/04/75	.20	.20	.85	(4)	1.25	159
a	Red omitted		*400.00*					
b	Ultramarine and bister omitted		*1,750.00*					
c	Tagging omitted		*11.00*					
	Tagged, Perf. 11							
1558	10¢ Collective Bargaining	03/13/75	.20	.20	1.75	(8)	1.00	153
	Imperfs. of #1558 exist from printer's waste							

	Issue	Date	Un	U	PB	#	FDC	Q(M)
	American Bicentennial: Contributors to the Cause, Tagged, Perf. 11 x 10.5							
1559	8¢ Sybil Ludington Riding Horse	03/25/75	.20	.20	1.50	(10)	1.00	63
a	Back inscription omitted		*200.00*					
1560	10¢ Salem Poor Carrying Musket	03/25/75	.20	.20	2.10	(10)	1.50	158
a	Back inscription omitted		*200.00*					
1561	10¢ Haym Salomon Figuring Accounts	03/25/75	.20	.20	2.10	(10)	1.00	167
a	Back inscription omitted		*200.00*					
b	Red omitted		*250.00*					
1562	18¢ Peter Francisco Shouldering Cannon	03/25/75	.35	.20	3.60	(10)	1.00	45
	American Bicentennial, Battle of Lexington & Concord, Tagged, Perf. 11							
1563	10¢ "Birth of Liberty," by Henry Sandham	04/19/75	.20	.20	2.50	(12)	1.00	144
a	Vertical pair, imperf. horizontally		*425.00*					
	American Bicentennial, Tagged, Perf. 11							
1564	10¢ "Battle of Bunker Hill," by John Trumbull	06/17/75	.20	.20	2.50	(12)	1.00	140
	American Bicentennial, Military Uniforms, Tagged, Perf. 11							
1565	10¢ Soldier with Flintlock Musket, Uniform Button	07/04/75	.20	.20			1.00	45
1566	10¢ Sailor with Grappling Hook, First Navy Jack, 1775	07/04/75	.20	.20			1.00	45
1567	10¢ Marine with Musket, Full-Rigged Ship	07/04/75	.20	.20			1.00	45
1568	10¢ Militiaman with Musket, Powder Horn	07/04/75	.20	.20			1.00	45
a	Block of 4, #1565-1568		.85	.90	2.50	(12)	2.50	
	Space, Tagged, Perf. 11							
1569	10¢ Apollo and Soyuz after Link-up and Earth	07/15/75	.20	.20			5.00	81
1570	10¢ Spacecraft before Link-up, Earth and Project Emblem	07/15/75	.20	.20			3.00	81
a	Attached pair, #1569-1570		.45	.40	2.50	(12)		
b	As "a", tagging omitted		*30.00*	—				
c	As "a," vertical pair, imperf. horizontally		*2,250.00*					
	Tagged, Perf. 11 x 10.5							
1571	10¢ International Women's Year	08/26/75	.20	.20	1.30	(6)	1.00	146
	Postal Service Bicentennial, Tagged, Perf. 11 x 10.5							
1572	10¢ Stagecoach and Trailer Truck	09/03/75	.20	.20			1.00	42
1573	10¢ Old and New Locomotives	09/03/75	.20	.20			1.00	42
1574	10¢ Early Mail Plane and Jet	09/03/75	.20	.20			1.00	42
1575	10¢ Satellite for Mailgrams	09/03/75	.20	.20			1.00	42
a	Block of 4, #1572-1575		.85	.90	2.50	(12)	2.50	
b	As "a," red "10¢" omitted		*7,500.00*					
	Tagged, Perf. 11							
1576	10¢ World Peace Through Law	09/29/75	.20	.20	.85	(4)	1.25	147
a	Tagging omitted		10.00					
b	Horizontal pair, imperf. vert.		*7,500.00*					
	Banking and Commerce, Tagged, Perf. 11							
1577	10¢ Engine Turning, Indian Head Penny and Morgan Silver Dollar	10/06/75	.25	.20			1.00	73
	Banking and Commerce continued, **Tagged, Perf. 11**							
1578	10¢ Seated Liberty Quarter, $20 Gold Piece and Engine Turning	10/06/75	.25	.20			1.00	73
a	Attached pair, #1577-1578		.50	.40	1.20	(4)	1.75	
b	Brown and blue omitted		*2,250.00*					
c	As "a," brown, blue and yel. omitted		*2,750.00*					
	Holiday Celebrations: Christmas, Tagged, Perf. 11							
1579	(10¢) Madonna and Child, by Domenico Ghirlandaio	10/14/75	.20	.20	2.50	(12)	1.00	739
a	Imperf., pair		*100.00*					
	Plate flaw ("d" damaged)		5.00	—				
	Holiday Celebrations: Holiday, Perf. 11.2							
1580	(10¢) Christmas Card, by Louis Prang, 1878	10/14/75	.20	.20	2.50	(12)	1.00	879
a	Imperf., pair		*100.00*					
c	Perf. 10.9		.25	.20	3.50	(12)		
	Perf. 10.5 x 11.3							
1580B	(10¢) Christmas Card, by Louis Prang, 1878	10/14/75	.65	.20	15.00	(12)		
	Americana, Tagged, Perf. 11 x 10.5 (Designs 18.5 x 22.5mm; #1590-1590a, 17.5 x 20mm							
1581	1¢ Inkwell & Quill	12/08/77	.20	.20	.25	(4)	1.00	
a	Untagged (Bureau precanceled)		4.50	1.50	22.50	(4)		
d	Tagging omitted		4.50					
1582	2¢ Speaker's Stand	12/08/77	.20	.20	.25	(4)	1.00	
a	Untagged (Bureau precanceled)		4.50	1.50	22.50	(4)		
b	Cream paper, dull gum, *1981*		.20	.20	.25	(4)		
c	Tagging omitted		4.50					
1583	Not assigned							
1584	3¢ Early Ballot Box	12/08/77	.20	.20	.30	(4)	1.00	
a	Untagged (Bureau precanceled)		.75	.50				
b	Tagging omitted		7.50					
1585	4¢ Books, Bookmark, Eyeglasses	12/08/77	.20	.20	.40	(4)	1.00	
a	Untagged (Bureau precanceled)		1.05	.75	13.50	(4)		
1586-1589	Not assigned							
1590	9¢ Capitol Dome, single (1591) from booklet (1623a)	03/11/77	.45	.20			1.00	
	Americana, Perf. 10 x 9.75							
1590A	Single (1591) from booklet (1623c)		20.00	15.00				
	#1590 is on white paper; #1591 is on gray paper.							
	Americana, Perf. 11 x 10.5							
1591	9¢ Capitol Dome	11/24/75	.20	.20	.85	(4)	1.00	
a	Untagged (Bureau precanceled)		1.75	1.00	50.00	(4)		
b	Tagging omitted		5.00					
1592	10¢ Contemplation of Justice	11/17/77	.20	.20	.90	(4)	1.00	
a	Untagged (Bureau precanceled)		9.50	5.00	95.00	(4)		
b	Tagging omitted		7.50					
1593	11¢ Printing Press	11/13/75	.20	.20	.90	(4)	1.00	
a	Tagging omitted		4.00					
1594	12¢ Torch, Statue of Liberty	04/08/81	.25	.20	1.60	(4)	1.00	
a	Tagging omitted		7.50					
1595	13¢ Liberty Bell, single from booklet		.30	.20			1.00	
a	Booklet pane of 6	10/31/75	2.25	*1.00*			2.00	
b	Booklet pane of 7 + label		2.25	*1.00*			2.75	
c	Booklet pane of 8		2.25	*1.00*			2.50	
d	Booklet pane of 5 + label	04/02/76	1.75	*1.00*			2.25	
e	Vertical pair, imperf. between		*1,250.00*					

1559

1560

Contributors To The Cause
U.S. 10c
Haym Salomon Financial Hero

1561

1562

1563

1564

YOUTHFUL HEROINE
On the dark night of April 26, 1777, 16-year-old Sybil Ludington rode her horse "Star" alone through the Connecticut countryside rallying her father's militia to repel a raid by the British on Danbury.

GALLANT SOLDIER
The conspicuously courageous actions of black foot soldier Salem Poor at the Battle of Bunker Hill on June 17, 1775, earned him citations for his bravery and leadership ability.

FINANCIAL HERO
Businessman and broker Haym Salomon was responsible for raising most of the money needed to finance the American Revolution and later to save the new nation from collapse.

FINANCIAL HERO
Businessman and broker Haym Salomon was responsible for raising most of the money needed to finance the American Revolution and later to save the new nation from collapse.

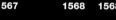

1565 1566

1567 1568 1568a

1569

US 10c
APOLLO SOYUZ 1975
APOLLO SOYUZ SPACE TEST PROJECT
UNITED STATES 1975
10c

1570 1570a

1571

1572 1573

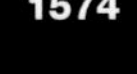

1574 1575 1575a

1576

1577 1578 1578a

1579

1580

1581

1582

1584

1585

1591

1592

1593

1594

1595

1596

1597

1599

1603 1604

1605

1606

1608

1610

1611

1612

1613

1614

1615

1615C

1622

1623a

1629 1630 1631 1631a

1632

	Issue	Date	Un	U	PB/LP	#	FDC	Q(M)
	Americana continued, **Perf. 11.2** (Designs 17.5 x 20mm; #1606, 1608, 1610-1619, 1622-1623, 1625, 1811, 1813, 1816)							
1596	13¢ Eagle and Shield	12/01/75	.25	.20	3.25	(12)	1.00	
a	Imperf., pair		*45.00*	—				
b	Yellow omitted		*125.00*					
d	Line perforated		*27.50*	—	*375.00*	(12)		
1597	15¢ Ft. McHenry Flag	06/30/78	.30	.20	1.90	(6)	1.00	
a	Small block tagging		.30	.20	1.90	(6)	1.00	
b	Gray omitted		*475.00*					
d	Tagging omitted		3.00					
	Americana, Booklet, Perf. 11 x 10.5							
1598	15¢ Ft. McHenry Flag (1597), single from booklet		.40	.20			1.00	
a	Booklet pane of 8	06/30/78	4.25	*.80*			2.50	
1599	16¢ Head, Statue of Liberty	03/31/78	.35	.20	1.90	(4)	1.00	
1600-1602	Not assigned							
1603	24¢ Old North Church	11/14/75	.50	.20	2.25	(4)	1.00	
a	Tagging omitted		11.00					
1604	28¢ Ft. Nisqually	08/11/78	.55	.20	2.40	(4)	1.00	
	Dull gum		1.10		10.00	(4)		
1605	29¢ Sandy Hook Lighthouse	04/14/78	.60	.20	3.00	(4)	1.50	
	Dull gum		2.00		15.00	(4)		
1606	30¢ Morris Township School No.2	08/27/79	.55	.20	2.40	(4)	1.25	
a	Tagging omitted		15.00					
1607	Not assigned							
	Americana, Perf. 11							
1608	50¢ Iron "Betty" Lamp	09/11/79	.85	.20	3.75	(4)	1.50	
a	Black omitted		*275.00*					
b	Vertical pair, imperf. horizontally		*1,750.00*					
c	Tagging omitted		16.00					
1609	Not assigned							
1610	$1 Rush Lamp and Candle	07/02/79	2.00	.20	8.50	(4)	3.00	
a	Brown omitted		*250.00*					
b	Tan, orange and yellow omitted		*275.00*					
c	Brown inverted		*22,500.00*					
d	Tagging omitted		*15.00*					
1611	$2 Kerosene Table Lamp	11/16/78	3.75	.75	16.00	(4)	5.00	
1612	$5 Railroad Conductor's Lantern	08/23/79	8.50	1.75	36.00	(4)	12.50	
	Americana, Coil, Perf. 10 Vertically							
1613	3.1¢ Six String Guitar	10/25/79	.20	.20	1.25	(2)	1.00	
a	Untagged (Bureau precanceled)		.35	.35	5.25	(2)		
b	Imperf., pair		*1,300.00*		*3,000.00*	(2)		
1614	7.7¢ Saxhorns	11/20/76	.20	.20	.90	(2)	1.00	
a	Untagged (Bureau precanceled)		.40	.30	3.25	(2)		
b	As "a," imperf., pair		*1,600.00*		*3,000.00*	(2)		
1615	7.9¢ Drum	04/23/76	.20	.20	.75	(2)	1.00	
a	Untagged (Bureau precanceled)		.40	.40				
b	Imperf., pair		*575.00*					
1615C	8.4¢ Steinway Grand Piano	07/13/78	.20	.20	3.25	(2)	1.00	
d	Untagged (Bureau precanceled)		.50	.40	4.25	(2)		
e	As "d," pair, imperf. between			50.00	*125.00*	(2)		
f	As "d," imperf., pair			17.50	*27.50*	(2)		
1616	9¢ slate green Capitol Dome (1591)	03/05/76	.20	.20	.90	(2)	1.00	
a	Imperf., pair		*150.00*		*350.00*	(2)		
b	Untagged (Bureau precanceled)		1.15	.75	42.50	(2)		
c	As "b," imperf., pair			*700.00*	—	(2)		

	Issue	Date	Un	U	PB/LP	#	FDC	Q(M)
	Americana, Coil, Perf. 10 Vertically continued							
1617	10¢ purple Contemplation of Justice (1592)	11/04/77	.20	.20	1.00	(2)	1.00	
	Dull gum		.30		2.50	(2)		
a	Untagged (Bureau precanceled)		42.50	1.35	*1,150.00*	(2)		
b	Imperf., pair		*60.00*		*125.00*	(2)		
1618	13¢ brown Liberty Bell (1595)	11/25/75	.25	.20	.75	(2)	1.00	
a	Untagged (Bureau precanceled)		5.75	.75	90.00	(2)		
b	Imperf., pair		25.00		*50.00*	(2)		
1618C	15¢ Ft. McHenry Flag (1597)	06/30/78	.50	.20			1.00	
d	Imperf., pair		20.00					
e	Pair, imperf. between		*150.00*					
f	Gray omitted		*35.00*					
i	Tagging omitted		20.00					
1619	16¢ blue Head of Liberty (1599)	03/31/78	.35	.20	1.50	(2)	1.00	
a	Huck Press printing (white background with a bluish tinge, fraction of a millimeter smaller)		.50	.20				
1620-1621	Not assigned							
	Americana, Perf. 11 x 10.75							
1622	13¢ Flag over Independence Hall	11/15/75	.25	.20	5.75	(20)	1.00	
a	Horizontal pair, imperf. between		50.00					
b	Imperf., pair		*450.00*					
e	Horizontal pair, imperf. vertically		—					
f	Tagging omitted		4.00					
	Americana, Perf. 11.25							
1622C	13¢ Star Flag over Independence Hall		1.00	.25	20.00	(6)		
d	Vertical pair, imperf.		*135.00*					
	Americana, Booklet, Engr., Perf. 11 x 10.5							
1623	13¢ Flag over Capitol, single from booklet (1623a)	03/11/77	.25	.20			1.50	
a	Booklet pane of 8, (1 #1590 and 7 #1623)		2.25	*1.25*			25.00	
d	Attached pair, #1590 and 1623		.70	*1.00*				
	Americana, Booklet, Perf. 10 x 9.75							
1623B	13¢ Single from booklet		.80	.80				
c	Booklet pane of 8, (1 #1590A and 7 #1623B)		25.00	—			15.00	
e	Attached pair, #1590A and 1623B		21.00	21.00				
	#1623, 1623B issued only in booklets. All stamps are imperf. at one side or imperf. at one side and bottom.							
1624	Not assigned							
	Coil, Perf. 10 Vertically							
1625	13¢ Flag over Independence Hall (1622)	11/15/75	.25	.20			1.00	
a	Imperf. pair		22.50					
	American Bicentennial: The Spirit of '76, Tagged, Perf. 11							
1629	13¢ Drummer Boy	01/01/76	.25	.20			1.25	73
1630	13¢ Old Drummer	01/01/76	.25	.20			1.25	73
1631	13¢ Fifer	01/01/76	.25	.20			1.25	73
a	Strip of 3, #1629-1631		.75	.75	3.50	(12)	2.00	
b	As "a," imperf.		*950.00*					
c	Imperf., pair, #1631		*800.00*					
	Tagged, Perf. 11							
1632	13¢ *Interphil 76*	01/17/76	.20	.20	1.00	(4)	1.00	158

	Issue	Date	Un	U	FDC	Q(M)
	American Bicentennial: State Flags, Tagged, Perf. 11					
1633	13¢ Delaware	02/23/76	.25	.20	1.50	9
1634	13¢ Pennsylvania	02/23/76	.25	.20	1.50	9
1635	13¢ New Jersey	02/23/76	.25	.20	1.50	9
1636	13¢ Georgia	02/23/76	.25	.20	1.50	9
1637	13¢ Connecticut	02/23/76	.25	.20	1.50	9
1638	13¢ Massachusetts	02/23/76	.25	.20	1.50	9
1639	13¢ Maryland	02/23/76	.25	.20	1.50	9
1640	13¢ South Carolina	02/23/76	.25	.20	1.50	9
1641	13¢ New Hampshire	02/23/76	.25	.20	1.50	9
1642	13¢ Virginia	02/23/76	.25	.20	1.50	9
1643	13¢ New York	02/23/76	.25	.20	1.50	9
1644	13¢ North Carolina	02/23/76	.25	.20	1.50	9
1645	13¢ Rhode Island	02/23/76	.25	.20	1.50	9
1646	13¢ Vermont	02/23/76	.25	.20	1.50	9
1647	13¢ Kentucky	02/23/76	.25	.20	1.50	9
1648	13¢ Tennessee	02/23/76	.25	.20	1.50	9
1649	13¢ Ohio	02/23/76	.25	.20	1.50	9
	American Bicentennial: State Flags continued, **Tagged, Perf. 11**					
1650	13¢ Louisiana	02/23/76	.25	.20	1.50	9
1651	13¢ Indiana	02/23/76	.25	.20	1.50	9
1652	13¢ Mississippi	02/23/76	.25	.20	1.50	9
1653	13¢ Illinois	02/23/76	.25	.20	1.50	9
1654	13¢ Alabama	02/23/76	.25	.20	1.50	9
1655	13¢ Maine	02/23/76	.25	.20	1.50	9
1656	13¢ Missouri	02/23/76	.25	.20	1.50	9
1657	13¢ Arkansas	02/23/76	.25	.20	1.50	9
1658	13¢ Michigan	02/23/76	.25	.20	1.50	9
1659	13¢ Florida	02/23/76	.25	.20	1.50	9
1660	13¢ Texas	02/23/76	.25	.20	1.50	9
1661	13¢ Iowa	02/23/76	.25	.20	1.50	9
1662	13¢ Wisconsin	02/23/76	.25	.20	1.50	9
1663	13¢ California	02/23/76	.25	.20	1.50	9
1664	13¢ Minnesota	02/23/76	.25	.20	1.50	9
1665	13¢ Oregon	02/23/76	.25	.20	1.50	9
1666	13¢ Kansas	02/23/76	.25	.20	1.50	9
1667	13¢ West Virginia	02/23/76	.25	.20	1.50	9

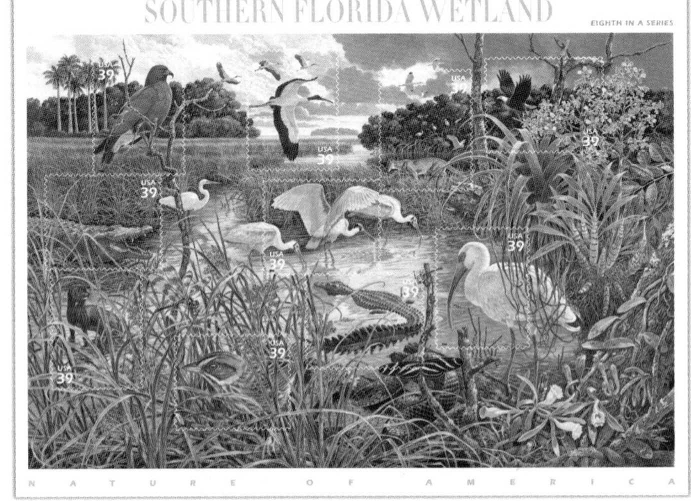

NATURE OF AMERICA: SOUTHERN FLORIDA WETLAND

The Nature of America series continues in 2006 with its eighth issuance featuring a southern Florida wetland. The stamp pane depicts a wetland community where freshwater mingles with salt water along the coast; both freshwater and coastal species are included in the painting by John D. Dawson. Wetlands—places where shallow water constantly saturates the soil or regularly inundates it—may take the form of marshes, swamps, bogs, strands, and riparian forests. The seasonal ebb and flow of water does much to determine the kinds of life-forms found in a wetland. In southern Florida, plants and animals are adapted to water-level changes that correspond to alternating wet and dry seasons; although some species require freshwater habitats and others are more salt tolerant. Florida's subtropical wetlands include some of the most extensive saw grass marshes and mangrove swamps in the world. Insects such as dragonflies and butterflies thrive here, along with hundreds of species of birds—great egrets, roseate spoonbills, eagles snail kites, and Cape Sable seaside sparrows. Reptiles include the American alligator and the American crocodile. One of the rarest animals shown on the stamp pane is a mammal: the Florida panther, a long-tailed cat reaching more than six feet in length. A variety of trees, such as royal palms and West Indian mahoganies, flourish on natural rises known as hammocks. Other trees fringe coastal areas, especially in the southwest: Here, the exposed roots of salt-tolerant mangroves shelter marine organisms and help stabilize the shores of this unique and fragile realm.

1633 1634 1635 1636 1637

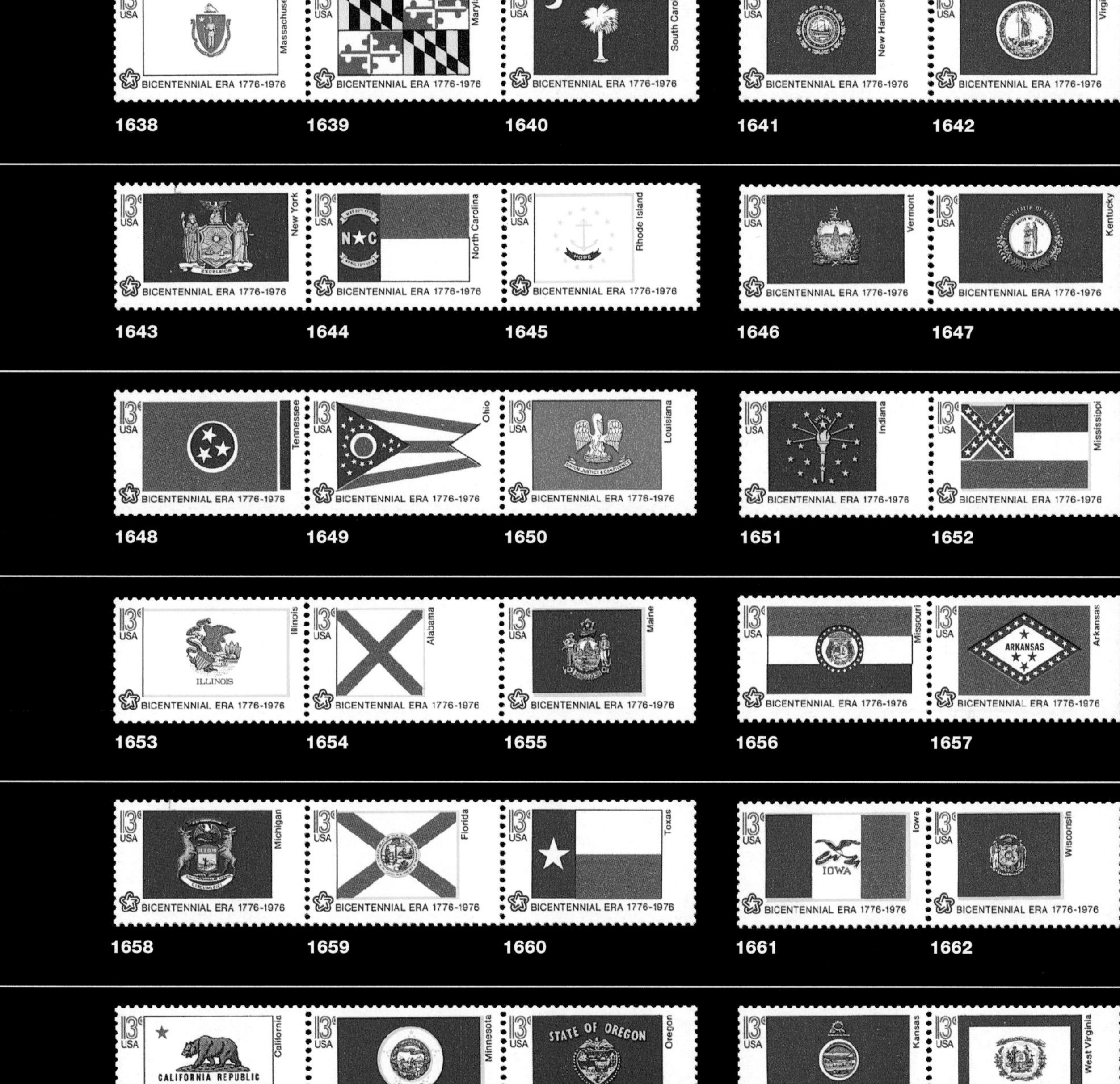

1638 1639 1640 1641 1642

1643 1644 1645 1646 1647

1648 1649 1650 1651 1652

1653 1654 1655 1656 1657

1658 1659 1660 1661 1662

1663 1664 1665 1666 1667

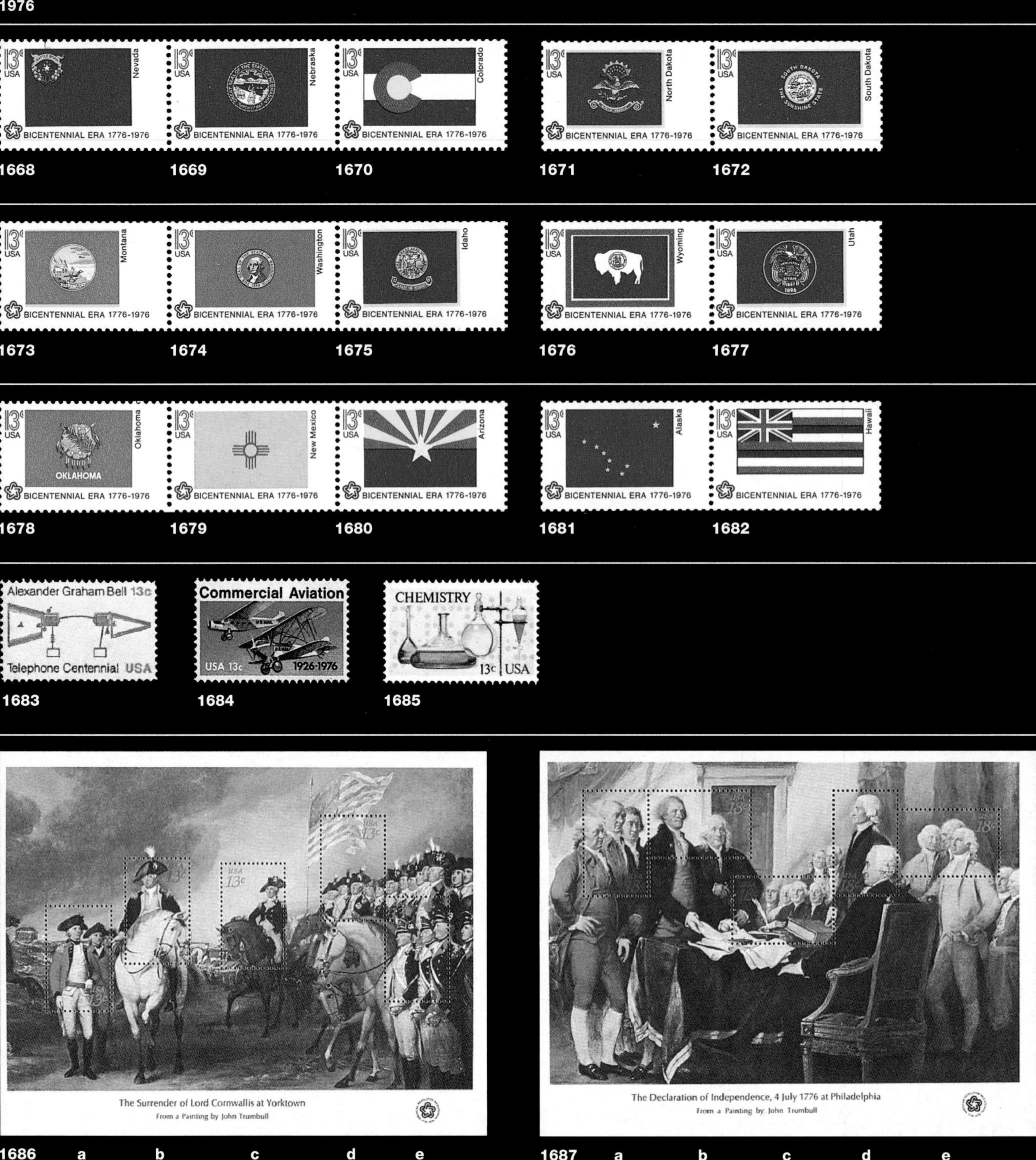

1668 1669 1670 1671 1672

1673 1674 1675 1676 1677

1678 1679 1680 1681 1682

1683 1684 1685

1686 a b c d e

1687 a b c d e

Issue		Date	Un	U	PB	#	FDC	Q(M)
	American Bicentennial: State Flags continued, **Tagged, Perf. 11**							
1668	13¢ Nevada	02/23/76	.25	.20			1.50	9
1669	13¢ Nebraska	02/23/76	.25	.20			1.50	9
1670	13¢ Colorado	02/23/76	.25	.20			1.50	9
1671	13¢ North Dakota	02/23/76	.25	.20			1.50	9
1672	13¢ South Dakota	02/23/76	.25	.20			1.50	9
1673	13¢ Montana	02/23/76	.25	.20			1.50	9
1674	13¢ Washington	02/23/76	.25	.20			1.50	9
1675	13¢ Idaho	02/23/76	.25	.20			1.50	9
1676	13¢ Wyoming	02/23/76	.25	.20			1.50	9
1677	13¢ Utah	02/23/76	.25	.20			1.50	9
1678	13¢ Oklahoma	02/23/76	.25	.20			1.50	9
1679	13¢ New Mexico	02/23/76	.25	.20			1.50	9
1680	13¢ Arizona	02/23/76	.25	.20			1.50	9
1681	13¢ Alaska	02/23/76	.25	.20			1.50	9
1682	13¢ Hawaii	02/23/76	.25	.20			1.50	9
a	Pane of 50, #1633-1682		15.00	—			27.50	
	Tagged, Perf. 11							
1683	13¢ Telephone Centennial	03/10/76	.25	.20	1.10	(4)	1.00	158
a	Black and purple omitted		*500.00*					
1684	13¢ Commercial Aviation	03/19/76	.25	.20	2.75	(10)	1.50	156
1685	13¢ Chemistry	04/06/76	.25	.20	3.25	(12)	1.50	158

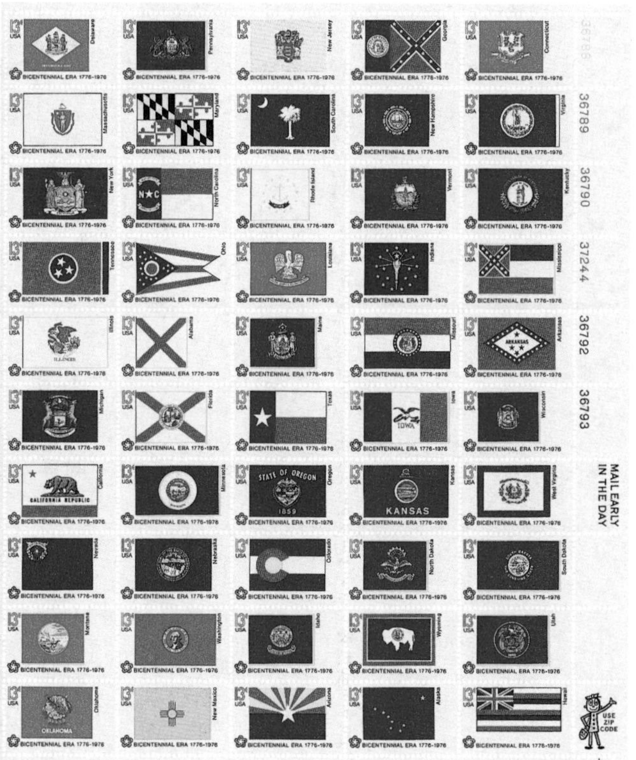

Example of 1682a

Issue		Date	Un	U	PB	#	FDC	Q(M)
	American Bicentennial, Souvenir Sheets, Tagged, Perf. 11							
1686	13¢ The Surrender of Lord Cornwallis at Yorktown, by John Trumbull, sheet of 5	05/29/76	3.25	—			7.50	2
a	13¢ Two American Officers		.45	.40				2
b	13¢ Gen. Benjamin Lincoln		.45	.40				2
c	13¢ George Washington		.45	.40				2
d	13¢ John Trumbull, Col. David Cobb, General Friedrich von Steuben, Marquis de Lafayette and Thomas Nelson		.45	.40				2
e	13¢ Alexander Hamilton, John Laurens and Walter Stewart		.45	.40				2
f	"USA/13¢" omitted on "b," "c" and "d," imperf.		—	*2,000.00*				
g	"USA/13¢" omitted on "a" and "e"		*450.00*	—				
h	Imperf. (untagged)			*2,250.00*				
i	"USA/13¢" omitted on "b," "c" and "d"		*450.00*					
j	"USA/13¢" double on "b"		—					
k	"USA/13¢" omitted on "c" and "d"		*750.00*					
l	"USA/13¢" omitted on "e"		*550.00*					
m	"USA/13¢" omitted, imperf. (untagged)			—				
1687	18¢ The Declaration of Independence, 4 July 1776 at Philadelphia, by John Trumbull, sheet of 5	05/29/76	4.25	—			7.50	2
a	18¢ John Adams, Roger Sherman and Robert R. Livingston		.55	.55				2
b	18¢ Thomas Jefferson and Benjamin Franklin		.55	.55				2
c	18¢ Thomas Nelson, Jr., Francis Lewis, John Witherspoon and Samuel Huntington		.55	.55				2
d	18¢ John Hancock and Charles Thomson		.55	.55				2
e	18¢ George Read, John Dickinson and Edward Rutledge		.55	.55				2
f	Design and marginal inscriptions omitted		*3,250.00*					
g	"USA/18¢" omitted on "a" and "c"		*600.00*					
h	"USA/18¢" omitted on "b," "d" and "e"		*450.00*					
i	"USA/18¢" omitted on "d"		*475.00*	*475.00*				
j	Black omitted in design		*2,000.00*					
k	"USA/18¢" omitted, imperf. (untagged)		*2,000.00*					
m	"USA/18¢" omitted on "b" and "e"		*500.00*					

	Issue	Date	Un	U	PB	#	FDC	Q(M)
	American Bicentennial, Souvenir Sheets continued, **Tagged, Perf. 11**							
1688	24¢ Washington Crossing the Delaware, by Emanuel Leutze/ Eastman Johnson, sheet of 5	05/29/76	5.25	—			7.50	2
a	24¢ Boatmen		.70	.70				2
b	24¢ George Washington		.70	.70				2
c	24¢ Flagbearer		.70	.70				2
d	24¢ Men in Boat		.70	.70				2
e	24¢ Steersman and Men on Shore		.70	.70				2
f	"USA/24¢" omitted, imperf.		*1,500.00*					
g	"USA/24¢" omitted on "d" and "e"		*450.00*	*450.00*				
h	Design and marginal inscriptions omitted		*2,750.00*					
i	"USA/24¢" omitted on "a," "b" and "c"		*500.00*	500.00				
j	Imperf. (untagged)		*1,750.00*					
k	"USA/24¢" inverted on "d" and "e"		—					
l	As "i," imperf., tagging omitted		*3,250.00*	—				
m	Tagging omitted on "e" and "f"		—					
n	As (1688), perfs. inverted		*450.00*					
1689	31¢ Washington Reviewing His Ragged Army at Valley Forge, by William T. Trego, sheet of 5	05/29/76	6.25	—			7.50	2
a	31¢ Two Officers		.85	.85				2
b	31¢ George Washington		.85	.85				2
c	31¢ Officer and Brown Horse		.85	.85				2
d	31¢ White Horse and Officer		.85	.85				2
e	31¢ Three Soldiers		.85	.85				2
f	"USA/31¢" omitted, imperf.		*1,500.00*					
g	"USA/31¢" omitted on "a" and "c"		*400.00*					
h	"USA/31¢" omitted on "b," "d" and "e"		*500.00*	—				
i	"USA/31¢" omitted on "e"		*450.00*					
j	Black omitted in design		*1,500.00*					
k	Imperf. (untagged)			*2,000.00*				
l	"USA/31¢" omitted on "b" and "d"		600.00					
m	"USA/31¢" omitted on "a," "c" and "e"		—					
n	As "m," imperf. (untagged)		—					
p	As "h," imperf. (untagged)			*2,000.00*				
q	As "g," imperf. (untagged)		*2,750.00*					
r	"USA/31¢" omitted on "d" & "e"		*600.00*					
s	As "f", untagged		*2,250.00*					
t	"USA/13¢" omitted on "d"		*750.00*					
	American Bicentennial, Tagged, Perf. 11							
1690	13¢ Bust of Benjamin Franklin, Map of North America, 1776	06/01/76	.25	.20	1.10	(4)	1.00	165
a	Light blue omitted		*225.00*					
b	Tagging omitted		7.50					
	American Bicentennial: Declaration of Independence continued, **Tagged, Perf. 11**							
1691	13¢ Delegates	07/04/76	.30	.20			1.00	41
1692	13¢ Delegates and John Adams	07/04/76	.30	.20			1.00	41
1693	13¢ Roger Sherman, Robert R. Livingston, Thomas Jefferson and Benjamin Franklin	07/04/76	.30	.20			1.00	41
1694	13¢ John Hancock, Charles Thomson, George Read, John Dickinson and Edward Rutledge	07/04/76	.30	.20			1.00	41
a	Strip of 4, #1691-1694		1.20	1.10	7.75	(20)	2.00	
	Olympic Games, Tagged, Perf. 11							
1695	13¢ Diver and Olympic Rings	07/16/76	.30	.20			1.00	46
1696	13¢ Skier and Olympic Rings	07/16/76	.30	.20			1.00	46
1697	13¢ Runner and Olympic Rings	07/16/76	.30	.20			1.00	46
1698	13¢ Skater and Olympic Rings	07/16/76	.30	.20			1.00	46
a	Block of 4, #1695-1698		1.20	*1.40*	4.00	(12)	2.00	
b	As "a," imperf.		*625.00*					
	Tagged, Perf. 11							
1699	13¢ Clara Maass	08/18/76	.25	.20	3.25	(12)	1.25	131
a	Horizontal pair, imperf. vertically		*425.00*					
1700	13¢ Adolph S. Ochs	09/18/76	.25	.20	1.10	(4)	1.00	158
a	Tagging omitted		*50.00*	—				
	Holiday Celebrations: Christmas, Tagged, Perf. 11							
1701	13¢ Nativity, by John Singleton Copley	10/27/76	.25	.20	3.25	(12)	1.00	810
a	Imperf., pair		*90.00*					
	Holiday Celebrations: Holiday, Tagged, Perf. 11							
1702	13¢ "Winter Pastime," by Nathaniel Currier	10/27/76	.25	.20	2.75	(10)	1.00	482*
a	Imperf., pair		*100.00*					
	*Includes #1703 printing							
1703	13¢ as #1702	10/27/76	.25	.20	6.00	(20)	1.00	
a	Imperf., pair		*100.00*					
b	Vertical pair, imperf. between		*350.00*					
c	Tagging omitted		12.50					
	#1702 has overall tagging. Lettering at base is black and usually ½mm below design. As a rule, no "snowflaking" in sky or pond. Pane of 50 has margins on 4 sides with slogans. #1703 has block the size of the printed area. Lettering at base is gray-black and usually ¾mm below design. "Snowflaking" generally in sky and pond. Pane of 50 has margin only at right or left and no slogans.							
	American Bicentennial, Tagged, Perf. 11							
1704	13¢ Washington, Nassau Hall, Hessian Prisoners and 13-star Flag	01/03/77	.25	.20	2.75	(10)	1.00	150
a	Horizontal pair, imperf. vertically		*525.00*					
	Tagged, Perf. 11							
1705	13¢ Sound Recording	03/23/77	.25	.20	1.10	(4)	1.25	177

1688

a b c d e

1689

a b c d e

1690

1691 1692 1693 1694

1695 1696

1697 1698 1698a

1699

1700

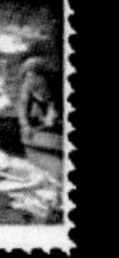

1701

1702

1703

1704

1705

1706 1707 1710 1712 1713

1716

1708 1709 1709a 1711 1714 1715 1715a

1717 1718 1721  1722 1723 1725

1719 1720 1720a 1724 1724a

1726  1727  1728  1729  1730  1731

1732

1733 1733b 1734 1735 1737 1738 1739 1740 1741 1742 1742a

	Issue	Date	Un	U	PB	#	FDC	Q(M)
	American Folk Art: Pueblo Pottery, Tagged, Perf. 11							
1706	13¢ Zia Pot	04/13/77	.25	.20			1.00	49
1707	13¢ San Ildefonso Pot	04/13/77	.25	.20			1.00	49
1708	13¢ Hopi Pot	04/13/77	.25	.20			1.00	49
1709	13¢ Acoma Pot	04/13/77	.25	.20			1.00	49
a	Block of 4, #1706-1709		1.00	1.00	2.75	(10)	2.00	
b	As "a," imperf. vertically		*2,250.00*					
	Tagged, Perf. 11							
1710	13¢ Solo Transatlantic Flight	05/20/77	.25	.20	3.25	(12)	2.75	209
a	Imperf. pair		*900.00*					
1711	13¢ Colorado Statehood	05/21/77	.25	.20	3.25	(12)	1.00	192
a	Horizontal pair, imperf. between		—					
b	Horizontal pair, imperf. vertically		*800.00*					
c	Perf. 11.2		.35	.25	20.00	(12)		
	Butterfly, Tagged, Perf. 11							
1712	13¢ Swallowtail	06/06/77	.25	.20			2.00	55
1713	13¢ Checkerspot	06/06/77	.25	.20			2.00	55
1714	13¢ Dogface	06/06/77	.25	.20			2.00	55
1715	13¢ Orange-Tip	06/06/77	.25	.20			2.00	55
a	Block of 4, #1712-1715		1.00	1.00	3.25	(12)	2.00	
b	As "a," imperf. horizontally		*15,000.00*					
	American Bicentennial, Tagged, Perf. 11							
1716	13¢ Marquis de Lafayette	06/13/77	.25	.20	1.10	(4)	1.00	160
1717	13¢ Seamstress	07/04/77	.25	.20			1.00	47
1718	13¢ Blacksmith	07/04/77	.25	.20			1.00	47
1719	13¢ Wheelwright	07/04/77	.25	.20			1.00	47
1720	13¢ Leatherworker	07/04/77	.25	.20			1.00	47
a	Block of 4, #1717-1720		1.00	1.00	3.25	(12)	2.00	
	Tagged, Perf. 11 x 10.5							
1721	13¢ Peace Bridge	08/04/77	.25	.20	1.10	(4)	1.00	164
	American Bicentennial, Tagged, Perf. 11							
1722	13¢ Herkimer at Oriskany, by Frederick Yohn	08/06/77	.25	.20	2.75	(10)	1.00	156
	Energy, Tagged, Perf. 11							
1723	13¢ Energy Conservation	10/20/77	.25	.20			1.25	79
1724	13¢ Energy Development	10/20/77	.25	.20			1.25	79
a	Attached pair, #1723-1724		.50	.50	3.25	(12)		
	Tagged, Perf. 11							
1725	13¢ First Civil Settlement Alta, California	09/09/77	.25	.20	1.10	(4)	1.00	154
	American Bicentennial: Articles of Confederation, Tagged, Perf. 11							
1726	13¢ Members of Continental Congress in Conference	09/30/77	.25	.20	1.10	(4)	1.00	168
	Tagged, Perf. 11							
1727	13¢ Talking Pictures	10/06/77	.25	.20	1.10	(4)	1.50	157
	American Bicentennial, Tagged, Perf. 11							
1728	13¢ Surrender of Burgoyne, at Saratoga	10/07/77	.25	.20	2.75	(10)	1.00	154

	Issue	Date	Un	U	PB	#	FDC	Q(M)
	Holiday Celebrations: Christmas, Tagged, Perf. 11							
1729	13¢ Washington at Valley Forge, by J.C. Leyendecker	10/21/77	.25	.20	5.75	(20)	1.00	882
a	Imperf., pair		*70.00*					
1730	13¢ Rural Mailbox	10/21/77	.25	.20	2.75	(10)	1.00	922
a	Imperf., pair		*250.00*					
	Tagged, Perf. 11							
1731	13¢ Carl Sandburg	01/06/78	.25	.20	1.25	(4)	1.00	157
a	Brown omitted		*2,250.00*					
1732	13¢ Capt. James Cook Alaska, by Nathaniel Dance	01/20/78	.25	.20			1.25	101
1733	13¢ *Resolution* and *Discovery* Hawaii, by John Webber	01/20/78	.25	.20			1.25	101
a	Vertical pair, imperf. horizontally		—					
b	Attached pair, #1732-1733		.50	.50	1.10	(4)		
c	As " b," imperf. between		*4,250.00*					
1734	13¢ Indian Head Penny	01/11/78	.25	.20	1.25	(4)	1.00	
a	Horizontal pair, imperf. vertically		*275.00*					
1735	(15¢) "A" Stamp	05/22/78	.30	.20	1.40	(4)	1.00	
a	Imperf., pair		*90.00*					
b	Vertical pair, imperf. horizontally		*650.00*					
c	Perf. 11.2		.35	.20	1.80	(4)		
	Booklet, Perf. 11 x 10.5 on 2 or 3 sides							
1736	(15¢) "A" orange Eagle (1735), single from booklet	05/22/78	.30	.20			1.00	
a	Booklet pane of 8	05/22/78	2.50	*1.50*			2.50	
b	Vert. pair, imperf. between		*900.00*					
	Booklet, Perf. 10							
1737	15¢ Roses, single from booklet	07/11/78	.30	.20			1.00	
a	Booklet pane of 8	07/11/78	2.50	*1.50*			2.50	
b	As "a," imperf.		*500.00*					
c	As "a," imperf.		*2,300.00*					
d	As "a," tagging omitted		*50.00*	—				
	#1736-1737 issued only in booklets. All stamps are imperf. on one side or on one side and bottom.							
	Windmills, Booklet, Tagged, Perf. 11 on 2 or 3 sides							
1738	15¢ Virginia, 1720	02/07/80	.30	.20			1.00	
1739	15¢ Rhode Island, 1790	02/07/80	.30	.20			1.00	
1740	15¢ Massachusetts, 1793	02/07/80	.30	.20			1.00	
1741	15¢ Illinois, 1860	02/07/80	.30	.20			1.00	
1742	15¢ Texas, 1890	02/07/80	.30	.20			1.00	
a	Booklet pane of 10, #1738-1742		3.50	*3.00*			3.50	
b	Strip of 5, #1730-1742		1.50	1.40				
	#1737-1742 issued only in booklets. All stamps are imperf. top or bottom, or top or bottom and right side.							
	Coil, Perf. 10 Vertically							
1743	(15¢) "A" orange Eagle (1735)	05/22/78	.30	.20	.75	(2)	1.00	
a	Imperf., pair		85.00		—	(2)		

	Issue	Date	Un	U	PB	#	FDC	Q(M)
	Black Heritage, Tagged, Perf. 10.5 x 11							
1744	13¢ Harriet Tubman and Cart Carrying Slaves	02/01/78	.25	.20	3.25	(12)	1.75	157
	American Folk Art: Quilts, Perf. 11							
1745	13¢ Basket design, red and orange	03/08/78	.25	.20			1.00	41
1746	13¢ Basket design, red	03/08/78	.25	.20			1.00	41
1747	13¢ Basket design, orange	03/08/78	.25	.20			1.00	41
1748	13¢ Basket design, brown	03/08/78	.25	.20			1.00	41
a	Block of 4, #1745-1748		1.00	1.00	3.25	(12)	2.00	
	American Dance, Tagged, Perf. 11							
1749	13¢ Ballet	04/26/78	.25	.20			1.00	39
1750	13¢ Theater	04/26/78	.25	.20			1.00	39
1751	13¢ Folk	04/26/78	.25	.20			1.00	39
1752	13¢ Modern	04/26/78	.25	.20			1.00	39
a	Block of 4, #1749-1752		1.00	1.00	3.25	(12)	2.00	
	American Bicentennial: French Alliance, Tagged, Perf. 11							
1753	13¢ King Louis XVI and Benjamin Franklin, by Charles Gabriel Sauvage	05/04/78	.25	.20	1.10	(4)	1.00	103
	Tagged, Perf. 10.5 x 11							
1754	13¢ Early Cancer Detection	05/18/78	.25	.20	1.10	(4)	1.00	152
	Performing Arts, Tagged, Perf. 11							
1755	13¢ Jimmie Rodgers with Guitar and Brakeman's Cap, Locomotive	05/24/78	.25	.20	4.00	(12)	1.00	95
1756	15¢ George M. Cohan, "Yankee Doodle Dandy" and Stars	07/03/78	.30	.20	4.00	(12)	1.25	152
	CAPEX '78 Souvenir Sheet, Tagged, Perf. 11							
1757	13¢ Souvenir sheet of 8	06/10/78	2.00	2.00	2.25	(8)	2.75	15
a	13¢ Cardinal		.25	.20				
b	13¢ Mallard		.25	.20				
c	13¢ Canada Goose		.25	.20				
d	13¢ Blue Jay		.25	.20				
e	13¢ Moose		.25	.20				
f	13¢ Chipmunk		.25	.20				
g	13¢ Red Fox		.25	.20				
h	13¢ Raccoon		.25	.20				
i	Yellow, green, red, brown and black (litho.) omitted		*7,000.00*					

	Issue	Date	Un	U	PB	#	FDC	Q(M)
	Tagged, Perf. 11							
1758	15¢ Photography	06/26/78	.30	.20	4.00	(12)	1.00	161
	Space, Tagged, Perf. 11							
1759	15¢ Viking Missions to Mars	07/20/78	.30	.20	1.35	(4)	1.00	159
a	Tagging omitted		*50.00*					
	Wildlife Conservation: American Owls, Tagged, Perf. 11							
1760	15¢ Great Gray Owl	08/26/78	.30	.20			1.25	47
1761	15¢ Saw-Whet Owl	08/26/78	.30	.20			1.25	47
1762	15¢ Barred Owl	08/26/78	.30	.20			1.25	47
1763	15¢ Great Horned Owl	08/26/78	.30	.20			1.25	47
a	Block of 4, #1760-1763		1.25	1.25	1.40	(4)	2.00	
	Wildlife Conservation: American Trees, Tagged, Perf. 11							
1764	15¢ Giant Sequoia	10/09/78	.30	.20			1.25	42
1765	15¢ White Pine	10/09/78	.30	.20			1.25	42
1766	15¢ White Oak	10/09/78	.30	.20			1.25	42
1767	15¢ Gray Birch	10/09/78	.30	.20			1.25	42
a	Block of 4, #1764-1767		1.25	1.25	4.00	(12)	2.00	
b	As "a," imperf. horizontally		*17,500.00*					
	Holiday Celebrations: Christmas, Perf. 11							
1768	15¢ Madonna and Child with Cherubim, by Andrea della Robbia	10/18/78	.30	.20	4.00	(12)	1.00	963
a	Imperf., pair		*90.00*					
	Holiday Celebrations: Holiday, Perf. 11							
1769	15¢ Child on Hobby Horse and Christmas Trees	10/18/78	.30	.20	4.00	(12)	1.00	917
a	Imperf., pair		*90.00*					
b	Vertical pair, imperf. horizontally		*1,700.00*					
	Tagged, Perf. 11							
1770	15¢ Robert F. Kennedy	01/12/79	.35	.20	1.75	(4)	1.50	159
a	Tagging omitted		*50.00*					
	Black Heritage, Tagged, Perf. 11							
1771	15¢ Martin Luther King, Jr., and Civil Rights Marchers	01/13/79	.40	.20	5.75	(12)	2.00	166
a	Imperf., pair		*1,500.00*					
	Tagged, Perf. 11							
1772	15¢ International Year of the Child	02/15/79	.30	.20	1.40	(4)	1.00	163
	Literary Arts, Tagged, Perf. 10.5 x 11							
1773	15¢ John Steinbeck, by Philippe Halsman	02/27/79	.30	.20	1.40	(4)	1.00	155
	Tagged, Perf. 10.5 x 11							
1774	15¢ Albert Einstein	03/04/79	.35	.20	1.75	(4)	3.00	157

1744

1745 1746

1747 1748 1748a

1750
1749 1752

1751 1752a

1753

1754

1755

1756

a b c d

1757 e f g h

1758

1759

1760 1761

1762 1763 1763a

1764 1765

1766 1767 1767a

1768

1769

1770

1771

1772

1773

1774

1775 1776 1779 1780 1783 1784

1777 1778 1778a 1781 1782 1782a 1785 1786 1786a 1787

1791 1792 1795 1796

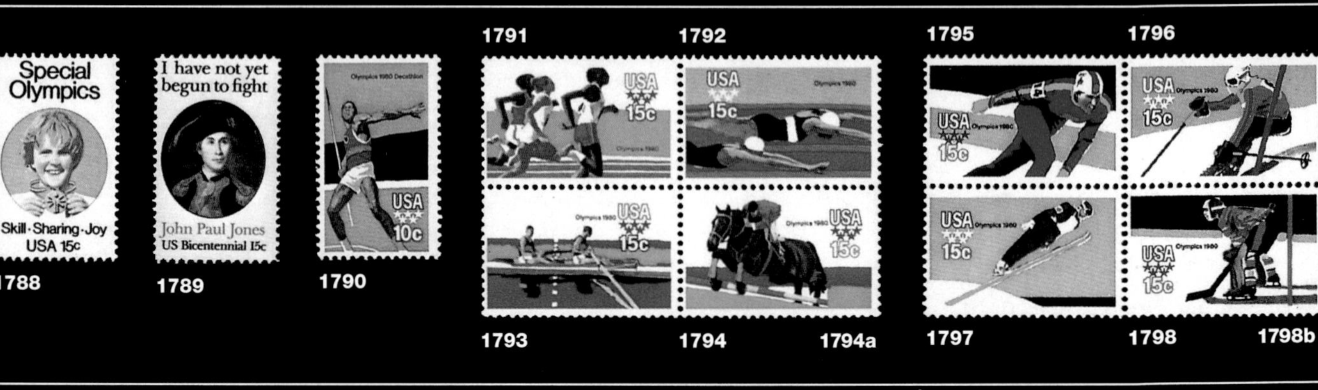

1788 1789 1790 1793 1794 1794a 1797 1798 1798b

1799 1800 1801 1802 1803 1804

1805 1807 1809

1806 1808 1810 1813 1816

Issue		Date	Un	U	PB	#	FDC	Q(M)
	American Folk Art: Pennsylvania Toleware, c.1800, **Tagged, Perf. 11**							
1775	15¢ Straight-Spout Coffeepot	04/19/79	.30	.20			1.00	44
1776	15¢ Tea Caddy	04/19/79	.30	.20			1.00	44
1777	15¢ Sugar Bowl	04/19/79	.30	.20			1.00	44
1778	15¢ Curved-Spout Coffeepot	04/19/79	.30	.20			1.00	44
a	Block of 4, #1775-1778		1.25	1.25	3.25	(10)	2.00	
b	As "a," imperf. horizontally		*4,000.00*					
	American Architecture, Tagged, Perf. 11							
1779	15¢ Virginia Rotunda, by Thomas Jefferson	06/04/79	.30	.20			1.00	41
1780	15¢ Baltimore Cathedral, by Benjamin Latrobe	06/04/79	.30	.20			1.00	41
1781	15¢ Boston State House, by Charles Bulfinch	06/04/79	.30	.20			1.00	41
1782	15¢ Philadelphia Exchange, by William Strickland	06/04/79	.30	.20			1.00	41
a	Block of 4, #1779-1782		1.25	*1.50*	1.45	(4)	2.00	
	Endangered Flora, Tagged, Perf. 11							
1783	15¢ Persistent Trillium	06/07/79	.30	.20			1.00	41
1784	15¢ Hawaiian Wild Broadbean	06/07/79	.30	.20			1.00	41
1785	15¢ Contra Costa Wallflower	06/07/79	.30	.20			1.00	41
1786	15¢ Antioch Dunes Evening Primrose	06/07/79	.30	.20			1.00	41
a	Block of 4, #1783-1786		1.25	1.25	4.00	(12)	2.00	
b	As "a," imperf.		*550.00*					
	Tagged, Perf. 11							
1787	15¢ Seeing Eye Dogs	06/15/79	.30	.20	6.50	(20)	1.25	162
a	Imperf., pair		*425.00*					
b	Tagging omitted		10.00					
1788	15¢ Special Olympics	08/09/79	.30	.20	3.25	(10)	1.25	166
	American Bicentennial, Tagged, Perf. 11 x 12							
1789	15¢ John Paul Jones	09/23/79	.30	.20	3.25	(10)	1.50	160
c	Vertical pair, imperf. horizontally		*175.00*					
	American Bicentennial, Perf. 11							
1789A	15¢ John Paul Jones	09/23/79	.55	.20	4.00	(10)		
d	Vertical pair, imperf. horizontally		*140.00*					
	American Bicentennial, Perf. 12							
1789B	15¢ John Paul Jones	09/23/79	*3,500.00*	*3,500.00*	*40,000.00*	*(10)*		
	Numerous varieties of printer's waste of #1789 exist							
	Olympic Games, Tagged, Perf. 11							
1790	10¢ Javelin Thrower	09/05/79	.20	.20	3.00	(12)	1.00	67
1791	15¢ Runner	09/28/79	.30	.20			1.25	47
1792	15¢ Swimmer	09/28/79	.30	.20			1.25	47
1793	15¢ Rowers	09/28/79	.30	.20			1.25	47
1794	15¢ Equestrian Contestant	09/28/79	.30	.20			1.25	47
a	Block of 4, #1791-1794		1.25	*1.50*	4.00	(12)	2.00	
b	As "a," imperf.		*1,500.00*					
	Olympic Games, Tagged, Perf. 11.25 x 10.5							
1795	15¢ Speed Skater	02/01/80	.35	.20			1.25	52
1796	15¢ Downhill Skier	02/01/80	.35	.20			1.25	52
1797	15¢ Ski Jumper	02/01/80	.35	.20			1.25	52
1798	15¢ Ice Hockey	02/01/80	.35	.20			1.25	52
b	Block of 4, #1795-1798		1.50	1.40	4.50	(12)	2.00	

Issue		Date	Un	U	PB	#	FDC	Q(M)
	Olympic Games, Tagged, Perf. 11							
1795A	15¢ Speed Skater	02/01/80	1.20	.60				
1796A	15¢ Downhill Skier	02/01/80	1.20	.60				
1797A	15¢ Ski Jumper	02/01/80	1.20	.60				
1798A	15¢ Ice Hockey	02/01/80	1.20	.60				
c	Block of 4, #1795A-1798A		5.00	3.50	16.00	(12)		
	Holiday Celebrations: Christmas, Tagged, Perf. 11							
1799	15¢ Virgin and Child with Cherubim, by Gerard David	10/18/79	.30	.20	4.00	(12)	1.25	874
a	Imperf., pair		*90.00*					
b	Vertical pair, imperf. horizontally		*650.00*					
c	pair, imperf. between		*1,200.00*					
	Holiday Celebrations: Holiday, Tagged, Perf. 11							
1800	15¢ Santa Claus, Tree Ornament Christmas	10/18/79	.30	.20	4.00	(12)	1.25	932
a	Green and yellow omitted		*550.00*					
b	Green, yellow and tan omitted		*550.00*					
	Performing Arts, Tagged, Perf. 11							
1801	15¢ Will Rogers and Rogers as a Cowboy Humorist	11/04/79	.30	.20	4.00	(12)	1.50	161
a	Imperf., pair		*200.00*					
	Tagged, Perf. 11							
1802	15¢ Vietnam Veterans	11/11/79	.30	.20	3.25	(10)	2.75	173
	Performing Arts, Tagged, Perf. 11							
1803	15¢ W.C. Fields and Fields as a Juggler	01/29/80	.30	.20	4.00	(12)	1.75	169
	Black Heritage, Tagged, Perf. 11							
1804	15¢ Benjamin Banneker and Banneker as Surveyor	02/15/80	.35	.20	4.50	(12)	2.00	160
a	Horizontal pair, imperf. vertically		*500.00*					
	Letter Writing, Tagged, Perf. 11							
1805	15¢ Letters Preserve Memories	02/25/80	.30	.20			1.00	39
1806	15¢ purple P.S. Write Soon	02/25/80	.30	.20			1.00	39
1807	15¢ Letters Lift Spirits	02/25/80	.30	.20			1.00	39
1808	15¢ green P.S. Write Soon	02/25/80	.30	.20			1.00	39
1809	15¢ Letters Shape Opinions	02/25/80	.30	.20			1.00	39
1810	15¢ red and blue P.S. Write Soon	02/25/80	.30	.20			1.00	39
a	Vertical Strip of 6, #1805-1810		1.85	*2.25*	13.00	(36)	2.50	
	Americana, Coil, Perf. 10 Vertically							
1811	1¢ dark blue, greenish Inkwelll and Quill (1581)	03/06/80	.20	.20	.40	(2)	1.00	
a	Imperf., pair		*175.00*		*275.00*	(2)		
1812	Not assigned							
1813	3.5¢ Weaver Violins	06/23/80	.20	.20	1.00	(2)	1.00	
a	Untagged (Bureau precanceled)		.20	.20	1.95	(2)		
b	Imperf., pair		*175.00*		*450.00*	(2)		
1814-1815	Not assigned							
1816	12¢ red brown, *beige* Torch from Statue of Liberty (1594)	04/08/81	.25	.20	1.50	(2)	1.00	
a	Untagged (Bureau precanceled)		1.15	1.15	47.50	(2)		
b	Imperf., pair		*175.00*		*325.00*	(2)		
1817	Not assigned							

	Issue	Date	Un	U	PB/LP	#	FDC	Q(M)
	Tagged, Perf. 11 x 10.5							
1818	(18¢) "B" Stamp Eagle	03/15/81	.35	.20	1.60	(4)	1.25	
	Booklet, Perf. 10							
1819	(18¢) "B" Stamp (1818), single from booklet	03/15/81	.40	.20			1.00	
a	Booklet pane of 8	03/15/81	3.75	*2.25*			3.00	
	Coil, Perf. 10 Vertically							
1820	(18¢) "B" Stamp (1818)	03/15/81	.40	.20	1.60	(2)	1.00	
a	Imperf., pair		*90.00*		*160.00*	(2)		
	Tagged, Perf. 10.5 x 11							
1821	15¢ Frances Perkins	04/10/80	.30	.20	1.30	(4)	1.00	164
	Tagged, Perf. 11							
1822	15¢ Dolley Madison	05/20/80	.30	.20	1.40	(4)	1.00	257
1823	15¢ Emily Bissell	05/31/80	.35	.20	1.75	(4)	1.00	96
a	Vertical pair, imperf. horizontally		*375.00*					
1824	15¢ Helen Keller/Anne Sullivan	06/27/80	.30	.20	1.30	(4)	1.00	154
1825	15¢ Veterans Administration	07/21/80	.30	.20	1.30	(4)	1.50	160
a	Horizontal pair, imperf. vertically		*450.00*					
	American Bicentennial, Tagged, Perf. 11							
1826	15¢ General Bernardo de Galvez, Battle of Mobile	07/23/80	.30	.20	1.30	(4)	1.00	104
a	Red, brown and blue omitted		*700.00*					
b	Bl., brn., red and yel. omitted		*1,250.00*					
	Coral Reefs, Tagged, Perf. 11							
1827	15¢ Brain Coral, Beaugregory Fish	08/26/80	.30	.20			1.00	51
1828	15¢ Elkhorn Coral, Porkfish	08/26/80	.30	.20			1.00	51
1829	15¢ Chalice Coral, Moorish Idol	08/26/80	.30	.20			1.00	51
1830	15¢ Finger Coral, Sabertooth Blenny	08/26/80	.30	.20			1.00	51
a	Block of 4, #1827-1830		1.25	1.10	4.00	(12)	2.00	
b	As "a," imperf.		*950.00*					
c	As "a," imperf. between, vertically		—					
d	As "a," imperf. vertically		*3,500.00*					

	Issue	Date	Un	U	PB	#	FDC	Q(M)
	Tagged, Perf. 11							
1831	15¢ Organized Labor	09/01/80	.30	.20	3.50	(12)	1.00	167
a	Imperf., pair		*325.00*					
	Literary Arts, Tagged, Perf. 10.5 x 11							
1832	15¢ Edith Wharton Reading Letter	09/05/80	.30	.20	1.30	(4)	1.00	163
	Tagged, Perf. 11							
1833	15¢ Education	09/12/80	.30	.20	1.90	(6)	1.50	160
a	Horizontal pair, imperf. vertically		*225.00*					
	American Folk Art: Pacific Northwest Indian Masks, Tagged, Perf. 11							
1834	15¢ Heiltsuk, Bella Bella Tribe	09/25/80	.35	.20			1.00	38
1835	15¢ Chilkat Tlingit Tribe	09/25/80	.35	.20			1.00	38
1836	15¢ Tlingit Tribe	09/25/80	.35	.20			1.00	38
1837	15¢ Bella Coola Tribe	09/25/80	.35	.20			1.00	38
a	Block of 4, #1834-1837		1.50	1.25	5.00	(10)	2.00	
	American Architecture, Tagged, Perf. 11							
1838	15¢ Smithsonian Institution, by James Renwick	10/09/80	.30	.20			1.00	38
1839	15¢ Trinity Church, by Henry Hobson Richardson	10/09/80	.30	.20			1.00	38
1840	15¢ Pennsylvania Academy of Fine Arts, by Frank Furness	10/09/80	.30	.20			1.00	38
1841	15¢ Lyndhurst, by Alexander Jefferson Davis	10/09/80	.30	.20			1.00	38
a	Block of 4, #1838-1841		1.25	*1.50*	1.50	(4)	1.75	
b	As "a", red omitted on #1838,1839		*400.00*					
	Holiday Celebrations: Christmas, Tagged, Perf. 11							
1842	15¢ Madonna and Child from Epiphany Window, Washington Cathedral	10/31/80	.30	.20	4.00	(12)	1.25	693
a	Imperf., pair		*60.00*					
	Pair with full vertical gutter between		—					
	Holiday Celebrations: Holiday, Tagged, Perf. 11							
1843	15¢ Wreath and Toys	10/31/80	.30	.20	6.50	(20)	1.25	719
a	Imperf., pair		*70.00*					
b	Buff omitted		*25.00*					
c	Vertical pair, imperf. horizontally		—					
d	Horizontal pair, imperf. between		*4,000.00*					

1818

Frances Perkins
USA 15c

1821

1822

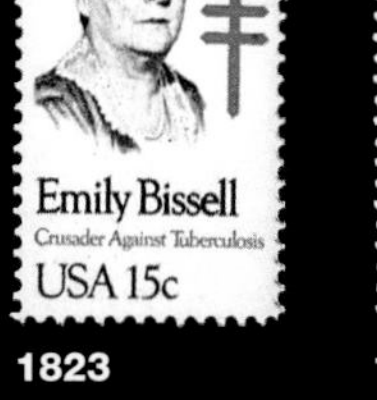

1823

1824

1825

1826

1827 1828

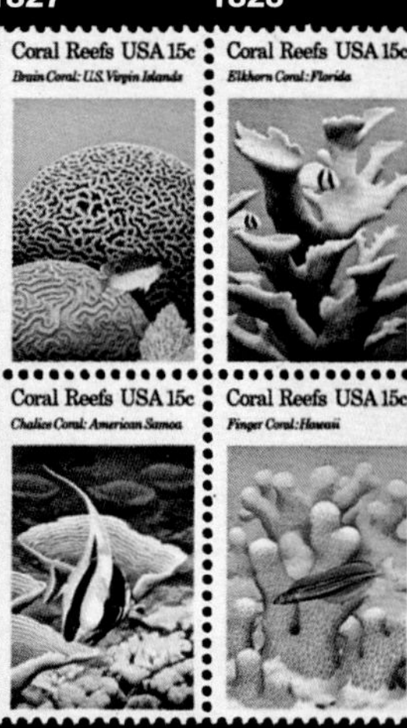

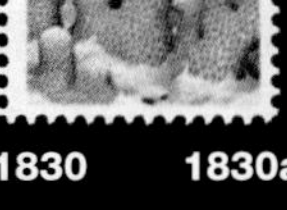

1829 1830 1830a

1831

1832

USA 15c
Learning
never ends

1833

1834 1835

Chilkat Tlingit
Indian Art USA 15c

1836 1837 1837a

1838 1839

1840 1841 1841a

1842

1843

1844

1845

1846

1847

1848

1849

1850

1851

1852

1853

1854

1855

1856

1857

1858

1859

1860

1861

1862

1863

1864

1865

1866

1867

1868

1869

1874

1875

1876 1877

1878 1879 1879a

1880 1881

1882 1883

1884 1885

1886 1887

1888 1889

1889a

1890

1891

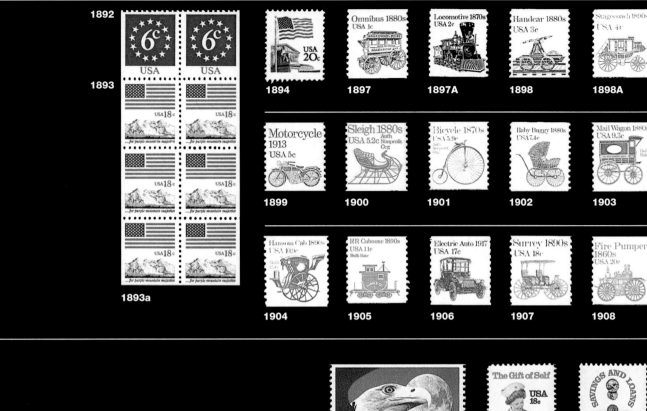

1892

1893

1893a

1894  1897  1897A  1898  1898A

1899  1900  1901  1902  1903

1904  1905  1906  1907  1908

1909

1910

1911

1912 1913 1914 1915

1921 1922

1916 1917 1918 1919 1919a

1920

1925 1926 1927 1928 1929 1930 1931 1931a

1932 1933 1934 1935 1936

1937 1938 1938a 1939 1940 1941

1942 1943 1944 1945 1945a 1946 1949 1950

1951 1952

Issue		Date	Un	U	PB	#	FDC	Q(M)
	Tagged, Perf. 11							
1925	18¢ International Year of the Disabled	06/29/81	.35	.20	1.50	(4)	1.00	100
a	Vertical pair, imperf. horizontally		*2,750.00*					
1926	18¢ Edna St. Vincent Millay	07/10/81	.35	.20	1.50	(4)	1.00	100
a	Black omitted		*300.00*	—				
1927	18¢ Alcoholism	08/19/81	.45	.20	10.00	(6)	2.50	98
a	Imperf., pair		*400.00*					
b	Vertical pair, imperf. horizontally		*2,500.00*					
	American Architecture, Tagged, Perf. 11							
1928	18¢ NYU Library, by Sanford White	08/28/81	.40	.20			1.00	42
1929	18¢ Biltmore House, by Richard Morris Hunt	08/28/81	.40	.20			1.00	42
1930	18¢ Palace of the Arts, by Bernard Maybeck	08/28/81	.40	.20			1.00	42
1931	18¢ National Farmer's Bank, by Louis Sullivan	08/28/81	.40	.20			1.00	42
a	Block of 4, #1928-1931		1.65	1.75	2.10	(4)	2.50	
	American Sports Personalities, Tagged, Perf. 10.5 x 11							
1932	18¢ Babe Zaharias Holding Trophy	09/22/81	.40	.20	3.00	(4)	6.50	102
1933	18¢ Bobby Jones Teeing off	09/22/81	.60	.20	3.25	(4)	10.00	99
	Tagged, Perf. 11							
1934	18¢ Frederic Remington	10/09/81	.35	.20	1.60	(4)	1.25	101
a	Vertical pair, imperf. between		*250.00*					
b	Brown omitted		*425.00*					
1935	18¢ James Hoban	10/13/81	.35	.20	1.60	(4)	1.00	101
1936	20¢ James Hoban	10/13/81	.35	.20	1.65	(4)	1.00	167
	American Bicentennial, Tagged, Perf. 11							
1937	18¢ Battle of Yorktown 1781	10/16/81	.35	.20			1.00	81
1938	18¢ Battle of the Virginia Capes 1781	10/16/81	.35	.20			1.00	81
a	Attached pair, #1937-1938		.90	.75	2.00	(4)	1.50	
b	As "a," black omitted		*375.00*					
	Holiday Celebrations: Christmas, Tagged, Perf. 11							
1939	20¢ Madonna and Child, by Botticelli	10/28/81	.40	.20	1.75	(4)	1.00	598
a	Imperf., pair		*110.00*					
b	Vertical pair, imperf. horizontally		*1,250.00*					
	Holiday Celebrations: Holiday, Tagged, Perf. 11							
1940	20¢ Felt Bear on Sleigh	10/28/81	.40	.20	1.75	(4)	1.00	793
a	Imperf., pair		*225.00*					
b	Vertical pair, imperf. horizontally		*3,000.00*					

Issue		Date	Un	U	PB/LP	#	FDC	Q(M)
	American Bicentennial, Tagged, Perf. 11							
1941	20¢ John Hanson	11/05/81	.40	.20	1.75	(4)	1.00	167
	Desert Plants, Tagged, Perf. 11							
1942	20¢ Barrel Cactus	12/11/81	.35	.20			1.00	48
1943	20¢ Agave	12/11/81	.35	.20			1.00	48
1944	20¢ Beavertail Cactus	12/11/81	.35	.20			1.00	48
1945	20¢ Saguaro	12/11/81	.35	.20			1.00	48
a	Block of 4, #1942-1945		1.50	1.25	1.90	(4)	2.50	
b	As "a," deep brown omitted		*4,250.00*					
c	#1945 vertical pair, imperf.		*3,500.00*					
	Tagged, Perf. 11 x 10.5							
1946	(20¢) "C" brown Eagle	10/11/81	.40	.20	2.00	(4)	1.00	
a	Tagging omitted		9.00					
	Coil, Perf. 10 Vertically							
1947	(20¢) "C" brown Eagle (1946)	10/11/81	.60	.20	1.50	(2)	1.00	
a	Imperf., pair		*1,000.00*		—	(2)		
	Booklet, Perf. 11							
1948	(20¢) "C" brown Eagle (1946), single from booklet	10/11/81	.40	.20			1.00	
a	Booklet pane of 10	10/11/81	4.50	*3.25*			*3.50*	
	Booklet, Tagged, Perf. 11							
1949	20¢ Bighorn Sheep, single from booklet	01/08/82	.55	.20			1.25	
a	Booklet pane of 10		5.50	*2.50*			*6.00*	
b	As "a," imperf. between		*110.00*					
c	Type II		.55	.20				
d	Type II, booklet pane of 10		11.00	—				
e	As #1949, tagging omitted		5.00	—				
f	As "e," booklet pane of 10		*50.00*	—				
	#1949 issued only in booklets. All stamps are imperf. at one side or imperf. at one side and bottom.							
	Tagged, Perf. 11							
1950	20¢ Franklin D. Roosevelt	01/30/82	.40	.20	1.75	(4)	1.00	164
	Love, Tagged, Perf. 11.25							
1951	20¢ Love	02/01/82	.40	.20	1.75	(4)	1.00	447
b	Imperf., pair		*250.00*					
c	Blue omitted		*225.00*					
d	Yellow omitted		*1,000.00*					
e	Purple omitted		—					
1951A	Perf. 11.25 x 10.5		.75	.25	3.50	(4)		
	American Bicentennial, Tagged, Perf. 11							
1952	20¢ George Washington	02/22/82	.40	.20	1.75	(4)	1.25	181

	Issue	Date	Un	U	PB #	FDC	Q(M)
	State Birds & Flowers, Tagged, Perf. 10.5 x 11.25						
1953	20¢ Alabama: Yellowhammer and Camellia	04/14/82	.50	.30		1.25	13
1954	20¢ Alaska: Willow Ptarmigan and Forget-Me-Not	04/14/82	.50	.30		1.25	13
1955	20¢ Arizona: Cactus Wren and Saguaro Cactus Blossom	04/14/82	.50	.30		1.25	13
1956	20¢ Arkansas: Mockingbird and Apple Blossom	04/14/82	.50	.30		1.25	13
1957	20¢ California: California Quail and California Poppy	04/14/82	.50	.30		1.25	13
1958	20¢ Colorado: Lark Bunting and Rocky Mountain Columbine	04/14/82	.50	.30		1.25	13
1959	20¢ Connecticut: Robin and Mountain Laurel	04/14/82	.50	.30		1.25	13
1960	20¢ Delaware: Blue Hen Chicken and Peach Blossom	04/14/82	.50	.30		1.25	13
1961	20¢ Florida: Mockingbird and Orange Blossom	04/14/82	.50	.30		1.25	13
1962	20¢ Georgia: Brown Thrasher and Cherokee Rose	04/14/82	.50	.30		1.25	13
1963	20¢ Hawaii: Hawaiian Goose and Hibiscus	04/14/82	.50	.30		1.25	13
1964	20¢ Idaho: Mountain Bluebird and Syringa	04/14/82	.50	.30		1.25	13

	Issue	Date	Un	U	PB #	FDC	Q(M)
	State Birds & Flowers continued, **Tagged, Perf. 10.5 x 11.25**						
1965	20¢ Illinois: Cardinal and Violet	04/14/82	.50	.30		1.25	13
1966	20¢ Indiana: Cardinal and Peony	04/14/82	.50	.30		1.25	13
1967	20¢ Iowa: Eastern Goldfinch and Wild Rose	04/14/82	.50	.30		1.25	13
1968	20¢ Kansas: Western Meadowlark and Sunflower	04/14/82	.50	.30		1.25	13
1969	20¢ Kentucky: Cardinal and Goldenrod	04/14/82	.50	.30		1.25	13
1970	20¢ Louisiana: Brown Pelican and Magnolia	04/14/82	.50	.30		1.25	13
1971	20¢ Maine: Chickadee and White Pine Cone and Tassel	04/14/82	.50	.30		1.25	13
1972	20¢ Maryland: Baltimore Oriole and Black-Eyed Susan	04/14/82	.50	.30		1.25	13
1973	20¢ Massachusetts: Black-Capped Chickadee and Mayflower	04/14/82	.50	.30		1.25	13
1974	20¢ Michigan: Robin and Apple Blossom	04/14/82	.50	.30		1.25	13
1975	20¢ Minnesota: Common Loon and Showy Lady Slipper	04/14/82	.50	.30		1.25	13
1976	20¢ Mississippi: Mockingbird and Magnolia	04/14/82	.50	.30		1.25	13
1977	20¢ Missouri: Eastern Bluebird and Red Hawthorn	04/14/82	.50	.30		1.25	13

BENJAMIN FRANKLIN

These four stamps celebrate the 300th anniversary of the birth of Benjamin Franklin (1706-1790), an American icon whose diverse accomplishments as a printer, postmaster, scientist, and statesman earned him a cherished place in the history of our nation. Each stamp features a collage representing one of four aspects of Franklin's life, career, and personal interests. ***Benjamin Franklin, Scientist:*** Remembered for the pursuits he called "philosophical amusements," Franklin was intensely curious about natural phenomena. His observations and experiments in areas such as electricity and meteorology resulted in interesting inventions, including a heating stove, the lightning rod, and an early electrical battery. ***Benjamin Franklin, Printer:*** From his childhood apprenticeship in Boston to his career in Philadelphia as an adult, Franklin enjoyed a lifelong association with printing. In addition to the *Pennsylvania Gazette* and *Poor Richard's Almanack* his presses also printed materials such as government pamphlets, religious tracts, currency, and books. ***Benjamin Franklin, Statesman:*** Deeply involved in politics and civic life, Franklin served in the Continental Congress and signed both the Declaration of Independence and the Constitution. Often considered America's first diplomat, Franklin negotiated an alliance with France and helped to secure a peace treaty with Great Britain. ***Benjamin Franklin, Postmaster:*** Franklin was vital to the organization of the American postal system, serving as postmaster of Philadelphia and a deputy postmaster for the American colonies before being appointed postmaster general by the Continental Congress in 1775. He marked postage-free letters with his unique personal signature: "B. Free Franklin."

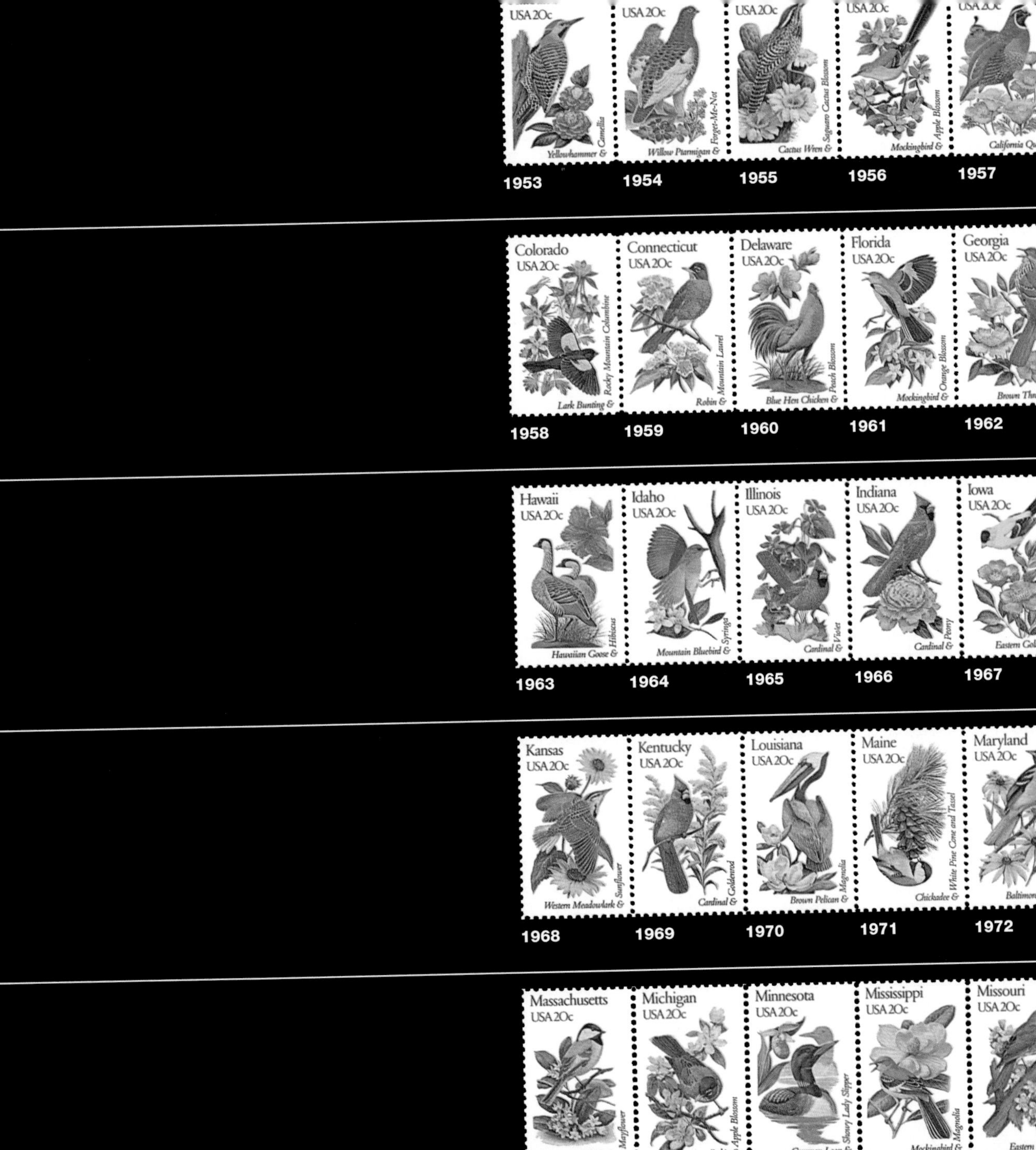

VISIT US ONLINE AT **THE POSTAL STORE**

AT **WWW.USPS.COM**

OR CALL **1 800 STAMP-24**

978 1979 1980 1981 1982

983 1984 1985 1986 1987

88 1989 1990 1991 1992

93 1994 1995 1996 1997

8 1999 2000 2001 2002

	Issue	Date	Un	U	PB	#	FDC	Q(M)
	State Birds & Flowers continued, **Tagged, Perf. 10.5 x 11.25**							
1978	20¢ Montana: Western Meadowlark & Bitterroot	04/14/82	.50	.30			1.25	13
1979	20¢ Nebraska: Western Meadowlark & Goldenrod	04/14/82	.50	.30			1.25	13
1980	20¢ Nevada: Mountain Bluebird & Sagebrush	04/14/82	.50	.30			1.25	13
1981	20¢ New Hampshire: Purple Finch & Lilac	04/14/82	.50	.30			1.25	13
b	Black omitted		*6,000.00*					
1982	20¢ New Jersey: American Goldfinch & Violet	04/14/82	.50	.30			1.25	13
1983	20¢ New Mexico: Roadrunner & Yucca Flower	04/14/82	.50	.30			1.25	13
1984	20¢ New York: Eastern Bluebird & Rose	04/14/82	.50	.30			1.25	13
1985	20¢ North Carolina: Cardinal & Flowering Dogwood	04/14/82	.50	.30			1.25	13
1986	20¢ North Dakota: Western Meadowlark & Wild Prairie Rose	04/14/82	.50	.30			1.25	13
1987	20¢ Ohio: Cardinal & Red Carnation	04/14/82	.50	.30			1.25	13
1988	20¢ Oklahoma: Scissor-tailed Flycatcher & Mistletoe	04/14/82	.50	.30			1.25	13
1989	20¢ Oregon: Western Meadowlark & Oregon Grape	04/14/82	.50	.30			1.25	13
1990	20¢ Pennsylvania: Ruffed Grouse & Mountain Laurel	04/14/82	.50	.30			1.25	13
1991	20¢ Rhode Island: Rhode Island Red & Violet	04/14/82	.50	.30			1.25	13
b	Black omitted		*6,000.00*					

	Issue	Date	Un	U	PB	#	FDC	Q(M)
	State Birds & Flowers continued, **Tagged, Perf. 10.5 x 11.25**							
1992	20¢ South Carolina: Carolina Wren & Carolina Jessamine	04/14/82	.50	.30			1.25	13
1993	20¢ South Dakota: Ring-Necked Pheasant & Pasqueflower	04/14/82	.50	.30			1.25	13
1994	20¢ Tennessee: Mockingbird & Iris	04/14/82	.50	.30			1.25	13
1995	20¢ Texas: Mockingbird & Bluebonnet	04/14/82	.50	.30			1.25	13
1996	20¢ Utah: California Gull & Sego Lily	04/14/82	.50	.30			1.25	13
1997	20¢ Vermont: Hermit Thrush & Red Clover	04/14/82	.50	.30			1.25	13
1998	20¢ Virginia: Cardinal & Flowering Dogwood	04/14/82	.50	.30			1.25	13
1999	20¢ Washington: American Goldfinch & Rhododendron	04/14/82	.50	.30			1.25	13
2000	20¢ West Virginia: Cardinal & Rhododendron Maximum	04/14/82	.50	.30			1.25	13
2001	20¢ Wisconsin: Robin & Wood Violet	04/14/82	.50	.30			1.25	13
b	Black omitted		*6,000.00*					
2002	20¢ Wyoming: Western Meadowlark & Indian Paintbrush	04/14/82	.50	.30			1.25	13
b	Pane of 50		25.00	—			30.00	
d	Pane of 50, imperf.		*27,500.00*					

KATHERINE ANNE PORTER

In 2006 the Literary Arts series honors writer Katherine Anne Porter (1890-1980). Considered a master prose stylist, Porter won both the National Book Award and the Pulitzer Prize for fiction in 1966 for *The Collected Stories of Katherine Anne Porter* (1965). Porter was born and raised in Texas where she first worked as a journalist. Strong-willed, intelligent, and gifted, she moved to New York City in 1919 where she met some Mexican artists. Inspired by her new friends, she traveled to Mexico City four times between 1920 and 1931, all the while writing essays, reviews, and several original pieces of fiction including "Flowering Judas." Set in Mexico, "Flowering Judas" was also the title of Porter's first collection of stories, which she published to critical praise in 1930. Perhaps the finest collection of her fiction is *Pale Horse, Pale Rider* (1939), which brought together three short novels. Although skilled in creating short fiction, Porter did not achieve significant financial success until the publication of her only full-length novel, *Ship of Fools* (1962), a best seller that was made into a full-length movie. Three years before her death, Porter published her final work, *The Never-Ending Wrong* (1977), a personal memoir of the Sacco-Vanzetti trial of 1921. Award-winning stamp artist Michael J. Deas based his painting of Porter on a 1936 photograph made by George Platt Lynes.

	Issue	Date	Un	U	PB/PNC/LP	#	FDC	Q(M)
	Tagged, Perf. 11							
2003	20¢ USA/ The Netherlands	04/20/82	.40	.20	3.50	(6)	1.00	109
a	Imperf., pair		*300.00*					
2004	20¢ Library of Congress	04/21/82	.40	.20	1.75	(4)	1.00	113
	Coil, Tagged, Perf. 10 Vertically							
2005	20¢ Consumer Education	04/27/82	.55	.20	22.50	(3)	1.00	
a	Imperf., pair		*100.00*		*400.00*	(2)		
b	Tagging omitted		*7.50*					
	Value for plate no. coil strip of 3 stamps is for most common plate nos. Other plate nos. and strips of 5 stamps may have higher values.							
	Knoxville World's Fair, Tagged, Perf. 11							
2006	20¢ Solar Energy	04/29/82	.45	.20			1.00	31
2007	20¢ Synthetic Fuels	04/29/82	.45	.20			1.00	31
2008	20¢ Breeder Reactor	04/29/82	.45	.20			1.00	31
2009	20¢ Fossil Fuels	04/29/82	.45	.20			1.00	31
a	Block of 4, #2006-2009		1.80	1.50	2.40	(4)	2.50	
	Tagged, Perf. 11							
2010	20¢ Horatio Alger	04/30/82	.40	.20	1.75	(4)	1.00	108
2011	20¢ Aging Together	05/21/82	.40	.20	1.75	(4)	1.00	173
	Performing Arts, Tagged, Perf. 11							
2012	20¢ John, Ethel and Lionel Barrymore	06/08/82	.40	.20	1.75	(4)	1.00	107
	Tagged, Perf. 11							
2013	20¢ Dr. Mary Walker	06/10/82	.40	.20	1.75	(4)	1.00	109
2014	20¢ International Peace Garden	06/30/82	.40	.20	1.75	(4)	1.00	183
a	Black and green omitted		*250.00*					
2015	20¢ America's Libraries	07/13/82	.40	.20	1.75	(4)	1.00	169
a	Vertical pair, imperf. horizontally		*275.00*					
b	Tagging omitted		*7.50*					
	Black Heritage, Tagged, Perf. 10.5 x 11							
2016	20¢ Jackie Robinson	08/02/82	1.10	.20	5.50	(4)	6.00	164
	Tagged, Perf. 11							
2017	20¢ Touro Synagogue	08/22/82	.45	.20	12.50	(20)	1.50	110
a	Imperf., pair		*2,500.00*					
2018	20¢ Wolf Trap Farm Park	09/01/82	.40	.20	1.75	(4)	1.00	111

	Issue	Date	Un	U	PB	#	FDC	Q(M
	American Architecture, Tagged, Perf. 11							
2019	20¢ Fallingwater, by Frank Lloyd Wright	09/30/82	.45	.20			1.00	4
2020	20¢ Illinois Institute of Technology, by Ludwig Mies van der Rohe	09/30/82	.45	.20			1.00	4
2021	20¢ Gropius House, by Walter Gropius	09/30/82	.45	.20			1.00	4
2022	20¢ Dulles Airport by Eero Saarinen	09/30/82	.45	.20			1.00	4
a	Block of 4, #2019-2022		2.00	1.75	2.50	(4)	2.50	
	Tagged, Perf. 11							
2023	20¢ St. Francis of Assisi	10/07/82	.40	.20	1.75	(4)	1.00	17
2024	20¢ Ponce de Leon	10/12/82	.50	.20	3.50	(6)	1.00	11
a	Imperf., pair		*450.00*					
	Holiday Celebrations: Holiday, Tagged, Perf. 11							
2025	13¢ Puppy and Kitten	11/03/82	.25	.20	1.40	(4)	1.25	23
a	Imperf., pair		*500.00*					
	Holiday Celebrations: Christmas, Tagged, Perf. 11							
2026	20¢ Madonna and Child, by Tiepolo	10/28/82	.40	.20	11.00	(20)	1.00	70
a	Imperf., pair		*150.00*					
	Holiday Celebrations: Holiday, Tagged, Perf. 11							
2027	20¢ Children Sledding	10/28/82	.50	.20			1.00	19
2028	20¢ Children Building a Snowman	10/28/82	.50	.20			1.00	19
2029	20¢ Children Skating	10/28/82	.50	.20			1.00	19
2030	20¢ Children Trimming a Tree	10/28/82	.50	.20			1.00	19
a	Block of 4, #2027-2030		2.10	1.50	2.50	(4)	2.50	
b	As "a," imperf.		*2,000.00*					
c	As "a," imperf. horizontally		*850.00*					
	Tagged, Perf. 11							
2031	20¢ Science & Industry	01/19/83	.40	.20	1.75	(4)	1.00	11
a	Black omitted		*1,250.00*					

2003

2004

2005

2006 2007

2008 2009 2009a

2010

2011

2012

2013

2014

2015

2016

2017

2018

2019 2020

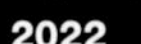
2021 2022 2022a

2023

2024

2025

2026

2027 2028

2029 2030 2030a

2031

2032 2033

2034 2035 2035a

2036

2037

2038

2039

2040

2041

2042

2043

2044

2045

2046

2047

2048 2049

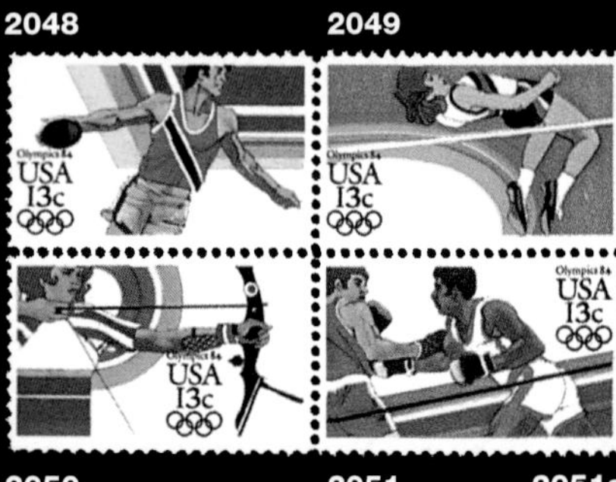

2050 2051 2051a

2052

2053

2054

2055 2056

2057 2058 2058a

VISIT US ONLINE AT ***THE POSTAL STORE***
AT ***WWW.USPS.COM***
OR CALL ***1 800 STAMP-24***

Issue		Date	Un	U	PB	#	FDC	Q(M)
	Balloons, Tagged, Perf. 11							
2032	20¢ Intrepid, 1861	03/31/83	.50	.20			1.00	57
2033	20¢ Hot Air Ballooning (wording lower right)	03/31/83	.50	.20			1.00	57
2034	20¢ Hot Air Ballooning (wording upper left)	03/31/83	.50	.20			1.00	57
2035	20¢ Explorer II, 1935	03/31/83	.50	.20			1.00	57
a	Block of 4, #2032-2035		2.00	1.50	2.25	(4)	2.50	
b	As "a," imperf.		*4,000.00*					
c	As "a," right stamp perf., otherwise imperf.		*4,500.00*					
	Tagged, Perf. 11							
2036	20¢ U.S./Sweden Treaty	03/24/83	.40	.20	1.75	(4)	1.00	118
2037	20¢ Civilian Conservation Corps	04/05/83	.40	.20	1.75	(4)	1.00	114
a	Imperf., pair		*3,000.00*					
2038	20¢ Joseph Priestley	04/13/83	.40	.20	1.75	(4)	1.00	165
2039	20¢ Voluntarism	04/20/83	.40	.20	3.00	(6)	1.00	120
a	Imperf., pair		*350.00*					
2040	20¢ Concord-German Immigration, Apr. 29	04/29/83	.40	.20	1.75	(4)	1.00	117
	Tagged, Perf. 11							
2041	20¢ Brooklyn Bridge	05/17/83	.40	.20	1.75	(4)	1.75	182
a	Tagging omitted		*7.00*					
b	All color omitted		*75.00*					
2042	20¢ Tennessee Valley Authority	05/18/83	.40	.20	10.00	(20)	1.00	114
2043	20¢ Physical Fitness	05/14/83	.40	.20	3.00	(6)	1.25	112
	Black Heritage, Tagged, Perf. 11							
2044	20¢ Scott Joplin	06/09/83	.50	.20	2.00	(4)	1.75	115
a	Imperf., pair		*450.00*					
	Tagged, Perf. 11							
2045	20¢ Medal of Honor	06/07/83	.55	.20	1.75	(4)	5.50	109
a	Red omitted		*250.00*					
	American Sports Personalities, Tagged, Perf. 10.5 x 11							
2046	20¢ Babe Ruth	07/06/83	1.40	.20	6.50	(4)	5.00	185
	Literary Arts, Tagged, Perf. 11							
2047	20¢ Nathaniel Hawthorne	07/08/83	.45	.20	2.10	(4)	1.00	111
	Olympic Games, Tagged, Perf. 11							
2048	13¢ Discus Thrower	07/28/83	.35	.20			1.25	99
2049	13¢ High Jumper	07/28/83	.35	.20			1.25	99
2050	13¢ Archer	07/28/83	.35	.20			1.25	99
2051	13¢ Boxers	07/28/83	.35	.20			1.25	99
a	Block of 4, #2048-2051		1.50	1.25	1.75	(4)	2.50	
	American Bicentennial, Tagged, Perf. 11							
2052	20¢ Signing of Treaty of Paris (John Adams, Benjamin Franklin and John Jay observing David Hartley)	09/02/83	.40	.20	1.75	(4)	1.00	104
	Tagged, Perf. 11							
2053	20¢ Civil Service	09/09/83	.40	.20	3.00	(6)	1.00	115
2054	20¢ Metropolitan Opera	09/14/83	.40	.20	1.75	(4)	1.50	113
	American Inventors, Tagged, Perf. 11							
2055	20¢ Charles Steinmetz and Curve on Graph	09/21/83	.50	.20			1.00	48
2056	20¢ Edwin Armstrong and Frequency Modulator	09/21/83	.50	.20			1.00	48
2057	20¢ Nikola Tesla and Induction Motor	09/21/83	.50	.20			1.00	48
2058	20¢ Philo T. Farnsworth and First Television Camera	09/21/83	.50	.20			1.00	48
a	Block of 4, #2055-2058		2.00	1.25	2.75	(4)	2.50	
b	As "a," black omitted		*350.00*					

JUDY GARLAND

The 12th stamp in the Legends of Hollywood series honors Judy Garland (1922-1969), considered by many to be one of the greatest entertainers of the 20th century. An all-around performer, she acted with equal effectiveness in comedy or drama, sang a varied repertoire with unparalleled skill, and partnered with the leading male dancers of her time, Gene Kelly and Fred Astaire among them. Her show business colleagues have been nearly unanimous in their praise of Garland's natural brilliance—indeed, she was a "star of stars." Garland triumphed in most media of her era. She appeared in 32 feature films, winning international fame as Dorothy, the girl who rides a tornado from her home in Kansas to an imaginary land in the 1939 musical *The Wizard of Oz*. In addition, she was a best-selling recording artist who released more than a dozen albums and nearly 100 singles and made hundreds of radio broadcasts. She starred in 30 of her own television shows and made guest appearances on almost as many others. Her live performances, widely regarded as her supreme showcase, frequently broke box office records for theaters, concert halls, and nightclubs. After her death on June 22, 1969, Judy Garland was lauded around the world for enriching the lives of her legion of fans. Many celebrated contemporary entertainers, Aretha Franklin, Barbra Streisand, and Bette Midler among them, have hailed Garland as an inspiration and influence.

	Issue	Date	Un	U	PB	#	FDC	Q(M)
	Streetcars, Tagged, Perf. 11							
2059	20¢ First American Streetcar	10/08/83	.50	.20			1.00	52
2060	20¢ Early Electric Streetcar	10/08/83	.50	.20			1.00	52
2061	20¢ “Bobtail” Horsecar	10/08/83	.50	.20			1.00	52
2062	20¢ St. Charles Streetcar	10/08/83	.50	.20			1.00	52
a	Block of 4, #2059-2062		2.00	1.40	2.60	(4)	2.50	
b	As “a,” black omitted		*400.00*					
c	As “a,” black omitted on #2059, 2061		—					
	Holiday Celebrations: Christmas, Tagged, Perf. 11							
2063	20¢ Niccolini-Cowper Madonna, by Raphael	10/28/83	.40	.20	1.75	(4)	1.00	716
	Holiday Celebrations: Holiday, Tagged, Perf. 11							
2064	20¢ Santa Claus	10/28/83	.40	.20	3.00	(6)	1.00	849
a	Imperf., pair		*150.00*					
	Tagged, Perf. 11							
2065	20¢ Martin Luther	11/11/83	.40	.20	1.75	(4)	1.50	165
2066	20¢ Alaska Statehood	01/03/84	.40	.20	1.75	(4)	1.00	120
	Olympic Games, Tagged, Perf. 10.5 x 11							
2067	20¢ Ice Dancing	01/06/84	.50	.20			1.00	80
2068	20¢ Downhill Skiing	01/06/84	.50	.20			1.00	80
2069	20¢ Cross-country Skiing	01/06/84	.50	.20			1.00	80
2070	20¢ Hockey	01/06/84	.50	.20			1.00	80
a	Block of 4, #2067-2070		2.10	1.50	3.00	(4)	2.50	
	Tagged, Perf. 11							
2071	20¢ Federal Deposit Insurance Corporation	01/12/84	.40	.20	1.75	(4)	1.00	104
	Love, Tagged, Perf. 11 x 10.5							
2072	20¢ Love	01/31/84	.40	.20	11.50	(20)	1.00	555
a	Horizontal pair, imperf. vertically		*175.00*					
b	Tagging omitted		*5.00*					
	Black Heritage, Tagged, Perf. 11							
2073	20¢ Carter G. Woodson	02/01/84	.40	.20	2.00	(4)	1.75	120
a	Horizontal pair, imperf. vertically		*1,250.00*					
	Tagged, Perf. 11							
2074	20¢ Soil and Water Conservation	02/06/84	.40	.20	1.75	(4)	1.00	107
2075	20¢ 50th Anniversary of Credit Union Act	02/10/84	.40	.20	1.75	(4)	1.00	107
	Orchids, Tagged, Perf. 11							
2076	20¢ Wild Pink	03/05/84	.50	.20			1.00	77
2077	20¢ Yellow Lady’s-Slipper	03/05/84	.50	.20			1.00	77
2078	20¢ Spreading Pogonia	03/05/84	.50	.20			1.00	77
2079	20¢ Pacific Calypso	03/05/84	.50	.20			1.00	77
a	Block of 4, #2076-2079		2.00	1.50	2.50	(4)	2.50	
	Tagged, Perf. 11							
2080	20¢ Hawaii Statehood	03/12/84	.40	.20	1.70	(4)	1.00	120
2081	20¢ National Archives	04/16/84	.40	.20	1.70	(4)	1.00	108
	Olympic Games, Tagged, Perf. 11							
2082	20¢ Diving	05/04/84	.55	.20			1.25	78
2083	20¢ Long Jump	05/04/84	.55	.20			1.25	78
2084	20¢ Wrestling	05/04/84	.55	.20			1.25	78
2085	20¢ Kayak	05/04/84	.55	.20			1.25	78
a	Block of 4, #2082-2085		2.40	1.90	3.50	(4)	2.50	
	Tagged, Perf. 11							
2086	20¢ Louisiana World Exposition	05/11/84	.50	.20	2.60	(4)	1.00	130
2087	20¢ Health Research	05/17/84	.40	.20	1.75	(4)	1.00	120
	Performing Arts, Tagged, Perf. 11							
2088	20¢ Douglas Fairbanks	05/23/84	.40	.20	11.00	(20)	1.00	117
a	Tagging omitted		*15.00*					
	American Sports Personalities, Tagged, Perf. 11							
2089	20¢ Jim Thorpe on Football Field	05/24/84	.40	.20	2.00	(4)	3.00	116
	Performing Arts, Tagged, Perf. 11							
2090	20¢ John McCormack	06/06/84	.40	.20	1.75	(4)	1.00	117

CHRISTMAS: MADONNA AND CHILD

The 2006 Christmas stamp features an oil-on-canvas entitled *Madonna and Child with Bird.* Dating to around 1765, the painting is attributed to Ignacio Chacón—an artist active from about 1745 to 1775 in Cuzco, Peru. Spanish colonial art flourished in the New World between the mid-16th and early 19th centuries, especially in Mexico and Peru. In Cuzco, the main art center in the Andes highlands, paintings were characterized by elements such as floral borders, vivid coloring, and *brocateado de oro* (gold-leaf overlay). Ignacio Chacón was a student and friend of Marcos Zapata, a master painter of the Cuzco School. Zapata’s students continued his personal interpretation of the mestizo-baroque style—a red, white, and blue color scheme embellished with *brocateado de oro*, which is readily apparent in Chacón’s *Madonna and Child with Bird.* Rendered in exquisite detail against a dark background, both figures are brightly clothed in red and white and cloaked in the Virgin’s sumptuous, gold-patterned blue mantle. Their halos, which are also enhanced with gold leaf overlay, radiate luminously behind their heads. A painted border of red, white, and blue flowers frames the entire composition.

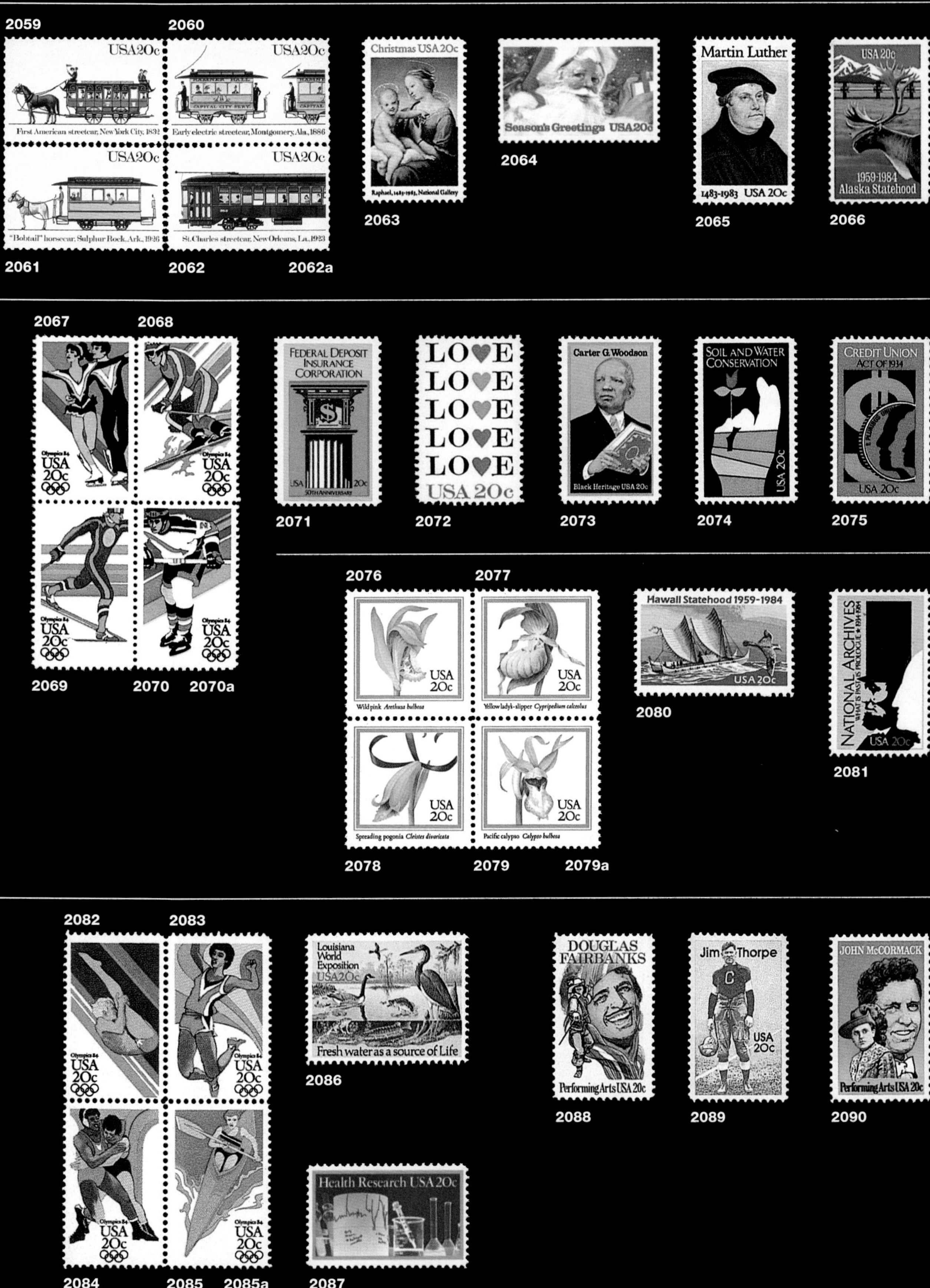
2059
2060
USA20c
First American streetcar, New York City, 1832
Early electric streetcar, Montgomery, Ala., 1886
"Bobtail" horsecar, Sulphur Rock, Ark., 1926
St. Charles streetcar, New Orleans, La., 1923
2061
2062
2062a
Christmas USA 20c
Raphael, 1483-1983, National Gallery
2063
Season's Greetings USA20c
2064
Martin Luther
1483-1983 USA 20c
2065
USA 20c
1959·1984
Alaska Statehood
2066
2067
2068
Olympics 84
USA
20c
2069
2070
2070a
FEDERAL DEPOSIT
INSURANCE
CORPORATION
USA 20c
50TH ANNIVERSARY
2071
LOVE
LOVE
LOVE
LOVE
LOVE
USA 20c
2072
Carter G. Woodson
Black Heritage USA 20c
2073
SOIL AND WATER
CONSERVATION
USA 20c
2074
CREDIT UNION
ACT OF 1934
USA 20c
2075
2076
2077
USA
20c
Wild pink Arethusa bulbosa
Yellow lady's-slipper Cypripedium calceolus
Spreading pogonia Cleistes divaricata
Pacific calypso Calypso bulbosa
2078
2079
2079a
Hawaii Statehood 1959-1984
USA 20c
2080
NATIONAL ARCHIVES
WHAT IS PAST IS PROLOGUE ★ 1934-1984
USA 20c
2081
2082
2083
Olympics 84
USA
20c
2084
2085
2085a
Louisiana
World
Exposition
USA20c
Fresh water as a source of Life
2086
Health Research USA 20c
2087
DOUGLAS
FAIRBANKS
Performing Arts USA 20c
2088
Jim Thorpe
USA
20c
2089
JOHN McCORMACK
Performing Arts USA 20c
2090

2091

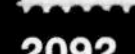

2092

2093 2094

2095 2096

2097

2098 2099

2100 2101 2101a

2102

2103

2104

2105

2106

2107

2108

2109

2110

2111

2114

2115b

2116

2117 2118 2119 2120 2121 2121a

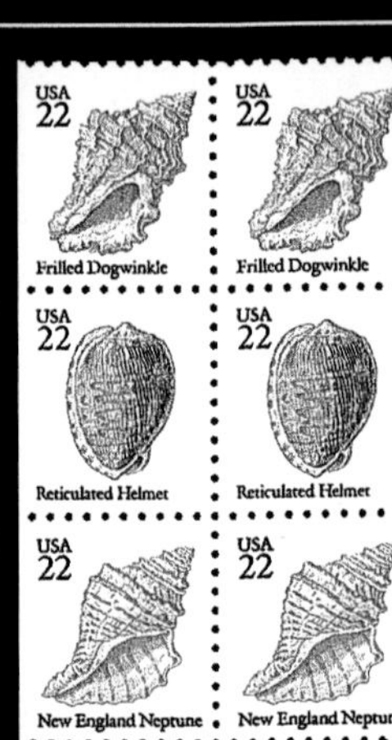

2122

	Issue	Date	Un	U	PB	#	FDC	Q(M)
	Tagged, Perf. 11							
2091	20¢ 25th Anniversary of St. Lawrence Seaway	06/26/84	.40	.20	1.75	(4)	1.00	120
2092	20¢ Migratory Bird Hunting and Preservation Act	07/02/84	.50	.20	2.50	(4)	1.00	124
a	Horizontal pair, imperf. vertically		*350.00*					
2093	20¢ Roanoke Voyages	07/13/84	.40	.20	1.75	(4)	1.00	120
	Pair with full horizontal gutter between		—					
	Literary Arts, Tagged, Perf. 11							
2094	20¢ Herman Melville	08/01/84	.40	.20	1.75	(4)	1.75	117
	Tagged, Perf. 11							
2095	20¢ Horace Moses	08/06/84	.45	.20	3.50	(6)	1.00	117
2096	20¢ Smokey the Bear	08/13/84	.40	.20	2.00	(4)	3.00	96
a	Horizontal pair, imperf. between		*275.00*					
b	Vertical pair, imperf. between		*225.00*					
c	Block of 4, imperf. between vertically and horizontally		*5,500.00*					
d	Horizontal pair, imperf. vertically		*1,500.00*					
	American Sports Personalities, Tagged, Perf. 11							
2097	20¢ Roberto Clemente	08/17/84	1.50	.20	7.00	(4)	9.00	119
a	Horizontal pair, imperf. vertically		*2,000.00*					
	American Dogs, Tagged, Perf. 11							
2098	20¢ Beagle and Boston Terrier	09/07/84	.50	.20			1.50	54
2099	20¢ Chesapeake Bay Retriever and Cocker Spaniel	09/07/84	.50	.20			1.50	54
2100	20¢ Alaskan Malamute and Collie	09/07/84	.50	.20			1.50	54
2101	20¢ Black and Tan Coonhound and American Foxhound	09/07/84	.50	.20			1.50	54
a	Block of 4, #2098-2101		2.00	1.90	3.00	(4)	3.00	
	Tagged, Perf. 11							
2102	20¢ Crime Prevention	09/26/84	.40	.20	1.75	(4)	1.25	120
2103	20¢ Hispanic Americans	10/31/84	.40	.20	1.75	(4)	1.75	108
a	Vertical pair, imperf. horizontally		*2,250.00*					
2104	20¢ Family Unity	10/01/84	.40	.20	12.50	(20)	1.00	118
a	Horizontal pair, imperf. vertically		*500.00*					
b	Tagging omitted		*7.50*					
2105	20¢ Eleanor Roosevelt	10/11/84	.40	.20	2.00	(4)	1.00	113
2106	20¢ A Nation of Readers	10/16/84	.40	.20	1.90	(4)	1.00	117
	Holiday Celebrations: Christmas, Tagged, Perf. 11							
2107	20¢ Madonna and Child, by Fra Filippo Lippi	10/30/84	.40	.20	1.70	(4)	1.00	751
	Holiday Celebrations: Holiday, Tagged, Perf. 11							
2108	20¢ Santa Claus	10/30/84	.40	.20	1.70	(4)	1.00	786
a	Horizontal pair, imperf. vertically		*925.00*					
	Tagged, Perf. 11							
2109	20¢ Vietnam Veterans' Memorial	11/10/84	.40	.20	2.25	(4)	3.50	105
	Performing Arts, Tagged, Perf. 11							
2110	22¢ Jerome Kern	01/23/85	.40	.20	1.75	(4)	1.00	125
a	Tagging omitted		*7.50*					

	Issue	Date	Un	U	PB/PNC	#	FDC	Q(M)
	Tagged, Perf. 11							
2111	(22¢) "D" Stamp	02/01/85	.55	.20	4.50	(6)	1.00	
a	Imperf., pair		*40.00*					
b	Vertical pair, imperf. horizontally		*1,350.00*					
	Coil, Perf. 10 Vertically							
2112	(22¢) "D" green Eagle (2111)	02/01/85	.60	.20	5.00	(3)	1.00	
a	Imperf., pair		*45.00*					
b	As "a," tagging omitted		*100.00*					
	Booklet, Perf. 11							
2113	(22¢) "D" green Eagle (2111), single from booklet	02/01/85	.80	.20			1.00	
a	Booklet pane of 10	02/01/85	8.50	*3.00*			*7.50*	
b	As "a," imperf. between horizontally		—					
	Tagged, Perf. 11							
2114	22¢ Flag Over Capitol	03/29/85	.40	.20	1.90	(4)	1.00	
	Pair with full horizontal gutter between		—					
	Coil, Perf. 10 Vertically							
2115	22¢ Flag Over Capitol (2114)	03/29/85	.40	.20	3.00	(3)	1.00	
a	Narrow block tagging		.40	.20	3.00	(3)		
b	Wide and tall block tagging		.40	.20	3.00	(3)	*1.00*	
c	Inscribed "T" at bottom	05/23/87	.50	.40				
	#2115b issued for test on prephosphored paper. Paper is whiter and colors are brighter than on 2115.							
	Booklet, Perf. 10 Horizontally							
2116	22¢ Flag over Capitol, single from booklet		.50	.20			1.00	
a	Booklet pane of 5	03/29/85	2.50	*1.25*			3.50	
	#2116 issued only in booklets. All stamps are imperf. at both sides or imperf. at both sides and bottom.							
	Seashells Booklet, Tagged, Perf. 10							
2117	22¢ Frilled Dogwinkle	04/04/85	.40	.20			1.00	
2118	22¢ Reticulated Helmet	04/04/85	.40	.20			1.00	
2119	22¢ New England Neptune	04/04/85	.40	.20			1.00	
2120	22¢ Calico Scallop	04/04/85	.40	.20			1.00	
2121	22¢ Lightning Whelk	04/04/85	.40	.20			1.00	
a	Booklet pane of 10		4.00	*3.00*			*7.50*	
b	As "a," violet omitted		*600.00*					
c	As "a," imperf. between vertically		*550.00*					
e	Strip of 5, #2117-2121		2.00	—				
	Express Mail Booklet, Perf. 10 Vertically							
2122	$10.75 Eagle and Moon, booklet single	04/29/85	19.00	7.50			40.00	
a	Booklet pane of 3		60.00	—			*95.00*	
b	Type II		21.00	10.00				
c	As "b," booklet pane of 3		65.00	—				
	#2122 issued only in booklets. All stamps are imperf. at top and bottom or at top, bottom and one side.							

	Issue	Date	Un	U	PNC	#	FDC	Q(M)
	Transportation, Coil, Tagged, Perf. 10 Vertically							
2123	3.4¢ School Bus 1920s	06/08/85	.20	.20	.90	(5)	1.00	
a	Untagged (Bureau precanceled)		.20	.20	4.25	(5)		
2124	4.9¢ Buckboard 1880s	06/21/85	.20	.20	.85	(5)	1.00	
a	Untagged (Bureau precanceled)		.20	.20	1.40	(5)		
2125	5.5¢ Star Route Truck 1910s	11/01/86	.20	.20	1.50	(5)	1.00	
a	Untagged (Bureau precanceled)		.20	.20	1.75	(5)		
2126	6¢ Tricycle 1880s	05/06/85	.20	.20	1.50	(5)	1.25	
a	Untagged (Bureau precanceled)		.20	.20	1.75	(5)		
b	As "a," imperf., pair		*225.00*					
2127	7.1¢ Tractor 1920s	02/06/87	.20	.20	2.10	(5)	1.00	
a	Untagged (Bureau precanceled "Nonprofit org.")		.20	.20	3.00	(5)	5.00	
b	Untagged (Bureau precanceled "Nonprofit 5-Digit ZIP + 4")	05/26/89	.20	.20	1.75	(5)		
2128	8.3¢ Ambulance 1860s	06/21/85	.20	.20	1.50	(5)	1.00	
a	Untagged (Bureau precanceled)		.20	.20	1.50	(5)		
2129	8.5¢ Tow Truck 1920s	01/24/87	.20	.20	3.00	(5)	1.25	
a	Untagged (Bureau precanceled)		.20	.20	2.75	(5)		
2130	10.1¢ Oil Wagon 1890s	04/18/85	.25	.20	2.50	(5)	1.25	
a	Untagged (Bureau precanceled, red)		.25	.25	2.25	(5)	1.25	
	Untagged (Bureau precanceled, black)		.25	.25	2.50	(5)		
b	As "a," red precancel, imperf., pair		15.00		200.00	(6)		
	As "a," black precancel, imperf., pair		85.00					
2131	11¢ Stutz Bearcat 1933	06/11/85	.25	.20	1.40	(5)	1.25	
2132	12¢ Stanley Steamer 1909	04/02/85	.25	.20	2.25	(5)	1.25	
a	Untagged (Bureau precanceled)		.25	.25	2.40	(5)		
b	As "a," type II		.40	.30	19.00	(5)		
	Type II has "Stanley Steamer 1909" .5 mm shorter (17.5 mm) than #2132 (18mm).							
2133	12.5¢ Pushcart 1880s	04/18/85	.25	.20	3.00	(5)	1.25	
a	Untagged (Bureau precanceled)		.25	.25	3.00	(5)		
b	As "a," imperf., pair		45.00					
2134	14¢ Iceboat 1880s	03/23/85	.30	.20	2.25	(5)	1.25	
a	Imperf., pair		100.00					
b	Type II		.30	.20	3.25	(5)		
2135	17¢ Dog Sled 1920s	08/20/86	.35	.20	3.25	(5)	1.25	
a	Imperf., pair		*400.00*					
2136	25¢ Bread Wagon 1880s	11/22/86	.45	.20	3.50	(5)	1.25	
a	Imperf., pair		10.00					
b	Pair, imperf. between		*650.00*					
c	Tagging omitted		*27.50*					
	Black Heritage, Tagged, Perf. 11							
2137	22¢ Mary McLeod Bethune	03/05/85	.60	.20	3.25	(4)	1.50	120
	American Folk Art: Duck Decoys, Tagged, Perf. 11							
2138	22¢ Broadbill Decoy	03/22/85	.80	.20			1.00	75
2139	22¢ Mallard Decoy	03/22/85	.80	.20			1.00	75
2140	22¢ Canvasback Decoy	03/22/85	.80	.20			1.00	75
2141	22¢ Redhead Decoy	03/22/85	.80	.20			1.00	75
a	Block of 4, #2138-2141		4.00	2.75	4.75	(4)	2.50	

	Issue	Date	Un	U	PB/PNC	#	FDC	Q(M)
	Tagged, Perf. 11							
2142	22¢ Winter Special Olympics	03/25/85	.40	.20	1.75	(4)	1.00	121
a	Vertical pair, imperf. horizontally		*475.00*					
	Love, Tagged, Perf. 11							
2143	22¢ Love	04/17/85	.40	.20	1.70	(4)	1.00	730
a	Imperf., pair		*1,500.00*					
	Tagged, Perf. 11							
2144	22¢ Rural Electrification Administration	05/11/85	.45	.20	17.50	(20)	1.00	125
2145	22¢ AMERIPEX '86	05/25/85	.40	.20	1.75	(4)	1.00	203
a	Red, black and blue omitted		*190.00*					
b	Red and black omitted		*1,250.00*					
2146	22¢ Abigail Adams	06/14/85	.40	.20	2.00	(4)	1.00	126
a	Imperf., pair		*250.00*					
2147	22¢ Frederic A. Bartholdi	07/18/85	.40	.20	1.90	(4)	1.00	130
2148	Not assigned							
	Coil Stamps, Perf. 10 Vertically							
2149	18¢ George Washington, Washington Monument	11/06/85	.35	.20	3.00	(5)	1.00	
a	Untagged (Bureau precanceled)		.35	.35	6.00	(5)		
b	Imperf., pair		*950.00*					
c	As "a," imperf. pair		*750.00*					
d	Tagging omitted		—	—				
e	As "a," tagged (error), dull gum		*2.00*	1.75	—			
2150	21.1¢ Sealed Envelopes	10/22/85	.40	.20	3.25	(5)	1.00	
a	Untagged (Bureau precanceled)		.40	.40	3.25	(5)		
b	As "a," tagged (error)		2.50	2.50	*30.00*	(5)		
2151	Not assigned							
	Tagged, Perf. 11							
2152	22¢ Korean War Veterans	07/26/85	.40	.20	2.50	(4)	2.50	120
2153	22¢ Social Security Act, 50th Anniversary	08/14/85	.40	.20	1.90	(4)	1.00	120
2154	22¢ World War I Veterans	08/26/85	.40	.20	2.25	(4)	1.50	120
	American Horses, Tagged, Perf. 11							
2155	22¢ Quarter Horse	09/25/85	1.25	.20			1.50	37
2156	22¢ Morgan	09/25/85	1.25	.20			1.50	37
2157	22¢ Saddlebred	09/25/85	1.25	.20			1.50	37
2158	22¢ Appaloosa	09/25/85	1.25	.20			1.50	37
a	Block of 4, #2155-2158		6.00	5.00	7.50	(4)	2.50	
	Tagged, Perf. 11							
2159	22¢ Public Education	10/01/85	.45	.20	2.75	(4)	1.00	120
	International Youth Year, Tagged, Perf. 11							
2160	22¢ YMCA Youth Camping	10/07/85	.65	.20			1.00	33
2161	22¢ Boy Scouts	10/07/85	.65	.20			2.00	33
2162	22¢ Big Brothers/Big Sisters	10/07/85	.65	.20			1.00	33
2163	22¢ Camp Fire	10/07/85	.65	.20			1.00	33
a	Block of 4, #2160-2163		3.00	2.25	4.00	(4)	2.50	

2123 2124 2125 2126 2127 2128 2129 2130

2131 2132 2133 2134 2135 2136

2138 2139

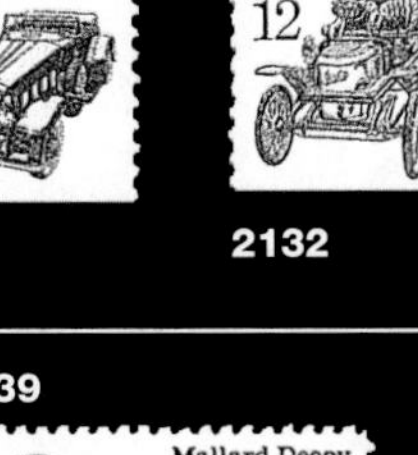

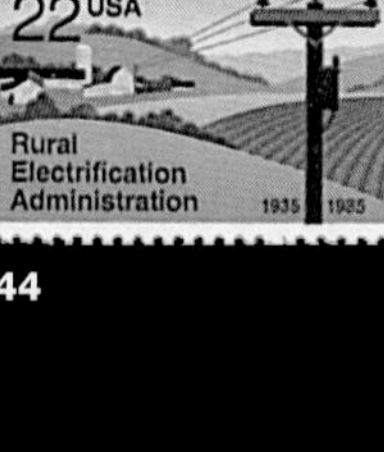

2137 2140 2141 2141a 2142 2143 2144

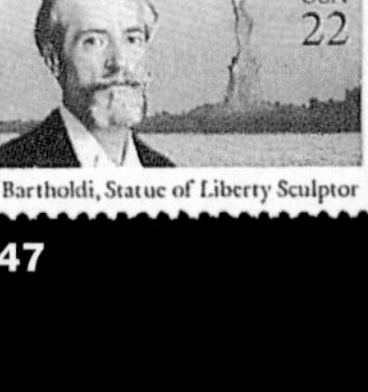

2145 2146 2147 2149 2150 2152

2155 2156 2160 2161

2153 2154 2157 2158 2158a 2159 2162 2163 2163a

2164 2165 2166 2167

2168 2169 2170 2171 2172 2173 2175

2176 2177 2178 2179 2180 2181 2182

2183 2184 2185 2186 2187 2188 2189

2190 2191 2192 2193 2194 2195 2196

2198 2199 2200 2201 2201a 2202 2203

	Issue	Date	Un	U	PB #	FDC	Q(M)
	Tagged, Perf. 11						
2164	22¢ Help End Hunger	10/15/85	.45	.20	2.00 (4)	1.00	120
	Holiday Celebrations: Christmas, Tagged, Perf. 11						
2165	22¢ Genoa Madonna, by Luca Della Robbia	10/30/85	.40	.20	1.75 (4)	1.00	759
a	Imperf., pair		*80.00*				
	Holiday Celebrations: Holiday, Tagged, Perf. 11						
2166	22¢ Poinsettia Plants	10/30/85	.40	.20	1.70 (4)	1.00	758
a	Imperf., pair		*120.00*				
	Tagged, Perf. 11						
2167	22¢ Arkansas Statehood	01/03/86	.75	.20	3.75 (4)	1.00	130
	Great Americans, Tagged, Perf. 11, 11.2 x 11.1						
2168	1¢ Margaret Mitchell	06/30/86	.20	.20	.25 (4)	2.00	
a	Tagging omitted		*5.00*				
2169	2¢ Mary Lyon	02/28/87	.20	.20	.30 (4)	1.00	
a	Untagged		.20	.20	.35 (4)		
2170	3¢ Paul Dudley White, MD	09/15/86	.20	.20	.50 (4)	1.00	
a	Untagged, dull gum		.20	.20	.50 (4)		
2171	4¢ Father Flanagan	07/14/86	.20	.20	.60 (4)	1.00	
a	Grayish violet, untagged		.20	.20	.40 (4)		
b	Deep grayish blue, untagged		.20	.20	.50 (4)		
2172	5¢ Hugo L. Black	02/27/86	.20	.20	1.00 (4)	1.00	
a	Tagging omitted		*80.00*				
2173	5¢ Luis Munoz Marin	02/18/90	.20	.20	.75 (4)	1.00	
a	Untagged		.20	.20	.60 (4)		
2174	Not assigned						
2175	10¢ Red Cloud	08/15/87	.25	.20	1.10 (4)	1.50	
a	Overall tagging	1990	.60	.25	10.00 (4)		
b	Tagging omitted		*12.50*				
c	Prephosphored coated paper (solid tagging)		.90	.20	4.00 (4)		
d	Prephosphored uncoated paper (mottled tagging)		.90	.20	4.00 (4)		
e	Carmine, prephosphored uncoated paper (mottled tagging)		.30	.20	1.50 (4)		
2176	14¢ Julia Ward Howe	02/12/87	.30	.20	1.50 (4)	1.00	
2177	15¢ Buffalo Bill Cody	06/06/88	.35	.20	10.00 (4)	1.75	
a	Overall tagging	1990	.30	—	3.25 (4)		
b	Prephosphored coated paper (solid tagging)		.40	—	3.25 (4)		
c	Tagging omitted		*15.00*	—			
2178	17¢ Belva Ann Lockwood	06/18/86	.35	.20	2.00 (4)	1.00	
a	Tagging omitted		*10.00*				
2179	20¢ Virginia Apgar	10/24/94	.40	.20	2.00 (4)	1.00	
a	Orange brown		.45	.20	2.25 (4)		
2180	21¢ Chester Carlson	10/21/88	.45	.20	2.50 (4)	1.00	
2181	23¢ Mary Cassatt	11/04/88	.45	.20	2.50 (4)	1.00	
a	Overall tagging, dull gum		.65	—	5.00 (4)		
b	Prephosphored coated paper (solid tagging)		.60	—	3.50 (4)		
c	Prephosphored uncoated paper (mottled tagging)		.65	.20	5.00 (4)		
d	Tagging omitted		*7.50*				
2182	25¢ Jack London	01/11/86	.50	.20	2.75 (4)	1.25	
a	Booklet pane of 10	05/03/88	5.00	*3.75*		6.00	
2183	28¢ Sitting Bull	09/14/89	.65	.20	3.50 (4)	1.50	
2184	29¢ Earl Warren	03/09/92	.65	.20	3.50 (4)	1.25	
	Great Americans, Tagged, Perf. 11.5 x 11						
2185	29¢ Thomas Jefferson	04/13/93	.65	.20	3.50 (4)	1.25	

	Issue	Date	Un	U	PB #	FDC	Q(M)
	Great Americans, Tagged, Perf. 11, 11.2 x 11.1						
2186	35¢ Dennis Chavez	04/03/91	.75	.20	4.25 (4)	1.25	
2187	40¢ Claire Lee Chennault	09/06/90	.85	.20	4.50 (4)	2.00	
a	Prephosphored coated paper (solid tagging)		1.00	.35	5.50 (4)		
b	Prephosphored coated paper (grainy solid tagging)		.85	.35			
c	Prephosphored uncoated paper (mottled tagging)		1.00	.20	10.00 (4)		
2188	45¢ Harvey Cushing, MD	06/17/88	1.00	.20	5.00 (4)	1.25	
a	Overall tagging	1990	2.25	.20	17.50 (4)		
b	Tagging omitted		*20.00*				
2189	52¢ Hubert H. Humphrey	06/03/91	1.10	.20	7.50 (4)	1.40	
a	Prephosphored uncoated paper (mottled tagging)		1.25	—	8.00 (4)		
2190	56¢ John Harvard	09/03/86	1.20	.20	7.00 (4)	2.50	
2191	65¢ H.H. 'Hap' Arnold	11/05/88	1.30	.20	6.50 (4)	2.50	
a	Tagging omitted		*20.00*				
	Perf. 11						
2192	75¢ Wendell Willkie	02/16/92	1.60	.20	7.50 (4)	2.50	
a	Prephosphored uncoated paper (mottled tagging)		1.75	—	9.00 (4)		
2193	$1 Bernard Revel	09/23/86	3.00	.50	15.00 (4)	3.50	
2194	$1 Johns Hopkins	06/07/89	2.25	.50	12.00 (4)	3.00	
b	Overall tagging	1990	2.50	.50	13.00 (4)		
c	Tagging omitted		*10.00*				
d	Dark blue, prephosphored coated paper (solid tagging)		2.50	.50	13.00 (4)		
e	Blue, prephosphored uncoated paper (mottled tagging)		2.75	.60	14.00 (4)		
f	Blue, prephosphored coated paper (grainy solid tagging)		2.75	.50	14.00 (4)		
2195	$2 William Jennings Bryan	03/19/86	4.25	.50	20.00 (4)	5.50	
a	Tagging omitted		*45.00*				
2196	$5 Bret Harte	08/25/87	9.00	1.00	42.50 (4)	15.00	
b	Prephosphored paper (solid tagging)		11.00	—	45.00 (4)		
	Great Americans, Booklet, Perf. 10 on 2 or 3 sides						
2197	25¢ Jack London (2182), single from booklet		.55	.20		1.00	
a	Booklet pane of 6	05/03/88	3.30	*2.50*		4.00	
b	Tagging omitted		*4.50*				
c	As "b," booklet pane of 6		*60.00*				
	United States — Sweden Stamp Collecting Booklet, Tagged, Perf. 10 Vertically on 1 or 2 sides						
2198	22¢ Handstamped Cover	01/23/86	.45	.20		1.00	17
2199	22¢ Boy Examining Stamp Collection	01/23/86	.45	.20		1.00	17
2200	22¢ #836 Under Magnifying Glass	01/23/86	.45	.20		1.00	17
2201	22¢ 1986 Presidents Miniature Sheet	01/23/86	.45	.20		1.00	17
a	Booklet pane of 4, #2198-2201		2.00	*1.75*		4.00	17
b	As "a," black omitted on #2198, 2201		45.00	—			
c	As "a," blue omitted on #2198-2200		*2,400.00*				
	#2198-2201 issued only in booklets. All stamps are imperf. at top and bottom or imperf. at top, bottom and right side.						
	Love, Tagged, Perf. 11						
2202	22¢ Love	01/30/86	.55	.20	2.75 (4)	1.00	947
	Black Heritage, Tagged, Perf. 11						
2203	22¢ Sojourner Truth and Truth Lecturing	02/04/86	.55	.20	2.75 (4)	1.75	130

	Issue	Date	Un	U	PB	#	FDC	Q(M)
	Tagged, Perf. 11							
2204	22¢ Republic of Texas, 150th Anniversary	03/02/86	.55	.20	2.75	(4)	1.75	137
a	Horizontal pair, imperf. vertically		*1,000.00*					
b	Dark red omitted		*2,500.00*					
c	Dark blue omitted		*8,000.00*					
	Fish, Booklet, Tagged, Perf. 10 Horizontally							
2205	22¢ Muskellunge	03/21/86	.60	.20			1.25	44
2206	22¢ Atlantic Cod	03/21/86	.60	.20			1.25	44
2207	22¢ Largemouth Bass	03/21/86	.60	.20			1.25	44
2208	22¢ Bluefin Tuna	03/21/86	.60	.20			1.25	44
2209	22¢ Catfish	03/21/86	.60	.20			1.25	44
a	Booklet pane of 5, #2205-2209		5.50	*2.75*			5.00	44
	#2205-2209 issued only in booklets. All stamps are imperf. at sides or imperf. at sides and bottom.							
	Tagged, Perf. 11							
2210	22¢ Public Hospitals	04/11/86	.40	.20	1.75	(4)	1.00	130
a	Vertical pair, imperf. horizontally		*300.00*					
b	Horizontal pair, imperf. vertically		*1,250.00*					
	Performing Arts, Tagged, Perf. 11							
2211	22¢ Duke Ellington and Piano Keys	04/29/86	.40	.20	1.90	(4)	2.25	130
a	Vertical pair, imperf. horizontally		*825.00*					
2212-2215 Not assigned								

	Issue	Date	Un	U	PB	#	FDC	Q(M)
	AMERIPEX '86, Presidents Miniature Sheets, Tagged, Perf. 11							
2216	Sheet of 9	05/22/86	5.00	—			4.00	6
a	22¢ George Washington		.50	.40			1.50	
b	22¢ John Adams		.50	.40			1.50	
c	22¢ Thomas Jefferson		.50	.40			1.50	
d	22¢ James Madison		.50	.40			1.50	
e	22¢ James Monroe		.50	.40			1.50	
f	22¢ John Quincy Adams		.50	.40			1.50	
g	22¢ Andrew Jackson		.50	.40			1.50	
h	22¢ Martin Van Buren		.50	.40			1.50	
i	22¢ William H. Harrison		.50	.40			1.50	
j	Blue omitted		*2,500.00*					
k	Black inscription omitted		*2,000.00*					
l	Imperf.		*10,500.00*					
2217	Sheet of 9	05/22/86	5.00	—			4.00	6
a	22¢ John Tyler		.50	.40			1.50	
b	22¢ James Polk		.50	.40			1.50	
c	22¢ Zachary Taylor		.50	.40			1.50	
d	22¢ Millard Fillmore		.50	.40			1.50	
e	22¢ Franklin Pierce		.50	.40			1.50	
f	22¢ James Buchanan		.50	.40			1.50	
g	22¢ Abraham Lincoln		.50	.40			1.50	
h	22¢ Andrew Johnson		.50	.40			1.50	
i	22¢ Ulysses S. Grant		.50	.40			1.50	

#2216

#2217

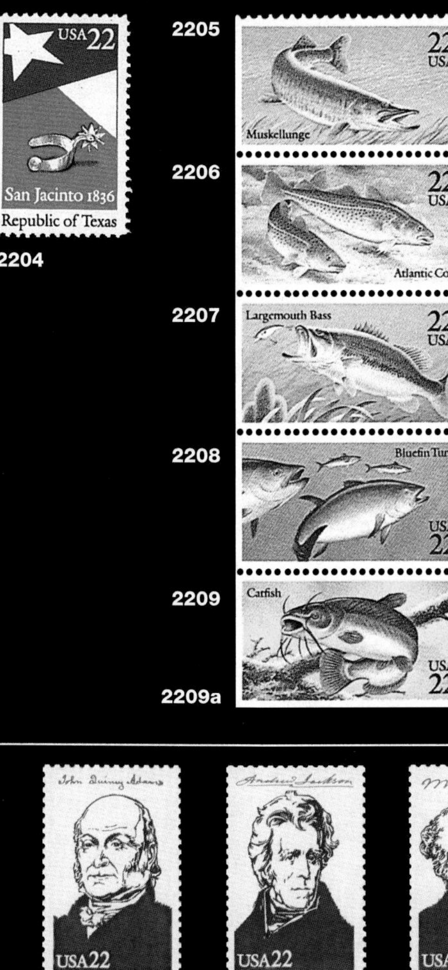

2204

2205

2206

2207

2208

2209

2209a

2210

2211

2216a

2216b

2216c

2216d

2216e

2216f

2216g

2216h

2216i

2217a

2217b

2217c

2217d

2217e

2217f

2217g

2217h

2217i

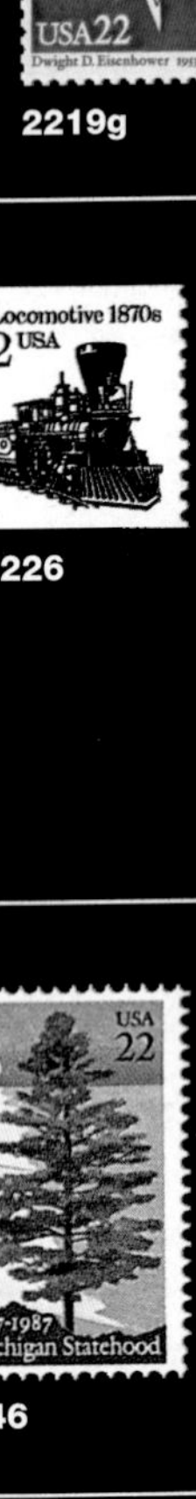

2218a 2218b 2218c 2218d 2218e 2218f 2218g 2218h

2218i 2219a 2219b 2219c 2219d 2219e 2219f 2219g

2220 2221

2219h 2219i 2224 2225 2226

2222 2223 2223a

2235 2236

2237 2238 2238a

2239

2240 2241

2242 2243 2243a

CHRISTMAS
22 USA
Perugino, National Gallery
GREETINGS
22 USA
Pan American Games Indianapolis 1987

2244 2245 2246

2247

	Issue	Date	Un	U	PB/PNC #	FDC	Q(M)
	AMERIPEX '86 continued, **Presidents Miniature Sheets, Tagged, Perf. 11**						
2218	Sheet of 9	05/22/86	5.00	—		4.00	6
a	22¢ Rutherford B. Hayes		.50	.40		1.50	
b	22¢ James A. Garfield		.50	.40		1.50	
c	22¢ Chester A. Arthur		.50	.40		1.50	
d	22¢ Grover Cleveland		.50	.40		1.50	
e	22¢ Benjamin Harrison		.50	.40		1.50	
f	22¢ William McKinley		.50	.40		1.50	
g	22¢ Theodore Roosevelt		.50	.40		1.50	
h	22¢ William H. Taft		.50	.40		1.50	
i	22¢ Woodrow Wilson		.50	.40		1.50	
j	Brown omitted		—				
k	Black inscription omitted		*2,500.00*				
2219	Sheet of 9	05/22/86	5.00	—		4.00	6
a	22¢ Warren G. Harding		.50	.40		1.50	
b	22¢ Calvin Coolidge		.50	.40		1.50	
c	22¢ Herbert Hoover		.50	.40		1.50	
d	22¢ Franklin D. Roosevelt		.50	.40		1.50	
e	22¢ White House		.50	.40		1.50	
f	22¢ Harry S. Truman		.50	.40		1.50	
g	22¢ Dwight D. Eisenhower		.50	.40		1.50	
h	22¢ John F. Kennedy		.50	.40		2.50	
i	22¢ Lyndon B. Johnson		.50	.40		1.50	
j	Blackish blue inscription omitted		*2,500.00*				
k	Tagging omitted		*4,000.00*				
	Arctic Explorers, Tagged, Perf. 11						
2220	22¢ Elisha Kent Kane	05/28/86	.65	.20		1.25	33
2221	22¢ Adolphus W. Greely	05/28/86	.65	.20		1.25	33
2222	22¢ Vilhjalmur Stefansson	05/28/86	.65	.20		1.25	33
2223	22¢ Robt. Peary, Matt. Henson	05/28/86	.65	.20		1.25	33
a	Block of 4, #2220-2223		2.75	2.25	4.50 (4)	3.75	
b	As "a," black omitted		*5,500.00*				
2224	22¢ Statue of Liberty	07/04/86	.40	.20	2.25 (4)	1.25	221

#2218

#2219

	Issue	Date	Un	U	PB/PNC #	FDC	Q(M)
	Transportation Coil, Tagged, Perf. 10 Vertically						
2225	1¢ Omnibus	11/26/86	.20	.20	.60 (5)	1.00	
a	Prephosphored uncoated paper (mottled tagging)		.20	.20	27.50 (5)		
b	Untagged, dull gum		.20	.20	.65 (5)		
c	Imperf., pair		*2,000.00*				
2226	2¢ Locomotive	03/06/87	.20	.20	.70 (5)	1.50	
a	Untagged, dull gum		.20	.20	.70 (5)		
2227	Not assigned						
2228	4¢ Stagecoach (1898A)	08/86	.20	.20	1.25 (5)		
a	Overall tagging		.70	.20	11.00 (5)		
b	Imperf., pair		250.00				
	On #2228, "Stagecoach 1890s" is 17mm long; on #1898A, it is 19.5mm long. On #2231, "Ambulance 1860s" is 18mm long; on #2128, it is 18.5mm long.						
2229-2230	Not assigned						
	Transportation Coil, Untagged, Perf. 10 Vertically						
2231	8.3¢ Ambulance (2128) (Bureau precanceled)	08/29/86	.20	.20	5.25 (5)		
2232-2234	Not assigned						
	American Folk Art: Navajo Art, Tagged, Perf. 11						
2235	22¢ Navajo Art, four "+" marks horizontally through middle	09/04/86	.80	.20		1.00	60
2236	22¢ Navajo Art, vertical diamond pattern	09/04/86	.80	.20		1.00	60
2237	22¢ Navajo Art, horizontal diamond pattern	09/04/86	.80	.20		1.00	60
2238	22¢ Navajo Art, jagged line horizontally through middle	09/04/86	.80	.20		1.00	60
a	Block of 4, #2235-2238		3.25	2.25	4.25 (4)	2.00	
b	As "a," black omitted		*375.00*				
	Literary Arts, Tagged, Perf. 11						
2239	22¢ T.S. Eliot	09/26/86	.55	.20	2.75 (4)	1.00	132
	American Folk Art: Wood Carved Figurines, Tagged, Perf. 11						
2240	22¢ Highlander Figure	10/01/86	.50	.20		1.00	60
2241	22¢ Ship Figurehead	10/01/86	.50	.20		1.00	60
2242	22¢ Nautical Figure	10/01/86	.50	.20		1.00	60
2243	22¢ Cigar Store Figure	10/01/86	.50	.20		1.00	60
a	Block of 4, #2240-2243		2.00	*1.50*	3.75 (4)	2.00	
b	As "a," imperf. vertically		*1,350.00*				
	Holiday Celebrations: Christmas, Tagged, Perf. 11						
2244	22¢ Madonna and Child	10/24/86	.40	.20	2.00 (4)	1.00	690
a	Imperf. pair		*650.00*				
	Holiday Celebrations: Holiday, Tagged, Perf. 11						
2245	22¢ Village Scene	10/24/86	.40	.20	1.90 (4)	1.00	882
	Tagged, Perf. 11						
2246	22¢ Michigan Statehood	01/26/87	.55	.20	2.75 (4)	1.00	167
	Pair with full vertical gutter between		—				
2247	22¢ Pan American Games	01/29/87	.40	.20	1.90 (4)	1.00	167
a	Silver omitted		*1,500.00*				

	Issue	Date	Un	U	PB/PNC	#	FDC	Q(M)
	Love, Tagged, Perf. 11.5 x 11							
2248	22¢ Love	01/30/87	.40	.20	1.90	(4)	1.00	812
	Black Heritage, Tagged, Perf. 11							
2249	22¢ Jean Baptiste Point Du Sable and Chicago Settlement	02/20/87	.50	.20	2.60	(4)	1.50	143
a	Tagging omitted		*10.00*					
	Performing Arts, Tagged, Perf. 11							
2250	22¢ Enrico Caruso	02/27/87	.40	.20	1.90	(4)	1.00	130
a	Black (engr.) omitted		*5,000.00*					
	Tagged, Perf. 11							
2251	22¢ Girl Scouts	03/12/87	.40	.20	1.90	(4)	2.50	150
a	All litho colors omitted		*2,500.00*					
	Transportation, Coil, Tagged, Perf. 10 Vertically							
	Untagged (5.3¢, 7.6¢,8.4¢,13¢, 13.2¢, 16.7¢, 20.5¢, 21¢, 24.1¢)							
2252	3¢ Conestoga Wagon 1800s	02/29/88	.20	.20	.90	(5)	1.00	
a	Untagged, dull gum		.20	.20	1.25	(5)		
2253	5¢ Milk Wagon 1900s	09/25/87	.20	.20	.90	(5)	1.00	
2254	5.3¢ Elevator 1900s, Bureau precanceled	09/16/88	.20	.20	1.10	(5)	1.00	
2255	7.6¢ Carreta 1770s, Bureau precanceled	08/30/88	.20	.20	2.25	(5)	1.00	
2256	8.4¢ Wheel Chair 1920s, Bureau precanceled	08/12/88	.20	.20	1.90	(5)	1.00	
a	Imperf., pair		*600.00*					
2257	10¢ Canal Boat 1880s	04/11/87	.20	.20	2.50	(5)	1.00	
a	Overall tagging, dull gum		.20	.20	4.00	(5)		
b	Prephosphored uncoated paper		.20	.20	3.25	(5)		
d	Tagging omitted		*27.50*					
2258	13¢ Patrol Wagon 1880s, Bureau precanceled	10/29/88	.30	.25	3.25	(5)	1.50	
2259	13.2¢ Coal Car 1870s, Bureau precanceled	07/19/88	.25	.25	2.75	(5)	1.00	
a	Imperf., pair		100.00					
2260	15¢ Tugboat 1900s	07/12/88	.25	.20	2.00	(5)	1.00	
a	Overall tagging		.25	.20	3.25	(5)		
b	Tagging omitted		*3.75*		*225.00*	*(5)*		
c	Imperf., pair		*700.00*					
2261	16.7¢ Popcorn Wagon 1902, Bureau precanceled	07/07/88	.30	.30	2.75	(5)	1.00	
a	Imperf., pair		*175.00*					
2262	17.5¢ Racing Car 1911	09/25/87	.40	.20	2.75	(5)	1.00	
a	Untagged (Bureau precanceled)		.50	.30	3.50	(5)		
b	Imperf., pair		*2,500.00*					
2263	20¢ Cable Car 1880s	10/28/88	.35	.20	3.50	(5)	1.00	
a	Imperf., pair		50.00					
b	Overall tagging		.35	.20	8.00	(5)		
2264	20.5¢ Fire Engine 1920s, Bureau precanceled	09/28/88	.40	.40	5.25	(5)	1.50	

	Issue	Date	Un	U	PB/PNC	#	FDC	Q(M)
	Transportation, Coil continued, **Untagged, Perf. 10 Vertically**							
2265	21¢ Railroad Mail Car 1920s, Bureau precanceled	08/16/88	.40	.40	3.50	(5)	1.00	
a	Imperf., pair		45.00					
2266	24.1¢ Tandem Bicycle 1890s, Bureau precanceled	10/26/88	.45	.45	4.00	(5)	1.50	
	Special Occasions Booklet, Tagged, Perf. 10 on 1, 2 or 3 sides							
2267	22¢ Congratulations!	04/20/87	.65	.20			1.00	1,222
2268	22¢ Get Well!	04/20/87	.80	.20			1.00	611
2269	22¢ Thank you!	04/20/87	.80	.20			1.00	611
2270	22¢ Love You, Dad!	04/20/87	.80	.20			1.00	611
2271	22¢ Best Wishes!	04/20/87	.80	.20			1.00	611
2272	22¢ Happy Birthday!	04/20/87	.65	.20			1.00	1,222
2273	22¢ Love You, Mother!	04/20/87	1.25	.20			1.00	611
2274	22¢ Keep In Touch!	04/20/87	.80	.20			1.00	611
a	Booklet pane of 10, #2268-2271, #2273-2274 and 2 each of #2267, #2272		10.00	*5.00*			5.00	611
	#2267-2274 issued only in booklets. All stamps are imperf. at one or two sides or imperf. at sides and bottom.							
	Tagged, Perf. 11							
2275	22¢ United Way	04/28/87	.40	.20	1.90	(4)	1.00	157
2276	22¢ Flag with Fireworks	05/09/87	.40	.20	1.90	(4)	1.00	
a	Booklet pane of 20	11/30/87	8.50	—			8.00	
b	As "a," vert. pair, imperf. between		*1,500.00*					
2277	(25¢) "E" Stamp	03/22/88	.45	.20	2.00	(4)	1.25	
2278	25¢ Flag with Clouds	05/06/88	.45	.20	1.90	(4)	1.25	
	Pair with full vertical gutter between		*125.00*					
	Coil, Perf. 10 Vertically							
2279	(25¢) "E" Earth	03/22/88	.45	.20	2.75	(5)	1.25	
a	Imperf., pair		*65.00*	—				
2280	25¢ Flag over Yosemite	05/20/88	.45	.20	3.50	(5)	1.25	
a	Prephosphored paper	02/14/89	.45	.20	3.50	(5)	1.25	
b	Imperf., pair, large block tagging		25.00					
c	Imperf., pair, prephosphored paper		10.00					
d	Tagging omitted		*7.50*					
e	Black trees		*100.00*	—	*550.00*	*(5)*		
f	Pair, imperf. between		*400.00*					
2281	25¢ Honeybee	09/02/88	.45	.20	3.75	(3)	1.25	
a	Imperf., pair		50.00					
b	Black (engr.) omitted		*60.00*					
c	Black (litho) omitted		*475.00*					
d	Pair, imperf. between		*750.00*					
e	Yellow (litho) omitted		*1,100.00*					
	Booklet, Perf. 10							
2282	(25¢) "E" Earth (#2277), single from booklet		.50	.20			1.25	
a	Booklet pane of 10	03/22/88	6.50	*3.50*			6.00	

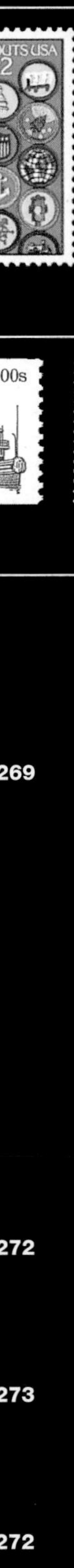

2248 2249 2250 2251 2252 2253 2254 2255 2256

2257 2258 2259 2260 2261 2262 2263 2264 2265

2266

2267 2268 2269 2270 2271 2272 2273 2274 2272 2267

2274a

2275 2276 2277 2278

2279 2280 2281

2282a

2283

2283c

2284 2285

2285b

2286 2287 2288 2289 2290

2291 2292 2293 2294 2295

2296 2297 2298 2299 2300

2301 2302 2303 2304 2305

2306 2307 2308 2309 2310

2311 2312 2313 2314 2315

Issue		Date	Un	U	PB #	FDC	Q(M)
	Booklet, Perf. 11						
2283	25¢ Pheasant, single from booklet		.50	.20		1.25	
a	Booklet pane of 10	04/29/88	6.00	*3.50*		6.00	
b	Single, red removed from sky		6.50	.20			
c	As "b," booklet pane of 10		*70.00*	—			
	#2283 issued only in booklets. All stamps have one or two imperf. edges. Imperf. and part perf. pairs and panes exist from printer's waste.						
	Booklet, Perf. 10						
2284	25¢ Grosbeak	05/28/88	.50	.20		1.25	
2285	25¢ Owl	05/28/88	.50	.20		1.25	
b	Booklet pane of 10, 5 each of #2284, 2285	05/28/88	5.00	*3.50*		6.00	
d	Pair, #2284, 2285		1.10	.25			
e	As "d," tagging omitted		*12.50*				
	#2284 and 2285 issued only in booklets. All stamps are imperf. at one side or imperf. at one side and bottom.						
2285A	25¢ Flag with Clouds	07/05/88	.50	.20			
c	Booklet pane of 6		3.00	*2.00*		4.00	
	North American Wildlife, Tagged, Perf. 11						
2286	22¢ Barn Swallow	06/13/87	*.85*	.20		1.50	13
2287	22¢ Monarch Butterfly	06/13/87	*.85*	.20		1.50	13
2288	22¢ Bighorn Sheep	06/13/87	*.85*	.20		1.50	13
2289	22¢ Broad-tailed Hummingbird	06/13/87	*.85*	.20		1.50	13
	North American Wildlife continued, **Tagged, Perf. 11**						
2290	22¢ Cottontail	06/13/87	*.85*	.20		1.50	13
2291	22¢ Osprey	06/13/87	*.85*	.20		1.50	13
2292	22¢ Mountain Lion	06/13/87	*.85*	.20		1.50	13
2293	22¢ Luna Moth	06/13/87	*.85*	.20		1.50	12
2294	22¢ Mule Deer	06/13/87	*.85*	.20		1.50	13
2295	22¢ Gray Squirrel	06/13/87	*.85*	.20		1.50	13
2296	22¢ Armadillo	06/13/87	*.85*	.20		1.50	13
2297	22¢ Eastern Chipmunk	06/13/87	*.85*	.20		1.50	13
2298	22¢ Moose	06/13/87	*.85*	.20		1.50	13
2299	22¢ Black Bear	06/13/87	*.85*	.20		1.50	13
2300	22¢ Tiger Swallowtail	06/13/87	*.85*	.20		1.50	13
2301	22¢ Bobwhite	06/13/87	*.85*	.20		1.50	13
2302	22¢ Ringtail	06/13/87	*.85*	.20		1.50	13
2303	22¢ Red-winged Blackbird	06/13/87	*.85*	.20		1.50	13
2304	22¢ American Lobster	06/13/87	*.85*	.20		1.50	13
2305	22¢ Black-tailed Jack Rabbit	06/13/87	*.85*	.20		1.50	13
2306	22¢ Scarlet Tanager	06/13/87	*.85*	.20		1.50	13
2307	22¢ Woodchuck	06/13/87	*.85*	.20		1.50	13
2308	22¢ Roseate Spoonbill	06/13/87	*.85*	.20		1.50	13
2309	22¢ Bald Eagle	06/13/87	*.85*	.20		1.50	13
2310	22¢ Alaskan Brown Bear	06/13/87	*.85*	.20		1.50	13
2311	22¢ Iiwi	06/13/87	*.85*	.20		1.50	13
2312	22¢ Badger	06/13/87	*.85*	.20		1.50	13
2313	22¢ Pronghorn	06/13/87	*.85*	.20		1.50	13
2314	22¢ River Otter	06/13/87	*.85*	.20		1.50	13
2315	22¢ Ladybug	06/13/87	*.85*	.20		1.50	13

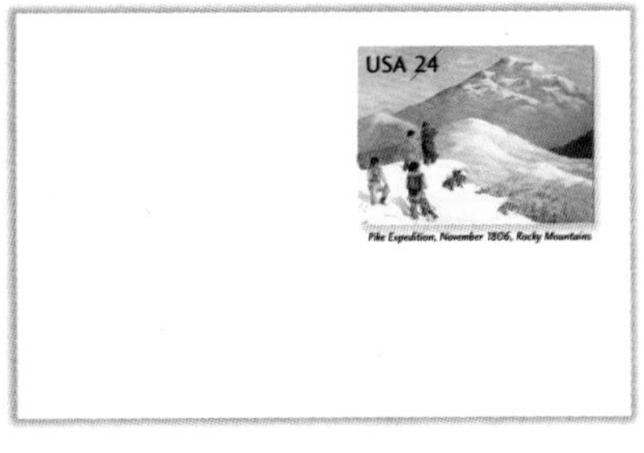

PIKES PEAK

The Pikes Peak stamped card commemorates the 200th anniversary of Capt. Zebulon Montgomery Pike's sighting of the famous Rocky Mountain peak that bears his name. Noted for its imposing appearance and for the majestic views from its 14,110-foot summit, Pikes Peak is a popular tourist destination near Colorado Springs, Colorado. It was declared a national historic landmark in 1961. In 1806, Pike (1779-1813), then a lieutenant in the Army, was commissioned to explore the watersheds of the Arkansas and Red Rivers, as well as the poorly defined southwestern border of the newly acquired Louisiana Territory. In July he and his men headed westward from Fort Belle Fontaine—located north of St. Louis on the Missouri River. As the expedition crossed the plains in mid-November, Pike became intrigued by a mountain "which appeared like a small blue cloud" in the distance. Shortly, the Front Range of the Rockies "appeared in full view." On November 24, Pike set out with three men to ascend the mountain that he called "Grand Peak." Three days later, from the summit of a neighboring peak, Pike realized that "Grand Peak" still lay several miles away. Harsh weather conditions prevented Pike from climbing the mountain that had captured his attention, nevertheless it became commonly known as "Pikes Peak" and eventually was formally named in his honor.

	Issue	Date	Un	U	PB #	FDC	Q(M)
	North American Wildlife continued, **Tagged, Perf. 11**						
2316	22¢ Beaver	06/13/87	.85	.20		1.50	13
2317	22¢ White-tailed Deer	06/13/87	.85	.20		1.50	13
2318	22¢ Blue Jay	06/13/87	.85	.20		1.50	13
2319	22¢ Pika	06/13/87	.85	.20		1.50	13
2320	22¢ Bison	06/13/87	.85	.20			
2321	22¢ Snowy Egret	06/13/87	.85	.20		1.50	13
2322	22¢ Gray Wolf	06/13/87	.85	.20		1.50	13
2323	22¢ Mountain Goat	06/13/87	.85	.20		1.50	13
2324	22¢ Deer Mouse	06/13/87	.85	.20		1.50	13
2325	22¢ Black-tailed Prairie Dog	06/13/87	.85	.20		1.50	13
2326	22¢ Box Turtle	06/13/87	.85	.20		1.50	13
2327	22¢ Wolverine	06/13/87	.85	.20		1.50	13
2328	22¢ American Elk	06/13/87	.85	.20		1.50	13
2329	22¢ California Sea Lion	06/13/87	.85	.20		1.50	13
2330	22¢ Mockingbird	06/13/87	.85	.20		1.50	13
2331	22¢ Raccoon	06/13/87	.85	.20		1.50	13
2332	22¢ Bobcat	06/13/87	.85	.20		1.50	13
2333	22¢ Black-footed Ferret	06/13/87	.85	.20		1.50	13
2334	22¢ Canada Goose	06/13/87	.85	.20		1.50	13
2335	22¢ Red Fox	06/13/87	.85	.20		1.50	13
a	Pane of 50, #2286-2335		47.50			50.00	

	Issue	Date	Un	U	PB #	FDC	Q(M)
	Ratification of the Constitution, Tagged, Perf. 11						
2336	22¢ Delaware	07/04/87	.60	.20	2.75 (4)	1.50	16
2337	22¢ Pennsylvania	08/26/87	.60	.20	2.75 (4)	1.50	18
2338	22¢ New Jersey	09/11/87	.60	.20	2.75 (4)	1.50	18
a	Black omitted		5,500.00				
2339	22¢ Georgia	01/06/88	.60	.20	2.75 (4)	1.50	16
2340	22¢ Connecticut	01/09/88	.60	.20	2.75 (4)	1.50	15
2341	22¢ Massachusetts	02/06/88	.60	.20	2.75 (4)	1.50	10
2342	22¢ Maryland	02/15/88	.60	.20	2.75 (4)	1.50	10
2343	25¢ South Carolina	05/23/88	.60	.20	2.75 (4)	1.50	16
2344	25¢ New Hampshire	06/21/88	.60	.20	2.75 (4)	1.50	15
2345	25¢ Virginia	06/25/88	.60	.20	2.75 (4)	1.50	16
2346	25¢ New York	07/26/88	.60	.20	2.75 (4)	1.50	18
2347	25¢ North Carolina	08/22/89	.60	.20	2.75 (4)	1.50	18
2348	25¢ Rhode Island	05/29/90	.60	.20	3.00 (4)	1.50	16
	Tagged, Perf. 11						
2349	22¢ Friendship with Morocco	07/18/87	.55	.20	1.75 (4)	1.00	15
a	Black omitted		275.00				
	Literary Arts, Tagged, Perf. 11						
2350	22¢ William Faulkner	08/03/87	.55	.20	2.75 (4)	1.00	15
	American Folk Art: Lace Making, Tagged, Perf. 11						
2351	22¢ Squash Blossoms	08/14/87	.45	.20		1.00	4
2352	22¢ Floral Piece	08/14/87	.45	.20		1.00	4
2353	22¢ Floral Piece	08/14/87	.45	.20		1.00	4
2354	22¢ Dogwood Blossoms	08/14/87	.45	.20		1.00	4
a	Block of 4, #2351-2354		1.90	1.90	3.25 (4)	2.50	
b	As "a," white omitted		850.00				

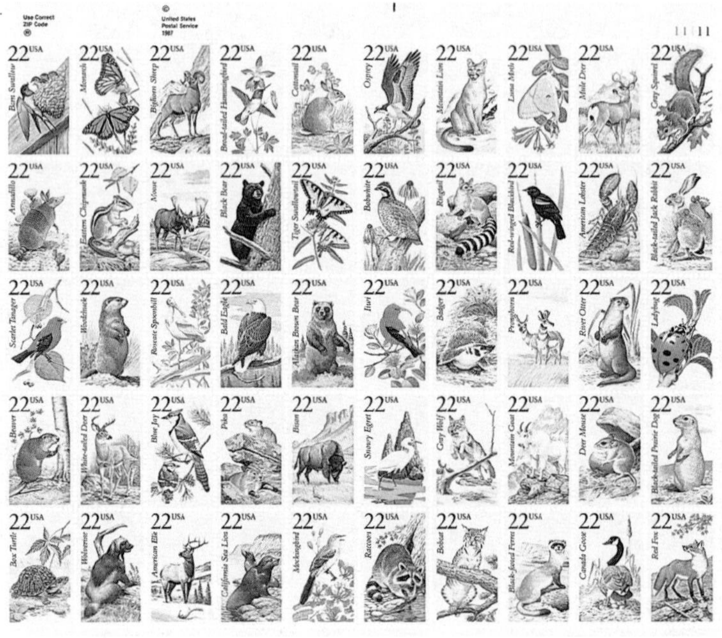

2335a

2316 2317 2318 2319 2320

2321 2322 2323 2324 2325

2326 2327 2328 2329 2330

2331 2332 2333 2334 2335

2336 2337 2338

2339 2340 2341

2342 2343 2344

2345  2346  2347

2348

2349

2350

2351 2352

2353 2354 2354a

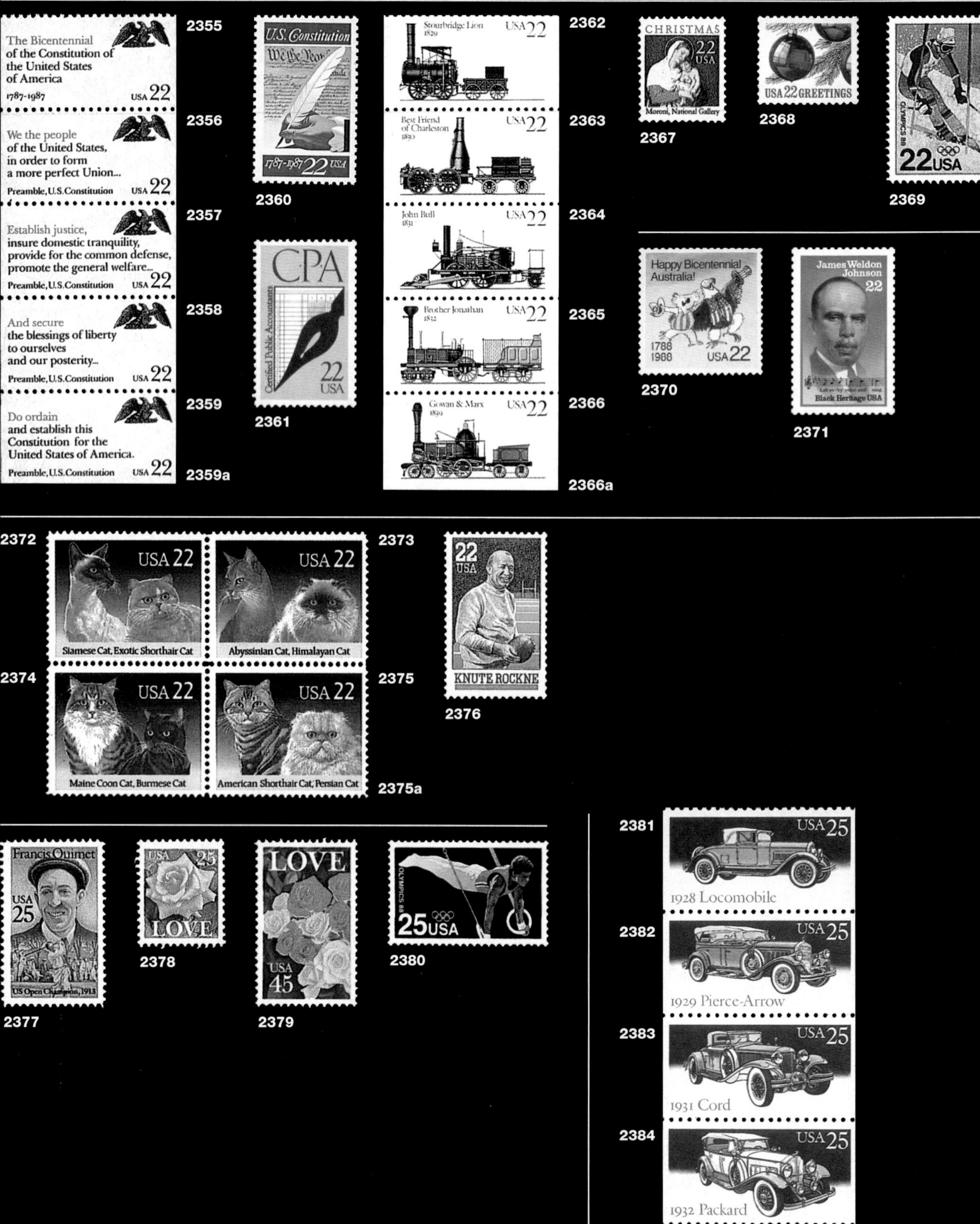

The Bicentennial of the Constitution of the United States of America
1787-1987
USA 22
We the people of the United States, in order to form a more perfect Union...
Preamble, U.S. Constitution
Establish justice, insure domestic tranquility, provide for the common defense, promote the general welfare...
And secure the blessings of liberty to ourselves and our posterity...
Do ordain and establish this Constitution for the United States of America.
U.S. Constitution
1787-1987 22 USA
CPA
Certified Public Accountants
Stourbridge Lion 1829
Best Friend of Charleston 1830
John Bull 1831
Brother Jonathan 1832
Gowan & Marx 1839
CHRISTMAS
Moroni, National Gallery
USA 22 GREETINGS
OLYMPICS 88
22USA
Happy Bicentennial Australia!
1788 1988
James Weldon Johnson
Black Heritage USA
Siamese Cat, Exotic Shorthair Cat
Abyssinian Cat, Himalayan Cat
Maine Coon Cat, Burmese Cat
American Shorthair Cat, Persian Cat
KNUTE ROCKNE
Francis Ouimet
US Open Champion, 1913
LOVE
USA 45
25USA
1928 Locomobile
1929 Pierce-Arrow
1931 Cord
1932 Packard
1935 Duesenberg

2355 2356 2357 2358 2359 2359a 2360 2361 2362 2363 2364 2365 2366 2366a 2367 2368 2369 2370 2371

2372 2373 2374 2375 2375a 2376

2377 2378 2379 2380

2381 2382 2383 2384 2385 2385a

	Issue	Date	Un	U	PB	#	FDC	Q(M)
	Drafting of the Constitution, Booklet, Tagged, Perf. 10 Horizontally							
2355	22¢ "The Bicentennial..."	08/28/87	.75	.20			1.25	117
2356	22¢ "We the people..."	08/28/87	.75	.20			1.25	117
2357	22¢ "Establish justice..."	08/28/87	.75	.20			1.25	117
2358	22¢ "And secure..."	08/28/87	.75	.20			1.25	117
2359	22¢ "Do ordain..."	08/28/87	.75	.20			1.25	117
a	Booklet pane of 5, #2355-2359		3.75	*2.25*			4.00	
	#2355-2359 issued only in booklets. All stamps are imperf. at sides or imperf. at sides and bottom.							
	Signing of the Constitution, Tagged, Perf. 11							
2360	22¢ Constitution and Signer's Hand-Holding Quill Pen	09/17/87	.55	.20	2.75	(4)	1.25	169
2361	22¢ Certified Public Accountants	09/21/87	*1.25*	.20	*6.00*	(4)	7.50	163
a	Black omitted		*725.00*					
	Locomotives Booklet, Tagged, Perf. 10 Horizontally							
2362	22¢ Stourbridge Lion, 1829	10/01/87	.55	.20			1.25	79
2363	22¢ Best Friend of Charleston, 1830	10/01/87	.55	.20			1.25	79
2364	22¢ John Bull, 1831	10/01/87	.55	.20			1.25	79
2365	22¢ Brother Jonathan, 1832	10/01/87	.55	.20			1.25	79
a	Red omitted		*1,100.00*	*225.00*				
2366	22¢ Gowan & Marx, 1839	10/01/87	.55	.20			1.25	79
a	Booklet pane of 5, #2362-2366		2.75	*2.50*			3.00	
	#2362-2366 issued only in booklets. All stamps are imperf. at sides or imperf. at sides and bottom.							
	Holiday Celebrations: Christmas, Tagged, Perf. 11							
2367	22¢ Madonna and Child, by Moroni	10/23/87	.45	.20	2.25	(4)	1.25	529
	Holiday Celebrations: Holiday, Tagged, Perf. 11							
2368	22¢ Christmas Ornaments	10/23/87	.45	.20	2.10	(4)	1.25	978
	Pair with full vertical gutter between		—					
	Olympic Games, Tagged, Perf. 11							
2369	22¢ Skier and Olympic Rings	01/10/88	.45	2.10	1.75	(4)	1.00	159

	Issue	Date	Un	U	PB	#	FDC	Q(M)
	Tagged, Perf. 11							
2370	22¢ Australia Bicentennial	01/10/88	.45	.20	2.10	(4)	1.75	146
	Black Heritage, Tagged, Perf. 11							
2371	22¢ James Weldon Johnson	02/02/88	.50	.20	2.60	(4)	1.75	97
	American Cats, Tagged, Perf. 11							
2372	22¢ Siamese and Exotic Shorthair	02/05/88	.60	.20			2.00	40
2373	22¢ Abyssinian and Himalayan	02/05/88	.60	.20			2.00	40
2374	22¢ Maine Coon and Burmese	02/05/88	.60	.20			2.00	40
2375	22¢ American Shorthair and Persian	02/05/88	.60	.20			2.00	40
a	Block of 4, #2372-2375		2.50	1.90	4.00	(4)	4.50	
	American Sports Personalities, Tagged, Perf. 11							
2376	22¢ Knute Rockne	03/09/88	.50	.20	2.60	(4)	4.00	97
2377	25¢ Francis Ouimet	06/13/88	.60	.20	3.00	(4)	4.50	153
	Love, Tagged							
2378	25¢ Love	07/04/88	.50	.20	2.25	(4)	1.00	841
a	Imperf., pair		*1,900.00*					
2379	45¢ Love	08/08/88	.85	.20	3.75	(4)	1.25	170
	Olympic Games, Tagged							
2380	25¢ Gymnast on Rings	08/19/88	.50	.20	2.25	(4)	1.25	157
	Classic Cars, Booklet, Tagged, Perf. 10 Horizontally							
2381	25¢ 1928 Locomobile	08/25/88	.80	.20			1.25	127
2382	25¢ 1929 Pierce-Arrow	08/25/88	.80	.20			1.25	127
2383	25¢ 1931 Cord	08/25/88	.80	.20			1.25	127
2384	25¢ 1932 Packard	08/25/88	.80	.20			1.25	127
2385	25¢ 1935 Duesenberg	08/25/88	.80	.20			1.25	127
a	Booklet pane of 5, #2381-2385		6.00	*2.25*			4.00	
	#2381-2385 issued only in booklets. All stamps are imperf. at sides or imperf. at sides and bottom.							

DR. ALBERT SABIN

In 2006 the Distinguished Americans series honors virologist Albert Sabin (1906-1993), whose successful efforts to develop a polio vaccine made him one of the most esteemed scientists in the world. For his dedication to fighting polio and other infectious diseases, he received numerous awards, including the National Medal of Science (1970) and the Presidential Medal of Freedom (1986). Born in Poland, Sabin immigrated with his family to the United States in 1921. After earning a medical degree from New York University and training at Bellevue Hospital, Dr. Sabin devoted himself to polio research, seeking a way to prevent the disabling and sometimes fatal disease caused by the poliovirus. "A scientist," Dr. Sabin once said, "cannot rest while knowledge which might be used to reduce suffering rests on the shelf." In 1939, Dr. Sabin moved to Ohio where he continued his research. By the mid-1950s he was ready to test a vaccine made from live but weakened poliovirus. In 1960, after extensive worldwide trials, his live-virus vaccine—which is administered orally—was approved for use in the United States. Today, Dr. Sabin's vision of a world without polio has almost been realized, thanks to an extraordinary international effort to make his vaccine available to all people.

	Issue	Date	Un	U	PB #	FDC	Q(M)
	Antarctic Explorers, Tagged, Perf. 11						
2386	25¢ Nathaniel Palmer	09/14/88	.65	.20		1.25	41
2387	25¢ Lt. Charles Wilkes	09/14/88	.65	.20		1.25	41
2388	25¢ Richard E. Byrd	09/14/88	.65	.20		1.25	41
2389	25¢ Lincoln Ellsworth	09/14/88	.65	.20		1.25	41
a	Block of 4, #2386-2389		2.75	2.00	4.50 (4)	3.00	
b	As "a," black omitted		*1,350.00*				
c	As "a," imperf. horizontally		*2,150.00*				
	American Folk Art: Carousel Animals, Tagged, Perf. 11						
2390	25¢ Deer	10/01/88	.65	.20		1.25	76
2391	25¢ Horse	10/01/88	.65	.20		1.25	76
2392	25¢ Camel	10/01/88	.65	.20		1.25	76
2393	25¢ Goat	10/01/88	.65	.20		1.25	76
a	Block of 4, #2390-2393		3.00	2.00	4.00 (4)	3.00	
	Tagged, Perf. 11						
2394	$8.75 Express Mail	10/04/88	13.50	8.00	54.00 (4)	27.50	
	Special Occasions, Booklet, Tagged, Perf. 11						
2395	25¢ Happy Birthday	10/22/88	.50	.20		1.25	120
2396	25¢ Best Wishes	10/22/88	.50	.20		1.25	120
a	Booklet pane of 6, 3 #2395 and 3 #2396 with gutter between		3.50	*3.25*		4.00	
2397	25¢ Thinking of You	10/22/88	.50	.20		1.25	120
2398	25¢ Love You	10/22/88	.50	.20		1.25	120
a	Booklet pane of 6, 3 #2397 and 3 #2398 with gutter between		3.50	*3.25*		4.00	
b	As "a," imperf. horizontally		—				
	#2395-2398a issued only in booklets. All stamps are imperf. on one side or on one side and top or bottom.						

	Issue	Date	Un	U	PB #	FDC	Q(M)
	Holiday Celebrations: Christmas, Tagged, Perf. 11.5						
2399	25¢ Madonna and Child, by Botticelli	10/20/88	.50	.20	2.25 (4)	1.25	822
a	Gold omitted		25.00				
	Holiday Celebrations: Holiday, Tagged, Perf. 11						
2400	25¢ One-Horse Open Sleigh and Village Scene	10/20/88	.50	.20	2.20 (4)	1.25	1,038
	Pair with full vertical gutter between			—			
	Tagged, Perf. 11						
2401	25¢ Montana Statehood	01/15/89	.55	.20	2.75 (4)	1.25	165
	Black Heritage, Tagged, Perf. 11						
2402	25¢ A. Philip Randolph	02/03/89	.50	.20	2.25 (4)	1.75	152
	Tagged, Perf. 11						
2403	25¢ North Dakota Statehood	02/21/89	.50	.20	2.25 (4)	1.00	163
2404	25¢ Washington Statehood	02/22/89	.50	.20	2.25 (4)	1.00	265
	Steamboats, Booklet, Tagged, Perf. 10 Horizontally on 1 or 2 sides						
2405	25¢ Experiment 1788-1790	03/03/89	.50	.20		1.25	41
2406	25¢ Phoenix 1809	03/03/89	.50	.20		1.25	41
2407	25¢ New Orleans 1812	03/03/89	.50	.20		1.25	41
2408	25¢ Washington 1816	03/03/89	.50	.20		1.25	41
2409	25¢ Walk in the Water 1818	03/03/89	.50	.20		1.25	41
a	Booklet pane of 5, #2405-2409		2.50	*1.75*		3.00	
	#2405-2409 issued only in booklets. All stamps are imperf. at sides or imperf. at sides and bottom.						
	Tagged, Perf. 11						
2410	25¢ World Stamp Expo '89	03/16/89	.50	.20	2.25 (4)	1.00	104
	Performing Arts, Tagged, Perf. 11						
2411	25¢ Arturo Toscanini	03/25/89	.50	.20	2.25 (4)	1.00	152

CROPS OF THE AMERICAS

Corn, chili peppers, beans, squashes, and sunflowers had been cultivated in the Americas for centuries when Europeans first arrived in the New World. Columbus and later explorers carried seeds from American crops to Europe; traders eventually took them to Africa and Asia. Over the years, American plants transformed diets in many lands. Today they enrich national cuisines from Mexico to China. These crops are popular and important parts of the world's food supply for a number of reasons. They can be grown in a variety of soils and climates, they develop quickly, and they produce heavy yields. They also come in several forms, including, for example, popcorn, sweet corn, and flour corn; chilies such as jalapeños, poblanos, and serranos; Hubbard and butternut squashes, zucchini, and pumpkins; and green, pinto, and lima beans. There are different kinds of sunflowers, too, and these are used for vegetable oil, edible kernels, birdseed, and garden flowers. Artist Steve Buchanan created each of the five stamp designs using, as reference, slide photographs made by his wife Rita Buchanan, a consultant for the stamp project. The slides document her research in the late 1970s on indigenous agricultural methods in the southwestern United States.

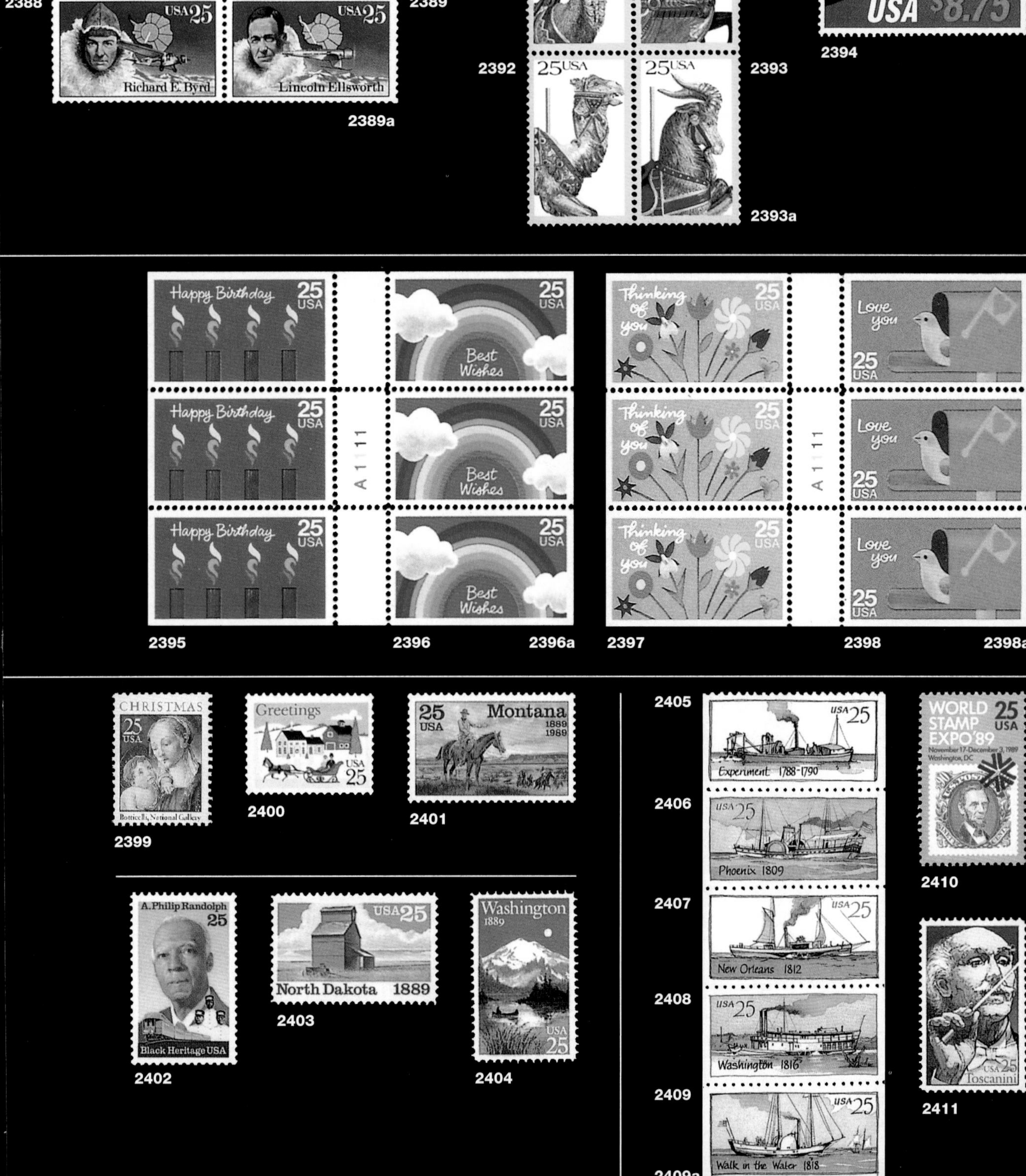
2386
Nathaniel Palmer
USA 25
2387
Lt. Charles Wilkes
USA 25
2388
Richard E. Byrd
USA 25
2389
Lincoln Ellsworth
USA 25
2389a
2390
2391
2392
2393
2393a
25 USA
2394
USA $8.75
Happy Birthday
25 USA
Best Wishes
A1111
2395
2396
2396a
Thinking of you
Love you
2397
2398
2398a
CHRISTMAS
Botticelli, National Gallery
2399
Greetings
2400
Montana 1889 1989
2401
A. Philip Randolph
Black Heritage USA
2402
North Dakota 1889
2403
Washington 1889
2404
2405
Experiment 1788-1790
2406
Phoenix 1809
2407
New Orleans 1812
2408
Washington 1816
2409
Walk in the Water 1818
2409a
WORLD STAMP EXPO '89
November 17-December 3, 1989
Washington, DC
2410
Toscanini
2411

2412 2413 2414 2415 2416 2417 2418

2419 2420 2421 2422 2423 2424 2425 2425a

2426 2427 2428

2433

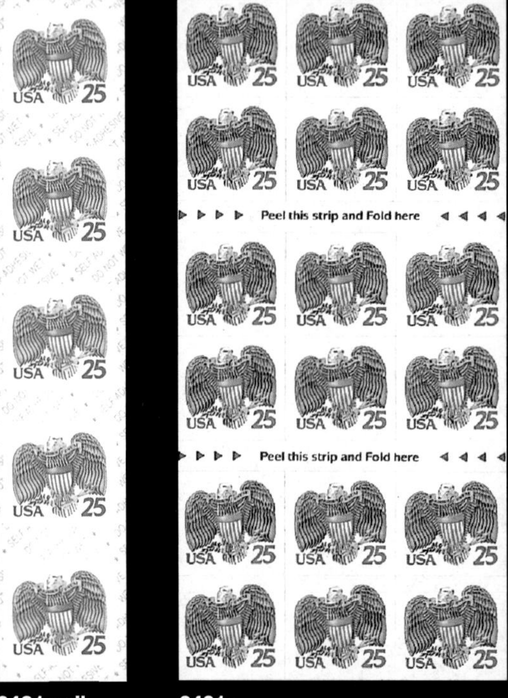

2431 2431 coil 2431a

2434 2435 2436 2437 2437a

	Issue	Date	Un	U	PB	#	FDC	Q(M)
	Constitution Bicentennial, Tagged, Perf. 11							
2412	25¢ U.S. House of Representatives	04/04/89	.50	.20	2.25	(4)	1.25	139
2413	25¢ U.S. Senate	04/06/89	.50	.20	2.75	(4)	1.25	138
2414	25¢ Executive Branch, George Washington	04/16/89	.50	.20	2.25	(4)	1.25	139
2415	25¢ Supreme Court, Chief Justice John Marshall	02/02/90	.50	.20	2.25	(4)	1.25	151
	Tagged, Perf. 11							
2416	25¢ South Dakota Statehood	05/03/89	.50	.20	2.25	(4)	1.00	165
	American Sports Personalities, Tagged, Perf. 11							
2417	25¢ Lou Gehrig	06/10/89	.50	.20	3.00	(4)	4.00	263
	Literary Arts, Tagged, Perf. 11							
2418	25¢ Ernest Hemingway	07/17/89	.50	.20	2.25	(4)	1.25	192
a	Vertical pair, imperf. horiz.		*1,850.00*					
	Space, Priority Mail, Tagged, Perf. 11 x 11.5							
2419	$2.40 Moon Landing	07/20/89	4.75	2.00	20.00	(4)	7.50	
a	Black (engr.) omitted		*2,250.00*					
b	Imperf., pair		*700.00*					
c	Black (litho.) omitted		*2,500.00*					
	Tagged, Perf. 11							
2420	25¢ Letter Carriers	08/30/89	.50	.20	2.25	(4)	1.25	188
	Constitution Bicentennial, Tagged, Perf. 11							
2421	25¢ Bill of Rights	09/25/89	.50	.20	3.25	(4)	1.00	192
a	Black omitted		*275.00*					
	Prehistoric Animals, Tagged, Perf. 11							
2422	25¢ Tyrannosaurus	10/01/89	.65	.20			1.50	102
2423	25¢ Pteranodon	10/01/89	.65	.20			1.50	102
2424	25¢ Stegosaurus	10/01/89	.65	.20			1.50	102
2425	25¢ Brontosaurus	10/01/89	.65	.20			1.50	102
a	Block of 4, #2422-2425		3.00	2.00	3.50	(4)	3.00	
b	As "a," black omitted		*625.00*					
	America/PUAS, Tagged, Perf. 11							
2426	25¢ Southwest Carved Figure (A.D. 1150-1350), Emblem of the Postal Union of the Americas	10/12/89	.60	.20	3.00	(4)	1.00	137
	Holiday Celebrations: Christmas, Tagged, Perf. 11.5							
2427	25¢ Madonna and Child, by Caracci	10/19/89	.50	.20	2.25	(4)	1.00	913
a	Booklet pane of 10		5.00	*3.50*			6.00	
b	Red (litho.) omitted		*750.00*					

	Issue	Date	Un	U	PB	#	FDC	Q(M)
	Holiday Celebrations: Holiday, Tagged, Perf. 11							
2428	25¢ Sleigh Full of Presents	10/19/89	.50	.20	2.25	(4)	1.00	900
a	Vertical pair, imperf. horizontally		*850.00*					
	Booklet, Perf. 11.5 on 2 or 3 sides							
2429	25¢ Single from booklet pane (#2428)	10/19/89	.50	.20			1.00	399
a	Booklet pane of 10		5.00	*3.50*			6.00	
b	As "a," imperf. horiz. between		—					
c	Vertical pair, imperf. horizontally		—					
d	As "a," red omitted		*3,500.00*					
e	Imperf., pair		—					
	In #2429, runners on sleigh are twice as thick as in #2428; bow on package at rear of sleigh is same color as package; board running underneath sleigh is pink.							
2430	Not assigned							
	Tagged, Self-Adhesive, Die-Cut							
2431	25¢ Eagle and Shield	11/10/89	.50	.20			1.25	75
a	Booklet pane of 18		11.00					
b	Vertical pair, no die-cutting between		*500.00*					
c	Die-cutting omitted, pair		*275.00*					
2432	Not assigned							
	World Stamp Expo '89 Souvenir Sheet, Tagged, Imperf.							
2433	Reproduction of #122, 90¢ Lincoln, and three essays of #122	11/17/89	12.00	9.00			7.00	2
a-d	Single stamp from sheet		2.00	1.50				
	20th UPU Congress, Classic Mail Transportation, Tagged, Perf. 11							
2434	25¢ Stagecoach	11/19/89	.50	.20			1.25	41
2435	25¢ Paddlewheel Steamer	11/19/89	.50	.20			1.25	41
2436	25¢ Biplane	11/19/89	.50	.20			1.25	41
2437	25¢ Depot-Hack Type Automobile	11/19/89	.50	.20			1.25	41
a	Block of 4, #2434-2437		2.00	1.75	3.75	(4)	2.50	
b	As "a," dark blue omitted		*500.00*					

Create Your Own Postage Stamp and Pictorial Postmarks

Make your own mark on history!
For information on how you can create or suggest your own idea for a postage stamp or pictorial postmark stop by your local post office and inquire about these free brochures. *Creating U.S. Postage Stamps* and *Celebrating with Pictorial Postmarks.*

	Issue	Date	Un	U	PB	#	FDC	Q(M)
	Souvenir Sheet, Tagged, Imperf.							
2438	Designs of #2434-2437	11/28/89	4.00	2.50			3.00	2
a-d	Single stamp from sheet		.75	.25				
	Tagged, Perf. 11							
2439	25¢ Idaho Statehood	01/06/90	.55	.20	2.75	(4)	1.25	173
	Love, Tagged, Perf. 12.5 x 13							
2440	25¢ Love	01/18/90	.50	.20	2.25	(4)	1.25	886
a	Imperf., pair		*750.00*					
	Booklet, Perf. 11.5							
2441	25¢ Love, single from booklet	01/18/90	.50	.20			1.00	995
a	Booklet pane of 10	01/18/90	5.00	*3.50*			6.00	
b	bright pink omitted, single		*175.00*					
c	As "a," bright pink omitted		*1,800.00*					
	Black Heritage, Tagged, Perf. 11							
2442	25¢ Ida B. Wells	02/01/90	.75	.20	3.75	(4)	2.00	153
	Booklet, Tagged, Perf. 11							
2443	15¢ Beach Umbrella, single from booklet	02/03/90	.30	.20			1.25	
a	Booklet pane of 10	02/03/90	3.00	*2.00*			4.25	
b	Blue omitted		*150.00*					
c	As "a," blue omitted		*1,500.00*					
	#2443 issued only in booklets. All stamps are imperf. at one side or imperf. at one side and bottom.							
	Tagged, Perf. 11							
2444	25¢ Wyoming Statehood	02/23/90	.50	.20	2.75	(4)	1.00	169
a	Black (engr.) omitted		*1,500.00*	—				
	Classic Films, Tagged, Perf. 11							
2445	25¢ The Wizard of Oz	03/23/90	1.50	.20			2.50	44
2446	25¢ Gone With the Wind	03/23/90	1.50	.20			2.50	44
2447	25¢ Beau Geste	03/23/90	1.50	.20			2.50	44
2448	25¢ Stagecoach	03/23/90	1.50	.20			2.50	44
a	Block of 4, #2445-2448		6.00	3.50	6.50	(4)	5.00	
	Literary Arts, Tagged, Perf. 11							
2449	25¢ Marianne Moore	04/18/90	.60	.20	2.75	(4)	1.25	150
2450	Not assigned							
	Transportation, Coil, Tagged, Perf. 9.8 Vertically Untagged (#2452B, 2452D, 2453, 2454, 2457, 2458)							
2451	4¢ Steam Carriage 1866	01/25/91	.20	.20	1.10	(5)	1.25	
a	Imperf., pair		*575.00*					
b	Untagged		.20	.20	1.10	(5)		
2452	5¢ Circus Wagon 1900s, intaglio printing	08/31/91	.20	.20	1.25	(5)	1.50	
a	Untagged, dull gum		.20	.20	1.25	(5)		
c	Imperf., pair		*650.00*					
2452B	5¢ Circus Wagon (2452), gravure printing	12/08/92	.20	.20	1.50	(5)	1.50	
f	Printed with luminescent ink		.20	.20	2.10	(5)		
2452D	5¢ Circus Wagon (2452), gravure printing	03/20/95	.20	.20	1.60	(5)	2.00	
e	Imperf., pair		150.00					
g	Printed with luminescent ink		.20	.20	1.90	(5)		
2453	5¢ Canoe 1800s, precanceled, intaglio printing	05/25/91	.20	.20	1.50	(5)	1.25	
a	Imperf., pair		*250.00*					
2454	5¢ Canoe 1800s, precanceled, gravure printing	10/22/91	.20	.20	1.40	(5)	1.25	
2455-2456	Not assigned							
2457	10¢ Tractor Trailer, Bureau precanceled, intaglio printing	05/25/91	.20	.20	2.10	(5)	1.25	
a	Imperf., pair		*140.00*					
	Transportation continued, **Coil, Untagged, Perf. 9.8 Vertically**							
2458	10¢ Tractor Trailer, Bureau precanceled, gravure printing	05/25/94	.30	.20	2.50	(5)	1.25	
2459-2462	Not assigned							
	Tagged, Perf. 9.8 Vertically							
2463	20¢ Cog Railway Car 1870s	06/09/95	.40	.20	4.00	(5)	1.25	
a	Imperf., pair		*95.00*					
2464	23¢ Lunch Wagon 1890s	04/12/91	.45	.20	3.75	(5)	1.25	
a	Prephosphored uncoated paper		.45	.20	4.50	(5)		
b	Imperf., pair		*125.00*					
2465	Not assigned							
2466	32¢ Ferryboat 1900s	06/02/95	.65	.20	5.50	(5)	1.25	
a	Imperf., pair		*550.00*					
b	Bright blue, prephosphored uncoated paper		6.00	4.50	140.00	(5)		
2467	Not assigned							
2468	$1 Seaplane 1914	04/20/90	1.75	.50	10.00	(5)	2.50	
a	Imperf., pair		*2,750.00*	—				
b	Prephosphored uncoated paper		1.75	.50	10.00	(5)		
c	Prephosphored coated paper		1.75	.50	10.00	(5)		
2469	Not assigned							
	Lighthouses, Booklet, Tagged, Perf. 10 Vertically on 1 or 2 sides							
2470	25¢ Admiralty Head, WA	04/26/90	1.40	.20			1.50	147
2471	25¢ Cape Hatteras, NC	04/26/90	1.40	.20			1.50	147
2472	25¢ West Quoddy Head, ME	04/26/90	1.40	.20			1.50	147
2473	25¢ American Shoals, FL	04/26/90	1.40	.20			1.50	147
2474	25¢ Sandy Hook, NJ	04/26/90	1.40	.20			1.50	147
a	Booklet pane of 5, #2470-2474		7.00	*2.00*			3.00	
b	As "a," white (USA 25) omitted		75.00	—				
	Untagged, Self-Adhesive, Die-Cut							
2475	25¢ Flag, single from pane	05/18/90	.50	.25			1.00	36
a	Pane of 12	05/18/90	6.00					
	Flora and Fauna, Untagged, Perf. 11, Perf. 11.2 (#2477)							
2476	1¢ American Kestrel	06/22/91	.20	.20	.20	(4)	1.00	
2477	1¢ American Kestrel	05/10/95	.20	.20	.20	(4)	1.00	
2478	3¢ Eastern Bluebird	06/22/91	.20	.20	.30	(4)	1.00	
	Tagged, Perf. 11.5 x 11							
2479	19¢ Fawn	03/11/91	.35	.20	1.75	(4)	1.00	
a	Tagging omitted		*10.00*					
b	Red omitted		*750.00*					
2480	30¢ Cardinal	06/22/91	.60	.20	2.75	(4)	1.25	
	Perf. 11							
2481	45¢ Pumpkinseed Sunfish	12/02/92	.90	.20	4.25	(4)	1.75	
a	Black omitted		*450.00*	—				
2482	$2 Bobcat	06/01/90	3.50	1.25	14.00	(4)	5.00	
a	Black omitted		*250.00*					
b	Tagging omitted		15.00					
	Booklet, Tagged, Perf. 10.9 x 9.8, Perf. 10 on 2 or 3 sides (#2477)							
2483	20¢ Blue Jay	06/15/95	.50	.20			1.25	
a	Booklet pane of 10		5.25	*2.25*				
	Booklet, Tagged, Perf. 10 on 2 or 3 sides							
2484	29¢ Wood Duck	04/12/91	.60	.20			1.00	
a	Booklet pane of 10		6.00	*3.75*			4.00	
b	Vertical pair, imperf. between		*200.00*					
c	As "b," booklet pane of 10		*1,000.00*					
d	Prephosphored coated paper		.50	.20				
	Booklet, Tagged, Perf. 11 on 2 or 3 sides							
2485	29¢ Red and multicolored	04/12/91	.60	.20			1.00	
a	Booklet pane of 10		6.00	*4.00*			4.00	
b	Vertical pair, imperf. between		*3,000.00*					
c	Imperf, pair		*2,500.00*					
	#2484-2485a issued only in booklets. All stamps are imperf. top or bottom, or top or bottom and right edge.							

20th Universal Postal Congress
A review of historical methods of delivering the mail in the United States is the theme of these four stamps issued in commemoration of the 20th Universal Postal Congress in Washington, D.C. from November 13 through December 15, 1989. The United States, as host nation to the Congress for the first time in ninety-two years, welcomed more than 1,000 delegates from most of the member nations of the Universal Postal Union to the major international event.
USA 25
20th Universal Postal Congress

2438

2439

2440

2442

2443

2444

2445

2446

2447

2448

2448a

2449

2451

2452

2452D

2453

2454

2457

2463

2464

2466

2468

2470

2471

2472

2473

2474

2474a

2475

2476

2477

2478

2479

2480

2481

2482

2483

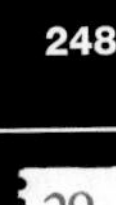

2484

2485

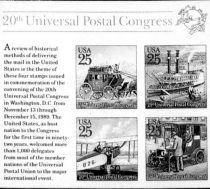

2486

2487 2488

2489

2490

2491

2492

2496 2497 2498 2499 2500 2500a

2501 2502 2503 2504 2505 2505a

2506 2507 2507a

2508 2509

2510 2511 2511a

2512

2513

2514

2515

2517 2519 2520

2521

2522

2523

2523A

2524

2525

2526

2528

No.	Issue	Date	Un	U	PB	#	FDC	Q(M)
	Booklet, Tagged, Perf. 10 x 11 on 2 or 3 sides							
2486	29¢ African Violet	10/08/93	.60	.20			1.00	
a	Booklet pane of 10		6.00	*4.00*			4.00	
2487	32¢ Peach	07/08/95	.65	.20			1.50	
2488	32¢ Pear	07/08/95	.65	.20			1.50	
a	Booklet pane, 5 each #2487-2488		6.50	*4.25*			7.50	
b	Pair, #2487-2488		1.30	.30				
	Booklet, Tagged, Self-Adhesive, Die-Cut							
2489	29¢ Red Squirrel	06/25/93	.60	.20			1.25	
a	Booklet pane of 18		11.00					
2490	29¢ Red Rose	08/19/93	.60	.20			1.25	
a	Booklet pane of 18		10.00					
2491	29¢ Pine Cone	11/05/93	.60	.20			1.25	
a	Booklet pane of 18		11.00					
b	Horizontal pair, no die cutting between		*225.00*					
c	Coil with plate #B1		—	5.00	8.00	(5)		
	Serpentine Die-Cut 11.3 x 11.7 on 2, 3 or 4 sides							
2492	32¢ Pink Rose	06/02/95	.65	.20			1.25	
a	Booklet pane of 20 plus label		13.00					
b	Booklet pane of 15 plus label		9.75					
c	Horizontal pair, no die cutting between		—					
d	As "a," 2 stamps and parts of 7 others printed on backing liner		—					
e	Booklet pane of 14		21.00					
g	Coil with plate #S111		—	3.75	7.00	(5)		
	Serpentine Die-Cut 8.8 on 2, 3 or 4 sides							
2493	32¢ Peach	07/08/95	.65	.20			1.25	
2494	32¢ Pear	07/08/95	.65	.20			1.25	
a	Booklet pane, 10 each #2493-2494		13.00					
b	Pair, #2493-2494		1.30					
	Coil, Serpentine Die-Cut 8.8 Vertically							
2495	32¢ Peach	07/08/95	.90	.20			1.25	
2495A	32¢ Pear	07/08/95	.90	.20			1.25	
b	Pair #2495-2495A		1.80		8.50	(5)		
	Olympians, Tagged, Perf. 11							
2496	25¢ Jesse Owens	07/06/90	.60	.20			1.25	36
2497	25¢ Ray Ewry	07/06/90	.60	.20			1.25	36
2498	25¢ Hazel Wightman	07/06/90	.60	.20			1.25	36
2499	25¢ Eddie Eagan	07/06/90	.60	.20			1.25	36
2500	25¢ Helene Madison	07/06/90	.60	.20			1.25	36
a	Strip of 5, #2496-2500		3.25	2.50	8.00	(10)	4.00	
	Indian Headdresses, Booklet, Tagged, Perf. 11 on 2 or 3 sides							
2501	25¢ Assiniboine Headdress	08/17/90	1.00	.20			1.25	124
2502	25¢ Cheyenne Headdress	08/17/90	1.00	.20			1.25	124
2503	25¢ Comanche Headdress	08/17/90	1.00	.20			1.25	124
2504	25¢ Flathead Headdress	08/17/90	1.00	.20			1.25	124
2505	25¢ Shoshone Headdress	08/17/90	1.00	.20			1.25	124
a	Booklet pane of 10, 2 each of #2501-2505		10.00	*5.00*			6.00	
b	As "a," black omitted		*3,500.00*					
c	Strip of 5		5.00	2.50				
	Micronesia/Marshall Islands, Tagged, Perf. 11							
2506	25¢ Canoe and Flag of the Federated States of Micronesia	09/28/90	.50	.20			1.25	76
2507	25¢ Stick Chart, Canoe and Flag of the Marshall Islands	09/28/90	.50	.20			1.25	76
a	Pair, #2506-2507		1.00	.60	2.50	(4)	2.00	
b	As "a," black omitted		*3.000.00*					
	Creatures of the Sea, Tagged, Perf. 11							
2508	25¢ Killer Whales	10/03/90	.55	.20			1.25	70
2509	25¢ Northern Sea Lions	10/03/90	.55	.20			1.25	70
2510	25¢ Sea Otter	10/03/90	.55	.20			1.25	70
2511	25¢ Common Dolphin	10/03/90	.55	.20			1.25	70
a	Block of 4, #2508-2511		2.25	1.90	2.50	(4)	3.00	
b	As "a," black omitted		*650.00*					
	America/PUAS, Tagged, Perf. 11							
2512	25¢ Grand Canyon	10/12/90	.55	.20	2.75	(4)	1.25	144
	Tagged, Perf. 11							
2513	25¢ Dwight D. Eisenhower	10/13/90	.90	.20	4.00	(4)	1.25	143
a	Imperf., pair		*2,250.00*					
	Holiday Celebrations: Christmas, Tagged, Perf. 11.5							
2514	25¢ Madonna and Child, by Antonello	10/18/90	.50	.20	2.25	(4)	1.25	729
a	Prephosphored coated paper (solid tagging)		.50	.20				
b	Booklet pane of 10		5.00	*3.25*			6.00	23
	Holiday Celebrations: Holiday, Tagged, Perf. 11							
2515	25¢ Christmas Tree	10/18/90	.50	.20	2.25	(4)	1.25	599
a	Vertical pair, imperf. horizontally		*1,100.00*					
	Booklet, Perf. 11.5 x 11 on 2 or 3 sides							
2516	Single (2515) from booklet pane	10/18/90	.50	.20			1.00	320
a	Booklet pane of 10	10/18/90	5.00	*3.25*			6.00	
	Tagged, Perf. 13							
2517	(29¢) "F" Stamp	01/22/91	.60	.20	2.75	(4)	1.25	
a	Imperf., pair		*700.00*					
b	Horizontal pair, imperf. vertically		*1,250.00*					
	Coil, Perf. 10 Vertically							
2518	(29¢) "F" Tulip (2517)	01/22/91	.60	.20	3.50	(5)	1.25	
a	Imperf., pair		*35.00*					
	Booklet, Perf. 11 on 2 or 3 sides							
2519	(29¢) "F", single from booklet		.60	.20			1.00	
a	Booklet pane of 10	01/22/91	6.50	*4.50*			7.25	
2520	(29¢) "F", single from booklet		1.75	.20			1.25	
a	Booklet pane of 10	01/22/91	18.00	*4.50*			8.00	
	#2519 has bull's-eye perforations that measure approximately 11.2. #2520 has less-pronounced black lines in the leaf, which is a much brighter green than on #2519.							
	Untagged, Perf. 11							
2521	(4¢) Makeup Rate	01/22/91	.20	.20	.40	(4)	1.25	
a	Vertical pair, imperf. horizontally		100.00					
b	Imperf., pair		65.00					
	Untagged, Self-Adhesive, Die-Cut							
2522	(29¢) F Flag, single from pane	01/22/91	.60	.25			1.25	
a	Pane of 12		7.25					
	Coil, Tagged, Perf. 10 Vertically							
2523	29¢ Flag Over Mt. Rushmore, intaglio printing	03/29/91	.60	.20	4.25	(5)	1.25	
b	Imperf., pair		20.00					
c	Blue, red and brown		5.00	—	*190.00*	(5)		
d	Prephosphored coated paper		5.00	—	*850.00*	(5)		
2523A	29¢ Flag Over Mt. Rushmore, gravure printing	07/04/91	.60	.20	4.00	(5)	1.25	
	Tagged, Perf. 11							
2524	29¢ Tulip	04/05/91	.60	.20	2.75	(4)	1.00	
	Tagged, Perf. 13 x 12.75							
2524A	29¢ Tulip		.75	.20	10.00	(4)		
	Coil, Rouletted 10 Vertically							
2525	29¢ Tulip	08/16/91	.60	.20	4.50	(5)	1.00	
	Perf. 10 Vertically							
2526	29¢ Tulip	03/03/92	.60	.20	4.50	(5)	1.00	
	Booklet, Tagged, Perf. 11 on 2 or 3 sides							
2527	29¢ Tulip (2524), single from bklt.		.60	.20			1.00	
a	Booklet pane of 10	04/05/91	6.00	*3.50*			4.00	
	Olympic Games, Booklet, Tagged, Perf. 11 on 2 or 3 sides							
2528	29¢ U.S. Flag, Olympic Rings, single from booklet	04/21/91	.60	.20			1.25	
a	Booklet pane of 10	04/21/91	6.00	*3.50*			5.00	

	Issue	Date	Un	U	PB	#	FDC	Q(M)
	Tagged, Perf. 9.8 Vertically							
2529	19¢ Fishing Boat	08/08/91	.40	.20	3.25	(5)	1.50	
a	New printing, Type II	1993	.40	.20	3.75	(5)		
b	As "a," untagged		1.00	.40	7.50	(5)		
	Tagged, Perf. 9.8							
2529C	19¢ Fishing Boat	06/25/94	.50	.20	5.25	(5)	1.50	
	Type II stamps have finer dot pattern, smoother edges along type. #2529C has only one loop of rope tying up the boat.							
	Ballooning, Booklet, Tagged, Perf. 10 on 2 or 3 sides							
2530	19¢ Overhead View of Balloon, single from booklet	05/17/91	.40	.20			1.25	
a	Booklet pane of 10	05/17/91	4.00	*2.75*			5.00	
	#2530 was issued only in booklets. All stamps are imperf. on one side or on one side and bottom.							
	Tagged, Perf. 11							
2531	29¢ Flags on Parade	05/30/91	.60	.20	2.75	(4)	1.00	
	Tagged, Self-Adhesive, Die-Cut, Imperf.							
2531A	29¢ Liberty Torch, single stamp from pane	06/25/91	.60	.25			1.25	
b	Pane of 18	06/25/91	11.00					
	Tagged, Perf. 11							
2532	50¢ Founding of Switzerland	02/22/91	1.00	.25	5.00	(4)	1.40	104
a	Vertical pair, imperf. horizontally		*2,500.00*					
2533	29¢ Vermont Statehood	03/01/91	.90	.20	4.50	(4)	1.50	180
	Tagged, Perf. 11							
2534	29¢ Savings Bonds	04/30/91	.60	.20	2.75	(4)	1.25	151
	Love, Tagged, Perf. 12.5 x 13							
2535	29¢ Love	05/09/91	.60	.20	2.75	(4)	1.25	631
a	Imperf. pair		*2,000.00*					
2535A	Perf. 11		.75	.20	4.00	(4)		
	Booklet, Perf. 11 on 2 or 3 sides							
2536	29¢ (2535), single from booklet		.60	.20			1.25	
a	Booklet pane of 10	05/09/91	6.00	*3.50*			5.00	
	Love, Perf. 11							
2537	52¢ Love	05/09/91	.90	.20	4.50	(4)	1.25	200
	Literary Arts, Tagged, Perf. 11							
2538	29¢ William Saroyan	05/22/91	.60	.20	2.75	(4)	1.50	161
	Olympic Games, Tagged, Perf. 11							
2539	$1 USPS Logo/Olympic Rings	09/29/91	1.90	.50	8.00	(4)	2.25	
	Tagged, Perf. 11							
2540	$2.90 Priority Mail	07/07/91	6.00	1.50	24.00	(4)	5.50	

	Issue	Date	Un	U	PB	#	FDC	Q(M)
	Untagged, Perf. 11							
2541	$9.95 Domestic Express Mail	06/16/91	20.00	6.00	80.00	(4)	15.00	
2542	$14 International Express Mail	08/31/91	25.00	10.00	100.00	(4)	27.50	
	Space, Tagged, Perf. 11 x 10.5							
2543	$2.90 Space Vehicle	06/03/93	5.50	1.75	25.00	(4)	6.00	
	Space, Tagged, Perf. 11.2							
2544	$3 Space Shuttle *Challenger*	06/22/95	5.75	1.75	21.00	(4)	6.00	
	Space, Tagged, Perf. 11							
2544A	$10.75 Space Shuttle *Endeavour*	08/04/95	20.00	7.50	77.50	(4)	15.00	
	Fishing Flies, Booklet, Tagged, Perf. 11 Horizontally							
2545	29¢ Royal Wulff	05/31/91	1.60	.20			1.25	149
2546	29¢ Jock Scott	05/31/91	1.60	.20			1.25	149
2547	29¢ Apte Tarpon Fly	05/31/91	1.60	.20			1.25	149
2548	29¢ Lefty's Deceiver	05/31/91	1.60	.20			1.25	149
2549	29¢ Muddler Minnow	05/31/91	1.60	.20			1.25	149
a	Booklet pane of 5, #2545-2549		8.00	*3.50*			3.00	
	#2545-2549 were issued only in booklets. All stamps are imperf. at sides or imperf. at sides and bottom.							
	Performing Arts, Tagged, Perf. 11							
2550	29¢ Cole Porter	06/08/91	.60	.20	2.75	(4)	1.25	150
a	Vertical pair, imperf. horizontally		*575.00*					
	Tagged, Perf. 11							
2551	29¢ Operations Desert Shield/ Desert Storm	07/02/91	.60	.20	2.75	(4)	2.50	200
a	Vertical pair, imperf. horizontally		*1,500.00*					
	Booklet, Perf. 11 Vertically on 1 or 2 sides							
2552	29¢ Operations Desert Shield/ Desert Storm (2551), single from booklet	07/02/91	.60	.20			2.50	200
a	Booklet pane of 5	07/02/91	3.00	*2.25*			4.75	40
	Olympic Games, Tagged, Perf. 11							
2553	29¢ Pole Vaulter	07/12/91	.60	.20			1.25	34
2554	29¢ Discus Thrower	07/12/91	.60	.20			1.25	34
2555	29¢ Women Sprinters	07/12/91	.60	.20			1.25	34
2556	29¢ Javelin Thrower	07/12/91	.60	.20			1.25	34
2557	29¢ Women Hurdlers	07/12/91	.60	.20			1.25	34
a	Strip of 5, #2553-2557		3.00	2.25	8.00	(10)	3.00	
	Tagged, Perf. 11							
2558	29¢ Numismatics	08/13/91	.60	.20	2.75	(4)	1.25	150

2529

2529C

2530

2531

2531A

2532

2533

2534

2535

2537

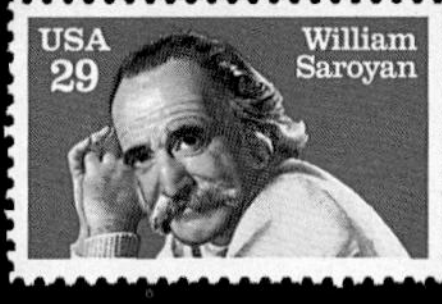

2538

2539

2540

2541

2542

2543

2544

2544A

2545

2546

2547

2548

2549

2549a

2550

2551

2553

2554

2555

2556

2557

2557a

2558

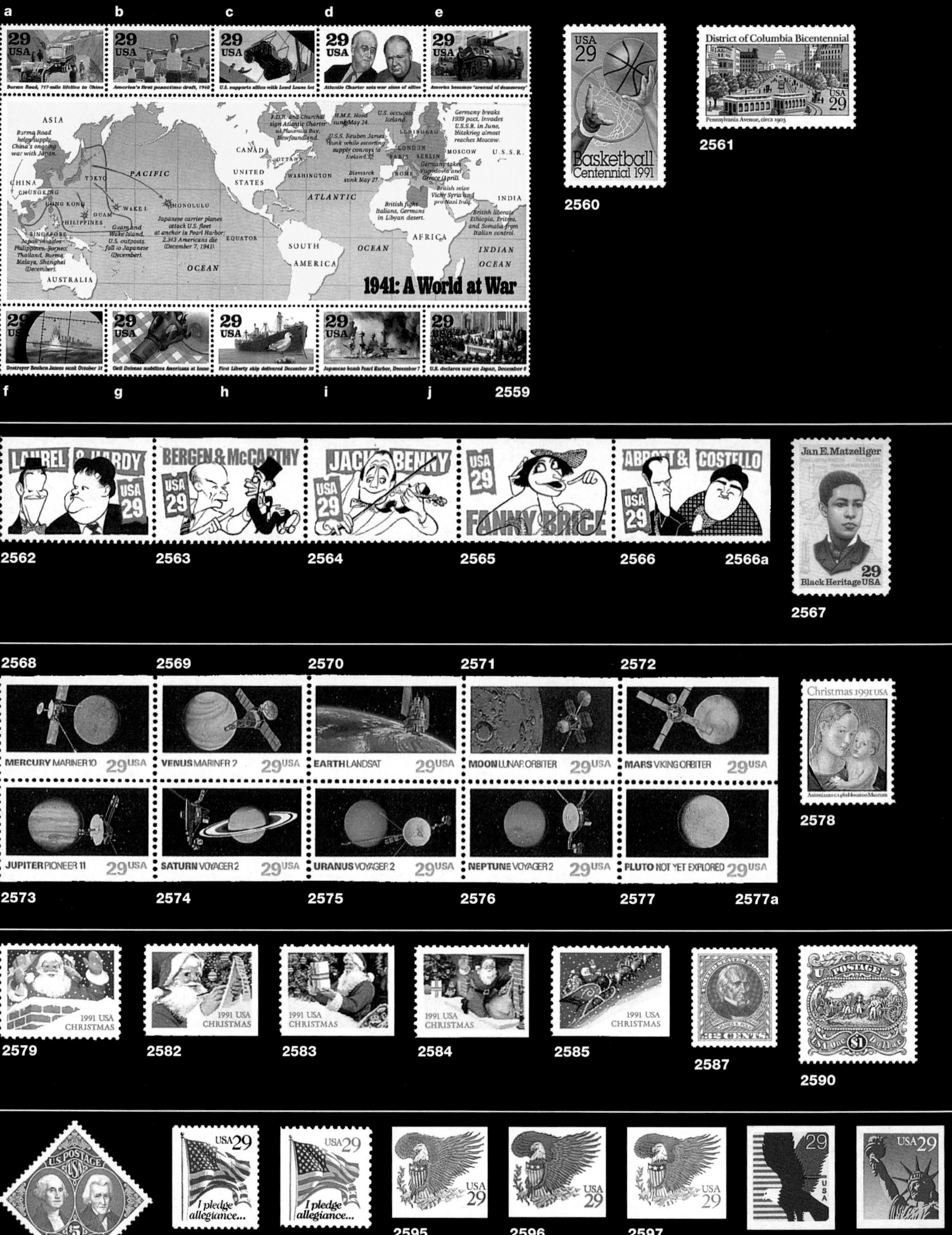
a
b
c
d
e
29 USA
Burma Road, 717-mile lifeline to China
America's first peacetime draft, 1940
U.S. supports allies with Lend Lease Act
Atlantic Charter sets war aims of allies
America becomes "arsenal of democracy"
ASIA
CANADA
UNITED STATES
PACIFIC
ATLANTIC
SOUTH AMERICA
AFRICA
INDIAN OCEAN
AUSTRALIA
U.S.S.R.
INDIA
CHINA
TOKYO
WASHINGTON
LONDON
BERLIN
MOSCOW
EQUATOR
OCEAN
1941: A World at War
Destroyer Reuben James sunk October 31
Civil Defense mobilizes Americans at home
First Liberty ship delivered December 30
Japanese bomb Pearl Harbor, December 7
U.S. declares war on Japan, December 8
f
g
h
i
j
2559
USA 29
Basketball Centennial 1991
2560
District of Columbia Bicentennial
Pennsylvania Avenue, circa 1903
USA 29
2561
LAUREL & HARDY
BERGEN & McCARTHY
JACK BENNY
FANNY BRICE
ABBOTT & COSTELLO
USA 29
2562
2563
2564
2565
2566
2566a
Jan E. Matzeliger
Black Heritage USA
29
2567
2568
2569
2570
2571
2572
MERCURY MARINER 10 29USA
VENUS MARINER 2 29USA
EARTH LANDSAT 29USA
MOON LUNAR ORBITER 29USA
MARS VIKING ORBITER 29USA
JUPITER PIONEER 11 29USA
SATURN VOYAGER 2 29USA
URANUS VOYAGER 2 29USA
NEPTUNE VOYAGER 2 29USA
PLUTO NOT YET EXPLORED 29USA
2573
2574
2575
2576
2577
2577a
Christmas 1991 USA
2578
1991 USA CHRISTMAS
2579
2582
2583
2584
2585
32 CENTS
2587
U POSTAGE S
USA One Dollar $1
2590
U.S. POSTAGE
FIVE DOLLARS
$5
2592
USA 29
I pledge allegiance...
2593
2594
USA 29
2595
2596
2597
29 USA
2598
USA 29
2599

	Issue	Date	Un	U	PB #	FDC	Q(M)
	World War II, 1941: A World at War, Miniature Sheet, Tagged, Perf. 11						
2559	Sheet of 10 and central label	09/03/91	7.50	5.00		7.00	15
a	29¢ Burma Road		.75	.45		1.50	15
b	29¢ America's First Peacetime Draft		.75	.45		1.50	15
c	29¢ Lend-Lease Act		.75	.45		1.50	15
d	29¢ Atlantic Charter		.75	.45		1.50	15
e	29¢ Arsenal of Democracy		.75	.45		1.50	15
f	29¢ Destroyer *Reuben James*		.75	.45		1.50	15
g	29¢ Civil Defense		.75	.45		1.50	15
h	29¢ Liberty Ship		.75	.45		1.50	15
i	29¢ Pearl Harbor		.75	.45		1.50	15
j	29¢ U.S. Declaration of War		.75	.45		1.50	15
k	29¢ Black omitted		*12,500.00*				
2560	29¢ Basketball	08/28/91	.60	.20	2.75 (4)	2.25	150
2561	29¢ District of Columbia	09/07/91	.60	.20	2.50 (4)	1.25	149
a	Black omitted		*110.00*				
	Comedians, Booklet, Tagged, Perf. 11 on 2 or 3 sides						
2562	29¢ Stan Laurel and Oliver Hardy	08/29/91	.65	.20		1.25	140
2563	29¢ Edgar Bergen and Dummy Charlie McCarthy	08/29/91	.65	.20		1.25	140
2564	29¢ Jack Benny	08/29/91	.65	.20		1.25	140
2565	29¢ Fanny Brice	08/29/91	.65	.20		1.25	140
2566	29¢ Bud Abbott and Lou Costello	08/29/91	.65	.20		1.25	140
a	Booklet pane of 10, 2 each of #2562-2566		9.00	*5.00*		3.00	
b	As "a," scarlet and bright violet omitted			*700.00*			
c	Strip of 5		3.25	2.50			
	#2562-2566 issued only in booklets. All stamps are imperf. at top or bottom, or at top or bottom and right side.						
	Black Heritage, Tagged, Perf. 11						
2567	29¢ Jan Matzeliger	09/15/91	.60	.20	2.75 (4)	1.75	149
a	Horizontal pair, imperf. vertically		*1,500.00*				
b	Vertical pair, imperf. horizontally		*1,450.00*				
c	Imperf., pair		*500.00*				
	Space, Booklet, Tagged, Perf. 11 on 2 or 3 sides						
2568	29¢ Mercury, Mariner 10	10/01/91	.85	.20		1.25	33
2569	29¢ Venus, Mariner 2	10/01/91	.85	.20		1.25	33
2570	29¢ Earth, Landsat	10/01/91	.85	.20		1.25	33
2571	29¢ Moon, Lunar Orbiter	10/01/91	.85	.20		1.25	33
2572	29¢ Mars, Viking Orbiter	10/01/91	.85	.20		1.25	33
2573	29¢ Jupiter, Pioneer 11	10/01/91	.85	.20		1.25	33
2574	29¢ Saturn, Voyager 2	10/01/91	.85	.20		1.25	33
2575	29¢ Uranus, Voyager 2	10/01/91	.85	.20		1.25	33
2576	29¢ Neptune, Voyager 2	10/01/91	.85	.20		1.25	33
2577	29¢ Pluto	10/01/91	.85	.20		1.25	33
a	Booklet pane of 10, #2568-2577		9.00	*3.50*		5.00	
	#2568-2577 issued only in booklets. All stamps are imperf. at top or bottom, or at top or bottom and right side.						
	Holiday Celebrations: Christmas, Tagged, Perf. 11						
2578	29¢ Madonna and Child, by Antoniazzo Romano	10/17/91	.60	.20	2.75 (4)	1.25	401
a	Booklet pane of 10		6.00	*3.25*			30
b	As "a," single, red and black omitted		*3,500.00*				
	Holiday Celebrations: Holiday, Tagged, Perf. 11						
2579	29¢ Santa Claus in Chimney	10/17/91	.60	.20	2.50 (4)	1.25	900
a	Horizontal pair, imperf. vertically		*275.00*				
b	Vertical pair, imperf. horizontally		*500.00*				

	Issue	Date	Un	U	PB #	FDC	Q(M)
	Holiday Celebrations: Holiday, Booklet, Perf. 11 on 2 or 3 sides						
2580	29¢ Santa Claus (2579), Type I, single from booklet	10/17/91	2.00	.20		1.25	
2581	29¢ Santa Claus (2579), Type II, single from booklet	10/17/91	2.00	.20		1.25	
a	Pair, #2580, 2581	10/17/91	4.00	.50			28
b	Booklet pane, 2 each		9.00	*1.25*		2.50	
	The extreme left brick in top row of chimney is missing from Type II, #2581.						
2582	29¢ Santa Claus Checking List, single from booklet	10/17/91	.60	.20		1.25	
a	Booklet pane of 4	10/17/91	2.40	*1.25*		2.50	28
2583	29¢ Santa Claus with Present Under Tree, single from booklet	10/17/91	.60	.20		1.25	
a	Booklet pane of 4	10/17/91	2.40	*1.25*		2.50	28
2584	29¢ Santa Claus at Fireplace, single from booklet	10/17/91	.60	.20		1.25	
a	Booklet pane of 4	10/17/91	2.40	*1.25*		2.50	28
2585	29¢ Santa Claus and Sleigh, single from booklet	10/17/91	.60	.20		1.25	
a	Booklet pane of 4	10/17/91	2.40	*1.25*		2.50	28
	#2582-2585 issued only in booklets. All stamps are imperf. at top or bottom, or at top or bottom and right side.						
	Tagged, Perf. 11.2						
2587	32¢ James K. Polk	11/02/95	.65	.20	3.25 (4)	1.25	
	Perf. 11.5						
2590	$1 Victory at Saratoga	05/05/94	1.90	.50	7.60 (4)	2.50	
2592	$5 Washington and Jackson	08/19/94	8.00	2.50	40.00 (4)	12.50	
	Tagged, Perf. 10 on 2 or 3 sides						
2593	29¢ Pledge of Allegiance	09/08/92	.60	.20		1.25	
a	Booklet of 10		6.00	*4.25*		5.00	
	Perf. 11 x 10 on 2 or 3 sides						
2593B	29¢ Pledge of Allegiance, shiny gum		1.40	.50			
c	Booklet pane of 10, shiny gum		14.00	*7.50*			
2594	29¢ Pledge of Allegiance	04/08/93	.60	.20			
a	Booklet of 10		6.00	4.25			
	Booklet, Tagged, Self-Adhesive, Die-Cut						
2595	29¢ Eagle and Shield (brown lettering)	09/25/92	.60	.25		1.50	
a	Pane of 17 + label		13.00				
b	Pair, no die-cutting		*150.00*				
c	Brown omitted		*375.00*				
d	As "a," no die-cutting		*1,250.00*				
2596	29¢ Eagle and Shield (green lettering)	09/25/92	.60	.25		1.50	
a	Pane of 17 + label		12.00				
2597	29¢ Eagle and Shield (red lettering)	09/25/92	.60	.25		1.50	
a	Pane of 17 + label		10.50				
2598	29¢ Eagle	02/04/94	.60	.20		1.25	
a	Booklet pane of 18		11.00				
b	Coil		—	3.75	6.75 (5)		
2599	29¢ Statue of Liberty	06/24/94	.60	.20		1.25	
a	Booklet pane of 18		11.00				
b	Coil		—	4.00	6.75 (5)		

	Issue	Date	Un	U	PB	#	FDC	Q(M)
	Coil, Untagged, Perf. 10 Vertically							
2602	10¢ Eagle and Shield (inscribed "Bulk Rate USA")	12/13/91	.20	.20	2.50	(5)	1.25	
2603	10¢ Eagle and Shield (inscribed "USA Bulk Rate")	05/29/93	.20	.20	3.00	(5)	1.25	
a	Imperf., pair		*25.00*					
b	Tagged (error), shiny gum		2.00	1.50	13.00	(5)		
2604	10¢ Eagle and Shield (metallic, inscribed "USA Bulk Rate")	05/29/93	.20	.20	3.25	(5)	1.25	
2605	23¢ Flag, Presorted First-Class	09/27/91	.45	.40	3.50	(5)	1.25	
	Perf. 11							
2606	23¢ USA	07/21/92	.45	.40	4.00	(5)	1.25	
2607	23¢ USA (Bureau) (In #2607, "23" is 7mm long)	10/09/92	.45	.40	4.00	(5)	1.25	
a	Tagged (error), shiny gum		5.00	4.50	140.00	(5)		
c	Imperf., pair		75.00					
2608	23¢ USA (violet)	05/14/93	.45	.40	4.25	(5)	1.25	
	Tagged							
2609	29¢ Flag Over White House	04/23/92	.60	.20	4.50	(5)	1.25	
a	Imperf., pair		15.00					
b	Pair, imperf. between		95.00					
	Olympic Games, Tagged, Perf. 11							
2611	29¢ Hockey	01/11/92	.60	.20			1.25	
2612	29¢ Figure Skating	01/11/92	.60	.20			1.25	
2613	29¢ Speed Skating	01/11/92	.60	.20			1.25	
2614	29¢ Skiing	01/11/92	.60	.20			1.25	
2615	29¢ Bobsledding	01/11/92	.60	.20			1.25	
a	Strip of 5, #2611-2615		3.00	2.50	7.00	(10)	3.50	32
	Tagged, Perf. 11							
2616	29¢ World Columbian Stamp Expo	01/24/92	.60	.20	2.75	(4)	1.25	149
a	Tagging omitted		8.50					
	Black Heritage, Tagged, Perf. 11							
2617	29¢ W.E.B. DuBois	01/31/92	.60	.20	2.75	(4)	1.75	150
	Love, Tagged, Perf. 11							
2618	29¢ Love	02/06/92	.60	.20	2.75	(4)	1.25	835
a	Horizontal pair, imperf. vertically		*700.00*					
2619	29¢ Olympic Baseball	04/03/92	.60	.20	2.75	(4)	2.00	160

	Issue	Date	Un	U	PB	#	FDC	Q(M)
	First Voyage of Christopher Columbus, Tagged, Perf. 11							
2620	29¢ Seeking Queen Isabella's Support	04/24/92	.60	.20			1.25	40
2621	29¢ Crossing The Atlantic	04/24/92	.60	.20			1.25	40
2622	29¢ Approaching Land	04/24/92	.60	.20			1.25	40
2623	29¢ Coming Ashore	04/24/92	.60	.20			1.25	40
a	Block of 4, #2620-2623		2.40	2.00	2.75	(4)	2.75	
	The Voyages of Columbus Souvenir Sheets, Perf. 10.5							
2624	First Sighting of Land, sheet of 3	05/22/92	2.00	1.25			2.10	1
a	1¢ deep blue		.20	.20			1.50	
b	4¢ ultramarine		.20	.20			1.50	
c	$1 salmon		1.75	1.00			2.00	
2625	Claiming a New World, sheet of 3	05/22/92	7.25	5.00			8.00	1
a	2¢ brown violet		.20	.20			1.50	
b	3¢ green		.20	.20			1.50	
c	$4 crimson lake		7.00	4.00			8.00	
2626	Seeking Royal Support, sheet of 3	05/22/92	1.60	1.00			1.75	1
a	5¢ chocolate		.20	.20			1.50	
b	30¢ orange brown		.60	.30			1.50	
c	50¢ slate blue		.90	.50			1.50	
2627	Royal Favor Restored, sheet of 3	05/22/92	5.75	3.50			6.25	1
a	6¢ purple		.20	.20			1.50	
b	8¢ magenta		.20	.20			1.50	
c	$3 yellow green		5.50	3.00			6.00	
2628	Reporting Discoveries, sheet of 3	05/22/92	4.00	3.00			4.50	1
a	10¢ black brown		.20	.20			1.50	
b	15¢ dark green		.30	.20			1.50	
c	$2 brown red		3.50	2.00			4.00	
2629	$5 Christopher Columbus, sheet of 1	05/22/92	8.75	6.00			10.00	1
a	$5 black		8.50	5.00				

COMMON BUCKEYE

In 2006 the U.S. Postal Service issued a new definitive stamp depicting the Common Buckeye (Junonia coenia), a butterfly named for the distinctive eye-spots on its wings. Frequenting a variety of open, sunny habitats such as beaches, fields, gardens, roadsides, and trails, Common Buckeyes fly year-round in the southern United States and Mexico. During warmer months they gradually disperse northward throughout much of the U.S. to southern Canada. Large-scale migrations occur in autumn along the East Coast as thousands of Common Buckeyes—along with other species such as Monarchs and Red Admirals—retreat south for the winter. Common Buckeyes often bask in the sun with their wings open, prominently displaying their colorful markings. The upper side is tawny brown to dark brown, punctuated with bold eyespots on each wing that may serve to scare away predators. These black, yellow-rimmed eyespots have iridescent purple or pink centers. Other marks include an orange band near the margin of each hind wing; two orange bars on the leading edge of each forewing; and a diagonal white band on each forewing. The wingspan ranges from 1.5 to 2.25 inches with males noticeably smaller than females. Renowned wildlife illustrator Steve Buchanan created an exquisitely detailed and precise artistic rendering of this handsome butterfly for the stamp.

2602

2603

2604

2605

2606

2607

2608

2609

2611

2612

2613

2614

2615 2615a

2616

2617

2618

2624

2625

2619

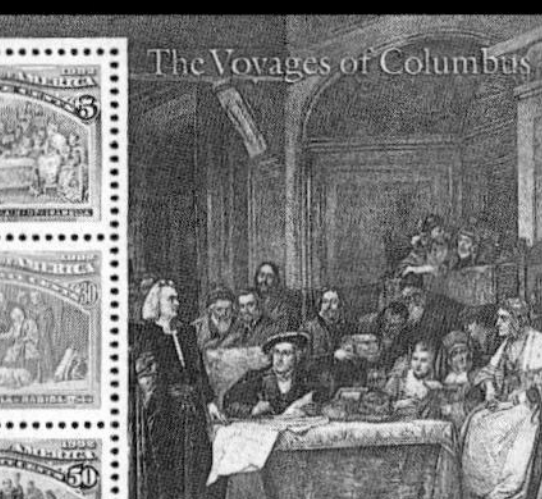

2626

2627

2620 2621

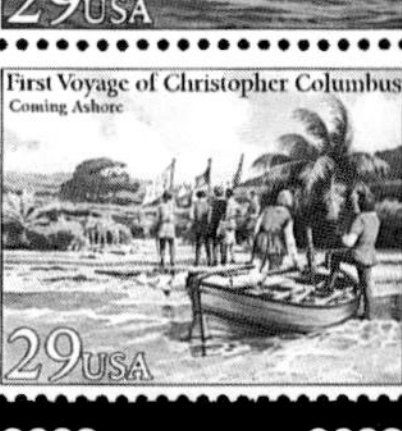

2622 2623 2623a

2628

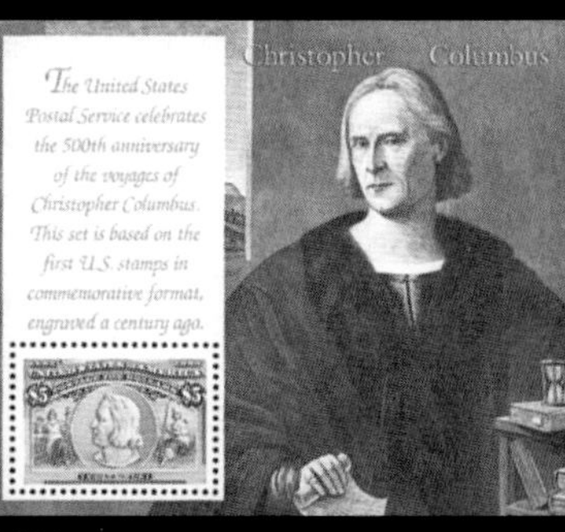

2629

2630

2631 2632 2633 2634 2634a

2635

2636

2637

2638

2639

2640

2641 2641a

2642

2643

2644

2645

2646 2646a

2647

2648

2649

2650

2651

2652

2653

2654

2655

2656

2657

2658

2659

2660

2661

2662

2663

2664

2665

USA 29 Common Sunflower

2666

	Issue	Date	Un	U	PB	#	FDC	Q(M)
	Tagged, Perf. 11							
2630	29¢ New York Stock Exchange Bicentennial	05/17/92	.60	.20	2.75	(4)	2.50	148
	Space, Tagged, Perf. 11							
2631	29¢ Cosmonaut, US Space Shuttle	05/29/92	.60	.20			1.50	37
2632	29¢ Astronaut, Russian Space Station	05/29/92	.60	.20			1.50	37
2633	29¢ Sputnik, Vostok, Apollo Command and Lunar Modules	05/29/92	.60	.20			1.50	37
2634	29¢ Soyuz, Mercury and Gemini Spacecraft	05/29/92	.60	.20			1.50	37
a	Block of 4, #2631-2634		2.40	1.90	3.25	(4)	2.75	
	Tagged, Perf. 11							
2635	29¢ Alaska Highway, 50th Anniversary	05/30/92	.60	.20	2.75	(4)	1.25	147
a	Black (engr.) omitted		*825.00*					
	Tagged, Perf. 11							
2636	29¢ Kentucky Statehood Bicentennial	06/01/92	.60	.20	2.75	(4)	1.25	160
	Olympic Games, Tagged, Perf. 11							
2637	29¢ Soccer	06/11/92	.60	.20			1.25	32
2638	29¢ Gymnastics	06/11/92	.60	.20			1.25	32
2639	29¢ Volleyball	06/11/92	.60	.20			1.25	32
2640	29¢ Boxing	06/11/92	.60	.20			1.25	32
2641	29¢ Swimming	06/11/92	.60	.20			1.25	32
a	Strip of 5, #2637-2641		3.00	2.50	6.50	(10)	3.00	

	Issue	Date	Un	U	PB	#	FDC	Q(M)
	Hummingbirds, Tagged, Perf. 11 Vertically on 1 or 2 sides							
2642	29¢ Ruby-Throated	06/15/92	.60	.20			1.25	88
2643	29¢ Broad-Billed	06/15/92	.60	.20			1.25	88
2644	29¢ Costa's	06/15/92	.60	.20			1.25	88
2645	29¢ Rufous	06/15/92	.60	.20			1.25	88
2646	29¢ Calliope	06/15/92	.60	.20			1.25	88
a	Booklet pane of 5, #2642-2646		3.00	*2.50*			3.00	
	Wildflowers, Tagged, Perf. 11							
2647	29¢ Indian Paintbrush	07/24/92	.75	.60			1.25	11
2648	29¢ Fragrant Water Lily	07/24/92	.75	.60			1.25	11
2649	29¢ Meadow Beauty	07/24/92	.75	.60			1.25	11
2650	29¢ Jack-in-the-Pulpit	07/24/92	.75	.60			1.25	11
2651	29¢ California Poppy	07/24/92	.75	.60			1.25	11
2652	29¢ Large-Flowered Trillium	07/24/92	.75	.60			1.25	11
2653	29¢ Tickseed	07/24/92	.75	.60			1.25	11
2654	29¢ Shooting Star	07/24/92	.75	.60			1.25	11
2655	29¢ Stream Violet	07/24/92	.75	.60			1.25	11
2656	29¢ Bluets	07/24/92	.75	.60			1.25	11
2657	29¢ Herb Robert	07/24/92	.75	.60			1.25	11
2658	29¢ Marsh Marigold	07/24/92	.75	.60			1.25	11
2659	29¢ Sweet White Violet	07/24/92	.75	.60			1.25	11
2660	29¢ Claret Cup Cactus	07/24/92	.75	.60			1.25	11
2661	29¢ White Mountain Avens	07/24/92	.75	.60			1.25	11
2662	29¢ Sessile Bellwort	07/24/92	.75	.60			1.25	11
2663	29¢ Blue Flag	07/24/92	.75	.60			1.25	11
2664	29¢ Harlequin Lupine	07/24/92	.75	.60			1.25	11
2665	29¢ Twinflower	07/24/92	.75	.60			1.25	11
2666	29¢ Common Sunflower	07/24/92	.75	.60			1.25	11

AMERICAN MOTORCYCLES

With the issuance of the American Motorcycles stamps, the U.S. Postal Service recognizes the role of motorcycles in American culture. The stamps feature digital illustrations by Steve Buchanan of a 1918 Cleveland, a 1940 Indian Four, a 1965 Harley-Davidson Electra-Glide, and a circa 1970 chopper. **Cleveland 1918:** Lightweight and affordable, this Cleveland was a popular motorcycle with a single-cylinder, 2.5-horsepower motor. Advertisements claimed that it could travel 75 miles on a single gallon of gas and reach speeds of up to 35 to 40 miles per hour. **Indian 1940:** The 1940 entry in a series of deluxe, four-cylinder motorcycles known as the Four, this streamlined bike from the Indian Motorcycle Company featured skirted fenders that partially covered the wheels, a controversial design innovation that soon became an Indian trademark. **Harley-Davidson 1965:** With its whitewall tires, extensive chrome, large fenders, and fiberglass saddlebags, this Harley-Davidson is considered by many to be one of the company's most iconic motorcycles. Known as the Electra-Glide, this model was first manufactured in 1965, when its new features included a push-button electric starter. **Chopper c.1970:** Especially prominent during the 1960s and 1970s, choppers are extensively customized motorcycles that earned their name from the process of removing, or "chopping," unwanted components. Typical chopper features include a stretched frame, raised handlebars, and long forks leading to the front wheel.

	Issue	Date	Un	U	PB	#	FDC	Q(M)
	Wildflowers continued, **Tagged, Perf. 11**							
2667	29¢ Sego Lily	07/24/92	.75	.60			1.25	11
2668	29¢ Virginia Bluebells	07/24/92	.75	.60			1.25	11
2669	29¢ Ohi'a Lehua	07/24/92	.75	.60			1.25	11
2670	29¢ Rosebud Orchid	07/24/92	.75	.60			1.25	11
2671	29¢ Showy Evening Primrose	07/24/92	.75	.60			1.25	11
2672	29¢ Fringed Gentian	07/24/92	.75	.60			1.25	11
2673	29¢ Yellow Lady's Slipper	07/24/92	.75	.60			1.25	11
2674	29¢ Passionflower	07/24/92	.75	.60			1.25	11
2675	29¢ Bunchberry	07/24/92	.75	.60			1.25	11
2676	29¢ Pasqueflower	07/24/92	.75	.60			1.25	11
2677	29¢ Round-Lobed Hepatica	07/24/92	.75	.60			1.25	11
2678	29¢ Wild Columbine	07/24/92	.75	.60			1.25	11
2679	29¢ Fireweed	07/24/92	.75	.60			1.25	11
2680	29¢ Indian Pond Lily	07/24/92	.75	.60			1.25	11
2681	29¢ Turk's Cap Lily	07/24/92	.75	.60			1.25	11
2682	29¢ Dutchman's Breeches	07/24/92	.75	.60			1.25	11
2683	29¢ Trumpet Honeysuckle	07/24/92	.75	.60			1.25	11
2684	29¢ Jacob's Ladder	07/24/92	.75	.60			1.25	11
2685	29¢ Plains Prickly Pear	07/24/92	.75	.60			1.25	11
2686	29¢ Moss Campion	07/24/92	.75	.60			1.25	11
2687	29¢ Bearberry	07/24/92	.75	.60			1.25	11
2688	29¢ Mexican Hat	07/24/92	.75	.60			1.25	11
2689	29¢ Harebell	07/24/92	.75	.60			1.25	11
2690	29¢ Desert Five Spot	07/24/92	.75	.60			1.25	11
2691	29¢ Smooth Solomon's Seal	07/24/92	.75	.60			1.25	11
2692	29¢ Red Maids	07/24/92	.75	.60			1.25	11
2693	29¢ Yellow Skunk Cabbage	07/24/92	.75	.60			1.25	11
2694	29¢ Rue Anemone	07/24/92	.75	.60			1.25	11
2695	29¢ Standing Cypress	07/24/92	.75	.60			1.25	11
2696	29¢ Wild Flax	07/24/92	.75	.60			1.25	11
a	Pane of 50, #2647-2696		37.50	—			30.00	
	World War II, 1942: Into the Battle, Miniature Sheet,Tagged, Perf. 11							
2697	Sheet of 10 and central label	08/17/92	7.50	5.00			7.00	
a	29¢ B-25s Take Off to Raid Tokyo		.75	.30			1.50	12
b	29¢ Food and Other Commodities Rationed		.75	.30			1.50	12
c	29¢ U.S. Wins Battle of the Coral Sea		.75	.30			1.50	12
d	29¢ Corregidor Falls to Japanese		.75	.30			1.50	12
e	29¢ Japan Invades Aleutian Islands		.75	.30			1.50	12
f	29¢ Allies Decipher Secret Enemy Codes		.75	.30			1.50	12
g	29¢ *Yorktown Lost*		.75	.30			1.50	12
h	29¢ Millions of Women Join War Effort		.75	.30			1.50	12
i	29¢ Marines Land on Guadalcanal		.75	.30			1.50	12
j	29¢ Allies Land in North Africa		.75	.30			1.50	12
k	Red (litho.) omitted		*5,000.00*					
	Literary Arts, Tagged, Perf. 11							
2698	29¢ Dorothy Parker	08/22/92	.60	.20	2.75	(4)	1.50	105
	Tagged, Perf. 11							
2699	29¢ Dr. Theodore von Karman	08/31/92	.60	.20	2.75	(4)	1.50	143

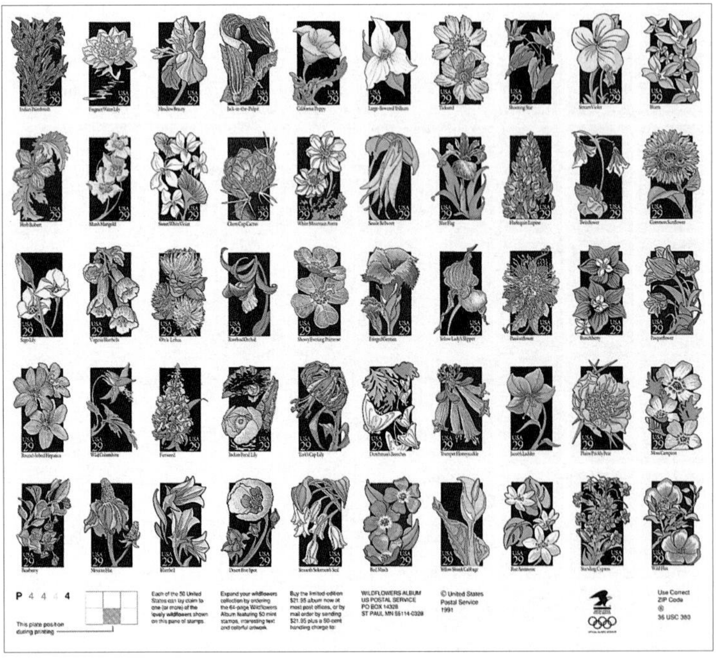

#2696a

Sego Lily
Virginia Bluebells
Ohi'a Lehua
Rosebud Orchid
Showy Evening Primrose
Fringed Gentian
Yellow Lady's Slipper
Passionflower
Bunchberry
Pasqueflower
2667
2668
2669
2670
2671
2672
2673
2674
2675
2676
Round-lobed Hepatica
Wild Columbine
Fireweed
Indian Pond Lily
Turk's Cap Lily
Dutchman's Breeches
Trumpet Honeysuckle
Jacob's Ladder
Plains Prickly Pear
Moss Campion
2677
2678
2679
2680
2681
2682
2683
2684
2685
2686
Bearberry
Mexican Hat
Harebell
Desert Five Spot
Smooth Solomon's Seal
Red Maids
Yellow Skunk Cabbage
Rue Anemone
Standing Cypress
Wild Flax
2687
2688
2689
2690
2691
2692
2693
2694
2695
2696
USA 29
a
b
c
d
e
B-25s take off to raid Tokyo April 18, 1942
Food and other commodities rationed, 1942
U.S. wins Battle of the Coral Sea May 1942
Corregidor falls to Japanese May 6, 1942
Japan invades Aleutian Islands June 1942
1942: Into the Battle
Note: Red areas controlled by enemy.
ASIA
CHINA
AUSTRALIA
PACIFIC
OCEAN
CANADA
UNITED STATES
ATLANTIC
OCEAN
SOUTH AMERICA
AFRICA
INDIAN OCEAN
INDIA
U.S.S.R.
Allies decipher secret enemy codes, 1942
Yorktown lost, U.S. wins at Midway, 1942
Millions of women join war effort, 1942
Marines land on Guadalcanal Aug. 7, 1942
Allies land in North Africa November 1942
29 USA
Dorothy Parker
American Writer 1893-1967
2698
Theodore von Kármán
Aerospace Scientist
USA 29
2699

2700 2701

2702 2703 2703a

2704

2705
2706
2707
2708
2709
2709a

2710

2711 2712

2713 2714 2714a

2720

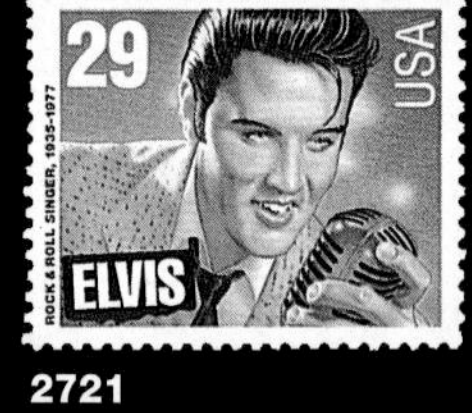

2721

2722

2723

2724 2725 2726 2727 2728

2729 2730

2737b

	Issue	Date	Un	U	PB	#	FDC	Q(M)
	Minerals, Tagged, Perf. 11							
2700	29¢ Azurite	09/17/92	.60	.20			1.25	37
2701	29¢ Copper	09/17/92	.60	.20			1.25	37
2702	29¢ Variscite	09/17/92	.60	.20			1.25	37
2703	29¢ Wulfenite	09/17/92	.60	.20			1.25	37
a	Block of 4, #2700-2703		2.40	2.00	2.75	(4)	2.75	
b	As "a," silver (litho.) omitted		*8,500.00*					
	Tagged, Perf. 11							
2704	29¢ Juan Rodriguez Cabrillo	09/28/92	.60	.20	2.75	(4)	1.25	85
a	Black (engr.) omitted		*3,500.00*					
	Wild Animals, Tagged, Perf. 11 Horizontally							
2705	29¢ Giraffe	10/01/92	.60	.20			1.25	80
2706	29¢ Giant Panda	10/01/92	.60	.20			1.25	80
2707	29¢ Flamingo	10/01/92	.60	.20			1.25	80
2708	29¢ King Penguins	10/01/92	.60	.20			1.25	80
2709	29¢ White Bengal Tiger	10/01/92	.60	.20			1.25	80
a	Booklet pane of 5, #2705-2709		3.00	*2.25*			3.25	
b	As "a," imperf.		*2,500.00*					
	Holiday Celebrations: Christmas, Tagged, Perf. 11.5 x 11							
2710	29¢ Madonna and Child by Giovanni Bellini	10/22/92	.60	.20	2.75	(4)	1.25	300
a	Booklet pane of 10		6.00	*3.50*			7.25	349
	Holiday Celebrations: Holiday, Tagged, Perf. 11.5 x 11							
2711	29¢ Horse and Rider	10/22/92	.75	.20			1.25	125
2712	29¢ Toy Train	10/22/92	.75	.20			1.25	125
2713	29¢ Toy Steamer	10/22/92	.75	.20			1.25	125
2714	29¢ Toy Ship	10/22/92	.75	.20			1.25	125
a	Block of 4, #2711-2714		3.00	1.10	3.75	(4)	2.75	
	Holiday Celebrations: Holiday, Booklet, Perf. 11 on 2 or 3 sides							
2715	29¢ Horse and Rider	10/22/92	.85	.20			1.25	102
2716	29¢ Toy Train	10/22/92	.85	.20			1.25	102
2717	29¢ Toy Steamer	10/22/92	.85	.20			1.25	102
2718	29¢ Toy Ship	10/22/92	.85	.20			1.25	102
a	Booklet pane of 4, #2715-2718		3.50	*1.25*			2.75	
2719	29¢ Toy Train (self-adhesive)	10/22/92	.60	.20			1.25	22
a	Booklet pane of 18		11.00					

	Issue	Date	Un	U	PB	#	FDC	Q(M)
	Lunar New Year, Tagged, Perf. 11							
2720	29¢ Year of the Rooster	12/30/92	.60	.20	2.50	(4)	2.25	
a	Prephosphored paper (mottled tagging) + block tagging		3.00	—				
b	Prephosphored paper		*50.00*	—				
	Legends of American Music: Rock & Roll/Rhythm & Blues (#2721-2730), **Tagged, Perf. 11**							
2721	29¢ Elvis Presley	01/08/93	.60	.20	2.75	(4)	1.75	517
	Perf. 10							
2722	29¢ *Oklahoma!*	03/30/93	.60	.20	4.00	(4)	1.25	150
2723	29¢ Hank Williams	06/09/93	.60	.20	4.00	(4)	1.25	152
	Perf. 11.2 x 11.5							
2723A	29¢ Hank Williams		22.50	10.00	140.00	(4)	—	
	Perf. 10							
2724	29¢ Elvis Presley	06/16/93	.70	.20			1.25	14
2725	29¢ Bill Haley	06/16/93	.70	.20			1.25	14
2726	29¢ Clyde McPhatter	06/16/93	.70	.20			1.25	14
2727	29¢ Ritchie Valens	06/16/93	.70	.20			1.25	14
2728	29¢ Otis Redding	06/16/93	.70	.20			1.25	14
2729	29¢ Buddy Holly	06/16/93	.70	.20			1.25	14
2730	29¢ Dinah Washington	06/16/93	.70	.20			1.25	14
a	Vertical strip of 7, #2724-2730		5.50		10.00	(10)	5.00	
	Booklet, Perf. 11 Horizontally							
2731	29¢ Elvis Presley	06/16/93	.60	.20			1.25	99
2732	29¢ Bill Haley (2725)	06/16/93	.60	.20			1.25	33
2733	29¢ Clyde McPhatter (2726)	06/16/93	.60	.20			1.25	33
2734	29¢ Ritchie Valens (2727)	06/16/93	.60	.20			1.25	33
2735	29¢ Otis Redding	06/16/93	.60	.20			1.25	66
2736	29¢ Buddy Holly	06/16/93	.60	.20			1.25	66
2737	29¢ Dinah Washington	06/16/93	.60	.20			1.25	66
a	Booklet pane, 2 #2731, 1 each #2732-2737		5.00	*2.25*			5.25	
b	Booklet pane of 4, #2731, 2735-2737		2.40	*1.50*			2.75	
2738-40		Not assigned						

HATTIE McDANIEL

Hattie McDaniel (1895-1952), the first African American to win an Academy Award, entertained America as a movie actress, singer, and radio and television performer. In 2006 the U.S. Postal Service pays tribute to her with a stamp in its Black Heritage series. McDaniel was born in Wichita, Kansas, and raised in Denver, Colorado. Showing signs of talent at an early age, she dropped out of school as a teenager to tour with vaudeville companies, traveling musical ensembles, and minstrel shows. In 1931 McDaniel arrived in Hollywood and soon began to appear in films. She is usually credited with appearing in more than 90 films, although some sources suggest that she may have appeared, albeit in uncredited roles, in as many as 300. She often appeared alongside some of the brightest stars of the era: Clark Gable in *Saratoga* (1937) and Katharine Hepburn in *Alice Adams* (1935). Other notable films include *Show Boat* (1936), *In This Our Life* (1942), and *Since You Went Away* (1944). The stamp features a portrait of McDaniel by Tim O'Brien of Brooklyn, New York. Based on a 1941 photograph, the portrait shows McDaniel in the dress she wore on February 29, 1940, when she won an Academy Award for Best Supporting Actress for her performance as Mammy in the 1939 film *Gone With the Wind*.

	Issue	Date	Un	U	PB	#	FDC	Q(M)
	Space, Tagged, Perf. 11 Vertically on 1 or 2 sides							
2741	29¢ Space Fantasy	01/25/93	.60	.20			1.25	140
2742	29¢ Space Fantasy	01/25/93	.60	.20			1.25	140
2743	29¢ Space Fantasy	01/25/93	.60	.20			1.25	140
2744	29¢ Space Fantasy	01/25/93	.60	.20			1.25	140
2745	29¢ Space Fantasy	01/25/93	.60	.20			1.25	140
a	Booklet pane of 5, #2741-2745		3.00	*2.25*			3.25	
	Black Heritage, Tagged, Perf. 11							
2746	29¢ Percy Lavon Julian	01/29/93	.60	.20	2.75	(4)	1.75	105
	Tagged, Perf. 11							
2747	29¢ Oregon Trail	02/12/93	.60	.20	2.75	(4)	1.25	110
a	Tagging omitted		20.00					
2748	29¢ World University Games	02/25/93	.60	.20	2.75	(4)	1.50	110
2749	29¢ Grace Kelly	03/24/93	.60	.20	2.75	(4)	3.00	173
	Circus, Tagged, Perf. 11							
2750	29¢ Clown	04/06/93	.60	.20			1.50	66
2751	29¢ Ringmaster	04/06/93	.60	.20			1.50	66
2752	29¢ Trapeze Artist	04/06/93	.60	.20			1.50	66
2753	29¢ Elephant	04/06/93	.60	.20			1.50	66
a	Block of 4, #2750-2753		2.40	1.75	5.75	(6)	3.00	
	Tagged, Perf. 11							
2754	29¢ Cherokee Strip	04/17/93	.60	.20	2.50	(4)	1.25	110
	Perf. 11							
2755	29¢ Dean Acheson	04/21/93	.60	.20	2.75	(4)	1.25	116
	Sporting Horses, Tagged, Perf. 11 x 11.5							
2756	29¢ Steeplechase	05/01/93	.60	.20			1.75	40
2757	29¢ Thoroughbred Racing	05/01/93	.60	.20			1.75	40
2758	29¢ Harness Racing	05/01/93	.60	.20			1.75	40
2759	29¢ Polo	05/01/93	.60	.20			1.75	40
a	Block of 4, #2756-2759		2.40	2.00	2.75	(4)	3.50	
b	As "a," black omitted		*1,000.00*					
	Garden Flowers, Tagged, Perf. 11 Vertically							
2760	29¢ Hyacinth	05/15/93	.60	.20			1.50	200
2761	29¢ Daffodil	05/15/93	.60	.20			1.50	200
2762	29¢ Tulip	05/15/93	.60	.20			1.50	200
2763	29¢ Iris	05/15/93	.60	.20			1.50	200
2764	29¢ Lilac	05/15/93	.60	.20			1.50	200
a	Booklet pane of 5, #2760-2764		3.00	*2.25*			3.00	
b	As "a," black omitted		*225.00*					
c	As "a," imperf.		*1,250.00*					
	World War II, 1943: Turning The Tide, Miniature Sheet, Tagged, Perf. 11							
2765	Sheet of 10 and central label	05/31/93	7.50	5.00			7.00	
a	29¢ Allied Forces Battle German U-boats		.75	.40			1.50	120
b	29¢ Military Medics Treat the Wounded		.75	.40			1.50	120
c	29¢ Sicily Attacked by Allied Forces		.75	.40			1.50	120
d	29¢ B-24s Hit Ploesti Refineries		.75	.40			1.50	120
e	29¢ V-Mail Delivers Letters from Home		.75	.40			1.50	120
f	29¢ Italy Invaded by Allies		.75	.40			1.50	120
g	29¢ Bonds and Stamps Help War Effort		.75	.40			1.50	120
h	29¢ "Willie and Joe" Keep Spirits High.		.75	.40			1.50	120
i	29¢ Gold Stars Mark World War II Losses		.75	.40			1.50	120
j	29¢ Marines Assault Tarawa		.75	.40			1.50	120
	American Sports Personalities, Tagged, Perf. 11							
2766	29¢ Joe Louis	06/22/93	.60	.20	2.75	(4)	3.00	160
	Legends of American Music: Broadway Musicals, Tagged, Perf. 11 Horizontally on 1 or 2 sides							
2767	29¢ *Show Boat*	07/14/93	.60	.20			1.25	129
2768	29¢ *Porgy & Bess*	07/14/93	.60	.20			1.25	129
2769	29¢ *Oklahoma!*	07/14/93	.60	.20			1.25	129
2770	29¢ *My Fair Lady*	07/14/93	.60	.20			1.25	129
a	Booklet pane of 4, #2767-2770		2.75	*2.25*			3.50	

2765 a b c d e

f g h i j

2741 2742 2743 2744 2745 2745a

2746

2747

2748

2749

2750 2751

2752 2753

2753a

2754

2755

2756 2757

2758 2759

2759a

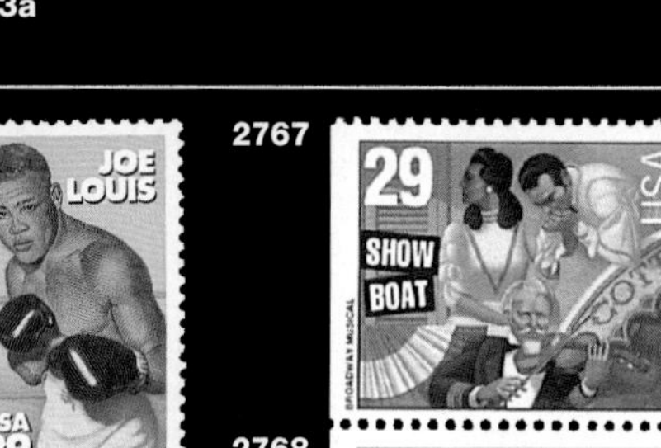

2766

2767

2768

2769

2770

2770a

2760 2761 2762 2763 2764 2764a

2773 2774 2774a

2775

2776

2777

2778

2778a

2781 2782 2782a

2783 2784 2784a

2785 2786

2787 2788 2788a

2789

2790

2791 2792

2793 2794 2794a

2795 2796

2797 2798 2798c

2803

2804

2805

2806

2806a

Issue		Date	Un	U	PB #	FDC	Q(M)
	Legends of American Music: Country & Western, Tagged, Perf. 10						
771	29¢ Hank Williams (2775)	09/25/93	.75	.20		1.25	25
772	29¢ Patsy Cline (2777)	09/25/93	.75	.20		1.25	25
773	29¢ The Carter Family (2776)	09/25/93	.75	.20		1.25	25
774	29¢ Bob Wills (2778)	09/25/93	.75	.20		1.25	25
a	Block or horiz. strip of 4, #2771-2774		3.00	1.75	3.25 (4)	3.00	
	Booklet, Perf. 11 Horizontally on 1 or 2 sides						
775	29¢ Hank Williams	09/25/93	.60	.20		1.25	170
776	29¢ The Carter Family	09/25/93	.60	.20		1.25	170
777	29¢ Patsy Cline	09/25/93	.60	.20		1.25	170
778	29¢ Bob Wills	09/25/93	.60	.20		1.25	170
a	Booklet pane of 4, #2775-2778		2.50	*2.00*		3.00	
	National Postal Museum, Tagged, Perf. 11						
779	Independence Hall, Benjamin Franklin, Printing Press, Colonial Post Rider	07/30/93	.60	.20		1.25	38
780	Pony Express Rider, Civil War Soldier, Concord Stagecoach	07/30/93	.60	.20		1.25	38
781	Biplane, Charles Lindbergh, Railway Mail Car, 1931 Model A Ford Mail Truck	07/30/93	.60	.20		1.25	38
782	California Gold Rush Miner's Letter, Barcode and Circular Date Stamp	07/30/93	.60	.20		1.25	38
a	Block or strip of 4, #2779-2782		2.40	2.00	2.50 (4)	2.75	
c	As "a," imperf.	*3,500.00*					
	American Sign Language, Tagged, Perf. 11.5						
783	29¢ Recognizing Deafness	09/20/93	.60	.20		1.25	42
784	29¢ American Sign Language	09/20/93	.60	.20		1.25	42
a	Pair, #2783-2784		1.20	.75	2.50 (4)	2.25	
	Classic Books, Tagged, Perf. 11						
785	29¢ *Rebecca of Sunnybrook Farm*	10/23/93	.60	.20		1.25	38
786	29¢ *Little House on the Prairie*	10/23/93	.60	.20		1.25	38
787	29¢ *The Adventures of Huckleberry Finn*	10/23/93	.60	.20		1.25	38
788	29¢ *Little Women*	10/23/93	.60	.20		1.25	38
a	Block or horiz. strip of 4, #2785-2788		2.40	2.00	5.00 (4)	2.75	
b	As "a," imperf.	*2,750.00*					

Issue		Date	Un	U	PB #	FDC	Q(M)
	Holiday Celebrations: Christmas, Tagged, Perf. 11						
2789	29¢ Madonna and Child by Giovanni Battista Cima	10/21/93	.60	.20	2.75 (4)	1.25	500
	Booklet, Perf. 11.5 x 11 on 2 or 3 sides						
2790	29¢ Madonna and Child (2789)	10/21/93	.60	.20		1.25	500
a	Booklet pane of 4		2.40	*1.75*		2.50	
	Perf. 11.5						
2791	29¢ Jack-in-the-Box	10/21/93	.60	.20		1.25	250
2792	29¢ Red-Nosed Reindeer	10/21/93	.60	.20		1.25	250
2793	29¢ Snowman	10/21/93	.60	.20		1.25	250
2794	29¢ Toy Soldier	10/21/93	.60	.20		1.25	250
a	Block or strip of 4, #2791-2794		2.40	2.00	4.00 (4)	2.75	
	Booklet, Perf. 11 x 10 on 2 or 3 sides						
2795	29¢ Toy Soldier (2794)	10/21/93	.85	.20		1.25	200
2796	29¢ Snowman (2793)	10/21/93	.85	.20		1.25	200
2797	29¢ Red-Nosed Reindeer (2792)	10/21/93	.85	.20		1.25	200
2798	29¢ Jack-in-the-Box (2791)	10/21/93	.85	.20		1.25	200
a	Booklet pane, 3 each #2795-2796, 2 each #2797-2798		8.50	*4.00*		6.50	
b	Booklet pane, 3 each #2797-2798, 2 each #2795-2796		8.50	*4.00*		6.50	
c	Block of 4		3.40	1.75			
	Self-Adhesive, Die-Cut						
2799	29¢ Snowman	10/28/93	.60	.20		1.25	120
a	Coil with plate		—	3.50	6.00 (5)		
2800	29¢ Toy Soldier	10/28/93	.60	.20		1.25	120
2801	29¢ Jack-in-the-Box	10/28/93	.60	.20		1.25	120
2802	29¢ Red-Nosed Reindeer	10/28/93	.60	.20		1.25	120
a	Booklet pane, 3 each #2799-2802		7.25				
b	Block of 4		2.40				
2803	29¢ Snowman	10/28/93	.60	.20		1.25	18
a	Booklet pane of 18		11.00				
	Tagged, Perf. 11						
2804	29¢ Northern Mariana Islands	11/04/93	.60	.20	2.50 (4)	1.25	88
	Tagged, Perf. 11.2						
2805	29¢ Columbus Landing in Puerto Rico	11/19/93	.60	.20	2.75 (4)	1.25	105
2806	29¢ AIDS Awareness	12/01/93	.60	.20	2.75 (4)	2.00	100
a	Booklet version		.60	.20		2.00	250
b	Booklet pane of 5		2.75	*3.00*		4.00	

LOVE: TRUE BLUE

In 2006 the U.S. Postal Service continued its popular Love series with the issuance of the .ove: True Blue stamp. This colorful new first-class tamp depicts two azure-blue birds perched on a ranch sharing a devoted gaze. The space between heir bodies forms a heart. Small heart-shaped leaves dd a graceful touch to the supporting branch. To create this orignal design, illustrator Craig Frazier arranged paper cutouts into a omposition and then created a digital file of the artwork and applied shades of blue to the birds, setting them against a yellow background. Frazier's previous projects for the Postal Service include the 2003 Nurturing Love stamped envelope and the 2005 Child Health stamp. Previous issuances in the Love series, which began in 1973 with a stamp designed by Robert Indiana, have featured a wide variety of designs and styles including abstracts, flowers, cherubs, hearts, love letters, and the word "LOVE" itself.

	Issue	Date	Un	U	PB	#	FDC	Q(M)
	Olympic Games, Tagged, Perf. 11.2							
2807	29¢ Slalom	01/06/94	.60	.20			1.25	36
2808	29¢ Luge	01/06/94	.60	.20			1.25	36
2809	29¢ Ice Dancing	01/06/94	.60	.20			1.25	36
2810	29¢ Cross-Country Skiing	01/06/94	.60	.20			1.25	36
2811	29¢ Ice Hockey	01/06/94	.60	.20			1.25	36
a	Strip of 5, #2807-2811		3.00	2.50	6.00	(10)	3.00	
	Tagged, Perf. 11.2							
2812	29¢ Edward R. Murrow	01/21/94	.60	.20	2.75	(4)	1.25	151
	Love, Tagged, Self-Adhesive, Die-Cut							
2813	29¢ Love Sunrise	01/27/94	.60	.20			1.25	358
a	Booklet of 18 (self-adhesive)		11.00					
b	Coil with plate		—	3.75	6.75	(5)		
	Love, Perf. 10.9 x 11.1 on 2 or 3 sides							
2814	29¢ Love Stamp	02/14/94	.70	.20			1.25	830
a	Booklet pane of 10		7.00	*3.50*			6.50	
	Tagged, Perf. 11.1							
2814C	29¢ Love Stamp	06/11/94	.70	.20	3.00	(4)	1.25	300
	Perf. 11.2							
2815	52¢ Love Birds	02/14/94	1.00	.20	5.00	(4)	1.50	273
	Black Heritage, Tagged, Perf. 11.2							
2816	29¢ Dr. Allison Davis	02/01/94	.60	.20	2.50	(4)	2.00	156
	Lunar New Year, Tagged, Perf. 11.2							
2817	29¢ Year of the Dog	02/05/94	.80	.20	3.50	(4)	1.75	105
	Tagged, Perf. 11.5 x 11.2							
2818	29¢ Buffalo Soldiers	04/22/94	.60	.20	2.50	(4)	2.75	186
	Stars of the Silent Screen, Tagged, Perf. 11.2							
2819	29¢ Rudolph Valentino	04/27/94	.90	.30			1.50	19
2820	29¢ Clara Bow	04/27/94	.90	.30			1.50	19
2821	29¢ Charlie Chaplin	04/27/94	.90	.30			1.50	19
2822	29¢ Lon Chaney	04/27/94	.90	.30			1.50	19
2823	29¢ John Gilbert	04/27/94	.90	.30			1.50	19
2824	29¢ Zasu Pitts	04/27/94	.90	.30			1.50	19
2825	29¢ Harold Lloyd	04/27/94	.90	.30			1.50	19
2826	29¢ Keystone Cops	04/27/94	.90	.30			1.50	19
2827	29¢ Theda Bara	04/27/94	.90	.30			1.50	19
2828	29¢ Buster Keaton	04/27/94	.90	.30			1.50	19
a	Block of 10 #2819-2828		9.00	4.00	10.00	(10)	6.50	

	Issue	Date	Un	U	PB	#	FDC	Q(M
	Garden Flowers, Booklet, Tagged, Perf. 10.9 Vertically							
2829	29¢ Lily	04/28/94	.60	.20			1.25	16
2830	29¢ Zinnia	04/28/94	.60	.20			1.25	16
2831	29¢ Gladiola	04/28/94	.60	.20			1.25	16
2832	29¢ Marigold	04/28/94	.60	.20			1.25	16
2833	29¢ Rose	04/28/94	.60	.20			1.25	16
a	Booklet pane of 5, #2829-2833		3.00	2.25			3.25	
b	As "a," imperf.	*1,750.00*						
c	As "a," black (engr.) omitted	*300.00*						
	1994 World Cup Soccer Championships, Tagged, Perf. 11.1							
2834	29¢ Soccer Player	05/26/94	.60	.20	2.50	(4)	1.25	20
2835	40¢ Soccer Player	05/26/94	.80	.20	3.20	(4)	1.40	30
2836	50¢ Soccer Player	05/26/94	1.00	.20	4.00	(4)	1.50	26
2837	Souvenir Sheet of 3, #2834-2836	05/26/94	3.00	2.00			3.00	6
a	29¢ Soccer Player							
b	40¢ Soccer Player							
c	50¢ Soccer Player							
	World War II, 1944: Road to Victory, Miniature, Sheet, Tagged, Perf. 10.							
2838	Sheet of 10 and central label	06/06/94	12.50	6.50			7.00	12
a	29¢ Allies Retake New Guinea		1.25	.50			1.50	12
b	29¢ Bombing Raids		1.25	.50			1.50	12
c	29¢ Allies in Normandy, D-Day		1.25	.50			1.50	12
d	29¢ Airborne Units		1.25	.50			1.50	12
e	29¢ Submarines Shorten War		1.25	.50			1.50	12
f	29¢ Allies Free Rome, Paris		1.25	.50			1.50	12
g	29¢ Troops Clear Siapan Bunkers		1.25	.50			1.50	12
h	29¢ Red Ball Express		1.25	.50			1.50	12
i	29¢ Battle for Leyte Gulf		1.25	.50			1.50	12
j	29¢ Battle of the Bulge		1.25	.50			1.50	12

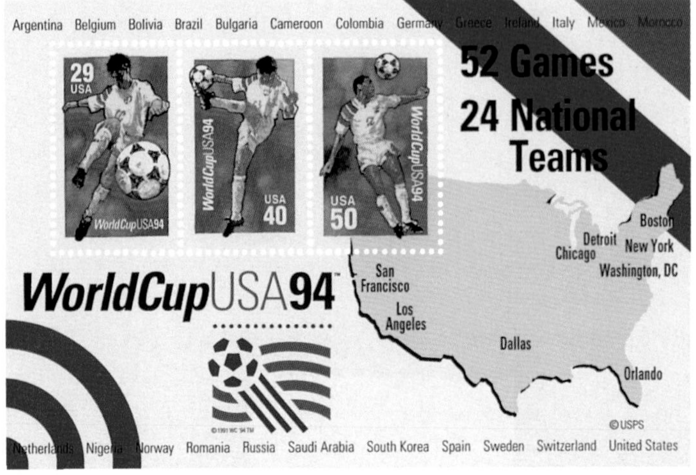

2837

2807 2808 2809 2810 2811 2811a
2812
Edward R.Murrow
2813 2814 2814C
LOVE
2815 2817
HAPPY NEW YEAR!
2816
BLACK HERITAGE
DR. ALLISON DAVIS
2818
29 USA Buffalo Soldiers
2819 2820 2821 2822 2823
RUDOLPH VALENTINO
CLARA BOW
CHARLIE CHAPLIN
LON CHANEY
JOHN GILBERT
ZASU PITTS
HAROLD LLOYD
KEYSTONE COPS
THEDA BARA
BUSTER KEATON
2824 2825 2826 2827 2828 2828a
Lily
Zinnia
Gladiola
Marigold
Rose
2829 2830 2831 2832 2833 2833a
WorldCupUSA94
2834 2835 2836
2838
a b c d e
Allied forces retake New Guinea, 1944
P-51s escort B-17s on bombing raids, 1944
Allies in Normandy, D-Day, June 6, 1944
Airborne units spearhead attacks, 1944
Submarines shorten war in Pacific, 1944
1944: Road to Victory
ASIA
U.S. Navy fliers deal mortal blow to Japanese naval aviation in Philippine Sea in June. Battle becomes known as "the Marianas Turkey Shoot."
Extent of Japanese control at end of 1944
PACIFIC
U.S. Marines and Army troops take Saipan, Tinian and Guam in fierce fighting in June, July and August.
U.S. aircraft and ship production hit wartime peak.
CANADA
UNITED STATES
WASHINGTON
President Roosevelt signs the "GI Bill of Rights," landmark legislation that will provide college and vocational training, housing and other benefits to millions of returning veterans.
Extent of German control at end of 1944
Landings in Normandy and in Southern France result in liberation of France.
Advancing GIs enter Germany in September, seizing Aachen and breaching the Siegfried Line.
Allied troops free Rome June 4.
American heavy bombers, escorted by long-range fighters, batter German industry.
MOSCOW
U.S.S.R.
Leningrad's 900-day siege ends in January.
Advancing Soviet armies drive Germans from Baltic nations, Byelorussia, Ukraine and Balkans.
CHINA
TOKYO
HONOLULU
SAIPAN
TINIAN
GUAM
PHILIPPINES
NEW GUINEA
EQUATOR
ATLANTIC
SOUTH AMERICA
OCEAN
AFRICA
INDIA
INDIAN OCEAN
Supplies flown from India to China over "the Hump" rise sharply in late 1944 as U.S.-led Allied forces regain territory in Burma.
Biggest fleet action in history, the Battle for Leyte Gulf in October, all but destroys Japanese naval power.
Note: Red areas controlled by enemy. (Several enemy bases and islands are not shown)
f g h i j
Allies free Rome, June 4; Paris, Aug. 25, 1944
U.S. troops clear Saipan bunkers, 1944
Red Ball Express speeds vital supplies, 1944
Battle for Leyte Gulf, October 23-26, 1944
Bastogne and Battle of the Bulge, Dec. 1944

839

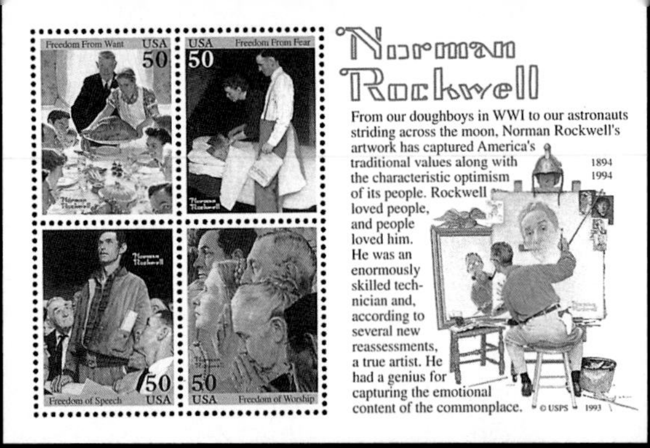

Norman Rockwell

From our doughboys in WWI to our astronauts striding across the moon, Norman Rockwell's artwork has captured America's traditional values along with the characteristic optimism of its people. Rockwell loved people, and people loved him. He was an enormously skilled technician and, according to several new reassessments, a true artist. He had a genius for capturing the emotional content of the commonplace.

a b

c d

2840

2841a

2842

848

2849

2850

2851

2852

2853

2853a

2854

2855

2856

2857

2858

2859

2860

2861

2862

2863 2864

2865 2866

2866a

2867 2868 2868a

Issue		Date	Un	U	PB #	FDC	Q(M)
	Norman Rockwell, Tagged, Perf. 10.9 x 11.1						
2839	29¢ Rockwell Self-Portrait	07/01/94	.60	.20	2.75 (4)	1.25	209
2840	Four Freedoms souvenir sheet	07/01/94	4.00	2.75		3.50	20
a	50¢ Freedom from Want		1.00	.65		1.50	20
b	50¢ Freedom from Fear		1.00	.65		1.50	20
c	50¢ Freedom of Speech		1.00	.65		1.50	20
d	50¢ Freedom of Worship		1.00	.65		1.50	20
	Space, Tagged, Perf. 11.2 x 11.1						
2841	29¢ First Moon Landing, 1969 sheet of 12	07/20/94	9.00	—		6.50	13
a	Single stamp		.75	.60		1.50	
	Space, Perf. 10.7 x 11.1						
2842	$9.95 First Moon Landing 25th Anniversary	07/20/94	20.00	12.50	82.50 (4)	17.50	101
	Locomotives, Booklet, Tagged, Perf. 11 Horizontally						
2843	29¢ Hudson's General	07/28/94	.70	.20		1.50	159
2844	29¢ McQueen's Jupiter	07/28/94	.70	.20		1.50	159
2845	29¢ Eddy's No. 242	07/28/94	.70	.20		1.50	159
2846	29¢ Ely's No. 10	07/28/94	.70	.20		1.50	159
2847	29¢ Buchanan's No. 999	07/28/94	.70	.20		1.50	159
a	Booklet pane of 5, #2843-2847		3.50	*2.00*		3.25	
	Tagged, Perf. 11.1 x 11						
2848	29¢ George Meany	08/16/94	.60	.20	2.50 (4)	1.25	151
	Legends of American Music: Popular Singers, Tagged, Perf. 10.1 x 10.2						
2849	29¢ Al Jolson	09/01/94	.75	.20		1.50	35
2850	29¢ Bing Crosby	09/01/94	.75	.20		1.50	35
2851	29¢ Ethel Waters	09/01/94	.75	.20		1.50	35
2852	29¢ Nat "King" Cole	09/01/94	.75	.20		1.50	35
2853	29¢ Ethel Merman	09/01/94	.75	.20		1.50	35
a	Vert. strip of 5, #2849-2853		3.75	2.00	7.00 (6)	4.50	
b	Pane of 20, imperf.	*4,600.00*					

Issue		Date	Un	U	PB #	FDC	Q(M)
	Legends of American Music: Jazz and Blues, Tagged, Perf. 11 x 10.8						
2854	29¢ Bessie Smith	09/17/94	.75	.20		1.25	25
2855	29¢ Muddy Waters	09/17/94	.75	.20		1.25	25
2856	29¢ Billie Holiday	09/17/94	.75	.20		1.25	25
2857	29¢ Robert Johnson	09/17/94	.75	.20		1.25	20
2858	29¢ Jimmy Rushing	09/17/94	.75	.20		1.25	20
2859	29¢ "Ma" Rainey	09/17/94	.75	.20		1.25	20
2860	29¢ Mildred Bailey	09/17/94	.75	.20		1.25	20
2861	29¢ Howlin' Wolf	09/17/94	.75	.20		1.25	20
a	Block of 9, #2854-2861 + 1 additional stamp		7.50	4.50	9.00(10)	6.00	
	Literary Arts, Tagged, Perf. 11						
2862	29¢ James Thurber	09/10/94	.60	.20	2.75 (4)	1.25	151
	Wonders of the Sea, Tagged, Perf. 11 x 10.9						
2863	29¢ Diver, Motorboat	10/03/94	.60	.20		1.25	56
2864	29¢ Diver, Ship	10/03/94	.60	.20		1.25	56
2865	29¢ Diver, Ship's Wheel	10/03/94	.60	.20		1.25	56
2866	29¢ Diver, Coral	10/03/94	.60	.20		1.25	56
a	Block of 4, #2963-2966		2.40	1.50	2.50 (4)	2.75	
b	As "a" imperf.		*1,500.00*				
	Cranes, Tagged, Perf. 10.8 x 11						
2867	29¢ Black-Necked Crane	10/09/94	.70	.20		1.25	78
2868	29¢ Whooping Crane	10/09/94	.70	.20		1.25	78
a	Pair, #2867-2868		1.40	.75	3.00 (4)	2.50	
b	Black and magenta (engr.) omitted		*1,750.00*				
c	As "a," double impression of (engr.) black & magenta		*5,000.00*				

HOLIDAY SNOWFLAKES

In 2006 the U.S. Postal Service celebrates the winter holiday season with four stamps featuring photographs of snowflakes. Falling from thousands of feet, these intricate ice crystals commonly begin as a piece of dust tumbling through the clouds. Gathering water molecules, they blossom into crystal forms in endlessly different patterns because of the constantly changing conditions of the atmosphere. Snowflakes generally take one of seven basic forms. For example, stellar, or starlike, snowflakes usually grow six primary branches that support arms, which often develop thin plates of ice at the ends. Bitter-cold conditions create crystals with more facets. The most symmetrical snowflakes occur during light snowfalls when there is cold weather and little wind.

If the air is warmer, crystals tend to stick together to form less symmetrical snowflakes, or they can take on a needlelike shape. In higher humidity, snowflakes may branch more, making them dendritic, or plantlike, in appearance. The stamps feature photographs taken by physicist Kenneth Libbrecht of two basic snowflake paterns—stellar dendrites, which form branching treelike arms, and sectored plates, which as their name suggests, form platelike arms. Because fallen snowflakes start to melt and lose their shape in mere minutes, Libbrecht quickly transferred the snowflakes from cardboard to a glass slide using a paintbrush. He then snapped the photos inside a temperature-regulated enclosure using a digital camera attached to a high-resolution microscope.

Issue		Date	Un	U	PB	#	FDC	Q(M)
	Classic Collections: Legends of the West, Tagged, Perf. 10.1 x 10							
2869	Sheet of 20	10/18/94	15.00	—			14.00	
a	29¢ Home on the Range		.75	.50			1.75	20
b	29¢ Buffalo Bill Cody		.75	.50			1.75	20
c	29¢ Jim Bridger		.75	.50			1.75	20
d	29¢ Annie Oakley		.75	.50			1.75	20
e	29¢ Native American Culture		.75	.50			1.75	20
f	29¢ Chief Joseph		.75	.50			1.75	20
g	29¢ Bill Pickett		.75	.50			1.75	20
h	29¢ Bat Masterson		.75	.50			1.75	20
i	29¢ John C. Fremont		.75	.50			1.75	20
j	29¢ Wyatt Earp		.75	.50			1.75	20
k	29¢ Nellie Cashman		.75	.50			1.75	20
l	29¢ Charles Goodnight		.75	.50			1.75	20
m	29¢ Geronimo		.75	.50			1.75	20
n	29¢ Kit Carson		.75	.50			1.75	20
o	29¢ Wild Bill Hickok		.75	.50			1.75	20
p	29¢ Western Wildlife		.75	.50			1.75	20
q	29¢ Jim Beckwourth		.75	.50			1.75	20
r	29¢ Bill Tilghman		.75	.50			1.75	20
s	29¢ Sacagawea		.75	.50			1.75	20
t	29¢ Overland Mail		.75	.50			1.75	20
2870	29¢ Sheet of 20 (recalled)	10/18/94	*225.00*	—				0.15
	Holiday Celebrations: Christmas, Tagged, Perf. 11.25							
2871	29¢ Madonna and Child by Elisabetta Sira	10/20/94	.70	.20	3.00	(4)	1.25	519
2871A	Perf. 9.8 x 10.8		.60	.20			1.25	
b	As "a," booklet pane of 10		6.25	*3.50*				50
c	Imperf., pair		*550.00*					
	Holiday Celebrations: Holiday, Perf. 11.25							
2872	29¢ Stocking	10/20/94	.60	.20	2.50	(4)	1.25	603
a	Booklet pane of 20		12.50	*3.00*				
	Booklet, Self-Adhesive, Die-Cut							
2873	29¢ Santa Claus	10/20/94	.60	.20	6.75	(5)	1.25	237
a	Booklet pane of 12		7.25					
2874	29¢ Cardinal in Snow	10/20/94	.60	.20			1.25	45
a	Booklet pane of 18		11.00					
	Bureau of Engraving and Printing, Souvenir Sheet, Tagged, Perf.11							
2875	$2.00 Sheet of 4	11/03/94	15.00	—			17.50	5
a	Single stamp		3.75	1.50				
	Lunar New Year, Tagged, Perf. 11.2 x 11.1							
2876	29¢ Year of the Boar	12/30/94	.70	.20	3.00	(4)	1.50	80
	Untagged, Perf. 11 x 10.8							
2877	(3¢) Dove Make-Up Rate	12/13/94	.20	.20	.30	(4)	1.25	
a	Imperf., pair		*150.00*					
	Perf. 10.8 x 10.9							
2878	(3¢) Dove Make-Up Rate	12/13/94	.20	.20	.30	(4)	1.25	
	Tagged, Perf. 11.2 x 11.1							
2879	(20¢) Old Glory Postcard Rate	12/13/94	.40	.20	7.00	(4)	1.25	
	Perf. 11 x 10.9							
2880	(20¢) Old Glory Postcard Rate	12/13/94	.75	.20	*10.00*	(4)	1.25	
	Perf. 11.2 x 11.1							
2881	(32¢) "G" Old Glory	12/13/94	.75	.20	*70.00*	(4)	1.25	
a	Booklet pane of 10		6.00	*3.75*			6.75	
	Perf. 11 x 10.9							
2882	(32¢) "G" Old Glory	12/13/94	.60	.20	4.00	(4)	1.25	
	Booklet, Perf. 10 x 9.9 on 2 or 3 sides							
2883	(32¢) "G" Old Glory	12/13/94	.65	.20			1.25	
a	Booklet pane of 10		6.50	*3.75*			6.75	
	Booklet, Perf. 10.9 on 2 or 3 sides							
2884	(32¢) "G" Old Glory	12/13/94	.65	.20			1.25	
a	Booklet pane of 10		6.50	*3.75*			6.75	
b	As "a," imperf.		*1,750.00*					
	Booklet, Perf. 11 x 10.9 on 2 or 3 sides							
2885	(32¢) "G" Old Glory	12/13/94	.85	.20			1.25	
a	Booklet pane of 10		8.50	*4.50*			6.75	
	Self-Adhesive, Die-Cut							
2886	(32¢) "G" Old Glory	12/13/94	.75	.20	5.50	(5)	1.25	
a	Booklet pane of 18		14.00					
b	Coil with plate		—	3.25				
2887	(32¢) "G" Old Glory	12/13/94	.75	.20			1.25	
a	Booklet pane of 18		14.00					
	Coil, Perf. 9.8 Vertically							
2888	(25¢) Old Glory First-Class Presort	12/13/94	.60	.50	4.50	(5)	1.25	
2889	(32¢) Black "G"	12/13/94	1.25	.20	11.50	(5)	1.25	
a	Imperf., pair		*300.00*					
2890	(32¢) Blue "G"	12/13/94	.65	.20	5.00	(5)	1.25	
2891	(32¢) Red "G"	12/13/94	.85	.20	5.75	(5)	1.25	
	Coil, Rouletted 9.8 Vertically							
2892	(32¢) Old Glory, red "G"	12/13/94	.75	.20	6.00	(5)	1.25	
	Coil, Untagged, Perf. 9.8 Vertically							
2893	(5¢) Old Glory, green	01/12/95	.30	.20	2.50	(5)		
	Coil, Tagged, Perf. 10.4							
2897	32¢ Flag Over Porch	05/19/95	.65	.20	4.25	(4)	1.25	
b	Imperf., vert. pair		*70.00*					
	American Scenes, Coil, Untagged, Perf. 9.8 Vertically							
2902	(5¢) Butte	03/10/95	.20	.20	1.50	(5)	1.25	
a	Imperf., pair		650.00					
	American Scenes, Coil, Untagged, Self-Adhesive, Serpentine Die-Cut 11.5 Vertically							
2902B	(5¢) Butte	06/15/96	.20	.20	1.50	(5)	1.25	550
	American Scenes, Coil, Perf. 9.8 Vertically							
2903	(5¢) Mountain, purple and multi	03/16/96	.25	.20	1.50	(5)	1.25	150
a	Tagged (error)		*4.00*	3.50	*85.00*	(5)		
2904	(5¢) Mountain, blue and multi	03/16/96	.20	.20	1.50	(5)	1.25	150
c	Imperf., pair		450.00					
	American Scenes, Coil, Self-Adhesive, Serpentine Die-Cut 11.2 Vertically							
2904A	(5¢) Mountain, purple and multi	06/15/96	.20	.20	1.75	(5)	1.25	
	American Scenes, Coil, Self-Adhesive, Serpentine Die-Cut 9.8 Vertically							
2904B	(5¢) Mountain, purple and multi	01/24/97	.20	.20	1.50	(5)	1.25	148
	American Transportation, Coil, Perf. 9.8 Vertically							
2905	(10¢) Automobile	03/10/95	.20	.20	2.40	(5)	1.25	
	American Transportation, Coil, Self-Adhesive, Serpentine Die-Cut 11.5 Vertically							
2906	(10¢) Automobile	06/15/96	.20	.20	2.50	(5)	1.25	450
2907	(10¢) Eagle and Shield	05/21/96	.35	.20	3.00	(5)	1.25	450

2869 a b c d e
f g h i j
k l m n o
p q r s t

2870g Recalled

2871

2872

2873

2874

2875

2876

2877

2878

2879

2880

2881

2882

2883

2884

2885

2886

2887

2888

2889

2890

2891

2892

2893

2897

2902

2903

2904

2905

2906

2907

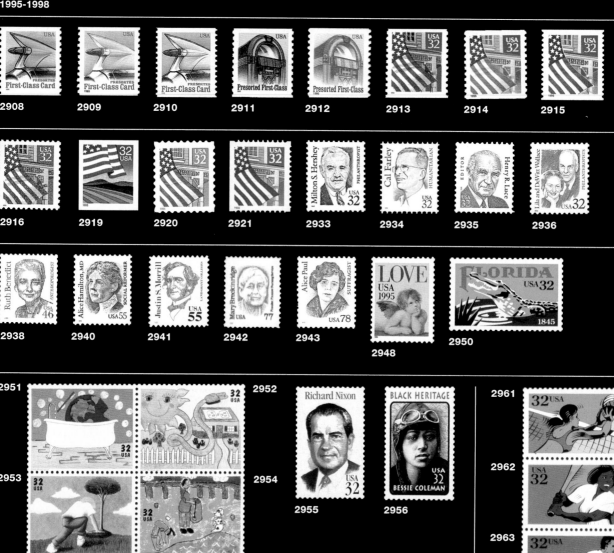

2908  2909  2910  2911  2912  2913  2914  2915

2916  2919  2920  2921  2933  2934  2935  2936

2938  2940  2941  2942  2943  2948  2950

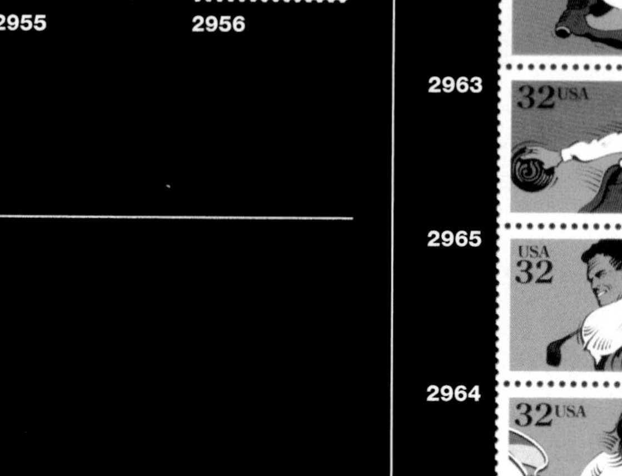

2951 2952 2953 2954 2954a 2955  2956

2961 2962 2963 2965 2964 2965a

2958 2966

Issue		Date	Un	U	PB #	FDC	Q(M)
	American Culture, Coil, Perf. 9.8 Vertically						
2908	(15¢) Auto Tail Fin, bureau printing	03/17/95	.30	.30	3.00 (5)	1.25	
2909	(15¢) Auto Tail Fin, private printing	03/17/95	.30	.30	2.75 (5)	1.25	
	American Culture, Coil, Self-Adhesive, Serpentine Die-Cut 11.5 Vertically						
2910	(15¢) Auto Tail Fin	06/15/96	.30	.30	2.90 (5)	1.25	
	American Culture, Coil, Perf. 9.8 Vertically						
2911	(25¢) Juke Box, bureau printing	03/17/95	.50	.50	4.25 (5)	1.25	
2912	(25¢) Juke Box, private printing	03/17/95	.50	.50	3.75 (5)	1.25	
	American Culture, Coil, Self-Adhesive, Serpentine Die-Cut 11.5 Vertically						
2912A	(25¢) Juke Box	06/15/96	.50	.50	4.50 (5)	1.25	550
	American Culture, Coil, Self-Adhesive, Serpentine Die-Cut 9.8 Vertically						
2912B	(25¢) Juke Box	01/24/97	.65	.50	4.00 (5)	1.25	20
	Coil, Tagged, Perf. 9.8 Vertically						
2913	32¢ Flag Over Porch	05/19/95	.65	.20	5.25 (5)	1.25	
a	Imperf., pair		35.00				
2914	32¢ Flag Over Porch	05/19/95	.65	.20	4.50 (3)	1.25	
	Coil, Self-Adhesive, Serpentine Die-Cut 8.7 Vertically						
2915	32¢ Flag Over Porch	04/18/95	1.25	.30	8.50 (5)	1.25	
	Coil, Self-Adhesive, Serpentine Die-Cut Perf. 9.8 Vertically						
2915A	32¢ Flag Over Porch	05/21/96	.65	.20	5.00 (5)	1.25	
	Coil, Self-Adhesive, Serpentine Die-Cut 11.5 Vertically						
2915B	32¢ Flag Over Porch	06/15/96	.75	*.90*	7.00 (5)	1.25	
	Coil, Self-Adhesive, Serpentine Die-Cut 10.9 Vertically						
2915C	32¢ Flag Over Porch	06/21/96	1.50	.40	17.50 (5)	2.00	
	Coil, Self-Adhesive, Serpentine Die-Cut 9.8 Vertically						
2915D	32¢ Flag Over Porch	01/24/97	1.25	*.90*	7.50 (5)	1.25	300
	Booklet, Perf. 10.8 x 9.8 on 2 or 3 adjacent sides						
2916	32¢ Flag Over Porch	05/19/95	.65	.20		1.25	
a	Booklet pane of 10		6.50	*3.25*		7.50	
b	As "a," imperf.		—				
	Booklet, Die-Cut						
2919	32¢ Flag Over Field	03/17/95	.65	.20		1.25	
a	Booklet pane of 18		12.00				
	Booklet, Self-Adhesive, Serpentine Die-Cut 8.7 on 2, 3 or 4 adjacent sides						
2920	32¢ Flag Over Porch	04/18/95	.65	.20		1.25	
a	Booklet pane of 20 + label		13.00				
b	Small date		5.50	.35			
c	As "b," booklet pane of 20 + label		*110.00*				
f	As #2920, pane of 15 + label		*10.00*				
h	As #2920, booklet pane of 15		*35.00*				
	Booklet, Self-Adhesive, Serpentine Die-Cut 11.3 on 3 sides						
2920D	32¢ Flag Over Porch	01/20/96	.70	.25			789
e	Booklet pane of 10		7.50				
	Booklet, Self-Adhesive, Serpentine Die-Cut Perf. 9.8 on 2 or 3 adjacent sides						
2921	32¢ Flag Over Porch	05/21/96	.75	.20		1.25	7,344
a	Booklet pane of 10		7.50				
b	As #2921, dated red "1997"		.75	.20			
c	As "a," dated red "1997"		7.50				
d	Booklet pane of 5 + label		7.00				
	Great Americans, Tagged, Perf. 11.2						
2933	32¢ Milton S. Hershey	09/13/95	.65	.20	3.00 (4)	1.25	
2934	32¢ Cal Farley	04/26/96	.65	.20	3.00 (4)	1.25	150
2935	32¢ Henry R. Luce	04/03/98	.65	.20	2.75 (4)	1.25	
2936	32¢ Lila and DeWitt Wallace	07/16/98	.65	.20	2.75 (4)	1.25	
2938	46¢ Ruth Benedict	10/20/95	.90	.20	4.50 (4)	1.40	
2940	55¢ Alice Hamilton, MD	07/11/95	1.10	.20	5.50 (4)	1.40	
	Tagged, Self-Adhesive, Serpentine Die-Cut 11.7 x 11.5						
2941	55¢ Justin S. Morrill	07/17/99	1.10	.20	4.40 (4)	1.40	
	Tagged, Self-Adhesive, Serpentine Die-Cut 11.7 x 11.5						
2942	77¢ Mary Breckinridge	11/09/98	1.50	.20	6.00 (4)	1.75	
	Tagged, Perf. 11.2						
2943	78¢ Alice Paul	08/18/95	1.60	.20	7.50 (4)	1.75	
a	Dull violet		1.60	.20	7.50 (4)		
b	P ale violet		1.75	.30	12.00 (4)		
	Love, Tagged, Perf. 11.2						
2948	(32¢) Love, Cherub from Sistine Madonna, by Raphael	02/01/95	.65	.20	3.00 (4)	1.50	215
	Love, Self-Adhesive, Die-Cut						
2949	(32¢) Love, Cherub from Sistine Madonna, by Raphael	02/01/95	.65	.20		1.50	1,221
a	Booklet pane of 20 + label		13.00				
b	Red (engr.) omitted		*400.00*				
c	As "a," red (engr.) omitted		*8,000.00*				
	Tagged, Perf. 11.1						
2950	32¢ Florida Statehood, 150th Anniversary	03/03/95	.65	.20	2.60 (4)	1.25	95
	Kids Care, Earth Day, Tagged, Perf. 11.1 x 11						
2951	32¢ Earth Clean-Up	04/20/95	.65	.20		1.25	13
2952	32¢ Solar Energy	04/20/95	.65	.20		1.25	13
2953	32¢ Tree Planting	04/20/95	.65	.20		1.25	13
2954	32¢ Beach Clean-Up	04/20/95	.65	.20		1.25	13
a	Block of 4, #2951-2954		2.60	1.75	2.60 (4)	2.75	
	Tagged, Perf. 11.2						
2955	32¢ Richard Nixon	04/26/95	.65	.20	3.00 (4)	1.25	80
a	Red (engr.) omitted		*1,250.00*				
	Black Heritage, Tagged, Perf. 11.2						
2956	32¢ Bessie Coleman	04/27/95	.75	.20	3.25 (4)	1.75	97
	Love, Tagged, Perf. 11.2						
2957	32¢ Love, Cherub from Sistine Madonna, by Raphael	05/12/95	.65	.20	3.00 (4)	1.25	315
2958	55¢ Love, Cherub from Sistine Madonna, by Raphael	05/12/95	1.10	.20	5.50 (4)	1.25	300
	Love, Booklet, Perf. 9.8 x 10.8						
2959	32¢ Love, Cherub from Sistine Madonna, by Raphael	05/12/95	.65	.20		1.25	
a	Booklet pane of 10		6.50	*3.25*		7.50	
	Love, Self-Adhesive, Die-Cut						
2960	55¢ Love, Cherub from Sistine Madonna, by Raphael	05/12/95	1.10	.20		1.40	
a	Booklet pane of 20 + label		22.50				
	Recreational Sports, Tagged, Perf. 11.2						
2961	32¢ Volleyball	05/20/95	.65	.20		1.50	6
2962	32¢ Softball	05/20/95	.65	.20		1.50	6
2963	32¢ Bowling	05/20/95	.65	.20		1.50	6
2964	32¢ Tennis	05/20/95	.65	.20		1.50	6
2965	32¢ Golf	05/20/95	.65	.20		1.50	6
a	Vertical strip of 5, #2961-2965		3.25	2.00	6.50(10)	3.25	
b	As "a," imperf.		*2,500.00*				
c	As "a," yellow omitted		*2,250.00*				
d	As "a," yellow, blue and magenta omitted		*2,250.00*				
	Tagged, Perf. 11.2						
2966	32¢ Prisoners of War and Missing in Action	05/29/95	.65	.20	2.40 (4)	2.00	125
	Pane of 20		12.50	—			

	Issue	Date	Un	U	PB #	FDC	Q(M)
	Legends of Hollywood, Tagged, Perf. 11.1						
2967	32¢ Marilyn Monroe	06/01/95	.85	.20	5.50 (4)	3.00	400
	pane of 20		25.00				
a	Imperf., pair		*550.00*				
	Tagged, Perf. 11.2						
2968	32¢ Texas Statehood	06/16/95	.75	.30	2.40 (4)	1.75	99
	Lighthouses, Tagged, Perf. 11.2 Vertically						
2969	32¢ Split Rock, Lake Superior	06/17/95	1.00	.30		2.00	
2970	32¢ St. Joseph, Lake Michigan	06/17/95	1.00	.30		2.00	
2971	32¢ Spectacle Reef, Lake Huron	06/17/95	1.00	.30		2.00	
2972	32¢ Marblehead, Lake Erie	06/17/95	1.00	.30		2.00	
2973	32¢ Thirty Mile Point, Lake Ontario	06/17/95	1.00	.30		2.00	
a	Booklet pane of 5, #2969-2973		5.00	*3.00*		5.00	120
	Tagged, Perf. 11.2						
2974	32¢ United Nations, 50th Anniversary	06/26/95	.65	.20	2.60 (4)	1.50	60
	Classic Collections: Civil War, Tagged, Perf. 10.1						
2975	Sheet of 20	06/29/95	30.00	—		16.00	300
a	32¢ *Monitor and Virginia*		1.25	.60		1.50	
b	32¢ Robert E. Lee		1.25	.60		1.50	
c	32¢ Clara Barton		1.25	.60		1.50	
d	32¢ Ulysses S. Grant		1.25	.60		1.50	
e	32¢ Battle of Shiloh		1.25	.60		1.50	
f	32¢ Jefferson Davis		1.25	.60		1.50	
g	32¢ David Farragut		1.25	.60		1.50	
h	32¢ Frederick Douglass		1.25	.60		1.50	
i	32¢ Raphael Semmes		1.25	.60		1.50	
j	32¢ Abraham Lincoln		1.25	.60		1.50	
k	32¢ Harriet Tubman		1.25	.60		1.50	
l	32¢ Stand Watie		1.25	.60		1.50	
m	32¢ Joseph E. Johnston		1.25	.60		1.50	
n	32¢ Winfield Hancock		1.25	.60		1.50	
o	32¢ Mary Chesnut		1.25	.60		1.50	
p	32¢ Battle of Chancellorsville		1.25	.60		1.50	
q	32¢ William T. Sherman		1.25	.60		1.50	
r	32¢ Phoebe Pember		1.25	.60		1.50	
s	32¢ “Stonewall” Jackson		1.25	.60		1.50	
t	32¢ Battle of Gettysburg		1.25	.60		1.50	

	Issue	Date	Un	U	PB #	FDC	Q(M)
	American Folk Art: Carousel Horses, Tagged, Perf. 11						
2976	32¢ Golden Horse with Roses	07/21/95	.65	.20		1.25	
2977	32¢ Black Horse with Gold Bridle	07/21/95	.65	.20		1.25	
2978	32¢ Horse with Armor	07/21/95	.65	.20		1.25	
2979	32¢ Brown Horse with Green Bridle	07/21/95	.65	.20		1.25	
a	Block of 4, #2976-2979		2.60	2.00	2.40 (4)	3.25	63
	Tagged, Perf. 11.1 x 11						
2980	32¢ Women's Suffrage	08/26/95	.65	.20	3.00 (4)	1.25	105
a	Black (engr.) omitted		*400.00*				
b	Imperf., pair		*1,500.00*				
	World War II, 1945: Victory at Last, Miniature Sheet, Tagged, Perf. 11.1						
2981	Block of 10 and central label	09/02/95	9.50	7.50		7.00	100
a	32¢ Marines Raise Flag on Iwo Jima		.95	.50		1.50	
b	32¢ Fierce Fighting Frees Manila by March 3, 1945		.95	.50		1.50	
c	32¢ Soldiers Advancing: Okinawa, the Last Big Battle		.95	.50		1.50	
d	32¢ Destroyed Bridge: U.S. and Soviets Link Up at Elbe River		.95	.50		1.50	
e	32¢ Allies Liberate Holocaust Survivors		.95	.50		1.50	
f	32¢ Germany Surrenders at Reims		.95	.50		1.50	
g	32¢ Refugees: By 1945, World War II Has Uprooted Millions		.95	.50		1.50	
h	32¢ Truman Announces Japan's Surrender		.95	.50		1.50	
i	32¢ Sailor Kissing Nurse: News of Victory Hits Home		.95	.50		1.50	
j	32¢ Hometowns Honor Their Returning Veterans		.95	.50		1.50	

2967 2968

2969 2970 2971 2972 2973 2973a

2974

2975

a b c d e

f g h i j

k l m n o

p q r s t

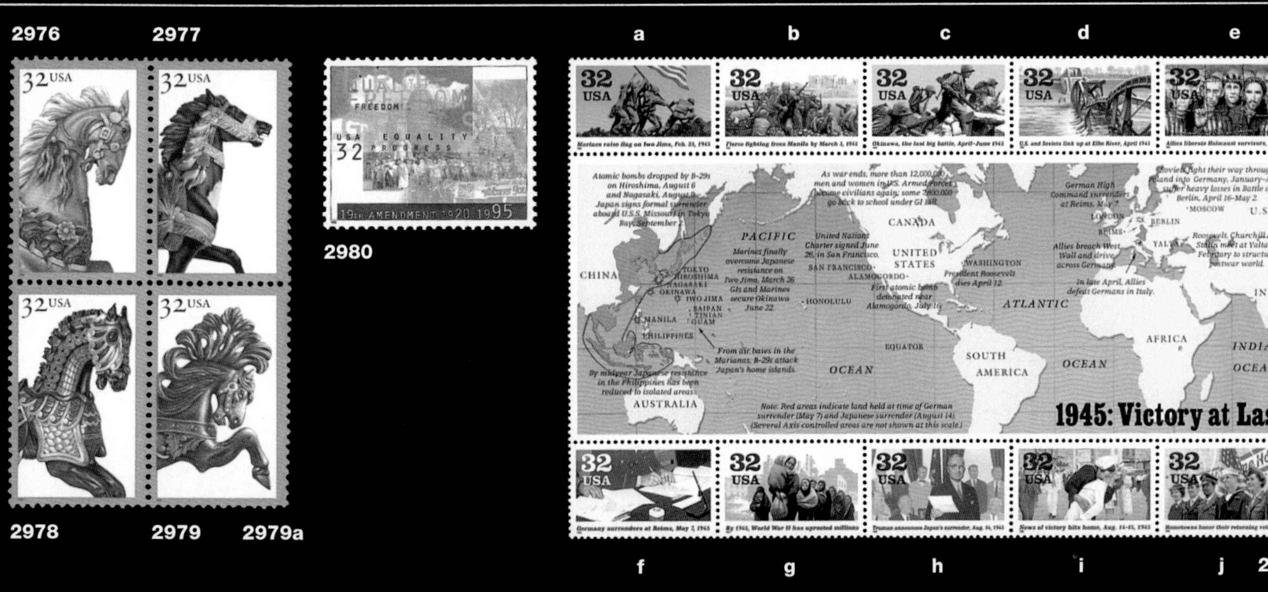

2976 2977

2978 2979 2979a

2980

a b c d e

f g h i j 2981

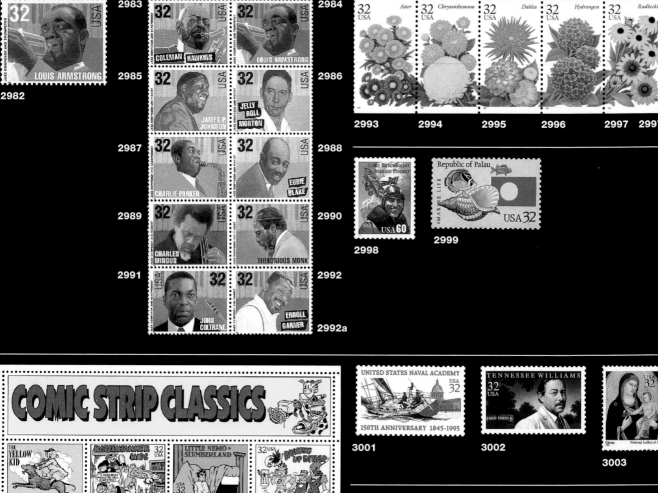

2982

2983 2984

2985 2986

2987 2988

2989 2990

2991 2992

2992a

2993 2994 2995 2996 2997 2997a

2998

2999

3000 a b c d
e f g h
i j k l
m n o p
q r s t

3001

3002

3003

3004 3005

3006 3007

3007a

	Issue	Date	Un	U	PB	#	FDC	Q(M)
	Legends of American Music: Jazz Musicians, Tagged, Perf. 11.1 x 11							
2982	32¢ Louis Armstrong, white denomination	09/01/95	.80	.20	3.20	(4)	1.75	150
2983	32¢ Coleman Hawkins	09/16/95	1.50	.20			1.50	15
2984	32¢ Louis Armstrong, black denomination	09/16/95	1.50	.20			1.50	15
2985	32¢ James P. Johnson	09/16/95	1.50	.20			1.50	15
2986	32¢ Jelly Roll Morton	09/16/95	1.50	.20			1.50	15
2987	32¢ Charlie Parker	09/16/95	1.50	.20			1.50	15
2988	32¢ Eubie Blake	09/16/95	1.50	.20			1.50	15
2989	32¢ Charles Mingus	09/16/95	1.50	.20			1.50	15
2990	32¢ Thelonious Monk	09/16/95	1.50	.20			1.50	15
2991	32¢ John Coltrane	09/16/95	1.50	.20			1.50	15
2992	32¢ Erroll Garner	09/16/95	1.50	.20			1.50	15
a	Vertical block of 10, #2983-2992		15.00	—	15.00	(10)	6.50	
	Pane of 20		30.00	—				
	Garden Flowers, Tagged, Perf. 10.9 Vertically							
2993	32¢ Aster	09/19/95	.65	.20			1.25	
2994	32¢ Chrysanthemum	09/19/95	.65	.20			1.25	
2995	32¢ Dahlia	09/19/95	.65	.20			1.25	
2996	32¢ Hydrangea	09/19/95	.65	.20			1.25	
2997	32¢ Rudbeckia	09/19/95	.65	.20			1.25	
a	Booklet pane of 5, #2993-2997		3.25	*2.25*			4.00	200
	Pioneers of Aviation, Tagged, Perf. 11.25							
2998	60¢ Eddie Rickenbacker, Aviator	09/25/95	1.40	.50	9.00	(4)	1.75	300
a	Large date, 2000		1.40	.50	9.00	(4)		
	Tagged, Perf. 11.1							
2999	32¢ Republic of Palau	09/29/95	.65	.20	3.00	(4)	1.25	85
	Classic Collections: Comic Strip Classics, Tagged, Perf. 10.1							
3000	Pane of 20	10/01/95	13.00	—			13.00	300
a	32¢ The Yellow Kid		.65	.20			2.00	
b	32¢ Katzenjammer Kids		.65	.20			2.00	
c	32¢ Little Nemo in Slumberland		.65	.20			2.00	
d	32¢ Bringing Up Father		.65	.20			2.00	
e	32¢ Krazy Kat		.65	.20			2.00	
f	32¢ Rube Goldberg's Inventions		.65	.20			2.00	

	Issue	Date	Un	U	PB	#	FDC	Q(M)
	Comic Strip Classics continued, **Tagged, Perf. 10.1**							
g	32¢ Toonerville Folks		.65	.20			2.00	
h	32¢ Gasoline Alley		.65	.20			2.00	
i	32¢ Barney Google		.65	.20			2.00	
j	32¢ Little Orphan Annie		.65	.20			2.00	
k	32¢ Popeye		.65	.20			2.00	
l	32¢ Blondie		.65	.20			2.00	
m	32¢ Dick Tracy		.65	.20			2.00	
n	32¢ Alley Oop		.65	.20			2.00	
o	32¢ Nancy		.65	.20			2.00	
p	32¢ Flash Gordon		.65	.20			2.00	
q	32¢ Li'l Abner		.65	.20			2.00	
r	32¢ Terry and the Pirates		.65	.20			2.00	
s	32¢ Prince Valiant		.65	.20			2.00	
t	32¢ Brenda Starr, Reporter		.65	.20			2.00	
	Tagged, Perf 10.9							
3001	32¢ U.S. Naval Academy, 150th Anniversary	10/10/95	.65	.20	2.60	(4)	2.00	80
	Literary Arts, Tagged, Perf 11.1							
3002	32¢ Tennessee Williams	10/13/95	.65	.20	2.60	(4)	1.25	80
	Holiday Celebrations: Christmas, Tagged, Perf. 11.2							
3003	32¢ Madonna and Child, by Giotto di Bondone	10/19/95	.65	.20	3.00	(4)	1.25	300
c	Black (engr., denom.) omitted		*225.00*					
	Booklet, Perf. 9.8 x 10.9							
3003A	32¢ Madonna and Child	10/19/95	.65	.20			1.25	
b	Booklet pane of 10		6.50	*4.00*			7.25	
	Holiday Celebrations: Holiday, Perf. 11.25							
3004	32¢ Santa Claus Entering Chimney	09/30/95	.65	.20			1.25	
3005	32¢ Child Holding Jumping Jack	09/30/95	.65	.20			1.25	
3006	32¢ Child Holding Tree	09/30/95	.65	.20			1.25	
3007	32¢ Santa Claus Working on Sled	09/30/95	.65	.20			1.25	
a	Block of 4, #3004-3007		2.60	1.25	3.00	(4)	3.25	75
b	Booklet pane of 10, 3 each #3004-3005, 2 each 3006-3007		6.50	*4.00*			7.25	
c	Booklet pane of 10, 2 each #3004-3005, 3 each 3006-3007		6.50	*4.00*			7.25	
d	As "a," imperf.		*600.00*					

BRYCE CANYON, UTAH

This international rate stamp in the Scenic American Landscapes series features a photograph of Bryce Canyon in southern Utah, where erosion has shaped the landscape into countless whimsical spires known as hoodoos. Bryce Canyon is the primary attraction at Bryce Canyon National Park, home to a colorful array of stunning geological formations. The park was recognized first as a national monument in 1923 and then, in 1924, as Utah National Park. The park, which now encompasses 35,835 acres, was given its current name in 1928. The section of Bryce Canyon that appears on the stamp is known as Bryce Amphitheater. The photograph was taken by Tom Till of Moab, Utah.

Issue		Date	Un	U	PB #	FDC	Q(M)
	Holiday Celebrations: Holiday continued, **Self-Adhesive, Serpentine Die-Cut 11.25 on 2, 3 or 4 sides**						
3008	32¢ Santa Claus Working on Sled	09/30/95	.75	.20		1.25	350
3009	32¢ Child Holding Jumping Jack	09/30/95	.75	.20		1.25	350
3010	32¢ Santa Claus Entering Chimney	09/30/95	.75	.20		1.25	350
3011	32¢ Child Holding Tree	09/30/95	.75	.20		1.25	350
a	Booklet pane of 20, 5 each #3008-3011 + label		15.00			3.25	
	Serpentine Die-Cut 11.3 x 11.6 on 2, 3 or 4 sides						
3012	32¢ Midnight Angel	10/19/95	.65	.20		1.25	
a	Booklet pane of 20 + label		13.00				
	Self-Adhesive, Die-Cut						
3013	32¢ Children Sledding	10/19/95	.65	.20		1.25	90
a	Booklet pane of 18		12.00				
	Self-Adhesive Coil, Serpentine Die-Cut 11.2 Vertically						
3014	32¢ Santa Claus Working on Sled	09/30/95	.65	.30		1.25	
3015	32¢ Child Holding Jumping Jack	09/30/95	.65	.30		1.25	
3016	32¢ Santa Claus Entering Chimney	09/30/95	.65	.30		1.25	
3017	32¢ Child Holding Tree	09/30/95	.65	.30		1.25	
a	Strip of 4, #3014-3017		2.60		8.50 (8)	2.50	
	Serpentine Die-Cut 11.6 Vertically						
3018	32¢ Midnight Angel	10/19/95	.65	.30	6.25 (5)	1.25	
	Antique Automobiles, Tagged, Perf. 10.1 x 11.1						
3019	32¢ 1893 Duryea	11/03/95	.90	.20		1.25	
3020	32¢ 1894 Haynes	11/03/95	.90	.20		1.25	
3021	32¢ 1898 Columbia	11/03/95	.90	.20		1.25	
3022	32¢ 1899 Winton	11/03/95	.90	.20		1.25	
3023	32¢ 1901 White	11/03/95	.90	.20		1.25	
a	Vertical or horizontal strip of 5, #3019-3023		4.50	2.00		3.00	30
	Tagged, Perf. 11.1						
3024	32¢ Utah Statehood	01/04/96	.75	.20	3.50 (4)	1.25	120
	Garden Flowers, Perf 10.9 Vertically						
3025	32¢ Crocus	01/19/96	.75	.20		1.25	
3026	32¢ Winter Aconite	01/19/96	.75	.20		1.25	
3027	32¢ Pansy	01/19/96	.75	.20		1.25	
3028	32¢ Snowdrop	01/19/96	.75	.20		1.25	
3029	32¢ Anemone	01/19/96	.75	.20		1.25	
a	Booklet pane of 5, #3025-3029		3.75	*2.50*		3.50	160
	Love, Tagged, Self-Adhesive, Serpentine Die-Cut 11.3 x 11.7						
3030	32¢ Love Cherub from Sistine Madonna, by Raphael	01/20/96	.65	.20		1.25	2,550
a	Booklet pane of 20 + label		13.00				
b	Booklet pane of 15 + label		10.00				
	Flora and Fauna, Untagged, Self-Adhesive, Serpentine Die-Cut 10.5						
3031	1¢ American Kestrel	11/19/99	.20	.20	.25 (4)	1.50	120
	Self-Adhesive, Serpentine Die-Cut 11.25						
3031A	1¢ American Kestrel	10/2000	.20	.20	.20 (4)		
	Perf. 11						
3032	2¢ Red-Headed Woodpecker	02/02/96	.20	.20	.25 (4)	1.25	311
3033	3¢ Eastern Bluebird	04/03/96	.20	.20	.25 (4)	1.25	317
	Tagged, Self-Adhesive, Serpentine Die-Cut 11.5 x 11.25						
3036	$1 Red Fox	08/14/98	2.00	.50	8.00 (4)	3.50	
a	Serpentine Die-Cut 11.75 x 11	2002	2.00	.50	8.00 (4)		
	Coil, Untagged, Perf. 9.75 Vertically						
3044	1¢ American Kestrel	01/20/96	.20	.20	.60 (5)	1.25	
a	Large date		.20	.20	.95 (5)		
	Coil, Untagged						
3045	2¢ Red-Headed Woodpecker	06/22/99	.20	.20	.80 (5)	1.25	100
	Booklet, Tagged, Self-Adhesive, Serpentine Die-Cut 10.4 x 10.8 on 3 sides						
3048	20¢ Blue Jay	08/02/96	.40	.20		1.25	491
a	Booklet pane of 10		4.00				
b	Booklet pane of 4		22.50				
c	Booklet pane of 6		37.50				
	Serpentine Die-Cut 11.3 x 11.7 on 2, 3 or 4 sides						
3049	32¢ Yellow Rose	10/24/96	.65	.20		1.25	2,900
a	Booklet pane of 20 and label		13.00				
b	Booklet pane of 4	12/96	2.60				
c	Booklet pane of 5	12/96	3.50				
d	Booklet pane of 6	12/96	4.00				
	Serpentine Die-Cut 11.2 on 2 or 3 sides						
3050	20¢ Ring-neck Pheasant	07/31/98	.50	.20		1.25	
a	Booklet pane of 10		5.00				
	Serpentine Die-Cut 10.5 x 11 on 3 sides						
3051	20¢ Ring-neck Pheasant	07/99	.60	.20			634
	Serpentine Die-Cut 10.5 x 11 on 3 sides						
3051A	20¢ Ring-neck Pheasant		4.50	.50			
b	Booklet pane of 5, 4 #3051, 1 #3051A turned sideways at top		7.00				
c	Booklet pane of 5, 4 #3051, 1 #3051A turned sideways at bottom		7.00				
	Serpentine Die-Cut 11.5 x 11.25 on 2, 3 or 4 sides						
3052	33¢ Coral Pink Rose	08/13/99	.90	.20		1.25	1,000
a	Booklet pane of 4		3.60				
b	Booklet pane of 5 + label		4.50				
c	Booklet pane of 6		5.50				
d	Booklet pane of 20		13.00				
	Serpentine Die-Cut 10.75 x 10.5 on 2 or 3 sides						
3052E	33¢ Coral Pink Rose	04/07/00	.65	.20		1.25	
f	Booklet pane of 20		13.00				
g	Black "33 USA" omitted		*400.00*				
	Coil, Serpentine Die-Cut 11.5 Vertically						
3053	20¢ Blue Jay	08/02/96	.50	.20	3.25 (5)	1.25	330
	Coil, Tagged, Self-Adhesive, Serpentine Die-Cut 9.75 Vertically						
3054	32¢ Yellow Rose	08/01/97	.65	.20	5.25 (5)	1.25	
a	Die-cutting omitted, pair		*90.00*				
3055	20¢ Ring-necked Pheasant	07/31/98	.40	.20	3.50 (5)	1.25	
a	Imperf., pair		*200.00*				
	Black Heritage, Tagged, Perf. 11.1						
3058	32¢ Ernest E. Just	02/01/96	.65	.20	2.60 (4)	1.75	92
	Tagged, Perf. 11.1						
3059	32¢ Smithsonian Institution	02/07/96	.65	.20	2.60 (4)	1.25	115
	Lunar New Year, Tagged, Perf. 11.1						
3060	32¢ Year of the Rat	02/08/96	.90	.20	4.25 (4)	1.50	93
a	Imperf., pair		*800.00*				
	Pioneers of Communication, Tagged, Perf. 11.1 x 11						
3061	32¢ Eadweard Muybridge	02/22/96	.65	.20		1.25	96
3062	32¢ Ottmar Mergenthaler	02/22/96	.65	.20		1.25	96
3063	32¢ Frederic E. Ives	02/22/96	.65	.20		1.25	96
3064	32¢ William Dickson	02/22/96	.65	.20		1.25	96
a	Block or strip of 4, #3061-3064		2.60	2.00	2.60 (4)	2.50	24
	Tagged, Perf. 11.1						
3065	32¢ Fulbright Scholarships	02/28/96	.75	.20	4.00 (4)	1.25	111
	Pioneers of Aviation, Tagged, Perf. 11.1						
3066	50¢ Jacqueline Cochran	03/09/96	1.00	.20	5.00 (4)	1.75	314
a	Black omitted		60.00				
	Tagged, Perf. 11.1						
3067	32¢ Marathon	04/11/96	.60	.20	2.40 (4)	2.00	209

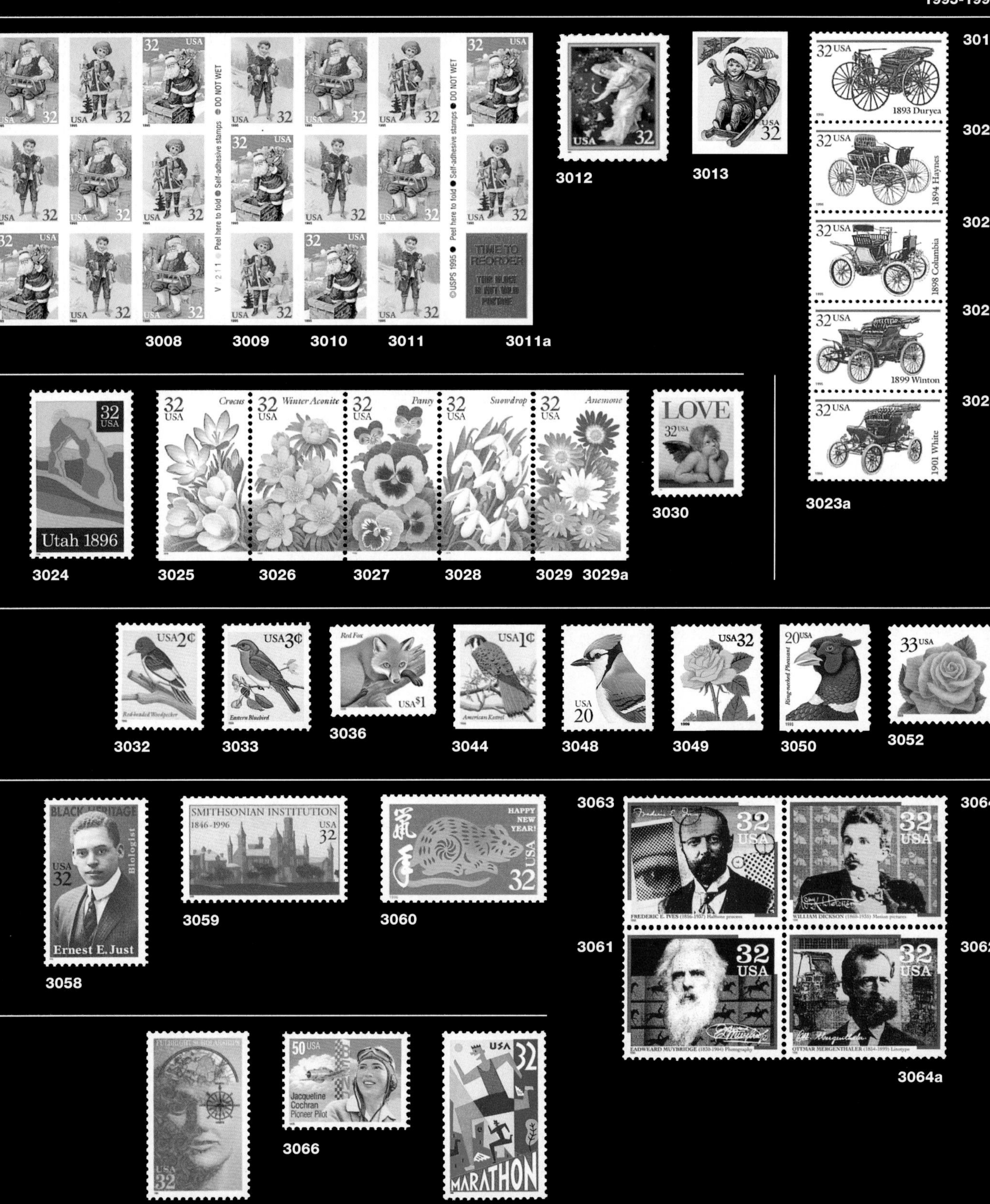

3008 3009 3010 3011 3011a 3012 3013 3019 3020 3021 3022 3023 3023a

3024 3025 3026 3027 3028 3029 3029a 3030

3032 3033 3036 3044 3048 3049 3050 3052

3058 3059 3060 3063 3064 3061 3062 3064a

3065 3066 3067

3068 a b c d e
f g h i j
k l m n o
p q r s t

3069

3070

3072 3073 3074 3075 3076 3076a

3077 3078

3079 3080 3080a

3081 3082

3083 3086

3085 3084 3086a

3087 3088

3090

	Issue	Date	Un	U	PB	#	FDC	Q(M)
	Classic Collections: Atlanta Centennial Olympic Games, Tagged, Perf. 10.1							
3068	Pane of 20	05/02/96	13.00	—			13.00	16
a	32¢ Decathlon		.65	.50			1.25	
b	32¢ Canoeing		.65	.50			1.25	
c	32¢ Women's running		.65	.50			1.25	
d	32¢ Women's diving		.65	.50			1.25	
e	32¢ Cycling		.65	.50			1.25	
f	32¢ Freestyle wrestling		.65	.50			1.25	
g	32¢ Women's gymnastic		.65	.50			1.25	
h	32¢ Women's sailboarding		.65	.50			1.25	
i	32¢ Shot put		.65	.50			1.25	
j	32¢ Women's soccer		.65	.50			1.25	
k	32¢ Beach volleyball		.65	.50			1.25	
l	32¢ Rowing		.65	.50			1.25	
m	32¢ Sprinting		.65	.50			1.25	
n	32¢ Women's swimming		.65	.50			1.25	
o	32¢ Women's softball		.65	.50			1.25	
p	32¢ Hurdles		.65	.50			1.25	
q	32¢ Swimming		.65	.50			1.25	
r	32¢ Gymnastics		.65	.50			1.25	
s	32¢ Equestrian		.65	.50			1.25	
t	32¢ Basketball		.65	.50			1.25	
	Artists, Tagged, Perf. 11.6 x 11.4							
3069	32¢ Georgia O'Keeffe	05/23/96	.85	.20	5.00	(4)	1.25	156
a	Imperf., pair		*150.00*					
	Tagged, Perf. 11.1							
3070	32¢ Tennessee Statehood	05/31/96	.65	.20	3.00	(4)	1.25	100
	Booklet, Self-Adhesive, Serpentine Die-Cut 9.9 x 10.8							
3071	32¢ Tennessee Statehood	05/31/96	.70	.30			1.25	60
a	Booklet pane of 20		14.00					
	American Indian Dances, Tagged, Perf. 11.1							
3072	32¢ Fancy Dance	06/07/96	.80	.20			1.25	
3073	32¢ Butterfly Dance	06/07/96	.80	.20			1.25	
3074	32¢ Traditional Dance	06/07/96	.80	.20			1.25	
3075	32¢ Raven Dance	06/07/96	.80	.20			1.25	
3076	32¢ Hoop Dance	06/07/96	.80	.20			1.25	
a	Strip of 5, #3072-3076		4.00	2.50	10.00	(10)	2.75	28

	Issue	Date	Un	U	PB	#	FDC	Q(M)
	Prehistoric Animals, Tagged, Perf. 11.1 x 11							
3077	32¢ Eohippus	06/08/96	.65	.20			1.50	
3078	32¢ Woolly Mammoth	06/08/96	.65	.20			1.50	
3079	32¢ Mastodon	06/08/96	.65	.20			1.50	
3080	32¢ Saber-tooth Cat	06/08/96	.65	.20			1.50	
a	Block or strip of 4, #3077-3080		2.60	2.00	2.60	(4)	2.75	22
	Pane of 20		13.00	—				
	Tagged, Perf. 11.1							
3081	32¢ Breast Cancer Awareness	06/15/96	.65	.20	2.60	(4)	1.25	96
	Pane of 20		13.00	—				
	Legends of Hollywood, Tagged, Perf. 11.1							
3082	32¢ James Dean	06/24/96	.65	.20	3.75	(4)	1.75	300
	Pane of 20		17.50	—				
a	Imperf., pair		*200.00*					
	Folks Heroes, Tagged, Perf. 11.1 x 11							
3083	32¢ Mighty Casey	07/11/96	.65	.20			1.25	
3084	32¢ Paul Bunyan	07/11/96	.65	.20			1.25	
3085	32¢ John Henry	07/11/96	.65	.20			1.25	
3086	32¢ Pecos Bill	07/11/96	.65	.20			1.25	
a	Block or strip of 4, #3083-3086		2.60	2.00	2.40	(4)	2.75	24
	Pane of 20		13.00	—				
	Centennial Olympic Games, Tagged, Perf. 11.1							
3087	32¢ Centennial Olympic Games	07/11/96	.80	.20	4.50	(4)	1.25	134
	Pane of 20		21.50	—				
3088	32¢ Iowa Statehood	08/01/96	.80	.20	3.75	(4)	1.25	103
	Booklet, Self-Adhesive, Serpentine Die-Cut 11.6 x 11.4							
3089	32¢ Iowa Statehood	08/01/96	.70	.30			1.25	60
a	Booklet pane of 20		14.00					
	Tagged, Perf. 11.2 x 11							
3090	32¢ Rural Free Delivery	08/07/96	.65	.20	2.60	(4)	1.25	134
	Pane of 20		13.00					

LADY LIBERTY AND U.S. FLAG

In 2006, the U.S. Postal Service issued a first-class definitive stamp featuring two of the most recognized symbols of the United States: the Statue of Liberty and the American flag. The statue is located on Liberty Island in New York Harbor. It was designed by French sculptor Frederic-Auguste Bartholdi, with assistance from engineer Alexandre-Gustave Eiffel (who also designed the Eiffel Tower in Paris). At the time of its dedication on October 28, 1886, the statue was the tallest structure in New York at some 305 feet. A gift from the people of France to the people of the United States in recognition of the friendship that had developed between the two nations during the American Revolution, the Statue of Liberty is a symbol of political freedom and democracy for millions of people around the world. Carl and Ann Purcell of Alexandria, Virginia, took separate photographs of the Statue of Liberty and the American flag and combined them to create the montage used as the stamp art.

No.	Issue	Date	Un	U	PB	#	FDC	Q(M)
	Riverboats, Tagged, Self-Adhesive, Serpentine Die-Cut 11 x 11.1							
3091	32¢ Robert E. Lee	08/22/96	.65	.20			1.25	160
3092	32¢ Sylvan Dell	08/22/96	.65	.20			1.25	160
3093	32¢ Far West	08/22/96	.65	.20			1.25	160
3094	32¢ Rebecca Everingham	08/22/96	.65	.20			1.25	160
3095	32¢ Bailey Gatzert	08/22/96	.65	.20			1.25	160
a	Vertical strip of 5, #3091-3095		3.25		6.50	(10)	3.50	
b	Strip of 5, #3091-3095 with special die-cutting		*80.00*	*50.00*	*160.00*	(10)	3.50	
	Legends of American Music: Big Band Leaders, Tagged, Perf. 11.1 x 11							
3096	32¢ Count Basie	09/11/96	.65	.20			1.25	92
3097	32¢ Tommy and Jimmy Dorsey	09/11/96	.65	.20			1.25	92
3098	32¢ Glenn Miller	09/11/96	.65	.20			1.25	92
3099	32¢ Benny Goodman	09/11/96	.65	.20			1.25	92
a	Block or strip of 4, #3096-3099		2.60	2.00	3.50	(4)	3.25	
	Legends of American Music: Songwriters, Tagged, Perf. 11.1 x 11							
3100	32¢ Harold Arlen	09/11/96	.70	.20			1.25	92
3101	32¢ Johnny Mercer	09/11/96	.70	.20			1.25	92
3102	32¢ Dorothy Fields	09/11/96	.70	.20			1.25	92
3103	32¢ Hoagy Carmichael	09/11/96	.70	.20			1.25	92
a	Block or strip of 4, #3100-3103		2.80	2.00	3.00	(4)	3.25	
	Literary Arts, Tagged, Perf. 11.1							
3104	23¢ F. Scott Fitzgerald	09/11/96	.55	.20	2.50	(4)	1.25	300
	Endangered Species, Tagged, Perf. 11.1 x 11							
3105	Pane of 15	10/02/96	10.50	—			7.50	15
a	32¢ Black-footed ferret		.70	.50			1.25	
b	32¢ Thick-billed parrot		.70	.50			1.25	
c	32¢ Hawaiian monk seal		.70	.50			1.25	
d	32¢ American crocodile		.70	.50			1.25	
e	32¢ Ocelot		.70	.50			1.25	
f	32¢ Schaus swallowtail butterfly		.70	.50			1.25	
g	32¢ Wyoming toad		.70	.50			1.25	
h	32¢ Brown pelican		.70	.50			1.25	
i	32¢ California condor		.70	.50			1.25	
j	32¢ Gilatrout		.70	.50			1.25	
k	32¢ San Francisco garter snake		.70	.50			1.25	
l	32¢ Woodland caribou		.70	.50			1.25	
m	32¢ Florida panther		.70	.50			1.25	
n	32¢ Piping plover		.70	.50			1.25	
o	32¢ Florida manatee		.70	.50			1.25	
	Tagged, Perf. 10.9 x 11.1							
3106	32¢ Computer Technology	10/08/96	.65	.20	3.00	(4)	1.75	94
	Holiday Celebrations: Christmas, Tagged, Perf. 11.1 x 11.2							
3107	32¢ Madonna and Child by Paolo de Matteis	10/08/96	.65	.20	3.00	(4)	1.25	848
	Holiday Celebrations: Holiday, Perf. 11.3							
3108	32¢ Family at Fireplace	10/08/96	.65	.20			1.25	226
3109	32¢ Decorating Tree	10/08/96	.65	.20			1.25	226
3110	32¢ Dreaming of Santa Claus	10/08/96	.65	.20			1.25	226
3111	32¢ Holiday Shopping	10/08/96	.65	.20			1.25	226
a	Block or strip of 4, #3108-3111		2.60	1.75	3.00	(4)	2.75	

No.	Issue	Date	Un	U	PB	#	FDC	Q(M)
	Holiday Celebrations: Christmas, Booklet, Self-Adhesive, Serpentine Die-Cut 10 on 2, 3 or 4 sides							
3112	32¢ Madonna and Child by Paolo de Matteis	10/08/96	.65	.20			1.25	848
a	Booklet pane of 20 + label		13.00					
b	Die-cutting omitted, pair		*75.00*					
	Holiday Celebrations: Holiday, Serpentine Die-Cut 11.8 x 11.5 on 2, 3 or 4 sides							
3113	32¢ Family at Fireplace	10/08/96	.65	.20			1.25	1,805
3114	32¢ Decorating Tree	10/08/96	.65	.20			1.25	1,805
3115	32¢ Dreaming of Santa Claus	10/08/96	.65	.20			1.25	1,805
3116	32¢ Holiday Shopping	10/08/96	.65	.20			1.25	1,805
a	Booklet pane, 5 ea #3113-3116		13.00				3.25	
b	Strip of 4, die-cutting omitted		*600.00*					
c	Block of 6, die-cutting omitted		*800.00*					
d	As "a," Die-cutting omitted		*2,250.00*					
	Die-Cut							
3117	32¢ Skaters	10/08/96	.65	.20			1.25	495
a	Booklet pane of 18		12.00					
	Holiday Celebrations, Tagged, Self-Adhesive, Serpentine Die-Cut 11.1							
3118	32¢ Hanukkah	10/22/96	.65	.20	2.60	(4)	1.75	104
	Cycling, Tagged, Perf. 11 x 11.1							
3119	32¢ Souvenier sheet of 2	11/01/96	2.00	2.00			4.00	
a	50¢ orange		1.00	1.00			2.00	
b	50¢ blue and green		1.00	1.00			2.00	
	Lunar New Year, Tagged, Perf. 11.2							
3120	32¢ Year of the Ox	01/05/97	.80	.20	3.20	(4)	1.50	106
	Black Heritage, Tagged, Self-Adhesive, Serpentine Die-Cut 11.4							
3121	32¢ Brig. Gen. Benjamin O. Davis Sr.	01/28/97	.65	.20	2.60	(4)	1.75	112
	Tagged, Self-Adhesive, Serpentine Die-Cut 11 on 2, 3 or 4 sides							
3122	32¢ Statue of Liberty, Type of 1994	02/01/97	.65	.20			1.25	2,855
a	Booklet panel of 20 + label		13.00					
b	Booklet pane of 4		2.60					
c	Booklet pane of 5 + label		3.50					
d	Booklet pane of 6		4.00					
	Self-Adhesive, Serpentine Die-Cut 11.5 x 11.8 on 2, 3 or 4 sides							
3122E	32¢ Statue of Liberty		1.10	.20				
f	Booklet pane of 20 + label		35.00					
g	Booklet pane of 6		7.00					
	Love, Tagged, Self-Adhesive, Serpentine Die-Cut 11.8 x 11.6 on 2, 3 or 4 sides							
3123	32¢ Love Swans	02/04/97	.65	.20			1.25	1,660
a	Booklet pane of 20 + label		13.00					
b	Die-cutting omitted, pair		*150.00*					
c	As "a," die-cutting omitted		*1,500.00*					
d	As "a," black omitted		*600.00*					
	Love, Serpentine Die-Cut 11.6 x 11.8 on 2, 3 or 4 sides							
3124	55¢ Love Swans	02/04/97	1.10	.20			1.50	814
a	Booklet pane of 20 + label		22.00					

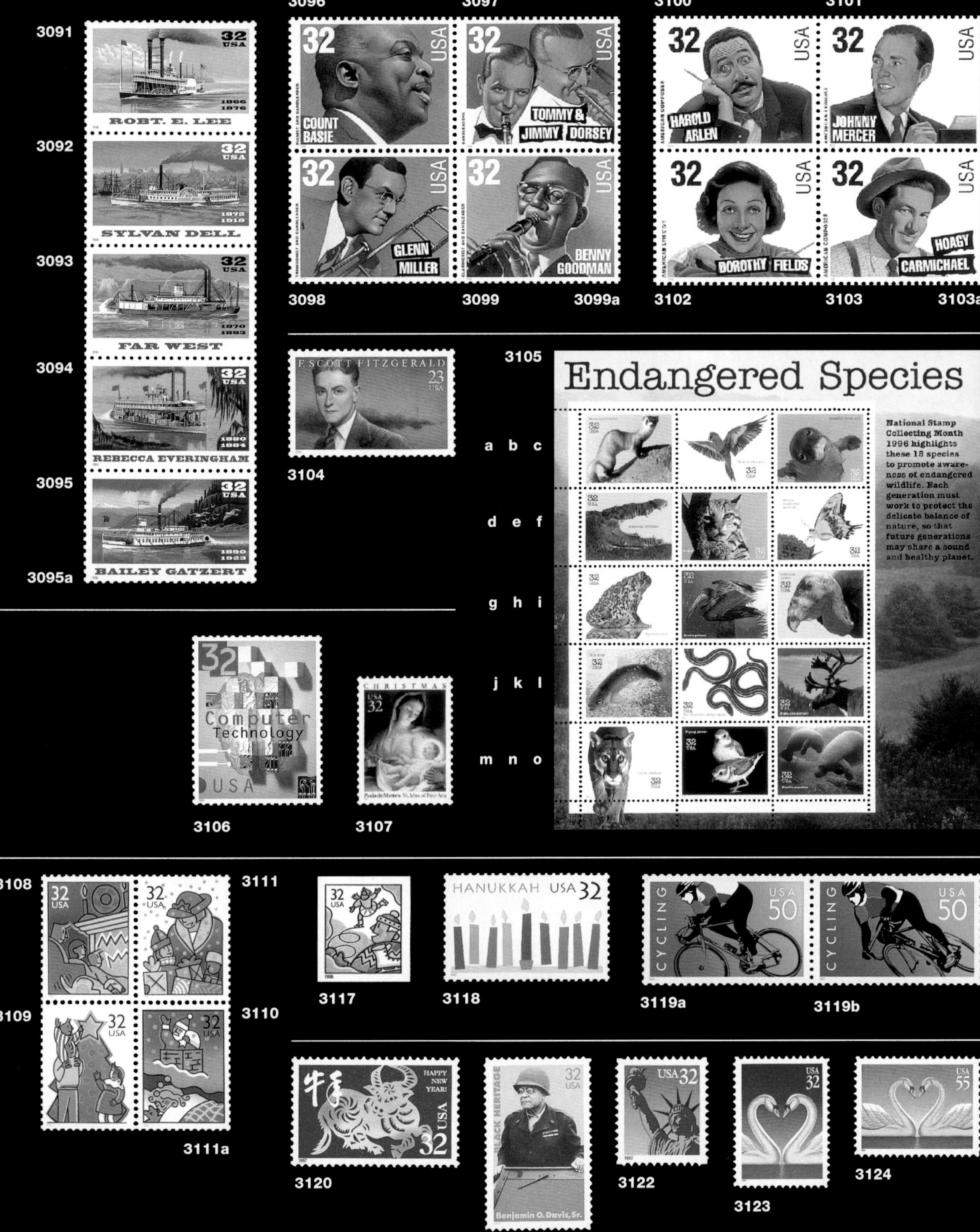

3091
32 USA
1866 1876
ROBT. E. LEE
3092
SYLVAN DELL
1872 1919
3093
FAR WEST
1870 1883
3094
REBECCA EVERINGHAM
1880 1884
3095
BAILEY GATZERT
1890 1923
3095a
3096
3097
COUNT BASIE
TOMMY & JIMMY DORSEY
GLENN MILLER
BENNY GOODMAN
3098
3099
3099a
3100
3101
HAROLD ARLEN
JOHNNY MERCER
DOROTHY FIELDS
HOAGY CARMICHAEL
3102
3103
3103a
F. SCOTT FITZGERALD
23 USA
3104
3105
Endangered Species
National Stamp Collecting Month 1996 highlights these 15 species to promote awareness of endangered wildlife. Each generation must work to protect the delicate balance of nature, so that future generations may share a sound and healthy planet.
a b c
d e f
g h i
j k l
m n o
Computer Technology
USA
3106
CHRISTMAS
3107
3108
3111
3109
3110
3111a
3117
HANUKKAH USA 32
3118
CYCLING
USA 50
3119a
3119b
HAPPY NEW YEAR!
USA 32
3120
BLACK HERITAGE
Benjamin O. Davis, Sr.
3121
USA 32
3122
3123
3124

HELPING CHILDREN LEARN
32USA

3125

3126

3127

3130

3131

3132

3133

3134

3135

3136

a	b	c	d	f	g	
			e		h	
	i	j	k	m	n	o

3137a

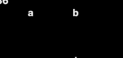

	Issue	Date	Un	U	PB #	FDC	Q(M)
	Tagged, Self-Adhesive, Serpentine Die-Cut 11.6 x 11.7						
3125	32¢ Helping Children Learn	02/18/97	.65	.20	2.60 (4)	1.25	122
	Merian Botanical Prints, Tagged, Self-Adhesive, Serpentine Die-Cut 10.9 x 10.2 on 2, 3 or 4 sides						
3126	32¢ Citron, Roth, Larvae, Pupa, Beetle	03/03/97	.65	.20		1.25	2,048
3127	32¢ Flowering Pineapple, Cockroaches	03/03/97	.65	.20		1.25	2,048
a	Booklet pane, 10 each #3126-3127 + label		13.00				
b	Pair, #3126-3127		1.30				
c	Vert. pair, die-cutting omitted		*500.00*				
	Serpentine Die-Cut 11.2 x 10.8 on 2 or 3 sides						
3128	32¢ Citron, Roth, Larvae, Pupa, Beetle	03/03/97	1.00	.20		1.25	30
b	Booklet pane, 2 each #3128-3129		6.00				
3129	32¢ Flowering Pineapple, Cockroaches	03/03/97	1.00	.20		1.25	30
b	Booklet pane of 5, 2 each #3128-3129, 1 #3129a		7.50				
c	Pair, #3128-3129		2.00				
	Pacific 97, Tagged, Perf. 11.2						
3130	32¢ Sailing Ship	03/13/97	.65	.20		1.30	130
3131	32¢ Stagecoach	03/13/97	.65	.20		1.30	130
a	Pair #3130-3131		1.30	.60	2.60 (4)	1.75	
	American Culture, Coil, Untagged, Self-Adhesive, Imperf.						
3132	25¢ Juke Box	03/14/97	1.00	.50	5.50 (5)	1.25	24
	Coil Stamps, Tagged, Serpentine Die-Cut 9.9 Vertically						
3133	32¢ Flag Over Porch	03/14/97	.85	.20	6.50 (5)	1.25	1
	Literary Arts, Tagged, Perf. 11.1						
3134	32¢ Thornton Wilder	04/17/97	.65	.20	2.60 (4)	1.25	98
	Tagged, Perf. 11.1						
3135	32¢ Raoul Wallenberg	04/24/97	.65	.20	2.60 (4)	2.00	96

	Issue	Date	Un	U	PB #	FDC	Q(M)
	The World of Dinosaurs, Tagged, Perf. 11 x 11.1						
3136	Sheet of 15	05/01/97	10.00	—		7.50	219
a	32¢ Ceratosaurus		.65	.50		1.25	
b	32¢ Camptosaurus		.65	.50		1.25	
c	32¢ Camarasaurus		.65	.50		1.25	
d	32¢ Brachiosaurus		.65	.50		1.25	
e	32¢ Goniopholis		.65	.50		1.25	
f	32¢ Stegosaurus		.65	.50		1.25	
g	32¢ Allosaurus		.65	.50		1.25	
h	32¢ Opisthias		.65	.50		1.25	
i	32¢ Edmontonia		.65	.50		1.25	
j	32¢ Einiosaurus		.65	.50		1.25	
k	32¢ Daspletosaurus		.65	.50		1.25	
l	32¢ Palaeosaniwa		.65	.50		1.25	
m	32¢ Corythosaurus		.65	.50		1.25	
n	32¢ Ornithominus		.65	.50		1.25	
o	32¢ Parasaurolophus		.65	.50		1.25	
	Looney Tunes, Tagged, Self-Adhesive, Serpentine Die-Cut 11						
3137	Bugs Bunny Pane of 10	05/22/97	6.50				265
a	32¢ single		.65	.20		2.00	
b	Booklet pane of 9		6.00				
c	Booklet pane of 1		.65				
	Die-cutting on #3137b does not extend through the backing paper.						
3138	Pane of 10	05/22/97	*140.00*				118
a	32¢ single		*2.00*				
b	Booklet pane of 9		—				
c	Booklet pane of 1, imperf.		—				
	Die-cutting on #3138b extends through the backing paper.						

3137b

	Issue	Date	Un	U	PB	#	FDC	Q(M)
	Pacific 97, Tagged, Perf. 10.5 x 10.4							
3139	Benjamin Franklin, Pane of 12	05/29/97	12.00	—			12.00	594
a	50¢ single		1.00	.50			2.00	
3140	George Washington, Pane of 12	05/30/97	14.50	—			12.00	593
a	60¢ single		1.20	.60			2.00	
	The Marshall Plan, 50th Anniversary, Tagged, Perf. 11.1							
3141	32¢ The Marshall Plan	06/04/97	.65	.20	2.60	(4)	1.25	45
	Classic Collections: Classic American Aircraft, Tagged, Perf. 10.1							
3142	Pane of 20	07/19/97	13.00	—			10.00	161
a	32¢ Mustang		.65	.50			1.25	
b	32¢ Model B		.65	.50			1.25	
c	32¢ Cub		.65	.50			1.25	
d	32¢ Vega		.65	.50			1.25	
e	32¢ Alpha		.65	.50			1.25	
f	32¢ B-10		.65	.50			1.25	
g	32¢ Corsair		.65	.50			1.25	
h	32¢ Stratojet		.65	.50			1.25	
i	32¢ Gee Bee		.65	.50			1.25	
j	32¢ Staggerwing		.65	.50			1.25	
	Classic Collections: Classic American Aircraft continued, **Tagged, Perf. 10.1**							
k	32¢ Flying Fortress		.65	.50			1.25	
l	32¢ Stearman		.65	.50			1.25	
m	32¢ Constellation		.65	.50			1.25	
n	32¢ Lightning		.65	.50			1.25	
o	32¢ Peashooter		.65	.50			1.25	
p	32¢ Tri-Motor		.65	.50			1.25	
q	32¢ DC-3		.65	.50			1.25	
r	32¢ 314 Clipper		.65	.50			1.25	
s	32¢ Jenny		.65	.50			1.25	
t	32¢ Wildcat			.50			1.25	

AMERICAN TREASURES: QUILTS OF GEE'S BEND

In 2006 the American Treasures stamp series features photographs of ten quilts created between circa 1940 and 2001 by African-American women in Gee's Bend, Alabama. Noted for their unexpected color combinations, bold patterns, and improvised designs, the quilts of Gee's Bend are also remarkable for the humble materials with which they are made. Until recently, necessity limited the quilters to fabric from everyday items such as flour sacks, old dresses, and worn-out denim and flannel work clothes. Stains, mended holes and tears, faded patches, and seams became integral parts of a quilt's design. Created for the practical purpose of keeping warm, the quilts also demonstrate ingenuity and improvisation. Having learned from their mothers, grandmothers, and other female relations the fundamental motifs and techniques for stitching pieces together, each quilter is then expected to find her own manner of expression. Gee's Bend, a community made up primarily of African Americans descended from slaves, is located southwest of Selma, on the Alabama River. For generations geography has isolated "Benders." Water surrounds the community on three sides, and only one long strip of roadway leads in from the northwest. Decades of separation have made it difficult for the residents of Gee's Bend to escape poverty, but isolation has also brought a priceless gift: the uninterrupted transmission of the quilting tradition.

3139

3140

3141

CLASSIC AMERICAN AIRCRAFT

CLASSIC COLLECTION

.32 x20 $6.40

Mustang 32USA
Model B 32USA
Cub 32USA
Vega 32USA
Alpha 32USA
B-10 32USA
Corsair 32USA
Stratojet 32USA
Gee Bee 32USA
Staggerwing 32USA
Flying Fortress 32USA
Stearman 32USA
Constellation 32USA
Lightning 32USA
Peashooter 32USA
Tri-Motor 32USA
DC-3 32USA
314 Clipper 32USA
Jenny 32USA
Wildcat 32USA

PLATE POSITION
S11111

© 1996 United States Postal Service

3142	a	b	c	d
	e	f	g	h
	i	j	k	l
	m	n	o	p
	q	r	s	t

3145 3146 3143 3144 3146a

3147 3148

3149 3150

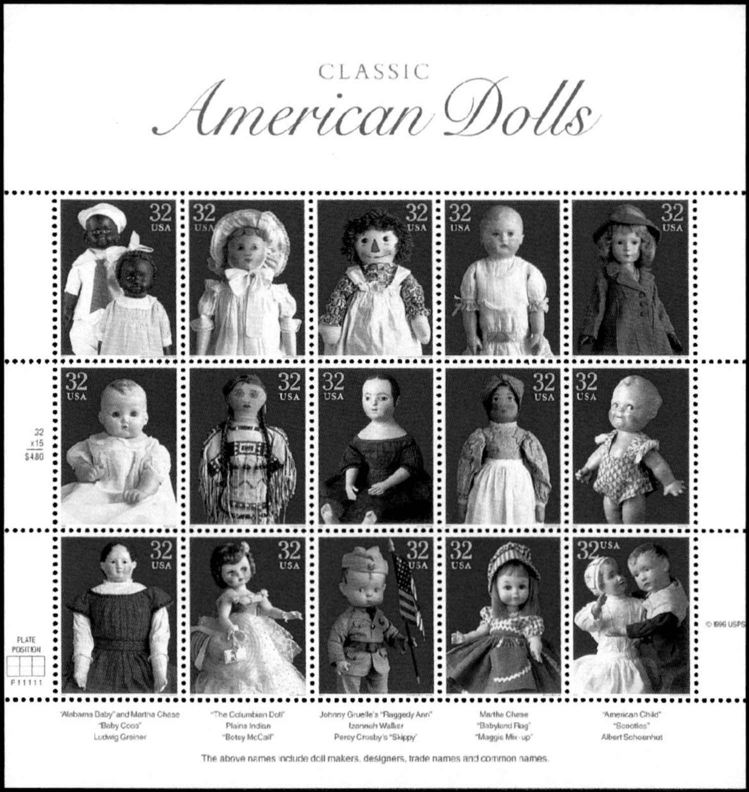

"Alabama Baby" and Martha Chase
"Baby Coos"
Ludwig Greiner

"The Columbian Doll"
Plains Indian
"Betsy McCall"

Johnny Gruelle's "Raggedy Ann"
Izannah Walker
Percy Crosby's "Skippy"

Martha Chase
"Babyland Rag"
"Maggie Mix-up"

"American Child"
"Scootles"
Albert Schoenhut

The above names include doll makers, designers, trade names and common names.

© 1996 USPS

3151 a b c d e

f g h i j

k l m n o

3152  3153

3154 3155

3156 3157 3157a

VISIT US ONLINE AT **THE POSTAL STORE**
AT **WWW.USPS.COM**
OR CALL **1-800-STAMP-24**

	Issue	Date	Un	U	PB	#	FDC	Q(M)
	Legendary Football Coaches, Tagged, Perf. 11.2							
3143	32¢ Bear Bryant	07/25/97	.65	.20			1.50	90
3144	32¢ Pop Warner	07/25/97	.65	.20			1.50	90
3145	32¢ Vince Lombardi	07/25/97	.65	.20			1.50	90
3146	32¢ George Halas	07/25/97	.65	.20			1.50	90
a	Block or strip of 4, #3143-3146		2.60	—	2.60	(4)	2.50	
	Legendary Football Coaches, Perf. 11							
3147	32¢ Vince Lombardi	08/05/97	.65	.30	3.00	(4)	1.50	20
3148	32¢ Bear Bryant	08/07/97	.65	.30	3.00	(4)	1.50	20
3149	32¢ Pop Warner	08/08/97	.65	.30	3.00	(4)	1.50	10
3150	32¢ George Halas	08/16/97	.65	.30	3.00	(4)	1.50	10
	Classic American Dolls, Tagged, Perf. 10.9 x 11.1							
3151	Pane of 15	07/28/97	13.50	—			8.00	105
a	32¢ "Alabama Baby," and doll by Martha Chase		.90	.60			1.25	
b	32¢ "Columbian Doll"		.90	.60			1.25	
c	32¢ Johnny Gruelle's "Raggedy Ann"		.90	.60			1.25	
d	32¢ Doll by Martha Chase		.90	.60			1.25	
e	32¢ "American Child"		.90	.60			1.25	
f	32¢ "Baby Coos"		.90	.60			1.25	
g	32¢ Plains Indian		.90	.60			1.25	
	Classic American Dolls continued, **Tagged, Perf. 10.9 x 11.1**							
h	32¢ Doll by Izannah Walker		.90	.60			1.25	
i	32¢ "Babyland Rag"		.90	.60			1.25	
j	32¢ "Scootles"		.90	.60			1.25	
k	32¢ Doll by Ludwig Greiner		.90	.60			1.25	
l	32¢ "Betsy McCall"		.90	.60			1.25	
m	32¢ Percy Crosby's "Skippy"		.90	.60			1.25	
n	32¢ "Maggie Mix-up"		.90	.60			1.25	
o	32¢ Dolls by Albert Schoenhut		.90	.60			1.25	
	Legends of Hollywood, Tagged, Perf. 11.1							
3152	32¢ Humphrey Bogart	07/31/97	.85	.20	3.50	(4)	1.50	195
	Tagged, Perf. 11.1							
3153	32¢ "The Stars and Stripes Forever"	08/21/97	.65	.20	3.00	(4)	1.25	323
	Legends of American Music: Opera Singers, Tagged, Perf. 11							
3154	32¢ Lily Pons	09/10/97	.65	.20			1.25	86
3155	32¢ Richard Tucker	09/10/97	.65	.20			1.25	86
3156	32¢ Lawrence Tibbett	09/10/97	.65	.20			1.25	86
3157	32¢ Rosa Ponselle	09/10/97	.65	.20			1.25	86
a	Block or strip of 4, #3154-3157		2.60	1.75	2.00	(4)	2.75	

WASHINGTON 2006
WORLD PHILATELIC EXHIBITION

For eight days beginning May 27, 2006, thousands of philatelists gathered in Washington, D.C., for Washington 2006 World Philatelic Exhibition. The U.S. Postal Service, continuing its tradition of commemorating philatelic exhibitions held in the United States, issued a souvenir sheet with reproductions of three stamps issued in 1923. These stamps depict well-known Washington sights—the Lincoln Memorial, the U.S. Capitol, and the statue "Freedom"—and appear on the sheet in their original denominations. The $1 Lincoln Memorial stamp was issued at Washington, D.C., and Springfield, Illinois, on February 12, 1923, the 114th anniversary of President Lincoln's birthday. The stamp features an engraving by Louis S. Schofield, of the Bureau of Engraving and Printing. The $2 U.S. Capitol stamp was issued at Washington, D.C., on March 20, 1923. Also engraved by Louis S. Schofield, this image is from a photograph of the East Front of the Capitol in the collection of the Bureau of Engraving and Printing. The $5 stamp was also issued at Washington, D.C., on March 20, 1923. Printed in two colors, the stamp features a John Eissler engraving of the head of "Freedom"—the magnificent statue by American sculptor Thomas Crawford that stands atop the Capitol dome. A favorite of collectors, this stamp is sometimes referred to as "America" (the word appears on the banner below the main design).

	Issue	Date	Un	U	PB	#	FDC	Q(M)
	Legends of American Music: Classical Composers & Conductors, Tagged, Perf. 11							
3158	32¢ Leopold Stokowski	09/12/97	.65	.20			1.25	3
3159	32¢ Arthur Fiedler	09/12/97	.65	.20			1.25	3
3160	32¢ George Szell	09/12/97	.65	.20			1.25	3
3161	32¢ Eugene Ormandy	09/12/97	.65	.20			1.25	3
3162	32¢ Samuel Barber	09/12/97	.65	.20			1.25	2
3163	32¢ Ferde Grofé	09/12/97	.65	.20			1.25	2
3164	32¢ Charles Ives	09/12/97	.65	.20			1.25	2
3165	32¢ Louis Moreau Gottschalk	09/12/97	.65	.20			1.25	2
a	Block of 8, #3158-3165		5.25	4.00	8.50	(8)	5.25	
	Tagged, Perf. 11.2							
3166	32¢ Padre Félix Varela	09/15/97	.65	.20	2.60	(4)	1.25	25
	Department of the Air Force, 50th Anniversary, Tagged, Perf. 11.2 x 11.1							
3167	32¢ Thunderbirds Aerial Demonstration Squadron	09/18/97	.65	.20	2.60	(4)	1.50	45
	Classic Movie Monsters, Tagged, Perf. 10.2							
3168	32¢ Lon Chaney as the Phantom of the Opera	09/30/97	.75	.20			1.50	145
3169	32¢ Bela Lugosi as Dracula	09/30/97	.75	.20			1.50	145
3170	32¢ Boris Karloff as Frankenstein's Monster	09/30/97	.75	.20			1.50	145
3171	32¢ Boris Karloff as the Mummy	09/30/97	.75	.20			1.50	145
3172	32¢ Lon Chaney, Jr. as the Wolf Man	09/30/97	.75	.20			1.50	145
a	Strip of 5, #3168-3172		3.75	2.25	7.50	(10)	3.75	
	Pane of 20		15.00	—				

Beginning with No. 3167, a hidden 3-D design can be seen on some stamps when they are viewed with a special viewer sold by the post office.

	Issue	Date	Un	U	PB	#	FDC	Q(M)
	Tagged, Self-Adhesive, Serpentine Die-Cut 11.4							
3173	32¢ First Supersonic Flight, 50th Anniversary	10/14/97	.65	.20	2.60	(4)	1.50	173
	Tagged, Perf. 11.1							
3174	32¢ Women in Military Service	10/18/97	.65	.20	2.60	(4)	1.50	37
	Holiday Celebrations, Tagged, Self-Adhesive, Serpentine Die-Cut 11							
3175	32¢ Kwanzaa	10/22/97	.65	.20	3.00	(4)	1.75	133
	Holiday Celebrations: Christmas, Booklet, Tagged, Self-Adhesive, Serpentine Die-Cut 9.9 on 2, 3 or 4 sides							
3176	32¢ Madonna and Child by Sano di Pietro	10/09/97	.65	.20			1.25	883
a	Booklet pane of 20 + label		13.00					
	Holiday Celebrations: Holiday, Booklet, Self-Adhesive, Serpentine Die-Cut 11.2 x 11.8 on 2, 3 or 4 sides							
3177	32¢ American Holly	10/30/97	.65	.20			1.25	1,621
a	Booklet pane of 20 + label		13.00					
b	Booklet pane of 4		2.60					
c	Booklet pane of 5 + label		3.25					
d	Booklet pane of 6		3.90					
	Space, Tagged, Perf. 11 x 11.1							
3178	$3 Mars Rover Sojourner	12/10/97	6.00	4.00			7.50	15
a	$3, single stamp		5.50	3.00				
	Lunar New Year, Tagged, Perf. 11.2							
3179	32¢ Year of the Tiger	01/05/98	.80	.20	3.75	(4)	1.50	51
	Tagged, Perf. 11.2							
3180	32¢ Winter Sports-Skiing	1/2/98	.65	.20	2.60	(4)	1.25	80
	Black Heritage, Tagged, Self-Adhesive, Serpentine Die-Cut 11.6 x 11.3							
3181	32¢ Madam C. J. Walker	1/28/98	.65	.20	2.60	(4)	1.75	45

OUR WEDDING

In 2006 the U.S. Postal Service introduced a new booklet of stamps designed especially for mailing wedding invitations and RSVPs. The Our Wedding booklet contains 20 one-ounce and 20 two-ounce first-class stamps. The one-ounce stamp is intended for use on the RSVP envelope often enclosed with a wedding invitation while the two-ounce stamp accommodates the heavier weight of an envelope containing a wedding invitation and the enclosures. The stamps, which were designed by artist Michael Osborne, feature an illustration of a white dove—a time-honored symbol of peace, love, and fidelity—and a heart, surrounded by calligraphic flourishes set against a lavender background (one-ounce denomination) and a light green background (two-ounce denomination). Reminiscent of a bygone era when letter writing was a form of art, the stamp design is based on Spencerian script, an elegant mid-19th century form of cursive penmanship that has grown popular again with commercial artists. To create the stamp art, Osborne consulted vintage etiquette and penmanship books that contain plates of calligraphic designs used to embellish correspondence (including love letters) during the 18th and 19th centuries.

3162 3163 3164 3165 3165a

3166 3167

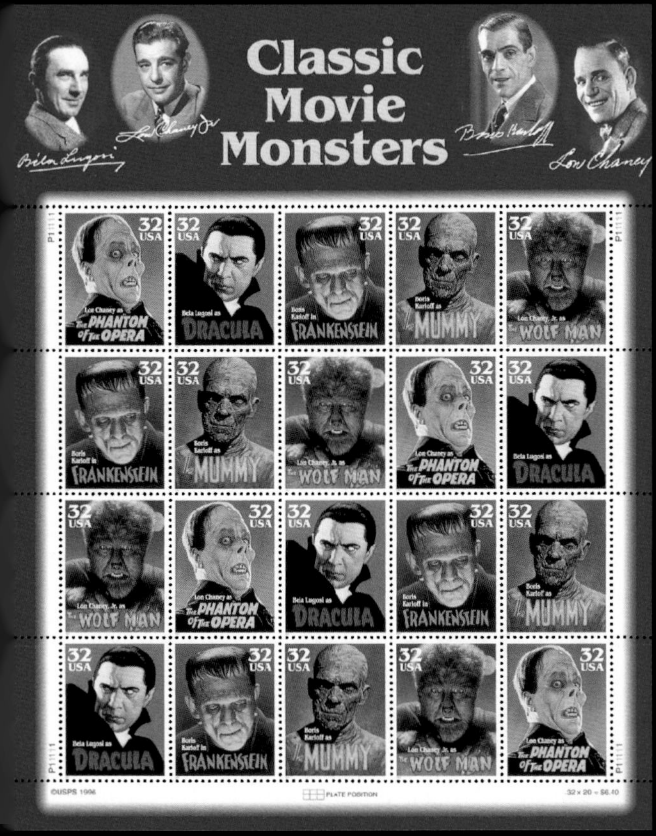

3173 3174

3175

3176

3177

3169 3170 3171 3172 3168

3179

3180  3181

3182	a	b	c	d	e
			f	g	h
				i	j
	k	l	m	n	o

3183	a	b			c
	d	e			f
	g	h	i	j	k
		l	m	n	o

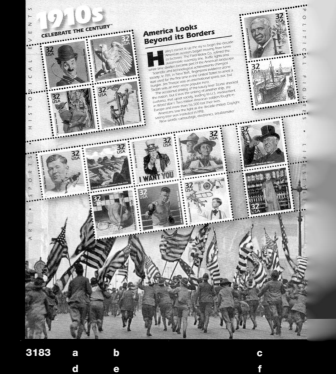

	Issue	Date	Un	U	PB #	FDC	Q(M)
	Celebrate The Century® 1900s, Tagged, Perf. 11.5						
3182	Pane of 15, 1900-1909	02/03/98	11.50	—		8.50	13
a	32¢ Model T Ford		.75	.65		1.50	
b	32¢ President Theodore Roosevelt		.75	.65		1.50	
c	32¢ Motion picture, "The Great Train Robbery"		.75	.65		1.50	
d	32¢ Crayola Crayons introduced, 1903		.75	.65		1.50	
e	32¢ St. Louis World's Fair, 1904		.75	.65		1.50	
f	32¢ Design used on Hunt's Remedy stamp (#RS56), Pure Food & Drugs Act, 1906		.75	.65		1.50	
g	32¢ Wright Brothers first flight, Kitty Hawk, 1903		.75	.65		1.50	
h	32¢ Boxing match shown in painting "Stag at Sharkey's," by George Bellows of the Ash Can School		.75	.65		1.50	
i	32¢ Immigrants arrive		.75	.65		1.50	
j	32¢ John Muir, preservationist		.75	.65		1.50	
k	32¢ "Teddy" Bear created		.75	.65		1.50	
l	32¢ W.E.B. Du Bois, social activist		.75	.65		1.50	
m	32¢ Gibson Girl		.75	.65		1.50	
n	32¢ First World Series, 1903		.75	.65		1.50	
o	32¢ Robie House, Chicago, designed by Frank Lloyd Wright		.75	.65		1.50	
	Celebrate The Century® 1910s, Tagged, Perf. 11.5						
3183	Pane of 15, 1910-1919	02/03/98	11.50	—		8.50	13
a	32¢ Charlie Chaplin as the Little Tramp		.75	.65		1.50	
b	32¢ Federal Reserve System created, 1913		.75	.65		1.50	
c	32¢ George Washington Carver		.75	.65		1.50	
d	32¢ Avant-garde art introduced at Armory Show, 1913		.75	.65		1.50	
e	32¢ First transcontinental telephone line, 1914		.75	.65		1.50	
f	32¢ Panama Canal opens, 1914		.75	.65		1.50	
g	32¢ Jim Thorpe wins decathlon at Stockholm Olympics, 1912		.75	.65		1.50	
h	32¢ Grand Canyon National Park, 1919		.75	.65		1.50	
i	32¢ U.S. enters World War I		.75	.65		1.50	
j	32¢ Boy Scouts started in 1910, Girl Scouts formed in 1912		.75	.65		1.50	
k	32¢ President Woodrow Wilson		.75	.65		1.50	
	Celebrate The Century® 1910s continued, **Tagged, Perf. 11.5**						
l	32¢ First crossword puzzle published, 1913		.75	.65		1.50	
m	32¢ Jack Dempsey wins heavyweight title, 1919		.75	.65		1.50	
n	32¢ Construction toys		.75	.65		1.50	
o	32¢ Child labor reform		.75	.65		1.50	
	Celebrate The Century® 1920s, Tagged, Perf. 11.5						
3184	Pane of 15, 1920-1929	05/28/98	11.50	—		8.50	13
a	32¢ Babe Ruth		.75	.65		1.50	
b	32¢ The Gatsby style		.75	.65		1.50	
c	32¢ Prohibition enforced		.75	.65		1.50	
d	32¢ Electric toy trains		.75	.65		1.50	
e	32¢ Nineteenth Amendment (women voting)		.75	.65		1.50	
f	32¢ Emily Post's Etiquette		.75	.65		1.50	
g	32¢ Margaret Mead, anthropologist		.75	.65		1.50	
h	32¢ Flappers do the Charleston		.75	.65		1.50	
i	32¢ Radio entertains America		.75	.65		1.50	
j	32¢ Art Deco style (Chrysler Building)		.75	.65		1.50	
k	32¢ Jazz flourishes		.75	.65		1.50	
l	32¢ Four Horsemen of Notre Dame		.75	.65		1.50	
m	32¢ Lindbergh flies the Atlantic		.75	.65		1.50	
n	32¢ American realism (*The Automat* by Edward Hopper)		.75	.65		1.50	
o	32¢ Stock Market crash, 1929		.75	.65		1.50	
	Celebrate The Century® 1930s, Tagged, Perf. 11.5						
3185	Pane of 15, 1930-1939	09/10/98	11.50	—		8.50	13
a	32¢ President Franklin D. Roosevelt		.75	.65		1.50	
b	32¢ The Empire State Building		.75	.65		1.50	
c	32¢ First Issue of Life Magazine, 1936		.75	.65		1.50	
d	32¢ First Lady Eleanor Roosevelt		.75	.65		1.50	
e	32¢ FDR's New Deal		.75	.65		1.50	
f	32¢ Superman arrives, 1938		.75	.65		1.50	
g	32¢ Household conveniences		.75	.65		1.50	
h	32¢ "Snow White and the Seven Dwarfs," 1937		.75	.65		1.50	
i	32¢ "Gone With the Wind," 1936		.75	.65		1.50	
j	32¢ Jesse Owens		.75	.65		1.50	
k	32¢ Streamline design		.75	.65		1.50	
l	32¢ Golden Gate Bridge		.75	.65		1.50	
m	32¢ America survives the Depression		.75	.65		1.50	
n	32¢ Bobby Jones wins golf Grand Slam, 1930		.75	.65		1.50	
o	32¢ The Monopoly Game		.75	.65		1.50	

Issue		Date	Un	U	PB #	FDC	Q(M)
	Celebrate The Century® 1940s, Tagged, Perf. 11.5						
3186	Pane of 15, 1940-1949	02/18/99	12.00	—		8.50	12.5
a	33¢ World War II		.80	.65		1.50	
b	33¢ Antibiotics save lives		.80	.65		1.50	
c	33¢ Jackie Robinson		.80	.65		1.50	
d	33¢ President Harry S. Truman		.80	.65		1.50	
e	33¢ Women support war effort		.80	.65		1.50	
f	33¢ TV entertains America		.80	.65		1.50	
g	33¢ Jitterbug sweeps nation		.80	.65		1.50	
h	33¢ Jackson Pollock, Abstract Expressionism		.80	.65		1.50	
i	33¢ GI Bill, 1944		.80	.65		1.50	
j	33¢ The Big Band Sound		.80	.65		1.50	
k	33¢ International style of architecture		.80	.65		1.50	
l	33¢ Postwar baby boom		.80	.65		1.50	
m	33¢ Slinky, 1945		.80	.65		1.50	
n	33¢ "A Streetcar Named Desire", 1947		.80	.65		1.50	
o	33¢ Orson Welles' "Citizen Kane"		.80	.65		1.50	
	Celebrate The Century® 1950s, Tagged, Perf. 11.5						
3187	Pane of 15, 1950-1959	05/26/99	12.00	—		8.50	12.5
a	33¢ Polio vaccine developed		.80	.65		1.50	
b	33¢ Teen fashions		.80	.65		1.50	
c	33¢ The "Shot Heard 'Round the World"		.80	.65		1.50	
d	33¢ U.S. launches satellites		.80	.65		1.50	
e	33¢ Korean War		.80	.65		1.50	
f	33¢ Desegregating public schools		.80	.65		1.50	
g	33¢ Tail fins and chrome		.80	.65		1.50	
h	33¢ Dr. Seuss' "The Cat in the Hat"		.80	.65		1.50	
i	33¢ Drive-in movies		.80	.65		1.50	
j	33¢ World Series rivals		.80	.65		1.50	
k	33¢ Rocky Marciano, undefeated boxer		.80	.65		1.50	
l	33¢ "I Love Lucy"		.80	.65		1.50	
m	33¢ Rock 'n' Roll		.80	.65		1.50	
n	33¢ Stock car racing		.80	.65		1.50	
o	33¢ Movies go 3-D		.80	.65		1.50	

Issue		Date	Un	U	PB #	FDC	Q(M)
	Celebrate The Century® 1960s, Tagged, Perf. 11.5						
3188	Pane of 15, 1960-1969	09/17/99	12.00	—		8.50	8
a	33¢ "I have a dream"		.80	.65		1.50	
b	33¢ Woodstock		.80	.65		1.50	
c	33¢ Man walks on the Moon		.80	.65		1.50	
d	33¢ Green Bay Packers		.80	.65		1.50	
e	33¢ Star Trek		.80	.65		1.50	
f	33¢ The Peace Corps		.80	.65		1.50	
g	33¢ The Vietnam War		.80	.65		1.50	
h	33¢ Ford Mustang		.80	.65		1.50	
i	33¢ Barbie Doll		.80	.65		1.50	
j	33¢ The Integrated Circuit		.80	.65		1.50	
k	33¢ Lasers		.80	.65		1.50	
l	33¢ Super Bowl I		.80	.65		1.50	
m	33¢ Peace Symbol		.80	.65		1.50	
n	33¢ Roger Maris, 61 in '61		.80	.65		1.50	
o	33¢ The Beatles						
	Celebrate The Century® 1970s, Tagged, Perf. 11.5						
3189	Pane of 15, 1970-1979	11/18/99	12.00	—		8.50	6
a	33¢ Earth Day celebrated		.80	.65		1.50	
b	33¢ TV series "All in the Family"		.80	.65		1.50	
c	33¢ "Sesame Street"		.80	.65		1.50	
d	33¢ Disco music		.80	.65		1.50	
e	33¢ Steelers win four Super Bowls		.80	.65		1.50	
f	33¢ U.S. celebrates 200th birthday		.80	.65		1.50	
g	33¢ Secretariat wins the Triple Crown		.80	.65		1.50	
h	33¢ VCRs transform entertainment		.80	.65		1.50	
i	33¢ Pioneer 10		.80	.65		1.50	
j	33¢ Women's Rights Movement		.80	.65		1.50	
k	33¢ 1970s fashions		.80	.65		1.50	
l	33¢ "Monday Night Football"		.80	.65		1.50	
m	33¢ America smiles		.80	.65		1.50	
n	33¢ Jumbo Jets		.80	.65		1.50	
o	33¢ Medical imaging		.80	.65		1.50	

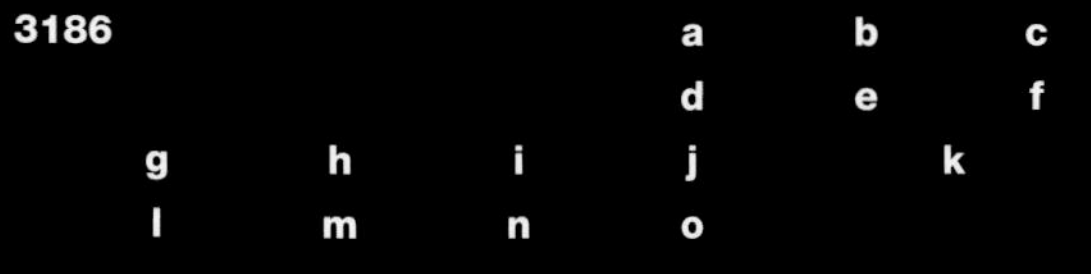

3186 a b c
d e f
g h i j k
l m n o

3187 a b c d e
f g h
i j
k l m n o

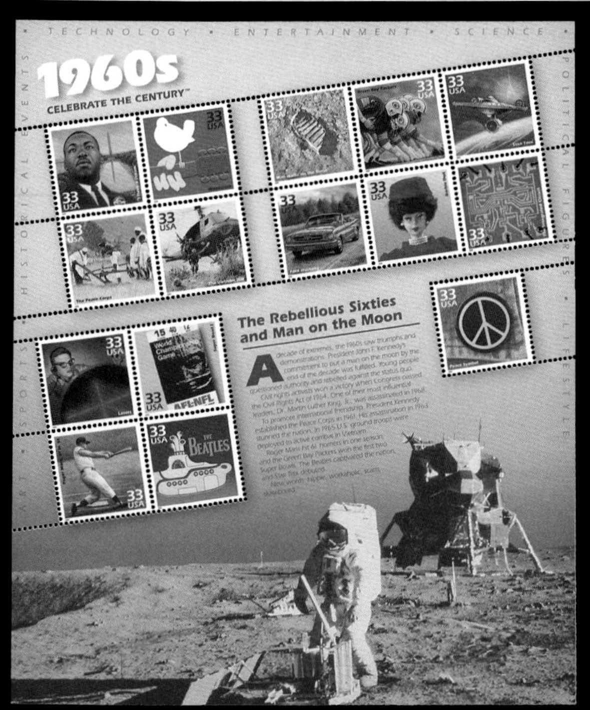

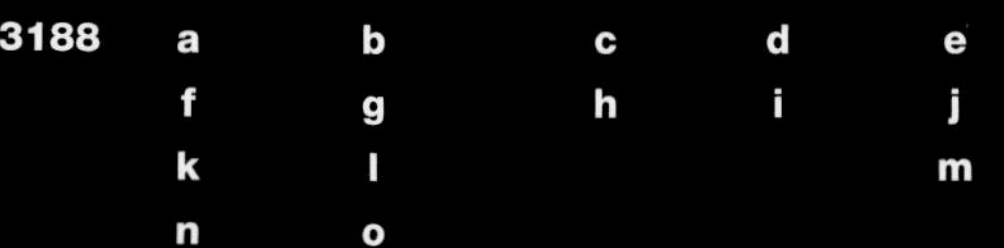

3188 a b c d e
f g h i j
k l m
n o

3189 a b c
d e f
g h i j k
l m n o

3190 a b c d e
f g h i j
k l m
n o

3191 a b c
d e f
g h i j k
l m n o

3192

3193 3194 3195 3196 3197 3197a

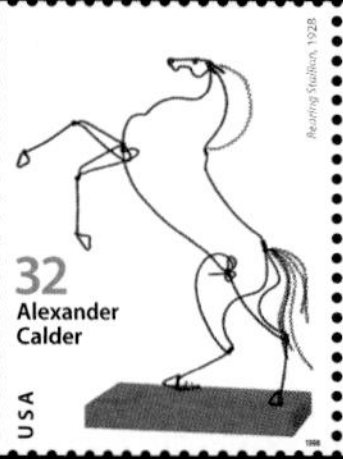

3198 3199 3200 3201 3202 3202a

3203

3204a

3206

3207A

3208A

Issue		Date	Un	U	PB	#	FDC	Q(M)
	Celebrate The Century® 1980s, Tagged, Perf. 11.5							
3190	Pane of 15, 1980-1989	01/12/00	12.00	—			8.50	6
a	33¢ Space Shuttle Program		.80	.65			1.50	
b	33¢ "Cats", Broadway show		.80	.65			1.50	
c	33¢ San Francisco 49ers		.80	.65			1.50	
d	33¢ Hostages Come Home		.80	.65			1.50	
e	33¢ Figure Skating		.80	.65			1.50	
f	33¢ Cable TV		.80	.65			1.50	
g	33¢ Vietnam Veterans Memorial		.80	.65			1.50	
h	33¢ Compact Discs		.80	.65			1.50	
i	33¢ Cabbage Patch Kids		.80	.65			1.50	
j	33¢ "The Cosby Show"		.80	.65			1.50	
k	33¢ Fall of the Berlin Wall		.80	.65			1.50	
l	33¢ Video Games		.80	.65			1.50	
m	33¢ "E.T. The Extra-Terrestrial"		.80	.65			1.50	
n	33¢ Personal Computers		.80	.65			1.50	
o	33¢ Hip-Hop Culture		.80	.65			1.50	
	Celebrate The Century® 1990s, Tagged, Perf. 11.5							
3191	Pane of 15, 1990-1999	05/02/00	12.00	—			8.50	8
a	33¢ New Baseball Records		.80	.65			1.50	
b	33¢ Gulf War		.80	.65			1.50	
c	33¢ "Seinfeld", television series		.80	.65			1.50	
d	33¢ Extreme Sports		.80	.65			1.50	
e	33¢ Improving Education		.80	.65			1.50	
f	33¢ Computer Art and Graphics		.80	.65			1.50	
g	33¢ Recovering Species		.80	.65			1.50	
h	33¢ Return to Space		.80	.65			1.50	
i	33¢ Special Olympics		.80	.65			1.50	
j	33¢ Virtual Reality		.80	.65			1.50	
k	33¢ "Jurassic Park"		.80	.65			1.50	
l	33¢ "Titanic"		.80	.65			1.50	
m	33¢ Sport Utility Vehicles		.80	.65			1.50	
n	33¢ World Wide Web		.80	.65			1.50	
o	33¢ Cellular Phones		.80	.65			1.50	

Issue		Date	Un	U	PB	#	FDC	Q(M)
	Tagged, Perf. 11.2 x 11							
3192	32¢ "Remember the Maine" Spanish-American War	02/15/98	.65	.20	2.60	(4)	1.75	30
	Flowering Trees, Tagged, Die-Cut, Perf. 11.3							
3193	32¢ Southern Magnolia	03/19/98	.65	.20			1.50	
3194	32¢ Blue Paloverde	03/19/98	.65	.20			1.50	
3195	32¢ Yellow Poplar	03/19/98	.65	.20			1.50	
3196	32¢ Prairie Crab Apple	03/19/98	.65	.20			1.50	
3197	32¢ Pacific Dogwood	03/19/98	.65	.20			1.50	
a	Strip of 5, #3193-3197	03/19/98	3.25		6.50	(10)	3.75	250
	Artists, Alexander Calder, Tagged, Perf. 10.2							
3198	32¢ Black Cascade	03/25/98	.65	.20			1.50	
3199	32¢ Untitled	03/25/98	.65	.20			1.50	
3200	32¢ Rearing Stallion	03/25/98	.65	.20			1.50	
3201	32¢ Portrait of a Young Man	03/25/98	.65	.20			1.50	
3202	32¢ Un Effet du Japonais	03/25/98	.65	.20			1.50	
a	Strip of 5, #3198-3202	03/25/98	3.25	2.25	6.50	(10)	3.75	80
	Holiday Celebrations, Tagged, Self-Adhesive, Serpentine Die-Cut 11.7 x 10.9							
3203	32¢ Cinco de Mayo	04/16/98	.65	.20	2.60	(4)	1.25	85
	Looney Tunes, Tagged, Self-Adhesive, Serpentine Die-Cut 11.1							
3204	Sylvester & Tweety Pane of 10	04/27/98	6.50					39
a	32¢ single		.65	.20			1.25	
b	Booklet pane of 9, #3204a		6.00					
c	Booklet pane of 1, #3204a		.65					
	Tagged, Self-Adhesive, Serpentine Die-Cut 10.8 x 10.9							
3206	32¢ Wisconsin Statehood	05/29/98	.65	.30	2.60	(4)	1.25	32
	American Scenes, Coil, Untagged, Perf. 10 Vertically							
3207	5¢ Wetlands (Nonprofit)	06/05/98	.20	.20	1.50	(5)	1.25	
	Coil, Self-Adhesive, Serpentine Die-Cut 9.8 Vertically							
3207A	5¢ Wetlands (Nonprofit)	12/04/98	.20	.20	1.50	(5)	1.25	650
	American Culture, Coil, Perf. 10 Vertically							
3208	25¢ Diner	06/05/98	.50	.50	3.75	(5)	1.25	400
	American Culture, Coil, Self-Adhesive, Serpentine Die-Cut 9.8 Vertically							
3208A	25¢ Diner	09/30/98	.50	.50	4.00	(5)	1.25	

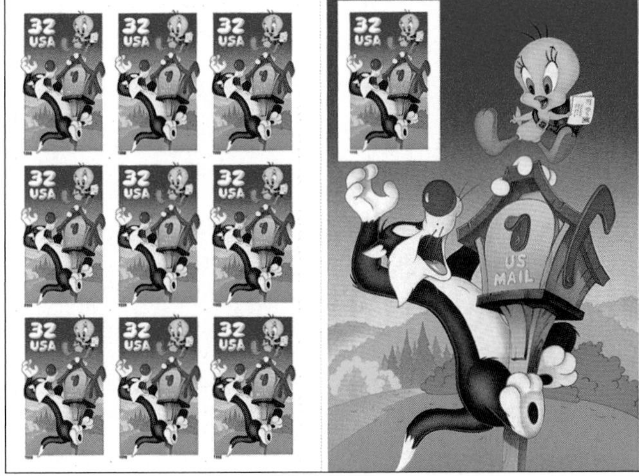

3204

	Issue	Date	Un	U	PB #	FDC	Q(M)
	1898 Trans-Mississippi Reissue, Tagged, Perf. 12 x 12.4						
3209	Pane of 9	06/18/98	9.00	5.00		6.50	2
a	1¢ Marquette on the Mississippi		.20	.20		1.50	
b	2¢ Mississippi River Bridge		.20	.20		1.50	
c	4¢ Indian Hunting Buffalo		.20	.20		1.50	
d	5¢ Fremont on the Rocky Mountains		.20	.20		1.50	
e	8¢ Troops Guarding Train		.20	.20		1.50	
f	10¢ Hardships of Emigration		.20	.20		1.50	
g	50¢ Western Mining Prospector		1.25	.60		2.00	
h	$1 Western Cattle in Storm		2.25	1.25		2.50	
i	$2 Farm in the West		4.25	2.50		4.50	
3210	Pane of 9 #3209h, single	06/18/98	18.00	—		15.00	2
	Tagged, Perf. 11.2						
3211	32¢ Berlin Airlift	06/26/98	.65	.20	2.60 (4)	1.25	30
	Legends of American Music: Folk Musicians, Tagged, Perf. 10.1 x 10.2						
3212	32¢ Huddle "Leadbelly" Ledbetter	06/26/98	.65	.20		1.25	
3213	32¢ Woody Guthrie	06/26/98	.65	.20		1.25	
3214	32¢ Sonny Terry	06/26/98	.65	.20		1.25	
3215	32¢ Josh White	6/26/98	.65	.20		1.25	
a	Block or strip of 4, #3212-3215	06/26/98	2.60	2.00	2.60 (4)	3.25	45
	Legends of American Music: Gospel Singers, Tagged, Perf. 10.1 x 10.3						
3216	32¢ Mahalia Jackson	07/15/98	.65	.20		1.25	
3217	32¢ Roberta Martin	07/15/98	.65	.20		1.25	
3218	32¢ Clara Ward	07/15/98	.65	.20		1.25	
3219	32¢ Sister Rosetta Tharpe	07/15/98	.65	.20		1.25	
a	Block or strip of 4, #3216-3219	07/15/98	2.60	2.00	3.50 (4)	3.25	45
	Tagged, Perf. 11.2						
3220	32¢ Spanish Settlement of the Southwest	07/11/98	.65	.20	2.60 (4)	1.25	4
	Literary Arts, Tagged, Perf. 11.2						
3221	32¢ Stephen Vincent Benét	07/22/98	.65	.20	2.60 (4)	1.25	3
	Tropical Birds, Tagged, Perf. 11.2						
3222	32¢ Antillean Euphonia	07/29/98	.65	.20		1.25	
3223	32¢ Green-throated Carib	07/29/98	.65	.20		1.25	
3224	32¢ Crested Honeycreeper	07/29/98	.65	.20		1.25	
3225	32¢ Cardinal Honeyeater	07/29/98	.65	.20		1.25	
a	Block of 4, #3222-3225		2.60	2.00	2.60 (4)	3.00	7
	Legends of Hollywood, Tagged, Perf. 11.1						
3226	32¢ Alfred Hitchcock	08/03/98	.75	.20	4.25 (4)	1.50	6
	Tagged, Self-Adhesive, Serpentine Die-Cut 11.7						
3227	32¢ Organ & Tissue Donation	08/05/98	.65	.20	2.60 (4)	1.25	5
	American Transportation, Coil, Untagged, Self-Adhesive, Serpentine Die-Cut 9.8 Vertically						
3228	(10¢) Green Bicycle	08/14/98	.20	.20	2.75 (5)	1.25	
	American Transportation, Coil, Untagged, Perf. 9.9 Vertically						
3229	(10¢) Green Bicycle	08/14/98	.20	.20	2.50 (5)	1.25	
	Bright Eyes, Tagged, Self-Adhesive, Serpentine Die-Cut 9.9						
3230	32¢ Dog	08/20/98	.75	.20		1.50	
3231	32¢ Goldfish	08/20/98	.75	.20		1.50	
3232	32¢ Cat	08/20/98	.75	.20		1.50	
3233	32¢ Parakeet	08/20/98	.75	.20		1.50	
3234	32¢ Hamster	08/20/98	.75	.20		1.50	
a	Strip of 5, #3230-3234		3.75		7.50 (8)	3.25	18

DC COMICS SUPER HEROES

With these 20 colorful stamps, the U.S. Postal Service salutes several stars from the world of DC Comics. Ever since Superman was introduced to readers in 1938, super heroes have been nearly synonymous with the comic book medium. Their fantastic adventures provide an escape from the everyday while simultaneously encouraging readers to feel that individuals can make a difference. Comic books aren't simply "kid stuff"—adults have always been among their readers, and the form has attracted its share of serious artists and writers. And super heroes have responded to social and political issues from the start, fighting corporate greed and political corruption during the Depression, for example, and then becoming patriotic defenders of national interests during World War II. Half of the stamps on the DC Comics Super Heroes pane show portraits of characters; the others show covers of individual comic books devoted to their exploits.

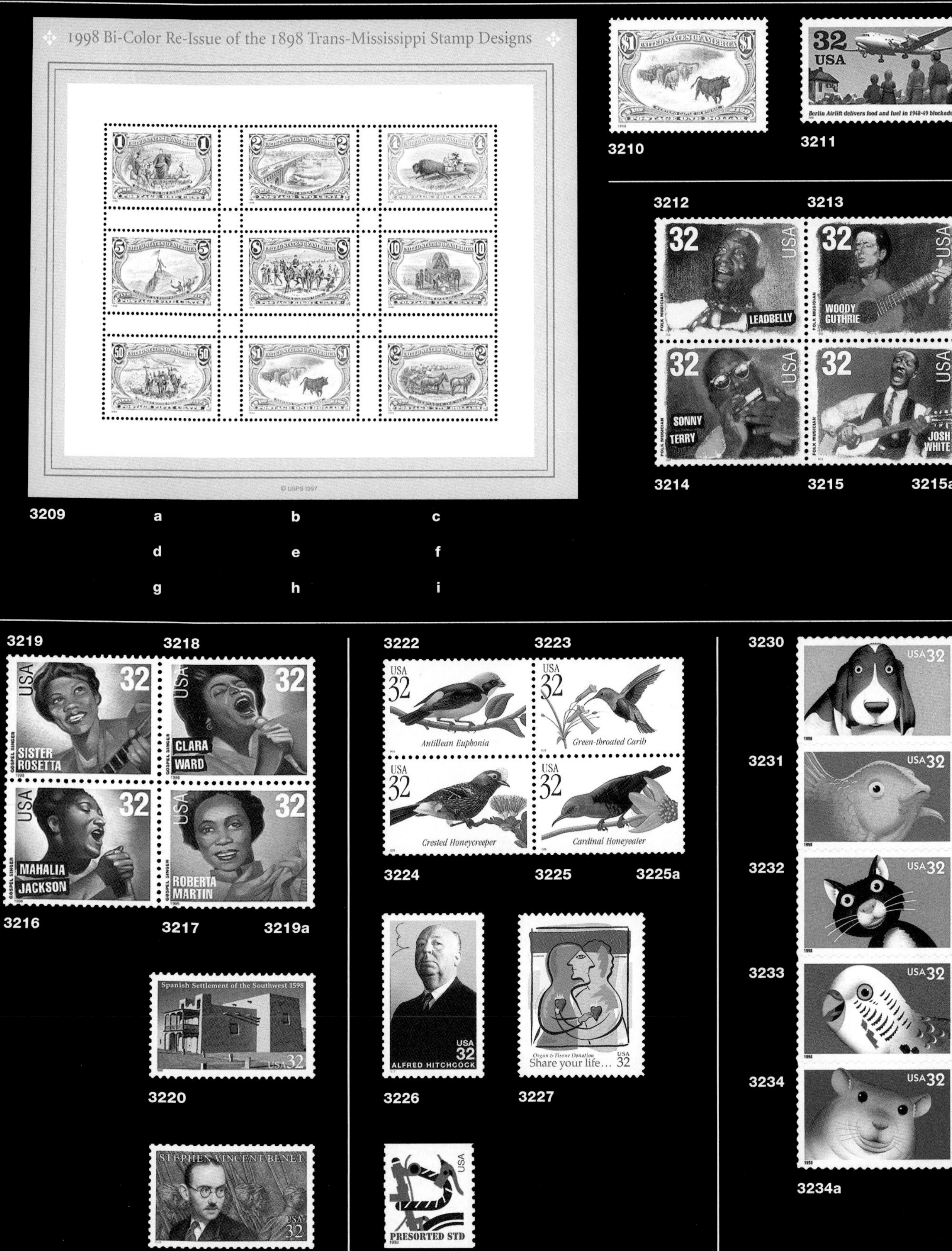

3209 a b c d e f g h i

3210

3211

3212 3213 3214 3215 3215a

3219 3218 3216 3217 3219a

3222 3223 3224 3225 3225a

3220

3226

3227

3221

3228

3230 3231 3232 3233 3234 3234a

KLONDIKE GOLD RUSH 1898
USA 32
3235
3236
FOUR CENTURIES OF
American Art
a b c d e
f g h i j
k l m n o
p q r s t
32 USA
BALLET
3237
3238
3239
3240
3241
3242
3242a
GIVING & SHARING An American Tradition
32 USA
3243
CHRISTMAS
32 USA
Florentine, 15th C.
National Gallery
3244
3245
GREETINGS
32 USA
GREETINGS
32 USA
3246
The "H" Rate make-up stamp
USA
3258
USA 22
3259
USA H
First-Class Rate
3260

	Issue	Date	Un	U	PB	#	FDC	Q(M)
	Tagged, Perf. 11.1							
235	32¢ Klondike Gold Rush	08/21/98	.65	.20	2.60	(4)	1.50	28
	Classic Collections: Four Centuries of American Art, Tagged, Perf. 10.2							
236	Pane of 20	08/27/98	15.00	—			9.00	4
a	32¢ "Portrait of Richard Mather," by John Foster		.75	.60			1.25	
b	32¢ "Mrs. Elizabeth Freake and Baby Mary," by The Freake Limner		.75	.60			1.25	
c	32¢ "Girl in Red Dress with Cat and Dog," by Ammi Phillips		.75	.60			1.25	
d	32¢ "Rubens Peale with a Geranium," by Rembrandt Peale		.75	.60			1.25	
e	32¢ "Long-billed Curlew, Numenius Longrostris," by John James Audubon		.75	.60			1.25	
f	32¢ "Boatmen on the Missouri," by George Caleb Bingham		.75	.60			1.25	
g	32¢ "Kindred Spirits," by Asher B. Durand		.75	.60			1.25	
h	32¢ "The Westwood Children," by Joshua Johnson		.75	.60			1.25	
i	32¢ "Music and Literature," by William Harnett		.75	.60			1.25	
j	32¢ "The Fog Warning," by Winslow Homer		.75	.60			1.25	
k	32¢ "The White Cloud, Head Chief of the Iowas," by George Catlin		.75	.60			1.25	
l	32¢ "Cliffs of Green River," by Thomas Moran		.75	.60			1.25	
m	32¢ "The Last of the Buffalo," by Alfred Bierstadt		.75	.60			1.25	
n	32¢ "Niagara," by Frederic Edwin Church		.75	.60			1.25	
o	32¢ "Breakfast in Bed," by Mary Cassatt		.75	.60			1.25	
p	32¢ "Nighthawks," by Edward Hopper		.75	.60			1.25	
q	32¢ "American Gothic," by Grant Wood		.75	.60			1.25	
r	32¢ "Two Against the White," by Charles Sheeler		.75	.60			1.25	
s	32¢ "Mahoning," by Franz Kline		.75	.60			1.25	
t	32¢ "No. 12" by Mark Rothko		.75	.60			1.25	
	Tagged, Perf. 10.9 x 11.1							
3237	32¢ Ballet	09/16/98	.65	.20	2.60	(4)	1.25	131
	Space, Tagged, Perf. 11.1							
3238	32¢ Space Discovery	10/01/98	.65	.20			1.25	
3239	32¢ Space Discovery	10/01/98	.65	.20			1.25	
3240	32¢ Space Discovery	10/01/98	.65	.20			1.25	
3241	32¢ Space Discovery	10/01/98	.65	.20			1.25	
3242	32¢ Space Discovery	10/01/98	.65	.20			1.25	
a	Strip of 5, #3238-3242		3.25	2.25	6.50	(10)	3.75	185
	Tagged, Self-Adhesive, Serpentine Die-Cut 11.1							
3243	32¢ Philanthropy, Giving and Sharing	10/07/98	.65	.20	2.60	(4)	1.25	50
	Holiday Celebrations: Christmas, Booklet, Self-Adhesive, Serpentine Die-Cut 10.1 x 9.9 on 2, 3 or 4 sides							
3244	32¢ The Madonna and Child by Hans Memling	10/15/98	.65	.20			1.25	925
a	Booklet pane of 20 + label		13.00					
	Holiday Celebrations: Holiday, Booklet, Self-Adhesive, Serpentine Die-Cut 11.3 x 11.7 on 2 or 3 sides							
3245	32¢ Evergreen Wreath	10/15/98	4.50	.20			1.25	
3246	32¢ Victorian Wreath	10/15/98	4.50	.20			1.25	
3247	32¢ Chili Pepper Wreath	10/15/98	4.50	.20			1.25	
3248	32¢ Tropical Wreath	10/15/98	4.50	.20			1.25	
a	Booklet pane of 4, #3245-3248		20.00				3.25	117
b	Booklet pane of 5, #3245, #3246, 3248, 2 #3247 and label		25.00					
c	Booklet pane of 6, #3247-3248, 2 each #3245-3246		30.00					
	Serpentine Die-Cut 11.4 x 11.5 on 2, 3 or 4 sides							
3249	32¢ Evergreen Wreath	10/15/98	1.00	.20			1.25	248
3250	32¢ Victorian Wreath	10/15/98	1.00	.20			1.25	248
3251	32¢ Chili Pepper Wreath	10/15/98	1.00	.20			1.25	248
3252	32¢ Tropical Wreath	10/15/98	1.00	.20			1.25	248
a	Serpentine die-cut 11.7 x 11.6 on 2, 3, or 4 sides		1.00	.20				
b	Block of 4, #3249-3252		4.00		4.50	(4)	3.00	
c	Booklet pane, 5 each #3249-3252		20.00					
	Untagged, Perf. 11.2							
3257	(1¢) Make-Up Rate Weathervane	11/09/98	.20	.20	.25	(4)	1.25	
a	Black omitted		150.00					
3258	(1¢) Make-Up Rate Weathervane	11/09/98	.20	.20	.25	(4)	1.25	
	#3257 is 18mm high, has thin letters, white USA, and black 1998. #3258 is 17mm high, has thick letters, pale blue USA, and blue 1998.							
	Tagged, Self-Adhesive, Serpentine Die-Cut 10.8							
3259	22¢ Uncle Sam	11/09/98	.45	.20	2.50	(4)	1.25	
a	Die-cut 10.8 x 10.5		2.50	.25				
	Perf. 11.2							
3260	(33¢) H-Series	11/09/98	.65	.20	2.60	(4)	1.25	

	Issue	Date	Un	U	PB #	FDC	Q(M)
	Space, Self-Adhesive, Serpentine Die-Cut 11.5						
3261	$3.20 Space Shuttle Landing	11/09/98	6.00	1.50	24.00 (4)	5.00	245
3262	$11.75 Express Mail	11/19/98	22.50	10.00	90.00 (4)	25.00	21
	Coil, Self-Adhesive, Serpentine Die-Cut 9.9 Vertically						
3263	22¢ Uncle Sam	11/09/98	.45	.20	3.50 (5)	1.25	
	Perf. 9.8 Vertically						
3264	33¢ Unce Sam's Hat	11/09/98	.65	.20	5.00 (5)	1.25	
	Self-Adhesive, Serpentine Die-Cut 9.9 Vertically						
3265	33¢ H-Series	11/09/98	.65	.20	5.50 (5)	1.25	
3266	33¢ Uncle Sam's Hat	11/09/98	.65	.20	5.00 (5)	1.50	
	Booklet, Self-Adhesive, Serpentine Die-Cut 9.9 on 2 or 3 sides						
3267	33¢ H-Series	11/09/98	.65	.20		1.25	
a	Booklet pane of 10		6.50				
	Self-Adhesive, Serpentine Die-Cut 11.25 on 3 sides						
3268	(33¢) Uncle Sam's Hat	11/09/98	.65	.20		1.25	
a	Booklet pane of 10		6.50				
b	Serpentine die-cut 11		.65	.20			
c	As "b", booklet pane of 20 + label		13.00				
	Self-Adhesive, Die-Cut 8 on 2, 3 or 4 sides						
3269	(33¢) Uncle Sam's Hat	11/09/98	.65	.20		1.25	
a	Booklet pane of 18		12.00				
	Coil, Untagged, Perf. 9.8 Vertically						
3270	10¢ Eagle with Shield	12/14/98	.20	.20	2.75 (5)	1.25	
a	Large date		.35	.20	7.00 (5)		
	Coil, Self-Adhesive, Serpentine Die-Cut 9.9 Vertically						
3271	10¢ Eagle with Shield	12/14/98	.20	.20	2.75 (5)	1.25	
a	Large date		.60	.20	3.25 (5)		
b	Tagged (error)		1.25	.75	10.50 (5)		
	Lunar New Year, Tagged, Perf. 11.2						
3272	33¢ Year of the Rabbit	01/05/99	.80	.20	3.25 (4)	1.50	51
	Black Heritage, Tagged, Self-Adhesive, Serpentine Die-Cut 11.4						
3273	33¢ Malcolm X	01/20/99	.85	.20	2.60 (4)	1.75	100
	Love, Booklet, Tagged, Self-Adhesive, Die-Cut						
3274	33¢ Love	01/28/99	.65	.20		1.25	1,500
a	Booklet pane of 20		13.00				
3275	55¢ Love	01/20/99	1.10	.20	4.40 (4)	1.50	300
	Tagged, Serpentine Die-Cut 11.4						
3276	33¢ Hospice Care	02/09/99	.65	.20	2.80 (4)	1.25	100
	Tagged, Perf. 11.2						
3277	33¢ City Flag	02/25/99	.70	.20	40.00 (4)	1.25	200
	Tagged, Self-Adhesive, Serpentine Die-Cut 11 on 2, 3 or 4 sides						
3278	33¢ City Flag	02/25/99	.65	.20	4.00 (4)	1.25	
a	Booklet pane of 4		2.60				
b	Booklet pane of 5 + label		3.25				
	Booklet, Serpentine Die-Cut 11.5 x 11.75 on 2, 3 or 4 sides						
3278F	33¢ City Flag		.85	.20			
g	Booklet pane of 20 + label		17.50				
	Self-Adhesive, Serpentine Die-Cut 9.8 on 2 or 3 sides						
3279	33¢ City Flag	02/25/99	.75	.20		1.25	
a	Booklet pane of 10		7.50				
	Coil, Perf. 9.9 Vertically						
3280	33¢ City Flag	02/25/99	.65	.20	5.00 (5)	1.25	
a	Large date		.75	.20	8.00 (5)		
	Coil, Self-Adhesive, Serpentine Die-Cut 9.8 Vertically						
3281	33¢ City Flag (large date)	02/25/99	.65	.20	5.00 (5)	1.25	
c	Small date		.65	.20	5.00 (5)		
3282	33¢ City Flag Rounded corners	02/25/99	.65	.20	5.00 (5)	1.25	

	Issue	Date	Un	U	PB #	FDC	Q(M)
	Booklet, Self-Adhesive, Serpentine Die-Cut 7.9 on 2, 3 or 4 sides						
3283	33¢ Flag and Chalkboard	03/13/99	.65	.20		1.25	30
a	Booklet pane of 18		12.00				
	Tagged, Perf. 11.2						
3286	33¢ Irish Immigration	02/26/99	.65	.20	2.60 (4)	1.50	4
	Performing Arts, Tagged, Perf. 11.2						
3287	33¢ Alfred Lunt & Lynn Fontanne	03/02/99	.65	.20	2.60 (4)	1.25	4
	Arctic Animals, Tagged, Perf. 11						
3288	33¢ Arctic Hare	03/12/99	.85	.20		1.25	1
3289	33¢ Arctic Fox	03/12/99	.85	.20		1.25	1
3290	33¢ Snowy Owl	03/12/99	.85	.20		1.25	1
3291	33¢ Polar Bear	03/12/99	.85	.20		1.25	1
3292	33¢ Gray Wolf	03/12/99	.85	.20		1.25	1
a	Strip of 5, #3288-3292		4.25			3.25	
	Nature of America: Sonoran Desert, Tagged, Self-Adhesive, Serpentine Die-Cut Perf. 11.2						
3293	Pane of 10	04/06/99	6.50			6.75	1
a	33¢ Cactus Wren, brittlebush, teddy bear cholla		.65	.50		1.25	
b	33¢ Desert tortoise		.65	.50		1.25	
c	33¢ White-winged dove		.65	.50		1.25	
d	33¢ Gambel quail		.65	.50		1.25	
e	33¢ Saguaro cactus		.65	.50		1.25	
f	33¢ Desert mule deer		.65	.50		1.25	
g	33¢ Desert cottontail, hedgehog cactus		.65	.50		1.25	
h	33¢ Gila monster		.65	.50		1.25	
i	33¢ Western diamondback rattlesnake, cactus mouse		.65	.50		1.25	
j	33¢ Gila woodpecker		.65	.50		1.25	
	Fruit Berries, Tagged, Self-Adhesive, Serpentine Die-Cut 11.25 x 11.5 on 2, 3 or 4 sides, Serpentine Die-Cut 11.5 x 11.75 on 2 or 3 sides (3294a-3297a)						
3294	33¢ Blueberries	04/10/99	.65	.50		1.25	
a	Dated "2000"	03/15/2000	.65	.50		1.25	
3295	33¢ Raspberries	04/10/99	.65	.50		1.25	
a	Dated "2000"	03/15/2000	.65	.50		1.25	
3296	33¢ Strawberries	04/10/99	.65	.50		1.25	
a	Dated "2000"	03/15/2000	.65	.50		1.25	
3297	33¢ Blackberries	04/10/99	.65	.50		1.25	
a	Dated "2000"	03/15/2000	.65	.50		1.25	
b	Booklet pane, 5 each #3294-3297 + label		13.00			3.25	
c	Block of 4, #3294-3297		2.60				
d	Booklet pane, 5 #3297e		15.00				
e	Block of 4, #3294a-3297a		2.60				
	Tagged, Self-Adhesive, Serpentine Die-Cut 9.5 x 10 on 2 or 3 sides						
3298	33¢ Blueberries	04/10/99	.75	.20		1.25	
3299	33¢ Raspberries	04/10/99	.75	.20		1.25	
3300	33¢ Strawberries	04/10/99	.75	.20		1.25	
3301	33¢ Blackberries	04/10/99	.75	.20		1.25	
a	Booklet pane of 4 #3298-#3301		3.00			3.25	
b	Booklet pane of 5 #3298, #3299, #3301 2 #3300 + label		3.75				
c	Booklet pane of 6 #3300, #3301, 2 #3298, #3299		4.50				
d	Block of 4, #3298-#3301		3.00				
	Coil, Serpentine Die-Cut 8.5 Vertically						
3302	33¢ Blueberries	04/10/99	.75	.20		1.25	
3303	33¢ Raspberries	04/10/99	.75	.20		1.25	
3304	33¢ Strawberries	04/10/99	.75	.20		1.25	
3305	33¢ Blackberries	04/10/99	.75	.20		1.25	
a	Strip of 4		3.00			3.25	

3261

3262

HAPPY NEW YEAR! USA 33

3272

3273

USA 33

3274

3275

Hospice Care usa 33

3276

3277

3278

3279

3283

3286

3287

3288

3289

3290

3291

3292

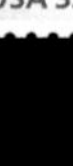

3292a

SONORAN DESERT

FIRST IN A SERIES

N A T U R E O F A M E R I C A

3293

e

c f j

a b d g h

3294 3296

3295 3297

3297c

3305a

3306a

3308

3309

3310 3311

3312 3313 3313a

3314

Prostate Cancer Awareness
Annual Checkups and Tests
USA 33

3315

3316

3317 3318 3319 3320 3320a

3321 3322

3323 3324 3324a

3325 3326

3327 3328 3328a

3329

3330

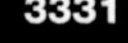
3331

3332

3333

3334

3335

3336

3337

3337a

3338

	Issue	Date	Un	U	PB #	FDC	Q(M)
	Looney Tunes, Tagged, Self-Adhesive, Serpentine Die-Cut 11.1						
3306	Pane of 10	04/16/99	6.50				
a	33¢ Daffy Duck		.65	.20		1.50	43
b	Booklet pane of 9 #3306a		5.85				
c	Booklet pane of 1 #3306a		.65				
3307	Pane of 10		*6.50*				0.5
a	33¢ Single		*.65*				
	Literary Arts, Tagged, Perf. 11.2						
3308	33¢ Ayn Rand	04/22/99	.65	.20	2.60 (4)	1.75	43
	Tagged, Self-Adhesive, Serpentine Die-Cut 11.6 x 11.3						
3309	33¢ Cinco De Mayo	04/27/99	.65	.20	2.60 (4)	1.25	113
	Tropical Flowers, Tagged, Self-Adhesive, Serpentine Die-Cut 10.9 on 2 or 3 sides						
3310	33¢ Bird of Paradise	05/01/99	.65	.20		1.25	
3311	33¢ Royal Poinciana	05/01/99	.65	.20		1.25	
3312	33¢ Gloriosa Lily	05/01/99	.65	.20		1.25	
3313	33¢ Chinese Hibiscus	05/01/99	.65	.20		1.25	
a	Block of 4 #3310-3313		2.60			3.25	375
b	Booklet pane of 5 #3313a		13.00				
	Tagged, Self-Adhesive, Perf. 11.5 Serpentine Die-Cut 11						
3314	33¢ John & William Bartram	05/18/99	.65	.20	2.60 (4)	1.25	145
3315	33¢ Prostate Cancer Awareness	05/28/99	.65	.20	2.60 (4)	1.25	78
	Tagged, Perf. 11.25						
3316	33¢ California Gold Rush 1849	06/18/99	.65	.20	2.60 (4)	1.25	89
	Aquarium Fish, Tagged, Self-Adhesive, Serpentine Die-Cut 11.5						
3317	33¢ Yellow fish, red fish, cleaner shrimp	06/24/99	.65	.20		1.25	39
a	Overall tagging		10.00	*10.00*			
3318	33¢ Fish, thermometer	06/24/99	.65	.20		1.25	39
a	Overall tagging		10.00	*10.00*			
3319	33¢ Red fish, blue & yellow fish	06/24/99	.65	.20		1.25	39
a	Overall tagging		10.00	*10.00*			
3320	33¢ Fish, heater/aerator	06/24/99	.65	.20		1.25	39
a	Overall tagging		10.00	*10.00*			
b	Strip of 4, #3317-3320		2.60		5.20 (8)	3.25	
	Extreme Sports, Tagged, Self-Adhesive, Serpentine Die-Cut 11						
3321	33¢ Skateboarding	06/25/99	.75	.20		1.25	38
3322	33¢ BMX Biking	06/25/99	.75	.20		1.25	38
3323	33¢ Snowboarding	06/25/99	.75	.20		1.25	38
3324	33¢ Inline Skating	06/15/99	.75	.20		1.25	38
a	Block of 4, #3321-3324		3.00		3.00 (4)	3.00	
	American Glass, Tagged, Perf. 11						
3325	33¢ Free-Blown Glass	06/29/99	.75	.20		1.25	29
3326	33¢ Mold-Blown Glass	06/29/99	.75	.20		1.25	29
3327	33¢ Pressed Glass	06/29/99	.75	.20		1.25	29
3328	33¢ Art Glass	06/29/99	.75	.20		1.25	29
a	Strip or block of 4, #3325-3328		3.00	—		3.00	
	Legends of Hollywood, Tagged, Perf. 11						
3329	33¢ James Cagney	07/22/99	.80	.20	3.25 (4)	1.50	76
	Pioneers of Aviation, Tagged, Self-Adhesive, Serpentine Die-Cut 9.75 x 10						
3330	55¢ Gen. William "Billy" L. Mitchell	07/30/99	1.10	.20	4.40 (4)	1.50	101
	Tagged, Self-Adhesive, Serpentine Die-Cut 11						
3331	33¢ Honoring Those Who Served	08/16/99	.65	.20	2.60 (4)	1.75	102
	Tagged, Perf. 11						
3332	45¢ Universal Postal Union	08/25/99	.90	.45	3.60 (4)	1.25	43
	All Aboard! Twentieth Century Trains, Tagged, Perf. 11						
3333	33¢ Daylight	08/26/99	.75	.20		1.50	24
3334	33¢ Congressional	08/26/99	.75	.20		1.50	24
3335	33¢ 20th Century Limited	08/26/99	.75	.20		1.50	24
3336	33¢ Hiawatha	08/26/99	.75	.20		1.50	24
3337	33¢ Super Chief	08/26/99	.75	.20		1.50	24
a	Strip of 5, #3333-3337		3.75	—	6.00 (8)	3.75	
	Tagged, Perf. 11						
3338	33¢ Frederick Law Olmstead	09/13/99	.65	.20	2.60 (4)	1.25	43

Let's Dance/Bailemos Stamped Cards

This booklet of 20 stamped cards would make a great addition to your collection. Or frame it and give it to someone who loves dancing the *Merengue, Salsa, Cha-cha-cha* or *Mambo*. Each design comes with its corresponding stamp affixed.

Item #457766 $9.75

For more information call 1 800 STAMP-24

	Issue	Date	Un	U	PB	#	FDC	Q(M)
	Legends of American Music: Hollywood Composers, Tagged, Perf. 11							
3339	33¢ Max Steiner	09/16/99	.65	.20			1.25	
3340	33¢ Dimitri Tiomkin	09/16/99	.65	.20			1.25	
3341	33¢ Bernard Herrmann	09/16/99	.65	.20			1.25	
3342	33¢ Franz Waxman	09/16/99	.65	.20			1.25	
3343	33¢ Alfred Newman	09/16/99	.65	.20			1.25	
3344	33¢ Erich Wolfgang Korngold	09/16/99	.65	.20			1.25	
a	Block of 6, #3339-3344		3.90	—	3.90	(6)	3.75	85
	Legends of American Music: Broadway Songwriters, Tagged, Perf. 11							
3345	33¢ Ira & George Gershwin	09/21/99	.65	.20			1.25	
3346	33¢ Lerner & Loewe	09/21/99	.65	.20			1.25	
3347	33¢ Lorenz Hart	09/21/99	.65	.20			1.25	
3348	33¢ Rodgers & Hammerstein	09/21/99	.65	.20			1.25	
3349	33¢ Meredith Willson	09/21/99	.65	.20			1.25	
3350	33¢ Frank Loesser	09/21/99	.65	.20			1.25	
a	Block of 6, #3345-3350		3.90	—	3.90	(6)	3.75	85
	Classic Collections: Insects & Spiders, Tagged, Perf. 11							
3351	33¢ Pane of 20	10/01/99	13.00	—			10.00	4
a	Black widow		.65	.20			1.25	
b	Elderberry longhorn		.65	.20			1.25	
c	Lady beetle		.65	.20			1.25	
d	Yellow garden spider		.65	.20			1.25	
e	Dogbane beetle		.65	.20			1.25	
f	Flower Fly		.65	.20			1.25	
g	Assassin bug		.65	.20			1.25	
h	Ebony jewelwing		.65	.20			1.25	
i	Velvet ant		.65	.20			1.25	
j	Monarch caterpillar		.65	.20			1.25	
k	Monarch butterfly		.65	.20			1.25	
l	Eastern Hercules beetle		.65	.20			1.25	
m	Bombardier beetle		.65	.20			1.25	
n	Dung beetle		.65	.20			1.25	
o	Spotted water beetle		.65	.20			1.25	
p	True katydid		.65	.20			1.25	
q	Spinybacked spider		.65	.20			1.25	
r	Periodical cicada		.65	.20			1.25	
s	Scorpionfly		.65	.20			1.25	
t	Jumping spider		.65	.20			1.25	

	Issue	Date	Un	U	PB	#	FDC	Q(M)
	Holiday Celebrations, Tagged, Self-Adhesive, Serpentine Die-Cut 11							
3352	33¢ Hanukkah	10/08/99	.65	.20	2.60	(4)	1.50	65
	Coil, Tagged, Perf. 9.75 Vertically							
3353	22¢ Uncle Sam	10/08/99	.45	.20	3.50	(5)	1.25	150
	Tagged, Perf. 11.25							
3354	33¢ NATO 50th Anniversary	10/13/99	.65	.20	2.60	(4)	1.25	45
	Holiday Celebrations: Christmas, Tagged, Self-Adhesive Booklet, Serpentine Die-Cut 11.25 on 2 or 3 sides							
3355	33¢ Madonna and child by Bartolomeo Vivarini	10/20/99	.65	.15			1.25	1,556
a	Booklet pane of 20		13.00					
	Holiday Celebrations: Holiday, Self-Adhesive, Serpentine Die-Cut 11.25							
3356	33¢ Red Deer	10/20/99	.75	.20			1.25	
3357	33¢ Blue Deer	10/20/99	.75	.20			1.25	
3358	33¢ Purple Deer	10/20/99	.75	.20			1.25	
3359	33¢ Green Deer	10/20/99	.75	.20			1.25	
a	Block or strip, #3356-3359		3.00		3.00	(4)	3.00	29
	Holiday Celebrations: Holiday, Booklet, Serpentine Die-Cut 11.25 on 2, 3 or 4 sides							
3360	33¢ Red Deer	10/20/99	.75	.20			1.25	
3361	33¢ Blue Deer	10/20/99	.75	.20			1.25	
3362	33¢ Purple Deer	10/20/99	.75	.20			1.25	
3363	33¢ Green Deer	10/20/99	.75	.20			1.25	
a	Booklet pane of 20		15.00				3.00	446
	Holiday Celebrations: Holiday, Booklet, Serpentine Die-Cut 11.5 x 11.25 on 2 or 3 sides							
3364	33¢ Red Deer	10/20/99	1.50	.20			1.25	
3365	33¢ Blue Deer	10/20/99	1.50	.20			1.25	
3366	33¢ Purple Deer	10/20/99	1.50	.20			1.25	
3367	33¢ Green Deer	10/20/99	1.50	.20			1.25	
a	Booklet pane of 4		6.50				3.00	30
b	Block pane of 5, #3364, #3366, #3367, 2 #3365 + label		8.00					
c	Block pane of 6, #3365, #3367, 2 #3364, #3366		10.00					
	Holiday Celebrations, Tagged, Self-Adhesive, Serpentine Die-Cut 11							
3368	33¢ Kwanzaa	10/29/99	.65	.20	2.60	(4)	1.75	95

3339 MAX STEINER — 3340 DIMITRI TIOMKIN

3341 BERNARD HERRMANN — 3342 FRANZ WAXMAN

3343 ALFRED NEWMAN — 3344 ERICH WOLFGANG KORNGOLD

3344a

3345 IRA & GEORGE GERSHWIN — 3346 LERNER & LOEWE

3347 LORENZ HART — 3348 RODGERS & HAMMERSTEIN

3349 MEREDITH WILLSON — 3350 FRANK LOESSER

3350a

INSECTS & SPIDERS

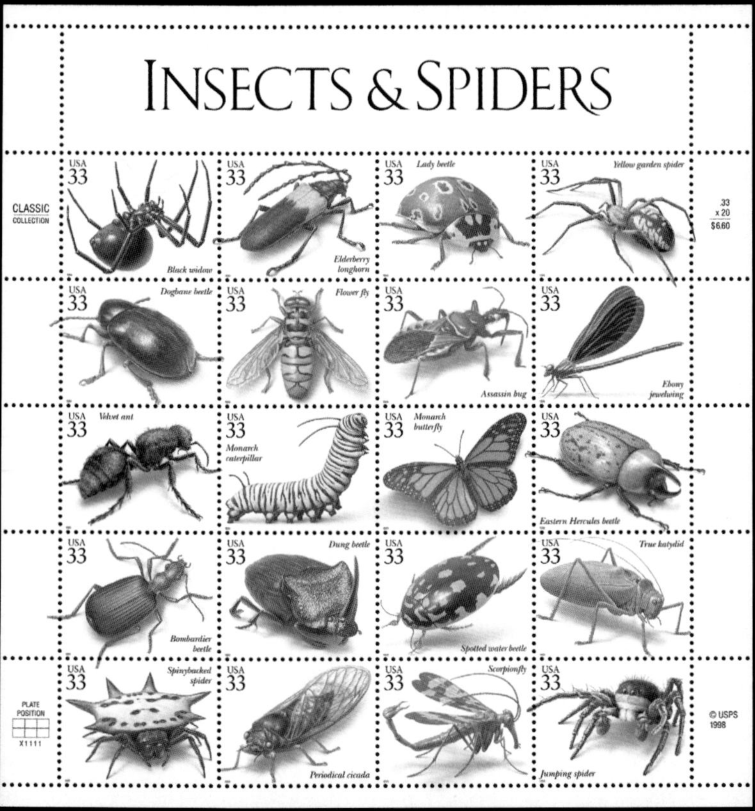

3351

a	b	c	d
e	f	g	h
i	j	k	l
m	n	o	p
q	r	s	t

3352 3353

3354 3355

3356 3357

3359 3358 3359a

3368

3369
HAPPY NEW YEAR!
3370
BLACK HERITAGE
Patricia Roberts Harris
3371
LOS ANGELES CLASS USA 33
3372
3376
USS HOLLAND USA 60
S CLASS USA 22
3373
3377
GATO CLASS USA $3.20
3374
LOS ANGELES CLASS USA 33
OHIO CLASS USA 55
3375
3377a
PACIFIC COAST RAIN FOREST
SECOND IN A SERIES
N A T U R E O F A M E R I C A
3378
a b c d e f g h i j
LOUISE NEVELSON
3379 3380 3381 3382 3383 3383a
AMERICAN SAMOA 33 USA
3389
Library of Congress 33
1800 USA
3390
33USA EAGLE NEBULA
33USA RING NEBULA
33USA LAGOON NEBULA
33USA EGG NEBULA
33USA GALAXY NGC1316
3384 3385 3386 3387 3388 3388a
33 USA
3391a

Issue		Date	Un	U	PB	#	FDC	Q(M)
	Tagged, Self-Adhesive, Serpentine Die-Cut 11.25							
3369	33¢ Year 2000	12/27/99	.65	.20	3.00	(4)	1.25	124
	Lunar New Year, Tagged, Perf. 11.25							
3370	33¢ Year of the Dragon	01/06/2000	.80	.20	3.25	(4)	1.50	106
	Black Heritage, Tagged, Self-Adhesive, Serpentine Die-Cut 11.5 x 11.25							
3371	33¢ Patricia Harris	01/27/2000	.65	.20	2.60	(4)	1.75	150
	U.S. Navy Submarines, Tagged, Perf. 11							
3372	33¢ Los Angeles Class	03/27/2000	.75	.20	3.00	(4)	1.50	65
3373	22¢ S Class	03/27/2000	1.00	.75			1.50	3
3374	33¢ Los Angeles Class	03/27/2000	1.50	1.00			1.50	3
3375	55¢ Ohio Class	03/27/2000	2.25	1.25			1.75	3
3376	60¢ USS Holland	03/27/2000	2.50	1.50			1.75	3
3377	$3.20 Gato Class	03/27/2000	14.00	5.00			6.00	3
a	Booklet Pane of 5, #3373-3377		21.50	—			8.00	
	Nature of America: Pacific Coast Rain Forest, Tagged, Self-Adhesive, Serpentine Die-Cut 11.25 x 11.5, 11.5 (Horiz. Stamps)							
3378	Pane of 10	03/29/2000	8.00				6.75	10
a	33¢ Harlequin duck		.80	.50			1.25	10
b	33¢ Dwarf oregongrape, snail eating ground beetle		.80	.50			1.25	10
c	33¢ American dipper, horizontal		.80	.50			1.25	10
d	33¢ Cutthroat trout, horizontal		.80	.50			1.25	10
e	33¢ Roosevelt elk		.80	.50			1.25	10
f	33¢ Winter wren		.80	.50			1.25	10
g	33¢ Pacific giant salamander, Rough-skinned newt		.80	.50			1.25	10
h	33¢ Western tiger swallowtail, horizontal		.80	.50			1.25	10
i	33¢ Douglass squirrel, foliose lichen		.80	.50			1.25	10
j	33¢ Foliose lichen, banana slug		.80	.50			1.25	10
	Artists: Louise Nevelson, Tagged, Perf. 11 x 11.25							
3379	33¢ Silent Music I	04/06/2000	.65	.20	6.50	(10)	1.25	11
3380	33¢ Royal Tide I	04/06/2000	.65	.20	6.50	(10)	1.25	11
3381	33¢ Black Chord	04/06/2000	.65	.20	6.50	(10)	1.25	11
3382	33¢ Nightsphere-Light	04/06/2000	.65	.20	6.50	(10)	1.25	11
3383	33¢ Dawn's Wedding Chapel I	04/06/2000	.65	.20	6.50	(10)	1.25	11
a	Strip of 5, #3379-3383		3.25	—	6.50	(10)		
	Space: Hubble Telescope, Tagged, Perf. 11							
3384	33¢ Eagle Nebula	04/10/2000	.65	.20	6.50	(10)	1.25	21
3385	33¢ Ring Nebula	04/10/2000	.65	.20	6.50	(10)	1.25	21
3386	33¢ Lagoon Nebula	04/10/2000	.65	.20	6.50	(10)	1.25	21
3387	33¢ Egg Nebula	04/10/2000	.65	.20	6.50	(10)	1.25	21
3388	33¢ Galaxy NGC 1316	04/10/2000	.65	.20	6.50	(10)	1.25	21
a	Strip of 5, #3384-3388		3.25	—	6.50	(10)	3.25	
b	As "a," imperf.		*1,250.00*					
	Tagged, Perf. 11							
3389	33¢ American Samoa	04/17/2000	.65	.20	2.60	(4)	1.25	16
3390	33¢ Library of Congress	04/24/2000	.65	.20	2.60	(4)	1.25	55
	Looney Tunes, Tagged, Self-Adhesive, Serpentine Die-Cut 11							
3391	Pane of 10	04/26/2000	9.00					30
a	33¢ Road Runner & Wile E. Coyote		.85	.20			1.25	
3392	Pane of 10		*12.50*					

BENJAMIN FRANKLIN STAMPED ENVELOPE

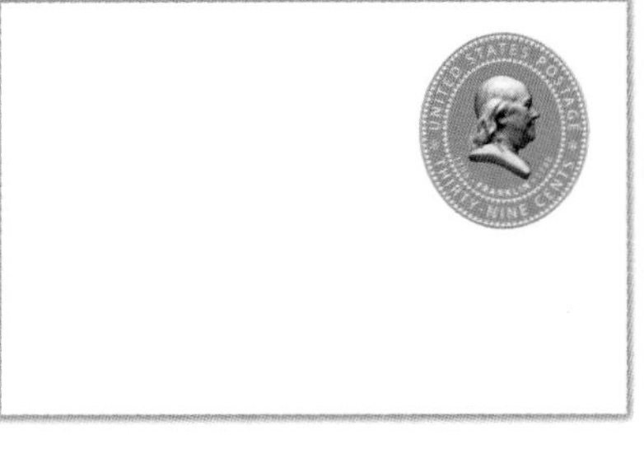

The U.S. Postal Service recognizes the 300th anniversary of the birth of Benjamin Franklin (1706-1790) with this stamped envelope featuring a photograph of a famous bust of the Founding Father by French sculptor Jean-Antoine Houdon (1741-1828). Houdon is considered by many to have been the foremost portrait sculptor of the 18th century. Born in Versailles, France, he studied and worked as a sculptor in Rome before returning to Paris, where he earned commissions from European royalty and major figures of the French Enlightenment. Houdon also sculpted several heroes of the American Revolution, including the Marquis de Lafayette, John Paul Jones, and Thomas Jefferson. In 1785 he traveled to America to sculpt the marble statue of George Washington that now stands in the Capitol building in Richmond, Virginia. The marble bust on this stamped envelope is part of the collection of the Philadelphia Museum of Art, which acquired it in 1996. Dated to 1779, it was created while Franklin was serving as minister to France. (Other versions of this bust exist in plaster and terra-cotta, and a similar marble bust of Franklin by Houdon, dated 1778, is part of the collection of the Metropolitan Museum of Art in New York.)

Bust of Benjamin Franklin, 1779, by Jean-Antoine Houdon. Philadelphia Museum of Art.

	Issue	Date	Un	U	PB	#	FDC	Q(M)
	Distinguished Soldiers, Tagged, Perf. 11							
3393	33¢ Maj. Gen. John L. Hines	08/16/00	.65	.20	2.60	(4)	1.25	14
3394	33¢ Gen. Omar N. Bradley	08/16/00	.65	.20	2.60	(4)	1.25	14
3395	33¢ Sgt. Alvin C. York	08/16/00	.65	.20	2.60	(4)	1.25	14
3396	33¢ Second Lt. Audie L. Murphy	08/16/00	.65	.20	2.60	(4)	1.25	14
a	Block Strip of 4, #3393-3396		2.60	—	2.60	(4)	3.25	
	Tagged, Perf. 11							
3397	33¢ Summer Sports	05/05/00	.65	.20	2.60	(4)	1.25	91
	Tagged, Self-Adhesive, Serpentine Die-Cut 11.5							
3398	33¢ Adoption	05/10/00	.75	.20	3.00	(4)	1.25	200
	Youth Team Sports, Tagged, Perf. 11							
3399	33¢ Basketball	05/27/00	.65	.20	2.60	(4)	1.25	22
3400	33¢ Football	05/27/00	.65	.20	2.60	(4)	1.25	22
3401	33¢ Soccer	05/27/00	.65	.20	2.60	(4)	1.25	22
3402	33¢ Baseball	05/27/00	.65	.20	2.60	(4)	1.25	22
a	Block strip of 4, #3399-3402		2.60	—	2.60	(4)	3.25	
	Classic Collections: The Stars and Stripes, Tagged, Perf. 10.5 x 11							
3403	Pane of 20	06/14/00	15.00				10.00	4
a	33¢ Sons of Liberty Flag, 1775		.75	.50			1.25	
b	33¢ New England Flag, 1775		.75	.50			1.25	
c	33¢ Forster Flag, 1775		.75	.50			1.25	
	The Stars and Stripes continued, **Tagged, Perf. 10.5 x 11**							
d	33¢ Continental Colors, 1776		.75	.50			1.25	
e	33¢ Francis Hopkinson Flag, 1777		.75	.50			1.25	
f	33¢ Brandywine Flag, 1777		.75	.50			1.25	
g	33¢ John Paul Jones Flag, 1779		.75	.50			1.25	
h	33¢ Pierre L'Enfant Flag, 1783		.75	.50			1.25	
i	33¢ Indian Peace Flag, 1803		.75	.50			1.25	
j	33¢ Easton Flag, 1814		.75	.50			1.25	
k	33¢ Star-Spangled Banner, 1814		.75	.50			1.25	
l	33¢ Bennington Flag, c. 1820		.75	.50			1.25	
m	33¢ Great Star Flag, 1837		.75	.50			1.25	
n	33¢ 29-Star Flag, 1847		.75	.50			1.25	
o	33¢ Fort Sumter Flag, 1861		.75	.50			1.25	
p	33¢ Centennial Flag, 1876		.75	.50			1.25	
q	33¢ 38-Star Flag, 1877		.75	.50			1.25	
r	33¢ Peace Flag, 1891		.75	.50			1.25	
s	33¢ 48-Star Flag, 1912		.75	.50			1.25	
t	33¢ 50-Star Flag, 1960		.75	.50			1.25	
	Fruit Berries, Tagged, Self-Adhesive, Serpentine Die-Cut 8.5 Horizontally							
3404	33¢ Blueberries	06/16/00	1.25	.20			1.25	
3405	33¢ Strawberries	06/16/00	1.25	.20			1.25	
3406	33¢ Blackberries	06/16/00	1.25	.20			1.25	
3407	33¢ Raspberries	06/16/00	1.25	.20			1.25	
a	Strip of 4, #3404-3407		5.00				3.25	83

Distinguished American Diplomats

DISTINGUISHED AMERICAN DIPLOMATS

Serving as our nation's representatives around the world, diplomats promote foreign policy, resolve disputes, and protect American citizens abroad. The accomplished diplomats featured on these stamps are remembered for their contributions to international relations—not only as negotiators and administrators but also as trailblazers, shapers of policy, peacemakers, and humanitarians. While serving as a diplomat in France during World War II, Hiram Bingham IV (1903-1988) defied U.S. policy by issuing visas that saved the lives of more than 2,000 Jews and other refugees. Frances E. Willis (1899-1983), who began her diplomatic career in 1927, was the first female Foreign Service Officer to rise through the ranks to become an ambassador and the first woman named Career Ambassador. A skilled troubleshooter, Robert D. Murphy (1894-1978) played a key role in the Allied invasion of North Africa during World War II. Our first postwar ambassador to Japan, he was also one of the first diplomats named Career Ambassador. Clifton R. Wharton, Sr. (1899-1990), the first black Foreign Service Officer, was also the first black diplomat to lead an American delegation to a European country and to become an ambassador by rising through the ranks. An expert on the Soviet Union, Charles E. Bohlen (1904-1974) was present at key wartime meetings with the Soviets, served as ambassador to Moscow during the 1950s, and advised every U.S. president between 1943 and 1968. Philip C. Habib (1920-1992), renowned for his diplomacy in some of the world's most dangerous flash points, was an authority on Southeast Asia, a peace negotiator in the Middle East, and a special envoy to Central America.

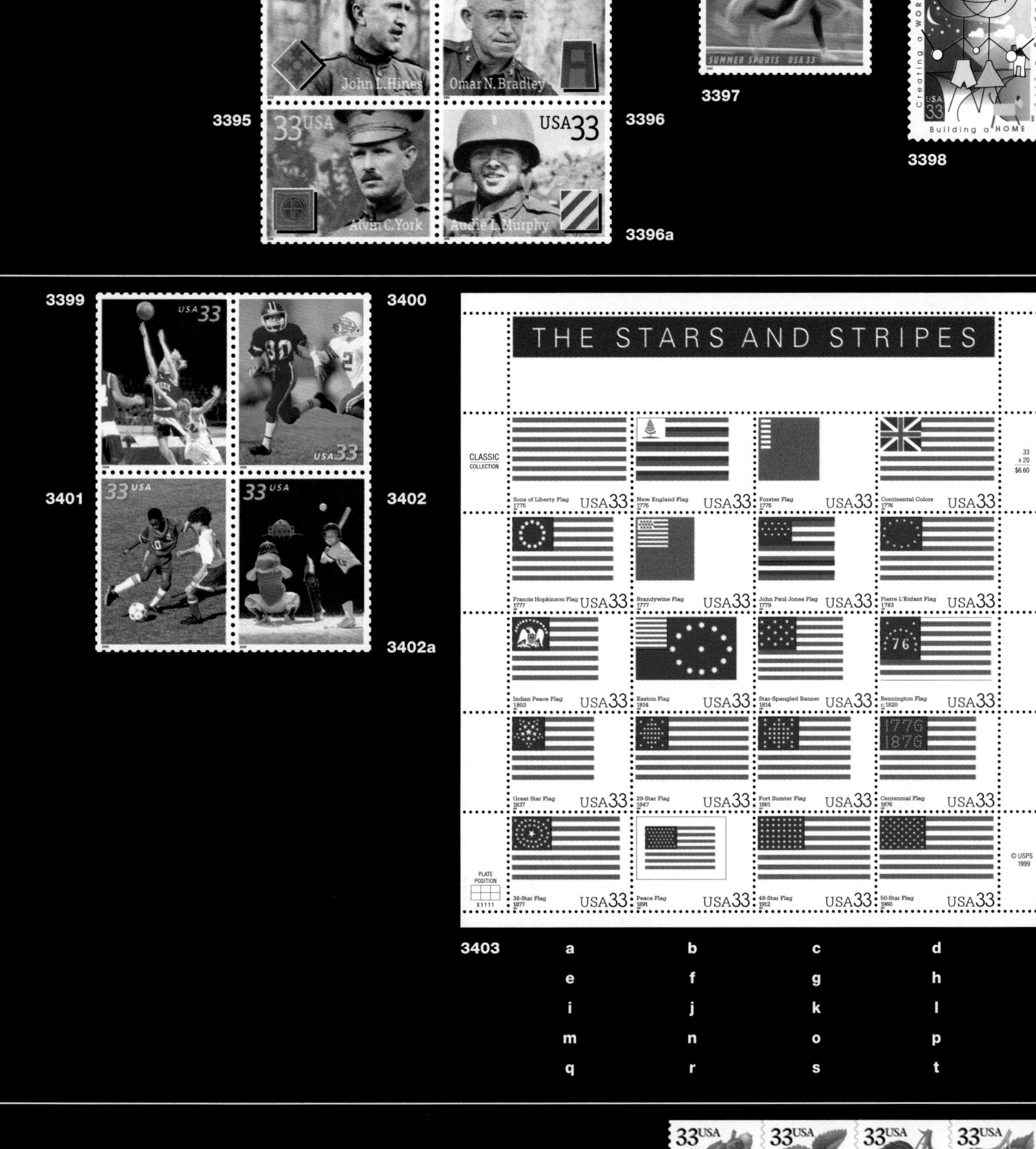
3393
3394
3395
3396
3396a
John L. Hines
Omar N. Bradley
Alvin C. York
Audie L. Murphy
33 USA
USA 33
3397
SUMMER SPORTS USA 33
3398
Adopting a CHILD
Shaping a LIFE
Building a HOME
Creating a WORLD
USA 33
3399
3400
3401
3402
3402a
USA 33
33 USA
THE STARS AND STRIPES
CLASSIC COLLECTION
.33 x 20 $6.60
Sons of Liberty Flag 1775
New England Flag 1775
Forster Flag 1775
Continental Colors 1776
Francis Hopkinson Flag 1777
Brandywine Flag 1777
John Paul Jones Flag 1779
Pierre L'Enfant Flag 1783
Indian Peace Flag 1803
Easton Flag 1814
Star-Spangled Banner 1814
Bennington Flag c.1820
Great Star Flag 1837
29-Star Flag 1847
Fort Sumter Flag 1861
Centennial Flag 1876
38-Star Flag 1877
Peace Flag 1891
48-Star Flag 1912
50-Star Flag 1960
PLATE POSITION
X1111
© USPS 1999
3403
a b c d
e f g h
i j k l
m n o p
q r s t
33 USA

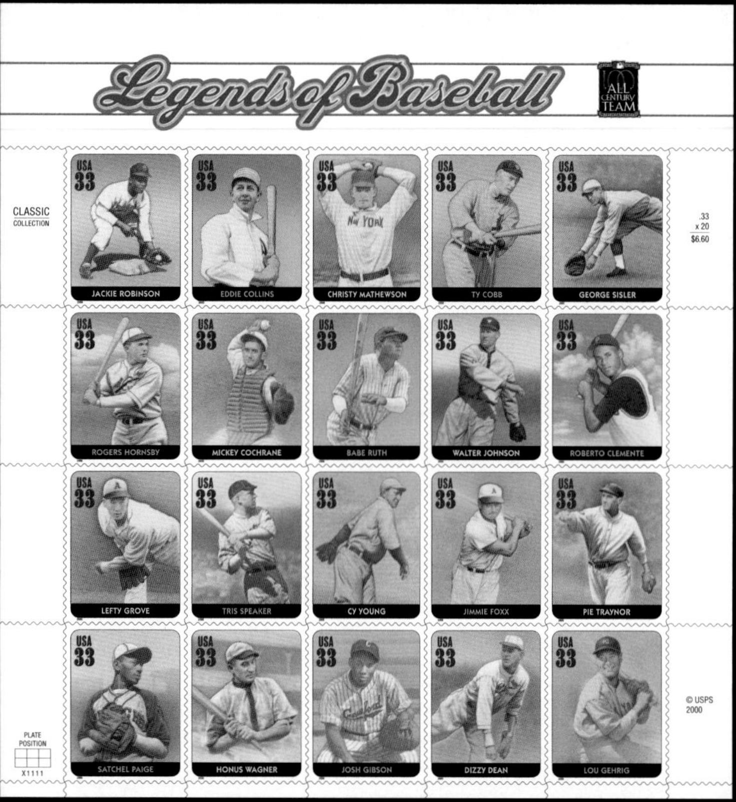

3408 a b c d e

f g h i j

k l m n o

p q r s t

3414 3415

3416 3417

3417a

3409 a b c

d e f

3410 a

e b

d c

3412

3411 a b

3413

	Issue	Date	Un	U	PB	#	FDC	Q(M)
	Classic Collections: Legends of Baseball, Tagged, Self-Adhesive, Serpentine Die-Cut 11.25							
3408	Pane of 20	07/06/00	13.00				10.00	11
a	33¢ Jackie Robinson		.65	.20			1.50	
b	33¢ Eddie Collins		.65	.20			1.50	
c	33¢ Christy Mathewson		.65	.20			1.50	
d	33¢ Ty Cobb		.65	.20			1.50	
e	33¢ George Sisler		.65	.20			1.50	
f	33¢ Rogers Hornsby		.65	.20			1.50	
g	33¢ Mickey Cochrane		.65	.20			1.50	
h	33¢ Babe Ruth		.65	.20			1.50	
i	33¢ Walter Johnson		.65	.20			1.50	
j	33¢ Roberto Clemente		.65	.20			1.50	
k	33¢ Lefty Grove		.65	.20			1.50	
l	33¢ Tris Speaker		.65	.20			1.50	
m	33¢ Cy Young		.65	.20			1.50	
n	33¢ Jimmie Foxx		.65	.20			1.50	
o	33¢ Pie Traynor		.65	.20			1.50	
p	33¢ Satchel Paige		.65	.20			1.50	
q	33¢ Honus Wagner		.65	.20			1.50	
r	33¢ Josh Gibson		.65	.20			1.50	
s	33¢ Dizzy Dean		.65	.20			1.50	
t	33¢ Lou Gehrig		.65	.20			1.50	
	Space, Tagged, Perf. 10.5 x 11							
3409	Probing the Vastness of Space	07/10/00	10.00	7.00			6.00	2
a	60¢ Hubble Space Telescope		1.60	1.00			1.50	
b	60¢ Radio interferometer very large array, New Mexico		1.60	1.00			1.50	
c	60¢ Optical and infrared telescopes, Keck Observatory, Hawaii		1.60	1.00			1.50	
d	60¢ Optical telescopes Cerro Tololo Observatory, Chile		1.60	1.00			1.50	

	Issue	Date	Un	U	PB	#	FDC	Q(M)
	Space, continued, **Tagged, Perf. 10.5 x 11**							
e	60¢ Optical telescope, Mount Wilson Observatory, California		1.60	1.00			1.50	
f	60¢ Radio telescope, Arecibo Observatory, Puerto Rico		1.60	1.00			1.50	
	Space, Perf. 10.75							
3410	Exploring the Solar System	07/11/00	15.00	10.00			9.00	2
a	$1 Sun and corona		2.75	1.75			2.00	
b	$1 Cross-section of sun		2.75	1.75			2.00	
c	$1 Sun and earth		2.75	1.75			2.00	
d	$1 Sun and solar flare		2.75	1.75			2.00	
e	$1 Sun and clouds		2.75	1.75			2.00	
	Space, Hologram, Untagged, Perf. 10.5, 10.75 (#3412)							
3411	Escaping the Gravity of Earth	07/09/00	20.00	10.00			9.50	2
a	$3.20 Space Shuttle and Space Station		9.00	4.00			3.75	
b	$3.20 Astronauts Working in Space		9.00	4.00			3.75	
3412	$11.75 Space Achievement and Exploration	07/07/00	32.50	17.50			17.50	2
a	$11.75 single		27.50	15.00				
3413	$11.75 Landing on the Moon	07/08/00	32.50	17.50			17.50	2
a	$11.75 single		27.50	15.00				
	Uncut sheet of 5 panes #3409-3412		100.00					
	Stampin' The Future™, Tagged, Self-Adhesive, Serpentine Die-Cut 11.25							
3414	33¢ By Zachary Canter	07/13/00	.65	.20	5.25	(8)	1.25	
3415	33¢ By Sarah Lipsey	07/13/00	.65	.20	5.25	(8)	1.25	
3416	33¢ By Morgan Hill	07/13/00	.65	.20	5.25	(8)	1.25	
3417	33¢ By Ashley Young	07/13/00	.65	.20	5.25	(8)	1.25	
a	Horizontal Strip of 4, #3414-3417		2.60		5.25	(8)	3.25	100

AMBER ALERT

The U.S. Postal Service continues its tradition of drawing attention to important social causes by issuing the AMBER Alert stamp to honor a program dedicated to the rapid recovery of abducted children. AMBER is an acronym for America's Missing: Broadcast Emergency Response. An AMBER Alert is issued when law enforcement officials have sufficient information regarding the circumstances of an abduction and believe that the kidnapped child is in imminent danger of serious injury or death. A description of the victim and the circumstances is relayed to area radio and television stations via the Emergency Alert System and is immediately broadcast to the general public. AMBER Alerts mobilize the community during the first critical hours following a kidnapping and provide the police with a wide network of eyes and ears to assist in the search. The AMBER Alert program originated in the Dallas-Fort Worth, Texas, area in 1996 after the kidnapping and subsequent murder of nine-year-old Amber Hagerman, for whom the program is named. Other states and communities soon began adopting similar plans, and by 2005 a national alert system coordinated by the U.S. Department of Justice extended across all 50 states. As of January 2006, nearly 250 children had been recovered as a direct result of these programs.

Issue		Date	Un	U	PB	#	FDC	Q(M)
	Distinguished Americans, Tagged, Perf. 11							
3420	10¢ Joseph W. Stilwell	08/24/00	.20	.20	.80	(4)	1.50	100
a	Imperf, pair		*500.00*					
	Distinguished Americans, Tagged, Self-Adhesive, Serpentine Die-Cut 11.25 x 10.75							
3422	23¢ Wilma Rudolph	07/14/04	.45	.20	1.80	(4)	1.25	
	Distinguished Americans, Tagged, Perf. 11							
3426	33¢ Claude Pepper	09/07/00	.65	.20	2.60	(4)	1.25	56
	Distinguished Americans, Tagged, Self-Adhesive, Serpentine Die-Cut 11							
3431	76¢ Hattie Caraway	02/21/01	1.50	.20	6.00	(4)	1.75	108
	Distinguished Americans, Tagged, Self-Adhesive, Serpentine Die-Cut 11.5 x 11							
3432	76¢ Hattie Caraway	02/21/01	*4.75*	*3.00*	*20.00*	(4)		108
	Distinguished Americans, Tagged, Self-Adhesive, Serpentine Die-Cut 11 x 11.75							
3433	83¢ Edna Ferber	07/29/02	1.60	.30	6.50	(4)	1.75	108
	Distinguished Americans, Tagged, Self-Adhesive, Serpentine Die-Cut 11.25							
3434	83¢ Edna Ferber	08/03	1.60	.30	6.50	(4)		108
	Distinguished Americans, Booklet, Self-Adhesive, Serpentine Die-Cut 11.25 x 10.75							
3436	23¢ Wilma Rudolph	07/14/04	.45	.20			1.25	
a	Booklet pane of 4		1.80					
	Tagged, Self-Adhesive, Serpentine Die-Cut 11							
3438	33¢ California Statehood	09/08/00	.75	.20	3.00	(4)	1.25	53
	Deep Sea Creatures, Tagged, Perf. 10 x 10.25							
3439	33¢ Fanfin Angelfish	10/02/00	.65	.20			1.25	17
3440	33¢ Sea Cucumber	10/02/00	.65	.20			1.25	17
3441	33¢ Fangtooth	10/02/00	.65	.20			1.25	17
3442	33¢ Amphipod	10/02/00	.65	.20			1.25	17
3443	33¢ Medusa	10/02/00	.65	.20			1.25	17
a	Vertical Strip 5, #3439-3443		3.25	—			3.75	
	Literary Arts, Tagged, Perf. 11							
3444	33¢ Thomas Wolfe	10/03/00	.65	.20	2.60	(4)	1.25	53
	Tagged, Self-Adhesive, Serpentine Die-Cut 11.25							
3445	33¢ White House	10/18/00	1.00	.20	4.00	(4)	1.25	125
	Legends of Hollywood, Tagged, Perf. 11							
3446	33¢ Edward G. Robinson	10/24/00	.75	.20	4.75	(4)	1.50	52
	American Culture, Coil, Untagged, Serpentine Die-Cut 11.5 Vertically							
3447	(10¢) The New York Public Library	11/09/00	.20	.20	3.00	(5)	1.25	100
	Tagged, Perf. 11.25							
3448	(34¢) Flag Over Farm	12/15/00	.65	.20	2.60	(4)	1.25	25
	Self-Adhesive, Serpentine Die-Cut 11.25							
3449	(34¢) Flag Over Farm	12/15/00	.65	.20	2.60	(4)	1.25	200
	Booklet, Self-Adhesive, Serpentine Die-Cut 8 on 2, 3 or 4 sides							
3450	(34¢) Flag Over Farm	12/15/00	.75	.20			1.25	
a	Booklet Pane of 18		14.00					300
	Booklet, Tagged, Self-Adhesive, Serpentine Die-Cut 11 on 2, 3 or 4 sides							
3451	34¢ Statue of Liberty	12/15/00	.65	.20	2.60	(4)	1.25	1.5
	Booklet pane of 20		13.00					
	Coil, Perf. 9.75 Vertically							
3452	34¢ Statue of Liberty	12/15/00	.65	.20	5.00	(5)	1.25	200
	Coil, Self-Adhesive, Serpentine Die-Cut 10 Vertically							
3453	34¢ Statue of Liberty	12/15/00	.65	.20	5.00	(5)	1.25	

Issue		Date	Un	U	PB	#	FDC	Q(M)
	Booklet, Tagged, Self-Adhesive, Serpentine Die-Cut 10.25 x 10.75 on 2 or 3 sides							
3454	(34¢) Purple Flower	12/15/00	1.00	.20			1.25	375
3455	(34¢) Tan Flower	12/15/00	1.00	.20			1.25	375
3456	(34¢) Green Flower	12/15/00	1.00	.20			1.25	375
3457	(34¢) Red Flower	12/15/00	1.00	.20			1.25	375
a	Block of 4		4.00				3.25	
b	Booklet pane of 4		4.00					
c	Booklet pane of 6		6.00					
	Booklet, Self-Adhesive, Serpentine Die-Cut 11.5 x 11.75 on 2 or 3 sides							
3458	34¢ Purple Flower	12/15/00	1.50	.25			1.25	125
3459	34¢ Tan Flower	12/15/00	1.50	.25			1.25	125
3460	34¢ Green Flower	12/15/00	1.50	.25			1.25	125
3461	34¢ Red Flower	12/15/00	1.50	.25			1.25	125
a	Block of 4		6.00				3.25	
b	Booklet pane of 20, 2 each #3461a		*30.00*					
c	Booklet pane of 20, 3 each #3461a		*35.00*					
	Coil, Serpentine Die-Cut 8.5 Vertically							
3462	34¢ Green Flower	12/15/00	2.00	.20			1.25	125
3463	34¢ Red Flower	12/15/00	2.00	.20			1.25	125
3464	34¢ Tan Flower	12/15/00	2.00	.20			1.25	125
3465	34¢ Purple Flower	12/15/00	2.00	.20			1.25	125
a	Strip of 4		8.00		11.50	(5)	3.25	
	Coil, Tagged, Self-Adhesive, Serpentine Die-Cut 9.75 Vertically							
3466	34¢ Statue of Liberty	01/07/01	.65	.20	5.00	(5)	1.25	240
	Tagged, Perf. 11.25 x 11							
3467	21¢ American Buffalo	09/20/01	.50	.20	5.00	(4)	1.25	25
	Self-Adhesive, Serpentine Die-Cut 11							
3468	21¢ American Buffalo	02/22/01	.40	.20	1.60	(4)	1.25	25
	Self-Adhesive, Serpentine Die-Cut 11.25 x 11.75							
3468A	23¢ George Washington	09/20/01	.45	.20	1.80	(4)	1.25	25
	Perf. 11.25							
3469	34¢ Flag Over Farm	02/07/01	.75	.20	25.00	(4)	1.25	200
	Self-Adhesive, Serpentine Die-Cut 11.25							
3470	34¢ Flag Over Farm	03/06/01	.65	.20	2.60	(4)	1.25	204
	Self-Adhesive, Serpentine Die-Cut 10.75							
3471	55¢ Art Deco Eagle	02/22/01	1.10	.20	4.40	(4)	1.50	100
3471A	57¢ Art Deco Eagle	09/20/01	1.10	.20	4.40	(4)	1.50	100
	Self-Adhesive, Serpentine Die-Cut 11.25 x 11.5							
3472	$3.50 U. S. Capitol	01/29/01	7.00	2.00	28.00	(4)	6.25	125
	Self-Adhesive, Serpentine Die-Cut 11.25 x 11.5							
3473	$12.25 Washington Monument	01/29/01	22.50	10.00	90.00	(4)	15.00	35
	Coil, Self-Adhesive, Serpentine Die-Cut 8.5 Vertically							
3475	21¢ Buffalo	02/22/01	.50	.20	3.50	(5)	1.25	680
3475A	23¢ George Washington	09/20/01	.50	.20	2.50	(5)	1.25	680
	Perf. 9.75 Vertically							
3476	34¢ Statue of Liberty	02/07/01	.65	.20	5.00	(5)	1.25	379.8
	Self-Adhesive, Serpentine Die-Cut 9.75 Vertically							
3477	34¢ Statue of Liberty	02/07/01	.65	.20	5.00	(5)	1.25	281
	Coil, Self-Adhesive, Serpentine Die-Cut 8.5 Vertically							
3478	34¢ Green Flower	02/07/01	.65	.20			1.25	200
3479	34¢ Red Flower	02/07/01	.65	.20			1.25	200
3480	34¢ Tan Flower	02/07/01	.65	.20			1.25	200
3481	34¢ Purple Flower	02/07/01	.65	.20			1.25	200
a	Strip of 4, #3478-3481		2.60		4.50	(5)	3.25	
	Booklet, Self-Adhesive, Tagged, Serpentine Die-Cut 11.25 on 3 sides							
3482	20¢ George Washington	02/22/01	.40	.20			1.25	20.5
a	Booklet pane of 10		4.00					
b	Booklet pane of 4		1.60					
c	Booklet pane of 6		2.40					

3420  3422  3426  3431  3433  3438

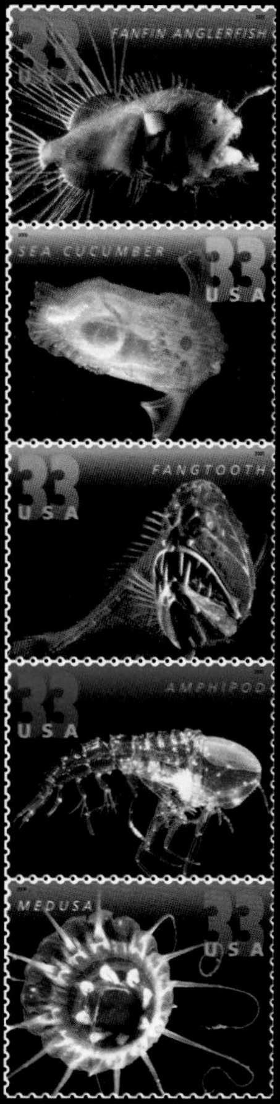

3439 3440 3441 3442 3443 3443a

3444  3445  3446  3447

3454 3455

3448 3451 3466 3468

3456 3457 3457a

3478 3479

3470

3471

3472

3473

3480 3481 3481a

3482

3491 3492 3492a

3497

3499

3500

3501

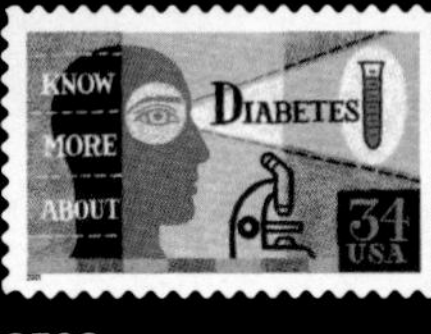

3503

3504

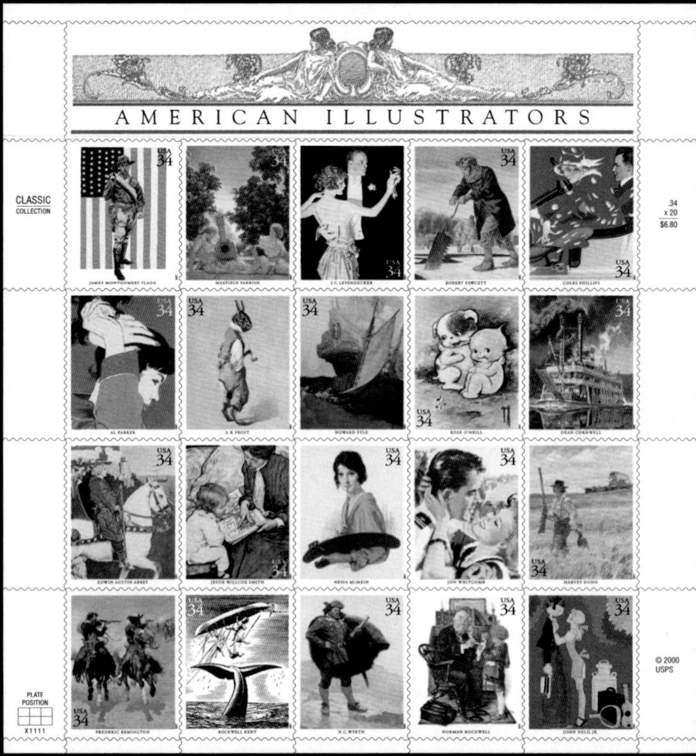

3505 a b c d

3502 a b c d e

f g h i j

k l m n o

p q r s t

3506 a b c d e f

Issue		Date	Un	U	PB	#	FDC	Q(M)
	Booklet, Serpentine Die-Cut 10.5 x 11.25 on 3 sides							
3483	20¢ George Washington	02/22/01	1.75	1.50			1.25	
a	Booklet pane of 4		*9.00*					
b	Booklet pane of 6		*15.00*					
c	Booklet pane of 10		*16.00*					
	Serpentine Die-Cut 11.25 on 3 sides							
3484	20¢ George Washington	09/20/01	.40	.20				
b	Booklet pane of 4		1.60					
c	Booklet pane of 6		2.40					
d	Booklet pane of 10		4.00					
3484A	20¢ George Washington	09/20/01	*1.75*	1.50				
	Serpentine Die-Cut 11 on 2, 3 or 4 sides							
3485	34¢ Statue of Liberty	02/07/01	.65	.20			1.25	
a	Booklet pane of 10		6.50					
b	Booklet pane of 20		13.00					
c	Booklet pane of 4		3.00					
	Self-Adhesive, Serpentine Die-Cut 10.25 x 10.75 on 2 or 3 sides							
3487	34¢ Purple Flower	02/07/01	.75	.20			1.25	
3488	34¢ Tan Flower	02/07/01	.75	.20			1.25	
3489	34¢ Green Flower	02/07/01	.75	.20			1.25	
3490	34¢ Red Flower	02/07/01	.75	.20			1.25	
a	Block of 4		3.00					
b	Booklet pane of 4		3.00					
c	Booklet pane of 6		3.00					
	Serpentine Die-Cut 11.25 on 2, 3 or 4 sides							
3491	34¢ Apple	03/06/01	.75	.20			1.25	3
3492	34¢ Orange	03/06/01	.75	.20			1.25	3
a	Pair		1.30				2.25	
b	Booklet pane of 20		13.00					
	Serpentine Die-Cut 11.5 x 10.75 on 2 or 3 sides							
3493	34¢ Apple	05/01	.75	.20				101
3494	34¢ Orange	05/01	.75	.20				101
a	Pair		1.50					
b	Booklet pane of 4		3.00					
c	Booklet pane of 6		4.50					
	Serpentine Die-Cut 8 on 2 or 3 sides							
3495	34¢ Orange	12/17/01	.65	.20			1.25	101
a	Booklet pane of 18		12.00					
	Love, Booklet, Tagged, Self-Adhesive, Serpentine Die-Cut 11.25 on 2, 3 or 4 sides							
3496	34¢ Rose and Love Letter	01/19/01	.65	.20			1.25	500
a	Booklet pane of 20		15.00					
	Love, Serpentine Die-Cut 11.25 on 2, 3 or 4 sides							
3497	34¢ Rose and Love Letter	02/14/01	.75	.20			1.25	2
a	Booklet pane of 20		15.00					
	Love, Self-Adhesive, Serpentine Die-Cut 11.5 x 10.75 on 2 or 3 sides							
3498	34¢ Rose and Love Letter	02/14/01	.80	.20			1.25	80
a	Booklet pane of 4		3.25					
b	Booklet pane of 6		4.80					
	Love, Serpentine Die-Cut 11.25							
3499	55¢ Rose and Love Letter	02/14/01	1.10	.20	4.50	(4)	1.50	180
	Lunar New Year, Tagged, Perf. 11.25							
3500	34¢ Year of the Snake	01/20/01	.70	.20	2.60	(4)	1.50	55

Issue		Date	Un	U	PB	#	FDC	Q(M)
	Black Heritage, Tagged, Self-Adhesive, Serpentine Die-Cut 11.5 x 11.25							
3501	34¢ Roy Wilkins	01/24/01	.65	.20	2.60	(4)	1.25	200
	Classic Collections: American Illustrators, Tagged, Self-Adhesive, Serpentine Die-Cut 11.25							
3502	Pane of 20	02/01/01	17.50				9.50	145
a	34¢ James Montgomery Flagg		.85	.60			1.25	
b	34¢ Maxfield Parrish		.85	.60			1.25	
c	34¢ J. C. Leyendecker		.85	.60			1.25	
d	34¢ Robert Fawcett		.85	.60			1.25	
e	34¢ Coles Phillips		.85	.60			1.25	
f	34¢ Al Parker		.85	.60			1.25	
g	34¢ A. B. Frost		.85	.60			1.25	
h	34¢ Howard Pyle		.85	.60			1.25	
i	34¢ Rose O'Neill		.85	.60			1.25	
j	34¢ Dean Cornwell		.85	.60			1.25	
k	34¢ Edwin Austin Abbey		.85	.60			1.25	
l	34¢ Jessie Willcox Smith		.85	.60			1.25	
m	34¢ Neysa McMein		.85	.60			1.25	
n	34¢ Jon Whitcomb		.85	.60			1.25	
o	34¢ Harvey Dunn		.85	.60			1.25	
p	34¢ Frederic Remington		.85	.60			1.25	
q	34¢ Rockwell Kent		.85	.60			1.25	
r	34¢ N. C. Wyeth		.85	.60			1.25	
s	34¢ Norman Rockwell		.85	.60			1.25	
t	34¢ John Held, Jr.		.85	.60			1.25	
	Tagged, Self-Adhesive, Serpentine Die-Cut 11.25 x 11.5							
3503	34¢ Diabetes Awareness	03/16/01	.65	.20	2.60	(4)	1.25	100
	Tagged, Perf. 11							
3504	34¢ The Nobel Prize	03/22/01	.65	.20	2.60	(4)	1.50	35
	The Pan-American Inverts, Untagged, Perf. 12.25 x 12 Tagged, Perf. 12 (#3505d)							
3505	34¢ Pane of 7	03/29/01	7.75	—			6.00	2
a	1¢ green		.45	.20			1.25	
b	2¢ carmine		.45	.20			1.25	
c	4¢ deep red brown		.45	.20			1.25	
d	80¢ red & blue		1.60	.35			1.75	
	Nature of America: Great Plains Prairie, Tagged, Self-Adhesive, Serpentine Die-Cut 10							
3506	Pane of 10	04/19/01	8.00				7.00	90
a	34¢ Pronghorns, Canada geese		.75	.20				
b	34¢ Burrowing owls, American buffalo		.75	.20				
c	34¢ American buffalo, Black-tailed prairie dogs, wild alfalfa		.75	.20				
d	34¢ Black-tailed prairie dog, American buffalo		.75	.20				
e	34¢ Painted lady butterfly, American buffalo, prairie coneflowers, prairie wild roses		.75	.20				
f	34¢ Western meadowlark, camel cricket, prairie coneflowers, prairie wild roses		.75	.20				
g	34¢ Badger, harvester ants		.75	.20				
h	34¢ Eastern short-horned lizard, plains pocket gopher		.75	.20				
i	34¢ Plains spadefoot, dung beetle, prairie wild roses		.75	.20				
j	34¢ Two-stripped grasshopper, Ord's kangaroo rat		.75	.20				

	Issue	Date	Un	U	PB	#	FDC	Q(M)
	Peanuts Comic Strip, Tagged, Self-Adhesive, Serpentine Die-Cut 11.25 x 11.5							
3507	34¢ Snoopy	05/17/01	.75	.20	3.00	(4)	1.50	125
	Tagged, Self-Adhesive, Serpentine Die-Cut 11.25 x 11.5							
3508	34¢ Honoring Veterans	05/23/01	.65	.20	2.60	(4)	1.75	200
	Artists, Tagged, Perf. 11.25							
3509	34¢ Frida Kahlo	06/21/01	.65	.20	2.60	(4)	1.25	55
	Baseball's Legendary Playing Fields, Self-Adhesive, Serpentine Die-Cut, Perf. 11.25 x 11.5							
3510	34¢ Ebbets Field, Brooklyn	06/27/01	.80	.60			1.50	
3511	34¢ Tiger Stadium, Detroit	06/27/01	.80	.60			1.50	
3512	34¢ Crosley Field, Cincinnati	06/27/01	.80	.60			1.50	
3513	34¢ Yankee Stadium, New York City	06/27/01	.80	.60			1.50	
3514	34¢ Polo Grounds, New York City	06/27/01	.80	.60			1.50	
3515	34¢ Forbes Field, Pittsburgh	06/27/01	.80	.60			1.50	
3516	34¢ Fenway Park, Boston	06/27/01	.80	.60			1.50	
3517	34¢ Comiskey Park, Chicago	06/27/01	.80	.60			1.50	
3518	34¢ Shibe Park, Philadelphia	06/27/01	.80	.60			1.50	
3519	34¢ Wrigley Field, Chicago	06/27/01	.80	.60			1.50	
a	Block of 10, #3510-3519		8.00		8.00	(10)	6.50	125
	American Culture, Untagged, Self-Adhesive, Serpentine Die-Cut 8.5 Vertically							
3520	10¢ *Atlas* Statue	06/29/01	.20	.20	2.75	(5)	1.25	400
	Tagged, Perf. 11.25							
3521	34¢ Leonard Bernstein	07/10/01	.65	.20	2.60	(4)	1.25	55
	American Culture, Coil, Untagged, Self-Adhesive, Serpentine Die-Cut 11.5 Vertically							
3522	15¢ Woody Wagon	08/03/01	.30	.20	3.00	(5)	1.25	160
	Legends of Hollywood, Tagged, Self-Adhesive, Serpentine Die-Cut 11							
3523	34¢ Lucille Ball	08/06/01	.85	.20	3.40	(4)	1.50	110
	American Treasures: Amish Quilts, Tagged, Self-Adhesive, Serpentine Die-Cut 11.25 x 11.5							
3524	34¢ Diamond in the Square	08/09/01	.65	.20			1.25	
3525	34¢ Lone Star	08/09/01	.65	.20			1.25	
3526	34¢ Sunshine and Shadow	08/09/01	.65	.20			1.25	
3527	34¢ Double Ninepatch	08/09/01	.65	.20			1.25	
a	Block or strip of 4 #3524-3527		2.60		2.60	(4)	3.25	96
	Carnivorous Plants, Self-Adhesive, Serpentine Die-Cut 11.5							
3528	34¢ Venus Flytrap	08/23/01	.65	.20			1.25	
3529	34¢ Yellow Trumpet	08/23/01	.65	.20			1.25	
3530	34¢ Cobra Lily	08/23/01	.65	.20			1.25	
3531	34¢ English Sundew	08/23/01	.65	.20			1.25	
a	Block or strip of 4 #3528-3531		2.60		2.60	(4)	3.25	100

	Issue	Date	Un	U	PB	#	FDC	Q(M)
	Holiday Celebrations, Tagged, Self-Adhesive, Serpentine Die-Cut 11.25							
3532	34¢ Eid	09/01/01	.65	.20	2.60	(4)	1.25	75
	Tagged, Perf. 11							
3533	34¢ Enrico Fermi	09/29/01	.65	.20	2.60	(4)	1.25	30
	Looney Tunes, Tagged, Self-Adhesive, Serpentine Die-Cut 11							
3534	Pane of 10	10/01/01	6.50					
a	34¢ Porky Pig "That's all Folks!"		.65	.20			1.25	275
	Holiday Celebrations: Christmas, Tagged, Self-Adhesive, Serpentine Die-Cut 11.5 on 2, 3 or 4 sides							
3536	34¢ Madonna and Child by Lorenzo Costa	10/10/01	.65	.20			1.25	800
a	Booklet Pane of 20		13.00					
	Holiday Celebrations: Holiday, Tagged, Self-Adhesive, Serpentine Die-Cut 10.75 x 11 (Black inscriptions)							
3537	34¢ Santa wearing tan hood	10/10/01	.65	.20			1.25	
3538	34¢ Santa wearing blue hat	10/10/01	.65	.20			1.25	
3539	34¢ Santa wearing red hat	10/10/01	.65	.20			1.25	
3540	34¢ Santa wearing gold hood	10/10/01	.65	.20			1.25	
b	Block of 4 #3537-3540		2.60		2.60	(4)	3.25	125
	Holiday Celebrations: Holiday, Tagged, Self-Adhesive, Serpentine Die-Cut 11 on 2 or 3 sides (Red & green inscriptions)							
3541	34¢ Santa wearing tan hood	10/10/01	.65	.20			1.25	
3542	34¢ Santa wearing blue hat	10/10/01	.65	.20			1.25	
3543	34¢ Santa wearing red hat	10/10/01	.65	.20			1.25	
3544	34¢ Santa wearing gold hood	10/10/01	.65	.20			1.25	
a	Block of 4 #3541-3544		2.60		2.60	(4)	3.25	201
	Tagged, Self-Adhesive, Serpentine Die-Cut 11 x 11.25							
3545	34¢ James Madison	10/18/01	.65	.20	2.60	(4)	1.25	32
	Holiday Celebrations, Tagged, Self-Adhesive, Serpentine Die-Cut 11.25							
3546	34¢ We Give Thanks	10/19/01	.65	.20	2.60	(4)	1.25	69
	Holiday Celebrations, Tagged, Self-Adhesive, Serpentine Die-Cut 11							
3547	34¢ Hanukkah	10/21/01	.65	.20	2.60	(4)	1.25	49
3548	34¢ Kwanzaa	10/21/01	.65	.20	2.60	(4)	1.25	40
	Tagged, Self-Adhesive, Serpentine Die-Cut 11.25 on 2, 3 or 4 sides							
3549	34¢ United We Stand	10/24/01	.65	.20			1.50	70
a	Booklet pane of 20		13.00					
	Tagged, Self-Adhesive, Serpentine Die-Cut 10.5 x 10.75 on 2 or 3 sides							
3549B	34¢ United We Stand	01/02	.65	.20			1.50	70
c	Booklet pane of 4		2.60					
d	Booklet pane of 6		3.90					

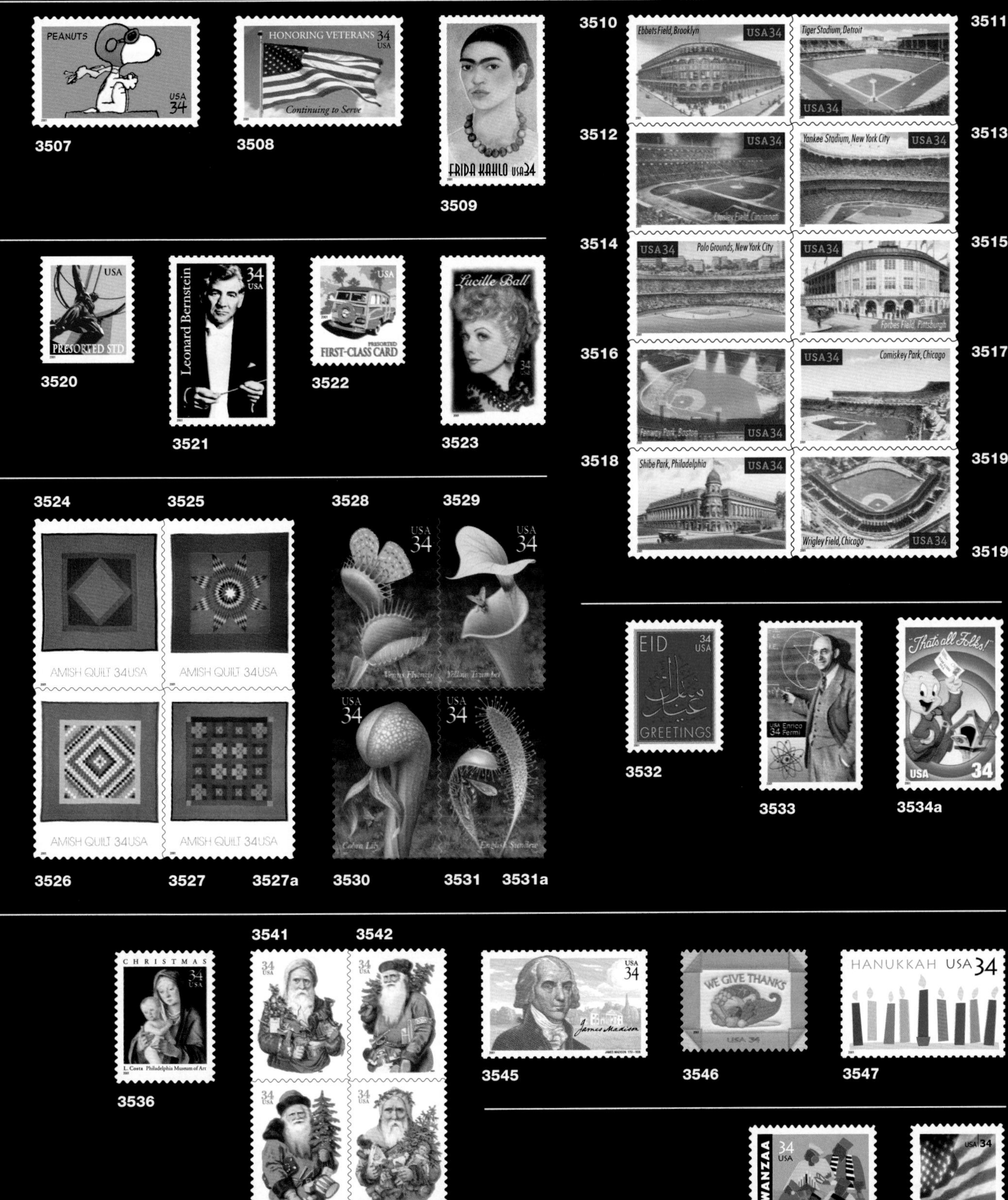

3507 3508 3509 3510 3511 3512 3513 3514 3515 3516 3517 3518 3519 3519a

3520 3521 3522 3523

3524 3525 3526 3527 3527a 3528 3529 3530 3531 3531a

3532 3533 3534a

3536 3541 3542 3543 3544 3544a 3545 3546 3547

3548 3549

3552 3553

3554 3555 3555a

3556

3557

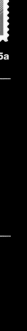

3558

3559

3610a					
	3561	3562	3563	3564	3565
	3566	3567	3568	3569	3570
	3571	3572	3573	3574	3575
	3576	3577	3578	3579	3580
	3581	3582	3583	3584	3585
	3586	3587	3588	3589	3590
	3591	3592	3593	3594	3595
	3596	3597	3598	3599	3600
	3601	3602	3603	3604	3605
	3606	3607	3608	3609	3610

No.	Issue	Date	Un	U	PB	#	FDC	Q(M)
	Coil, Tagged, Self-Adhesive, Serpentine Die-Cut 9.75 Vertically							
3550	34¢ United We Stand	10/24/01	.65	.20	5.00	(5)	1.50	
	Tagged, Self-Adhesive, Serpentine Die-Cut 11.25							
3551	57¢ Rose and Love Letter	11/19/01	1.10	.20	4.40	(4)	1.50	100
	Winter Olympics, Tagged, Self-Adhesive, Serpentine Die-Cut 11.5 x 10.75							
3552	34¢ Ski Jumping	01/08/02	.65	.20	2.60	(4)	1.25	79.64
3553	34¢ Snowboarding	01/08/02	.65	.20	2.60	(4)	1.25	79.64
3554	34¢ Ice Hockey	01/08/02	.65	.20	2.60	(4)	1.25	79.64
3555	34¢ Figure Skating	01/08/02	.65	.20	2.60	(4)	1.25	79.64
a	Block or strip of 4	01/08/02	2.60		2.60	(4)	3.25	
	Tagged, Self-Adhesive, Serpentine Die-Cut 11 x 10.75							
3556	34¢ Mentoring a Child	01/10/02	.65	.20	2.60	(4)	1.25	132.6
	Black Heritage, Tagged, Self-Adhesive, Serpentine Die-Cut 10.25 x 10.5							
3557	34¢ Langston Hughes	02/01/02	.65	.20	2.60	(4)	1.25	120
	Tagged, Self-Adhesive, Serpentine Die-Cut 11							
3558	34¢ Happy Birthday	02/08/02	.65	.20	2.60	(4)	1.25	79.6
	Lunar New Year, Tagged, Self-Adhesive, Serpentine Die-Cut 10.5 x 10.25							
3559	34¢ Year of the Horse	02/11/02	.75	.20	3.00	(4)	1.25	70
	Tagged, Self-Adhesive, Serpentine Die-Cut 10.5 x 11							
3560	34¢ U.S. Military Academy	03/16/02	.65	.20	2.60	(4)	1.50	55
	Greetings From America, Tagged, Self-Adhesive, Serpentine Die-Cut 10.75							
3561	34¢ Alabama	04/04/02	.65	.20			1.25	190
3562	34¢ Alaska	04/04/02	.65	.20			1.25	190
3563	34¢ Arizona	04/04/02	.65	.20			1.25	190
3564	34¢ Arkansas	04/04/02	.65	.20			1.25	190
3565	34¢ California	04/04/02	.65	.20			1.25	190
3566	34¢ Colorado	04/04/02	.65	.20			1.25	190
3567	34¢ Connecticut	04/04/02	.65	.20			1.25	190
3568	34¢ Delaware	04/04/02	.65	.20			1.25	190
3569	34¢ Florida	04/04/02	.65	.20			1.25	190
3570	34¢ Georgia	04/04/02	.65	.20			1.25	190
3571	34¢ Hawaii	04/04/02	.65	.20			1.25	190
3572	34¢ Idaho	04/04/02	.65	.20			1.25	190
3573	34¢ Illinois	04/04/02	.65	.20			1.25	190
3574	34¢ Indiana	04/04/02	.65	.20			1.25	190
3575	34¢ Iowa	04/04/02	.65	.20			1.25	190
	Greetings From America continued							
3576	34¢ Kansas	04/04/02	.65	.20			1.25	190
3577	34¢ Kentucky	04/04/02	.65	.20			1.25	190
3578	34¢ Louisiana	04/04/02	.65	.20			1.25	190
3579	34¢ Maine	04/04/02	.65	.20			1.25	190
3580	34¢ Maryland	04/04/02	.65	.20			1.25	190
3581	34¢ Massachusetts	04/04/02	.65	.20			1.25	190
3582	34¢ Michigan	04/04/02	.65	.20			1.25	190
3583	34¢ Minnesota	04/04/02	.65	.20			1.25	190
3584	34¢ Mississippi	04/04/02	.65	.20			1.25	190
3585	34¢ Missouri	04/04/02	.65	.20			1.25	190
3586	34¢ Montana	04/04/02	.65	.20			1.25	190
3587	34¢ Nebraska	04/04/02	.65	.20			1.25	190
3588	34¢ Nevada	04/04/02	.65	.20			1.25	190
3589	34¢ New Hampshire	04/04/02	.65	.20			1.25	190
3590	34¢ New Jersey	04/04/02	.65	.20			1.25	190
3591	34¢ New Mexico	04/04/02	.65	.20			1.25	190
3592	34¢ New York	04/04/02	.65	.20			1.25	190
3593	34¢ North Carolina	04/04/02	.65	.20			1.25	190
3594	34¢ North Dakota	04/04/02	.65	.20			1.25	190
3595	34¢ Ohio	04/04/02	.65	.20			1.25	190
3596	34¢ Oklahoma	04/04/02	.65	.20			1.25	190
3597	34¢ Oregon	04/04/02	.65	.20			1.25	190
3598	34¢ Vermont	04/04/02	.65	.20			1.25	190
3599	34¢ Rhode Island	04/04/02	.65	.20			1.25	190
3600	34¢ South Carolina	04/04/02	.65	.20			1.25	190
3601	34¢ South Dakota	04/04/02	.65	.20			1.25	190
3602	34¢ Tennessee	04/04/02	.65	.20			1.25	190
3603	34¢ Texas	04/04/02	.65	.20			1.25	190
3604	34¢ Utah	04/04/02	.65	.20			1.25	190
3605	34¢ Vermont	04/04/02	.65	.20			1.25	190
3606	34¢ Virginia	04/04/02	.65	.20			1.25	190
3607	34¢ Washington	04/04/02	.65	.20			1.25	190
3608	34¢ West Virginia	04/04/02	.65	.20			1.25	190
3609	34¢ Wisconsin	04/04/02	.65	.20			1.25	190
3610	34¢ Wyoming	04/04/02	.65	.20			1.25	190
a	Pane of 50, #3561-3610		32.50					

	Issue	Date	Un	U	PB	#	FDC	Q(M)
	Nature of America: Longleaf Pine Forest, Tagged, Self-Adhesive, Serpentine Die-Cut 10.5 x 10.75, 10.75 x 10.5							
3611	34¢ Wildlife and Flowers, Pane of 10	04/26/02	8.00				7.00	70
a	Bachman's sparrow		.75	.20			1.25	
b	Northern bobwhite, yellow pitcher plants		.75	.20			1.25	
c	Fox squirrel, red-bellied woodpecker		.75	.20			1.25	
d	Brown-headed nuthatch		.75	.20			1.25	
e	Broadhead skink, yellow pitcher plants, pipeworts		.75	.20			1.25	
f	Eastern towhee, yellow pitcher plants, Savannah meadow beauties, toothache grass		.75	.20			1.25	
g	Gray fox, gopher tortoise, horiz.		.75	.20			1.25	
h	Blind click beetle, sweetbay, pine woods treefrog		.75	.20			1.25	
i	Rosebud orchid, pipeworts, southern toad, yellow pitcher plants		.75	.20			1.25	
j	Grass-pink orchid, yellow-sided skimmer, pipeworts, yellow pitcher plants, horiz.		.75	.20			1.25	70
	American Design, Coil, Untagged, Perf. 10 Vertically							
3612	5¢ American Toleware	05/31/02	.20	.20	1.60	(5)	1.25	300
	Untagged, Self-Adhesive, Serpentine Die-Cut 11							
3613	3¢ Star (year at lower left)	06/07/02	.20	.20	.25	(4)	1.25	
	Self-Adhesive, Serpentine Die-Cut 10							
3614	3¢ Star (year at lower right)	06/07/02	.20	.20	.25	(4)	1.25	
	Coil, Perf. 10 Vertically							
3615	3¢ Star (year at lower left)	06/07/02	.20	.20	1.00	(5)	1.25	
	Tagged, Perf. 11.25							
3616	23¢ George Washington (green)	06/07/02	.45	.20	1.80	(4)	1.00	25
	Coil, Self-Adhesive, Serpentine Die-Cut 8.5 Vertically							
3617	23¢ George Washington (gray green)	06/07/02	.45	.20	3.00	(5)	1.00	
	Booklet, Self-Adhesive Serpentine Die-Cut 11.25 on 3 sides							
3618	23¢ George Washington (green)	06/07/02	.45	.20			1.00	496
a	Booklet pane of 4		1.80					
	Self-Adhesive, Serpentine Die-Cut 10. 5 x 11.25 on 3 sides							
3619	23¢ George Washington (green)	06/07/02	1.75	1.25				41
a	Booklet pane of 4		*6.00*					
	Tagged, Perf. 11.25 x 11							
3620	(37¢) U.S. Flag (First Class)	06/07/02	.75	.20	5.00	(4)	1.25	
	Self-Adhesive, Serpentine Die-Cut 11.25 x 11							
3621	(37¢) U.S. Flag (First Class)	06/07/02	.75	.20	2.80	(4)	1.25	
	Coil, Self-Adhesive, Serpentine Die-Cut 10 Vertically							
3622	(37¢) U.S. Flag (First Class)	06/07/02	.75	.20	5.25	(5)	1.25	
	Booklet, Self-Adhesive, Serpentine Die-Cut 11.25 on 2, 3 or 4 sides							
3623	(37¢) U.S. Flag (First Class)	06/07/02	.75	.20			1.25	
a	Booklet pane of 20		15.00					
	Booklet, Self-Adhesive, Serpentine Die-Cut 10.5 x 10.75 on 2 or 3 sides							
3624	(37¢) U.S. Flag (First Class)	06/07/02	.75	.20			1.25	
a	Booklet pane of 4		3.00					
	Booklet, Self-Adhesive, Serpentine Die-Cut 8 on 2, 3 or 4 sides							
3625	(37¢) U.S. Flag (First Class)	06/07/02	.75	.20			1.25	
a	Booklet pane of 18		13.50					
	Antique Toys, Booklet, Self-Adhesive, Serpentine Die-Cut 11 on 2, 3 or 4 sides							
3626	(37¢) Toy Mail Wagon	06/07/02	.75	.20			1.25	120
3627	(37¢) Toy Locomotive	06/07/02	.75	.20			1.25	120
3628	(37¢) Toy Taxicab	06/07/02	.75	.20			1.25	120
3629	(37¢) Toy Fire Pumper	06/07/02	.75	.20			1.25	120
a	Block of 4		3.00				3.25	

	Issue	Date	Un	U	PB	#	FDC	Q(M)
	Tagged, Perf. 11.25							
3629F	37¢ U.S. Flag	11/24/03	.75	.20	3.50	(4)	1.25	12
	Self-Adhesive, Serpentine Die-Cut 11.25 x 11							
3630	37¢ U.S. Flag	06/07/02	.75	.20	3.00	(4)	1.25	30
	Coil, Perf. 10 Vertically							
3631	37¢ U.S. Flag	06/07/02	.75	.20	5.25	(5)	1.25	
	Coil, Self-Adhesive, Serpentine Die-Cut 9.75 Vertically							
3632	37¢ U.S. Flag	06/07/02	.75	.20	4.75	(5)	1.25	
	Coil, Self-Adhesive, Serpentine Die-Cut 10.25 Vertically							
3632A	37¢ U.S. Flag	08/07/03	.75	.20	5.25	(5)	1.25	
	Coil, Self-Adhesive, Serpentine Die-Cut 11.75 Vertically							
3632C	37¢ U.S. Flag	06/07/02	.75	.20	5.25	(5)	1.25	
	Coil, Self-Adhesive, Serpentine Die-Cut 8.5 Vertically							
3633	37¢ U.S. Flag	06/07/02	.75	.20	5.25	(5)	1.25	
3633A	37¢ U.S. Flag	04/03	.75	.20	5.50	(5)	1.25	
3633B	37¢ U.S. Flag	06/07/05	.75	.20	5.25	(5)	1.25	
	Booklet, Serpentine Die-Cut 11 on 3 sides							
3634	37¢ U.S. Flag	06/07/02	.75	.20			1.25	
a	Booklet pane of 10		7.50					
	Booklet, Self-Adhesive, Serpentine Die-Cut 11.25 on 2, 3 or 4 sides							
3635	37¢ U.S. Flag	06/07/02	.75	.20			1.25	
a	Booklet pane of 20		15.00					
	Booklet, Serpentine Die-Cut 10.5 x 10.75 on 2 or 3 sides							
3636	37¢ U.S. Flag	06/07/02	.75	.20			1.25	
a	Booklet pane of 4		3.00					
	Booklet, Tagged, Self-Adhesive, Serpentine Die-Cut 11.25 x 11 on 2 or 3 sides							
3636D	37¢ U.S. Flag (type of 2002)	07/04	.70	.20			1.25	
	Booklet, Self-Adhesive, Serpentine Die-Cut 8 on 2, 3 or 4 sides							
3637	37¢ U.S. Flag	02/04/03	.75	.20			1.25	
a	Booklet pane of 18		13.50					
	Antique Toys, Coil, Tagged, Self-Adhesive, Serpentine Die-Cut 8.5 Horizontally							
3638	37¢ Toy Locomotive	07/26/02	.75	.20			1.25	
3639	37¢ Toy Mail Wagon	07/26/02	.75	.20			1.25	
3640	37¢ Toy Fire Pumper	07/26/02	.75	.20			1.25	
3641	37¢ Toy Taxicab	07/26/02	.75	.20			1.25	
a	Strip of 4		3.00				3.25	
	Antique Toys, Booklet, Self-Adhesive, Serpentine Die-Cut 11 on 2, 3 or 4 sides							
3642	37¢ Toy Mail Wagon	07/26/02	.75	.20			1.25	
a	Serpentine Die-Cut 11 x 11.25 on 2 or 3 sides dated "2003"		.75	.20			1.25	
3643	37¢ Toy Locomotive	07/26/02	.75	.20			1.25	
a	Serpentine Die-Cut 11 x 11.25 on 2 or 3 sides dated "2003"		.75	.20			1.25	
3644	37¢ Toy Taxicab	07/26/02	.75	.20			1.25	
a	Serpentine Die-Cut 11 x 11.25 on 2 or 3 sides dated "2003"		.75	.20			1.25	
3645	37¢ Toy Fire Pumper	07/26/02	.75	.20			1.25	
a	Block of 4 #3642-#3645		3.00				3.25	
	Tagged, Self-Adhesive, Serpentine Die-Cut 11 x 11.25							
3646	60¢ Coverlet Eagle	07/12/02	1.25	.25	5.00	(4)	1.50	10[illegible]
	Tagged, Self-Adhesive, Serpentine Die-Cut 11.25							
3647	$3.85 Jefferson Memorial	07/30/02	7.50	2.00	30.00	(4)	7.00	6[illegible]
	Tagged, Self-Adhesive, Serpentine Die-Cut 11 x 10.75							
3647A	$3.85 Jefferson Memorial (2003)	11/03	7.50	2.00	30.00	(4)	7.00	6[illegible]
	Tagged, Self-Adhesive, Serpentine Die-Cut 11.25							
3648	$13.65 Capitol Dome	07/30/02	27.50	10.00	110.00	(4)	25.00	2[illegible]

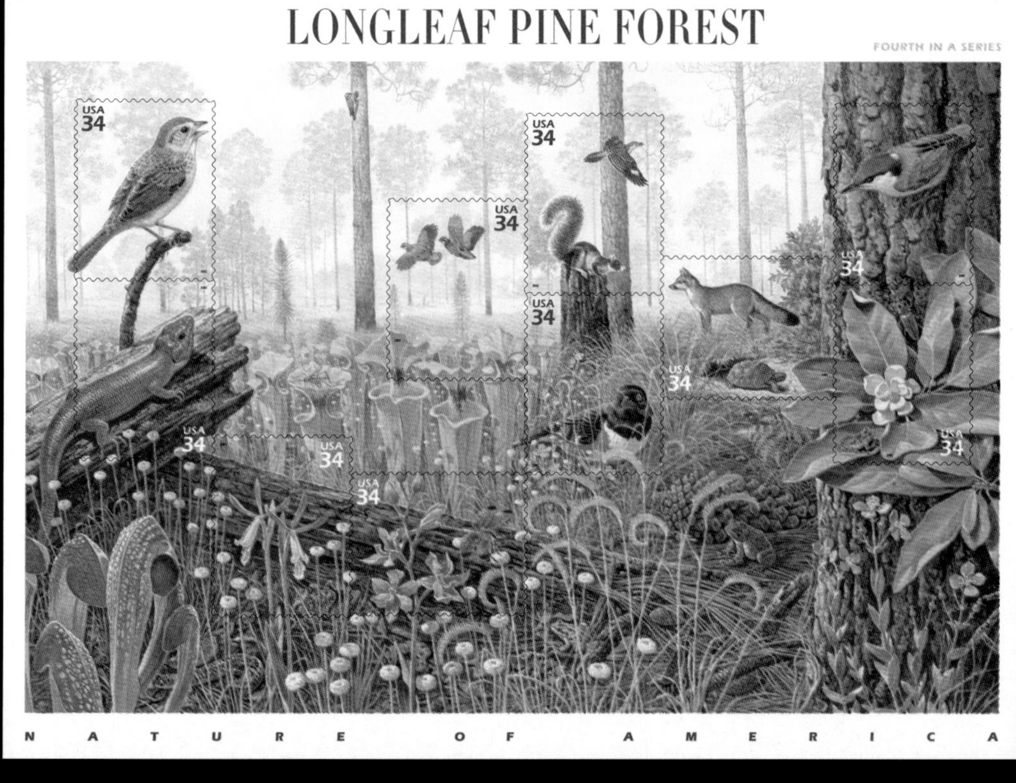

3611 a b c d
e f g h
i j

3612

3613

3616

3620

3626 3627

3628 3629
3629a

3630

3646

3647

3648

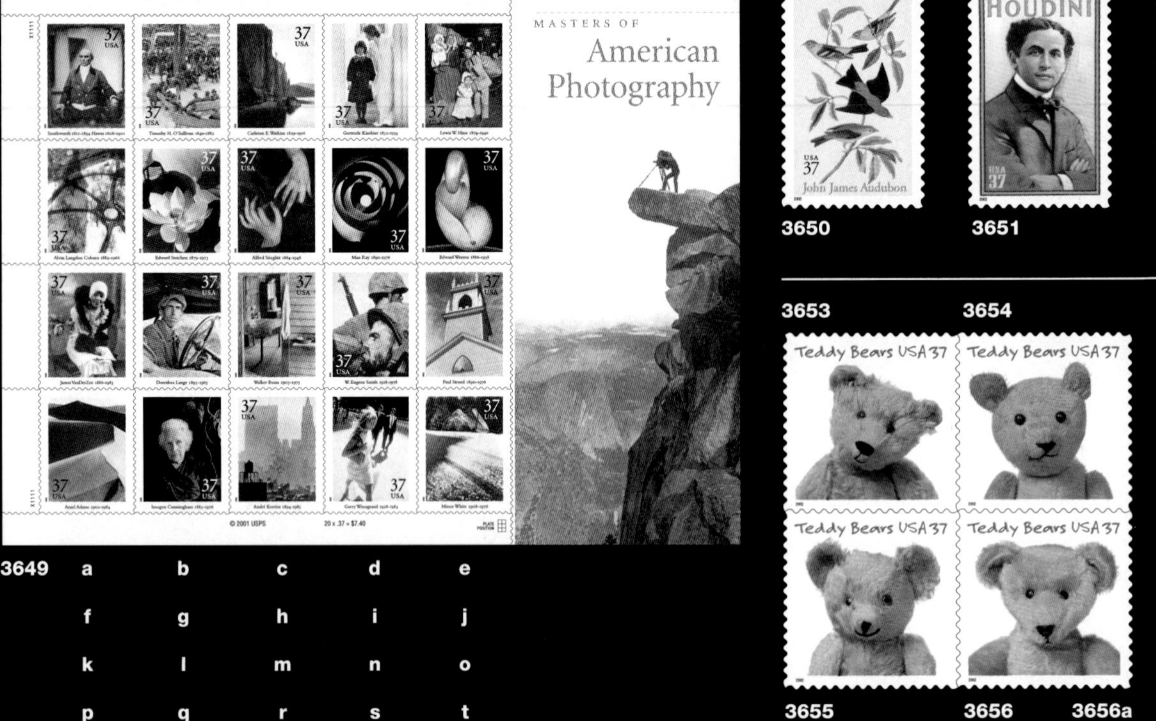

3649 a b c d e
f g h i j
k l m n o
p q r s t

3650 3651 3652

3653 3654

3655 3656 3656a

3657

3658

3659

3660

3661 3662

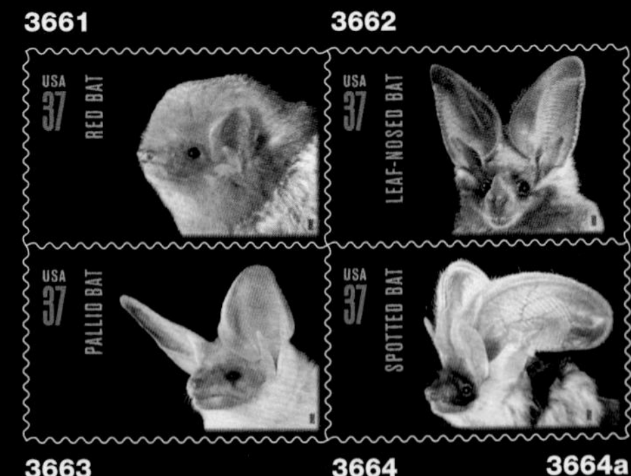

3663 3664 3664a

3668 3666

3667 3665 3668a

3669

3670 3671

	Issue	Date	Un	U	PB	#	FDC	Q(M)
	Masters of American Photography, Tagged, Self-Adhesive Serpentine Die-Cut 10.5 x 10.75							
3649	37¢ Pane of 20	06/13/02	15.00				10.00	63
a	Southworth & Hawes		.75	.50			1.25	
b	Timothy H. O'Sullivan		.75	.50			1.25	
c	Carleton E. Watkins		.75	.50			1.25	
d	Gertrude Käsebier		.75	.50			1.25	
e	Lewis W. Hine		.75	.50			1.25	
f	Alvin Langdon Coburn		.75	.50			1.25	
g	Edward Steichen		.75	.50			1.25	
h	Alfred Stieglitz		.75	.50			1.25	
i	Man Ray		.75	.50			1.25	
j	Edward Weston		.75	.50			1.25	
k	James VanDerZee		.75	.50			1.25	
l	Dorothea Lange		.75	.50			1.25	
m	Walker Evans		.75	.50			1.25	
n	W. Eugene Smith		.75	.50			1.25	
o	Paul Strand		.75	.50			1.25	
p	Ansel Adams		.75	.50			1.25	
q	Imogen Cunningham		.75	.50			1.25	
r	André Kertész		.75	.50			1.25	
s	Garry Winogrand		.75	.50			1.25	
t	Minor White		.75	.50			1.25	
	American Treasures, Self-Adhesive, Serpentine Die-Cut 10.75							
3650	37¢ John James Audubon	06/27/02	.75	.20	3.00	(4)	1.25	70
	Tagged, Self-Adhesive, Serpentine Die-Cut 11.25							
3651	37¢ Harry Houdini	07/03/02	.75	.20	3.00	(4)	1.50	61
	Artists, Tagged, Self-Adhesive, Serpentine Die-Cut 10.5 x 10.75							
3652	37¢ Andy Warhol	08/09/02	.75	.20	3.00	(4)	1.25	61

	Issue	Date	Un	U	PB	#	FDC	Q(M)
	Tagged, Self-Adhesive, Serpentine Die-Cut 10.5							
3653	37¢ Bruin Teddy Bear	08/15/02	1.00	.20			1.25	
3654	37¢ "Stick" Teddy Bear	08/15/02	1.00	.20			1.25	
3655	37¢ Gund Teddy Bear	08/15/02	1.00	.20			1.25	
3656	37¢ Ideal Teddy Bear	08/15/02	1.00	.20			1.25	
a	Block or vertical strip of 4		4.00		4.00	(4)	3.25	211
	Love, Tagged, Booklet, Self-Adhesive, Serpentine Die-Cut 11 on 2, 3 or 4 sides							
3657	37¢ Love	08/16/02	.75	.20			1.25	805
a	Booklet pane of 20		15.00					
	Love, Self-Adhesive, Serpentine Die-Cut 11							
3658	60¢ Love	08/16/02	1.25	.25	5.00	(4)	1.50	75
	Literary Arts, Tagged, Self-Adhesive, Serpentine Die-Cut 11							
3659	37¢ Ogden Nash	08/19/02	.75	.20	3.00	(4)	1.25	60
	Tagged, Self-Adhesive, Serpentine Die-Cut 11.5 x 11.75							
3660	37¢ Duke Kahanamoku	08/24/02	.75	.20	3.00	(4)	1.25	63
	American Bats, Tagged, Self-Adhesive, Serpentine Die-Cut 10.75							
3661	37¢ Red Bat	09/13/02	.75	.20			1.25	
3662	37¢ Leaf-nosed Bat	09/13/02	.75	.20			1.25	
3663	37¢ Pallid Bat	09/13/02	.75	.20			1.25	
3664	37¢ Spotted Bat	09/13/02	.75	.20			1.25	
a	Block or horizontal strip of 4		3.00		3.00	(4)	3.25	111
	Women in Journalism, Tagged, Self-Adhesive, Serpentine Die-Cut 11 x 10.5							
3665	37¢ Nellie Bly	09/14/02	.75	.20			1.25	
3666	37¢ Ida M. Tarbell	09/14/02	.75	.20			1.25	
3667	37¢ Ethel L. Payne	09/14/02	.75	.20			1.25	
3668	37¢ Marguerite Higgins	09/14/02	.75	.20			1.25	
a	Block or horizontal strip of 4		3.00		3.00	(4)	3.25	61
3669	37¢ Irving Berlin	09/15/02	.75	.20	3.00	(4)	1.25	61
	Tagged, Self-Adhesive, Serpentine Die-Cut 10.75 x 10.5							
3670	37¢ Neuter & Spay (Kitten)	09/20/02	1.00	.20			2.25	85
3671	37¢ Neuter & Spay (Puppy)	09/20/02	1.00	.20			2.25	85
a	Horizontal or vertical pair		2.00		4.00	(4)		

	Issue	Date	Un	U	PB	#	FDC	Q(M)
	Holiday Celebrations, Tagged, Self-Adhesive, Serpentine Die-Cut 11							
3672	37¢ Hanukkah (type of 1996)	10/10/02	.75	.20	3.00	(4)	1.25	35
3673	37¢ Kwanzaa (type of 1997)	10/10/02	.75	.20	3.00	(4)	1.25	48
3674	37¢ Eid (type of 2001)	10/10/02	.75	.20	3.00	(4)	1.25	35
	Holiday Celebrations: Christmas, Tagged, Self-Adhesive, Serpentine Die-Cut 11 x 11.25 on 2, 3 or 4 sides							
3675	37¢ Madonna and Child by Gossaert	10/10/02	.75	.20			1.25	536
a	Booklet pane of 20		15.00					
	Holiday Celebrations: Holiday, Tagged, Self-Adhesive, Serpentine Die-Cut 11							
3676	37¢ Snowman w/red & green plaid scarf	10/28/02	.75	.20			1.25	125
3677	37¢ Snowman w/blue plaid scarf	10/28/02	.75	.20			1.25	125
3678	37¢ Snowman w/pipe	10/28/02	.75	.20			1.25	125
3679	37¢ Snowman w/top hat	10/28/02	.75	.20			1.25	125
a	Block or vertical strip of 4, #3676-3679		3.00		3.00	(4)	3.25	
	Coil, Self-Adhesive, Serpentine Die-Cut 8.5 Vertically							
3680	37¢ Snowman w/blue plaid scarf	10/28/02	.75	.20			1.25	
3681	37¢ Snowman w/pipe	10/28/02	.75	.20			1.25	
3682	37¢ Snowman w/top hat	10/28/02	.75	.20			1.25	
3683	37¢ Snowman w/red & green plaid scarf	10/28/02	.75	.20			1.25	
a	Strip of 4, #3680-3683		3.00		5.50	(5)	3.25	
	Booklet, Self-Adhesive, Serpentine Die-Cut 10.75 x 11 on 2 or 3 sides							
3684	37¢ Snowman w/red & green plaid scarf	10/28/02	.75	.20			1.25	4
3685	37¢ Snowman w/blue plaid scarf	10/28/02	.75	.20			1.25	4
3686	37¢ Snowman w/pipe	10/28/02	.75	.20			1.25	4
3687	37¢ Snowman w/top hat	10/28/02	.75	.20			1.25	4
a	Block of 4, #3684-3687		3.00				3.25	
b	Booklet pane of 20, 5 #3687a + label		15.00					
	Colors of #3684-3687 are deeper and designs are slightly smaller than #3676-3679							
	Booklet, Self-Adhesive, Serpentine Die-Cut 11 on 2 or 3 sides							
3688	37¢ Snowman w/red & green plaid scarf	10/28/02	.75	.20			1.25	
3689	37¢ Snowman w/blue plaid scarf	10/28/02	.75	.20			1.25	
3690	37¢ Snowman w/pipe	10/28/02	.75	.20			1.25	
3691	37¢ Snowman w/top hat	10/28/02	.75	.20			1.25	
a	Block of 4 #3688-3691		3.00				3.25	
	Legends of Hollywood, Tagged, Self-Adhesive, Serpentine Die-Cut 10.75							
3692	37¢ Cary Grant	10/15/02	.90	.20	3.60	(4)	1.50	80
	American Scenes, Coil, Tagged, Self-Adhesive, Serpentine Die-Cut 8.5 Vertically							
3693	(5¢) Sea Coast	10/21/02	.20	.20	1.50	(5)	1.25	1,000
	Tagged, Perf, 11							
3694	37¢ Hawaiian Missionary	10/24/02	3.00	2.50			3.25	6
a	37¢-2¢ of 1851 (Hawaii Scott 1)		.75	.50			1.25	
b	37¢-5¢ of 1851 (Hawaii Scott 2)		.75	.50			1.25	
c	37¢-13¢ of 1851 (Hawaii Scott 3)		.75	.50			1.25	
d	37¢-13¢ of 1852 (Hawaii Scott 4)		.75	.50			1.25	
	Tagged, Self-Adhesive, Serpentine Die-Cut 11							
3695	37¢ Happy Birthday (type of 2002)	10/25/02	.70	.20	2.80	(4)	1.25	50

	Issue	Date	Un	U	PB	#	FDC	Q(M)
	Greetings From America (type of 2002), **Tagged, Self-Adhesive, Serpentine Die-Cut 10.75**							
3696	37¢ Alabama	10/25/02	.75	.60			1.25	200
3697	37¢ Alaska	10/25/02	.75	.60			1.25	200
3698	37¢ Arizona	10/25/02	.75	.60			1.25	200
3699	37¢ Arkansas	10/25/02	.75	.60			1.25	200
3700	37¢ California	10/25/02	.75	.60			1.25	200
3701	37¢ Colorado	10/25/02	.75	.60			1.25	200
3702	37¢ Connecticut	10/25/02	.75	.60			1.25	200
3703	37¢ Delaware	10/25/02	.75	.60			1.25	200
3704	37¢ Florida	10/25/02	.75	.60			1.25	200
3705	37¢ Georgia	10/25/02	.75	.60			1.25	200
3706	37¢ Hawaii	10/25/02	.75	.60			1.25	200
3707	37¢ Idaho	10/25/02	.75	.60			1.25	200
3708	37¢ Illinois	10/25/02	.75	.60			1.25	200
3709	37¢ Indiana	10/25/02	.75	.60			1.25	200
3710	37¢ Iowa	10/25/02	.75	.60			1.25	200
3711	37¢ Kansas	10/25/02	.75	.60			1.25	200
3712	37¢ Kentucky	10/25/02	.75	.60			1.25	200
3713	37¢ Louisiana	10/25/02	.75	.60			1.25	200
3714	37¢ Maine	10/25/02	.75	.60			1.25	200
3715	37¢ Maryland	10/25/02	.75	.60			1.25	200
3716	37¢ Massachusetts	10/25/02	.75	.60			1.25	200
3717	37¢ Michigan	10/25/02	.75	.60			1.25	200
3718	37¢ Minnesota	10/25/02	.75	.60			1.25	200
3719	37¢ Mississippi	10/25/02	.75	.60			1.25	200
3720	37¢ Missouri	10/25/02	.75	.60			1.25	200
3721	37¢ Montana	10/25/02	.75	.60			1.25	200
3722	37¢ Nebraska	10/25/02	.75	.60			1.25	200
3723	37¢ Nevada	10/25/02	.75	.60			1.25	200
3724	37¢ New Hampshire	10/25/02	.75	.60			1.25	200
3725	37¢ New Jersey	10/25/02	.75	.60			1.25	200
3726	37¢ New Mexico	10/25/02	.75	.60			1.25	200
3727	37¢ New York	10/25/02	.75	.60			1.25	200
3728	37¢ North Carolina	10/25/02	.75	.60			1.25	200
3729	37¢ North Dakota	10/25/02	.75	.60			1.25	200
3730	37¢ Ohio	10/25/02	.75	.60			1.25	200
3731	37¢ Oklahoma	10/25/02	.75	.60			1.25	200
3732	37¢ Oregon	10/25/02	.75	.60			1.25	200
3733	37¢ Pennsylvania	10/25/02	.75	.60			1.25	200
3734	37¢ Rhode Island	10/25/02	.75	.60			1.25	200
3735	37¢ South Carolina	10/25/02	.75	.60			1.25	200
3736	37¢ South Dakota	10/25/02	.75	.60			1.25	200
3737	37¢ Tennessee	10/25/02	.75	.60			1.25	200
3738	37¢ Texas	10/25/02	.75	.60			1.25	200
3739	37¢ Utah	10/25/02	.75	.60			1.25	200
3740	37¢ Vermont	10/25/02	.75	.60			1.25	200
3741	37¢ Virginia	10/25/02	.75	.60			1.25	200
3742	37¢ Washington	10/25/02	.75	.60			1.25	200
3743	37¢ West Virginia	10/25/02	.75	.60			1.25	200
3744	37¢ Wisconsin	10/25/02	.75	.60			1.25	200
3745	37¢ Wyoming	10/25/02	.75	.60			1.25	200
a	Pane of 50, #3696-3745		37.50					

3672

3673

3674

3675

3676  3677 

3678  3679  

3679a

3692

3693

The "Hawaiian Missionary" Stamps of 1851-1853

The first official Hawaiian post office was established in December 1850. Postmaster Henry M. Whitney had stamps printed locally in three denominations. Philatelists call these rare stamps "Hawaiian Missionaries" because virtually all were used by Christian missionaries on outbound mail. Only 28 covers with Missionary stamps are known to exist; only the Dawson cover (right) bears the 2¢ stamp. The two 13¢ stamps were unusual as they prepaid postage in two countries–Hawaii and the U.S.

"Hawaiian Missionary" stamp 1851 USA37

"Hawaiian Missionary" stamp 1851 USA37

"Hawaiian Missionary" stamp 1851 USA37

"Hawaiian Missionary" stamp 1852 USA37

3694 a b c d

3695

3696

3746 3747

3748

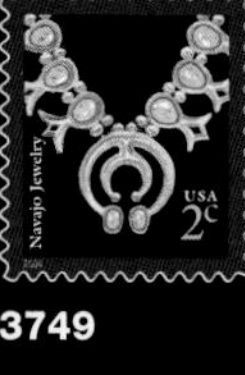

3749

3750

3750A

3751

3757 3759

3766 3771

3773 3774

3772

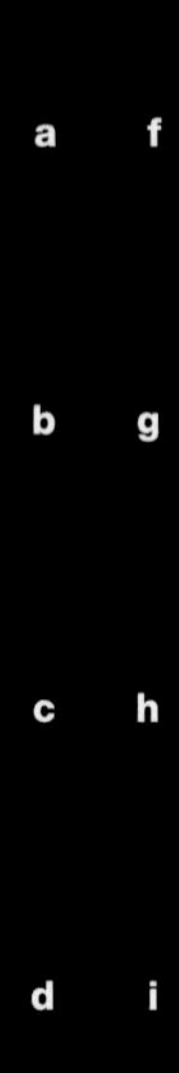

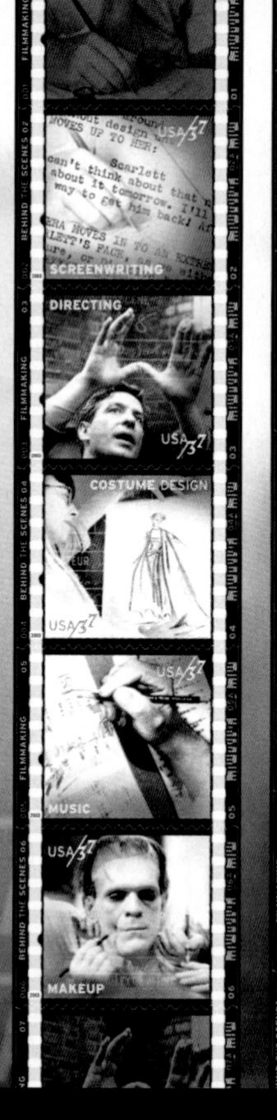

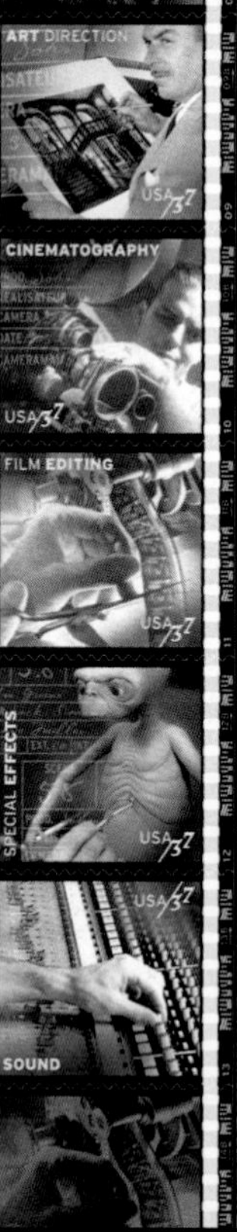

AMERICAN
FILM MAKING:
BEHIND the SCENES
"Thousands and thousands of details...
go into the making of a film. It is the sum
total of all these things that either
makes a great picture or destroys it."
DAVID O. SELZNICK, Producer

3776

3777

3778

3779 3780 3780a

	Issue	Date	Un	U	PB	#	FDC	Q(M)
	Black Heritage, Tagged, Self-Adhesive, Serpentine Die-Cut 11.5							
3746	37¢ Thurgood Marshall	01/07/03	.75	.20	3.00	(4)	1.25	150
	Lunar New Year, Tagged, Self-Adhesive, Serpentine Die-Cut 11.5							
3747	37¢ Year of the Ram	01/15/03	.75	.20	3.00	(4)	1.25	70
	Literary Arts, Tagged, Self-Adhesive, Serpentine Die-Cut 10.75							
3748	37¢ Zora Neale Hurston	01/24/03	.75	.20	3.00	(4)	1.25	70
	American Design, Untagged, Self-Adhesive, Serpentine Die-Cut 11							
3749	2¢ Navajo Jewelry	08/20/04	.20	.20	.20	(4)	1.25	100
	American Design, Untagged, Self-Adhesive, Serpentine Die-Cut 11.25 x 11.5							
3749A	2¢ Navajo Jewelry type of 2004	12/08/05	.20	.20	.20	(4)	1.25	100
	American Design, Untagged, Self-Adhesive, Serpentine Die-Cut 10.75 x 10.25							
3750	4¢ Chippendale Chair	03/05/04	.20	.20	.35	(4)	1.25	100
	American Design, Serpentine Die-Cut 11.25 x 11.75							
3750A	5¢ Toleware Coffeepot	06/25/04	.20	.20	.40	(4)	1.25	100
	American Design, Tagged, Serpentine Die-Cut 11.25 x 11							
3751	10¢ American Clock	01/24/03	.20	.20	.80	(4)	1.25	150
	American Design, Coil, Untagged, Perf. 10 Vertically							
3757	1¢ Tiffany Lamp	03/01/03	.20	.20	.60	(5)	1.25	210
	Untagged, Perf. 9.75 Vertically							
3759	3¢ Silver Coffeepot	09/16/05	.20	.20	1.00	(5)	1.25	210
	American Culture, Tagged, Self-Adhesive, Serpentine Die-Cut 11.25 x 11							
3766	$1 Wisdom	02/28/03	2.00	.40	8.00	(4)	2.50	100
	Coil, Untagged, Perf. 10 Vertically							
3769	(10¢) New York Public Library Lion (type of 2000)	02/04/03	.20	.20			1.25	170
	Coil, Untagged, Self-Adhesive, Serpentine Die-Cut 11, Vertically							
3770	(10¢) Atlas Statue dated "2003" (type of 2001)	11/03	.20	.20	2.75	(5)		400
	Tagged, Self-Adhesive, Serpentine Die-Cut 11							
3771	80¢ Special Olympics	02/13/03	1.60	.35	6.40	(4)	1.75	60
	American Filmmaking: Behind the Scenes Tagged, Self-Adhesive, Serpentine Die-Cut 11, Horizontally							
3772	37¢ Pane of 10	02/25/03	7.00				7.00	70
a	Screenwriting (script from Gone With the Wind)		.70	.50			1.25	
b	Directing (John Cassavetes)		.70	.50			1.25	
c	Costume Design (Edith Head)		.70	.50			1.25	
	American Filmmaking: Behind the Scenes continued, **Tagged, Self-Adhesive, Serpentine Die-Cut 11, Horizontally**							
d	Music (Max Steiner working on score)		.70	.50			1.25	
e	Makeup (Jack Pierce-Boris Karloff for Frankenstein)		.70	.50			1.25	
f	Art Direction (Perry Ferguson for Citizen Kane)		.70	.50			1.25	
g	Cinematography (Paul Hill for *Nagana*)		.70	.50			1.25	
h	Film Editing (J. Watson Webb for The Razor's Edge)		.70	.50			1.25	
i	Special Effects (Mark Siegel for E.T. Extra-Terrestriah)		.70	.50			1.25	
j	Sound (Gary Summers)		.70	.50			1.25	
	Tagged, Self-Adhesive, Serpentine Die-Cut 11.75 x 11.5							
3773	37¢ Ohio Statehood	03/01/03	.75	.20	3.00	(4)	1.25	50
	Tagged, Self-Adhesive, Serpentine Die-Cut 12 x 11.5							
3774	37¢ Pelican Island Natural Wildlife Refuge	03/14/03	.75	.20	3.00	(4)	1.25	55
	Coil, Untagged, Perf. 9.75 Vertically							
3775	(5¢) Sea Coast	03/19/03	.20	.20	1.50	(5)	1.25	200
	Old Glory, Booklet, Tagged, Self-Adhesive, Serpentine Die-Cut 10 x 9.75							
3776	37¢ Uncle Sam on Bicycle with Liberty Flag	04/03/03	.75	.50			1.25	
3777	37¢ 1888 Presidential Campaign	04/03/03	.75	.50			1.25	
3778	37¢ 1893 Silk Bookmark	04/03/03	.75	.50			1.25	
3779	37¢ Modern Hand Fan	04/03/03	.75	.50			1.25	
3780	37¢ Carving of Woman with Flag & Sword 19th Century	04/03/03	.75	.50			1.25	
a	Horizontal strip of 5 #3776-3780		3.75				4.00	60
b	Booklet pane, 2 #3780a		7.50					

	Issue	Date	Un	U	PB	#	FDC	Q(M)
	Tagged, Self-Adhesive, Serpentine Die-Cut 11.75 x 11.5							
3781	37¢ Cesar E. Chavez	04/23/03	.75	.20	3.00	(4)	1.25	75
	Tagged, Self-Adhesive, Serpentine Die-Cut 10.75							
3782	37¢ Louisiana Purchase	04/30/03	.75	.40	3.00	(4)	1.25	54
	Booklet, Tagged, Self-Adhesive, Serpentine Die-Cut 11							
3783	37¢ First Flight	05/22/03	.75	.40			1.25	85
a	Booklet pane of 9		6.75					
b	Booklet pane of 1		.75					
	Tagged, Self-Adhesive, Serpentine Die-Cut 11.25 x 10.75							
3784	37¢ Purple Heart	05/30/03	.75	.20	3.00	(4)	1.25	120
	Tagged, Self-Adhesive, Serpentine Die-Cut 10.75 x 10.25							
3784A	37¢ Purple Heart	05/30/03	.75	.20	3.00	(4)		
	Coil, Untagged, Self-Adhesive, Serpentine Die-Cut 9.5 x 10							
3785	(5¢) Sea Coast	06/03	.20	.20	1.50	(5)		50
	Legends of Hollywood, Tagged, Self-Adhesive, Serpentine Die-Cut 10.75							
3786	37¢ Audrey Hepburn	06/11/03	.90	.20	3.60	(4)	1.25	80
	Lighthouses, Tagged, Self-Adhesive, Serpentine Die-Cut 10.75							
3787	37¢ Old Cape Henry, Virginia	06/13/03	.95	.20			1.25	
3788	37¢ Cape Lookout, North Carolina	06/13/03	.95	.20			1.25	
3789	37¢ Morris Island, South Carolina	06/13/03	.95	.20			1.25	
3790	37¢ Tybee Island, Georgia	06/13/03	.95	.20			1.25	
3791	37¢ Hillsboro Inlet, Florida	06/13/03	.95	.20			1.25	
a	Strip of 5, #3587-3791		5.00				4.00	125
	American Eagle, (dated "2003"), **Untagged, Coil, Serpentine Die-Cut 11.75 Vertically**							
3792	(25¢) gray background & gold eagle	06/26/03	.50	.20			1.25	
3793	(25¢) gold background & red eagle	06/26/03	.50	.20			1.25	
3794	(25¢) dull blue background & gold eagle	06/26/03	.50	.20			1.25	
3795	(25¢) gold background & Prussian blue eagle	06/26/03	.50	.20			1.25	
3796	(25¢) green background & gold eagle	06/26/03	.50	.20			1.25	
3797	(25¢) gold background & gray eagle	06/26/03	.50	.20			1.25	
3798	(25¢) Prussian blue background & gold eagle	06/26/03	.50	.20			1.25	
3799	(25¢) gold background & dull blue eagle	06/26/03	.50	.20			1.25	
3800	(25¢) red background & gold eagle	06/26/03	.50	.20			1.25	
3801	(25¢) gold background & green eagle	06/26/03	.50	.20			1.25	
a	Strip of 10, #3792-3801		5.00				6.00	310

	Issue	Date	Un	U	PB	#	FDC	Q(M)
	American Eagle (dated "2005"), **Coil, Serpentine Die-Cut 11.5 Vertically**							
3792a	(25¢) gray background & gold eagle	08/05/05	.50	.20			1.25	
3793a	(25¢) gold background & red eagle	08/05/05	.50	.20			1.25	
3794a	(25¢) dull blue background & gold eagle	08/05/05	.50	.20			1.25	
3795a	(25¢) gold background & Prussian blue eagle	08/05/05	.50	.20			1.25	
3796a	(25¢) green background & gold eagle	08/05/05	.50	.20			1.25	
3797a	(25¢) gold background & gray eagle	08/05/05	.50	.20			1.25	
3798a	(25¢) Prussian blue background & gold eagle	08/05/05	.50	.20			1.25	
3799a	(25¢) gold background & dull blue eagle	08/05/05	.50	.20			1.25	
3800a	(25¢) red background & gold eagle	08/05/05	.50	.20			1.25	
3801a	(25¢) gold background & green eagle	08/05/05	.50	.20			1.25	
c	Strip of 10, #3792a-3801a		5.00				6.00	
	Nature of America: Arctic Tundra, Tagged, Self-Adhesive, Serpentine Die-Cut 10.75 x 10.5, 10.5 x 10.75							
3802	Pane of 10	07/02/03	7.50				7.50	60
a	37¢ Gyrfalcon		.75	.50			1.25	
b	37¢ Gray wolf		.75	.50			1.25	
c	37¢ Common raven		.75	.50			1.25	
d	37¢ Musk oxen & caribou		.75	.50			1.25	
e	37¢ Grizzly bears, caribou		.75	.50			1.25	
f	37¢ Caribou, willow ptarmigans		.75	.50			1.25	
g	37¢ Arctic ground squirrel		.75	.50			1.25	
h	37¢ Willow ptarmigan, bearberry		.75	.50			1.25	
i	37¢ Arctic grayling		.75	.50			1.25	
j	37¢ Singing vole, thin-legged wolf spider, lingonberry, Labrador tea		.75	.50			1.25	
	Tagged, Self-Adhesive, Serpentine Die-Cut 11.5 x 11.75							
3803	37¢ Korean War Veterans Memorial	07/27/03	.75	.20	3.00	(4)	1.25	87
	American Treasures, Booklet, Tagged, Self-Adhesive, Serpentine Die-Cut 10.75 on 2 or 3 sides							
3804	37¢ Mary Cassatt— Young Mother	08/07/03	.75	.20			1.25	
3805	37¢ Mary Cassatt— Children Playing on the Beach	08/07/03	.75	.20			1.25	
3806	37¢ Mary Cassatt— On a Balcony	08/07/03	.75	.20			1.25	
3807	37¢ Mary Cassatt— Child in a Straw Hat	08/07/03	.75	.20			1.25	
a	Block of 4, #3804-3807		3.00				3.25	779

3781

3782

3783

3784

3786

3787 3788 3789 3790 3791 3791a

a

3797 3798 3799 3800 3801 3792 3793 3794 3795 3796

3802

a

b

c d f e

g

j h i

3803

3804 3805

3806 3807 3807a

3808 3809

3810 3811 3812 3813

3811a

3820

3821 3822

3823 3824

3824a

3829

3831 a b c

d e

f g h i j

	Issue	Date	Un	U	PB	#	FDC	Q(M)
	Early Football Heroes, Tagged, Self-Adhesive, Serpentine Die-Cut 11.5 x 11.75							
3808	37¢ Bronko Nagurski	08/08/03	.75	.20			1.25	
3809	37¢ Ernie Nevers	08/08/03	.75	.20			1.25	
3810	37¢ Walter Camp	08/08/03	.75	.20			1.25	
3811	37¢ Red Grange	08/08/03	.75	.20			1.25	
a	Block of 4, #3808-3811		3.00		3.00	(4)	3.25	70
	Tagged, Self-Adhesive, Serpentine Die-Cut 11							
3812	37¢ Roy Acuff	09/13/03	.75	.20	3.00	(4)	1.25	52
3813	37¢ District of Columbia	09/23/03	.75	.20	3.00	(4)	1.25	72
	Reptiles and Amphibians, Tagged, Self-Adhesive, Serpentine Die-Cut 11							
3814	37¢ Scarlet Kingsnake	10/07/03	.75	.20			1.25	
3815	37¢ Blue-Spotted Salamander	10/07/03	.75	.20			1.25	
3816	37¢ Reticulate Collared Lizard	10/07/03	.75	.20			1.25	
3817	37¢ Ornate Chorus Frog	10/07/03	.75	.20			1.25	
3818	37¢ Ornate Box Turtle	10/07/03	.75	.20			1.25	
a	Vert. strip of 5, #3814-3818		3.75		7.00	(10)	4.00	100
	Tagged, Self-Adhesive, Serpentine Die-Cut 11							
3819	23¢ George Washington (type of 2002)	10//03	.45	.20	1.80	(4)	1.25	200
	Holiday Celebrations: Christmas, Booklet, Tagged, Self-Adhesive, Serpentine Die-Cut 11 x 11.25 on 2 or 3 sides							
3820	37¢ Madonna and Child by Gossaert (type of 2002)	10/23/03	.75	.20			1.25	
a	Booklet pane of 20		15.00					700
	Holiday Celebrations: Holiday, Music Makers, Self-Adhesive, Serpentine Die-Cut 11.75 x 11							
3821	37¢ Reindeer with Pan Pipes	10/23/03	.75	.20			1.25	
3822	37¢ Santa Claus with Drum	10/23/03	.75	.20			1.25	
3823	37¢ Santa Claus with Trumpet	10/23/03	.75	.20			1.25	
3824	37¢ Reindeer with Horn	10/23/03	.75	.20			1.25	
a	Block of 4, #3821-3824		3.00		3.00	(4)	3.25	125

	Issue	Date	Un	U	PB	#	FDC	Q(M)
	Holiday Celebrations: Holiday, Music Makers, Booklet, Self-Adhesive, Serpentine Die-Cut 10.5 x 10.75 on 2 or 3 sides							
3825	37¢ Reindeer with Pan Pipes	10/23/03	.75	.20			1.25	
3826	37¢ Santa Claus with Drum	10/23/03	.75	.20			1.25	
3827	37¢ Santa Claus with Trumpet	10/23/03	.75	.20			1.25	
3828	37¢ Reindeer with Horn	10/23/03	.75	.20			1.25	
a	Block of 4, #3825-3828		3.00				3.25	200
	Coil, Tagged, Self-Adhesive, Serpentine Die-Cut 8.5 Vertically							
3829	37¢ Snowy Egret	10/24/03	.75	.20	5.25	(5)	1.25	2,000
	Die-Cut 9.5 Vertically							
3829A	37¢ Snowy Egret	03/04	.75	.20	5.25	(5)	1.25	2,000
	Booklet, Self-Adhesive, Serpentine Die-Cut 11.5 x 11 on 2, 3 or 4 sides							
3830	37¢ Snowy Egret	03/30/04	.75	.20			1.25	2,000
a	Booklet pane of 20		15.00					
	Nature of America: Pacific Coral Reef, Tagged, Self-Adhesive, Serpentine Die-Cut 10.75							
3831	Pane of 10	01/02/04	7.50				7.50	76
a	37¢ Emperor angelfish, blue coral, mound coral		.75	.20			1.25	
b	37¢ Humphead wrasse, Moorish idol		.75	.20			1.25	
c	37¢ Bumphead parrotfish		.75	.20				
d	37¢ Black-spotted puffer, threadfin butterflyfish, staghorn coral		.75	.20			1.25	
e	37¢ Hawksbill turtle, palette surgeonfish		.75	.20			1.25	
f	37¢ Pink anemonefish, magnificent sea anemone		.75	.20			1.25	
g	37¢ Snowflake moray eel, Spanish dancer		.75	.20			1.25	
h	37¢ Lionfish		.75	.20			1.25	
i	37¢ Triton's trumpet		.75	.20			1.25	
j	37¢ Oriental sweetlips, bluestreak cleaner wrasse, mushroom coral		.75	.20			1.25	

	Issue	Date	Un	U	PB	#	FDC	Q(M)
	Lunar New Year, Tagged, Self-Adhesive, Serpentine Die-Cut 10.75							
3832	37¢ Year of the Monkey	01/13/04	.75	.20	3.00	(4)	1.25	80
	Love, Booklet, Tagged, Self-Adhesive, Serpentine Die-Cut 10.75 on 2, 3 or 4 sides							
3833	37¢ Candy Hearts	01/14/04	.75	.20			1.25	
a	Booklet pane of 20		15.00					750
	Black Heritage, Tagged, Self-Adhesive, Serpentine Die-Cut 10.75							
3834	37¢ Paul Robeson	01/20/04	.75	.20	3.00	(4)	1.25	150
	Tagged, Self-Adhesive, Serpentine Die-Cut 10.75 x 10.5							
3835	37¢ Theodor "Dr. Seuss" Geisel	03/02/04	.75	.20	3.00	(4)	1.25	172
	Garden Flowers (Wedding), **Tagged, Booklet, Self-Adhesive, Serpentine Die-Cut 10.75 on 2, 3 or 4 sides**							
3836	37¢ White Lilacs & Pink Roses	03/04/04	.75	.20			1.25	1,500
	Self-Adhesive, Serpentine Die-Cut 11.5 x 11							
3837	60¢ Pink Roses	03/04/04	1.25	.25	5.00	(4)	1.50	60
	Tagged, Self-Adhesive, Serpentine Die-Cut 10.75							
3838	37¢ US Air Force Academy	04/01/04	.75	.20	3.00	(4)	1.25	60
3839	37¢ Henry Mancini	04/13/04	.75	.20	3.00	(4)	1.25	80
	American Choreographers, Tagged, Self-Adhesive, Serpentine Die-Cut 10.75							
3840	37¢ Martha Graham	05/04/04	.75	.20	3.00	(4)	1.25	
3841	37¢ Alvin Ailey	05/04/04	.75	.20	3.00	(4)	1.25	
3842	37¢ Agnes de Mille	05/04/04	.75	.20	3.00	(4)	1.25	
3843	37¢ George Balanchine	05/04/04	.75	.20	3.00	(4)	1.25	
a	Horizontal strip of 4		3.00		6.00	(8)	3.25	57
	American Eagle (types of 2003), **Coil, Untagged, Perf. 9.75 Vertically**							
3844	(25¢) Gray Background & Gold Eagle	05/12/04	.50	.20			1.25	
3845	(25¢) Gold Background & Green Eagle	05/12/04	.50	.20			1.25	
3846	(25¢) Red Background & Gold Eagle	05/12/04	.50	.20			1.25	
3847	(25¢) Gold Background & Dull Blue Eagle	05/12/04	.50	.20			1.25	
3848	(25¢) Prussian Blue Background & Gold Eagle	05/12/04	.50	.20			1.25	
3849	(25¢) Gold Background & Gray Eagle	05/12/04	.50	.20			1.25	
3850	(25¢) Green Background & Gold Eagle	05/12/04	.50	.20			1.25	
3851	(25¢) Gold Background & Prussian Blue Eagle	05/12/04	.50	.20			1.25	
	American Eagle (types of 2003) continued, **Coil, Untagged, Perf. 9.75 Vertically**							
3852	(25¢) Dull Blue Background & Gold Eagle	05/12/04	.50	.20			1.25	
3853	(25¢) Gold Background & Red Eagle	05/12/04	.50	.20			1.25	
a	Strip of 10 #3844-3853		5.00		7.50	(11)	6.00	700
	Lewis & Clark Expedition Bicentennial, Tagged, Self-Adhesive, Serpentine Die-Cut 10.75							
3854	37¢ Lewis & Clark Bicentennial	05/14/04	.75	.20	3.00	(4)	1.25	
	Booklet, Serpentine Die-Cut 10.5 x 10.75							
3855	37¢ Meriwether Lewis	05/14/04	.90	.45			2.40	
3856	37¢ William Clark	05/14/04	.90	.45			2.40	
a	Horiz. or vert. pair #3855-3856		1.80					62
b	Booklet pane of 5 each #3855-3856		9.00					20
	Artists: Isamu Noguchi, Tagged, Self-Adhesive, Serpentine Die-Cut 10.5 x 10.75							
3857	37¢ Akari 25N	05/18/04	.75	.20			1.25	
3858	37¢ Margaret La Farge	05/18/04	.75	.20			1.25	
3859	37¢ Black Sun	05/18/04	.75	.20			1.25	
3860	37¢ Mother and Child	05/18/04	.75	.20			1.25	
3861	37¢ Figure	05/18/04	.75	.20			1.25	
a	Horizontal strip of 5 #3857-3860		3.75		4.50	(6)	4.00	57
	Tagged, Self-Adhesive, Serpentine Die-Cut 10.75							
3862	37¢ National WWII Memorial	05/29/04	.75	.20	3.00	(4)	1.25	96
	Olympic Games, Tagged, Self-Adhesive, Serpentine Die-Cut 10.75							
3863	37¢ 2004 Olympic Games Athens	06/09/04	.75	.20	3.00	(4)	1.25	71
	Coil, Untagged, Perf. 9.75 Vertically							
3864	(5¢) Sea Coast (type of 2002)	06/11/04	.20	.20			1.25	
	The Art of Disney: Friendship, Tagged, Self-Adhesive, Serpentine Die-Cut 10.5 x 10.75							
3865	37¢ Goofy, Mickey Mouse, Donald Duck	06/23/04	.75	.20	3.00	(4)	1.25	
3866	37¢ Bambi, Thumper	06/23/04	.75	.20	3.00	(4)	1.25	
3867	37¢ Mufasa, Simba	06/23/04	.75	.20	3.00	(4)	1.25	
3868	37¢ Jiminy Cricket, Pinocchio	06/23/04	.75	.20	3.00	(4)	1.25	
a	Block or vert. strip of 4		3.00		3.00	(4)	3.25	284
	Tagged, Self-Adhesive, Serpentine Die-Cut 10.5							
3869	37¢ USS *Constellation*	06/30/04	.75	.20	3.00	(4)	1.25	45
	Tagged, Self-Adhesive, Serpentine Die-Cut 10.5 x 10.75							
3870	37¢ R. Buckminster Fuller	07/12/04	.75	.20	3.00	(4)	1.25	60
	Literary Arts, Tagged, Self-Adhesive, Serpentine Die-Cut 10.75							
3871	37¢ James Baldwin	07/23/04	.75	.20	3.00	(4)	1.25	50

3832

3833

3834

3835

3836

3837

3838

3839

3840

3841

3842

3843

3843a

3854

3855

3856

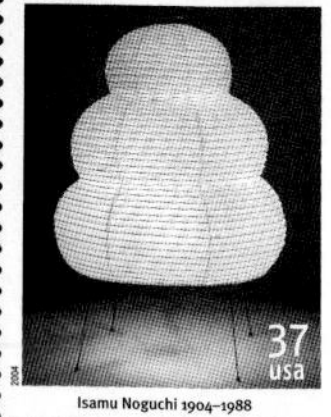

3857

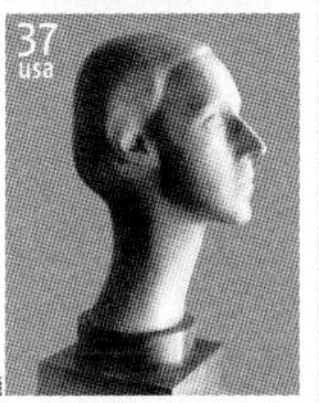

3858

3859

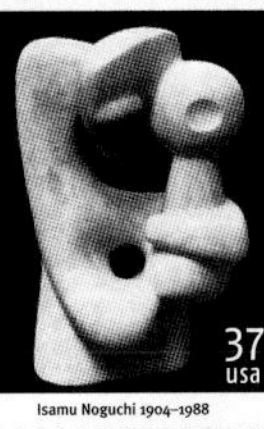

3860

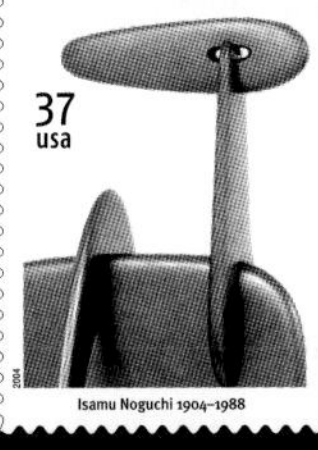

3861

3861a

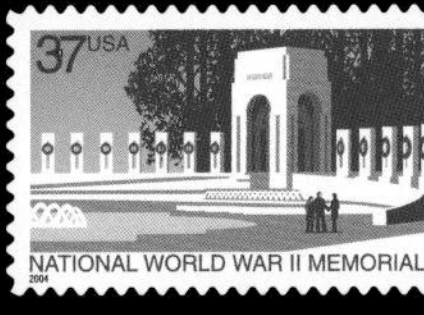

3862

363

3865

3866

3867

3868

3868a

3869

3870

3871

3872

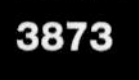

3873 a b c d e

f g h i j

3876

3877

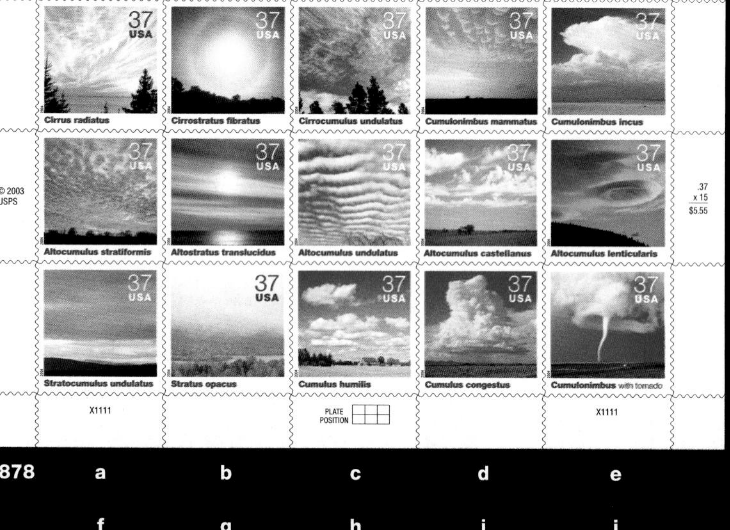

3878 a b c d e

f g h i j

k l m n o

3879

3880

3881

3882

3883 3884

3885 3886 3886a

VISIT US ONLINE AT ***THE POSTAL STORE***
AT ***WWW.USPS.COM***
OR CALL ***1 800 STAMP-24***

	Issue	Date	Un	U	PB	#	FDC	Q(M)
	American Treasures, Tagged, Booklet, Self-Adhesive, Serpentine Die-Cut 10.75 on 2 or 3 sides							
3872	37¢ Martin Johnson Heade	08/12/04	.70	.20	2.80	(4)	1.25	
a	Booklet of pane of 20		14.00					794
	Art of the American Indian, Tagged, Self-Adhesive, Serpentine Die-Cut 10.75 x 11							
3873	37¢ Pane of 10	08/21/04	7.50				7.00	87
a	Mimbres Bowl		.70	.20			1.25	
b	Kutenai Parfleche		.70	.20			1.25	
c	Tlingit Sculptures		.70	.20			1.25	
d	Ho-Chunk Bag		.70	.20			1.25	
e	Seminole Doll		.70	.20			1.25	
f	Mississippian Effigy		.70	.20			1.25	
g	Acoma Pot		.70	.20			1.25	
h	Navajo Weaving		.70	.20			1.25	
i	Seneca Carving		.70	.20			1.25	
j	Luiseño Basket		.70	.20			1.25	
	Coil, Untagged, Self-Adhesive, Serpentine Die-Cut 10 Vertically							
3874	(5¢) Sea Coast (type of 2002)	08/04	.20	.20	1.50	(5)		
	Coil, Untagged, Self-Adhesive, Serpentine Die-Cut 11.5 Vertically							
3875	(5¢) Sea Coast (type of 2002)	08/04	.20	.20	1.50	(5)		
	Legends of Hollywood, Tagged, Self-Adhesive, Serpentine Die-Cut 10.75							
3876	37¢ John Wayne	09/09/04	.70	.20	2.80	(4)	1.25	100
	Tagged, Self-Adhesive, Serpentine Die-Cut 11							
3877	37¢ Sickle Cell Awareness	09/29/04	.70	.20	2.80	(4)	1.25	96
	Cloudscapes, Tagged, Self-Adhesive, Serpentine Die-Cut 11							
3878	37¢ Pane of 15	10/04/04	11.25				9.00	125
a	Cirrus radiatus		.70	.20			1.25	
b	Cirrostratus fibratus		.70	.20			1.25	
c	Cirrocumulus undulatus		.70	.20			1.25	
d	Cumulonimbus mammatus		.70	.20			1.25	
e	Cumulonimbus incus		.70	.20			1.25	
f	Altocumulus stratiformis		.70	.20			1.25	
g	Altostratus translucidus		.70	.20			1.25	
h	Altocumulus undulatus		.70	.20			1.25	
i	Altocumulus castellanus		.70	.20			1.25	
j	Altocumulus lenticularis		.70	.20			1.25	
k	Stratocumulus undulatus		.70	.20			1.25	
l	Stratus opacus		.70	.20			1.25	
m	Cumulus humilis		.70	.20			1.25	
n	Cumulus congestus		.70	.20			1.25	
o	Cumulonimbus with tornado		.70	.20			1.25	

	Issue	Date	Un	U	PB	#	FDC	Q(M)
	Holiday Celebrations: Christmas, Tagged, Self-Adhesive, Serpentine Die-Cut 10.75 x 11 on 2 or 3 sides							
3879	37¢ Madonna and Child by Lorenzo Monaco	10/14/04	.70	.20			1.25	776
a	Booklet pane of 20		15.00					
	Holiday Celebrations: Tagged, Self-Adhesive, Serpentine Die-Cut 10.75							
3880	37¢ Hanukkah	10/15/04	.70	.20	2.80	(4)	1.25	43
3881	37¢ Kwanzaa	10/16/04	.70	.20	2.80	(4)	1.25	60
	Tagged, Self-Adhesive, Serpentine Die-Cut 11							
3882	37¢ Moss Hart	10/25/04	.70	.20	2.80	(4)	1.25	45
	Holiday Celebrations: Holiday Ornaments, Tagged, Self-Adhesive, Serpentine Die-Cut 11.25 x 11							
3883	37¢ Purple Santa	11/16/04	.70	.20	2.80	(4)	1.25	
3884	37¢ Green Santa	11/16/04	.70	.20	2.80	(4)	1.25	
3885	37¢ Blue Santa	11/16/04	.70	.20	2.80	(4)	1.25	
3886	37¢ Red Santa	11/16/04	.70	.20	2.80	(4)	1.25	
a	Block or strip of 4 #3883-3886		3.00					
	Holiday Celebrations: Holiday Ornaments, Booklet, Serpentine Die-Cut 10.25 x 10.75 on 2 or 3 sides							
3887	37¢ Purple Santa	11/16/04	.70	.20	3.00	(4)	1.25	
3888	37¢ Green Santa	11/16/04	.70	.20	3.00	(4)	1.25	
3889	37¢ Blue Santa	11/16/04	.70	.20	3.00	(4)	1.25	
3890	37¢ Red Santa	11/16/04	.70	.20	3.00	(4)	1.25	
a	Block or strip of 4 #3887-3890		3.00					
	Holiday Celebrations: Holiday Ornaments, Booklet, Serpentine Die-Cut 8 on 2, 3 or 4 sides							
3891	37¢ Purple Santa	11/16/04	.70	.20	2.80	(4)	1.25	
3892	37¢ Green Santa	11/16/04	.70	.20	2.80	(4)	1.25	
3893	37¢ Blue Santa	11/16/04	.70	.20	2.80	(4)	1.25	
3894	37¢ Red Santa	11/16/04	.70	.20	2.80	(4)	1.25	
a	Block or strip of 4 #3891-3894		3.00					
b	Pane of 18, 6 each #3891,#3893, 3 each #3892, #3894		13.50					

	Issue	Date	Un	U	PB	#	FDC	Q(M)
	Lunar New Year, Tagged, Self-Adhesive, Serpentine Die-Cut 10.75							
3895	37¢ Pane of 24	01/06/05	18.00					
a	Year of the Rat		.75	.20			1.25	
b	Year of the Ox		.75	.20			1.25	
c	Year of the Tiger		.75	.20			1.25	
d	Year of the Rabbit		.75	.20			1.25	
e	Year of the Dragon		.75	.20			1.25	
f	Year of the Snake		.75	.20			1.25	
g	Year of the Horse		.75	.20			1.25	
h	Year of the Ram		.75	.20			1.25	
i	Year of the Monkey		.75	.20			1.25	
j	Year of the Rooster		.75	.20			1.25	
k	Year of the Dog		.75	.20			1.25	
l	Year of the Boar		.75	.20			1.25	
	Black Heritage, Tagged, Self-Adhesive, Serpentine Die-Cut 10.75							
3896	37¢ Marian Anderson	01/27/05	.75	.20	3.00	(4)	1.25	
	Tagged, Self-Adhesive, Serpentine Die-Cut 10.75							
3897	37¢ Ronald Reagan	02/09/05	.75	.20	3.00	(4)	1.25	
	Love, Tagged, Self-Adhesive, Serpentine Die-Cut 10.75 x 11 on 2, 3 or 4 sides							
3898	37¢ Love Bouquet	02/18/05	.75	.20			1.25	
a	Booklet pane of 20		15.00					
	Northeast Deciduous Forest, Tagged, Self-Adhesive, Serpentine Die-Cut 10.75							
3899	37¢ Pane of 10	03/03/05	7.50					
a	Eastern buckmoth, vert.		.75	.20			1.25	
b	Red-shouldered hawk		.75	.20			1.25	
c	Eastern red bat		.75	.20			1.25	
d	White-tailed deer		.75	.20			1.25	
e	Black bear		.75	.20			1.25	
f	Long-tailed weasel, vert.		.75	.20			1.25	
g	Wild turkey		.75	.20			1.25	
h	Ovenbird, vert.		.75	.20			1.25	
i	Red eft		.75	.20			1.25	
j	Eastern chipmunk		.75	.20			1.25	
	Garden Flowers, Tagged, Self-Adhesive, Serpentine Die-Cut 10.75 x 11 on 2, 3 or 4 sides							
3900	37¢ Hyacinth	03/15/05	.75	.20			1.25	
3901	37¢ Daffodil	03/15/05	.75	.20			1.25	
3902	37¢ Tulip	03/15/05	.75	.20			1.25	
3903	37¢ Iris	03/15/05	.75	.20			1.25	
a	Block of 4 #3900-3903		3.00					
b	Booklet pane, 5 ea. #3900-3903		15.00					
	Literary Arts, Tagged, Self-Adhesive, Serpentine Die-Cut 10.75							
3904	37¢ Robert Penn Warren	04/22/05	.75	.20	3.00	(4)	1.25	
	Tagged, Self-Adhesive, Serpentine Die-Cut 10.75							
3905	37¢ Edgar Y. "Yip" Harburg	04/28/05	.75	.20	3.00	(4)	1.25	

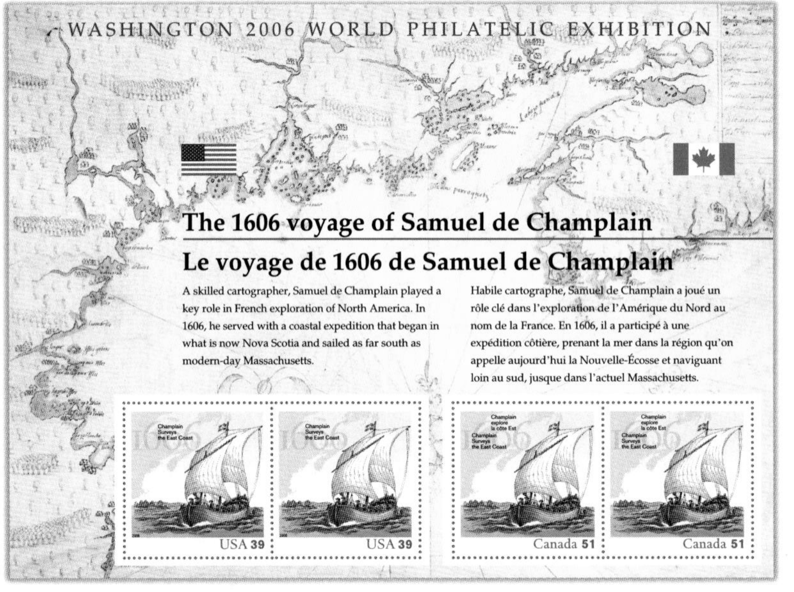

THE 1606 VOYAGE OF SAMUEL DE CHAMPLAIN

Canada Post and the U.S. Postal Service jointly issued this souvenir sheet commemorating the 400th anniversary of the explorations of Samuel de Champlain at the Washington 2006 World Philatelic Exhibition. The sheet features two 51-cent Canadian stamps and two 39-cent U.S. stamps. A skilled cartographer, Samuel de Champlain (c.1570-1635) played a key role in French exploration of North America. In 1606, he accompanied lieutenant governor Jean de Biencourt de Poutrincourt on a mission to explore southward along the Atlantic coast. Beginning in what is now Nova Scotia, the expedition reached as far south as modern-day Cape Cod. A remarkable draftsman, Champlain created highly detailed maps and drawings and wrote accounts of his travels, including descriptions of his encounters with local tribes. His works document the cultures and geography of the east coast of North America during the early 17th century, and his maps are considered the first scientific documents relating to Canada. On each stamp is a scene of a French sailing ship exploring the coastline of North America and a caption that reads "Champlain Surveys the East Coast." The two Canadian stamps also include this caption in French.

3896

3897

3898

395

a b c
d e f
g h i
j k l

3900 3901

3902 3903

Hyacinth USA 37
Daffodil USA 37
Tulip USA 37
Iris USA 37

3904

3906
3907
BARBARA McCLINTOCK
GENETICIST
usa 37
JOSIAH WILLARD GIBBS
THERMODYNAMICIST
usa 37
JOHN von NEUMANN
MATHEMATICIAN
usa 37
RICHARD FEYNMAN
PHYSICIST
usa 37
3908
3909
3909a
Henry Fonda
USA 37
3911
Masterworks of Modern American Architecture
Guggenheim Museum
NEW YORK, NY
37
Chrysler Building
NEW YORK, NY
37
Vanna Venturi House
PHILADELPHIA, PA
37
TWA Terminal
NEW YORK, NY
37
Walt Disney Concert Hall
LOS ANGELES, CA
37
860–880 Lake Shore Drive
CHICAGO, IL
37
National Gallery of Art
WASHINGTON, DC
37
Glass House
NEW CANAAN, CT
37
Yale Art + Architecture
NEW HAVEN, CT
37
High Museum of Art
ATLANTA, GA
37
Exeter Academy Library
EXETER, NH
37
Hancock Center
CHICAGO, IL
37
3910 a b c d
e f g h
i j k l
3912
3913
37 usa
37 usa
37 usa
37 usa
3914
3915
3915a
3916
3917
247
USA37
PBY Catalina
USA37
3918
3919
F6F Hellcat
USA37
P-47 Thunderbolt
USA37
3920
3921
Ercoupe 415
USA37
P-80 Shooting Star
USA37
3922
3923
B-24 Liberator
USA37
B-29 Superfortress
USA37
3924
3925
35 Bonanza
USA37
YB-49 Flying Wing
USA37
3926
3927
RIO GRANDE USA 37
RIO GRANDE USA 37
RIO GRANDE USA 37
RIO GRANDE USA 37
3928
3929
3929a
Presidential Libraries
FIFTY YEARS 37 USA
3930

	Issue	Date	Un	U	PB	#	FDC	Q(M)
	American Scientists, Tagged, Self-Adhesive, Serpentine Die-Cut 10.75							
3906	37¢ Barbara McClintock	05/04/05	.75	.20			1.25	
3907	37¢ Josiah Willard Gibbs	05/04/05	.75	.20			1.25	
3908	37¢ John von Neumann	05/04/05	.75	.20			1.25	
3909	37¢ Richard Feynman	05/04/05	.75	.20	3.00	(4)	1.25	
a	Block or strip of 4		3.00					
	Modern American Architecture, Tagged, Self-Adhesive, Serpentine Die-Cut 10.75 x 11							
3910	37¢ Pane of 12	05/19/05	9.00					
a	Guggenheim Museum, New York		.75	.20			1.25	
b	Chrysler Building, New York		.75	.20			1.25	
c	Vanna Venturi House, Philadelphia		.75	.20			1.25	
d	TWA Terminal, New York		.75	.20			1.25	
e	Walt Disney Concert Hall, Los Angeles		.75	.20			1.25	
f	860-880 Lake Shore Drive, Chicago		.75	.20			1.25	
g	National Gallery of Art, Washington, DC		.75	.20			1.25	
h	Glass House, New Canaan, CT		.75	.20			1.25	
i	Yale Art & Architecture Building, New Haven, CT		.75	.20			1.25	
j	High Museum of Art, Atlanta		.75	.20			1.25	
k	Exeter Academy Library, Exeter, NH		.75	.20			1.25	
l	Hancock Center, Chicago		.75	.20			1.25	
	Legends of Hollywood, Tagged, Self-Adhesive, Serpentine Die-Cut 11 x 10.75							
3911	37¢ Henry Fonda	05/20/05	.75	.20	3.00	(4)	1.25	
	The Art of Disney, Tagged, Self-Adhesive, Serpentine Die-Cut 10.5 x 10.75							
3912	37¢ Pluto, Mickey Mouse	06/30/05	.75	.20	3.00	(4)	1.25	
3913	37¢ Mad Hatter, Alice	06/30/05	.75	.20	3.00	(4)	1.25	
3914	37¢ Flounder, Ariel	06/30/05	.75	.20	3.00	(4)	1.25	
3915	37¢ Snow White, Dopey	06/30/05	.75	.20	3.00	(4)	1.25	
a	Block or vert. strip of 4		3.00		3.00	(4)	3.25	

	Issue	Date	Un	U	PB	#	FDC	Q(M)
	Advances in Aviation, Tagged, Self-Adhesive, Serpentine Die-Cut 10.75 x 10.5							
3916	37¢ Boeing 247	07/29/05	.75	.20			1.25	
3917	37¢ Consolidated PBY Catalina	07/29/05	.75	.20			1.25	
3918	37¢ Grumman F6F Hellcat	07/29/05	.75	.20			1.25	
3919	37¢ Republic P-47 Thunderbolt	07/29/05	.75	.20			1.25	
3920	37¢ Engineering and Research Corporation Ercoupe 415	07/29/05	.75	.20			1.25	
3921	37¢ Lockheed P-80 Shooting Star	07/29/05	.75	.20			1.25	
3922	37¢ Consolidated B-24 Liberator	07/29/05	.75	.20			1.25	
3923	37¢ Boeing B-29 Superfortress	07/29/05	.75	.20			1.25	
3924	37¢ Beechcraft 35 Bonanza	07/29/05	.75	.20			1.25	
3925	37¢ Northrop YB-49 Flying Wing	07/29/05	.75	.20			1.25	
a	Block of 10		7.50		7.50	(10)		
	American Treasures: new Mexico Rio Grande Blankets, Tagged, Self-Adhesive, Serpentine Die-Cut 10.75 on 2 or 3 sides							
3926	37¢ Spanish design	07/30/05	.75	.20			1.25	
3927	37¢ Mexican design	07/30/05	.75	.20			1.25	
3928	37¢ Pueblo design	07/30/05	.75	.20			1.25	
3929	37¢ Navajo design	07/30/05	.75	.20			1.25	
a	Block of 4		3.00					
b	Booklet pane of 5 ea.		15.00					
	Tagged, Self-Adhesive, Serpentine Die-Cut 10.75							
3930	37¢ Presidential Libraries	08/04/05	.75	.20	3.00	(4)	1.25	

2006 OLYMPIC WINTER GAMES

With this stamp featuring an illustration of a downhill skier, the U.S. Postal Service continues its tradition of honoring the spirit of athleticism and international unity inspired by the Olympic Games. First recorded in Greece in 776 B.C., the games began as a tribute to the Olympian gods who, it was believed, bestowed on humans the gifts of strength and fleetness of foot. The stamp was issued to coincide with the XXth Olympic Winter Games, which were held February 10-26, 2006, in Torino, Italy. Prompted by a growing cadre of snow-sport enthusiasts, the first Olympic Winter Games—initially called International Sports Week—were held in 1924 at a small Alpine resort in Chamonix, France. The event attracted more than 250 athletes from 16 countries, spurring the International Olympic Committee (IOC) to agree to stage winter games separately from summer competitions. At the 2006 Olympic Winter Games, some 2,500 athletes—a word derived from the Greek word for "prize-seekers"—competed on snow and ice in front of an estimated 1.5 million spectators. Stamps featuring Olympic themes have been popular with collectors since the first modern Olympiad in 1896, when Greece issued 12 Olympic-themed commemorative stamps. Beginning in 1932, numerous U.S. stamps have honored the Olympic Games held in both winter and summer.

36 U.S.C. Sec. 220506. Official Licensed Product of the United States Olympic Committee.

	Issue	Date	Un	U	PB	#	FDC	Q(M)
	America on the Move: 50s Sporty Cars, Tagged, Self-Adhesive, Serpentine Die-Cut 10.75 on 2 or 3 sides							
3931	37¢ 1953 Studebaker Starliner	08/20/05	.75	.20			1.25	
3932	37¢ 1954 Kaiser Darren	08/20/05	.75	.20			1.25	
3933	37¢ 1953 Chevrolet Corvette	08/20/05	.75	.20			1.25	
3934	37¢ 1952 Nash Healey	08/20/05	.75	.20			1.25	
3935	37¢ 1955 Ford Thunderbird	08/20/05	.75	.20			1.25	
a	Vertical strip of 5 #3931-3935		3.75					
b	Booklet pane of 4 ea.		15.00					
	American Sports Personalities, Tagged, Self-Adhesive, Serpentine Die-Cut 10.75							
3936	37¢ Arthur Ashe	08/27/05	.75	.20	3.00	(4)	1.25	
	To Form a More Perfect Union, Tagged, Self-Adhesive, Serpentine Die-Cut 10.75 x 10.5							
3937	37¢ Pane of 10	08/30/05	7.50					
a	1948 Executive Order 9981		.75	.20			1.25	
b	1965 Voting Rights Act		.75	.20			1.25	
c	1960 Lunch Counter Sit-ins		.75	.20			1.25	
d	1957 Little Rock Nine		.75	.20			1.25	
	To Form a More Perfect Union, continued, **Tagged, Self-Adhesive, Serpentine Die-Cut 10.75 x 10.5**							
e	1955 Montgomery Bus Boycott		.75	.20			1.25	
f	1961 Freedom Riders		.75	.20			1.25	
g	1964 Civil Rights Act		.75	.20			1.25	
h	1963 March on Washington		.75	.20			1.25	
i	1965 Selma March		.75	.20			1.25	
j	1954 Brown v. Board of Education		.75	.20			1.25	
	Tagged, Self-Adhesive, Serpentine Die-Cut 10.5 x 11							
3938	37¢ Child Health	09/07/05	.75	.20	3.00	(4)	1.25	
	Let's Dance/Bailemos, Tagged, Self-Adhesive, Serpentine Die-Cut 10.75							
3939	37¢ Merengue	09/17/05	.75	.20			1.25	
3940	37¢ Salsa	09/17/05	.75	.20			1.25	
3941	37¢ Cha cha cha	09/17/05	.75	.20			1.25	
3942	37¢ Mambo	09/17/05	.75	.20			1.25	
a	Vert. strip of 4		3.00		6.00	(8)	3.25	
	Legends of Hollywood, Tagged, Self-Adhesive, Serpentine Die-Cut 10.75							
3943	37¢ Greta Garbo	09/23/05	.75	.20	3.00	(4)	1.25	

FAVORITE CHILDREN'S BOOK ANIMALS

Eight cherished animal characters from children's literature enliven the Favorite Children's Book Animals stamp pane issued by the U.S. Postal Service in 2006. Children and adults alike will delight in the spirited and colorful stamps that feature The Very Hungry Caterpillar (Eric Carle), Maisy (Lucy Cousins), Curious George (Margret and H.A. Rey), Olivia (Ian Falconer), Wild Thing (Maurice Sendak), Wilbur (Garth Williams), Frederick (Leo Lionni), and Fox in Socks (Dr. Seuss). These stamps mark the first ever collaboration between Royal Mail in the United Kingdom and the U.S. Postal Service. After choosing children's book animals as the theme for the stamps, the two postal authorities agreed to share two characters—the Very Hungry Caterpillar and Maisy—but to work independently on the rest of the issuance. The results are two unique stamp panes that celebrate cherished animals from children's books treasured by readers on both sides of the Atlantic.

3931
3932
3933
3934
3935

3935a

USA 37
Arthur Ashe

3936

3937 a b
c d
e f
g h i j

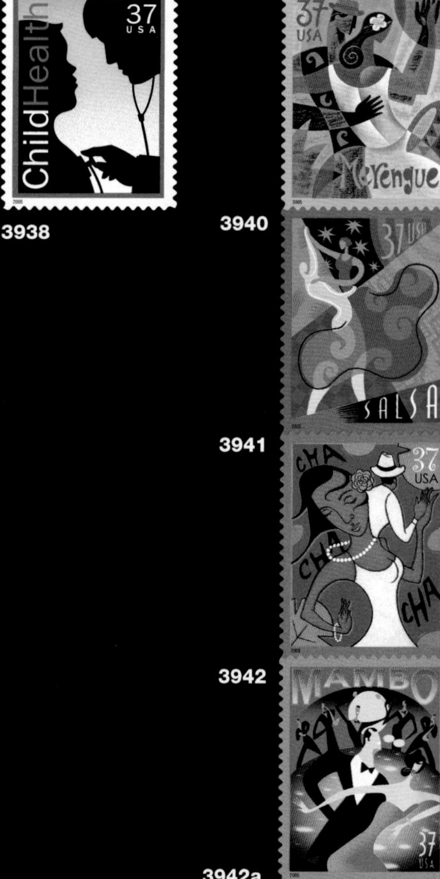

3938
3939
3940
3941
3942
3942a

USA 37
GRETA GARBO

3943

3965

VISIT US ONLINE AT **THE POSTAL STORE**

AT **WWW.USPS.COM**

OR CALL **1 800 STAMP-24**

Issue		Date	Un	U	PB	#	FDC	Q(M)
	Jim Henson and the Muppets, Tagged, Self-Adhesive, Serpentine Die-Cut 10.5, 10.5 x 10.75							
3944	37¢ Pane of 11	09/28/05	8.25				8.75	
a	Kermit the Frog		.75	.20			1.25	
b	Fozzie Bear		.75	.20			1.25	
c	Sam the Eagle and Flag		.75	.20			1.25	
d	Miss Piggy		.75	.20			1.25	
e	Statler and Waldorf		.75	.20			1.25	
f	The Swedish Chef and Fruit		.75	.20			1.25	
g	Animal		.75	.20			1.25	
h	Dr. Bunsen Honeydew and Beaker		.75	.20			1.25	
i	Rowlf the Dog		.75	.20			1.25	
j	The Great Gonzo and Camilla the Chicken		.75	.20			1.25	
k	Jim Henson		.75	.20			1.25	
	Constellations, Tagged, Self-Adhesive, Serpentine Die-Cut 10.75							
3945	37¢ Leo	10/03/05	.75	.20	3.00	(4)	1.25	
3946	37¢ Orion	10/03/05	.75	.20	3.00	(4)	1.25	
3947	37¢ Lyra	10/03/05	.75	.20	3.00	(4)	1.25	
3948	37¢ Pegasus	10/03/05	.75	.20	3.00	(4)	1.25	
a	Block or vert. strip of 4		3.00		3.00	(4)	3.25	
	Holiday Celebrations: Holiday, Christmas Cookies, Tagged, Self-Adhesive, Serpentine Die-Cut 10.75 x 11							
3949	37¢ Santa Claus	10/20/05	.75	.20	3.00	(4)	1.25	
3950	37¢ Snowmen	10/20/05	.75	.20	3.00	(4)	1.25	
3951	37¢ Angel	10/20/05	.75	.20	3.00	(4)	1.25	
3952	37¢ Elves	10/20/05	.75	.20	3.00	(4)	1.25	
a	Block or vert. strip of 4		3.00		3.00	(4)	3.25	
	Booklet, Self-Adhesive, Serpentine Die-Cut 10.75 x 11 on 2 or 3 sides							
3953	37¢ Santa Claus	10/20/05	.75	.20	3.00	(4)	1.25	
3954	37¢ Snowmen	10/20/05	.75	.20	3.00	(4)	1.25	
3955	37¢ Angel	10/20/05	.75	.20	3.00	(4)	1.25	
3956	37¢ Elves	10/20/05	.75	.20	3.00	(4)	1.25	
a	Block or vert. strip of 4		3.00		3.00	(4)	3.25	
	Booklet, Self-Adhesive, Serpentine Die-Cut 10.5 x 10.75 on 2 or 3 sides							
3957	37¢ Santa Claus	10/20/05	.75	.20	3.00	(4)	1.25	
3958	37¢ Snowmen	10/20/05	.75	.20	3.00	(4)	1.25	
3959	37¢ Angel	10/20/05	.75	.20	3.00	(4)	1.25	
3960	37¢ Elves	10/20/05	.75	.20	3.00	(4)	1.25	
a	Block or vert. strip of 4		3.00		3.00	(4)	3.25	

Issue		Date	Un	U	PB	#	FDC	Q(M)
	Distinguished Marines, Tagged, Self-Adhesive, Serpentine Die-Cut 11 x 10.5							
3961	37¢ Lt. Gen. John A. Lejeune	11/10/05	.75	.20	3.00	(4)	1.25	
3962	37¢ Lt. Gen. Lewis B. Puller	11/10/05	.75	.20	3.00	(4)	1.25	
3963	37¢ Sgt. John Basilone	11/10/05	.75	.20	3.00	(4)	1.25	
3964	37¢ Sgt. Major Daniel J. Daly	11/10/05	.75	.20	3.00	(4)	1.25	
a	Block or horiz. strip of 4		3.00		3.25	(4)	3.25	
	Tagged, Perf. 11.25							
3965	39¢ Flag and Statue of Liberty	12/08/05	.80	.20	3.20	(4)	1.25	
	Self-Adhesive, Serpentine Die-Cut 11.25 x 11							
3966	(39¢) Flag and Statue of Liberty	12/08/05	.80	.20	3.20	(4)	1.25	
	Coil, Perf. 9.75 Vertically							
3967	(39¢) Flag and Statue of Liberty	12/08/05	.80	.20	5.75	(5)	1.25	
	Self-Adhesive, Serpentine Die-Cut 8.5 Vertically							
3968	(39¢) Flag and Statue of Liberty	12/08/05	.80	.20	5.75	(5)	1.25	
	Tagged, Coil, Serpentine Die-Cut 10.25 Vertically							
3969	(39¢) Flag and Statue of Liberty, dated "2006"	12/08/05	.80	.20	5.75	(5)	1.25	
	Self-Adhesive, Serpentine Die-Cut 9.5 Vertically							
3970	(39¢) Flag and Statue of Liberty	12/08/05	.80	.20	5.75	(5)	1.25	
	Booklet, Serpentine Die-Cut 11.25 x 11 on 2 or 3 sides							
3971	(39¢) Flag and Statue of Liberty	12/08/05	.80	.20			1.25	
a	Booklet pane of 20		16.00					
	Self-Adhesive, Serpentine Die-Cut 11.25 x 10.75 on 2 or 3 sides							
3972	(39¢) Flag and Statue of Liberty	12/08/05	.80	.20			1.25	
a	Booklet pane of 20		16.00					
	Self-Adhesive, Serpentine Die-Cut 11.25 x 11 on 2 or 3 sides							
3974	(39¢) Flag and Statue of Liberty	12/08/05	.80	.20			1.25	
a	Booklet pane of 4		3.20					
	Self-Adhesive, Serpentine Die-Cut 8 on 2, 3 or 4 sides							
3975	(39¢) Flag and Statue of Liberty	12/08/05	.80	.20			1.25	
a	Booklet pane of 18		14.50					

SUGAR RAY ROBINSON

In 2006 the U.S. Postal Service paid tribute to six-time world champion boxer Sugar Ray Robinson (1921-1989) by issuing a commemorative stamp in his honor. In his prime, Robinson was virtually unbeatable in the ring. He reigned as the undefeated world welterweight champion from December 20, 1946, until February 14, 1951, when he won the world middleweight title for the first of five times. According to The Ring Record Book, he fought a total of 201 bouts, winning 174 (109 by knockout) against only 19 losses, 6 draws, and 2 no contests. No boxer could stop Robinson; heat exhaustion contributed to the only technical knockout he ever suffered. During and after his long boxing career Robinson received numerous awards and honors: He won his first fighter of the year award from The Ring magazine in 1942 and his second in 1951. He received the Edward J. Neil trophy for fighter of the year in 1950. His portrait appeared on the cover of the June 25, 1951, issue of TIME magazine—the caption read "Sugar Ray Robinson: Rhythm in his feet and pleasure in his work." In 1967 he was elected to the Boxing Hall of Fame. In 1999 a panel of experts named him "fighter of the century."

Sugar Ray Robinson licensed by CMG Worldwide, Indianapolis, IN.

	Issue	Date	Un	U	PB	#	FDC	Q(M)
	Semi-Postal, Tagged, Self-Adhesive, Serpentine Die-Cut 11							
B1	(32¢ + 8¢) Breast Cancer Research	07/29/1998	.75	.25	3.00	(4)	1.50	618
	The 8¢ surtax went for cancer research. After the 1999 first class postage rate increase the surcharge became 7¢; 2001 it became 6¢. In March, 2002 the stamp sold for 45¢ but the face value remained 34¢ until June at which time the face value rose to 37¢. Sales were suspended Jan. 1, 2004 but were resumed Feb. 2, 2004 when congress extended the sales period through Dec. 31, 2005.							

	Issue	Date	Un	U	PB	#	FDC	Q(M
	Semi-Postal, Tagged, Self-Adhesive, Serpentine Die-Cut 11.25							
B2	(34¢ + 11¢) Heroes of 2001	06/07/02	.80	.50	3.25	(4)	2.00	25
	The 11¢ surtax went for assistance to families of emergency relief personnel killed or permanently disabled in the line of duty in connection with the terrorists attacks of Sept. 11, 2001. The face value became 37¢ and the surtax 8¢ June 30, 2002.							
	Semi-Postal, Tagged, Self-Adhesive, Serpentine Die-Cut 11							
B3	(37¢ + 8¢) Stop Family Violence	10/08/03	.90	.55	3.60	(4)	1.60	12

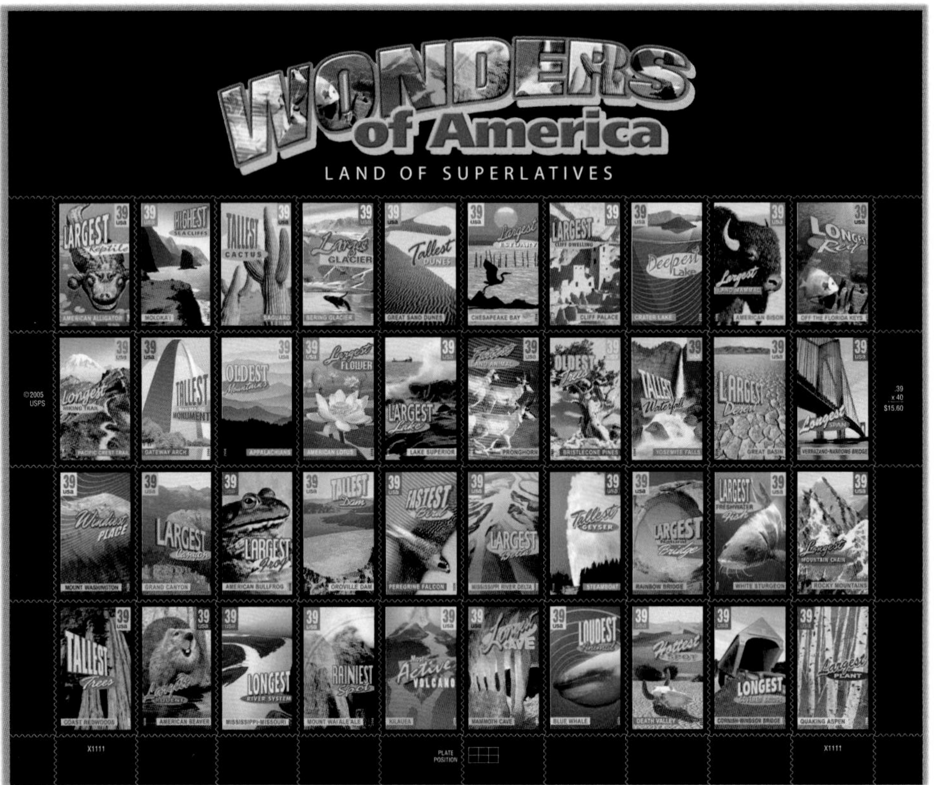

WONDERS OF AMERICA: LAND OF SUPERLATIVES

The United States is a land of superlatives, rich in natural and man-made wonders. Forty of the most remarkable places, structures, plants, and animals in America appear on this stamp pane. Among the many extraordinary places shown on the stamps are Kentucky's Mammoth Cave, the longest known cave; Oregon's Crater Lake, the deepest in the country; and the largest canyon, the aptly named Grand Canyon in Arizona. Record-holders from the animal kingdom—the American alligator, largest reptile in North America, and the peregrine falcon, fastest bird in the world—share the spotlight with superlatives from the plant world: the saguaro, tallest cactus in the U.S., and the American lotus whose flower may reach ten inches in diameter. Man-made wonders include the largest cliff dwelling, a centuries-old, multistor pueblo known today as Cliff Palace, in southwestern Colorado and Gateway Arch, in St. Louis, Missouri, the nation's tallest man made monument. The Wonders of America pane offers just a sampling of the many superlatives found all across the nation. Th stamp art is by Lonnie Busch, who illustrated the 50 Greeting from America stamps in 2002.

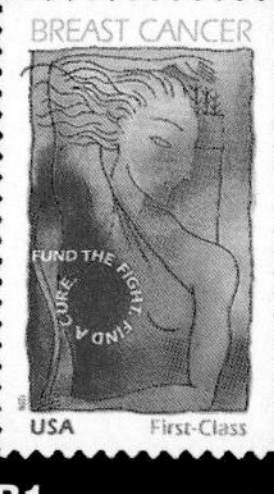
BREAST CANCER
FUND THE FIGHT. FIND A CURE.
USA
First-Class

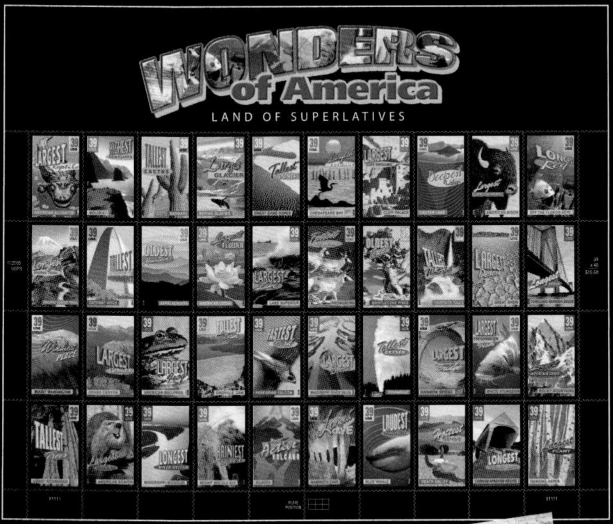

B1

FIRST-CLASS +
HEROES
USA
2001

B2

FIRST-CLASS + USA
STOP!
FAMILY
VIOLENCE

B3

1

2

3

5

6

8

9

11

12

13

14

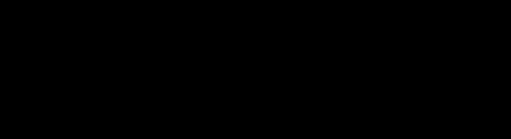

Newspaper/Periodical

1865-1897

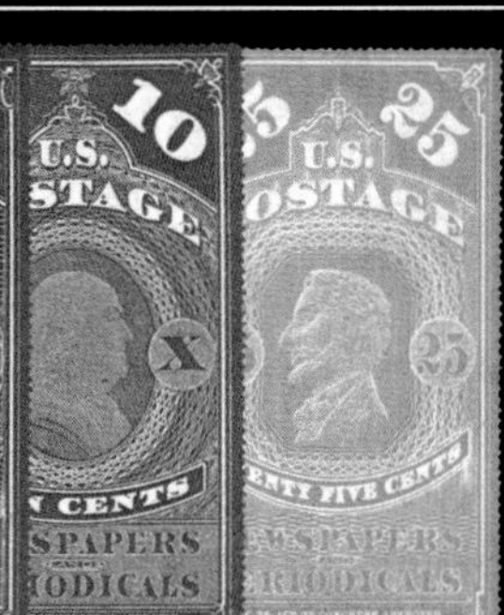

PR1 PR2 PR3

PR15

PR18

PR24

PR25

PR26

PR27

PR28

PR29

PR30

PR78

PR79

PR90

PR116

PR118

PR119

PR120

PR121

PR122

PR123

PR124

PR125

Confederate States of America

Issue		Date	Un	U
	Imperf., Lithographed, Soft Porous Paper			
	5¢ Jefferson Davis	1861	250.00	150.00
	10¢ Thomas Jefferson	1861	280.00	190.00
	2¢ Andrew Jackson	1862	750.00	650.00
	5¢ Jefferson Davis (6)	1862	180.00	110.00
	10¢ Thomas Jefferson	1862	1,400.00	500.00
	Imperf., Typographed, Hard Medium Paper			
	5¢ Jefferson Davis, (London print)	1862	10.00	27.50
	Imperf., Typographed, Thin to Thick Paper			
7	5¢ Jefferson Davis (6) (Local print)	1862	13.00	20.00
	Imperf., Engraved, Soft Porous Paper			
8	2¢ Andrew Jackson	1863	70.00	*350.00*
9	10¢ Jefferson Davis	1863	850.00	525.00
10	10¢ Jefferson Davis (9), (with rect. frame showing parts of lines outside at least 3 sides of frame)	1863	5,000.00	1,600.00
	Imperf., Engraved, Thick or Thin Paper			
11	10¢ Jefferson Davis, die A	1863	9.00	16.00
12	10¢ Jefferson Davis die B (11), with extra line outside corner ornament	1863	11.00	18.00
13	20¢ George Washington	1863	37.50	*400.00*
	Imperf., Typographed			
14	1¢ John C. Calhoun This stamp was never put into use	1862	100.00	

Newspaper/Periodical

Issue		Date	Un	U
	Typographed, Perf. 12: Colored Border, Thin Hard Paper			
PR1	5¢ Washington	1865	550.00	*1,250.00*
PR2	10¢ Franklin	1865	260.00	*1,000.00*
PR3	25¢ Lincoln	1865	300.00	*2,000.00*
	White Border, Yellowish Paper			
PR4	5¢ Washington	1865	175.00	—
	White Border, Hard White Paper			
PR5	5¢ Washington	1875	150.00	
	Colored Border, Hard White Paper			
PR6	10¢ Franklin	1875	165.00	
PR7	25¢ Lincoln	1875	200.00	
	White Border, Soft Porous Paper			
PR8	5¢ Washington	1881	450.00	
	Engraved, Perf. 12, Thin Hard Paper			
PR9	2¢ Statue of Freedom	1875	150.00	25.00
PR10	3¢ Statue of Freedom	1875	150.00	27.50
PR11	4¢ Statue of Freedom	1875	150.00	25.00
PR12	6¢ Statue of Freedom	1875	175.00	27.50
PR13	8¢ Statue of Freedom	1875	200.00	40.00
PR14	9¢ Statue of Freedom	1875	325.00	87.50
PR15	10¢ Statue of Freedom	1875	225.00	32.50
PR16	12¢ "Justice"	1875	450.00	82.50
PR17	24¢ "Justice"	1875	500.00	100.00
PR18	36¢ "Justice"	1875	600.00	110.00
PR19	48¢ "Justice"	1875	900.00	175.00
PR20	60¢ "Justice"	1875	800.00	100.00
PR21	72¢ "Justice"	1875	1,000.00	230.00
PR22	84¢ "Justice"	1875	1,400.00	330.00
PR23	96¢ "Justice"	1875	1,100.00	225.00
PR24	$1.92 Ceres	1875	1,250.00	225.00
PR25	$3 "Victory"	1875	1,500.00	250.00
PR26	$6 Clio	1875	2,500.00	475.00
PR27	$9 Minerva	1875	3,500.00	525.00
PR28	$12 Vesta	1875	4,000.00	675.00
PR29	$24 "Peace"	1875	4,000.00	700.00
PR30	$36 "Commerce"	1875	4,250.00	850.00
PR31	$48 Hebe	1875	5,500.00	1,000.00
PR32	$60 Indian Maiden	1875	5,750.00	1,100.00
	Special Printing, Perf. 12, Hard White Paper			
PR33	2¢ Statue of Freedom	1875	550.00	
PR34	3¢ Statue of Freedom	1875	550.00	
PR35	4¢ Statue of Freedom	1875	600.00	
PR36	6¢ Statue of Freedom	1875	800.00	
PR37	8¢ Statue of Freedom	1875	850.00	
PR38	9¢ Statue of Freedom	1875	950.00	
PR39	10¢ Statue of Freedom	1875	1,200.00	
PR40	12¢ "Justice"	1875	1,500.00	
PR41	24¢ "Justice"	1875	2,000.00	
PR42	36¢ "Justice"	1875	2,500.00	
PR43	48¢ "Justice"	1875	3,250.00	
PR44	60¢ "Justice"	1875	3,500.00	
PR45	72¢ "Justice"	1875	4,000.00	
PR46	84¢ "Justice"	1875	4,500.00	
PR47	96¢ "Justice"	1875	*7,500.00*	
PR48	$1.92 Ceres	1875	*20,000.00*	
PR49	$3 "Victory"	1875	*45,000.00*	
PR50	$6 Clio	1875	*80,000.00*	
PR51	$9 Minerva	1875	*115,000.00*	
PR52	$12 Vesta	1875	*115,000.00*	
PR53	$24 "Peace"	1875	—	
PR54	$36 "Commerce"	1875	*250,000.00*	
PR55	$48 Hebe	1875	—	
PR56	$60 Indian Maiden	1875	—	
	Soft Porous Paper, Perf. 12			
PR57	2¢ Statue of Freedom	1879	50.00	6.50
PR58	3¢ Statue of Freedom	1879	55.00	8.00
PR59	4¢ Statue of Freedom	1879	55.00	8.00
PR60	6¢ Statue of Freedom	1879	85.00	16.50
PR61	8¢ Statue of Freedom	1879	90.00	16.50
PR62	10¢ Statue of Freedom	1879	90.00	16.50
PR63	12¢ "Justice"	1879	400.00	65.00
PR64	24¢ "Justice"	1879	400.00	65.00
PR65	36¢ "Justice"	1879	800.00	185.00
PR66	48¢ "Justice"	1879	750.00	140.00
PR67	60¢ "Justice"	1879	625.00	120.00
PR68	72¢ "Justice"	1879	1,200.00	230.00
PR69	84¢ "Justice"	1879	1,200.00	175.00
PR70	96¢ "Justice"	1879	900.00	125.00
PR71	$1.92 Ceres	1879	450.00	105.00
PR72	$3 "Victory"	1879	550.00	115.00
PR73	$6 Clio	1879	950.00	175.00
PR74	$9 Minerva	1879	725.00	125.00
PR75	$12 Vesta	1879	750.00	160.00
PR76	$24 "Peace"	1879	775.00	200.00
PR77	$36 "Commerce"	1879	850.00	220.00
PR78	$48 Hebe	1879	900.00	300.00
PR79	$60 Indian Maiden	1879	825.00	280.00
	Special Printing of 1879			
PR80	2¢ Statue of Freedom	1883	1,250.00	
	Perf. 12			
PR81	1¢ Statue of Freedom	1885	50.00	7.50
PR82	12¢ "Justice"	1885	165.00	18.00
PR83	24¢ "Justice"	1885	165.00	20.00
PR84	36¢ "Justice"	1885	225.00	32.50
PR85	48¢ "Justice"	1885	300.00	47.50
PR86	60¢ "Justice"	1885	375.00	70.00
PR87	72¢ "Justice"	1885	375.00	75.00
PR88	84¢ "Justice"	1885	725.00	175.00
PR89	96¢ "Justice"	1885	600.00	135.00
	Soft Wove Paper, Perf. 12			
PR90	1¢ Stat. of Freedom	1894	325.00	*650.00*
PR91	2¢ Stat. of Freedom	1894	375.00	
PR92	4¢ Stat. of Freedom	1894	475.00	—
PR93	6¢ Stat. of Freedom	1894	4,250.00	
PR94	10¢ Stat. of Freedom	1894	900.00	
PR95	12¢ "Justice"	1894	2,500.00	*1,500.00*
PR96	24¢ "Justice"	1894	2,750.00	*1,750.00*
PR97	36¢ "Justice"	1894	*50,000.00*	
PR98	60¢ "Justice"	1894	*60,000.00*	*7,500.00*
PR99	96¢ "Justice"	1894	*50,000.00*	
PR100	$3 "Victory"	1894	*60,000.00*	
PR101	$6 Clio	1894	*60,000.00*	—
PR102	1¢ Stat. of Freedom	1895	150.00	40.00
PR103	2¢ Stat. of Freedom	1895	150.00	40.00
PR104	5¢ Stat. of Freedom	1895	225.00	70.00
PR105	10¢ Stat. of Freedom	1895	425.00	160.00
PR106	25¢ "Justice"	1895	600.00	200.00
PR107	50¢ "Justice"	1895	1,500.00	350.00
PR108	$2 "Victory"	1895	1,500.00	250.00
PR109	$5 Clio	1895	1,850.00	650.00
PR110	$10 Vesta	1895	2,250.00	750.00
PR111	$20 "Peace"	1895	3,000.00	1,250.00
PR112	$50 "Commerce"	1895	2,750	350.00
PR113	$100 Indian Maiden	1895	3,250.00	1,500.00
	Wmkd. 191, Perf. 12			
PR114	1¢ Stat. of Freedom	1895	7.50	*15.00*
PR115	2¢ Stat. of Freedom	1896	7.50	*15.00*
PR116	5¢ Stat. of Freedom	1896	10.00	*20.00*
PR117	10¢ Stat. of Freedom	1895	8.50	*15.00*
PR118	25¢ "Justice"	1895	13.50	*35.00*
PR119	50¢ "Justice"	1895	15.00	*40.00*
PR120	$2 "Victory"	1897	22.50	*60.00*
PR121	$5 Clio	1896	37.50	*90.00*
PR122	$10 Vesta	1896	35.00	*90.00*
PR123	$20 "Peace"	1896	40.00	*100.00*
PR124	$50 "Commerce"	1897	55.00	*120.00*
PR125	$100 Indian Maiden	1896	55.00	*150.00*

	Issue	Date	Un	U	PB #	FDC	Q(M)
	Unwmk., Engr., Perf. 11						
	For prepayment of postage on all mailable matter sent by airmail. All unwatermarked.						
C1	6¢ Curtiss Jenny	12/10/18	60.00	30.00	725.00 (6)	*32,500.00*	3
	Double transfer		90.00	45.00			
C2	16¢ Curtiss Jenny	07/11/18	75.00	35.00	1,000.00 (6)	*32,500.00*	4
C3	24¢ Curtiss Jenny	05/13/18	75.00	35.00	400.00 (4)	*27,500.00*	2
a	Center Inverted		*225,000.00*		*1,750,000.00* (4)		0.0001
	Unwmk., Perf. 11						
C4	8¢ Airplane Radiator and Wooden Propeller	08/15/23	22.50	14.00	225.00 (6)	450.00	6
C5	16¢ Air Service Emblem	08/17/23	75.00	30.00	1,550.00 (6)	650.00	5
C6	24¢ De Havilland Biplane	08/21/23	85.00	30.00	2,050.00 (6)	850.00	5
C7	10¢ Map of U.S. and Two Mail Planes	02/13/26	2.50	.35	35.00 (6)	70.00	42
	Double transfer		5.75	1.10			
C8	15¢ olive brown (C7)	09/18/26	2.75	2.50	35.00 (6)	85.00	16
C9	20¢ yellow green (C7)	01/25/27	7.00	2.00	75.00 (6)	100.00	18
C10	10¢ Lindbergh's "Spirit of St. Louis"	06/18/27	7.00	2.50	90.00 (6)	25.00	20
a	Booklet pane of 3	05/26/28	80.00	*65.00*		875.00	
C11	5¢ Beacon on Rocky Mountains	07/25/28	4.75	.75	175.00 (8)	50.00	107
	Recut frame line at left		6.50	1.25			
a	Vertical pair, imperf. between		*7,000.00*				
C12	5¢ Winged Globe	02/10/30	9.00	.50	135.00 (6)	12.00	98
a	Horizontal pair, imperf. between		*4,500.00*				
	Graf Zeppelin, Unwmk., Perf. 11						
C13	65¢ Zeppelin over Atlantic Ocean	04/19/30	240.00	160.00	2,250.00 (6)	1,200.00	0.09
C14	$1.30 Zeppelin Between Continents	04/19/30	450.00	375.00	5,600.00 (6)	1,100.00	0.07
C15	$2.60 Zeppelin Passing Globe	04/19/30	700.00	575.00	8,000.00 (6)	1,200.00	0.06
	Unwmk., Perf. 10.5 x 11						
C16	5¢ violet (C12)	08/19/31	5.00	.60	75.00 (4)	175.00	57
C17	8¢ olive bister (C12)	09/26/32	2.25	.40	27.50 (4)	15.00	77
	Century of Progress, Unwmk., Perf. 11						
C18	50¢ Zeppelin, Federal Building at Chicago Exposition and Hangar at Friedrichshafen	10/02/33	60.00	60.00	500.00 (6)	200.00	0.3
	Beginning with #C19, unused values are for never-hinged stamps.						
	Unwmk., Perf. 10.5 x 11						
C19	6¢ dull orange (C12)	06/30/34	3.50	.25	20.00 (4)	*190.00*	302
	Trans-Pacific, Unwmk., Perf. 11						
C20	25¢ "China Clipper" over the Pacific	11/22/35	1.40	1.00	20.00 (6)	40.00	10
C21	20¢ "China Clipper" over the Pacific	02/15/37	12.00	1.75	100.00 (6)	45.00	13
C22	50¢ carmine (C21)	02/15/37	12.00	5.00	100.00 (6)	50.00	9
C23	6¢ Eagle Holding Shield, Olive Branch and Arrows	05/14/38	.50	.20	6.50 (4)	15.00	350
	Ultramarine and carmine		*150.00*	*1,500.00*	*1,500.00* (4)		
a	Vertical pair, imperf. horizontally		*325.00*		1,250.00 (4)		
b	Horizontal pair, imperf. vertically		*12,500.00*		*37,500.00* (4)		

	Issue	Date	Un	U	PB/LP #	FDC	Q(M)
	Transatlantic, Unwmk., Perf. 11						
C24	30¢ Winged Globe	05/16/39	12.00	1.50	130.00 (6)	47.50	20
	Unwmk., Perf. 11 x 10.5						
C25	6¢ Twin-Motor Transport Plane	06/25/41	.20	.20	.60 (4)	3.75	4,747
a	Booklet pane of 3	03/18/43	5.00	*1.50*		25.00	
	Singles of #C25a are imperf. at sides or imperf. at sides and bottom.						
b	Horizontal pair, imperf. between		*2,250.00*				
C26	8¢ olive green (C25)	03/21/44	.20	.20	1.10 (4)	3.75	1,745
C27	10¢ violet (C25)	08/15/41	1.25	.20	5.50 (4)	8.00	67
C28	15¢ brn. carmine (C25)	08/19/41	2.25	.35	10.00 (4)	10.00	78
C29	20¢ bright green (C25)	08/27/41	2.25	.30	10.00 (4)	12.50	42
C30	30¢ blue (C25)	09/25/41	2.25	.35	10.00 (4)	20.00	60
C31	50¢ orange (C25)	10/29/41	11.00	3.25	50.00 (4)	40.00	11
C32	5¢ DC-4 Skymaster	09/25/46	.20	.20	.45 (4)	2.00	865
	Unwmk., Perf. 10.5 x 11						
C33	5¢ DC-4 Skymaster	03/26/47	.20	.20	.60 (4)	2.00	972
	Unwmk., Perf. 11 x 10.5						
C34	10¢ Pan American Union Bldg., Washington, D.C. and Martin 2-0-2	08/30/47	.25	.20	1.10 (4)	2.00	208
a	Dry printing		.40	.20	1.75 (4)		
C35	15¢ Statue of Liberty, N.Y. Skyline and Lockheed Constellation	08/20/47	.35	.20	1.50 (4)	1.75	756
a	Horizontal pair, imperf. between		*2,250.00*				
b	Dry printing		.55	.20	2.50 (4)		
C36	25¢ San Francisco-Oakland Bay Bridge and Boeing Stratocruiser	07/30/47	.90	.20	3.75 (4)	2.25	133
a	Dry printing		1.10	.20	4.75 (4)		
	Unwmk., Perf. 10 Horizontally						
C37	5¢ carmine (C33)	01/15/48	1.00	.80	10.00 (2)	1.75	33
	Unwmk., Perf. 11 x 10.5						
C38	5¢ New York City	07/31/48	.20	.20	3.50 (4)	1.75	38
	Unwmk., Perf. 10.5 x 11						
C39	6¢ carmine (C33)	01/18/49	.20	.20	.50 (4)	1.50	5,070
a	Booklet pane of 6	11/18/49	10.00	*5.00*		10.00	
b	Dry printing		.50	.20	2.25 (4)		
c	As "a," dry printing		20.00	—			
	Unwmk., Perf. 11 x 10.5						
C40	6¢ Alexandria, Virginia	05/11/49	.20	.20	.50 (4)	1.50	75
	Coil, Unwmk., Perf. 10 Horizontally						
C41	6¢ carmine (C33)	08/25/49	3.00	.20	14.00 (2)	1.25	260
	Universal Postal Union, Unwmk., Perf. 11 x 10.5						
C42	10¢ Post Office Dept. Bldg.	11/18/49	.20	.20	1.40 (4)	1.75	21
C43	15¢ Globe and Doves Carrying Messages	10/07/49	.30	.25	1.25 (4)	2.75	37
C44	25¢ Boeing Stratocruiser and Globe	11/30/49	.60	.40	4.00 (4)	3.75	16
C45	6¢ Wright Brothers	12/17/49	.20	.20	.65 (4)	2.75	80
C46	80¢ Diamond Head, Honolulu, Hawaii	03/26/52	5.00	1.25	22.50 (4)	17.50	19
C47	6¢ Powered Flight	05/29/53	.20	.20	.55 (4)	1.50	78
C48	4¢ Eagle in Flight	09/03/54	.20	.20	1.25 (4)	1.00	50

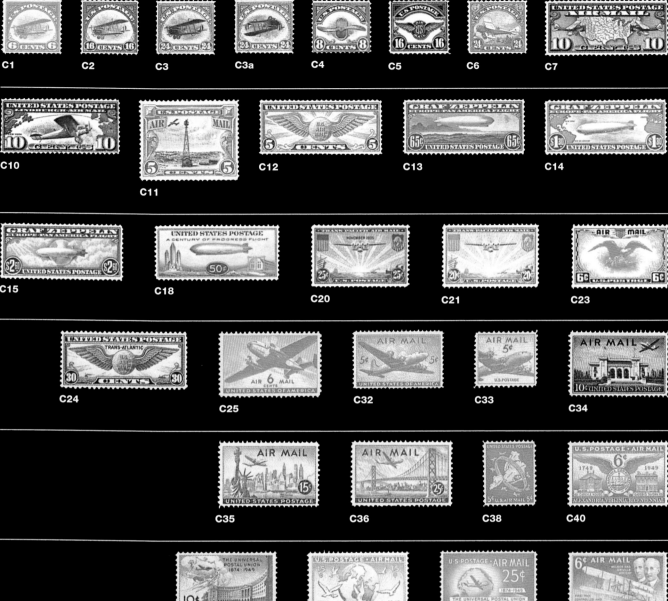

C1  C2  C3  C3a  C4  C5  C6  C7

C10  C11  C12  C13  C14

C15  C18  C20  C21  C23

C24  C25  C32  C33  C34

C35  C36  C38  C40

C42 C43 C44  C45

C46 C47 C48

C49

C51

C53

C54

C55

C56

C57

C58

C59

C61

C62

C63

C64

C66

C67

C68

C69

C70

C71

C72

C74

C75

C76

C77

C78

C79

C80

C81

C84

C85

C86

C87

C88

C89

C90

	Issue	Date	Un	U	PB/LP	#	FDC	Q(M)
	Unwmk., Perf. 11 x 10.5							
C49	6¢ Air Force	08/01/57	.20	.20	.65	(4)	1.75	63
C50	5¢ rose red (C48)	07/31/58	.20	.20	1.25	(4)	1.00	72
	Unwmk., Perf. 10.5 x 11							
C51	7¢ Jet Airliner	07/31/58	.20	.20	.60	(4)	1.00	1,327
a	Booklet pane of 6		10.00	*7.00*			9.00	221
	Coil, Perf. 10 Horizontally							
C52	7¢ blue (C51)	07/31/58	2.00	.20	14.00	(2)	1.00	157
	Unwmk., Perf. 11 x 10.5							
C53	7¢ Alaska Statehood	01/03/59	.20	.20	.60	(4)	1.25	90
	Unwmk., Perf. 11							
C54	7¢ Balloon Jupiter	08/17/59	.20	.20	.70	(4)	1.75	79
	Unwmk., Perf. 11 x 10.5							
C55	7¢ Hawaii Statehood	08/21/59	.20	.20	.60	(4)	1.00	85
	Unwmk., Perf. 11							
C56	10¢ Pan American Games	08/27/59	.25	.25	1.25	(4)	1.00	39
C57	10¢ Liberty Bell	06/10/60	1.00	.70	4.50	(4)	1.25	40
C58	15¢ Statue of Liberty	11/20/59	.35	.20	1.50	(4)	1.25	98
C59	25¢ Abraham Lincoln	04/22/60	.50	.20	2.00	(4)	1.25	
a	Tagged	12/29/66	.60	.30	2.50	(4)	50.00	
	Unwmk., Perf. 10.5 x 11							
C60	7¢ carmine (C61)	08/12/60	.20	.20	.60	(4)	1.00	1,289
	Pair with full horizontal gutter between		125.00					
a	Booklet pane of 6	08/19/60	11.00	*8.00*			8.00	
b	Vertical pair, imperf. between		*5,500.00*					
	Coil, Unwmk., Perf. 10 Horizontally							
C61	7¢ Jet Airliner	10//22/60	4.00	.25	35.00	(2)	1.00	87
	Unwmk., Perf. 11							
C62	13¢ Liberty Bell	06/28/61	.40	.20	1.65	(4)	1.00	
a	Tagged	02/15/67	.75	.50	5.00	(4)	50.00	
C63	15¢ Statue of Liberty	01/13/61	.30	.20	1.25	(4)	1.00	
a	Tagged	01/11/67	.35	.20	1.50	(4)	50.00	
b	As "a," horiz. pair, imperf. vertically		*12,500.00*					
	#C63 has a gutter between the two parts of the design; C58 does not.							
	Unwmk., Perf. 10.5 x 11							
C64	8¢ Jetliner over Capitol	12/05/62	.20	.20	.65	(4)	1.00	
a	Tagged	08/01/63	.20	.20	.65	(4)	2.00	
b	Booklet pane of 5 + label		7.00	*3.00*			3.50	
c	As "b," tagged	1964	2.00	*.75*				
	Coil, Perf. 10 Horizontally							
C65	8¢ carmine (C64)	12/05/62	.40	.20	3.75	(2)	1.00	
a	Tagged	01/14/65	.35	.20	1.50	(2)		
	Unwmk., Perf. 11							
C66	15¢ Montgomery Blair	05/03/63	.60	.55	2.60	(4)	1.50	42
	Unwmk., Perf. 11 x 10.5							
C67	6¢ Bald Eagle	07/12/63	.20	.20	1.60	(4)	1.00	
a	Tagged	02/15/67	4.00	3.00	55.00	(4)	50.00	
	Unwmk., Perf. 11							
C68	8¢ Amelia Earhart	07/24/63	.20	.20	1.00	(4)	3.50	64
	Tagged, Perf. 11							
C69	8¢ Robert H. Goddard	10/05/64	.40	.20	1.75	(4)	3.00	62
	Unwmk., Perf. 11							
C70	8¢ Alaska Purchase	03/30/67	.25	.20	1.25	(4)	1.25	56
	Perf. 11							
C71	20¢ "Columbia Jays," by Audubon, (See also #1241)	04/26/67	.80	.20	3.50	(4)	2.00	50
a	Tagging omitted		*10.00*					

	Issue	Date	Un	U	PB/LP	#	FDC	Q(M)
	Unwmk., Perf. 11 x 10.5							
C72	10¢ 50-Star Runway	01/05/68	.20	.20	.90	(4)	1.00	
b	Booklet pane of 8		2.00	*.75*			3.75	
c	Booklet pane of 5 + label	01/06/68	3.75	*.75*			125.00	
	Coil, Perf. 10 Vertically							
C73	10¢ carmine (C72)	01/05/68	.30	.20	1.75	(2)	1.00	
a	Imperf., pair		*600.00*		*900.00*	(2)		
	Perf. 11							
C74	10¢ U.S. Air Mail Service	05/15/68	.25	.20	1.75	(4)	1.50	60
b	Tagging omitted		*10.00*					
C75	20¢ USA and Jet	11/22/68	.35	.20	1.75	(4)	1.25	
a	Tagging omitted		*12.50*					
C76	10¢ Moon Landing	09/09/69	.25	.20	1.10	(4)	5.00	152
a	Rose red omitted		*525.00*	—				
	Perf. 10.5 x 11							
C77	9¢ Delta Wing Plane	05/15/71	.20	.20	.90	(4)	1.00	
	Perf. 11 x 10.5							
C78	11¢ Silhouette of Jet	05/07/71	.20	.20	.90	(4)	1.00	
a	Booklet pane of 4 + 2 labels		1.25	*.75*			2.25	
b	Untagged (Bureau precanceled)		.85	.85				
c	Tagging omitted (not Bureau precanceled)		7.50					
C79	13¢ Winged Airmail Envelope	11/16/73	.25	.20	1.10	(4)	1.00	
a	Booklet pane of 5 + label	12/27/73	1.50	*.75*			2.25	
b	Untagged (Bureau precanceled)		.85	.85				
	Perf. 11							
C80	17¢ Statue of Liberty	07/13/71	.35	.20	1.60	(4)	1.25	
a	Tagging omitted		10.00	—				
C81	21¢ USA and Jet	05/21/71	.40	.20	2.00	(4)	1.00	
a	Tagging omitted		*10.00*					
	Coil, Perf. 10 Vertically							
C82	11¢ carmine (C78)	05/07/71	.25	.20	.80	(2)	1.00	
a	Imperf., pair		*250.00*		*425.00*	(2)		
C83	13¢ carmine (C79)	12/27/73	.30	.20	1.10	(2)	1.00	
a	Imperf., pair		75.00		150.00	(2)		
	National Parks Centennial, Perf. 11							
C84	11¢ Kii Statue and Temple at City of Refuge Historical National Park, Honaunau, Hawaii	05/03/72	.20	.20	.90	(4)	1.00	78
a	Blue and green omitted		*750.00*					
	Olympic Games, Perf. 11 x 10.5							
C85	11¢ Skiers and Olympic Rings	08/17/72	.20	.20	2.50	(10)	1.00	96
	Progress in Electronics, Perf. 11							
C86	11¢ DeForest Audions	07/10/73	.20	.20	.95	(4)	1.00	59
a	Vermilion and green omitted		*900.00*					
b	Tagging omitted		*25.00*					
	Perf. 11							
C87	18¢ Statue of Liberty	01/11/74	.35	.30	1.50	(4)	1.00	
a	Tagging omitted		*17.50*					
C88	26¢ Mount Rushmore National Memorial	01/02/74	.50	.20	2.25	(4)	1.50	
a	Tagging omitted		*25.00*					
C89	25¢ Plane and Globes	01/02/76	.50	.20	2.25	(4)	1.00	
C90	31¢ Plane, Globes and Flag	01/02/76	.60	.20	2.60	(4)	1.25	
a	Tagging omitted		*15.00*					

	Issue	Date	Un	U	PB	#	FDC	Q(M)
	Pioneers of Aviation, Perf. 11							
C91	31¢ Wright Brothers, Flyer A	09/23/78	.65	.30			3.00	157
C92	31¢ Wright Brothers, Flyer A and Shed	09/23/78	.65	.30			3.00	157
a	Vert. pair, #C91-92		1.30	1.20	3.00	(4)	4.00	
b	As "a," ultramarine and black omitted		*700.00*					
c	As "a," black omitted		—					
d	As "a," black, yellow, magenta, blue and brown omitted		*2,250.00*					
	Pioneers of Aviation, Tagged, Perf. 11							
C93	21¢ Octave Chanute and Biplane Hang-Glider	03/29/79	.70	.35			3.00	29
C94	21¢ Biplane Hang-Glider and Chanute	03/29/79	.70	.35			3.00	29
a	Attached pair, #C93-C94		1.40	1.20	3.25	(4)	4.00	
b	As "a," ultramarine and black omitted		*4,500.00*					
C95	25¢ Wiley Post and "Winnie Mae"	11/20/79	1.10	.45			3.00	32
C96	25¢ NR-105-W, Post in Pressurized Suit and Portrait	11/20/79	1.10	.45			3.00	32
a	Vert. pair, #C95-C96		2.25	1.50	4.75	(4)	4.00	
	Olympic Games, Tagged, Perf. 11							
C97	31¢ High Jumper	11/01/79	.70	.30	9.50	(12)	1.50	47
	Tagged, Perf. 11							
C98	40¢ Philip Mazzei	10/13/80	.80	.20	10.00	(12)	1.50	81
b	Imperf., pair		*3,500.00*					
d	Tagging omitted		*10.00*					
	Tagged, Perf. 10.5 x 11.25							
C98A	40¢ Philip Mazzei	1982	7.50	1.50	125.00	(12)		
	Pioneers of Aviation, Tagged, Perf. 11							
C99	28¢ Blanche Stuart Scott and Biplane	12/30/80	.60	.20	8.50	(12)	1.50	20
a	Imperf., pair		*2,750.00*					
C100	35¢ Glen Curtiss and "Pusher" Biplane	12/30/80	.65	.20	9.00	(12)	1.50	23
	Olympic Games, Tagged, Perf. 11							
C101	28¢ Gymnast	06/17/83	1.00	.30			1.75	43
C102	28¢ Hurdler	06/17/83	1.00	.30			1.75	43
C103	28¢ Basketball Player	06/17/83	1.00	.30			1.75	43
C104	28¢ Soccer Player	06/17/83	1.00	.30			1.75	43
a	Block of 4, #C101-C104		4.25	2.50	5.50	(4)	3.75	
b	As "a," imperf., vert.		*7,500.00*					
	Olympic Games, Perf. 11.2 Bullseye							
C105	40¢ Shotputter	04/08/83	.90	.40			1.75	67
a	Perf. 11 line		1.00	.45				
C106	40¢ Gymnast	04/08/83	.90	.40			1.75	67
a	Perf. 11 line		1.00	.45				
	Olympic Games continued, **Perf. 11.2 Bullseye**							
C107	40¢ Swimmer	04/08/83	.90	.40			1.75	67
a	Perf. 11 line		1.00	.45				
C108	40¢ Weightlifter	04/08/83	.90	.40			1.75	67
a	Perf. 11 line		1.00	.45			5.00	
b	Block of 4, #C105-C108		4.25	3.00	5.00	(4)		
c	Block of 4, #C105a-C108a		5.00	4.00	7.50	(4)		
d	Block of 4, imperf.		*1,100.00*					
	Olympic Games, Tagged, Perf. 11							
C109	35¢ Fencer	11/04/83	.90	.55			1.75	
C110	35¢ Bicyclist	11/04/83	.90	.55			1.75	
C111	35¢ Volleyball Players	11/04/83	.90	.55			1.75	
C112	35¢ Pole Vaulter	11/04/83	.90	.55			1.75	
a	Block of 4, #C109-C112		4.00	3.25	7.00	(4)	4.50	175
	Pioneers of Aviation, Tagged, Perf. 11							
C113	33¢ Alfred Verville and Airplane Diagram	02/13/85	.65	.20	3.25	(4)	1.50	168
a	Imperf., pair		*850.00*					
C114	39¢ Lawrence and Elmer Sperry	02/13/85	.80	.25	3.75	(4)	1.50	168
a	Imperf., pair		*1,750.00*					
C115	44¢ Transpacific Airmail	02/15/85	.85	.25	4.00	(4)	1.75	209
a	Imperf., pair		*800.00*					
	Tagged, Perf. 11							
C116	44¢ Junipero Serra	08/22/85	1.00	.35	8.50	(4)	2.00	164
a	Imperf., pair		*1,500.00*					
C117	44¢ New Sweden	03/29/88	1.00	.25	6.75	(4)	1.50	137
	Pioneers of Aviation, Tagged, Perf. 11							
C118	45¢ Samuel P. Langley	05/14/88	.90	.20	4.25	(4)	1.50	406
a	Overall tagging		3.00	.50	30.00	(4)		
C119	36¢ Igor Sikorsky	06/23/88	.70	.25	3.25	(4)	2.00	179
	Tagged, Perf. 11.5 x 11							
C120	45¢ French Revolution	07/14/89	.95	.20	4.75	(4)	1.50	38
	America/PUAS, Perf. 11							
C121	45¢ Southeast Carved Wood Figure, Emblem of the Postal Union of the Americas and Spain	10/12/89	.90	.20	5.25	(4)	1.50	39
	20th UPU Congress, Tagged, Perf. 11							
C122	45¢ Hypersonic Airliner	11/27/89	1.00	.50			1.75	27
C123	45¢ Air-Cushion Vehicle	11/27/89	1.00	.50			1.75	27
C124	45¢ Surface Rover	11/27/89	1.00	.50			1.75	27
C125	45¢ Shuttle	11/27/89	1.00	.50			1.75	27
a	Block of 4, #C122-C125		4.25	3.25	5.50	(4)	6.50	
b	As "a," light blue (engr.) omitted		*750.00*					

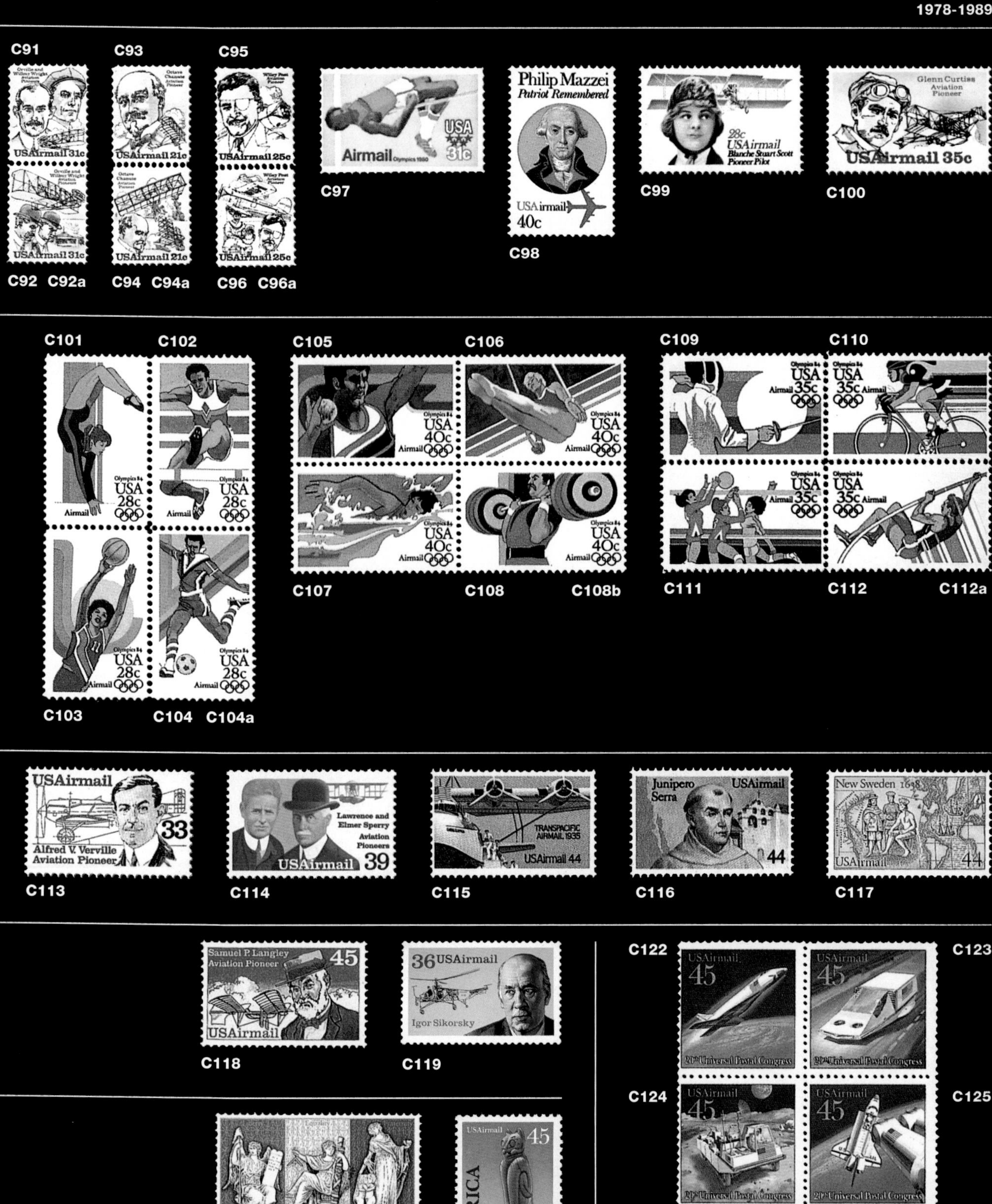

C91 C93 C95 C97 C98 C99 C100

C92 C92a C94 C94a C96 C96a

C101 C102 C103 C104 C104a

C105 C106 C107 C108 C108b

C109 C110 C111 C112 C112a

C113 C114 C115 C116 C117

C118 C119

C122 C123 C124 C125 C125a

C120 C121

20th Universal Postal Congress
A glimpse at several potential mail delivery methods of the future is the theme of these four stamps issued by the U.S. in commemoration of the convening of the 20th Universal Postal Congress in Washington, D.C. from November 13 through December 14, 1989. The United States, as host nation to the Congress for the first time in ninety-two years, welcomed more than 1,000 delegates from most of the member nations of the Universal Postal Union to the major international event.
©USPS 1989

C126

C127

C128

C129

C130

C131

C133

C134

C135

C136

C137

C138

CE1

CE2

E1

E3

E4

E6

E7

E12

E13

E14

E18

E20

E21

E22

E23

#	Issue	Date	Un	U	PB #	FDC	Q(M)
	20th UPU Congress Souvenir Sheet, Tagged, Imperf.						
C126	Designs of #C122-C125	11/24/1989	4.75	3.75		6.50	2
a-d	Single stamp from sheet		1.00	.50			
	America/PUAS, Tagged, Perf. 11 (See also #2512)						
C127	45¢ Tropical Coast	10/12/1990	.90	.20	6.75 (4)	1.50	48
	Pioneers of Aviation, Tagged, Perf. 11						
C128	50¢ Harriet Quimby and Early Plane	04/27/1991	1.00	.25	5.50 (4)	1.50	250
a	Vertical pair, imperf. horizontally		1,750.00				
b	Perf. 11.2	04/27/1991	1.10	.25	6.00 (4)		
C129	40¢ William T. Piper and Piper Cub Airplane	05/17/1991	.80	.20	4.00 (4)	1.50	182
	Tagged, Perf. 11						
C130	50¢ Antarctic Treaty	06/21/1991	1.00	.35	5.00 (4)	1.50	113
	America/PUAS, Tagged, Perf. 11						
C131	50¢ Eskimo and Bering Land Bridge	10/12/1991	1.00	.35	5.25 (4)	1.50	15
	Tagged, Perf. 11.2						
C132	40¢ William T. Piper, (type of 1991)	1993	1.50	.35	40.00 (4)		100
	Scenic American Landscapes, Tagged, Self-Adhesive, Perf. 11						
C133	48¢ Niagara Falls	05/12/1999	.95	.20	4.00 (4)	1.50	101
	Scenic American Landscapes, Tagged, Self-Adhesive, Serpentine Die-Cut 11						
C134	40¢ Rio Grande	07/30/1999	.80	.60	3.20 (4)	1.50	101
	Scenic American Landscapes, Tagged, Self-Adhesive, Serpentine Die-Cut 11.25 x 11.5						
C135	60¢ Grand Canyon	01/20/2000	1.25	.25	5.00 (4)	1.50	101
C136	70¢ Nine-Mile Prairie	03/06/2001	1.40	.30	5.60 (4)	1.50	85
	Scenic American Landscapes, Tagged, Self-Adhesive, Serpentine Die-Cut 11						
C137	80¢ Mount McKinley	04/17/2001	1.60	.35	6.40 (4)	1.75	85
	Scenic American Landscapes, Tagged, Self-Adhesive, Serpentine Die-Cut 11.25 x 11.5						
C138	60¢ Acadia National Park	05/30/2001	1.25	.25	5.00 (4)	1.50	100
a	Overall tagging	03/2003	1.25	.25	5.00 (4)	1.50	
b	As "a," with "2005"	01/2005	1.25	.25	5.00 (4)	1.50	

#	Issue	Date	Un	U	PB #	FDC
	Airmail Special Delivery					
	Unwmk. Perf. 11					
CE1	16¢ Great Seal of the United States	08/30/1934	.60	.70	17.50 (6)	25.00
	For imperforate variety see #771					
CE2	16¢ red and blue	02/10/1936	.40	.25	7.50 (4)	17.50
a	Horizontal pair, imperf. vertically		*3,750.00*			
	Special Delivery					
	1885, Unwmkd., Perf. 12					
E1	10¢ Messenger Running	10/01/1885	450.00	60.00	*15,000.00* (8)	*8,500.00*
E2	10¢ blue Messenger Running (E3)	09/06/1888	400.00	25.00	*12,500.00* (8)	
E3	10¢ Messenger Running	01/24/1893	250.00	35.00	*10,000.00* (8)	
E4	10¢ Messenger Running (Line under "Ten Cents")	10/10/1894	850.00	45.00	*17,500.00* (6)	
	Wmkd. (191), **Perf. 12**					
E5	10¢ bl. Messenger Running (E4)	08/16/1895	200.00	6.00	4,500.00 (6)	
	Double transfer		—	22.50		
	Line of color through "POSTAL DELIVERY"		275.00	25.00		
	Dots in curved frame above messenger		225.00	10.00		
	Special Delivery, Wmkd. (191), **Perf. 12**					
E6	10¢ ultramarine Messenger on Bicycle	12/09/1902	160.00	8.00		
a	Blue		160.00	80.00	*2,500.00* (6)	
	Damaged transfer under "N" of "CENTS"		190.00	9.00		
E7	10¢ Mercury Helmet and Olive Branch	12/12/1908	70.00	45.00	*1,000.00* (6)	
	Wmkd. (190), **Perf. 12**					
E8	10¢ ultramarine Messenger on Bicycle (E6)	01/1911	100.00	7.50	*1,850.00* (6)	
b	Violet blue		100.00	7.50	*1,700.00* (6)	
	Top frame line missing		140.00	15.00		
	Perf. 10					
E9	10¢ ultramarine Messenger on Bicycle (E6)	09/1914	180.00	10.00	*3,000.00* (6)	
a	Blue		225.00	12.00	*4,000.00* (6)	
	Unwmkd., Perf. 10					
E10	10¢ ultramarine Messenger on Bicycle (E6)	10/19/1916	300.00	40.00	*5,250.00* (6)	
a	Blue		325.00	40.00	*4,750.00* (6)	
	Unwmkd., Perf. 11					
E11	10¢ ultramarine Messenger on Bicycle (E6)	05/02/1917	20.00	.75	225.00 (6)	
c	Blue		55.00	2.50	600.00 (6)	
E12	10¢ Postman and Motorcycle	07/12/1922	40.00	.60	450.00 (6)	425.00
a	Deep ultramarine		45.00	.70	500.00 (6)	
E13	15¢ Postman and Motorcycle	04/11/1925	27.50	1.75	350.00 (6)	240.00
E14	20¢ Post Office Truck	04/25/1925	2.00	1.00	35.00 (6)	95.00
	Unwmkd., Perf. 11 x 10.5					
E15	10¢ gray violet Postman and Motorcycle (E12)	11/29/1927	.65	.25	3.75 (4)	110.00
c	Horizontal pair, imperf. between		300.00			
E16	15¢ orange Postman and Motorcycle (E13)	08/13/1931	.70	.25	2.75 (4)	125.00
	Beginning with #E17, unused values are for never-hinged stamps.					
E17	13¢ Postman and Motorcycle	10/30/1944	.60	.20	2.75 (4)	12.00
E18	17¢ Postman and Motorcycle	10/30/1944	2.75	1.75	22.50 (4)	12.00
E19	20¢ blk. Post Office Truck (E14)	11/30/1951	1.25	.20	5.50 (4)	5.00
E20	20¢ Delivery of Letter	10/13/1954	.40	.20	2.00 (4)	3.00
E21	30¢ Delivery of Letter	09/03/1957	.50	.20	2.25 (4)	2.25
	Unwmkd., Perf. 11					
E22	45¢ Arrows	11/21/1969	1.25	.25	5.50 (4)	3.50
E23	60¢ Arrows	05/10/1971	1.25	.20	5.50 (4)	3.50

	Issue	Date	Un	U	PB	#	FDC	Q(M)
	Registration Stamp							
	Issued for the prepayment of registry; not usable for postage. Sale discontinued May 28, 1913.							
	Wmkd. (190), **Perf. 12**							
F1	10¢ Bald Eagle	12/01/1911	70.00	9.00	*1,600.00*	(6)	*8,000.00*	
	Certified Mail Stamp							
	For use on First-Class mail for which no indemnity value was claimed, but for which proof of mailing and proof of delivery were available at less cost than registered mail.							
	Unwmkd., Perf. 10.5 x 11							
FA1	15¢ Letter Carrier	06/06/1955	.45	.30	4.25	(4)	3.25	54
	Postage Due Stamps							
	For affixing by a postal clerk to any mail to denote amount to be collected from addressee because of insufficient prepayment of postage.							
	Printed by American Bank Note Co., Design of #J2, Unwmkd., Perf. 12							
J1	1¢ brown	1879	85.00	12.50	*1,500.00*	(10)		
J2	2¢ brown	1879	400.00	12.50				
J3	3¢ brown	1879	100.00	5.00	*1,750.00*	(10)		
J4	5¢ brown	1879	700.00	50.00				
J5	10¢ brown	09/19/1879	900.00	60.00				
a	Imperf., pair		*2,750.00*					
J6	30¢ brown	09/19/1879	375.00	55.00	*4,750.00*	(10)		
J7	50¢ brown	09/19/1879	600.00	75.00	*12,000.00*	(10)		
	Special Printing, Soft Porous Paper, Unwmkd., Perf. 12							
J8	1¢ deep brown	1879	*20,000.00*					
J9	2¢ deep brown	1879	*14,000.00*					
J10	3¢ deep brown	1879	*19,000.00*					
J11	5¢ deep brown	1879	*12,500.00*					
J12	10¢ deep brown	1879	*7,500.00*					
J13	30¢ deep brown	1879	*7,500.00*					
J14	50¢ deep brown	1879	*7,500.00*					
	Design of #J19, Unwmkd., Perf. 12							
J15	1¢ red brown	1884	70.00	6.00	*1,400.00*	(10)		
J16	2¢ red brown	1884	85.00	5.00	*1,600.00*	(10)		
J17	3¢ red brown	1884	1,100.00	250.00				
J18	5¢ red brown	1884	600.00	35.00				
J19	10¢ Figure of Value	1884	600.00	30.00	*13,500.00*	(10)		
J20	30¢ red brown	1884	200.00	55.00	*3,250.00*	(10)		
J21	50¢ red brown	1884	1,750.00	200.00				

	Issue	Date	Un	U	PB	#	FDC	Q(M)
	Design of #J25, Unwmkd., Perf. 12							
J22	1¢ bright claret	1891	35.00	1.50	*625.00*	(10)		
J23	2¢ bright claret	1891	37.50	1.50	*700.00*	(10)		
J24	3¢ bright claret	1891	75.00	15.00	*1,100.00*	(10)		
J25	5¢ Figure of Value	1891	100.00	15.00	*1,400.00*	(10)		
J26	10¢ bright claret	1891	170.00	25.00	*2,400.00*	(10)		
J27	30¢ bright claret	1891	600.00	200.00	*8,750.00*	(10)		
J28	50¢ bright claret	1891	600.00	185.00	*9,750.00*	(10)		
	Design of #J33, Unwmkd., Perf. 12							
J29	1¢ vermilion	1894	2,100.00	650.00				
J30	2¢ vermilion	1894	800.00	300.00	6,750.00	(6)		
J31	1¢ deep claret	08/14/1894	70.00	8.00	525.00	(6)		
J32	2¢ deep claret	07/20/1894	60.00	6.00	475.00	(6)		
J33	3¢ Figure of Value	04/27/1895	200.00	40.00	2,150.00	(6)		
J34	5¢ deep claret	04/27/1895	325.00	45.00	2,600.00	(6)		
J35	10¢ deep claret	09/24/1894	350.00	30.00	2,600.00	(6)		
J36	30¢ deep claret	04/27/1895	525.00	175.00	4,250.00	(6)		
a	Carmine		600.00	200.00	*4,750.00*	(6)		
b	Pale rose		425.00	140.00	3,600.00	(6)		
J37	50¢ deep claret	04/27/1895	1,800.00	600.00				
a	Pale rose		1,650.00	650.00	*12,500.00*	(6)		
	Design of #J33, Wmkd. (191), **Horizontally or Vertically, Perf. 12**							
J38	1¢ deep claret	08/29/1895	12.50	.75	250.00	(6)		
J39	2¢ deep claret	09/14/1895	12.50	.70	250.00	(6)		
J40	3¢ deep claret	10/30/1895	85.00	3.00	800.00	(6)		
J41	5¢ deep claret	10/15/1895	95.00	3.00	900.00	(6)		
J42	10¢ deep claret	09/14/1895	95.00	5.00	900.00	(6)		
J43	30¢ deep claret	08/21/1897	600.00	55.00	*5,750.00*	(6)		
J44	50¢ deep claret	03/17/1896	425.00	40.00	*4,500.00*	(6)		
	Design of #J33, Wmkd. (190), **Perf. 12**							
J45	1¢ deep claret	08/30/1910	40.00	3.50				
a	Rose carmine		35.00	3.50	500.00	(6)		
J46	2¢ deep claret	11/25/1910	40.00	1.50				
a	Rose carmine		35.00	1.50	500.00	(6)		
J47	3¢ deep claret	08/31/1910	625.00	40.00	750.00	(6)		
J48	5¢ deep claret	08/31/1910	120.00	9.00				
a	Rose carmine		115.00	9.00	1,100.00	(6)		
J49	10¢ deep claret	08/31/1910	130.00	15.00	1,450.00	(6)		
J50	50¢ deep claret	09/23/1912	1,100.00	140.00	*10,000.00*	(6)		

YOSEMITE NATIONAL PARK, CALIFORNIA

The U.S. Postal Service continues its Scenic American Landscapes series with an international rate stamp featuring a photograph of the Gates of the Valley in Yosemite National Park in California. Established on October 1, 1890, the park encompasses 747,956 acres in the Sierra Nevada. With the impressive Yosemite Valley as its centerpiece, the park includes a breathtaking range of geographical features, such as waterfalls, lakes, glaciers, expansive meadows, groves of giar sequoias, and granite monoliths such as El Capita and Half Dome. Each year nearly four million peopl enjoy the spectacular sights of Yosemit Approximately 800 miles of marked trails can b found in the park. Nearly 95 percent of Yosemite ha been designated wilderness. The photograph appearing on th stamp was taken by Galen Rowell of Emeryville, California.

F1

FA1

J2

J19

J25

J33

J69

J78

J88

J98

J101

Disney materials © Disney.

The Art of Disney: Romance

This is the third pane in The Art of Disney series honoring the art of romance as imagined by animators at Disney. Fall in love with Cinderella and Prince Charming. Be wooed by Beauty and the Beast. Feel the attraction of Lady and the Tramp. Open up your heart to Mickey Mouse and Minnie Mouse.

Pane of 20, with four designs, nine positions, plate no. in two corners.

Item #568040 $7.80

To order this item and other related philatelic products call 1 800 STAMP-24 or visit us on-line at www.usps.com.

Issue		Date	Un	U	PB	#	FDC	Q(M)
	Design of #J33, Perf. 10							
J52	1¢ carmine lake	1914	75.00	12.50	650.00	(6)		
a	Dull rose		85.00	12.50	700.00	(6)		
J53	2¢ carmine lake	1914	52.50	.50	500.00	(6)		
a	Dull rose		57.50	1.00	700.00	(6)		
b	Vermillion		60.00	.75	550.00	(6)		
J54	3¢ carmine lake	1914	1,100.00	57.50				
a	Dull rose		1,100.00	57.50	*9,000.00*	(6)		
J55	5¢ carmine lake	1914	45.00	3.50				
a	Dull rose		45.00	2.50	400.00	(6)		
J56	10¢ carmine lake	1914	70.00	2.50	700.00	(6)		
a	Dull rose		80.00	4.00	850.00	(6)		
J57	30¢ carmine lake	1914	240.00	20.00	2,750.00	(6)		
J58	50¢ carmine lake	1914	*15,000.00*	1,200.00	*100,000.00*	(6)		
	Design of #J33, Unwmkd., Perf. 10							
J59	1¢ rose	1916	4,250.00	550.00	*31,500.00*	(6)		
	Experimental Bureau precancel, New Orleans			*250.00*				
J60	2¢ rose	1916	230.00	60.00	2,000.00	(6)		
	Design of #J33, Unwmkd., Perf. 11							
J61	1¢ carmine rose	1917	3.00	.25				
b	Deep claret		3.00	.25	45.00	(6)		
J62	2¢ carmine rose	1917	3.00	.25				
b	Deep claret		3.00	.25	45.00	(6)		
J63	3¢ carmine rose	1917	12.50	.35				
b	Deep claret		12.50	.25	105.00	(6)		
J64	5¢ carmine	1917	12.50	.35				
b	Deep claret		12.50	.25	105.00	(6)		
J65	10¢ carmine rose	1917	20.00	.40				
b	Deep claret		20.00	.40	11.00	(6)		
J66	30¢ carmine rose	1917	87.50	1.00				
b	Deep claret		87.50	1.00	725.00	(6)		
J67	50¢ carmine rose	1917	125.00	.50				
b	Deep claret		125.00	.30	900.00	(6)		
J68	½¢ dull red	04/13/25	1.00	.25	12.50	(6)		
	Design of #J69, Unwmkd., Perf. 11							
J69	½¢ Figure of Value	1930	4.50	1.40	42.50	(6)		
J70	1¢ carmine	1930	3.00	.25	30.00	(6)		
J71	2¢ carmine	1930	4.00	.25	45.00	(6)		
J72	3¢ carmine	1930	21.00	2.00	275.00	(6)		
J73	5¢ carmine	1930	19.00	3.00	250.00	(6)		
J74	10¢ carmine	1930	40.00	1.50	450.00	(6)		
J75	30¢ carmine	1930	140.00	3.00	1,100.00	(6)		
J76	50¢ carmine	1930	190.00	1.50	1,700.00	(6)		
	Design of #J78							
J77	$1 carmine	1930	30.00	.25	225.00	(6)		
a	$1 scarlet		25.00	.25	275.00	(6)		
J78	$5 "FIVE" on $	1930	37.50	.25	300.00	(6)		
a	$5 scarlet		32.50	.25	250.00	(6)		
b	As "a," wet printing		35.00	.25	275.00	(6)		

Issue		Date	Un	U	PB	#	FDC	Q(M)
	Design of #J69, Unwmkd., Perf. 11 x 10.5							
J79	½¢ dull carmine	1931	.90	.20				
a	½¢ scarlet		.90	.20	20.00	(4)		
J80	1¢ dull carmine	1931	.20	.20				
a	Scarlet		.20	.20	1.50	(4)		
J81	2¢ dull carmine	1931	.20	.20				
a	Scarlet		.20	.20	1.50	(4)		
J82	3¢ dull carmine	1931	.25	.20				
a	Scarlet		.25	.20	2.25	(4)		
b	Scarlet, wet printing		.30	.20	2.50	(4)		
J83	5¢ dull carmine	1931	.40	.20				
a	Scarlet		.40	.20	3.00	(4)		
J84	10¢ dull carmine	1931	1.10	.20				
a	Scarlet		1.10	.20	6.50	(4)		
b	scarlet, wet printing		1.25	.20	7.00	(4)		
J85	30¢ dull carmine	1931	7.50	.25				
a	Scarlet		7.50	.25	35.00	(4)		
J86	50¢ dull carmine	1931	9.00	.25				
a	Scarlet		9.00	.25	52.50	(4)		
	Design of #J78, Perf. 10.5 x 11							
J87	$1 scarlet	1956	30.00	.25	190.00	(4)		
	Beginning with #J88, unused values are for never-hinged stamps.							
	Designs of #J88, #J98 and #J101, Unwmkd., Perf. 11 x 10.5							
J88	½¢ Figure of Value	06/19/59	1.50	1.10	175.00	(4)		
J89	1¢ carmine rose	06/19/59	.20	.20	.35	(4)		
a	"1 CENT" omitted		250.00					
b	Pair, one without "1 CENT"		*500.00*					
J90	2¢ carmine rose	06/19/59	.20	.20	.45	(4)		
J91	3¢ carmine rose	06/19/59	.20	.20	.50	(4)		
a	Pair, one without "3 CENTS"		*675.00*					
J92	4¢ carmine rose	06/19/59	.20	.20	.60	(4)		
J93	5¢ carmine rose	06/19/59	.20	.20	.65	(4)		
a	Pair, one without "5 CENTS"		*1,500.00*					
J94	6¢ carmine rose	06/19/59	.20	.20	.70	(4)		
a	Pair, one without "6 CENTS"		*850.00*					
J95	7¢ carmine rose	06/19/59	.20	.20	.80	(4)		
J96	8¢ carmine rose	06/19/59	.20	.20	.90	(4)		
a	Pair, one without "8 CENTS"		*850.00*					
J97	10¢ carmine rose	06/19/59	.20	.20	1.00	(4)		
J98	30¢ Figure of Value	06/19/59	.75	.20	3.50	(4)		
J99	50¢ carmine rose	06/19/59	1.10	.20	5.00	(4)		
	Design of #J101							
J100	$1 carmine rose	06/19/59	2.00	.20	8.50	(4)		
J101	$5 Outline Figure of Value	06/19/59	9.00	.20	40.00	(4)		
	Design of #J98, Perf. 11 x 10.5							
J102	11¢ carmine rose	01/02/78	.25	.20	2.00	(4)		
J103	13¢ carmine rose	01/02/78	.25	.20	2.00	(4)		
J104	17¢ carmine rose	06/10/85	.40	.35	22.50	(4)		

	Issue	Un	U
	Official Stamps		
	Thin, Hard Paper, Unwmkd., Perf. 12		
	The franking privilege having been abolished as of July 1, 1873, these stamps were provided for each of the departments of government for the prepayment on official matter. These stamps were supplanted on May 1, 1879, by penalty envelopes and on July 5, 1884, were declared obsolete.		
	Issues of 1873		
	Department of Agriculture: Yellow		
O1	1¢ Franklin	210.00	160.00
	Ribbed paper	225.00	160.00
O2	2¢ Jackson	180.00	70.00
O3	3¢ Washington	175.00	13.00
O4	6¢ Lincoln	180.00	52.50
O5	10¢ Jefferson	380.00	180.00
	Golden yellow	390.00	185.00
	Olive yellow	400.00	190.00
O6	12¢ Clay	380.00	240.00
	Golden yellow	400.00	250.00
	Olive yellow	420.00	255.00
O7	15¢ Webster	350.00	210.00
	Golden yellow	375.00	220.00
	Olive yellow	400.00	230.00
O8	24¢ Scott	350.00	200.00
	Golden yellow	375.00	210.00
O9	30¢ Hamilton	450.00	250.00
	Golden yellow	475.00	260.00
	Olive yellow	500.00	275.00
	Executive Dept.: Carmine		
O10	1¢ Franklin	800.00	425.00
O11	2¢ Jackson	500.00	210.00
O12	3¢ Washington	575.00	175.00
O13	6¢ Lincoln	750.00	500.00
O14	10¢ Jefferson	1,000.00	575.00
	Dept. of the Interior: Vermilion		
O15	1¢ Franklin	55.00	8.50
	Ribbed paper	60.00	9.50
O16	2¢ Jackson	50.00	10.00
O17	3¢ Washington	70.00	5.25
O18	6¢ Lincoln	55.00	7.50
O19	10¢ Jefferson	55.00	16.00
O20	12¢ Clay	70.00	9.00
O21	15¢ Webster	140.00	18.00
	Double transfer of left side	200.00	26.00
O22	24¢ Scott	110.00	15.00
O23	30¢ Hamilton	175.00	15.00
O24	90¢ Perry	250.00	40.00
	Dept. of Justice: Purple		
O25	1¢ Franklin	175.00	90.00
O26	2¢ Jackson	240.00	90.00
O27	3¢ Washington	240.00	25.00
O28	6¢ Lincoln	230.00	35.00

	Issue	Un	U
	Dept. of Justice: Purple continued		
O29	10¢ Jefferson	240.00	75.00
O30	12¢ Clay	200.00	60.00
O31	15¢ Webster	375.00	160.00
O32	24¢ Scott	1,000.00	350.00
O33	30¢ Hamilton	1,000.00	275.00
	Double transfer at top	1,100.00	300.00
O34	90¢ Perry	1,750.00	600.00
	Navy Dept.: Ultramarine		
O35	1¢ Franklin	100.00	42.50
a	1¢ dull blue	105.00	45.00
O36	2¢ Jackson	100.00	20.00
a	Dull blue	105.00	18.00
	Gray blue	105.00	18.00
O37	3¢ Washington	125.00	11.50
a	Dull blue	120.00	12.50
O38	6¢ Lincoln	90.00	17.50
a	Dull blue	90.00	17.50
	Vertical line through "N" of "NAVY"	175.00	25.00
O39	7¢ Stanton	550.00	200.00
a	7¢ dull blue	550.00	200.00
O40	10¢ Jefferson	130.00	35.00
	Plate scratch	*250.00*	—
O41	12¢ Clay	140.00	35.00
	Double transfer of left side	350.00	180.00
O42	15¢ Webster	275.00	60.00
O43	24¢ Scott	325.00	70.00
a	24¢ dull blue	300.00	—
O44	30¢ Hamilton	250.00	40.00
O45	90¢ Perry	900.00	300.00
a	Double impression		*20,000.00*
	Post Office Dept.: Black		
O47	1¢ Figure of Value	20.00	10.00
O48	2¢ Figure of Value	25.00	7.50
a	Double impression	600.00	400.00
O49	3¢ Figure of Value	8.00	1.25
	Cracked plate	—	—
O50	6¢ Figure of Value	25.00	6.50
	Vertical ribbed paper	—	11.00
O51	10¢ Figure of Value	100.00	45.00
O52	12¢ Figure of Value	90.00	9.00
O53	15¢ Figure of Value	100.00	15.00
O54	24¢ Figure of Value	120.00	18.50
O55	30¢ Figure of Value	120.00	18.50
O56	90¢ Figure of Value	140.00	17.50

	Issue	Un	U
	Dept. of State: Green, Perf. 12		
O57	1¢ Franklin	200.00	60.00
O58	2¢ Jackson	225.00	85.00
O59	3¢ Washington	150.00	20.00
O60	6¢ Lincoln	150.00	25.00
O61	7¢ Stanton	210.00	55.00
	Ribbed paper	225.00	60.00
O62	10¢ Jefferson	190.00	45.00
	Short transfer	230.00	57.50
O63	12¢ Clay	275.00	110.00
O64	15¢ Webster	290.00	75.00
O65	24¢ Scott	450.00	200.00
O66	30¢ Hamilton	425.00	150.00
O67	90¢ Perry	1,000.00	300.00
O68	$2 Seward	1,250.00	1,250.00
O69	$5 Seward	6,000.00	10,000.00
O70	$10 Seward	4,500.00	*5,500.00*
O71	$20 Seward	4,000.00	2,500.00
	Treasury Dept.: Brown		
O72	1¢ Franklin	70.00	5.50
	Double transfer	80.00	6.75
O73	2¢ Jackson	80.00	5.50
	Double transfer	—	9.00
	Cracked plate	67.50	—
O74	3¢ Washington	60.00	1.50
	Shaded circle outside right frame line	—	—
O75	6¢ Lincoln	70.00	3.00
	Dirty plate	70.00	4.50
O76	7¢ Stanton	150.00	27.50
O77	10¢ Jefferson	150.00	9.00
O78	12¢ Clay	160.00	6.50
O79	15¢ Webster	150.00	9.00
O80	24¢ Scott	550.00	75.00
O81	30¢ Hamilton	225.00	10.00
	Short transfer top right	275.00	20.00
O82	90¢ Perry	240.00	11.00
	War Dept.: Rose		
O83	1¢ Franklin	150.00	12.00
O84	2¢ Jackson	140.00	12.00
	Ribbed paper	145.00	14.00
O85	3¢ Washington	150.00	4.00
O86	6¢ Lincoln	475.00	7.50
O87	7¢ Stanton	130.00	77.50
O88	10¢ Jefferson	75.00	17.50
O89	12¢ Clay	200.00	10.00
	Ribbed paper	225.00	11.00
O90	15¢ Webster	50.00	12.00
	Ribbed paper	55.00	15.00
O91	24¢ Scott	50.00	10.00
O92	30¢ Hamilton	60.00	9.00
O93	90¢ Perry	125.00	42.50

O3

O7

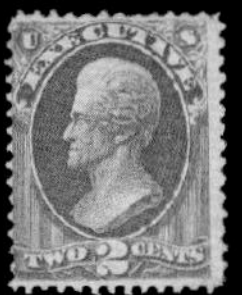
O11

O14

O16

O18

O25

O34

O37

O44

O47

O52

O57

O74

O76

O87

O91

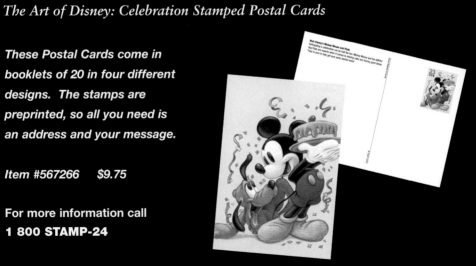

O121

O124

O125

O126

O127

O129A

O139

O140

O143

O146A

O151

O152

O153

O154

O155

O156

O157

O158

O159

VISIT US ONLINE AT ***THE POSTAL STORE***

AT ***WWW.USPS.COM***

OR CALL ***1 800 STAMP-24***

	Issue	Date	Un	U
	Soft Porous Paper			
	Dept. of Agriculture: Yellow			
O94	1¢ Franklin, issued without gum	1879	5,000.00	
O95	3¢ Washington		450.00	75.00
	Dept. of the Interior: Vermilion			
O96	1¢ Franklin	1879	250.00	230.00
O97	2¢ Jackson	1879	7.50	2.50
O98	3¢ Washington	1879	7.00	1.50
O99	6¢ Lincoln	1879	12.00	6.50
O100	10¢ Jefferson	1879	100.00	65.00
O101	12¢ Clay	1879	190.00	100.00
O102	15¢ Webster	1879	350.00	240.00
	Double transfer		400.00	—
O103	24¢ Scott	1879	4,250.00	—
O104-05	Not assigned			
	Dept. of Justice: Bluish Purple			
O106	3¢ Washington	1879	120.00	75.00
O107	6¢ Lincoln		300.00	190.00
	Post Office Dept.: Black			
O108	3¢ Figure of Value	1879	25.00	6.50
	Treasury Dept.: Brown			
O109	3¢ Washington	1879	70.00	7.50
O110	6¢ Lincoln	1879	110.00	40.00
O111	10¢ Jefferson	1879	200.00	65.00
O112	30¢ Hamilton	1879	1,750.00	325.00
O113	90¢ Perry	1879	2,750.00	400.00
	War Dept.: Rose Red			
O114	1¢ Franklin	1879	5.50	4.00
O115	2¢ Jackson	1879	8.00	3.50
O116	3¢ Washington	1879	8.00	1.50
	Double transfer		12.00	5.00
a	Imperf. pair		*5,000.00*	
b	Double impression		*6,500.00*	
O117	6¢ Lincoln	1879	8.00	2.50
O118	10¢ Jefferson	1879	45.00	40.00
O119	12¢ Clay	1879	35.00	11.00
O120	30¢ Hamilton	1879	130.00	75.00
	Official Postal Savings Mail These stamps were used to prepay postage on official correspondence of the Postal Savings Division of the Post Office Department. Discontinued Sept. 23, 1914.			
	Engr., Wmkd. (191)			
O121	2¢ Postal Savings	12/22/1910	15.00	1.75
	Double transfer		20.00	3.50
O122	50¢ dark green	02/01/1911	145.00	50.00
O123	$1 ultramarine	02/01/1911	150.00	12.50
	Wmkd. (190)			
O124	1¢ dark violet	03/27/1911	9.00	1.50
O125	2¢ Postal Savings (O121)		50.00	5.50
O126	10¢ carmine	02/01/1911	19.00	1.60
	Penalty Mail Stamps Stamps for use by government departments were reinstituted in 1983. Now known as Penalty Mail stamps, they help provide a better accounting of actual mail costs for official departments and agencies, etc.			
	Beginning with #O127, unused values are for never-hinged stamps.			
	Engr., Unwmkd., Perf. 11			
O127	1¢ red, blue & blk	01/12/1983	.20	.20
O128	4¢ red, blue & blk	01/12/1983	.20	.25
O129	13¢ red, blue & blk	01/12/1983	.45	.75
O129A	14¢ red, blue & blk	05/15/1985	.45	.50
O130	17¢ red, blue & blk	01/12/1983	.60	.40
O131, O134, O137, O142	Not assigned			
O132	$1 red, blue & blk	01/12/1983	2.25	1.00
O133	$5 red, blue & blk	01/12/1983	9.00	*12.00*
	Coil, Perf. 10 Vertically			
O135	20¢ red, blue & blk	01/12/1983	1.75	2.00
a	Imperf. pair		*2,000.00*	
O136	22¢ red, blue & blk	05/15/1985	1.00	*2.00*
	Perf. 11			
O138	"D" postcard rate (14¢)	02/04/1985	5.25	*10.00*
	Coil, Perf. 10 Vertically			
O138A	15¢ red, blue & blk	06/11/1988	.45	.50
O138B	20¢ red, blue & blk	05/19/1988	.45	.30
O139	"D" (22¢) red, blue & blk	02/04/1985	5.25	3.00
O140	"E" (25¢) red, blue & blk	03/22/1988	.75	*2.00*
O141	25¢ red, blue & blk	06/11/1988	.65	.50
	Litho., Perf. 11			
O143	1¢ red, blue & blk	07/05/1989	.20	.20
	Coil, Litho., Perf. 10 Vertically			
O144	"F" (29¢) red, blue & blk	01/22/1991	.80	.50
O145	29¢ red, blue & blk	05/24/1991	.65	.30
	Litho., Perf. 11			
O146	4¢ red, blue & blk	04/06/1991	.20	*.30*
O146A	10¢ red, blue & blk	10/19/1993	.25	*.30*
O147	19¢ red, blue & blk	05/24/1991	.40	*.50*
O148	23¢ red, blue & blk	05/241991	.45	.30
O151	$1 red, blue & blk	09/1993	2.50	.75
	Coil, Perf. 9.8 Vertically			
O152	(32¢) red, blue & blk	12/13/1994	.65	.50
O153	32¢ red, blue & blk	05/09/1995	1.25	.50
	Coil, Perf. 11.2			
O154	1¢ red, blue & blk	05/09/1995	.20	*.50*
O155	20¢ red, blue & blk	05/09/1995	.45	*.50*
O156	23¢ red, blue & blk	05/09/1995	.55	.50
	Coil, Litho., Perf. 9.75 Vertically			
O157	33¢ red, blue & blk	10/08/1999	.65	—
	Coil, Tagged, Litho., Perf. 9.75 Vertically			
O158	34¢ red, blue & blk	02/27/2001	.65	.50
	Coil, Tagged, Photo., Perf. 10 Vertically			
O159	37¢ red, blue & blk	08/02/2002	.70	.50

Variable Rate Coil Stamps

These are coil postage stamps printed without denominations. The denomination is imprinted by the dispensing equipment called a Postage and Mailing Center (PMC). Denominations can be set between 1¢ and $99.99. In 1993, the minimum denomination was adjusted to 19¢ (the postcard rate at the time).

Date of Issue: August 20, 1992
Printing: Intaglio

Date of Issue: February 19, 1994
Printing: Gravure

Date of Issue: January 26, 1996
Printing: Gravure

	Issue	Date	Un	U	PB #	FDC Q(M)
	Parcel Post Stamps					
	Engr., Wmkd. (190), **Perf. 12**					
	Issued for the prepayment of postage on parcel post packages only. Beginning July 1, 1913 these stamps were valid for all postal purposes.					
Q1	1¢ Post Office Clerk	07/01/13	5.75	1.75	110.00 (6)	*1,500.00*
	Double transfer		9.50	4.00		
Q2	2¢ City Carrier	07/01/13	6.75	1.40	145.00 (6)	*1,750.00*
a	Lake		*1,750.00*			
b	Carmine lake		*350.00*			
Q3	3¢ Railway Postal Clerk	04/05/13	13.50	6.50	235.00 (6)	*3,500.00*
	Retouched at lower right corner		26.00	14.50		
	Double transfer		26.00	14.50		
Q4	4¢ Rural Carrier	07/01/13	37.50	3.50	1,000.00 (6)	*3,500.00*
	Double transfer		—	—		
Q5	5¢ Mail Train	07/01/13	32.50	2.50	975.00 (6)	*3,500.00*
	Double transfer		45.00	6.25		
Q6	10¢ Steamship and Mail Tender	07/01/13	52.50	3.50	1,000.00 (6)	*12,500.00*
Q7	15¢ Automobile Service	07/01/13	67.50	15.00	2,300.00 (6)	—
Q8	20¢ Aeroplane Carrying Mail	1913	150.00	30.00	6,500.00 (6)	
Q9	25¢ Manufacturing	1913	67.50	8.50	2,400.00 (6)	
Q10	50¢ Dairying	03/15/13	300.00	50.00	22,500.00 (6)	
Q11	75¢ Harvesting		110.00	40.00	3,000.00 (6)	
Q12	$1 Fruit Growing	01/03/13	375.00	45.00	*18,000.00* (6)	

	Issue	Date	Un	U	PB #	FDC Q(M)
	Special Handling Stamps					
	Issued for use on parcel post packages to secure the same expeditious handling accorded first class mail matter.					
	Unwmkd., Perf. 11					
QE1	10¢ Special Handling	1955	1.50	1.00	32.50 (6)	
a	Wet printing	06/25/28	3.00	1.00	22.50 (6)	45.00
QE2	15¢ Special Handling	1955	1.60	.90	42.50 (6)	
a	Wet printing	06/25/28	3.25	.90	32.50 (6)	45.00
QE3	20¢ Special Handling	1955	2.50	1.50	47.50 (6)	
a	Wet printing	06/25/28	4.00	1.50	37.50 (6)	45.00
QE4	25¢ Special Handling	1929	18.00	7.50	260.00 (6)	
a	25¢ deep grn.	04/11/25	30.00	5.50	330.00 (6)	225.00
	"A" and "T" of "STATES" joined at top		50.00	22.50		
	"T" and "A" of "POSTAGE" joined at top		75.00	45.00		
	Parcel Post Postage Due Stamps					
	Issued for affixing by a postal clerk to any parcel post package to denote the amount to be collected from the addressee because of insufficient prepayment of postage. Beginning July 1, 1913 these stamps were valid for use as regular postage due stamps.					
	Engr., Wmkd. (190), **Perf. 12**					
JQ1	1¢ Figure of Value	11/27/13	10.50	4.50	550.00 (6)	
JQ2	2¢ dark green	12/09/13	85.00	17.50	*3,750.00* (6)	
JQ3	5¢ dark green	11/27/13	14.00	5.50	600.00 (6)	
JQ4	10¢ dark green	12/12/13	175.00	45.00	*9,750.00* (6)	
JQ5	25¢ Figure of Value	12/16/13	100.00	5.00	*5,000.00* (6)	

THE ART OF DISNEY: ROMANCE

This stamp pane—the third honoring the art of Disney—honors the art of romance as imagined by Walt Disney and his studio animators. Now, with help from a few beloved Disney characters, it's easy to add a dash of romance to your cards and letters with stamps that feature Cinderella and Prince Charming; Beauty and the Beast; Lady and Tramp; and Mickey Mouse and Minnie Mouse. Everyone dreams of living a rags-to-riches fairy tale and dancing with that special someone. As Cinderella and Prince Charming learn, one waltz can lead to a moment of realization: "So this is love." This is the evening the Beast has awaited, but can he tell Belle of his love? He knows his heart, but does she yet know her own? These lovers are as uncertain as they are hopeful—emotions and a tale "as old as time." First dates can be full of risks—and ordering spaghetti only complicates matters. Fortunately for Lady and Tramp, a plate of pasta leads to a memorable kiss, turning a simple dinner out into a wonderful "Bella Notte." Mickey Mouse and Minnie Mouse have been sweethearts for many years, yet they still have that first-date feeling. Seeing this celebrated couple, we can all take heart; they prove that sometimes the course of love can indeed run smooth.

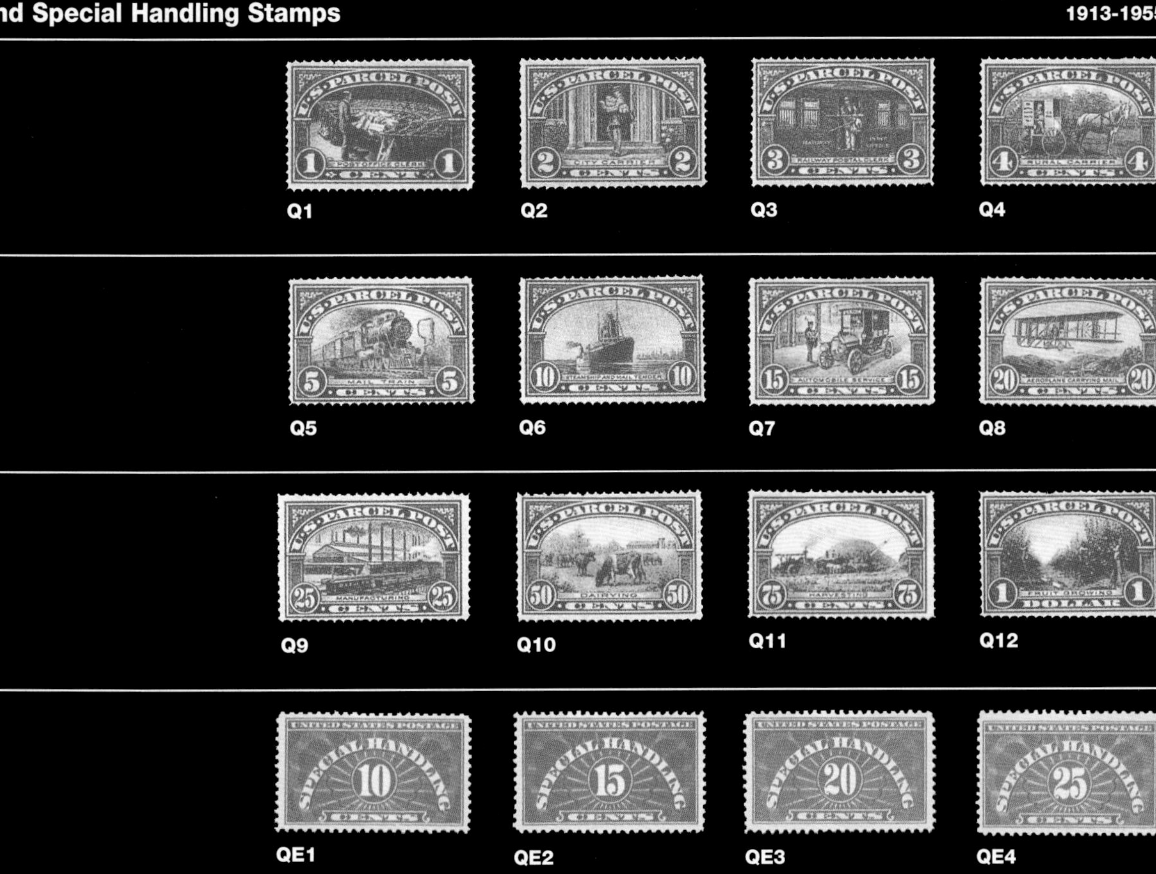

Q1 Q2 Q3 Q4

Q5 Q6 Q7 Q8

Q9 Q10 Q11 Q12

QE1 QE2 QE3 QE4

JQ1 JQ5

Create Your Own Postage Stamp and Pictorial Postmarks

Make your own mark on history!

For information on how you can create or suggest your own idea for a postage stamp or pictorial postmark stop by your local post office and inquire about these free brochures. *Creating U.S. Postage Stamps* and *Celebrating with Pictorial Postmarks.*

RW1

RW3

RW10

RW13

RW15

RW16

RW23

RW26

RW33

RW36

RW38

RW39

RW46

History of the Federal Duck Stamp Contest

The first Federal Duck Stamp, designed by Jay "Ding" Darling in 1934 at President Franklin D. Roosevelt's request, depicts two mallards about to land on a marsh pond. In subsequent years, other noted wildlife artists were asked to submit designs. The first contest in 1949 was open to any U.S. artist who wished to enter. The number of entries rose to 2,099 in 1981. This is the only art competition of its kind sponsored by the U.S. Government. A panel of noted art, waterfowl, and philatelic authorities is appointed by the Secretary of the Interior to judge each competition. Winners receive no compensation for their work, other than a pane of stamps carrying their design. The U.S. Fish and Wildlife Service mails contest regulations to interested artists each spring.

	Issue	Date	Un	U	PB	#	Q(M)
	Department of Agriculture, Unwmkd., Perf 11						
RW1	$1 Mallards Alighting	1934	800.00	140.00	16,500.00	(6)	0.6
a	Imperf. pair		—				
b	Vert. pair, imperf. horiz.		—				
RW2	$1 Canvasbacks	1935	700.00	160.00	11,500.00	(6)	0.4
RW3	$1 Canada Geese	1936	350.00	75.00	4,000.00	(6)	0.6
RW4	$1 Scaup Ducks	1937	300.00	60.00	3,000.00	(6)	0.8
RW5	$1 Pintail Drake and Hen Alighting	1938	425.00	60.00	4,000.00	(6)	1
	Department of the Interior, Unwmkd., Perf 11						
RW6	$1 Green-winged Teal	1939	250.00	45.00	2,500.00	(6)	1
RW7	$1 Black Mallards	1940	225.00	45.00	2,250.00	(6)	1
RW8	$1 Ruddy Ducks	1941	225.00	45.00	2,250.00	(6)	1
RW9	$1 Baldpates	1942	225.00	45.00	2,250.00	(6)	1
RW10	$1 Wood Ducks	1943	90.00	35.00	625.00	(6)	1
RW11	$1 White-fronted Geese	1944	110.00	30.00	650.00	(6)	1
RW12	$1 Shoveller Ducks	1945	95.00	25.00	450.00	(6)	2
RW13	$1 Redhead Ducks	1946	50.00	16.00	300.00	(6)	2
RW14	$1 Snow Geese	1947	50.00	16.00	350.00	(6)	2
RW15	$1 Buffleheads in Flight	1948	52.50	16.00	375.00	(6)	2
RW16	$2 Goldeneye Ducks	1949	65.00	15.00	450.00	(6)	2
RW17	$2 Trumpeter Swans	1950	85.00	12.00	575.00	(6)	2
RW18	$2 Gadwall Ducks	1951	85.00	12.00	575.00	(6)	2
RW19	$2 Harlequin Ducks	1952	85.00	12.00	575.00	(6)	2
RW20	$2 Blue-winged Teal	1953	85.00	12.00	575.00	(6)	2
RW21	$2 Ring-necked Ducks	1954	85.00	10.50	575.00	(6)	2
RW22	$2 Blue Geese	1955	85.00	10.50	575.00	(6)	2
a	Black inscription inverted		*5,500.00*	—			

	Issue	Date	Un	U	PB	#	Q(M)
	Department of the Interior continued, **Unwmkd., Perf 11**						
RW23	$2 American Merganser	1956	85.00	10.50	575.00	(6)	2
RW24	$2 American Eider	1957	85.00	10.50	575.00	(6)	2
a	Black inscription inverted		*3,500.00*	—			
RW25	$2 Canada Geese	1958	85.00	10.50	575.00	(6)	2
RW26	$3 Labrador Retriever Carrying Mallard Drake	1959	120.00	11.00	550.00	(4)	2
RW27	$3 Redhead Ducks	1960	90.00	10.50	450.00	(4)	2
RW28	$3 Mallard Hen and Ducklings	1961	90.00	10.50	450.00	(4)	1
RW29	$3 Pintail Drakes	1962	110.00	10.50	575.00	(4)	1
RW30	$3 Pair of Brant Landing	1963	110.00	10.50	500.00	(4)	1
RW31	$3 Hawaiian Nene Geese	1964	105.00	10.50	2,200.00	(6)	2
RW32	$3 Three Canvasback Drakes	1965	105.00	10.50	550.00	(4)	2
RW33	$3 Whistling Swans	1966	105.00	10.50	550.00	(4)	2
RW34	$3 Old Squaw Ducks	1967	125.00	10.50	600.00	(4)	2
RW35	$3 Hooded Mergansers	1968	65.00	10.50	325.00	(4)	2
RW36	$3 White-winged Scoters	1969	65.00	8.00	300.00	(4)	2
RW37	$3 Ross's Geese	1970	65.00	8.00	300.00	(4)	2
RW38	$3 Three Cinnamon Teal	1971	42.50	7.75	200.00	(4)	2
RW39	$5 Emperor Geese	1972	25.00	7.00	110.00	(4)	2
RW40	$5 Steller's Eiders	1973	18.00	7.00	90.00	(4)	2
RW41	$5 Wood Ducks	1974	18.00	6.00	75.00	(4)	2
RW42	$5 Canvasbacks Decoy, 3 Flying Canvasbacks	1975	15.00	6.00	60.00	(4)	2
RW43	$5 Canada Geese	1976	15.00	6.00	55.00	(4)	2
RW44	$5 Pair of Ross's Geese	1977	15.00	6.00	55.00	(4)	2
RW45	$5 Hooded Merganser Drake	1978	12.50	6.00	55.00	(4)	2
RW46	$7.50 Green-winged Teal	1979	14.00	7.00	55.00	(4)	2

Migratory Bird Hunting and Conservation Stamps (commonly known as "Duck Stamps") are sold as hunting permits. While they are sold at many Post Offices, they are not usable for postage.

DUCK STAMP DOLLARS
BUY WETLANDS
FOR WATERFOWL.
IT IS UNLAWFUL TO HUNT
WATERFOWL UNLESS YOU
SIGN YOUR NAME IN INK
ON THE FACE OF THIS STAMP.

RW26-34

BUY DUCK STAMPS
SAVE WETLANDS
SEND IN *ALL* BIRD BANDS
SIGN YOUR DUCK STAMP
IT IS UNLAWFUL TO HUNT WATERFOWL UNLESS YOU
SIGN YOUR NAME IN INK ON THE FACE OF THIS STAMP

RW37-53

TAKE PRIDE IN AMERICA
BUY DUCK STAMPS
SAVE WETLANDS
SEND IN ALL BIRD BANDS
SIGN YOUR DUCK STAMPS
IT IS UNLAWFUL TO HUNT WATERFOWL OR USE THIS STAMP
AS A NATIONAL WILDLIFE ENTRANCE PASS UNLESS YOU
SIGN YOUR NAME IN INK ON THE FACE OF THIS STAMP

RW57

TAKE PRIDE IN AMERICA
BUY DUCK STAMPS
SAVE WETLANDS
SEND IN ALL BIRD BANDS
IT IS UNLAWFUL TO HUNT WATERFOWL OR USE THIS STAMP
AS A NATIONAL WILDLIFE REFUGE ENTRANCE PASS UNLESS
YOU SIGN YOUR NAME IN INK ON THE FACE OF THIS STAMP.

RW58-present

	Issue	Date	Un	U	PB	#	Q(M)
	Department of the Interior continued, **Unwmkd., Perf 11**						
RW47	$7.50 Mallards	1980	14.00	7.00	55.00	(4)	2
RW48	$7.50 Ruddy Ducks	1981	14.00	7.00	55.00	(4)	2
RW49	$7.50 Canvasbacks	1982	15.00	7.00	55.00	(4)	2
a	Orange & violet omitted		*7,500.00*				
RW50	$7.50 Pintails	1983	15.00	7.00	60.00	(4)	2
RW51	$7.50 Widgeons	1984	15.00	7.00	62.50	(4)	2
RW52	$7.50 Cinnamon Teal	1985	15.00	8.00	60.00	(4)	
RW53	$7.50 Fulvous Whistling Duck	1986	15.00	7.00	60.00	(4)	2
a	Black omitted		*3,750.00*				
	Perf. 11.5 x 11						
RW54	$10 Redheads	1987	17.50	9.50	65.00	(4)	2
RW55	$10 Snow Goose	1988	17.00	10.00	75.00	(4)	1
RW56	$12.50 Lesser Scaup	1989	19.00	10.00	82.50	(4)	1
RW57	$12.50 Black Bellied Whistling Duck	1990	19.00	10.00	82.50	(4)	1
a	Back inscription omitted		*375.00*				
RW58	$15 King Eiders	1991	27.50	11.00	120.00	(4)	1
a	Black omitted		*12,500.00*				
RW59	$15 Spectacled Eider	1992	27.50	11.00	120.00	(4)	1
RW60	$15 Canvasbacks	1993	27.50	11.00	120.00	(4)	1
a	Black omitted		*3,000.00*				
	Perf. 11.25 x 11						
RW61	$15 Red-breasted Merganser	1994	27.50	11.00	120.00	(4)	1
RW62	$15 Mallards	1995	27.50	11.00	120.00	(4)	1
RW63	$15 Surf Scoters	1996	25.00	11.00	110.00	(4)	1
RW64	$15 Canada Goose	1997	25.00	11.00	110.00	(4)	1
	Perf. 11.25						
RW65	$15 Barrow's Goldeneye	1998	30.00	11.00	140.00	(4)	1
	Self-Adhesive, Die-Cut Perf. 10						
RW65A	$15 Barrow's Goldeneye	1998	25.00	11.00			1
	Department of the Interior continued						
	Perf. 11.25						
RW66	$15 Greater Scaup	1999	25.00	11.00	110.00	(4)	1
	Perf. 10, Self-Adhesive, Die-Cut						
RW66A	$15 Greater Scaup	1999	22.50	10.00			1
	Perf. 11.25						
RW67	$15 Mottled Duck	2000	25.00	11.00	110.00	(4)	1
	Perf. 10, Self-Adhesive, Die-Cut						
RW67A	$15 Mottled Duck	2000	22.50	10.00			1
	Perf. 11.25						
RW68	$15 Northern Pintail	2001	25.00	11.00	100.00	(4)	1
	Self-Adhesive, Die-Cut Perf. 10						
RW68A	$15 Northern Pintail	2001	22.50	10.00			1
	Perf. 11.25						
RW69	$15 Black Scoters	2002	25.00	11.00	100.00	(4)	1
	Self-Adhesive, Serpentine Die-Cut 11 x 10.75						
RW69A	$15 Black Scoters	2002	22.50	10.00			1
	Perf. 11						
RW70	$15 Snow Geese	2003	25.00	11.00	100.00	(4)	1
b	Imperf., pair		*7,500.00*				
c	Black inscription omitted		*4,500.00*				
	Self-Adhesive, Serpentine Die-Cut 11 x 10.75						
RW70A	$15 Snow Geese	2003	22.50	10.00			1
	Perf. 11						
RW71	$15 Redheads	2004	25.00	10.00	100.00	(4)	1
	Self-Adhesive, Serpentine Die-Cut 11 x 10.75						
RW71A	$15 Redheads	2004	22.50	10.00			1
	Perf. 11						
RW72	$15 Hooded Mergansers	2005	22.50	11.00	100.00	(4)	1
	Self-Adhesive, Serpentine Die-Cut 11 x 10.75						
RW72A	$15 Hooded Mergansers	2005	22.50	11.00			1

RW49

RW54

RW57

RW58

RW59

RW60

RW61

RW62

RW63

RW65

RW66

RW67

RW68

RW69

RW70

RW71

RW72

VISIT US ONLINE AT ***THE POSTAL STORE***
AT ***WWW.USPS.COM***
OR CALL ***1 800 STAMP-24***

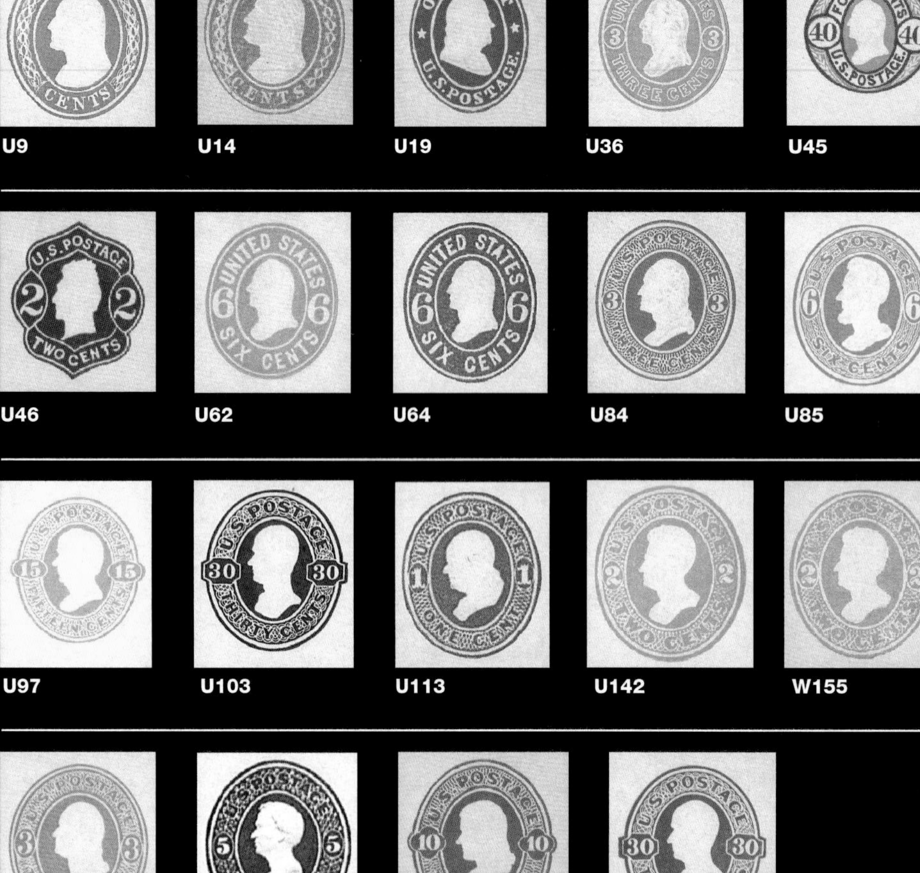

U9 U14 U19 U36 U45

U46 U62 U64 U84 U85

U97 U103 U113 U142 W155

U159 U172 U190 U204

U218

U250

Issue		Un	U

Represented below is only a partial listing of stamped envelopes. At least one example is listed for most die types; most die types exist on several colors of envelope paper. Values are for cut squares; prices for entire envelopes are higher. Color in italic is the color of the envelope paper; when no color is specified, envelope paper is white. "W" with catalog number indicates wrapper instead of envelope.

Issue		Un	U
	1853-1861		
U1	3¢ red Washington (top label 13mm wide)	400.00	35.00
U2	3¢ red Washington (top label 13mm wide), *buff*	97.50	25.00
U3	3¢ red Washington (top label 15½mm wide)	1,300.00	45.00
U4	3¢ red Washington, (top label 15½mm wide), *buff*	350.00	40.00
U5	3¢ red Washington, (label has octagonal ends)	6,250.00	550.00
U6	3¢ red Washington, (label has octagonal ends), *buff*	4,750.00	75.00
U7	3¢ red Washington, (label 20mm wide)	5,500.00	125.00
U8	3¢ red Washington, (label 20mm wide), *buff*	*8,750.00*	150.00
U9	3¢ red (label 14½mm)	40.00	4.00
U10	3¢ red (label 14½mm), *buff*	22.50	4.00
U11	6¢ red Washington	325.00	80.00
U12	6¢ red Washington, *buff*	160.00	80.00
U13	6¢ green Washington	400.00	125.00
U14	6¢ green Washington, *buff*	225.00	100.00
U15	10¢ green Washington (label 15½mm wide)	550.00	100.00
U16	10¢ green Washington, (label 15½mm wide), buff	190.00	75.00
U17	10¢ green Washington, (label 20mm)	550.00	140.00
U18	10¢ green Washington, (label 20mm), buff	400.00	90.00
U19	1¢ blue Franklin (period after "POSTAGE"), *buff*	40.00	15.00
U21A	1¢ blue Franklin, *orange*, entire	*2,750.00*	
U23	1¢ blue Franklin (bust touches inner frame line), *orange*	750.00	350.00
U24	1¢ blue Franklin (no period after "POSTAGE"), *amber*	375.00	125.00
U26	3¢ red Washington	35.00	20.00
U27	3¢ red Washington, *buff*	26.00	13.00
U28	3¢ + 1¢ (U12 and U9)	375.00	275.00
U29	3¢ + 1¢ (U12 and U9), *buff*	375.00	275.00
U30	6¢ red Washington, no label	3,500.00	1,500.00
U31	6¢ red Washington, no label, *buff*	4,000.00	1,500.00
U32	10¢ green Washington, no label	1,650.00	450.00
U33	10¢ green Washington, no label, *buff*	1,650.00	375.00

Issue		Un	U
	1861-1870		
U34	3¢ pink Washington (outline lettering)	32.50	6.00
U35	3¢ pink Washington (outline lettering), *buff*	32.50	6.00
U36	3¢ pink Washington, blue (letter sheet)	82.50	52.50
U38	6¢ pink Washington	125.00	80.00
U39	6¢ pink Washington, *buff*	82.50	62.50
U40	10¢ yellow green Washington	47.50	30.00
U41	10¢ yellow green Washington, *buff*	47.50	30.00
U42	12¢ red & brown Washington, *buff*	250.00	160.00
U43	20¢ red & blue Washington, *buff*	300.00	200.00
U44	24¢ Washington, *buff*	240.00	200.00
U45	40¢ black & red Washington, *buff*	375.00	350.00
U46	2¢ black Jackson ("U.S. POSTAGE" downstroke, tail of "2" unite near point)	52.50	21.00
U49	2¢ black Jackson ("POSTAGE" downstrokeand tail of "2" touch but do not merge), *orange*	2,500.00	
U50	2¢ black Jackson ("U.S. POST." 24-25mm wide), *buff*	17.50	9.50
U52	2¢ black Jackson ("U.S. POST." 24-25mm wide), *orange*	18.00	9.50
U54	2¢ black Jackson ("U.S. POST." 25½-26½mm), *buff*	18.00	9.50
U56	2¢ black Jackson ("U.S. POST." 25½-26½mm), *orange*	21.00	8.50
U58	3¢ pink Washington	10.50	1.60
U59	3¢ pink Washington, *buff*	9.50	1.25
U60	3¢ brown Washington	75.00	40.00
U61	3¢ brown Washington, *buff*	60.00	30.00
U62	6¢ pink Washington	110.00	29.00
U63	6¢ pink Washington, *buff*	55.00	27.50
U64	6¢ purple Washington	75.00	26.00
U65	6¢ purple Washington, *buff*	60.00	20.00
U66	9¢ lemon Washington, *buff*	450.00	250.00
U67	9¢ orange Washington, *buff*	160.00	90.00
U68	12¢ brown Washington, *buff*	325.00	275.00
U69	12¢ red brown Washington, *buff*	150.00	55.00
U70	18¢ red Washington, *buff*	95.00	95.00
U71	24¢ blue Washington, *buff*	100.00	95.00
U72	30¢ green Washington, *buff*	125.00	80.00
U73	40¢ rose Washington, *buff*	125.00	*250.00*
U74	1¢ blue Franklin (bust points to end of "N" of "ONE")	45.00	30.00
U75	1¢ blue Franklin (bust points to end of "N" of "ONE"), *amber*	37.50	27.50
U76	1¢ blue Franklin (bust points to end of "N" of "ONE"), *orange*	20.00	15.00

Issue		Un	U
	1870-1871		
U78	2¢ brown Jackson (bust narrow at back; small, thick numerals)	40.00	16.00
U79	2¢ brown Jackson (bust narrow at back; small, thick numerals), *amber*	20.00	9.00
U80	2¢ brown Jackson (bust narrow at back; small, thick numerals), *orange*	12.00	6.50
U82	3¢ green Washington ("ponytail" projects below bust)	8.50	1.00
U83	3¢ green Washington ("ponytail" projects below bust), *amber*	7.25	2.00
U84	3¢ green Washington ("ponytail" projects below bust), *cream*	10.50	4.25
U85	6¢ dark red Lincoln (neck very long at back)	32.50	16.00
U86	6¢ dark red Lincoln (neck very long at back), *amber*	40.00	20.00
U87	6¢ dark red Lincoln (neck very long at back), *cream*	40.00	20.00
U88	7¢ vermillion Stanton (figures "7" normal), *amber*	52.50	*190.00*
U89	10¢ olive black Jefferson	975.00	900.00
U90	10¢ olive black Jefferson, *amber*	975.00	900.00
U91	10¢ brown Jefferson	92.50	72.50
U92	10¢ brown Jefferson, *amber*	110.00	52.50
U93	12¢ plum Clay (ear partly covered, chin prominent)	125.00	82.50
U94	12¢ plum Clay (ear partly covered, chin prominent), *amber*	125.00	110.00
U95	12¢ plum Clay (ear partly covered, chin prominent), *cream*	275.00	250.00
U96	15¢ red orange Webster (has side whiskers)	82.50	77.50
U97	15¢ red orange Webster (has side whiskers), *amber*	210.00	*300.00*
U98	15¢ red orange Webster (has side whiskers), *cream*	325.00	350.00
U99	24¢ purple Scott (locks of hair project, top of head)	140.00	*140.00*
U100	24¢ purple Scott (locks of hair project, top of head), *amber*	200.00	*325.00*
U101	24¢ purple Scott (locks of hair project, top of head), *cream*	275.00	*500.00*
U102	30¢ black Hamilton (back of bust very narrow)	80.00	*110.00*
U103	30¢ black Hamilton (back of bust very narrow), *amber*	250.00	*500.00*
U104	30¢ black Hamilton (back of bust very narrow), *cream*	225.00	*500.00*
U105	90¢ carmine Perry (front of bust very narrow, pointed)	175.00	*350.00*
U106	90¢ carmine Perry (front of bust very narrow, pointed), *amber*	300.00	*450.00*
U107	90¢ carmine Perry (front of bust very narrow, pointed), *cream*	225.00	*2,500.00*

Issue		Un	U
	1874-1886		
U108	1¢ dark blue Franklin (circle in “O” of “Postage”)	210.00	70.00
U109	1¢ dark blue Franklin (circle in “O” of “Postage”), *amber*	190.00	75.00
U110	1¢ dark blue Franklin (circle in “O” of “Postage”), *cream*	1,750.00	
U111	1¢ dark blue Franklin (circle in “O” of “Postage”), *orange*	25.00	17.50
U113	1¢ light blue Franklin (lower part of bust points to end of “E” in “ONE”)	1.90	1.00
U114	1¢ light blue (lower part of bust points to end of “E” in “Postage”), *amber*	4.50	4.00
	1874-1886		
U115	1¢ blue Franklin (lower part of bust points to end of “E” in “ONE”), *cream*	5.25	4.50
U116	1¢ blue Franklin (lower part of bust points to end of “E” in “ONE”), *orange*	.80	.40
U117	1¢ light blue Franklin (lower part of bust points to end of “E” in “ONE”), *blue*	8.50	5.25
U118	1¢ light blue Franklin (lower part of bust points to end of “E” in “ONE”), *fawn*	8.50	5.25
U119	1¢ light blue Franklin (lower part of bust points to end of “E” in “ONE”), *manila*	9.00	3.25
U121	1¢ light blue Franklin (lower part of bust points to end of “E” in “ONE”), *amber manila*	19.00	10.00
U122	2¢ brown Jackson (bust narrow at back; numerals thin)	140.00	40.00
U123	2¢ brown Jackson (bust narrow at back; numerals thin), *amber*	72.50	40.00
U124	2¢ brown Jackson (bust narrow at back; numerals thin), *cream*	1,250.00	
U125	2¢ brown Jackson (bust narrow at back; numerals thin), *orange*	*25,000.00*	
U128	2¢ brown Jackson (numerals in long ovals)	57.50	35.00
U129	2¢ brown Jackson (numerals in long ovals), *amber*	82.50	40.00
U130	2¢ brown Jackson (numerals in long ovals), *cream*	*50,000.00*	
U132	2¢ brown Jackson, (left numeral touches oval)	82.50	29.00
U133	2¢ brown Jackson, (left numeral touches oval), *amber*	350.00	70.00

Issue		Un	U
	1875-1881		
U134	2¢ brown Jackson (numerals in long ovals and “O” of “TWO” has center netted instead of plain)	1,500.00	160.00
U135	2¢ brown Jackson (numerals in long ovals and “O” of “TWO” has center netted instead of plain), *amber*	525.00	125.00
U136	2¢ brown Jackson (numerals in long ovals and “O” of “TWO” has center netted instead of plain), *orange*	57.50	29.00
U139	2¢ brown Jackson (bust broad; numerals short, thick)	62.50	37.50
U140	2¢ brown Jackson (bust broad; numerals short, thick), *amber*	97.50	62.50
U142	2¢ vermillion Jackson (bust broad; numerals short, thick)	9.00	5.00
U143	2¢ vermillion Jackson (bust broad; numerals short, thick), *amber*	9.00	3.00
U144	2¢ vermillion Jackson (bust broad; numerals short, thick), *cream*	19.00	7.00
U146	2¢ vermillion Jackson (bust broad; numerals short, thick), *blue*	140.00	40.00
U147	2¢ vermillion Jackson (bust broad; numerals short, thick), *fawn*	9.50	5.00
U149	2¢ vermillion Jackson (similar to U139-147 but circles around ovals much heavier)	62.50	32.50
U150	2¢ vermillion Jackson (similar to U139-147 but circles around ovals much heavier), *amber*	42.50	17.50
U151	2¢ vermillion Jackson (similar to U139-147 but circles around ovals much heavier), *blue*	13.00	10.00
U152	2¢ vermillion Jackson (similar to U139-147 but circles around ovals much heavier), *fawn*	13.00	4.75
U153	2¢ vermillion Jackson (similar to U139-147 but middle stroke of “N” is thin)	77.50	27.50
U154	2¢ vermillion Jackson (similar to U139-147 but middle stroke of “N” as thin as verticals), *amber*	400.00	90.00
W155	2¢ vermillion Jackson (similar to U139-147 but middle stroke of “N” as thin as verticals), *manilla*	24.00	11.00
U156	2¢ vermillion Jackson (bottom of bust cut almost semi-circularly)	1,650.00	160.00
U157	2¢ vermillion Jackson (bottom of bust cut almost semi-circularly), *amber*	*57,500.00*	*35,000.00*

Issue		Un	U
	1875-1881		
U159	3¢ green Washington (thin letters, long numerals)	37.50	6.75
U160	3¢ green Washington (thin letters, long numerals), *amber*	37.50	10.50
U161	3¢ green Washington (thin letters, long numerals), *cream*	42.50	15.00
U163	3¢ green Washington (thick letters, “ponytail” does not project below bust)	1.50	.30
U164	3¢ green Washington (thick letters, “ponytail” does not project below bust), *amber*	1.60	.70
U165	3¢ green Washington (thick letters, “ponytail” does not project below bust), cream	9.50	6.50
U166	3¢ green Washington (thick letters, “ponytail” does not project below bust), *blue*	8.50	6.25
U167	3¢ green Washington (thick letters, “ponytail” does not project below bust), *fawn*	5.25	3.50
U168	3¢ green Washington (top of head egg-shaped; “ponytail” knot projects as point)	1,500.00	80.00
U169	3¢ green Washington (top of head egg-shaped; “ponytail” knot projects as point), *amber*	325.00	110.00
U170	3¢ green Washington (top of head egg-shaped; “ponytail” knot projects as point), *blue*	*12,500.00*	*3,750.00*
U171	3¢ green Washington (top of head egg-shaped; “ponytail” knot projects as point), *fawn*	*45,000.00*	*3,250.00*
U172	5¢ blue Taylor, (numerals have thick, curved tops)	15.00	8.50
U173	5¢ blue Taylor, die 1, (numerals have thick, curved tops), *amber*	15.00	9.50
U174	5¢ blue Taylor, die 1, (numerals have thick, curved tops), *cream*	125.00	42.50
U175	5¢ blue Taylor, die 1, (numerals have thick, curved tops), *blue*	40.00	16.00
U176	5¢ blue Taylor, die 1, (numerals have thick, curved tops), *blue*	160.00	60.00
U177	5¢ blue Taylor, die 2, (numerals have long, thin tops)	12.00	7.50
U178	5¢ blue Taylor, die 2, (numerals have long, thin tops), *amber*	11.00	8.00
U179	5¢ blue Taylor, die 2, (numerals have long, thin tops), *blue*	32.50	11.00
U180	5¢ blue Taylor, die 2, (numerals have long, thin tops), *fawn*	140.00	47.50

Issue		Un	U
	1875-1886		
U181	6¢ red Lincoln (neck short at back)	10.00	6.75
U182	6¢ red Lincoln (neck short at back), *amber*	15.00	6.75
U183	6¢ red Lincoln (neck short at back), *cream*	55.00	17.50
U184	6¢ red Lincoln (neck short at back), *fawn*	24.00	13.50
U185	7¢ vermillion Stanton (figures turned up at ends)	*1,800.00*	
U186	7¢ vermillion Stanton (figures turned up at ends), *amber*	150.00	65.00
U187	10¢ brown Jefferson (very large head)	45.00	22.50
U188	10¢ brown Jefferson (very large head), *amber*	82.50	35.00
U189	10¢ chocolate Jefferson (knot of "ponytail" stands out)	8.00	4.25
U190	10¢ chocolate Jefferson (knot of "ponytail" stands out), *amber*	9.00	7.25
U191	10¢ brown Jefferson (knot of "ponytail" stands out), *oriental buff*	18.00	8.25
U192	10¢ brown Jefferson (knot of "ponytail" stands out), *blue*	18.00	8.25
U193	10¢ brown Jefferson (knot of "ponytail" stands out), *manila*	19.00	10.00
U194	10¢ brown Jefferson (knot of "ponytail" stands out), *amber manila*	21.00	9.00
U195	12¢ plum Clay (ear prominent, chin receding)	475.00	100.00
U196	12¢ plum Clay (ear prominent, chin receding), *amber*	275.00	175.00
U197	12¢ plum Clay (ear prominent, chin receding), *cream*	225.00	150.00
U198	15¢ orange Webster (no side whiskers)	55.00	40.00
U199	15¢ orange Webster (no side whiskers), *amber*	160.00	100.00
U200	15¢ orange Webster (no side whiskers), *cream*	600.00	350.00
U201	24¢ purple Scott (hair does not project)	175.00	150.00
U202	24¢ purple Scott (hair does not project), *amber*	190.00	125.00
U203	24¢ purple Scott (hair does not project), *cream*	175.00	125.00
U204	30¢ black Hamilton (back of bust rather broad)	62.50	27.50
U205	30¢ black Hamilton (back of bust rather broad), *amber*	72.50	60.00
U206	30¢ black Hamilton (back of bust rather broad), *cream*	400.00	375.00
U207	30¢ black Hamilton (back of bust rather broad), *oriental buff*	100.00	82.50
U208	30¢ black Hamilton (back of bust rather broad), *blue*	110.00	82.50

Issue		Un	U
	1881-1884		
U209	30¢ black Hamilton (back of bust rather broad), *manila*	95.00	80.00
U210	30¢ black Hamilton (back of bust rather broad), *amber manila*	175.00	85.00
U211	90¢ carmine Perry (front of bust broad, sloping)	110.00	85.00
U212	90¢ carmine Perry (front of bust broad, sloping), *amber*	225.00	300.00
U213	90¢ carmine Perry (front of bust broad, sloping), *cream*	1,750.00	
U214	90¢ carmine Perry (front of bust broad, sloping), *oriental buff*	200.00	275.00
U215	90¢ carmine Perry (front of bust broad, sloping), *blue*	190.00	250.00
U216	90¢ carmine Perry (front of bust broad, sloping), *manila*	175.00	250.00
U217	90¢ carmine Perry (front of bust broad, sloping), *amber manila*	150.00	200.00
U218	3¢ red Post Rider, Train (1 line under "POSTAGE")	52.50	25.00
U219	3¢ green Post Rider, Train (1 line under "POSTAGE")	45.00	17.50
U220	3¢ red Post Rider, Train (2 lines under "POSTAGE")	*42,500.00*	
U221	3¢ green Post Rider, Train (2 lines under "POSTAGE")	52.50	25.00
U222	5¢ brown Garfield	5.25	2.75
U223	5¢ brown Garfield, *amber*	5.50	3.25
U224	5¢ brown Garfield, *oriental buff*	140.00	75.00
U225	5¢ brown Garfield, *blue*	82.50	35.00
U226	5¢ brown Garfield, *fawn*	375.00	
U227	2¢ red Washington	4.50	2.25
U228	2¢ red Washington, *amber*	5.75	2.75
U229	2¢ red Washington, *blue*	8.50	5.00
U230	2¢ red Washington, *fawn*	9.25	5.25
U231	2¢ red Washington (four clear wavy lines in oval)	4.75	2.25
U232	2¢ red Washington (four clear wavy lines in oval), *amber*	5.75	3.75
U233	2¢ red Washington (four clear wavy lines in oval), *blue*	9.25	7.25
U234	2¢ red Washington (four clear wavy lines in oval), *fawn*	7.00	4.75
U236	2¢ red Washington (wavy lines in oval thick, blurred)	13.00	4.00
U237	2¢ red Washington (wavy lines in oval thick, blurred), *amber*	16.00	10.00
U238	2¢ red Washington (wavy lines in oval thick, blurred), *blue*	29.00	10.00
U239	2¢ red Washington (wavy lines in oval thick, blurred), *fawn*	17.00	10.00

Issue		Un	U
	1884-1886		
U240	2¢ red Washington (3½ links over left "2")	100.00	47.50
U241	2¢ red Washington (3½ links over left "2"), *amber*	1,000.00	325.00
U242	2¢ red Washington (3½ links over left "2"), *fawn*		*37,500.00*
U243	2¢ red Washington (2 links below right "2")	140.00	75.00
U244	2¢ red Washington (2 links below right "2"), *amber*	350.00	80.00
U245	2¢ red Wash. (2 links below right "2"), *blue*	500.00	210.00
U246	2¢ red Wash. (2 links below right "2"), *fawn*	450.00	150.00
U247	2¢ red Washington (round "O" in "TWO")	3,000.00	600.00
U248	2¢ red Washington (round "O" in "TWO"), *amber*	5,000.00	1,050.00
U249	2¢ red Washington (round "O" in "TWO"), *fawn*	1,250.00	425.00
U250	4¢ green Jackson, die 1 (left numeral 2¾mm wide)	4.00	3.50
U251	4¢ green Jackson, die 1, (left numeral 2¾mm wide), *amber*	5.00	3.50
U252	4¢ green Jackson, die 1, (left numeral 2¾mm wide), *oriental buff*	13.00	9.00
U253	4¢ green Jackson, die 1, (left numeral 2¾mm wide), *blue*	13.00	6.50
U254	4¢ green Jackson, die 1, (left numeral 2¾mm wide), *manila*	16.00	7.50
U255	4¢ green Jackson, die 1, (left numeral 2¾mm wide), *amber manila*	24.00	10.00
U256	4¢ green Jackson, die 2, (left numeral 3¼mm wide)	11.00	5.00
U257	4¢ green Jackson, die 2, (left numeral 3¼mm wide), *amber*	15.00	7.00
U258	4¢ green Jackson, die 2, (left numeral 3¼mm wide), *manila*	15.00	7.50
U259	4¢ green Jackson, die 2, (left numeral 3¼mm wide), amber *manila*	15.00	7.50
U260	2¢ brown Washington (four clear wavy lines in oval)	17.00	5.75
U261	2¢ brown Washington (four clear wavy lines in oval), *amber*	17.00	6.50
U262	2¢ brown Washington (four clear wavy lines in oval), *blue*	21.00	10.00
U263	2¢ brown Washington (four clear wavy lines in oval), *fawn*	17.00	9.25
U265	2¢ brown Washington (wavy lines in oval thick, blurred)	19.00	6.25

	Issue	Un	U
	1884-1894		
U266	2¢ brown Washington (wavy lines in oval thick, blurred), *amber*	67.50	40.00
U267	2¢ brown Washington (wavy lines in oval thick, blurred), *blue*	25.00	9.00
U268	2¢ brown Washington (wavy lines in oval thick, blurred), *fawn*	18.00	11.00
U270	2¢ brown Washington (2 links below right "2")	140.00	50.00
U271	2¢ brown Washington (2 links below right "2"), *amber*	500.00	110.00
U272	2¢ brown Washington (2 links below right "2"), *fawn*	*10,000.00*	*3,000.00*
U273	2¢ brown Washington (round "O" in "TWO")	300.00	110.00
U274	2¢ brown Washington (round "O" in "TWO"), *amber*	300.00	90.00
U275	2¢ brown Washington (round "O" in "TWO"), *blue*		*20,000.00*
U276	2¢ brown Washington (round "O" in "TWO"), *fawn*	1,050.00	700.00
U277	2¢ brown Washington (extremity of bust below "ponytail" forms point)	.50	.20
U278	2¢ brown Washington (extremity of bust below "ponytail" forms point), *amber*	.65	.50
U279	2¢ brown Washington (extremity of bust below "ponytail" forms point), *oriental buff*	5.00	2.10
U280	2¢ brown Washington (extremity of bust below "ponytail" forms point), *blue*	3.00	2.10
U281	2¢ brown Washington (extremity of bust below "ponytail" forms point), *fawn*	3.75	2.40
U282	2¢ brown Washington (extremity of bust below "ponytail" forms point), *manila*	13.00	4.00
U284	2¢ brown Washington (extremity of bust below "ponytail" forms point), *amber manila*	9.00	5.75
U288	2¢ brown Washington (extremity of bust is rounded)	375.00	50.00
U289	2¢ brown Washington (extremity of bust is rounded), *amber*	18.00	13.00
U290	2¢ brown Washington (extremity of bust is rounded), *blue*	1,900.00	300.00
U291	2¢ brown Washington (extremity of bust is rounded), *fawn*	32.50	20.00
U293	2¢ green Grant	27.50	17.00
U294	1¢ blue Franklin, no wavy lines	.55	.20
U295	1¢ dark blue Franklin, no wavy lines	7.50	2.50
U296	1¢ blue Franklin, no wavy lines, *manila*	3.50	1.25
U297	1¢ dark blue Franklin, *amber*	47.50	22.50
U300	1¢ blue Franklin, no wavy lines, *amber*	.65	.35

	Issue	Un	U
	1894-1894		
U302	1¢ dark blue Franklin, *manila*	27.50	11.00
U304	1¢ blue Franklin, *amber manila*	12.50	5.00
U305	2¢ green Washington ("G" has no bar)	19.00	10.50
U306	2¢ green Washington ("G" has no bar), *amber*	42.50	16.00
U307	2¢ green Washington ("G" has no bar), *oriental buff*	92.50	32.50
U308	2¢ green Washington ("G" has no bar), *blue*	*9,000.00*	1,250.00
U309	2¢ green Washington ("G" has no bar), *manila*	*17,500.00*	750.00
U310	2¢ green Washington ("G" has no bar), *amber manila*	—	1,250.00
U311	2¢ green Washington ("G" has bar, ear indicated by 1 heavy line)	.35	.20
U312	2¢ green Washington ("G" has bar, ear indicated by 1 heavy line), amber	.45	.20
U313	2¢ greenWashington ("G" has bar, ear indicated by 1 heavy line), *oriental buff*	.60	.25
U314	2¢ green Washington ("G" has bar, ear indicated by 1 heavy line), *blue*	.65	.30
U315	2¢ green Washington ("G" has bar, ear indicated by 1 heavy line), *manila*	1.75	.50
U317	2¢ green Washington ("G" has bar, ear indicated by 1 heavy line), *amber manila*	2.75	1.90
U318	2¢ green Washington (like U314 but ear indicated by 2 curved lines)	150.00	12.50
U319	2¢ green Washington (like U314 but ear indicated by 2 curved lines), *amber*	190.00	25.00
U320	2¢ green Washington (like U314 but ear indicated by 2 curved lines), *oriental buff*	175.00	40.00
U321	2¢ green Washington (like U314 but ear indicated by 2 curved lines), *blue*	190.00	65.00
U322	2¢ green Washington (like U314 but ear indicated by 2 curved lines), *manila*	275.00	65.00
U323	2¢ green Washington (like U314 but ear indicated by 2 curved lines), *amber manila*	575.00	80.00
U324	4¢ carmine Jackson	3.25	2.00
U325	4¢ carmine Jackson, *amber*	3.75	3.50
U326	4¢ carmine Jackson, *oriental buff*	8.00	3.50
U327	4¢ carmine Jackson, *blue*	6.50	4.00
U328	4¢ carmine Jackson, *manila*	9.00	7.00
U329	4¢ carmine Jackson, *amber manila*	7.50	3.25

	Issue	Un	U
	1894-1899		
U330	5¢ blue Grant (space between beard and collar)	4.00	4.00
U331	5¢ blue Grant (space between beard and collar), *amber*	5.50	2.50
U332	5¢ blue Grant (space between beard and collar), *oriental buff*	6.00	4.00
U333	5¢ blue Grant (space between beard and collar), *blue*	10.50	6.00
U334	5¢ blue Grant (collar touches beard)	27.50	12.50
U335	5¢ blue Grant (collar touches beard), *amber*	15.00	7.50
U336	30¢ red brown Hamilton (back of bust rather broad)	60.00	47.50
U337	30¢ red brown Hamilton (back of bust rather broad), *amber*	60.00	47.50
U338	30¢ red brown Hamilton (back of bust rather broad), *oriental buff*	60.00	47.50
U339	30¢ red brown Hamilton (back of bust rather broad), *blue*	60.00	47.50
U340	30¢ red brown Hamilton (back of bust rather broad), *manila*	60.00	47.50
U341	30¢ red brown Hamilton (back of bust rather broad), *amber manila*	60.00	47.50
U342	90¢ purple Perry (front of bust broad, sloping)	77.50	*85.00*
U343	90¢ purple Perry (front of bust broad, sloping), *amber*	92.50	85.00
U344	90¢ purple Perry (front of bust broad, sloping), *oriental buff*	92.50	85.00
U345	90¢ purple Perry (front of bust broad, sloping), *blue*	92.50	*90.00*
U346	90¢ purple Perry (front of bust broad, sloping), *manila*	100.00	*92.50*
U347	90¢ purple Perry (front of bust broad, sloping), *amber manila*	100.00	*92.50*
U348	1¢ deep blue Columbus & Liberty	2.25	1.25
U349	2¢ violet Columbus & Liberty	1.75	.50
U350	5¢ chocolate Columbus & Liberty	8.50	7.50
U351	10¢ slate brown Columbus & Liberty	35.00	30.00
U352	1¢ green Franklin, no wavy lines	1.10	.20
U353	1¢ green Franklin, no wavy lines, *amber*	5.50	1.50
U354	1¢ green Franklin, no wavy lines, *oriental buff*	14.50	2.75
U355	1¢ green Franklin, no wavy lines, *blue*	14.50	7.50
U356	1¢ green Franklin, no wavy lines, *manila*	2.40	.95
U358	2¢ carmine Washington, (bust points to first notch of inner oval)	3.00	1.75
U359	2¢ carmine Washington, (bust points to first notch of inner oval), *amber*	24.00	14.50

U294

U314

U348

U351

U358

U368

U374

U377

U379

U386

U390

U393

U398

U400

U406

U416

U429

U447

U468

W485

U522

U523

U524

VISIT US ONLINE AT ***THE POSTAL STORE***
AT ***WWW.USPS.COM***
OR CALL ***1 800 STAMP-24***

U530

U531

U541

U542

U543

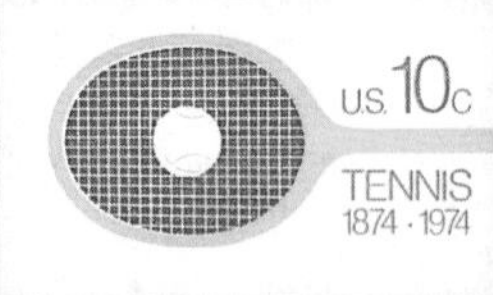

U569

U576

U581

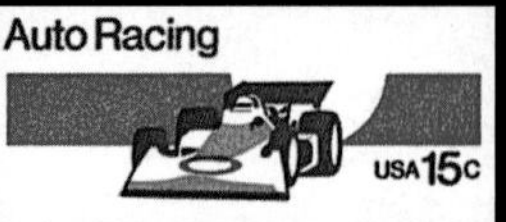
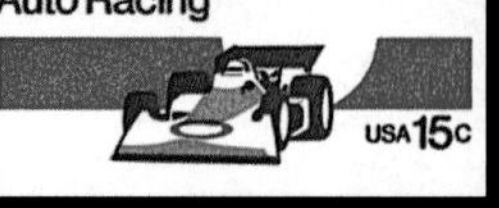

U587

U601

U609

U610

U611

U614

U616

U617

U631

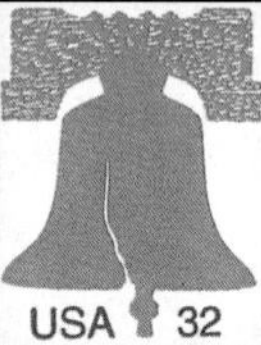

U632

Issue		Un	U
1899-1903			
U360	2¢ carmine Washington, bust points to first notch of inner oval), *amber*	24.00	12.50
U361	2¢ carmine Washington, bust points to first notch of inner oval), *blue*	65.00	35.00
U362	2¢ carmine Washington, bust points to middle of second notch of inner oval, "ponytail")	.35	.20
U363	2¢ carmine Washington, bust points to middle of second notch of inner oval, "ponytail"), *amber*	1.40	.20
U364	2¢ carmine Washington, bust points to middle of second notch of inner oval, "ponytail"), *oriental buff*	1.20	.20
U365	2¢ carmine Washington, bust points to middle of second notch of inner oval, "ponytail"), *blue*	1.50	.55
U367	2¢ carmine Washington, (same as U362 but hair flowing; no ribbon "ponytail")	6.00	2.75
U368	2¢ carmine Washington, (same as U362 but hair flowing; no ribbon "ponytail"), *amber*	9.00	6.75
U369	2¢ carmine Washington, (same as U362 but hair flowing; no ribbon "ponytail"), *oriental buff*	25.00	12.50
U370	2¢ carmine Washington, (same as U362 but hair flowing; no ribbon "ponytail"), *blue*	12.50	10.00
U371	4¢ brown Lincoln (bust pointed, undraped)	20.00	12.00
U372	4¢ brown Lincoln (bust pointed, undraped), *amber*	20.00	13.00
U373	4¢ brown Lincoln, (broad bust and draped)	*13,500.00*	1,250.00
U374	4¢ brown (head larger; inner oval has no notches)	15.00	8.00
U375	4¢ brown (head larger; inner oval has no notches), *amber*	65.00	25.00
U377	5¢ blue Grant (like U331, U335 but smaller)	13.00	10.00
U378	5¢ blue Grant (like U331, U335 but smaller), *amber*	17.00	10.50
U379	1¢ green Franklin, horizontal oval	.70	.20
U380	1¢ green Franklin, horizontal oval, *amber*	15.00	2.00
U381	1¢ green Franklin, horizontal oval, *oriental buff*	18.00	2.50
U382	1¢ green Franklin, horizontal oval, *blue*	22.50	2.50
U383	1¢ green Franklin, horizontal oval, *manila*	4.00	.90

Issue		Un	U
1903-1916			
U385	2¢ carmine Washington (1 short, 2 long vertical lines at right of "CENTS")	.40	.20
U386	2¢ carmine Washington (1 short, 2 long vertical lines at right of "CENTS"), *amber*	2.00	.20
U387	2¢ carmine Washington (1 short, 2 long vertical lines at right of "CENTS"), *oriental buff*	2.00	.30
U388	2¢ carmine Washington (1 short, 2 long vertical lines at right of "CENTS"), *blue*	1.50	.50
U390	4¢ chocolate Grant	22.50	11.00
U391	4¢ chocolate Grant, *amber*	22.50	12.50
U393	5¢ blue Lincoln	22.50	12.50
U394	5¢ blue Lincoln, *amber*	22.50	12.50
U395	2¢ carmine Washington, recut die (lines at end of "TWO CENTS" all short), *blue*	.60	.20
U396	2¢ carmine Washington, recut die (lines at end of "TWO CENTS" all short), *amber*	8.00	1.00
U397	2¢ carmine Washington, recut die (lines at end of "TWO CENTS" all short), *oriental buff*	5.50	1.10
U398	2¢ carmine Washington, recut die (lines at end of "TWO CENTS" all short), *blue*	4.00	.90
U400	1¢ green Franklin, oval, die 1 (wide "D" in "UNITED")	.30	.20
U401	1¢ green Franklin, oval, die 1 (wide "D" in "UNITED"), *amber*	2.00	.40
U402	1¢ green Franklin, oval, die 1 (wide "D" in "UNITED"), *oriental buff*	10.00	1.00
U403	1¢ green Franklin, oval, die 1 (wide "D" in "UNITED"), *blue*	10.00	1.50
U404	1¢ green Franklin, oval, die 1 (wide "D" in "UNITED"), *manila*	3.00	1.90
U406	2¢ brown red Washington, die 1 (oval "O" in "TWO" and "C" in "CENTS")	.85	.20
U407	2¢ brown red Washington, die 1 (oval "O" in "TWO" and "C" in "CENTS"), *amber*	6.00	2.00
U408	2¢ brown red Washington, die 1 (oval "O" in "TWO" and "C" in "CENTS"), *oriental buff*	8.50	1.50
U409	2¢ brown red Washington, die 1 (oval "O" in "TWO" and "C" in "CENTS"), *blue*	5.50	2.00

Issue		Un	U
1916-1932			
U411	2¢ carmine Washington, die 1 (oval "O" in "TWO" and "C" in "CENTS"), *blue*	.25	.20
U412	2¢ carmine Washington, die 1 (oval "O" in "TWO" and "C" in "CENTS"), *amber*	.25	.20
U413	2¢ carmine Washington, die 1 (oval "O" in "TWO" and "C" in "CENTS"), *oriental buff*	.45	.20
U414	2¢ carmine Washington, die 1 (oval "O" in "TWO" and "C" in "CENTS"), *blue*	.50	.20
U416	4¢ black Washington, die 2 ("F" is 1¾mm from left "4")	5.00	3.00
U417	4¢ black Washington, die 2 ("F" is 1¾mm from left "4"), *amber*	7.00	2.50
U418	5¢ blue Washington, die 2 (short "F" in FIVE")	6.50	2.25
U419	5¢ blue Washington, die 2 (short "F" in FIVE"), *amber*	16.00	11.00
U420	1¢ green Franklin, round, die 1 ("UNITED" nearer inner circle than outer circle)	.20	.20
U421	1¢ green Franklin, round, die 1 ("UNITED" nearer inner circle than outer circle), *amber*	.50	.30
U422	1¢ green Franklin, round, die 1 ("UNITED" nearer inner circle than outer circle), *oriental buff*	2.25	.90
U423	1¢ green Franklin, round, die 1 ("UNITED" nearer inner circle than outer circle), *blue*	.45	.35
U424	1¢ green Franklin, round, die 1 ("UNITED" nearer inner circle than outer circle), *manila*	6.50	4.00
U426	1¢ green Franklin, round, die 1 ("UNITED" nearer inner circle than outer circle), glazed, *brown*	45.00	15.00
U428	1¢ green Franklin, round, die 1 ("UNITED" nearer inner circle than outer circle), unglazed, *brown*	16.00	7.50

Issue		Un	U
	1915-1921		
U429	2¢ carmine Washington, die 1 (letters broad, numerals vertical, "E" closer than "N" to inner circle)	.20	.20
U430	2¢ carmine Washington, die 1 (letters broad, numerals vertical, "E" closer than "N" to inner circle), *amber*	.25	.20
U431	2¢ carmine Washington, die 1 (letters broad, numerals vertical, "E" closer than "N" to inner circle), *oriental buff*	2.25	.65
U432	2¢ carmine Washington, die 1 (letters broad, numerals vertical, "E" closer than "N" to inner circle), *blue*	.25	.20
U436	3¢ purple Washington, die 1 (as 2¢)	.30	.20
U437	3¢ purple Washington, die 1 (as 2¢), *amber*	.35	.20
U438	3¢ dark violet Washington, die 1 (as 2¢), *oriental buff*	25.00	1.65
U439	3¢ purplet Washington, die 1 (as 2¢), *blue*	.30	.20
U440	4¢ black Franklin, die 1, ("UNITED" closer to inner circle)	1.50	.60
U441	4¢ black Franklin, die 1, ("UNITED" closer to inner circle), *amber*	3.00	.85
U442	4¢ black Franklin, die 1, ("UNITED" closer to inner circle), *blue*	3.25	.85
U443	5¢ blue Washington, die 1, (letters are broad)	3.25	2.75
U444	5¢ blue Washington, die 1, (letters are broad), *amber*	3.75	1.60
U445	5¢ blue Washington, die 1, (letters are broad), *blue*	4.00	3.25
U446	2¢ on 3¢ dark violet Washington, die 1, black surcharge	15.00	10.00
U447	2¢ on 3¢ dark violet Washington, die 1, rose surcharge	9.00	6.50
U448	2¢ on 3¢ dark violet Washington, die 1, black surcharge	2.50	2.00
U449	2¢ on 3¢ dark violet Washington, die 1, black surcharge, *amber*	7.00	6.00
U450	2¢ on 3¢ dark violet Washington, die 1 black surcharge, *oriental buff*	17.50	14.00
U451	2¢ on 3¢ dark violet Washington, die 1, black surcharge, *blue*	14.00	10.00
U452	2¢ on 1¢ green Franklin, die 1, ("UNITED" nearer inner circle than outer circle)	3,750.00	

Issue		Un	U
	1921		
U453	2¢ on 2¢ carmine Washington, die 3, (round "O" and "C", coarse lettering)	5,000.00	
U454	2¢ on 2¢ carmine Washington, die 6, ("T" and "S" far apart at bottom)	150.00	
U455	2¢ on 2¢ carmine Washington, die 1, (letters broad, numerals vertical, "E" closer than "N" to inner circle), *amber*	2,250.00	
U456	2¢ on 2¢ carmine Washington, die 2, ("U" far from left circle), *oriental buff*	300.00	
U457	2¢ on 2¢ carmine Washington, die 6, ("T" and "S" far apart at bottom), *blue*	400.00	
U458	2¢ on 3¢ dark violet Washington, die 1, black surcharge, (bars 2mm apart)	.50	.35
U459	2¢ on 3¢ dark violet Washington, die 6, ("T" and "S" far apart at bottom), *amber*	3.00	1.00
U460	2¢ on 3¢ dark violet Washington, die 6, ("T" and "S" far apart at bottom), *oriental buff*	4.00	2.00
U461	2¢ on 3¢ dark violet Washington, die 1, (letters broad, numerals vertical, "E" closer than "N" to inner circle), *blue*	6.00	1.00
U462	2¢ on 4¢ chocolate Grant	625.00	260.00
U463	2¢ on 4¢ chocolate Grant, *amber*	1,250.00	350.00
U464	2¢ on 5¢ blue Washington, die 1, (letters are broad)	1,400.00	
U465	2¢ on 1¢ green Franklin, die 1, (letters are broad)	1,750.00	
U466	2¢ on 2¢ carmne Franklin, die 1, (letters are broad)	*15,000.00*	
U467	2¢ on 3¢ green Washington, die 2 (thick letters, "ponytail" does not project below bust), *blue*	425.00	
U468	2¢ on 3¢ dark violet Washington, die 1, black surcharge, (bars 1½mm apart)	.70	.45
U469	2¢ on 3¢ dark violet Washington, die 1, (letters broad, numerals vertical, "E" closer than "N" to inner circle), *amber*	3.50	2.25
U470	2¢ on 3¢ dark violet Washington, die 1, (letters broad, numerals vertical, "E" closer than "N" to inner circle), *oriental buff*	5.50	2.50
U471	2¢ on 3¢ dark violet Washington, die 1, (letters broad, numerals vertical, "E" closer than "N" to inner circle), *blue*	7.00	1.75

Issue		Un	U
	1921-1925		
U472	2¢ on 4¢ chocolate Grant	14.00	8.00
U473	2¢ on 4¢ chocolate Grant, *amber*	16.00	10.00
U474	2¢ on 1¢ on 3¢ dark violet Washington, die 1, double surcharge, (letters broad, numerals vertical, "E" closer than "N" to inner circle)	300.00	
U475	2¢ on 1¢ on 3¢ dark violet Washington, die 1, double surcharge, (letters broad, numerals vertical, "E" closer than "N" to inner circle), *amber*	300.00	
U476	2¢ on 3¢ dark violet Washington, die 1, double surcharge, (letters broad, numerals vertical, "E" closer than "N" to inner circle), *amber*	300.00	
U477	2¢ on 3¢ dark violet Washington, die 1, double surcharge, (letters broad, numerals vertical, "E" closer than "N" to inner circle)	140.00	
U478	2¢ on 3¢ dark violet Washington, die 1, double surcharge, (letters broad, numerals vertical, "E" closer than "N" to inner circle), *amber*	350.00	
U479	2¢ on 3¢ dark violet Washington, (bk) die 1, double surcharge, (letters broad, numerals vertical, "E" closer than "N" to inner circle), *amber*	450.00	
U480	2¢ on 3¢ dark violet Washington, (bk) die 7, double surcharge, (letters broad, numerals vertical, "E" closer than "N" to inner circle), *amber*	*6,000.00*	
U481	1½¢ brown Washington, die 1 (letters broad, numerals vertical, "E" closer than "N" to inner circle)	.20	.20
U482	1½¢ brown Washington, die 1 (letters broad, numerals vertical, "E" closer than "N" to inner circle), *amber*	.90	.40
U483	1½¢ brown Washington, die 1 (letters broad, numerals vertical, "E" closer than "N" to inner circle), *blue*	1.50	.95
U484	1½¢ brown Washington, die 1 (letters broad, numerals vertical, "E" closer than "N" to inner circle), *manila*	6.00	3.00
W485	1½¢ brown Washington, *manila*	.80	.20
U486	1½¢ on 2¢ green Washington, ("G" has bar, ear indicated by 1 heavy line)	900.00	
U487	1½¢ on 2¢ green Washington, ("G" has bar, ear indicated by 1 heavy line), *amber*	1,400.00	

Issue		Un	U
	1925		
U488	1½¢ on 1¢ green Franklin, (no wavy lines)	675.00	
U489	1½¢ on 1¢ green Franklin, (no wavy lines), *amber*	125.00	60.00
U490	1½¢ on 1¢ green Franklin, die 1, (wide "D" in "UNITED")	6.50	3.50
U491	1½¢ on 1¢ green Franklin, die 4, (sharp angle at back of bust), *amber*	7.50	2.25
U492	1½¢ on 1¢ green Franklin, die 2, (narrow "D" in "UNITED"), *oriental buff*	600.00	150.00
U493	1½¢ on 1¢ green Franklin, die 4, (sharp angle at back of bust), *blue*	125.00	70.00
U494	1½¢ on 1¢ green Franklin, die 1, (wide "D" in "UNITED"), *manila*	400.00	100.00
U495	1½¢ on 1¢ green Franklin, die 1, ("UNITED" nearer inner circle than outer circle)	.75	.25
U496	1½¢ on 1¢ green Franklin, die 1, ("UNITED" nearer inner circle than outer circle), *amber*	20.00	12.50
U497	1½¢ on 1¢ green Franklin, die 1, ("UNITED" nearer inner circle than outer circle), *oriental buff*	4.00	1.90
U498	1½¢ on 1¢ green Franklin, die 1, ("UNITED" nearer outer circle than inner circle), *blue*	1.50	.75
U499	1½¢ on 1¢, green Franklin, ("UNITED" nearer inner circle than outer circle), unglazed, *manila*	12.50	6.00
U500	1½¢ on 1¢, green Franklin, ("UNITED" nearer inner circle than outer circle), unglazed, *brown*	82.50	30.00
U500	1½¢ on 1¢, green Franklin, round, die 1 ("UNITED" nearer inner circle than outer circle), unglazed, *brown*	82.50	30.00
U501	1½¢ on 1¢, green Franklin, round, die 1 ("UNITED" nearer inner circle than outer circle), glazed, *brown*	82.50	30.00
U502	1½¢ on 2¢, carmine Washington, die 1 (letters broad, numerals vertical, "E" closer than "N" to inner circle)	300.00	—
U503	1½¢ on 2¢, carmine Washington, die 5 ("T" and "S" of CENTS close at bottom), *oriental buff*	400.00	—

Issue		Un	U
	1920-1925		
U504	1½¢ on 2¢, carmine Washington, die 1 (letters broad, numerals vertical, "E" closer than "N" to inner circle), *blue*	450.00	—
U505	1½¢ on 1½¢, brown Washington, die 1 (letters broad, numerals vertical, "E" closer than "N" to inner circle), *blue*	500.00	
U506	1½¢ on 1½¢, brown Washington, die 8 (large head, clean letters, all "T"s long top strokes), *blue*	500.00	
U507	1½¢ on 1½¢, brown Washington, die 8 (large head, clean letters, all "T"s long top strokes), *blue*	3,250.00	
U508	1½¢ on 1¢ green Franklin, no wavy lines, *amber*	70.00	
U509	1½¢ on 1¢ green Franklin, horizontal oval, *amber*	15.00	10.00
U510	1½¢ on 1¢ green Franklin, oval, die 1, (wide "D" in "UNITED")	2.75	1.25
U511	1½¢ on 1¢ green Franklin, oval, die 1, (wide "D" in "UNITED"), *amber*	250.00	100.00
U512	1½¢ on 1¢ green Franklin, oval, die 1, (wide "D" in "UNITED"), *oriental buff*	8.50	4.00
U513	1½¢ on 1¢ green Franklin, oval, die 1, (wide "D" in "UNITED"), *blue*	6.00	4.00
U514	1½¢ on 1¢ green Franklin, oval, die 1, (wide "D" in "UNITED")	32.50	9.00
U515	1½¢ on 1¢ green Franklin, die 1, (wide "D" in "UNITED"), *manila*	.35	.20
U516	1½¢ on 1¢ green Franklin, die 4, ("UNITED" nearer to outer circle), *amber*	47.50	25.00
U517	1½¢ on 1¢ green Franklin, die 4, ("UNITED" nearer to inner circle), *oriental buff*	6.00	1.25
U518	1½¢ on 1¢ green Franklin, die 4, ("UNITED" nearer to outer circle), *blue*	5.50	1.25
U519	1½¢ on 1¢ green Franklin, die 4, ("UNITED" nearer to inner circle), *manila*	30.00	10.00
U520	1½¢ on 1¢ green Washington, die 1, (letters broad, numerals vertical, "E" closer than "N" to inner circle)	350.00	—
U521	1½¢ on 1¢ green Franklin, die 3, (knob of hair at back of neck)	4.50	3.50
U522	2¢ carmine Liberty Bell, die 1	1.10	.50
U523	1¢ olive green Mount Vernon	1.00	.80
U524	1½¢ chocolate Mount Vernon	2.00	1.50
U525	2¢ carmine Mount Vernon	.40	.20
U526	3¢ violet Mount Vernon	2.00	.35

Issue		Un	U
	1926-1971		
U527	4¢ black Mount Vernon	18.00	*20.00*
U528	5¢ dark blue Mount Vernon	4.00	3.50
U529	6¢ orange Washington, die 7, both numerals slope to right	6.00	4.00
U530	6¢ orange Washington, die 7, both numerals slope to right, *amber*	12.00	10.00
U531	6¢ orange Washington, die 7, both numerals slope to right, *blue*	12.00	10.00
U532	1¢ green Franklin, die 1, (thick "I" in thick circle)	5.50	1.75
U533	2¢ carmine Washington, die 3, (thin "2" in thin circle, short "N" in UNITED, thin crossbar in "A" of STATES)	.75	.25
U534	3¢ dark violet Washington, die 4, (thin "3" in thin circle, short "N" in UNITED, thin crossbar in "A" of STATES)	.40	.20
U535	1½¢ brown Washington	5.50	3.50
U536	4¢ red violet Franklin, die 1 (thick "I" in thick circle)	.80	.20
U537	2¢ + 2¢ carmine Washington, die 1, (letters broad, numerals vertical, "E" closer than "N" to inner circle)	3.50	1.50
U538	2¢ + 2¢ carmine Washington, die 1, (thick "2" in thick circle)	.75	*1.25*
U539	3¢ + 1¢ purple, Washington, die 1, (thick "3" in thick circle)	15.00	11.00
U540	3¢ + 1¢ dark violet Washington, die 3, (thin "3" in thin circle)	.50	*1.00*
U541	1¼¢ turquoise Franklin	.75	.50
U542	2½¢ dull blue Washington	.85	.50
U543	4¢ brown Pony Express Rider	.60	.30
U544	5¢ dark blue Lincoln	.85	.20
U545	4¢ + 1¢ red violet Franklin	1.40	*1.25*
U546	5¢ maroon New York World's Fair	.60	.40
U547	1¼¢ brown Liberty Bell		.20
U548	1 4/10¢ brown Liberty Bell		.20
U548A	1 6/10¢ orange Liberty Bell		.20
U549	4¢ bright blue Old Ironsides	.75	.20
U550	5¢ bright purple Eagle	.75	.20
U551	6¢ light green Statue of Liberty, tagged	.70	.20
U552	4¢ + 2¢ bright blue Old Ironsides	3.75	2.00
U553	5¢ + 1¢ bright purple Eagle	3.50	2.75
U554	6¢ blue Herman Melville	.50	.20
U555	6¢ light blue Youth Conference	.75	.20
U556	1 7/10¢ deep lilac Liberty Bell		.20

Issue		Date	Un	U
U557	8¢ ultramarine Eagle	05/06/71	.40	.20
U561	6¢ + (2¢) light green Statue of Liberty	05/16/71	1.00	1.25
U562	6¢ + (2¢) light blue Youth Conference	05/16/71	2.00	2.50
U563	8¢ rose red Bowling	08/21/71	.70	.20
U564	8¢ Aging Conference	11/15/71	.50	.20
U565	8¢ ultramarine and rose red Transpo '72	05/02/72	.50	.20
U566	8¢ + 2¢ bright ultramarine Eagle	12/01/73	.40	*1.25*
U567	10¢ emerald Liberty Bell	12/05/73	.40	.20
U568	1 8/10¢ blue green Volunteer Yourself	08/23/74		.20
U569	10¢ Tennis Centenary	08/31/74	.65	.20
U571	10¢ Compass Rose	10/13/75	.30	.20
U572	13¢ Quilt Pattern	02/02/76	.35	.20
U573	13¢ Sheaf of Wheat	03/15/76	.35	.20
U574	13¢ Mortar and Pestle	06/30/76	.35	.20
U575	13¢ Tools	08/06/76	.35	.20
U576	13¢ Liberty Tree	11/08/75	.30	.20
U577	2¢ red Nonprofit Star and Pinwheel	09/10/76		.20
U578	2.1¢ yellow green Nonprofit	06/03/77		.20
U579	2.7¢ green Nonprofit	07/05/78		.20
U580	15¢ orange Eagle, A	05/22/78	.40	.20
U581	15¢ red Uncle Sam	06/03/78	.40	.20
U582	13¢ emerald bi-centennial	10/15/76	.35	.20
U583	13¢ Golf	04/07/77	.65	.20
U584	13¢ Energy Conservation	10/20/77	.40	.20
U585	13¢ Energy Development	10/20/77	.40	.20
U586	15¢ on 16¢ blue USA	07/28/78	.35	.20
U587	15¢ Auto Racing	10/02/78	.35	.20
U588	15¢ on 13¢ Liberty Tree	11/28/78	.35	.20
U589	3.1¢ ultramarine Nonprofit	05/18/79		.50
U590	3.5¢ purple Violins	06/23/80		.50
U591	5.9¢ brown nonprofit	02/17/82		.50
U592	(18¢) violet Eagle, B	03/15/81	.45	.25
U593	18¢ dark blue Star	04/02/81	.45	.25
U594	(20¢) brown Eagle, C	10/11/81	.45	.25
U595	15¢ Veterinary Medicine	07/24/79	.50	.20
U596	15¢ Summer Olympic Games	12/10/79	.60	.20
U597	15¢ blue and rose claret Highwheeler Bicycle	05/16/80	.40	.20
U598	15¢ America's Cup	09/15/80	.40	.20
U599	15¢ brown, green and yellow Honeybee	10/10/80	.35	.20

Issue		Date	Un	U
U600	18¢ red and blue Blind Veterans	08/13/81	.45	.20
U601	20¢ Capitol Dome	11/13/81	.45	.20
U602	20¢ dark blue, black and magenta Great Seal of US	06/15/82	.45	.20
U603	20¢ purple and black Purple Heart	08/06/82	.65	.20
U604	5.2¢ orange Nonprofit	03/21/83		.20
U605	20¢ red, blue and black Paralyzed Veterans	08/03/83	.45	.20
U606	20¢ Small Business	05/07/84	.50	.20
U607	22¢ deep green Eagle, D	02/01/85	.55	.30
U608	22¢ violet brown Bison	02/25/85	.55	.20
U609	6¢ nonprofit *USS Constitution*	05/03/85		.20
U610	8.5¢ nonprofit *Mayflower*	12/04/86		.20
U611	25¢ dark red and deep blue Stars	03/26/88	.60	.20
U612	8.4¢ nonprofit *US Frigate Constellation*	04/12/88		.20
U613	25¢ Snowflake	09/08/88	1.00	*20.00*
U614	25¢ dark red and deep blue Stars (Philatelic Mail)	03/10/89	.50	.25
U615	25¢ dark red and blue Stars (lined paper)	07/10/89	.50	.25
U616	25¢ dark red and bright blue, Love	09/22/89	.50	*.75*
U617	25¢ ultramarine Space hologram	12/03/89	.90	.60
U618	25¢ Football hologram	09/09/90	.90	.60
U619	29¢ ultramarine and rose Star	01/24/91	.60	.30
U620	11.1¢ Birds	05/03/91		.50
U621	29¢ light blue, maroon and bright rose, Love	05/09/91	.60	.60
U622	29¢ Magazine Industry	10/07/91	.60	.50
U623	29¢ ultramarine and rose Star	07/20/91	.60	.30
U624	29¢ Country Geese	11/08/91	.60	.60
U625	29¢ Space Shuttle, (type of 1989), die-cut	01/21/92	.90	.50
U626	29¢ Western Americana, die-cut	04/10/92	.60	.30
U627	29¢ Protect the Environment	04/22/92	.60	.30
U628	19.8¢ Bulk Rate star precanceled	05/19/92		.40

Issue		Date	Un	U
U629	29¢ Disabled Americans	07/22/92	.60	.30
U630	29¢ Kitten, die-cut	10/02/93	.90	.50
U631	29¢ brown and black Football	09/17/94	.60	.50
U632	32¢ greenish blue and blue Liberty Bell, embossed	01/03/95	.65	.30
U633	(32¢) Old Glory, #6¾	1995	.65	.30
U634	(32¢) Old Glory, #10	1995	.65	.30
U635	(5¢) green and red brown Nonprofit	03/10/95		.50
U636	(10¢) Graphic Eagle	03/10/95		.20
U637	32¢ red, *light blue,* Spiral Heart	05/12/95	.65	.30
U638	32¢ greenish blue and blue Liberty Bell	05/16/95	.65	.30
U639	32¢ Space Shuttle, (type of 1989), die-cut	09/22/95	.65	.35
U640	32¢ Save Our Environment	04/20/96	.60	.30
U641	32¢ multicolored 1996 Paralympic Games	05/02/96	.60	.30
U642	33¢ yellow, blue and red Flag	01/11/99	.65	.30
U643	33¢ red and blue Flag	01/11/99	.65	.30
U644	33¢ Victorian, Love	01/28/99	.65	.30
U645	33¢ Lincoln	06/05/99	.65	.30
U646	34¢ blue gray and gray Federal Eagle, tagged	01/07/01	.65	.30
U647	34¢ Lovebirds, tagged	01/14/01	.65	.30
U648	34¢ Community Colleges, tagged	02/20/01	.65	.30
U649	37¢ red, blue and gray Ribbon Star	06/07/02	.75	.35
U650	(10¢) Presorted Graphic Eagle	08/08/02		.20
U651	37¢ Nuturing, Love	01/25/03	.75	.35
U652	$3.85 Jefferson Memorial	01/25/03	7.75	6.25
U653	37¢ Goofy, Mickey Mouse, Donald Duck	06/23/04	2.50	2.10
U654	37¢ Bambi, Thumper	06/23/04	2.50	2.10
U655	37¢ Mufasa, Simba	06/23/04	2.50	2.10
U656	37¢ Jiminy Cricket, Pinocchio	06/23/04	2.50	2.10
U657	37¢ White lilacs & pink roses	03/03/05	2.50	2.50

U634

U635

U636

U637

U639

U640

U641

U642

U643

U644

U645

U646

U647

U648

U649

U650

U651

U657

VISIT US ONLINE AT ***THE POSTAL STORE***
AT ***WWW.USPS.COM***
OR CALL ***1 800 STAMP-24***

UC1

UC3

UC7

UC8

UC14

UC21

UC25

UC26

UC30

UC39

UC46

UC48

UC52

UC53

UC56

Olympics 84
USA
30c

UC57

UC59

UC63

	Issue	Date	Un	U
UC1	5¢ blue Airplane, die 1 (vertical rudder is not semi-circular)	01/12/29	3.50	2.00
	1933 wmk., entire		*750.00*	*750.00*
	1937 wmk., entire		—	*2,500.00*
	Bi-colored border omitted, entire		1,300.00	
UC2	5¢ blue, die 2 (vertical rudder is semi-circular)	01/12/29	11.50	5.00
	1929 wmk., entire		—	*1,500.00*
	1933 wmk., entire		*650.00*	—
UC3	6¢ orange Airplane, die 2a ("6" is 6½mm wide)	07/01/34	1.50	.40
UC4	6¢ orange Airplane, die 2b ("6" is 6mm wide)	1942	2.75	2.00
UC5	6¢ orange, Airplane, die 2c ("6" is 5½mm wide)	1944	.75	.30
UC6	6¢ orange, Airplane, die 3 (vertical) rudder leans forward)	1942	1.00	.35
a	6¢ orange, Airplane, blue, entire		*3,500.00*	*2,400.00*
UC7	8¢ olive green Airplane	09/26/32	13.00	3.50
UC8	6¢ on 2¢ carmine Washington, (letters broad, numerals vertical, "E" closer than "N" to inner circle)	1945	1.25	.65
UC9	6¢ on 2¢ Mount Vernon	1945	70.00	35.00
UC10	5¢ on 6¢ orange Airplane	1946	2.75	1.50
a	Double surcharge	1946	60.00	
UC11	5¢ on 6¢ orange Airplane, die 2b ("6" is 6mm wide)	1946	9.00	5.50
UC13	5¢ on 6¢ orange Airplane, die 3 (vertical) rudder leans forward)	1946	.80	.60
a	Double surcharge		60.00	
UC14	5¢ carmine DC-4, die 1 (end of wing on right is smooth curve)	09/25/46	.75	.20
UC15	5¢ carmine DC-4, die 2 (end of wing on right is a straight line)	1946	.85	.25
UC16	10¢ red, DC-4 2-line back inscription, entire, *pale blue*	04/29/47	8.50	6.00
a	"Air Letter" on face, 4-line inscription on back		17.50	14.00
	Die-cutting reversed		275.00	
UC17	5¢ carmine Postage Centenary	05/21/47	.40	.25
UC18	6¢ carmine DC-4, type I (6's lean right)	09/22/50	.40	.25
a	Type II (6's upright)		.75	.25
UC19	6¢ on 5¢ carmine DC-4, die 1, (end of wing on right is smooth curve)	1951	.85	.50
UC20	6¢ on 5¢ carmine DC-4, die 2, (end of wing on right is a straight line)	1951	.85	.50
a	6¢ on 6¢ carmine, entire		*1,500.00*	
b	Double surcharge		*500.00*	—
UC21	6¢ on 5¢ carmine DC-4 die 1, (end of wing on right is smooth curve)	1952	27.50	17.50
UC22	6¢ on 5¢ carmine DC-4 die 2, (end of wing on right is a straight line)	08/29/52	4.00	2.50
a	Double surcharge		200.00	
UC23	6¢ on 5¢ carmine Postage Centenary	1952	2,500.00	
UC25	6¢ red Eagle	05/02/56	.75	.50
UC26	7¢ blue DC-4, type of 1946	07/31/58	.65	.50
UC27	6¢ + 1¢ orange Airplane die 2a ("6" is 6½mm wide)	1958	350.00	250.00
UC28	6¢ + 1¢ orange DC-4, die 2b ("6" is 6mm wide)	1958	80.00	80.00
UC29	6¢ + 1¢ orange Airplane, die 2c ("6" is 5½mm wide)	1958	50.00	50.00
UC30	6¢ + 1¢ carmine DC-4, type I	1958	1.00	.50
UC31	6¢ + 1¢ red Eagle	1958	1.00	.50
UC32	10¢ blue and red Jet Airliner, *blue,* type II (back inscription in 2 lines)	05/1959	6.00	5.00
a	Type I, entire		10.00	5.00
UC33	7¢ blue Jet Airliner, embossed	11/21/58	.60	.25
UC34	7¢ carmine Jet Airliner	08/18/60	.60	.25
UC35	11¢ red and blue Jet Airliner and Globe, *blue,* entire	06/16/61	2.75	2.25
a	Red omitted		*950.00*	
	Die-cutting reversed		35.00	
UC36	8¢ red Jet Airliner, embossed	11/17/62	.55	.20
UC37	8¢ red Jet Airliner in Triangle	01/07/65	.45	.20
a	Tagged		3.50	.30
UC38	11¢ red and dark blue, John Kennedy, *blue,* entire	05/29/65	3.25	2.75
UC39	13¢ red and dark blue, John Kennedy, *blue,* entire	05/29/67	3.00	2.75
a	Red omitted		*750.00*	
UC40	10¢ red Jet Airliner in Triangle, embossed	01/08/68	.50	.20
UC41	8¢ + 2¢ red Jet Airliner in Triangle	02/05/68	.65	.20
UC42	13¢ Human Rights, tagged, entire	12/03/68	8.00	4.00
	Die-cutting reversed		75.00	
UC43	11¢ red and blue Jet Plane in Circle, embossed	05/06/71	.50	.20
UC44	15¢ gray, red, white and blue Birds in Flight	05/28/71	1.50	1.10
UC45	10¢ + (1¢) red Jet Airliner in Triangle, embossed	06/28/71	1.50	.20
UC46	15¢ red, white and blue Birds in Flight, tagged	02/10/73	.75	.40
UC47	13¢ rose red Bird in Flight	12/01/73	.30	.20
UC48	18¢ red and blue USA, entire	01/04/74	.90	.30
UC49	18¢ red and blue USA, *blue,* entire, tagged	04/04/74	.90	.40
UC50	22¢ red and blue USA, *blue,* entire, tagged	01/16/76	.90	.40
UC51	22¢ blue USA, *blue,* entire, tagged	11/03/78	.70	.25
	Die-cutting reversed		25.00	
UC52	22¢ Summer Olympic Games, *bluish,* entire tagged	12/05/79	1.50	.25
UC53	30¢ blue, red, and brown USA, Tour the United States, *blue,* entire, tagged	12/29/80	.65	*1.00*
a	Red "30" omitted		70.00	
UC54	30¢ yellow, magenta, blue and black USA, Tour the United States, *blue,* entire, tagged	09/21/81	.65	*1.00*
	Die-cutting reversed		20.00	
UC55	30¢ Made in USA, *blue,* entire, tagged	09/16/82	.65	*1.00*
UC56	30¢ World Communications Year, *blue,* entire, tagged	01/07/83	.65	*1.00*
	Die-cutting reversed		25.00	
UC57	30¢ Olympic Games, *blue,* entire, tagged	10/14/83	.65	*1.50*
UC58	36¢ Landsat, *blue,* entire, tagged	02/14/85	.70	*1.00*
UC59	36¢ Tourism Week, blue, entire, tagged	05/21/85	.70	*1.00*
UC60	36¢ Mark Twain/ Halley's Comet, entire, tagged	12/04/85	1.00	*1.50*
UC61	39¢ Envelope entire, tagged	05/09/88	.80	*1.00*
UC62	39¢ Montgomery Blair/ Lincoln, entire, tagged	11/20/89	.80	*1.00*
UC63	45¢ Eagle, *blue,* entire, tagged	05/17/91	.90	*1.00*
a	White paper		.90	*1.00*

Issue		Date	Un	U
UC64	50¢ Thaddeus Lowe, Balloonist, *blue,* entire, tagged	09/23/1995	1.00	1.00
UC65	60¢ Voyageurs Nat'l Park, Minnesota *blue,* entire, tagged	05/15/1999	1.25	1.00
	Official Envelopes			
	Post Office Department			
	Numeral 9mm high			
UO1	2¢ black, *lemon*	1873	24.00	10.00
UO2	3¢ black, *lemon*		16.00	6.50
	Numeral 9½mm high			
UO4	6¢ black, *lemon*	1873	26.00	16.00
	Numeral 9¼mm high			
UO5	2¢ black, *lemon*	1874	10.50	4.25
UO6	2¢ black		140.00	35.00
UO7	3¢ black, *lemon*		3.25	.85
UO8	3¢ black		3,000.00	2,250.00
UO9	3¢ black, *amber*		125.00	37.50
UO10	3¢ black, *blue*		*45,000.00*	
UO11	3¢ blue, *blue*	1875	*45,000.00*	
	Numeral 10½mm high			
UO12	6¢ black, *lemon*	1875	16.00	6.50
UO13	6¢ black		3,000.00	1,500.00
	Postal Service			
UO14	black	1877	7.00	4.50
UO15	black, *amber*		210.00	32.50
UO16	blue, *amber*		200.00	35.00
UO17	blue, *blue*		9.00	6.75
	War Department			
UO18	1¢ dark red Franklin	1873	700.00	300.00
UO19	2¢ dark red Jackson		2,250.00	400.00
UO20	3¢ dark red Washington		72.50	42.50
UO21	3¢ dark red Washington, *amber*		*40,000.00*	
UO22	3¢ dark red Washington, *cream*		900.00	250.00
UO23	6¢ dark red Lincoln		325.00	90.00
UO24	6¢ dark red Lincoln, *cream*		8,250.00	425.00
UO25	10¢ dark red Jefferson		*17,500.00*	2,250.00

Issue		Date	Un	U
UO26	12¢ dark red Clay	1873	175.00	50.00
UO27	15¢ dark red Webster		160.00	55.00
UO28	24¢ dark red Scott		175.00	50.00
UO29	30¢ dark red Hamilton		550.00	150.00
UO30	1¢ dark red Franklin		200.00	
UO34	3¢ vermilion Washington		100.00	40.00
UO35	3¢ vermilion Washington, *amber*		125.00	
UO36	3¢ vermilion Washington, *cream*		17.00	12.50
UO37	6¢ vermilion Lincoln		100.00	
UO39	10¢ vermilion Jefferson		350.00	
UO40	12¢ vermilion Clay		175.00	
UO41	15¢ vermilion Webster		250.00	
UO42	24¢ vermilion Scott		450.00	
UO43	30¢ vermilion Hamilton		500.00	
UO44	1¢ red Franklin	1875	190.00	85.00
UO47	2¢ red Jackson		140.00	—
UO48	2¢ red Jackson, *amber*		37.50	16.00
UO49	2¢ red Jackson, *orange*		62.50	16.00
UO51	3¢ red Washington		17.00	10.00
UO52	3¢ red Washington, *amber*		21.00	10.00
UO53	3¢ red Washington, *cream*		7.00	3.75
UO54	3¢ red Washington, *blue*		3.75	2.75
UO55	3¢ red Washington, *fawn*		6.00	2.75
UO56	6¢ red Lincoln		65.00	30.00
UO57	6¢ red Lincoln, *amber*		95.00	40.00
UO58	6¢ red Lincoln, *cream*		225.00	85.00
UO59	10¢ red Jefferson		250.00	80.00
UO60	10¢ red Jefferson, *amber*		1,250.00	
UO61	12¢ red		65.00	40.00
UO62	12¢ red, *amber*		800.00	
UO63	12¢ red, *cream*		700.00	
UO64	15¢ red		250.00	140.00
UO65	15¢ red, *amber*		950.00	
UO66	15¢ red, *cream*		800.00	
UO67	30¢ red		190.00	40.00
UO68	30¢ red, *amber*		950.00	
UO69	30¢ red, *cream*		1,000.00	
	Postal Savings Envelopes			
UO70	1¢ green	1911	75.00	22.50
UO71	1¢ green, *oriental buff*		200.00	67.50
UO72	2¢ carmine		12.50	4.00

Issue		Date	Un	U
	Penalty Mail Envelopes			
UO73	20¢ blue Great Seal, embossed	01/12/1983	1.25	*30.00*
UO74	22¢ blue Great Seal, embossed	02/26/1985	.90	*22.50*
UO75	22¢ blue Great Seal	03/02/1987	1.25	*25.00*
UO76	(25¢) black and blue "E" Great Seal		1.25	*25.00*
UO77	25¢ black and blue Great Seal, embossed	04/11/1988	.80	*20.00*
UO78	25¢ black and blue Great Seal	1988	.90	*25.00*
UO79	45¢ black and blue Great Seal (stars illegible)	03/17/1990	1.25	—
UO80	65¢ black and blue Great Seal (stars illegible)	03/17/1990	1.75	—
UO81	45¢ black and blue Great Seal, (stars clear)	08/10/1990	1.25	—
UO82	65¢ black and blue Great Seal, (stars clear)	08/10/1990	1.60	—
UO83	(29¢) "F" black and blue Great Seal, watermarked	01/22/1991	1.25	*25.00*
UO84	29¢ black and blue, Great Seal, watermarked	04/06/1991	.75	*20.00*
UO85	29¢ black and blue Great Seal, watermarked	04/17/1991	.70	*20.00*
UO86	52¢ blue and red Consular Service	07/10/1992	1.60	—
UO87	75¢ blue and red Consular Service	07/10/1992	3.00	—
UO88	32¢ blue and red Great Seal, embossed	05/09/1995	.80	*20.00*
UO89	33¢ blue and red Great Seal	02/22/1999	.70	*20.00*
UO90	34¢ blue and red Great Seal, type of 1995, tagged	02/27/2001	.85	20.00
UO91	37¢ blue and red Great Seal, type of 1995, tagged	08/02/2002	.90	—

UC64

UC65

UO1

UO16

UO20

UO73

UO84

UO88

Postal and Stamped Cards

UX5 UX6 UX11 UX14

UX16

UX18

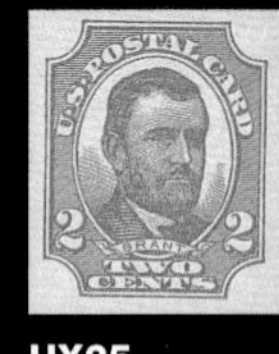

UX25

UX27

UX28

UX37

UX43

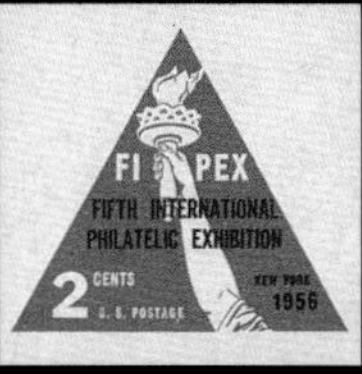

UX44

UX45

UX46

UX48

UX50

Postal and Stamped Cards

Represented below is a listing of postal cards. Values are for entire cards. Color in italic is color of card. Cards preprinted with written address or message usually sell for much less.

Issue		Date	Un	U
UX1	1¢ brown Liberty, wmkd. (90 x 60mm)	05/1873	375.00	20.00
UX3	1¢ brown Liberty, wmkd. (53 x 36mm), *buff*	07/06/1873	80.00	2.50
UX4	1¢ black Liberty, wmkd., USPOD in monogram, *buff*	09/28/1875	3,000.00	400.00
UX5	1¢ black Liberty, *buff*	09/30/1875	82.50	.45
UX6	2¢ blue Liberty, *buff*	12/01/1879	35.00	25.00
a	2¢ dark blue, *buff*		32.50	25.00
UX7	1¢ black Liberty, inscribed "Nothing But The Address", *buff*	10/17/1881	70.00	.40
a	23 teeth below "One Cent"		1,350.00	65.00
b	Printed on both sides		*800.00*	*400.00*
UX8	1¢ brown Jefferson, large "one-cent" wreath, *buff*	08/24/1885	55.00	1.25
c	1¢ dark chocolate, *buff*		175.00	40.00
UX9	1¢ black Jefferson, *buff*	12/01/1886	25.00	.55
a	1¢ black, *dark buff*		75.00	5.00
UX10	1¢ black Grant, *buff*	12/16/1891	45.00	1.50
UX11	1¢ blue Grant, *grayish white*		22.50	3.00
UX12	1¢ black Jefferson, small wreath, *buff*	01/02/1894	45.00	.65
UX13	2¢ blue Liberty, *cream*	01/25/1897	190.00	85.00
UX14	1¢ black Jefferson, large wreath, *buff*	12/01/1897	40.00	.45
UX15	1¢ black John Adams, *buff*	03/31/1898	47.50	15.00
UX16	2¢ black Liberty, *buff*		14.00	*17.00*
UX17	1¢ black McKinley, *buff*	1902	*9,000.00*	
UX18	1¢ black McKinley, (in oval), *buff*	1902	16.00	.35
UX19	1¢ black McKinley, (triangles in top corners), *buff*	1907	45.00	.50
UX20	1¢ black McKinley, (correspondence space at left), *buff*	01/02/1908	57.50	4.25
UX21	1¢ blue McKinley, (shaded background), *bluish*	1910	105.00	13.00
a	1¢ bronze blue, *bluish*		300.00	50.00
UX22	1¢ blue McKinley, (white background), *bluish*	04/13/1910	19.00	.35
UX23	1¢ red Lincoln, *cream*	01/21/1911	10.00	5.50
UX24	1¢ red McKinley, *cream*	08/10/1911	10.00	.35
UX25	2¢ red Grant, *cream*	10/27/1911	1.50	16.00
UX26	1¢ green Lincoln, *cream*	07/29/1913	13.00	7.50
UX27	1¢ green Jefferson, die I (end of ponytail small) *buff*	06/04/1914	.25	.25
a	1¢ green, *cream*		4.50	.65
UX27C	1¢ green Jefferson, die I	1916	*4,000.00*	190.00
UX27D	1¢ dark green Jefferson, die II (end of ponytail large and rounded)	12/22/1916	*12,000.00*	160.00
UX28	1¢ green Lincoln, *cream*	03/14/1917	.60	.30
a	1¢ green, *dark buff*		1.50	.60
UX29	2¢ red Jefferson, die I (coarse impression), *buff*	10/22/1917	42.50	2.10
a	2¢ lake, *cream*		50.00	4.00
c	2¢ vermilion, *buff*		925.00	75.00
UX30	2¢ red Jefferson, die II (fine lines), *cream*	01/23/1918	30.00	1.60
	Surcharged in one line by canceling machine			
UX31	1¢ on 2¢ red Jefferson, die II (fine lines), *cream*	01/23/1918	*4,500.00*	*4,500.00*
	Surcharged in two lines by canceling machine.			
UX32	1¢ on 2¢ red Jefferson, die I (coarse impression), *buff*	1920	52.50	12.50
a	1¢ on 2¢ vermilion, *buff*		150.00	60.00
b	Double surcharge		150.00	100.00
UX33	1¢ on 2¢ red Jefferson, die I (coarse impression), *cream*		12.50	2.00
a	Inverted surcharge		100.00	100.00
b	Double surcharge		100.00	75.00
	Surcharged in two lines by press printing			
UX34	1¢ on 2¢ red Jefferson, die I (coarse impression), *buff*	1920	550.00	52.50
UX35	1¢ on 2¢ red Jefferson, *cream*		225.00	37.50
UX36	1¢ on 2¢ red Grant, *cream*			*50,000.00*
UX37	3¢ red McKinley, *buff*	02/01/1926	4.50	*15.00*
a	3¢ red, *yellow*		5.25	*15.00*
UX38	2¢ carmine rose Franklin, *buff*	11/16/1951	.35	.25
a	Double impression		500.00	
	Surcharged by canceling machine in light green			
UX39	2¢ on 1¢ green Jefferson, *buff*	01/01/1952	.50	.35
a	Surcharge vertical		8.00	*10.00*
b	Double surcharge		20.00	*25.00*
UX40	2¢ on 1¢ green Lincoln, *cream*	03/22/1952	.65	.45
a	Surcharge vertical		7.00	5.50
	Surcharged typographically in dark green			
UX41	2¢ on 1¢ green Jefferson, *buff*	1952	4.50	2.00
a	Inverted surcharge lower left		77.50	125.00
UX42	2¢ on 1¢ green Lincoln, *cream*	1952	5.00	2.50
b	Surcharged on back		160.00	
UX43	2¢ carmine Lincoln, *buff*	07/31/1952	.30	*1.00*
UX44	2¢ deep carmine and dark violet blue FIPEX, *buff*	05/04/1956	.25	*1.00*
a	Dark violet blue omitted		650.00	600.00
UX45	4¢ deep red and ultramarine Statue of Liberty, *buff*	11/16/1956	1.50	*90.00*
UX46	3¢ purple Statue of Liberty, *buff*	08/01/1958	.50	.20
a	"N GOD WE TRUST"		14.00	*25.00*
UX47	2¢ + 1¢ carmine rose Franklin, *buff*	1958	225.00	600.00
UX48	4¢ red violet Lincoln	11/19/1962	.50	.20
UX49	7¢ blue and red World Vacationland	08/30/1963	4.00	*65.00*
UX50	4¢ red and blue U.S. Customs	02/22/1964	.50	*1.00*
a	Blue omitted		650.00	
UX51	4¢ dull blue and red Social Security		.40	*1.00*
b	Blue omitted		*700.00*	650.00
UX52	4¢ blue & red Coast Guard	08/04/1965	.30	*1.00*
UX53	4¢ bright blue and black Bureau of the Census	10/21/1965	.30	*1.00*
UX54	8¢ blue and red World Vacationland	12/04/1967	4.00	*65.00*
UX55	5¢ emerald Lincoln	01/04/1968	.30	*.60*
UX56	5¢ rose and red green Women Marines	07/26/1968	.35	*1.00*
UX57	5¢ blue, yellow, red and black Weather Services	09/01/1970	.30	*1.00*
a	Yellow, black omitted		*1,000.00*	*850.00*
b	Blue omitted		*1,000.00*	
c	Black omitted		*1,000.00*	*850.00*
UX58	6¢ brown Paul Revere	05/15/1971	.30	*1.00*
a	Double impression		*300.00*	
UX59	10¢ blue and red World Vacationland	06/10/1971	4.50	*60.00*

	Issue	Date	Un	U
UX60	6¢ blue and multicolored America's Hospitals	09/16/71	.30	1.00
a	Blue, yellow omitted		1,000.00	
UX61	6¢ black USF *Constellation*	06/29/72	.85	10.00
a	Address side blank		300.00	
UX62	6¢ black Gloucester, MA, *buff*	06/29/72	.40	10.00
UX63	6¢ black Monument Valley, *buff*	06/29/72	.40	6.00
UX64	6¢ blue John Hanson	09/01/72	.50	1.00
UX65	6¢ magenta Liberty	09/14/73	.25	1.00
UX66	8¢ orange Samuel Adams	12/16/73	.50	1.00
UX67	12¢ multicolored Visit USA/ Ship's Figurehead	01/04/74	.35	45.00
UX68	7¢ emerald Charles Thomson	09/14/05	.30	10.00
UX69	9¢ yellow brown John Witherspoon	11/10/75	.30	1.00
UX70	9¢ blue Caesar Rodney	07/01/76	.30	1.00
	Historic Preservation (UX71, UX73)			
UX71	9¢ multicolored Federal Court House	07/20/77	.25	1.00
UX72	9¢ green Nathan Hale	10/14/77	.25	1.00
UX73	10¢ Cincinnati Music Hall	05/12/78	.30	1.00
UX74	(10¢) brown orange John Hancock	05/19/78	.30	1.00
UX75	10¢ John Hancock	06/20/78	.30	1.00
UX76	14¢ Coast Guard Eagle	08/04/78	.40	30.00
UX77	10¢ Molly Pitcher	09/08/78	.30	1.60
UX78	10¢ George Rogers Clark	02/23/79	.30	1.50
UX79	10¢ Casimir Pulaski	11/11/79	.30	1.50
UX80	10¢ Olympic Summer Games	09/17/80	.60	1.50
	Historic Preservation (UX81, UX83)			
UX81	10¢ Iolani Palace	10/01/79	.30	1.50
UX82	14¢ Olympic Winter Games	01/15/80	.60	20.00
UX83	10¢ Salt Lake Temple	04/05/80	.25	1.50
UX84	10¢ Landing of Rochambeau	07/11/80	.25	1.50
UX85	10¢ Battle of Kings Mountain	10/07/80	.25	1.50
UX86	19¢ Drake's Golden Hinde	11/21/80	.70	35.00
UX87	10¢ Battle of Cowpens	01/07/81	.25	17.50
UX88	(12¢) violet Eagle	03/15/81	.30	.65
UX89	12¢ light blue Isaiah Thomas	05/05/81	.30	.60
UX90	12¢ Nathanael Greene	09/08/81	.30	15.00
UX91	12¢ Lewis and Clark	09/23/81	.30	25.00
UX92	13¢ buff Robert Morris	01/11/81	.30	.60
UX93	13¢ buff Robert Morris	11/10/81	.30	.60
UX94	13¢ "Swamp Fox" Francis Marion	04/03/82	.30	1.00
UX95	13¢ LaSalle Claims Louisiana	04/07/82	.30	1.00
	Historic Preservation (UX96, UX97)			
UX96	13¢ Academy of Music	06/18/82	.30	1.00
UX97	13¢ Old Post Office, St. Louis, Missouri	10/14/82	.30	1.00
UX98	13¢ Landing of Ogelthorpe	02/12/83	.30	1.00
UX99	13¢ Old Post Office, Washington, DC	04/19/83	.30	1.00
UX100	13¢ Olympic Yachting	08/05/83	.30	1.00
UX101	13¢ *Ark* and *Dove*, Maryland	03/25/84	.30	1.00
UX102	13¢ Olympic Torch	04/30/84	.30	1.25
UX103	13¢ Frederic Baraga	06/29/84	.30	1.00
UX104	13¢ Dominguez Adobe	09/16/84	.30	1.00
UX105	(14¢) pale green Charles Carroll	02/01/85	.45	.60
UX106	14¢ green Charles Carroll	03/06/85	.45	.50
UX107	25¢ Clipper *Flying Cloud*	02/27/85	.70	22.50
UX108	14¢ bright apple green George Wythe	06/20/85	.30	.75
UX109	14¢ Settlement of Connecticut	04/18/86	.30	1.50
UX110	14¢ Stamp Collecting	05/23/86	.30	1.25
UX111	14¢ Francis Vigo	05/24/86	.30	1.25
UX112	14¢ Settling of Rhode Island	06/26/86	.30	1.50
UX113	14¢ Wisconsin Territory	07/03/86	.30	1.00
UX114	14¢ National Guard	12/12/86	.30	1.25
UX115	14¢ Self-Scouring Plow	05/22/87	.30	1.25
UX116	14¢ Constitutional Convention	05/25/87	.30	.75
UX117	14¢ Stars and Stripes	06/14/87	.30	.60
UX118	14¢ Take Pride in America	09/22/87	.30	1.25
	Historic Preservation (UX119, UX121)			
UX119	14¢ Timberline Lodge	09/28/87	.30	1.25
UX120	15¢ Bison and Prairie	03/28/88	.30	.60
UX121	15¢ Blair House	05/04/88	.30	.75
UX122	28¢ *Yorkshire*	06/29/88	.60	20.00
UX123	15¢ Iowa Territory	07/02/88	.30	.75
UX124	15¢ Settling of Ohio, Northwest Territory	07/15/88	.30	.75
	Historic Preservation (UX125, UX128)			
UX125	15¢ Hearst Castle	09/20/88	.30	.75
UX126	15¢ The Federalist Papers	10/27/88	.30	.75
UX127	15¢ Hawk and Desert	01/13/89	.30	.75
UX128	15¢ Healy Hall, Georgetown University	01/23/89	.30	.75
UX129	15¢ America the Beautiful, Great Blue Heron	03/17/89	.30	.75
UX130	15¢ Settling of Oklahoma	04/22/89	.30	.75
UX131	21¢ America the Beautiful, Canadian Geese	05/05/89	.40	17.50
UX132	15¢ America the Beautiful, Seagull and Seashore	06/17/89	.30	.75
UX133	15¢ America the Beautiful, Deer and Waterfall	08/26/89	.30	.75
	Historic Preservation (UX134)			
UX134	15¢ Hull House, Chicago	09/16/89	.30	.75
UX135	15¢ America the Beautiful, Independence Hall, PA	09/25/89	.30	.75
UX136	15¢ America the Beautiful, Inner Harbor, Baltimore	10/07/89	.30	.75
UX137	15¢ America the Beautiful, 59th St. Bridge, NY	11/08/89	.30	.75
UX138	15¢ America the Beautiful, Capitol, Washington DC	11/26/89	.30	.75
	#UX139-UX142 issued in sheets of 4 plus 2 inscribed labels, rouletted 9½ on 2 or 3 sides			
UX139	15¢ (UX135)	12/01/89	3.25	4.00
UX140	15¢ (UX136)	12/01/89	3.25	4.00
UX141	15¢ (UX137)	12/01/89	3.25	4.00
UX142	15¢ (UX138)	12/01/89	3.25	4.00
a	Sheet of 4, #UX139-UX142		14.00	
UX143	15¢ The White House	11/30/89	1.50	2.50
UX144	15¢ Jefferson Memorial	12/02/89	1.50	2.00
UX145	15¢ Rittenhouse Paper Mill, Germantown, PA	03/13/90	.30	.40
UX146	15¢ World Literacy Year	03/22/90	.30	.75
UX147	15¢ George Caleb Bingham	05/04/90	1.50	2.50
	Historic Preservation (UX148-UX152)			
UX148	15¢ Isaac Royall House	06/16/90	.30	.75
UX150	15¢ Stanford University	09/30/90	.30	.75
UX151	15¢ Constitution Hall	10/11/90	1.50	2.00
UX152	15¢ Chicago Orchestra Hall	10/19/90	.30	.75
UX153	19¢ Flag	01/24/91	.40	.60
	Historic Preservation (UX154, UX155, UX157			
UX154	19¢ Carnegie Hall	04/01/91	.40	.75
UX155	19¢ Old Red, UT-Galveston	06/14/91	.40	.75
UX156	19¢ Bill of Rights	09/25/91	.40	.75
UX157	19¢ Notre Dame	10/15/91	.40	.75
UX158	30¢ Niagara Falls	08/21/90	.75	9.00
	Historic Preservation (UX159-UX162)			
UX159	19¢ The Old Mill	10/29/91	.40	.75
UX160	19¢ Wadsworth Atheneum	01/16/92	.40	.75
UX161	19¢ Cobb Hall	01/23/92	.40	.75
UX162	19¢ Waller Hall	02/01/92	.40	.75
UX163	19¢ America's Cup	05/06/92	1.75	3.00
UX164	19¢ Columbia River Gorge	05/09/92	.40	.75
	Historic Preservation (UX165-UX172)			
UX165	19¢ Ellis Island	05/11/92	.40	.75
UX166	19¢ National Cathedral	01/06/93	.40	.75
UX167	19¢ Wren Building	02/08/93	.40	.75
UX168	19¢ Holocaust Memorial	03/23/93	1.75	3.00
UX169	19¢ Fort Recovery	06/13/93	.40	.75
UX170	19¢ Playmakers Theatre	09/14/93	.40	.75
UX171	19¢ O'Kane Hall	09/17/93	.40	.75
UX172	19¢ Beecher Hall	10/09/93	.40	.75

UX70

UX79

UX81

Salt Lake Temple USA 10c
HISTORIC PRESERVATION

UX83

UX94

UX109

UX112

UX113

UX115

UX116

UX118

UX119

UX131

UX143

UX144

UX143 (picture side)

UX144 (picture side)

UX174

UX175

UX176

UX177

UX178

UX198

UX199

UX200

UX219A

UX220

UX221

UX241

UX262

UX263

UX264

UX280

UX282

UX283

UX285

UX290

UX292

UX293

UX298

UX299

UX301

UX302

UX303

UX305

UX306

VISIT US ONLINE AT ***THE POSTAL STORE***

AT ***WWW.USPS.COM***

OR CALL ***1 800 STAMP-24***

Issue		Date	Un	U
UX173	19¢ Massachusetts Hall	10/14/93	.40	.75
UX174	19¢ Lincoln's Home	02/12/94	.40	.75
	Historic Preservation (UX175, UX177)			
UX175	19¢ Wittenberg University	03/11/94	.40	.75
UX176	19¢ Canyon de Chelly	08/11/94	.40	.75
UX177	19¢ St. Louis Union Station	09/03/94	.40	.75
	Legends of the West (UX178-UX197)			
UX178	19¢ Home on the Range		1.10	3.00
UX179	19¢ Buffalo Bill		1.10	3.00
UX180	19¢ Jim Bridger		1.10	3.00
UX181	19¢ Annie Oakley		1.10	3.00
UX182	19¢ Native American Culture		1.10	3.00
UX183	19¢ Chief Joseph		1.10	3.00
UX184	19¢ Bill Pickett (revised)		1.10	3.00
UX185	19¢ Bat Masterson		1.10	3.00
UX186	19¢ John Fremont		1.10	3.00
UX187	19¢ Wyatt Earp		1.10	3.00
UX188	19¢ Nellie Cashman		1.10	3.00
UX189	19¢ Charles Goodnight		1.10	3.00
UX190	19¢ Geronimo		1.10	3.00
UX191	19¢ Kit Carson		1.10	3.00
UX192	19¢ Wild Bill Hickok		1.10	3.00
UX193	19¢ Western Wildlife		1.10	3.00
UX194	19¢ Jim Beckwourth		1.10	3.00
UX195	19¢ Bill Tilghman		1.10	3.00
UX196	19¢ Sacagawea		1.10	3.00
UX197	19¢ Overland Mail		1.10	3.00
a	pack of 20	10/18/94	22.00	
	Scenic America (UX198, UX199)			
UX198	20¢ Red Barn	01/03/95	.40	.60
UX199	20¢ Old Glory	1995	3.25	2.50
	Civil War (UX200-UX219)			
UX200	20¢ Monitor and Virginia		1.75	3.00
UX201	20¢ Robert E. Lee		1.75	3.00
UX202	20¢ Clara Barton		1.75	3.00
UX203	20¢ Ulysses S. Grant		1.75	3.00
UX204	20¢ Battle of Shiloh		1.75	3.00
UX205	20¢ Jefferson Davis		1.75	3.00
UX206	20¢ David Farragut		1.75	3.00
UX207	20¢ Frederick Douglas		1.75	3.00
UX208	20¢ Raphael Semmes		1.75	3.00
UX209	20¢ Abraham Lincoln		1.75	3.00
UX210	20¢ Harriet Tubman		1.75	3.00
UX211	20¢ Stand Watie		1.75	3.00
UX212	20¢ Joseph E. Johnson		1.75	3.00
UX213	20¢ Winfield Hancock		1.75	3.00
UX214	20¢ Mary Chestnut		1.75	3.00
UX215	20¢ Battle of Chancellorsville		1.75	3.00
UX216	20¢ William T. Sherman		1.75	3.00
UX217	20¢ Phoebe Pember		1.75	3.00
UX218	20¢ Stonewall Jackson		1.75	3.00
UX219	20¢ Battle of Gettysburg		1.75	3.00
a	pack of 20	06/29/95	35.00	
UX219A	50¢ Soaring Eagle	08/24/95	1.25	9.00
UX220	20¢ American Clipper Ships	09/03/95	.40	.75

Issue		Date	Un	U
	Comic Strip Characters (UX221-UX240)			
UX221	20¢ The Yellow Kid		2.50	3.00
UX222	20¢ Katzenjammer Kids		2.50	3.00
UX223	20¢ Little Nemo in Slumberland		2.50	3.00
UX224	20¢ Bringing Up Father		2.50	3.00
UX225	20¢ Krazy Kat		2.50	3.00
UX226	20¢ Rube Goldberg's Inventions		2.50	3.00
UX227	20¢ Toonerville Folks		2.50	3.00
UX228	20¢ Gasoline Alley		2.50	3.00
UX229	20¢ Barney Google		2.50	3.00
UX230	20¢ Little Orphan Annie		2.50	3.00
UX231	20¢ Popeye		2.50	3.00
UX232	20¢ Blondie		2.50	3.00
UX233	20¢ Dick Tracey		2.50	3.00
UX234	20¢ Alley Oop		2.50	3.00
UX235	20¢ Nancy		2.50	3.00
UX236	20¢ Flash Gordan		2.50	3.00
UX237	20¢ Li'l Abner		2.50	3.00
UX238	20¢ Terry and the Pirates		2.50	3.00
UX239	20¢ Prince Valiant		2.50	3.00
UX240	20¢ Brenda Starr Reporter		2.50	3.00
a	pack of 20	10/01/95	50.00	
	Scenic America			
UX241	20¢ Winter Scene		.40	.40
	Olympic Games (UX242-UX261)			
UX242	20¢ Men's Cycling		2.75	3.00
UX243	20¢ Women's Diving		2.75	3.00
UX244	20¢ Women's Running		2.75	3.00
UX245	20¢ Women's Canoeing		2.75	3.00
UX246	20¢ Decathlon		2.75	3.00
UX247	20¢ Women's Soccer		2.75	3.00
UX248	20¢ Men's Shot Put		2.75	3.00
UX249	20¢ Women's Sailboarding		2.75	3.00
UX250	20¢ Women's Gymnastics		2.75	3.00
UX251	20¢ Freestyle Wrestling		2.75	3.00
UX252	20¢ Women's Softball		2.75	3.00
UX253	20¢ Women's Swimming		2.75	3.00
UX254	20¢ Men's Sprints		2.75	3.00
UX255	20¢ Men's Rowing		2.75	3.00
UX256	20¢ Beach Volleyball		2.75	3.00
UX257	20¢ Men's Basketball		2.75	3.00
UX258	20¢ Equestrian		2.75	3.00
UX259	20¢ Men's Gymnastics		2.75	3.00
UX260	20¢ Men's Swimming		2.75	3.00
UX261	20¢ Men's Hurdles		2.75	3.00
a	pack of 20	05/02/96	55.00	
	Historic Preservation (UX262, UX263)			
UX262	20¢ St. John's College	06/01/96	.50	.75
UX263	20¢ Princeton University	09/20/96	.50	.75
	Endangered Species (UX264-UX278)			
UX264	20¢ Florida Panther		3.50	1.75
UX265	20¢ Black-footed Ferret		3.50	1.75
UX266	20¢ American Crocodile		3.50	1.75
UX267	20¢ Piping Plover		3.50	1.75
UX268	20¢ Gila Trout		3.50	1.75
UX269	20¢ Florida Manatee		3.50	1.75
UX270	20¢ Schaus Swallowtail Butterfly		3.50	1.75
UX271	20¢ Woodland Caribou		3.50	1.75
UX272	20¢ Thick-billed Parrot		3.50	1.75
UX273	20¢ San Francisco Garter Snake		3.50	1.75
UX274	20¢ Ocelot		3.50	1.75

Issue		Date	Un	U
	Endangered Species continued, (UX264-UX278)			
UX275	20¢ Wyoming Toad		3.50	1.75
UX276	20¢ California Condor		3.50	1.75
UX277	20¢ Hawaiian Monk Seal		3.50	1.75
UX278	20¢ Brown Pelican		3.50	1.75
a	pack of 20	10/02/96	55.00	
UX279	20¢ Love Swans	02/04/97	.80	1.10
	Historic Preservation (UX280, UX284)			
UX280	20¢ City College of New York	05/07/97	.50	.75
UX281	20¢ Bugs Bunny	05/22/97	1.25	2.00
UX282	20¢ Pacific 97 Golden Gate Bridge in Daylight	06/02/97	.40	.80
UX283	50¢ Pacific 97 Golden Gate Bridge at Sunset	06/03/97	1.10	2.50
UX284	20¢ Fort McHenry	09/07/97	.40	.75
	Classic Movie Monsters (UX285-UX289)			
UX285	20¢ Lon Chaney as Phantom of the Opera		1.50	1.40
UX286	20¢ Bela Lugosi as Dracula		1.50	1.40
UX287	20¢ Boris Karloff as Frankenstein's Monster		1.50	1.40
UX288	20¢ Boris Karloff as The Mummy		1.50	1.40
UX289	20¢ Lon Chaney, Jr. as The Wolfman		1.50	1.40
a	booklet of 20	09/30/97	30.00	
	Historic Preservation (UX290, UX292)			
UX290	20¢ University of Mississippi	04/20/98	.50	.75
UX291	20¢ Sylvester & Tweety	04/27/98	1.40	2.00
UX292	20¢ Girard College	05/01/98	.50	.75
	Tropical Birds (UX293-UX296)			
UX293	20¢ Antillean Euphonia		1.00	1.75
UX294	20¢ Green-throated Carib		1.00	1.75
UX295	20¢ Crested Honeycreeper		1.00	1.75
UX296	20¢ Cardinal Honeyeater		1.00	1.75
a	booklet of 20	07/28/1998	20.00	
UX297	20¢ American Ballet	09/16/1998	1.25	1.40
	Historic Preservation (UX298, UX299)			
UX298	20¢ Northeastern University	10/03/1998	.50	.75
UX299	20¢ Brandeis University	10/17/1998	.50	.75
UX300	20¢ Love	01/28/1999	1.25	1.50
	Historic Preservation (UX301-UX303, UX305)			
UX301	20¢ University of Wisconsin-Madison	02/05/1999	.50	.50
UX302	20¢ Washington and Lee University	02/11/1999	.50	.50
UX303	20¢ Redwood Library & Athenæum	03/11/1999	.50	.50
UX304	Daffy Duck	04/16/1999	1.40	1.40
UX305	20¢ Mount Vernon	05/14/1999	.50	.50
	Scenic America			
UX306	20¢ Block Island Lighthouse	07/24/1999	.40	.45

	Issue	Date	Un	U
	Trains (UX307-UX311)			
UX307	Super Chief		1.25	1.00
UX308	Hiawatha		1.25	1.00
UX309	Daylight		1.25	1.00
UX310	Congressional		1.25	1.00
UX311	20th Century Limited		1.25	1.00
a	booklet of 20	08/26/1999	22.50	
	Historic Preservation (UX312, UX313, UX316)			
UX312	20¢ Univ. of Utah	02/28/2000	.40	*.50*
UX313	20¢ Ryman Auditorium	03/18/2000	.40	*.50*
UX314	20¢ Road Runner & Wilie E. Coyote	04/26/2000	1.40	1.40
UX315	20th Adoption	05/10/2000	1.40	1.50
UX316	20¢ Middlebury College	05/19/2000	.40	*.50*
	Stars and Stripes (UX317-UX336)			
UX317	20¢ Sons of Liberty Flag, 1775		1.50	1.25
UX318	20¢ New England Flag, 1775		1.50	1.25
UX319	20¢ Forster Flag, 1775		1.50	1.25
UX320	20¢ Continental Colors, 1776		1.50	1.25
UX321	20¢ Francis Hopkinson Flag, 1777		1.50	1.25
UX322	20¢ Brandywine Flag, 1777		1.50	1.25
UX323	20¢ John Paul Jones Flag, 1779		1.50	1.25
UX324	20¢ Pierre L'Enfant Flag, 1783		1.50	1.25
UX325	20¢ Indian Peace Flag, 1803		1.50	1.25
UX326	20¢ Easton Flag, 1814		1.50	1.25
UX327	20¢ Star Spangled Banner, 1814		1.50	1.25
UX328	20¢ Bennington Flag, c. 1820		1.50	1.25
UX329	20¢ Great Star Flag, 1837		1.50	1.25
UX330	20¢ 29-Star Flag, 1847		1.50	1.25
UX331	20¢ Fort Sumter Flag, 1861		1.50	1.25
UX332	20¢ Sentennial Flag, 1876		1.50	1.25
UX333	20¢ 38-Star Flag, 1877		1.50	1.25
UX334	20¢ Peace Flag, 1891		1.50	1.25
UX335	20¢ 48-Star Flag, 1912		1.50	1.25
UX336	20¢ 50-Star Flag, 1960		1.50	1.25
a	five sheets of four	06/14/2000	30.00	25.00
	Legends of Baseball (UX337-UX356)			
UX337	20¢ Jackie Robinson		1.50	1.25
UX338	20¢ Eddie Collins		1.50	1.25
UX339	20¢ Christy Matthewson		1.50	1.25
UX340	20¢ Ty Cobb		1.50	1.25
UX341	20¢ George Sisler		1.50	1.25
UX342	20¢ Rogers Hornsby		1.50	1.25
UX343	20¢ Mickey Cochrane		1.50	1.25
UX344	20¢ Babe Ruth		1.50	1.25
UX345	20¢ Walter Johnson		1.50	1.25
UX346	20¢ Roberto Clemente		1.50	1.25
UX347	20¢ Lefty Grove		1.50	1.25
UX348	20¢ Tris Speaker		1.50	1.25
UX349	20¢ Cy Young		1.50	1.25
UX350	20¢ Jimmie Foxx		1.50	1.25
UX351	20¢ Pie Traynor		1.50	1.25
UX352	20¢ Satchel Paige		1.50	1.25
UX353	20¢ Honus Wagner		1.50	1.25
UX354	20¢ Josh Gibson		1.50	1.25
UX355	20¢ Dizzy Dean		1.50	1.25
UX356	20¢ Lou Gehrig		1.50	1.25
a	booklet of 20	07/06/2000	30.00	

	Issue	Date	Un	U
	Holiday Celebrations: Holiday Deer (UX357-UX360)			
UX357	20¢ gold & blue		1.25	1.25
UX358	20¢ gold & red		1.25	1.25
UX359	20¢ gold & purple		1.25	1.25
UX360	20¢ gold & green		1.25	1.25
a	sheet of four	10/12/2000	5.00	
	Historic Preservation (UX361-UX364)			
UX361	20¢ Yale University	03/30/2001	.40	.60
UX362	20¢ Univ. of Carolina Carolina	04/26/2001	.40	*.75*
UX363	20¢ Northwestern University	04/28/2001	.40	*.75*
UX364	20¢ University of Portland	05/01/2001	.40	*.65*
	Legendary Playing Fields (UX365-UX374)			
UX365	21¢ Ebbets Field		1.75	1.40
UX366	21¢ Tiger Stadium		1.75	1.40
UX367	21¢ Crosley Field		1.75	1.40
UX368	21¢ Yankee Stadium		1.75	1.40
UX369	21¢ Polo Grounds		1.75	1.40
UX370	21¢ Forbes Field		1.75	1.40
UX371	21¢ Fenway Park		1.75	1.40
UX372	21¢ Comiskey Park		1.75	1.40
UX373	21¢ Shibe Park		1.75	1.40
UX374	21¢ Wrigley Field		1.75	1.40
a	booklet of 10	06/27/2001	22.50	
	Scenic America (UX375)			
UX375	21¢ White Barn	09/20/2001	.45	.45
UX376	21¢ That's All Folks!	10/01/2001	1.50	1.50
	Holiday Celebrations: Holiday Santas (UX377-UX380)			
UX377	21¢ Santa with tan hood		1.25	1.00
UX378	21¢ Santa with blue hat		1.25	1.00
UX379	21¢ Santa with red hat		1.25	1.00
UX380	21¢ Santa with gold hood		1.25	1.00
a	sheet of four	10/10/2001	5.00	
UX381	23¢ Carlsbad Caverns National Park	06/07/2002	.50	.50
	Teddy Bears (UX382-UX385)			
UX382	23¢ Ideal Bear		1.10	1.00
UX383	23¢ Gund Bear		1.10	1.00
UX384	23¢ Bruin Bear		1.10	1.00
UX385	23¢ "Stick" Bear		1.10	1.00
a	pack of five	08/15/2002	5.00	
	Holiday Celebrations: Holiday Snowmen			
UX386	23¢ Snowman w/red & green scarf		1.25	1.00
UX387	23¢ Snowman w/blue plaid scarf		1.25	1.00
UX388	Snowman w/pipe		1.25	1.00
UX389	Snowman w/top hat		1.25	1.00
a	pack of five	10/28/2002	5.00	
	Old Glory (UX390-UX394)			
UX390	23¢ Uncle Sam on Bicycle with Liberty Flag		1.10	1.00
UX391	23¢ 1888 Presidential Campaign		1.10	1.00
UX392	23¢ 1893 Silk Bookmark		1.10	1.00
UX393	23¢ 1888 Modern Hand Fan		1.10	1.00
UX394	23¢ 1888 Carving of Woman with Flag & Sword 19th Century		1.10	1.00
a	booklet of 20	04/03/2003	22.50	
	Lighthouses (UX395-UX399)			
UX395	23¢ Old Cape Henry, Virginia		1.10	1.00
UX396	23¢ Cape Lookout, North Carolina		1.10	1.00

	Issue	Date	Un	U
	Lighthouses continued, (UX395-UX399)			
UX397	23¢ Morris Island, South Carolina		1.10	1.0
UX398	23¢ Cape Lookout, North Carolina		1.10	1.0
UX396	23¢ Tybee Island, Georgia		1.10	1.0
UX399	23¢ Hillsboro Inlet, Florida		1.10	1.0
a	booklet of 20	06/13/2003	22.50	
	Historic Preservation			
UX400	23¢ Ohio University	10/10/2003	.50	.5
	Holiday Celebrations: Holiday, Music Makers (UX401-UX404)			
UX401	23¢ Reindeer with Pan Pipes		1.00	1.0
UX402	23¢ Santa Claus with Drum		1.00	1.0
UX403	23¢ Santa Claus with Trumpet		1.00	1.0
UX404	23¢ Reindeer with Horn		1.00	1.0
a	sheet of four	10/23/2003	4.00	
	Historic Preservation (UX405, UX406)			
UX405	23¢ Columbia Univ.	03/25/2004	.50	.5
UX406	23¢ Harriton House	06/10/2004	.50	.5
	Disney Characters (UX407-UX410)			
UX407	23¢ Bambi, Thumper		1.00	1.0
UX408	23¢ Mufasa, Simba		1.00	1.0
UX409	23¢ Goofy, Mickey Mouse, Donald Duck		1.00	1.0
UX410	23¢ Jiminy Cricket, Pinocchio		1.00	1.0
a	booklet of 20	06/23/2004	20.00	
	Art of the American Indian (UX411-UX420)			
UX411	23¢ Mimbres Bowl		1.00	1.0
UX412	23¢ Kutenai Parfleche		1.00	1.0
UX413	23¢ Tlinget Scultures		1.00	1.0
UX414	23¢ Ho-Chunk Bag		1.00	1.0
UX415	23¢ Seminole Doll		1.00	1.0
UX416	23¢ Mississippian Effigy		1.00	1.0
UX417	23¢ Acoma Pot		1.00	1.0
UX418	23¢ Navajo Weaving		1.00	1.0
UX419	23¢ Seneca Carving		1.00	1.0
UX420	23¢ Luiseño Basket		1.00	1.0
a	booklet of 20	08/21/2004	20.00	
	Cloudscapes (UX421-UX435)			
UX421	23¢ Cirrus radiatus		1.00	1.0
UX422	23¢ Cirrostratus fibratus		1.00	1.0
UX423	23¢ Cirrocumulus undulatus		1.00	1.0
UX424	23¢ Cumulonimbus mammatus		1.00	1.0
UX425	23¢ Cumulonimbus incus		1.00	1.0
UX426	23¢ Altocumulus stratiformis		1.00	1.0
UX427	23¢ Altostratus translucidus		1.00	1.0
UX428	23¢ Altocumulus undulatus		1.00	1.0
UX429	23¢ Altocumulus castellanus		1.00	1.0
UX430	23¢ Altocumulus lenticularis		1.00	1.0
UX431	23¢ Stratocumulus undulatus		1.00	1.0
UX432	23¢ Stratus opacus		1.00	1.0
UX433	23¢ Cumulus humilis		1.00	1.0
UX434	23¢ Cumulus congestus		1.00	1.0
UX435	23¢ Cumulonimbus with tornado		1.00	1.0
a	booklet of 20	10/04/2004	20.00	
	The Art of Disney: Celebration (UX436-UX439)			
UX436	23¢ Pluto, Mickey Mouse	06/30/05	1.00	1.0
UX437	23¢ Mad Hatter	06/30/05	1.00	1.0
UX438	23¢ Flounder, Ariel	06/30/05	1.00	1.0
UX439	23¢ Snow White, Dopey	06/30/05	1.00	1.0
a	Booklet of 20		20.00	

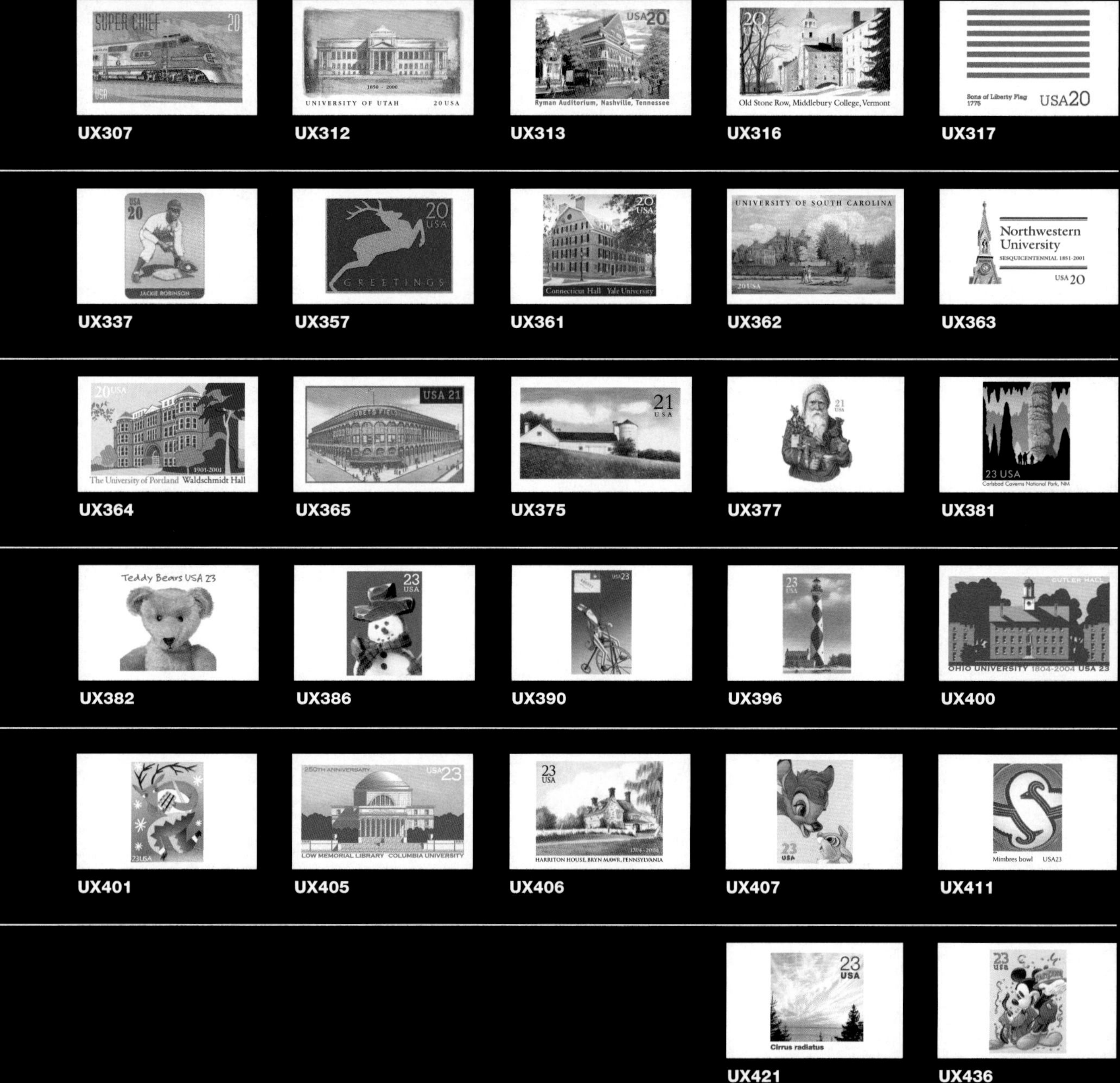
SUPER CHIEF
20
USA
UX307
UNIVERSITY OF UTAH
1850 - 2000
20 USA
UX312
USA20
Ryman Auditorium, Nashville, Tennessee
UX313
20
Old Stone Row, Middlebury College, Vermont
UX316
Sons of Liberty Flag 1775
USA20
UX317
USA 20
JACKIE ROBINSON
UX337
20 USA
GREETINGS
UX357
20 USA
Connecticut Hall Yale University
UX361
UNIVERSITY OF SOUTH CAROLINA
20 USA
UX362
Northwestern University
SESQUICENTENNIAL 1851-2001
USA 20
UX363
20 USA
1901-2001
The University of Portland Waldschmidt Hall
UX364
USA 21
EBBETS FIELD
UX365
21 USA
UX375
21 USA
UX377
23 USA
Carlsbad Caverns National Park, NM
UX381
Teddy Bears USA 23
UX382
23 USA
UX386
USA23
UX390
23 USA
UX396
CUTLER HALL
OHIO UNIVERSITY 1804-2004 USA 23
UX400
23USA
UX401
250TH ANNIVERSARY
USA23
LOW MEMORIAL LIBRARY COLUMBIA UNIVERSITY
UX405
23 USA
1704-2004
HARRITON HOUSE, BRYN MAWR, PENNSYLVANIA
UX406
23 USA
UX407
Mimbres bowl USA23
UX411
23 USA
Cirrus radiatus
UX421
23 USA
UX436

UX440

UX445

UXC1

UXC2

UXC4

UXC5

UXC6

UXC7

UXC8

UXC9

UXC10

UXC11

UXC12

UXC13

UXC19

UXC20

UXC23

UXC25

UXC27

UXC28

UY12

UY41

UY43

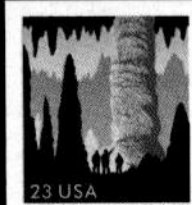

UY44

UZ6

Issue		Date	Un	U
	America on the Move: 50s Sporty Cars			
UX440	23¢ Ford Thunderbird	08/20/05	1.00	1.00
UX441	23¢ Nash Healey	08/20/05	1.00	1.00
UX442	23¢ Chevrolet Corvette	08/20/05	1.00	1.00
UX443	23¢ Studebaker Starliner	08/20/05	1.00	1.00
UX444	23¢ Kaiser Darrin	08/20/05	1.00	1.00
a	Booklet of 20		20.00	
	Let's Dance			
UX445	23¢ Cha cha cha	09/17/05	1.00	1.00
UX446	23¢ Mambo	09/17/05	1.00	1.00
UX447	23¢ Salsa	09/17/05	1.00	1.00
UX448	23¢ Merengue	09/17/05	1.00	1.00
a	Booklet of 20		20.00	
	Airmail Postal Cards			
UXC1	4¢ red orange Eagle in Flight	01/10/1949	.50	.75
UXC2	5¢ red Eagle in Flight (type of 1954), buff	07/31/1958	1.75	.75
UXC3	5¢ UXC2 redrawn, bi-colored border	06/18/1960	6.50	2.00
UXC4	6¢ red Bald Eagle	02/15/1963	1.10	2.50
UXC5	11¢ Visit The USA	05/27/1966	.65	20.00
UXC6	6¢ Virgin Islands	03/31/1967	.75	10.00
a	Red, yellow omitted		1,700.00	
UXC7	6¢ Boy Scout World Jamboree	08/04/1967	.75	15.00
a	blue omitted		11,000.00	
UXC8	13¢ Visit The USA	09/08/1967	1.50	25.00
UXC9	8¢ Stylized Eagle, precanceled w/3 red lines	03/01/1968	.75	2.50
UXC10	9¢ Stylized Eagle, precanceled w/3 red lines	05/15/1971	.50	1.25
UXC11	15¢ Visit The USA	06/10/1971	1.75	45.00
UXC12	9¢ black Grand Canyon, buff	06/29/1972	.75	1.50
UXC13	15¢ black Niagara Falls, buff	06/29/1972	.75	75.00
UXC14	11¢ Stylized Eagle	01/04/1974	1.10	20.00
UXC15	18¢ Eagle Weather Vane		1.10	20.00
UXC16	21¢ Angel Weather Vane	12/17/1975	.85	20.00
UXC17	21¢ Curtiss Jenny	09/16/1978	1.00	20.00
UXC18	21¢ Olympic Gymnast	12/01/1979	1.25	20.00
UXC19	28¢ First Transpacific Flight	01/02/1981	1.00	20.00
UXC20	28¢ Gliders	03/05/1982	1.00	20.00
UXC21	28¢ Olympic Speed Skater	12/29/1983	1.00	20.00
UXC22	33¢ China Clipper	02/15/1985	1.00	20.00
	Scenic American Landscapes (UXC27-UXC28)			
UXC23	33¢ AMERIPEX '86	02/01/1986	1.00	20.00
UXC24	36¢ DC-3	05/14/1988	.85	20.00
UXC25	40¢ Yankee Clipper	06/28/1991	.90	20.00
UXC27	55¢ Mt. Rainier	05/15/1999	1.25	20.00
UXC28	70¢ Badlands	02/22/2001	1.40	10.00

Issue		Date	Un	U
	Paid Reply Postal Cards Prices are: Un=unsevered, U=severed card			
UY1	1¢ + 1¢ black Grant	10/25/1892	37.50	9.00
UY2	2¢ + 2¢ blue Liberty		20.00	20.00
UY3	1¢ + 1¢ black Grant	09/1898	62.50	12.50
UY4	1¢ + 1¢ black Sherman	03/31/1904	52.50	6.50
UY5	1¢ + 1¢ blue Washington	09/14/1910	160.00	25.00
UY6	1¢ + 1¢ green George and Martha Washington, double frame line	10/27/1911	160.00	25.00
UY7	1¢ + 1¢ green George and Martha Washington, single frame line	09/18/1915	1.25	.50
UY8	2¢ + 2¢ red George and Martha Washington, *buff*	08/02/1918	82.50	40.00
UY9	1¢ on 2¢ + 1¢ on 2¢ red George and Martha Washington, *buff, (canceling machine type)*	04/1920	20.00	11.00
UY10	1¢ on 2¢ + 1¢ on 2¢ red George and Martha Washington, *buff, (press printed type)*	04/1920	350.00	200.00
UY11	2¢ + 2¢ red Liberty	03/18/1924	2.00	35.00
UY12	3¢ + 3¢ red McKinley	02/01/1926	10.00	25.00
UY13	2¢ + 2¢ carmine Washington, *buff*	12/29/1951	1.25	2.00
UY14	2¢ on 1¢ + 2¢ on 1¢ green George and Martha Washington, *buff, (canceling machine type)*	01/01/1952	1.00	2.00
UY15	2¢ on 1¢ + 2¢ on 1¢ green George and Martha Washington, *buff, (press printed type)*	1952	110.00	45.00
UY16	4¢ + 4¢ carmine and dark violet blue Statue of Liberty	11/16/1956	1.25	75.00
UY17	3¢ + 3¢ purple Statue of Liberty, *buff*	07/31/1958	3.00	2.00
UY18	4¢ + 4¢ red violet Lincoln	11/19/1962	3.00	2.50
UY19	7¢ + 7¢ blue and red World Vacationland	08/30/1963	2.50	60.00
UY20	8¢ + 8¢ blue and red World Vacationland	12/04/1967	2.50	60.00
UY21	5¢ + 5¢ emerald Lincoln	01/04/1968	1.25	2.00
UY22	6¢ + 6¢ brown Paul Revere	05/15/1971	.85	2.00
UY23	6¢ + 6¢ blue John Hanson	09/01/1972	1.00	2.00

Issue		Date	Un	U
UY24	8¢ + 8¢ orange Samuel Adams	09/01/1972	.75	2.00
UY25	7¢ + 7¢ emerald Charles Thomson	09/14/1975	.75	8.00
UY26	9¢ + 9¢ yellow brown John Witherspoon	11/10/1975	.75	2.00
UY27	9¢ + 9¢ blue Caesar Rodney	07/01/1976	1.00	2.00
UY28	9¢ + 9¢ green Nathan Hale	10/14/1977	1.00	2.00
UY29	(10¢ + 10¢) brown orange John Hancock	05/19/1978	9.00	9.00
UY30	10¢ + 10¢ brown orange John Hancock	06/20/1978	1.00	.25
UY31	(12¢ + 12¢) violet Eagle	03/15/1981	1.00	2.00
UY32	12¢ + 12¢ light blue Isaiah Thomas	05/05/1981	5.00	2.00
UY33	(13¢ + 13¢) buff Robert Morris	10/11/1981	1.50	2.00
UY34	13¢ + 13¢ buff Robert Morris	11/10/1981	.85	.20
UY35	(14¢ + 14¢) pale green Charles Carroll	02/01/1985	2.50	2.00
UY36	14¢ + 14¢ pale green Charles Carroll	03/06/1985	1.00	2.00
UY37	14¢ + 14¢ bright green George Wythe	06/20/1985	.75	2.00
UY38	14¢ + 14¢ black, blue & red Stars and Stripes	09/01/1987	.75	2.00
UY39	15¢ + 15¢ Bison and Prairie	07/11/1988	.75	1.00
UY40	19¢ + 19¢ Flag	03/27/1991	.80	1.00
	Scenic America (UY41, UY43, UY44)			
UY41	20¢ + 20¢ Red Barn	02/01/1995	.80	1.25
UY42	20¢ + 20¢ Block Island Lighthouse	11/10/1999	.85	1.25
UY43	21¢ + 21¢ White Barn	09/20/2001	.90	1.25
UY44	23¢ + 23¢ Carlsbad Caverns	06/07/2002	1.00	1.25
	Official Mail Postal Cards			
UZ1	1¢ black Numeral	07/1913	600.00	450.00
UZ2	13¢ blue Great Seal	01/12/1983	.75	90.00
UZ3	14¢ blue Great Seal	02/26/1985	.75	80.00
UZ4	15¢ blue Great Seal	06/10/1988	.75	90.00
UZ5	19¢ blue Great Seal	05/24/1991	.75	90.00
UZ6	20¢ Official Mail	05/09/1995	.90	90.00

American Commemorative Cancellations

The Postal Service offers American Commemorative Cancellations (formerly known as Souvenir Pages) for new stamps. The series began with a page for the Yellowstone Park Centennial stamp issued March 1, 1972. The pages feature one or more stamps tied by the first day cancel, along with technical data and information on the subject of the issue. More than just collectors' items, American Commemorative Cancellations make wonderful show and conversation pieces. These pages are issued in limited editions. Number in parentheses ( ) indicates the number of stamps on page if there are more than one.

The identifying numbers used below are based on the Postal Service's numbering system for American Commemorative Cancellations; therefore, they do not follow the Scott numbering system.

1972

72-00	Family Planning	400.00
72-01	Yellowstone Park	80.00
72-01a	Yellowstone Park with DC cancel	—
72-02	2¢ Cape Hatteras	65.00
72-03	14¢ Fiorello LaGuardia	65.00
72-04	11¢ City of Refuge Park	70.00
72-05	6¢ Wolf Trap Farm Park	22.50
72-06	Colonial Craftsmen (4)	12.50
72-07	15¢ Mount McKinley	17.50
72-08	6¢-15¢ Olympic Games (4)	9.00
72-08E	Olympic Games with broken red circle on 6¢ stamp	—
72-09	PTA	4.50
72-10	Wildlife Conservation (4)	6.00
72-11	Mail Order	4.50
72-12	Osteopathic Medicine	4.50
72-13	Tom Sawyer	6.00
72-14	7¢ Benjamin Franklin	4.75
72-15	Christmas (2)	5.50
72-16	Pharmacy	6.00
72-17	Stamp Collecting	4.50

1973

73-01	$1 Eugene O'Neill	10.00
73-01E	$1 Eugene O'Neill picture perf. error	—
73-02	Love	5.50
73-03	Pamphleteer Printing	3.50
73-04	George Gershwin	4.50
73-05	Broadside	4.50
73-06	Copernicus	4.25
73-07	Postal Employees	4.75
73-08	Harry S. Truman	3.75
73-09	Post Rider	4.50
73-10	21¢ Amadeo Gianninni	3.50
73-11	Boston Tea Party (4)	4.75
73-12	6¢-15¢ Electronics (4)	5.75
73-13	Robinson Jeffers	3.50
73-14	Lyndon B. Johnson	2.75
73-15	Henry O. Tanner	4.00
73-16	Willa Cather	3.25
73-17	Colonial Drummer	3.25
73-18	Angus Cattle	2.75
73-19	Christmas (2)	5.00
73-20	13¢ Winged Envelope airmail	2.00
73-21	10¢ Crossed Flags	2.25
73-22	10¢ Jefferson Memorial	2.25
73-23	13¢ Winged Envelope airmail coil (2)	2.50

1972

74-01	26¢ Mount Rushmore airmail	4.00
74-02	ZIP Code	3.25
74-02E	ZIP Code with date error 4/4/74	—
74-03	18¢ Statue of Liberty airmail	4.50
74-04	18¢ Elizabeth Blackwell	2.00
74-05	VFW	2.50
74-06	Robert Frost	3.50
74-07	Expo '74	4.00
74-08	Horse Racing	4.00
74-09	Skylab	4.50
74-10	UPU (8)	4.75
74-11	Mineral Heritage (4)	4.75
74-12	Fort Harrod	2.25
74-13	Continental Congress (4)	3.50
74-14	Chautauqua	2.50
74-15	Kansas Wheat	1.90
74-16	Energy Conservation	2.00
74-17	6.3¢ Liberty Bell coil (2)	2.25
74-18	Sleepy Hollow	3.00
74-19	Retarded Children	2.00
74-20	Christmas (3)	4.25

1975

75-01	Benjamin West	2.25
75-02	Pioneer/Jupiter	5.00
75-03	Collective Bargaining	2.25
75-04	8¢ Sybil Ludington	2.25
75-05	Salem Poor	3.00
75-06	Haym Salomon	2.25
75-07	18¢ Peter Francisco	2.25
75-08	Mariner 10	4.25
75-09	Lexington & Concord	2.50
75-10	Paul Dunbar	3.00
75-11	D.W. Griffith	2.50
75-12	Bunker Hill	2.50
75-13	Military Uniforms (4)	5.00
75-14	Apollo Soyuz (2)	5.00
75-15	International Women's Year	2.00
75-16	Postal Service Bicentennial (4)	3.00
75-17	World Peace Through Law	2.00
75-18	Banking & Commerce (2)	3.00
75-19	Christmas (2)	3.00
75-20	3¢ Francis Parkman	2.50
75-21	11¢ Printing Press	1.75
75-22	24¢ Old North Church	1.90
75-23	Flag over Independence Hall (2)	2.00
75-24	9¢ Freedom to Assemble (2)	2.25
75-25	Liberty Bell coil (2)	2.00
75-26	Eagle & Shield	2.50

1976

76-01	Spirit of '76 (3)	3.25
76-01E	Spirit of '76 with cancellation error Jan. 2, 1976 (3)	—
76-02	25¢ and 31¢ Plane and Globes airmails (2)	2.25
76-03	Interphil '76	2.50
76-04	State Flags, DE to VA (10)	5.50
76-05	State Flags, NY to MS (10)	5.50
76-06	State Flags, IL to WI (10)	5.50
76-07	State Flags, CA to SD (10)	5.50
76-08	State Flags, MT to HI (10)	5.50
76-09	9¢ Freedom to Assemble coil (2)	1.75
76-10	Telephone Centennial	1.75
76-11	Commercial Aviation	1.75
76-12	Chemistry	1.75
76-13	7.9¢ Drum coil (2)	1.90
76-14	Benjamin Franklin	1.75
76-15	Bicentennial souvenir sheet	7.00
76-15E	13¢ Bicentennial souvenir sheet with perforation and numerical errors	7.00
76-16	18¢ Bicentennial souvenir sheet	7.00
76-17	24¢ Bicentennial souvenir sheet	7.00
76-18	31¢ Bicentennial souvenir sheet	7.00
76-19	Declaration of Independence (4)	3.50
76-20	Olympics (4)	3.50
76-21	Clara Maass	2.75
76-22	Adolph S. Ochs	2.25
76-23	Christmas (3)	2.25
76-24	7.7¢ Saxhorns coil (2)	1.75

1977

77-01	Washington at Princeton	1.75
77-02	Flag over Capitol booklet pane (9¢ and 13¢) Perf. 10 (8)	14.00
77-03	Sound Recording	2.00
77-04	Pueblo Pottery (4)	3.00
77-05	Lindbergh Flight	2.25
77-06	Colorado Centennial	1.90
77-07	Butterflies (4)	2.25
77-08	Lafayette	1.50
77-09	Skilled Hands (4)	2.25
77-10	Peace Bridge	1.60
77-11	Battle of Oriskany	1.60
77-12	Alta, CA, First Civil Settlement	1.60
77-13	Articles of Confederation	1.60
77-14	Talking Pictures	2.00
77-15	Surrender at Saratoga	2.25
77-16	Energy (2)	1.60
77-17	Christmas, Mailbox and Christmas, Valley Forge, Omaha cancel (2)	1.60
77-18	Same, Valley Forge cancel	—
77-19	10¢ Petition for Redress coil (2)	2.25
77-20	10¢ Petition for Redress sheet (2)	2.25
77-21	1¢-4¢ Americana (5)	2.00

1978

78-01	Carl Sandburg	2.00
78-02	Indian Head Penny	2.00
78-03	Captain Cook Anchorage cancel (2)	2.00
78-04	Captain Cook, Honolulu cancel (2)	2.00
78-05	Harriet Tubman	3.00
78-06	American Quilts (4)	2.50
78-07	16¢ Statue of Liberty sheet and coil (2)	1.90
78-08	29¢ Sandy Hook Lighthouse	1.90
78-09	American Dance (4)	2.75
78-10	French Alliance	1.90
78-11	Early Cancer Detection	2.25
78-12	"A" (15¢) sheet and coil (2)	3.25
78-13	Jimmie Rodgers	3.00
78-14	CAPEX '78 (8)	5.50
78-15	Oliver Wendell Holmes coil	3.50
78-16	Photography	1.90
78-17	Fort McHenry Flag sheet and coil (2)	2.00
78-18	George M. Cohan	1.60
78-19	Rose booklet single	2.00
78-20	8.4¢ Piano coil (2)	2.00
78-21	Viking Missions	3.75
78-22	28¢ Ft. Nisqually	2.00
78-23	American Owls (4)	2.50
78-24	31¢ Wright Brothers airmails (2)	2.50
78-25	American Trees (4)	2.75
78-26	Christmas, Madonna	2.00
78-27	Christmas, Hobby Horse	2.00
78-28	$2 Kerosene Lamp	4.50

1979

79-01	Robert F. Kennedy	2.00
79-02	Martin Luther King, Jr.	3.50
79-03	International Year of the Child	2.00
79-04	John Steinbeck	2.50
79-05	Albert Einstein	3.00
79-06	21¢ Octave Chanute airmails (2)	2.50
79-07	Pennsylvania Toleware (4)	2.50
79-08	American Architecture (4)	2.25
79-09	Endangered Flora (4)	2.50
79-10	Seeing Eye Dogs	1.90
79-11	Candle & Holder	3.50
79-12	Special Olympics	1.90
79-13	$5 Lantern	9.00
79-14	30¢ Schoolhouse	2.50
79-15	10¢ Summer Olympics (2)	2.25
79-16	50¢ Whale Oil Lamp	3.00
79-17	John Paul Jones	2.00
79-18	Summer Olympics (4)	3.75
79-19	Christmas, Madonna	2.25
79-20	Christmas, Santa Claus	2.25
79-21	3.1¢ Guitar coil (2)	3.50
79-22	31¢ Summer Olympics airmail	3.00
79-23	Will Rogers	2.25
79-24	Vietnam Veterans	2.75
79-25	25¢ Wiley Post airmails (2)	3.00

1980

80-01 W.C. Fields 2.75
80-02 Winter Olympics (4) 3.50
80-03 Windmills booklet pane (10) 4.00
80-04 Benjamin Banneker 2.75
80-05 Letter Writing (6) 2.00
80-06 1¢ Ability to Write (2) 1.75
80-07 Frances Perkins 1.50
80-08 Dolley Madison 2.25
80-09 Emily Bissell 1.90
80-10 3.5¢ Violins coil (2) 2.50
80-11 Helen Keller/ Anne Sullivan 1.75
80-12 Veterans Administration 1.50
80-13 General Bernardo de Galvez 1.75
80-14 Coral Reefs (4) 2.75
80-15 Organized Labor 2.25
80-16 Edith Wharton 2.25
80-17 Education 2.25
80-18 Indian Masks (4) 2.50
80-19 American Architecture (4) 2.00
80-20 40¢ Philip Mazzei airmail 2.00
80-21 Christmas, Madonna 2.25
80-22 Christmas, Antique Toys 2.25
80-23 Sequoyah 1.50
80-24 28¢ Blanche Scott airmail 1.60
80-25 35¢ Glenn Curtiss airmail 1.60

1981

81-01 Everett Dirksen 1.50
81-02 Whitney M. Young 2.75
81-03 "B" (18¢ sheet and coil (3) 2.00
81-04 "B" (18¢) booklet pane (8) 2.00
81-05 12¢ Torch Sheet and coil (3) 2.25
81-06 Flowers block (4) 2.00
81-07 Flag and Anthem sheet and coil (3) 2.00
81-08 Flag and Anthem booklet pane (8 - 6¢ and 18¢) 2.00
81-09 American Red Cross 1.50
81-10 George Mason 1.50
81-11 Savings & Loans 1.50
81-12 Wildlife booklet pane (10) 2.00
81-13 Surrey coil (2) 1.75
81-14 Space Achievement (8) 6.75
81-15 17¢ Rachel Carson (2) 1.50
81-16 35¢ Charles Drew, MD 1.75
81-17 Professional Management 1.50
81-18 17¢ Electric Auto coil (2) 1.75
81-19 Wildlife Habitat (4) 2.00
81-20 Disabled 1.50
81-21 Edna St. Vincent Millay 1.75
81-22 Alcoholism 2.25
81-23 American Architecture (4) 2.50
81-24 Babe Zaharias 7.00
81-25 Bobby Jones 8.00
81-26 Frederic Remington 2.25
81-27 "C" (20¢) sheet and coil (3) 2.50
81-28 "C" (18¢) booklet pane (10) 2.50
81-29 18¢ and 20¢ Hoban (2) 1.50
81-30 Yorktown/ Virginia Capes (2) 2.00
81-31 Christmas, Madonna 2.00
81-32 Christmas, Bear on Sleigh 2.25
81-33 John Hanson 1.50
81-34 Fire Pumper coil (2) 3.25
81-35 Desert Plants (4) 2.00
81-36 9.3¢ Mail Wagon coil (3) 2.50
81-37 Flag over Supreme Court sheet and coil (3) 3.00
81-38 Flag over Supreme Court booklet pane (6) 2.50

1982

82-01 Sheep booklet pane (10) 3.00
82-02 Ralph Bunche 4.00
82-03 13¢ Crazy Horse (2) 1.75
82-04 37¢ Robert Millikan 1.50
82-05 Franklin D. Roosevelt 1.50
82-06 Love 1.50
82-07 5.9¢ Bicycle coil (4) 4.75
82-08 George Washington 2.25
82-09 10.9¢ Hansom Cab coil (2) 2.75
82-10 Birds & Flowers, AL-GE (10) 7.00
82-11 Birds & Flowers, HI-MD (10) 7.00
82-12 Birds & Flowers, MA-NJ (10) 7.00
82-13 Birds & Flowers, NM-SC (10) 7.00
82-14 Birds & Flowers, SD-WY (10) 7.00
82-15 USA/Netherlands 1.50
82-16 Library of Congress 1.50
82-17 Consumer Education coil (2) 2.25
82-18 Knoxville World's Fair (4) 1.50
82-19 Horatio Alger 1.25
82-20 2¢ Locomotive coil (2) 2.25
82-21 Aging Together 1.25
82-22 The Barrymores 2.50
82-23 Mary Walker 1.50
82-24 Peace Garden 1.50
82-25 America's Libraries 1.50
82-26 Jackie Robinson 12.50
82-27 4¢ Stagecoach coil (3) 2.50
82-28 Touro Synagogue 1.75
82-29 Wolf Trap Farm Park 1.50
82-30 American Architecture (4) 1.75
82-31 Francis of Assisi 1.40
82-32 Ponce de Leon 1.40
82-33 13¢ Kitten & Puppy (2) 2.00
82-34 Christmas, Madonna 2.25
82-35 Christmas, Seasons Greetings (4) 2.25
82-36 2¢ Igor Stravinsky (2) 2.00

1983

83-01 1¢, 4¢, 13¢ Penalty Mail (5) 2.50
83-02 17¢ Penalty Mail (4) 2.25
83-03 Penalty Mail coil (2) 3.25
83-04 $1 Penalty Mail 4.00
83-05 $5 Penalty Mail 9.50
83-06 Science & Industry 1.50
83-07 5.2¢ Antique Sleigh coil (4) 2.75
83-08 Sweden/USA Treaty 1.50
83-09 3¢ Handcar coil (3) 2.00
83-10 Balloons (4) 1.75
83-11 Civilian Conservation Corps 1.25
83-12 40¢ Olympics airmails (4) 2.75
83-13 Joseph Priestley 1.50
83-14 Volunteerism 1.25
83-15 Concord/German Immigration 1.50
83-16 Physical Fitness 1.50
83-17 Brooklyn Bridge 2.00
83-18 TVA 1.50
83-19 4¢ Carl Schurz (5) 1.50
83-20 Medal of Honor 3.25
83-21 Scott Joplin 2.50
83-22 Thomas H. Gallaudet 1.75
83-23 28¢ Olympics (4) 3.00
83-24 5¢ Pearl S. Buck (4) 1.50
83-25 Babe Ruth 10.00
83-26 Nathaniel Hawthorne 1.50
83-27 3¢ Henry Clay (7) 1.50
83-28 13¢ Olympics (4) 3.00
83-29 $9.35 Eagle booklet single 75.00
83-30 $9.35 Eagle booklet pane (3) 125.00
83-31 1¢ Omnibus coil (3) 1.75
83-32 Treaty of Paris 1.25
83-33 Civil Service 1.25
83-34 Metropolitan Opera 1.75
83-35 Inventors (4) 1.75
83-36 1¢ Dorothea Dix (3) 2.25
83-37 Streetcars (4) 2.25
83-38 5¢ Motorcycle coil (4) 3.75
83-39 Christmas, Madonna 1.50
83-40 Christmas, Santa Claus 1.50
83-41 35¢ Olympics airmails (4) 2.75
83-42 Martin Luther 2.25
83-43 Flag over Supreme Court booklet pane (10) 2.50

1984

84-01 Alaska Statehood 1.50
84-02 Winter Olympics (4) 2.25
84-03 FDIC 1.50
84-04 Harry S. Truman 1.50
84-05 Love 1.50
84-06 Carter G. Woodson 2.25
84-07 11¢ RR Caboose coil (2) 2.25
84-08 Soil & Water Conservation 1.25
84-09 Credit Union Act 1.50
84-10 40¢ Lillian M. Gilbreth 1.50
84-11 Orchids (4) 2.25
84-12 Hawaii Statehood 2.00
84-13 7.4¢ Baby Buggy coil (3) 2.50
84-14 National Archives 1.25
84-15 20¢ Summer Olympics (4) 2.75
84-16 New Orleans World's Fair 1.25
84-17 Health Research 1.25
84-18 Douglas Fairbanks 3.00
84-19 Jim Thorpe 7.00
84-20 10¢ Richard Russell (2) 1.50
84-21 John McCormack 3.00
84-22 St. Lawrence Seaway 1.25
84-23 Migratory Bird Hunting and Pre-Conservation Stamp Act 3.00
84-24 Roanoke Voyages 1.25
84-25 Herman Melville 1.50
84-26 Horace Moses 1.25
84-27 Smokey Bear 7.00
84-28 Roberto Clemente 11.00
84-29 30¢ Frank C. Laubach 1.50
84-30 Dogs (4) 3.00
84-31 Crime Prevention 1.50
84-32 Family Unity 2.25
84-33 Eleanor Roosevelt 2.50
84-34 Nation of Readers 2.00
84-35 Christmas, Madonna 2.00
84-36 Christmas, Santa Claus 2.00
84-37 Hispanic Americans 1.25
84-38 Vietnam Veterans Memorial 3.25

1985

85-01 Jerome Kern 2.00
85-02 7¢ Abraham Baldwin (3) 1.75
85-03 "D" (22¢) sheet and coil (3) 1.50
85-04 "D" (22¢) booklet pane (10) 3.00
85-05 "D" (22¢) Penalty Mail sheet and coil (3) 1.50
85-06 11¢ Alden Partridge (2) 1.50
85-07 33¢ Alfred Verville airmail 1.25
85-08 39¢ Lawrence & Elmer Sperry airmail 1.75
85-09 44¢ Transpacific airmail 1.50
85-10 50¢ Chester Nimitz 1.75
85-11 Mary McLeod Bethune 2.75
85-12 39¢ Grenville Clark 1.50
85-13 14¢ Sinclair Lewis (2) 1.50
85-14 Duck Decoys (4) 3.25
85-15 14¢ Iceboat coil (2) 3.25
85-16 Winter Special Olympics 1.25
85-17 Flag over Capitol sheet and coil (3) 2.00
85-18 Flag over Capitol booklet pane (5) 2.50
85-19 12¢ Stanley Steamer coil (2) 2.75
85-20 Seashells booklet pane (10) 3.50
85-21 Love 2.25
85-22 10.1¢ Oil Wagon coil (3) 2.25
85-23 12.5¢ Pushcart coil (2) 2.50
85-24 John J. Audubon 1.75
85-25 $10.75 Eagle booklet single 30.00
85-26 $10.75 Eagle booklet pane (3) 65.00
85-27 6¢ Tricycle coil (4) 2.50
85-28 Rural Electrification Administration 1.25
85-29 14¢ and 22¢ Penalty Mail sheet and coil (4) 2.00
85-30 AMERIPEX '86 1.25
85-31 9¢ Sylvanus Thayer (3) 1.75
85-32 3.4¢ School Bus coil (7) 3.00
85-33 11¢ Stutz Bearcat coil (2) 2.50
85-34 Abigail Adams 1.25
85-35 4.9¢ Buckboard coil (5) 2.75
85-36 8.3¢ Ambulance coil (3) 2.75
85-37 Frederic Bartholdi 2.25
85-38 8¢ Henry Knox (3) 1.50
85-39 Korean War Veterans 2.00
85-40 Social Security Act 1.50
85-41 44¢ Father Junipero Serra airmail 1.50
85-42 World War I Veterans 1.75
85-43 6¢ Walter Lippmann (4) 1.50
85-44 Horses (4) 3.25
85-45 Public Education 1.50

85-46	International Youth Year (4)	2.50
85-47	Help End Hunger	1.60
85-48	21.1¢ Letters coil (2)	2.25
85-49	Christmas, Madonna	1.50
85-50	Christmas, Poinsettias	2.50
85-51	18¢ Washington/ Washington Monument coil (2)	2.25

1986

86-01	Arkansas Statehood	1.50
86-02	25¢ Jack London	1.50
86-03	Stamp Collecting booklet pane (4)	3.00
86-04	Love	2.00
86-05	Sojourner Truth	2.50
86-06	5¢ Hugo L. Black (5)	2.25
86-07	Republic of Texas (2)	1.75
86-08	$2 William Jennings Bryan	3.25
86-09	Fish booklet pane (5)	3.00
86-10	Public Hospitals	1.50
86-11	Duke Ellington	3.25
86-12	Presidents, Washington-Harrison (9)	3.75
86-13	Presidents, Tyler-Grant (9)	3.75
86-14	Presidents, Hayes-Wilson (9)	3.75
86-15	Presidents, Harding-Johnson (9)	3.75
86-16	Polar Explorers (4)	2.75
86-17	17¢ Belva Ann Lockwood (2)	1.50
86-18	1¢ Margaret Mitchell (3)	2.50
86-19	Statue of Liberty	2.25
86-20	4¢ Father Flanagan (3)	1.60
86-21	17¢ Dog Sled coil (2)	2.25
86-22	56¢ John Harvard	2.00
86-23	Navajo Blankets (4)	2.75
86-24	3¢ Paul Dudley White, MD (8)	1.50
86-25	$1 Bernard Revel	1.75
86-26	T.S. Eliot	2.50
86-27	Wood-Carved Figurines (4)	2.75
86-28	Christmas, Madonna	1.75
86-29	Christmas, Village Scene	1.75
86-30	5.5¢ Star Route Truck coil (4)	3.00
86-31	25¢ Bread Wagon coil	3.00

1987

87-01	8.5¢ Tow Truck coil (5)	1.50
87-02	Michigan Statehood	2.50
87-03	Pan American Games	2.50
87-04	Love	2.00
87-05	7.1¢ Tractor coil (5)	2.50
87-06	14¢ Julia Ward Howe (2)	1.50
87-07	Jean Baptiste Pointe Du Sable	4.00
87-08	Enrico Caruso	2.25
87-09	2¢ Mary Lyon (3)	1.50
87-10	Reengraved 2¢ Locomotive coil (6)	2.25
87-11	Girl Scouts	3.50
87-12	10¢ Canal Boat coil (5)	1.75
87-13	Special Occasions booklet pane (10)	3.75
87-14	United Way	1.50
87-15	Flag with Fireworks	1.50
87-16	Flag over Capitol coil, prephosphored paper (2)	2.25
87-17	Wildlife, Swallow-Squirrel (10)	4.00
87-18	Wildlife, Armadillo-Rabbit (10)	4.00
87-19	Wildlife, Tanager-Ladybug (10)	4.00
87-20	Wildlife, Beaver-Prairie Dog (10)	4.00
87-21	Wildlife, Turtle-Fox (10)	4.00
87-22	Delaware Statehood	2.00
87-23	U.S./Morocco Friendship	1.50
87-24	William Faulkner	1.50
87-25	Lacemaking (4)	3.50
87-26	10¢ Red Cloud (3)	1.75
87-27	$5 Bret Harte	8.00
87-28	Pennsylvania Statehood	1.50
87-29	Drafting of the Constitution booklet pane (5)	2.50
87-30	New Jersey Statehood	1.75
87-31	Signing of Constitution	1.50
87-32	Certified Public Accountants	3.25
87-33	5¢ Milk Wagon and 17.5¢ Racing Car coils (4)	2.75
87-34	Locomotives booklet pane (5)	6.75
87-35	Christmas, Madonna	1.50
87-36	Christmas, Ornaments	1.50
87-37	Flag with Fireworks booklet-pair	2.25

1988

88-01	Georgia Statehood	1.75
88-02	Connecticut Statehood	1.75
88-03	Winter Olympics	1.50
88-04	Australia Bicentennial	1.75
88-05	James Weldon Johnson	2.75
88-06	Cats (4)	3.75
88-07	Massachusetts Statehood	2.25
88-08	Maryland Statehood	2.25
88-09	3¢ Conestoga Wagon coil (8)	2.50
88-10	Knute Rockne	5.00
88-11	"E" (25¢) Earth sheet and coil (3)	2.75
88-12	"E" (25¢) Earth booklet pane (10)	3.25
88-13	"E" (25¢) Penalty Mail coil (2)	2.25
88-14	44¢ New Sweden airmail	1.75
88-15	Pheasant booklet pane (10)	3.25
88-16	Jack London booklet pane (6)	2.25
88-17	Jack London booklet pane (10)	4.25
88-18	Flag with Clouds	1.50
88-19	45¢ Samuel Langley airmail	1.75
88-19A	20¢ Penalty Mail coil (2)	1.75
88-20	Flag over Yosemite coil (2)	1.75
88-21	South Carolina Statehood	1.50
88-22	Owl & Grosbeak booklet pane (10)	3.00
88-23	15¢ Buffalo Bill Cody (2)	1.75
88-24	15¢ and 25¢ Penalty Mail coils (4)	2.25
88-25	Francis Ouimet	4.00
88-26	45¢ Harvey Cushing, MD	1.50
88-27	New Hampshire Statehood	1.75
88-28	36¢ Igor Sikorsky airmail	2.00
88-29	Virginia Statehood	2.00
88-30	10.1¢ Oil Wagon coil, precancel (3)	2.25
88-31	Love	2.00
88-32	Flag with Clouds booklet pane (6)	3.00
88-33	16.7¢ Popcorn Wagon coil (2)	2.50
88-34	15¢ Tugboat coil (2)	2.50
88-35	13.2¢ Coal Car coil (2)	2.75
88-36	New York Statehood	2.00
88-37	45¢ Love	1.75
88-38	8.4¢ Wheelchair coil (3)	2.50
88-39	21¢ Railroad Mail Car coil (2)	3.00
88-40	Summer Olympics	1.75
88-41	Classic Cars booklet pane (5)	3.75
88-42	7.6¢ Carreta coil (4)	2.25
88-43	Honeybee coil (2)	3.00
88-44	Antarctic Explorers (4)	2.75
88-45	5.3¢ Elevator coil (5)	2.25
88-46	20.5¢ Fire Engine coil (2)	3.00
88-47	Carousel Animals (4)	3.00
88-48	$8.75 Eagle	15.00
88-49	Christmas, Madonna	1.50
88-50	Christmas, Snow Scene	1.50
88-51	21¢ Chester Carlson	1.50
88-52	Special Occasions booklet pane (6), Love You, Thinking of You	9.25
88-53	Special Occasions booklet pane (6), Happy Birthday, Best Wishes	14.00
88-54	24.1¢ Tandem Bicycle coil (2)	2.50
88-55	20¢ Cable Car coil (2)	2.50
88-56	13¢ Patrol Wagon coil (2)	2.75
88-57	23¢ Mary Cassatt	1.50
88-58	65¢ H.H. "Hap" Arnold	2.25

1989

89-01	Montana Statehood	1.75
89-02	A. Philip Randolph	3.00
89-03	Flag over Yosemite coil, prephosphored paper (2)	1.75
89-04	North Dakota Statehood	1.50
89-05	Washington Statehood	1.50
89-06	Steamboats booklet pane (5)	3.50
89-07	World Stamp Expo '89	1.50
89-08	Arturo Toscanini	2.00
89-09	U.S. House of Representatives	1.50
89-10	U.S. Senate	1.50
89-11	Executive Branch	1.50
89-12	South Dakota Statehood	1.50
89-13	7.1¢ Tractor coil, precancel (4)	2.50
89-14	$1 Johns Hopkins	2.25
89-15	Lou Gehrig	10.00
89-16	1¢ Penalty Mail	2.25
89-17	45¢ French Revolution airmail	2.25
89-18	Ernest Hemingway	2.50
89-19	$2.40 Moon Landing	11.00
89-20	North Carolina Statehood	2.00
89-21	Letter Carriers	1.50
89-22	28¢ Sitting Bull	1.75
89-23	Drafting of the Bill of Rights	1.50
89-24	Prehistoric Animals (4)	5.50
89-25	25¢ and 45¢ PUAS/ America (2)	2.00
89-26	Christmas, Madonna	4.25
89-27	Christmas, Antique Sleigh	4.25
89-28	Eagle and Shield, self-adhesive	1.75
89-29	World Stamp Expo '89 souvenir sheet	7.00
89-30	Classic Mail Transportation (4)	2.75
89-31	Future Mail Transportation souvenir sheet	3.25
89-32	45¢ Future Mail Transportation airmails (4)	3.25
89-33	Classic Mail Transportation souvenir sheet	3.50

1990

90-01	Idaho Statehood	1.50
90-02	Love sheet and booklet pane (10)	3.00
90-03	Ida B. Wells	3.00
90-04	U.S. Supreme Court	1.50
90-05	15¢ Beach Umbrella booklet pane (10)	3.00
90-06	5¢ Luis Muñoz Marín (5)	2.00
90-07	Wyoming Statehood	2.25
90-08	Classic Films (4)	4.25
90-09	Marianne Moore	1.50
90-10	$1 Seaplane coil (2)	5.00
90-11	Lighthouses booklet pane (5)	5.00
90-12	Plastic Flag	2.75
90-13	Rhode Island Statehood	2.00
90-14	$2 Bobcat	4.00
90-15	Olympians (5)	4.75
90-16	Indian Headdresses booklet pane (10)	5.50
90-17	5¢ Circus Wagon coil (5)	3.25
90-18	40¢ Claire Lee Chennault	2.50
90-19	Federated States of Micronesia/ Marshall Islands (2)	2.25
90-20	Creatures of the Sea (4)	4.75
90-21	25¢ and 45¢ PUAS/America (2)	2.25
90-22	Dwight D. Eisenhower	2.50
90-23	Christmas, Madonna, sheet and booklet pane (10)	5.00
90-24	Christmas, Yule Tree, sheet and booklet pane (10)	5.00

1991

No.	Item	Price
91-01	"F" (29¢) Flower sheet and coil (3)	2.50
91-02	"F" (29¢) Flower booklet panes (20)	8.00
91-03	4¢ Makeup	2.00
91-04	"F" (29¢) Flag ATM booklet single	2.25
91-05	"F" (29¢) Penalty Mail coil (2)	2.50
91-06	4¢ Steam Carriage coil (7)	2.25
91-07	50¢ Switzerland	2.25
91-08	Vermont Statehood	2.50
91-09	19¢ Fawn (2)	2.25
91-10	Flag over Mount Rushmore coil (2)	2.50
91-11	35¢ Dennis Chavez	2.75
91-12	Flower sheet and booklet pane (10)	5.00
91-13	4¢ Penalty Mail (8)	2.00
91-14	Wood Duck booklet panes (10)	9.50
91-15	23¢ Lunch Wagon coil (2)	2.25
91-16	Flag with Olympic Rings booklet pane (10)	5.00
91-17	50¢ Harriet Quimby	2.25
91-18	Savings Bond	2.00
91-19	Love sheet and booklet pane, 52¢ Love (12)	6.00
91-20	19¢ Balloon booklet pane (10)	4.00
91-21	40¢ William Piper airmail	2.25
91-22	William Saroyan	2.75
91-23	Penalty Mail coil and 19¢ and 23¢ sheet (4)	2.50
91-24	5¢ Canoe and 10¢ Tractor Trailer coils (4)	2.25
91-25	Flags on Parade	2.50
91-26	Fishing Flies booklet pane (5)	5.25
91-27	52¢ Hubert H. Humphrey	2.00
91-28	Cole Porter	2.25
91-29	50¢ Antarctic Treaty airmail	2.75
91-30	1¢ Kestrel, 3¢ Bluebird and 30¢ Cardinal (3)	2.25
91-31	Torch ATM booklet single	2.50
91-32	Desert Shield/Desert Storm sheet and booklet pane (11)	5.00
91-33	Flag over Mount Rushmore coil, gravure printing (darker, 3)	2.25
91-34	Summer Olympics (5)	4.00
91-35	Flower coil, slit perforations (3)	2.25
91-36	Numismatics	2.50
91-37	Basketball	5.25
91-38	**through 91-47** are unassigned	
91-48	19¢ Fishing Boat coil (3)	2.50
91-49	Comedians booklet pane (10)	5.00
91-50	World War II miniature sheet (10)	6.50
91-51	District of Columbia	2.25
91-52	Jan Matzeliger	4.00
91-53	$1 USPS/Olympic Logo	3.00
91-54	Space Exploration booklet pane (10)	6.75
91-55	50¢ PUASP/America airmail	2.25
91-56	Christmas, Madonna sheet and booklet pane (10)	7.50
91-57	Christmas, Santa Claus sheet and booklet pane (11)	11.00
91-58	5¢ Canoe coil, gravure printing (red, 6)	3.00
91-59	29¢ Eagle and Shield, self-adhesive (3)	4.00
91-60	23¢ Flag presort	2.50
91-61	$9.95 Express Mail	22.50
91-62	$2.90 Priority Mail	7.50
91-63	$14.00 Express Mail International	30.00

1992

No.	Item	Price
92-01	Winter Olympic Games (5)	3.75
92-02	World Columbian Stamp Expo '92	2.50
92-03	W.E.B. DuBois	3.75
92-04	Love	2.50
92-05	75¢ Wendell Willkie	2.25
92-06	29¢ Flower coil, round perforations (2)	2.25
92-07	Earl Warren	3.00
92-08	Olympic Baseball	10.00
92-09	Flag over White House, coil (2)	2.50
92-10	First Voyage of Christopher Columbus (4)	3.75
92-11	New York Stock Exchange	2.50
92-12	Christopher Columbus	7.50
92-13	Columbus - Seeking Royal Support (3)	7.50
92-14	Columbus - First Sighting of Land (3)	7.50
92-15	Columbus - Claiming New World (3)	7.50
92-16	Columbus - Reporting Discoveries (3)	7.50
92-17	Columbus - Royal Favor Restored (3)	7.50
92-18	Space Adventures (4)	4.00
92-19	Alaska Highway	2.50
92-20	Kentucky Statehood	2.50
92-21	Summer Olympic Games (5)	3.75
92-22	Hummingbirds booklet pane (5)	5.00
92-22A	23¢ Presort USA (3)	2.50
92-23	Wildflowers (10)	6.50
92-24	Wildflowers (10)	6.50
92-25	Wildflowers (10)	6.50
92-26	Wildflowers (10)	6.50
92-27	Wildflowers (10)	6.50
92-28	World War II miniature sheet (10)	6.00
92-29	29¢ Variable Rate	2.75
92-30	Dorothy Parker	2.75
92-31	Theodore von Karman	3.50
92-32	Pledge of Allegiance (10)	7.00
92-33	Minerals (4)	4.00
92-34	Eagle and Shield (3)	3.75
92-35	Juan Rodriguez Cabrillo	2.50
92-36	Wild Animals booklet pane (5)	5.00
92-37	23¢ Presort (3)	2.75
92-38	Christmas Contemporary, sheet and booklet pane (8)	7.50
92-39	Christmas Traditional, sheet and booklet pane (11)	5.50
92-40	Pumpkinseed Sunfish	2.75
92-41	Circus Wagon	2.75
92-42	Year of the Rooster	7.75

1993

No.	Item	Price
93-01	Elvis	10.00
93-02	Space Fantasy (5)	6.00
93-03	Percy Lavon Julian	3.50
93-04	Oregon Trail	2.75
93-05	World University Games	2.75
93-06	Grace Kelly	6.00
93-07	Oklahoma!	2.25
93-08	Circus	4.50
93-09	Thomas Jefferson	2.75
93-10	Cherokee Strip	3.50
93-11	Dean Acheson	3.00
93-12	Sporting Horses	5.50
93-13	USA Coil	2.75
93-14	Garden Flowers, booklet pane (5)	3.50
93-15	Eagle and Shield, coil	3.75
93-16	World War II miniature sheet (10)	5.50
93-17	Futuristic Space Shuttle	8.00
93-18	Hank Williams, sheet	5.00
93-19	Rock & Roll/Rhythm & Blues, sheet single, booklet pane (8)	10.00
93-20	Joe Louis	7.50
93-21	Red Squirrel	2.75
93-22	Broadway Musicals, booklet pane (4)	4.50
93-23	National Postal Museum, strip (4)	3.25
93-24	Red Rose	2.50
93-25	American Sign Language, pair	2.75
93-26	Country & Western Music, sheet and booklet pane (4)	9.25
93-27	African Violets, booklet pane (10)	4.25
93-28	10¢ Official Mail	2.75
93-29	Contemporary Christmas, booklet pane (10), sheet and self-adhesive stamps	8.50
93-30	Traditional Christmas, sheet, booklet pane (4)	4.75
93-31	Classic Books, strip (4)	3.25
93-32	Mariana Islands	2.75
93-33	Pine Cone	2.50
93-34	Columbus' Landing in Puerto Rico	3.25
93-35	AIDS Awareness	4.75

1994

No.	Item	Price
94-01	Winter Olympics	5.00
94-02	Edward R. Murrow	3.25
94-03	Love, self-adhesive	3.25
94-04	Dr. Allison Davis	4.50
94-05	29¢ Eagle, self-adhesive	3.50
94-06	Year of the Dog	4.00
94-07	Love, booklet pane (10), single sheet	6.50
94-08	Postage and Mailing Center	5.50
94-09	Buffalo Soldiers	5.00
94-10	Silent Screen Stars	6.00
94-11	Garden Flowers, booklet pane (5)	6.00
94-12	Victory at Saratoga	4.75
94-13	10¢ Tractor Trailer gravure printing	5.00
94-14	World Cup Soccer	6.00
94-15	World Cup Soccer souvenir sheet	6.00
94-16	World War II miniature sheet (10)	5.50
94-17	Love, sheet stamp	3.25
94-18	Statue of Liberty	3.50
94-19	Fishing Boat, reissue	3.75
94-20	Norman Rockwell	9.00
94-21	$9.95 and 29¢ Moon Landing	15.00
94-22	Locomotives (5)	6.50
94-23	George Meany	3.25
94-24	$5.00 Washington/ Jackson	10.00
94-25	Popular Singers (5)	6.00
94-26	James Thurber	4.00
94-27	Jazz Singers/ Blues Singers (10)	9.00
94-28	Wonders of the Sea (4)	5.00
94-29	Chinese/Joint Issue (2)	4.00
94-30	Holiday Traditional (10)	8.50
94-31	Holiday Contemporary (4)	6.50
94-32	Holiday, self-adhesive	7.00
94-33	20¢ Virginia Apgar	4.50
94-34	BEP Centennial	15.00
94-35	Year of the Boar	5.50
94-G1	G1 (4) Rate Change	4.00
94-G2	G2 (6) Rate Change	4.00
94-G3	G3 (5) Rate Change	4.00
94-G4	G4 (2) Rate Change	8.00
94-36	Legends of West	12.00

1995

No.	Item	Price
95-01	Love (2)	3.50
95-02	Florida Statehood	2.75
95-03	Butte (7)	5.50
95-04	Automobile (4)	4.50
95-05	Flag Over Field, self-adhesive	2.75
95-06	Juke Box (2+2)	3.00
95-07	Tail Fin (2+2)	4.50
95-08	Circus Wagon (7)	5.00
95-09	Kids Care (4)	3.50
95-10	Richard Nixon	3.50
95-11	Bessie Coleman	4.50
95-12	Official Mail	3.00
95-13	Kestrel with cent sign	16.00
95-14	Love 1 oz. and 2 oz.	3.50

95-15	Flag Over Porch	5.50
95-16	Recreational Sports (5)	9.00
95-17	POW & MIA	4.50
95-18	Marilyn Monroe	12.00
95-19	Pink Rose	5.00
95-20	Ferry Boat (3)	4.00
95-21	Cog Railway Car (3)	4.00
95-22	Blue Jay (10)	5.00
95-23	Texas Statehood	4.00
95-24	Great Lake Lighthouses (5)	9.00
95-25	Challenger Shuttle	10.00
95-26	United Nations	2.75
95-27	Civil War (front and back)	14.50
95-28	Peach & Pear	4.50
95-29	Alice Hamilton	2.75
95-30	Carousel Horses	5.25
95-31	Endeavor Shuttle	22.50
95-32	Alice Paul	2.75
95-33	Women's Suffrage	2.75
95-34	Louis Armstrong	4.50
95-35	World War II	6.00
95-36	Milton Hershey	2.75
95-37	Jazz Musicians	7.00
95-38	Fall Garden Flowers (5)	6.00
95-39	Eddie Rickenbacker (airmail)	4.50
95-40	Republic of Palau	3.50
95-41	Holiday Contemporary/ Santa (4)	5.00
95-42	American Comic Strips	15.00
95-43	Naval Academy	4.50
95-44	Tennessee Williams	4.50
95-45	Holiday Children Sledding	4.75
95-46	Holiday Traditional sheet and booklet pane (10)	5.50
95-47	Holiday Midnight Angel	4.75
95-48	Ruth Bendict	3.25
95-49	James K. Polk	7.00
95-50	Antique Automobiles, strip (5)	6.00

1996

96-01	Utah Statehood	3.50
96-02	Garden Flowers	6.00
96-03	Love/Kestrel	16.00
96-04	Postage and Mailing Center (3)	6.00
96-05	Ernest E. Just	5.00
96-06	Woodpecker	3.75
96-07	Smithsonian Institution	3.75
96-08	Year of the Rat	6.00
96-09	Pioneers of Communication	7.00
96-10	Fulbright Scholarships	3.75
96-11	Jacqueline Cochran	3.75
96-12	Mountain	9.00
96-13	Bluebird	3.75
96-14	Marathon	3.75
96-15	Flag over Porch/ Eagle & Shield	4.50
96-16	Cal Farley	3.25
96-17	Classic Olympic Collection	5.00
96-18	Georgia O'Keefe Art	4.75
96-19	Tennessee	3.75
96-20	American Indian Dances	4.75
96-21	Prehistoric Animals	4.75
96-22	Breast Cancer Awareness	4.75
96-23	Flag over Porch/Juke Box/ Butte/Tail Fin Automobile/Mountain	5.50
96-24	James Dean	6.00
96-25	Folk Heroes	5.00
96-26	Olympic/Discus	5.00
96-27	Iowa	5.00
96-28	Blue Jay	5.00
96-29	Rural Free Delivery	4.00
96-30	Riverboats	5.50
96-31	Big Band Leaders	6.00
96-32	Songwriters	6.00
96-33	F. Scott Fitzgerald	4.00
96-34	Endangered Species	15.00
96-35	Computer Technology	4.00
96-36	Holiday, Family Scenes	6.00
96-37	Skaters	6.00
96-38	Hanukkah	5.00
96-39	Madonna and Child	6.00
96-40	Yellow Rose	6.00
96-41	Cycling	6.00

1997

97-01	Year of the Ox	6.00
97-02	Flag Over Porch/ Juke Box/ Mountain	5.50
97-03	Benjamin O. Davis Sr.	6.00
97-04	Statue of Liberty	5.50
97-05	Love Swans	5.50
97-06	Helping Children Learn	5.00
97-07	Merian Botanical Plants	5.50
97-08	Pacific 97 - Stagecoach and Ship	6.00
97-09	Linerless Flag Over Porch/ Juke Box	5.50
97-10	Thornton Wilder	5.00
97-11	Raoul Wallenberg	5.00
97-12	Dinosaurs	12.50
97-13	Pacific '97 - Franklin	10.00
97-14	Pacific '97 - Washington	10.00
97-15	Bugs Bunny	10.00
97-16	The Marshall Plan	5.00
97-17	Humphrey Bogart	6.00
97-18	Classic Aircraft	12.50
97-19	Classic American Dolls	10.00
97-20	Football Coaches	10.00
97-20A	George Halas	8.00
97-20B	Vince Lombardi	8.00
97-20C	Pop Warner	8.00
97-20D	Bear Bryant	8.00
97-21	Yellow Rose	7.00
97-22	"Stars and Stripes Forever"	6.00
97-23	Padre Félix Varela	6.00
97-24	Composers and Conducters	9.00
97-25	Opera Singers	8.00
97-26	Air Force	8.00
97-27	Movie Monsters	10.00
97-28	Supersonic Flight	8.00
97-29	Women in Military	6.00
97-30	Kwanzaa	7.50
97-31	Holiday Traditional, Madonna and Child	7.50
97-32	Holly	7.50
97-33	Mars Pathfinder	12.00

1998

98-01	Year of the Tiger	6.00
98-02	Winter Sports	6.00
98-03	Madam C. J. Walker	6.00
98-03A	Celebrate The Century® 1900s	10.00
98-03B	Celebrate The Century® 1910s	10.00
98-04	"Remember the Maine"	6.00
98-05	Flowering Trees	8.00
98-06	Alexander Calder	8.00
98-07	Henry R. Luce	5.50
98-08	Cinco De Mayo	6.00
98-09	Sylvester & Tweety	6.00
98-09A	Celebrate The Century® 1920s	10.00
98-10	Wisconsin	6.00
98-11	Trans-Mississippi Reissue of 1898	10.00
98-12	Trans-Mississippi (single stamp)	6.00
98-13	Folk Musicians	8.00
98-14	Berlin Airlift	5.50
98-15	Diner/Wetlands coil	5.50
98-16	Spanish Settlement of the Southwest	6.00
98-17	Gospel Singers	7.50
98-18	The Wallaces	5.50
98-19	Stephen Vincent Benét	6.00
98-20	Tropical Birds	8.00
98-21	Breast Cancer Research (semi-postal)	6.00
98-22	Ring-Neck Pheasant	7.00
98-23	Alfred Hitchcock	6.00
98-24	Organ Donations	6.00
98-24A	Red Fox	7.00
98-24B	Green Bicycle coil	6.00
98-25	Bright Eyes	7.50
98-26	Klondike Gold Rush	6.00
98-26A	Celebrate The Century® 1930s	10.00
98-27	American Art	10.00
98-28	Ballet	6.00
98-28A	Diner coil	5.50
98-29	Space Discovery	7.50
98-30	Philanthropy	6.00
98-31	Holiday Traditional	6.00
98-32	Holiday Contemporary	7.50
98-33	Hat Rate Change "H" Series/ Makeup Rate	7.00
98-34	Uncle Sam - Rate Change	6.00
98-35	Hat Rate Change "H" Series	7.50
98-36	Hat Rate Change "H" Series	7.50
98-37	Mary Breckinridge	4.50
98-38	Space Shuttle Landing	9.00
98-39	Shuttle Piggyback	17.50
98-40	Wetlands non-denominated nonprofit coil and Eagle & Shield non-denominated presort coil	6.50

1999

99-01	Year of the Hare	6.00
99-02	Malcolm X	6.00
99-03	33¢ Victorian - Love	7.50
99-04	55¢ Victorian - Love	6.50
99-05	Hospice Care	6.00
99-06	Celebrate The Century® 1940s	10.00
99-07	City Flag	6.50
99-08	Irish Immigration	6.00
99-09	Alfred Lunt and Lynn Fontanne	6.00
99-10	Arctic Animals	7.50
99-10A	Classroom Flag	6.00
99-11	Nature of America Sonoran Desert	10.00
99-11A	Fruit Berries	7.50
99-12	Daffy Duck	8.00
99-13	Ayn Rand	6.50
99-14	Cinco de Mayo	6.00
99-15	Tropical Flowers	7.50
99-16	Niagara Falls	6.50
99-17	John and William Bartram	6.00
99-18	Celebrate The Century® 1950s	10.00
99-19	Prostate Cancer	6.00
99-20	California Gold Rush	6.00
99-20A	Woodpecker Stamp	6.00
99-21	Aquarium Fish	7.50
99-22	Xtreme Sports	7.50
99-23	American Glass	7.50
99-24	Justin Morrill	5.50
99-25	James Cagney	7.50
99-26	Billy Mitchell	7.50
99-27	Rio Grande	6.00
99-28	Pink Coral Rose	7.00
99-29	Honoring Those Who Served	6.00
99-29A	UPU	6.00
99-30	All Aboard!	7.50
99-31	Frederick Law Olmsted	6.00
99-32	Hollywood Composers	7.50
99-33	Celebrate The Century® 1960s	10.00
99-34	Broadway Songwriters	7.50
99-35	Insects and Spiders	10.00
99-36	Hanukkah	6.00
99-37	Official Mail	6.00
99-38	Uncle Sam	6.00
99-39	Nato	6.00
99-40	Holiday Traditional, Madonna & Child	6.00
99-41	Holiday Contemporary, Deer	7.50
99-42	Kwanzaa	6.00
99-43	Celebrate The Century® 1970s	10.00
99-44	Kestrel	6.50

99-45 through 99-49 are unassigned

99-50	Year 2000	6.00

2000

No.	Title	Price
0-01	Year of the Dragon	6.00
0-02	Celebrate The Century® 1980s	10.00
0-03	Grand Canyon	6.00
0-04	Patricia Roberts Harris	6.00
0-05	Fruit Berries	6.00
0-06	U.S. Navy Submarine – *Los Angeles* Class	6.00
0-07	Pacific Coast Rain Forest	10.00
0-08	Louise Nevelson	7.50
0-09	Coral Pink Rose	7.00
0-10	Edwin Powell Hubble	7.50
0-11	American Somoa	6.00
0-12	Library of Congress	6.00
0-13	Wile E. Coyote/ Road Runner	7.50
0-14	Celebrate The Century® 1990s	10.00
0-15	Summer Sports	6.00
0-16	Adoption	6.00
0-17	Youth Team Sports	6.50
0-18	Distinguished Soldiers	8.00
0-19	The Stars and Stripes	10.00
0-20	Legends of Baseball	10.00
0-21	Stampin' The Future™	6.50
0-22	Joseph Stilwell	6.00
0-23	Claude Pepper	6.00
0-24	California Statehood	6.00
0-25	Edward G. Robinson	6.00
0-26	Deep Sea Creatures	7.50
0-27	Thomas Wolfe	6.00
0-28	White House	6.00
0-29	New York Public Library Lion Presort	6.00

2001

No.	Title	Price
1-01	Farm Flag (1 oz.)	6.00
1-02	Statue of Liberty	6.00
1-03	Flowers	7.50
1-04	Statute of Liberty	6.00
1-05	Love Letters (1 oz.)	6.00
1-06	Year of the Snake	6.00
1-07	Roy Wilkins	6.00
1-08	Washington Monument	20.00
1-09	U.S. Capitol	10.00
1-10	American Illustrators (front & back)	10.00
1-11	Farm Flag (1 oz.)	6.00
1-12	Statute of Liberty	7.50
1-13	Flowers	7.50
1-14	Love Letters (1 oz. & 2 oz.)	7.50
1-15	Hattie Caraway (3 oz.)	6.00
1-16	Buffalo (2 oz.)	6.00
1-17	George Washington	6.00
1-18	Art Deco Eagle (2 oz.)	6.00
1-19	Official Mail	6.00
1-20	Apple and Orange	6.00
1-21	Nine-Mile Prairie	6.00
1-22	Farm Flag (1 oz.)	6.00
1-23	Diabetes Awareness	6.00
1-24	The Nobel Prize	6.00
1-25	The Pan- American Inverts (front and back)	10.00
01-26	Mt. McKinley (Int'l PC)	7.50
01-27	Great Plains Prairie (front and back)	10.00
01-28	Peanuts	6.00
01-29	Honoring Veterans	6.00
01-30	Acadia National Park	7.50
01-31	Frida Kahlo	6.00
01-32	Baseball's Legendary Playing Fields (front and back)	12.50
01-33	Atlas Statue	6.00
01-34	Leonard Bernstein	6.00
01-35	Woody Wagon	6.00
01-36	Lucille Ball	6.00
01-37	The Amish Quilts	7.50
01-38	Carnivorous Plants	7.50
01-39	Holiday Celebration–Eid	6.00
01-40	Dr. Enrico Fermi	6.00
01-41	Bison (2 oz.)	6.00
01-42	George Washington	6.00
01-43	Art Deco Eagle (2 oz.)	6.00
01-44	"That's All Folks!"	6.00
01-45	Holiday Traditional: Lorenza Costa– Virgin and Child	6.00
01-46	Holiday Celebration: Santas	7.50
01-47	Holiday Celebration: Thanksgiving	6.00
01-48	James Madison	6.00
01-49	Kwanzaa	6.00
01-50	Hanukkah	6.00
01-51	Farm Flag (1 oz.)	6.00
01-52	Love Letters (2 oz.)	6.00
01-53	United We Stand	7.50

2002

No.	Title	Price
02-01	Winter Sports	7.50
02-02	Mentoring a Child	6.00
02-03	Langston Hughes	6.00
02-04	Happy Birthday	6.00
02-05	Year of the Horse	6.00
02-06	U.S. Military Academy	6.00
02-07	Greetings From America	37.50
02-08	Longleaf Pine Forest	10.00
02-09	American Toleware	6.00
02-10	U.S. Flag	7.50
02-11	Antique Toys	7.50
02-12	Star	6.00
02-13	U.S. Flag	7.50
02-14	George Washington	7.50
02-15	Heroes 2001	6.00
02-16	Masters of American Photography	10.00
02-17	John James Audubon	6.00
02-18	Harry Houdini	6.00
02-19	Eagle Coverlet	6.00
02-20	Antique Toys	7.50
02-21	Edna Ferber	7.50
02-22	Jefferson Memorial	10.00
02-23	Capitol at Dusk	21.00
02-24	Official Mail	6.00
02-25	Andy Warhol	6.00
02-26	Teddy Bears	7.50
02-27	Love (1 oz. & 2 oz.)	7.50
02-28	Ogden Nash	6.00
02-29	Duke Kahanamoku	6.00
02-30	American Bats	7.50
02-31	Women in Journalism	7.50
02-32	Irving Berlin	6.00
02-33	Neuter or Spay	7.50
02-34	Christmas: Gossaert	6.00
02-35	Eid	6.00
02-36	Kwanzaa	6.00
02-37	Hanukkah	6.00
02-38	Cary Grant	6.00
02-39	Sea Coast Nonprofit	6.00
02-40	Hawaiian Missionaries	7.50
02-41	Happy Birthday	6.00
02-42	Greetings From America	37.50
02-43	Holiday Celebrations: Snowmen	7.50

2003

No.	Title	Price
03-01	Thurgood Marshall	6.00
03-02	Year of the Ram	6.00
03-03	Zora Neale Hurston	6.00
03-04	American Clock	6.00
03-05	U.S. Flag	7.50
03-06	The New York Public Library Lion	6.00
03-07	Special Oylmpics	7.50
03-08	American Filmmaking: Behind the Scenes	10.00
03-09	Wisdom	7.50
03-10	Tiffany Lamp	6.00
03-11	Ohio Statehood	6.00
03-12	Pelican Island National Wildlife Refuge	6.00
03-13	Sea Coast	6.00
03-14	Old Glory	7.50
03-15	Cesar E. Chavez	6.00
03-16	Louisiana Purchase	6.00
03-17	First Flight	6.00
03-18	Purple Heart	6.00
03-19	Audrey Hepburn	6.00
03-20	Southeastern Lighthouses	7.50
03-21	American Eagle	6.00
03-22	Arctic Tundra	10.00
03-23	Korean War Veterans Memorial	6.00
03-24	Purple Heart	6.00
03-25	Mary Cassatt	7.50
03-26	Early Football Heroes	7.50
03-27	Antique Toys	7.50
03-28	Roy Acuff	6.00
03-29	District of Columbia	6.00
03-30	Reptiles and Amphibians	7.50
03-31	Stop Family Violence	6.00
03-32	Holiday Music Makers	7.50
03-33	Christmas: Gossaert	6.00
03-34	Snowy Egret	6.00
02-31A	American Eagle	10.00

2004

No.	Title	Price
04-01	Pacific Coral Reef	10.00
04-02	Lunar NewYear: Monkey	6.00
04-03	Love: Candy Hearts	6.00
04-04	Paul Robeson	6.00
04-05	Snowy Egret	6.00
04-06	Theodor "Dr. Seuss" Geisel	6.00
04-07	Garden Bouquet	6.00
04-08	Garden Botanical	6.00
04-09	Chippendale Chair	6.00
04-10	U.S. Air Force Academy	6.00
04-11	Sea Coast PSA Coil	6.00
04-12	Henry Mancini	6.00
04-13	American Choreographers	7.50
04-14	American Eagle	10.00
04-15	Lewis & Clark Prestige Booklet	10.00
04-16	Lewis & Clark Pane	10.00
04-17	Isamu Noguchi	7.50
04-18	National WWII Memorial	6.00
04-19	2004 Olympic Games	6.00
04-20	Sea Coast (5¢) Coil	6.00
04-21	Art of Disney: Friendship	7.50
04-22	American Toleware	6.00
04-23	USS *Constellation*	6.00
04-24	R. Buckminster Fuller	6.00
04-25	Wilma Rudolph	6.00
04-26	James Baldwin	6.00
04-27	Martin Johnson Heade	6.00
04-28	Navajo Jewelry	6.00
04-29	Art of American Indian	10.00
04-30	John Wayne	6.00
04-30a	Atlas Statue (10¢)	6.00
04-31	Sick Cell Awareness	6.00
04-32	Cloudscapes	10.00
04-33	Madonna & Child	6.00
04-34	Hanukkah	6.00
04-35	Kwanzaa	6.00
04-36	Moss Hart	6.00
04-37	Holiday Ornaments	10.00

2005

No.	Title	Price
05-01	Lunar New Year	18.00
05-02	Marian Anderson	6.00
05-03	Ronald Reagan	6.00
05-04	Love Bouquet	6.00
05-05	Northeast Deciduous Forest	10.00
05-06	Spring Flowers	7.50
05-07	Robert Penn Warren	6.00
05-08	Yip Harburg	6.00
05-09	American Scientists	7.50
05-10	Modern American Architecture	10.00
05-11	Henry Fonda	6.00
05-12	Art of Disney: Celebration	7.50
05-13	Advances in Aviation	15.00
05-14	New Mexico Rio Grande Blankets	—
05-15	Presidential Libraries	—
05-16	American Eagle	—
05-17	Sporty Cars	—
05-18	Arthur Ashe	—
05-19	Perfect Union	—
05-20	Child Health	—
05-21	Silver Coffee Pot	—
05-22	Let's Dance/Bailemos	—
05-23	Greta Garbo	—
05-24	Jim Henson & Muppets	—
05-25	Constellations	—
05-26	Holiday Cookies	—
05-27	Distinguished Marines	—
05-28	Lady Liberty Non-Denominated	—
05-29	Navajo Jewelry	—

American Commemorative Panels

The Postal Service offers American Commemorative Panels for each new commemorative stamp and special Holiday and Love stamp issued. The series began in 1972 with the Wildlife Commemorative Panel.

The panels feature mint stamps complemented by fine reproductions of steel line engravings and the stories behind the commemorated subjects.

The identifying numbers used below are based on the Postal Service's numbering system for American Commemorative Panels; therefore, they do not follow the Scott numbering system.

1972

No.	Panel	Price
1	Wildlife	4.75
2	Mail Order	4.75
3	Osteopathic Medicine	6.50
4	Tom Sawyer	5.00
5	Pharmacy	6.00
6	Christmas, Angels	8.00
7	Santa Claus	8.00
8	Stamp Collecting	5.50

1973

No.	Panel	Price
9	Love	6.75
10	Pamphleteers	5.50
11	George Gershwin	6.00
12	Posting a Broadside	5.50
13	Copernicus	5.50
14	Postal Employees	5.25
15	Harry S. Truman	6.50
16	Postrider	6.00
17	Boston Tea Party	15.00
18	Electronics	5.50
19	Robinson Jeffers	4.75
20	Lyndon B. Johnson	6.50
21	Henry O. Tanner	5.50
22	Willa Cather	5.00
23	Drummer	8.25
24	Angus Cattle	5.50
25	Christmas, Madonna	7.75
26	Christmas Tree, Needlepoint	7.75

1974

No.	Panel	Price
27	VFW	5.25
28	Robert Frost	5.25
29	Expo '74	6.00
30	Horse Racing	8.00
31	Skylab	8.50
32	Universal Postal Union	6.00
33	Mineral Heritage	7.00
34	First Kentucky Settlement	5.25
35	Continental Congress	7.00
36	Chautauqua	5.75
37	Kansas Wheat	5.75
38	Energy Conservation	5.00
39	Sleepy Hollow	5.75
40	Retarded Children	5.00
41	Christmas, Currier & Ives	7.50
42	Christmas, Angel Altarpiece	7.50

1975

No.	Panel	Price
43	Benjamin West	5.50
44	Pioneer	8.50
45	Collective Bargaining	4.75
46	Contributors to the Cause	6.25
47	Mariner 10	9.00
48	Lexington & Concord	5.50
49	Paul Laurence Dunbar	6.00
50	D.W. Griffith	5.75
51	Bunker Hill	5.75
52	Military Uniforms	5.00
53	Apollo Soyuz	8.25
54	World Peace Through Law	5.00
55	Women's Year	5.75
56	Postal Service Bicentennial	5.50
57	Banking and Commerce	6.25
58	Early Christmas, Card	7.00
59	Christmas, Madonna	7.00

1976

No.	Panel	Price
60	Spirit of '76	8.00
61	*Interphil* 76	7.00
62	State Flags	15.00
63	Telephone	6.75
64	Commercial Aviation	9.25
65	Chemistry	7.00
66	Benjamin Franklin	7.00
67	Declaration of Independence	7.00
68	12th Winter Olympics	7.50
69	Clara Maass	8.00
70	Adolph S. Ochs	9.00
71	Christmas, Winter Pastime	8.00
72	Christmas, Nativity	8.75

1977

No.	Panel	Price
73	Washington at Princeton	9.00
74	Sound Recording	16.00
75	Pueblo Art	45.00
76	Solo Transatlantic Lindbergh Flight	45.00
77	Colorado	11.00
78	Butterflies	12.00
79	Lafayette	10.50
80	Skilled Hands	10.50
81	Peace Bridge	10.50
82	Battle of Oriskany	10.50
83	Alta, CA, Civil Settlement	11.00
84	Articles of Confederation	15.00
85	Talking Pictures	13.50
86	Surrender at Saratoga	15.00
87	Energy	12.00
88	Christmas, Valley Forge	18.00
89	Christmas, Mailbox	24.00

1978

No.	Panel	Price
90	Carl Sandburg	6.50
91	Captain Cook	12.00
92	Harriet Tubman	9.50
93	Quilts	14.00
94	Dance	10.00
95	French Alliance	10.00
96	Early Cancer Detection	8.25
97	Jimmie Rodgers	11.00
98	Photography	8.00
99	George M. Cohan	12.50
100	Viking Missions	27.50
101	Owls	27.50
102	Trees	26.00
103	Christmas, Madonna	10.50
104	Christmas, Hobby Horse	10.50

1979

No.	Panel	Price
105	Robert F. Kennedy	7.25
106	Martin Luther King, Jr.	7.50
107	International Year of the Child	6.50
108	John Steinbeck	6.00
109	Albert Einstein	7.25
110	Pennsylvania Toleware	6.75
111	Architecture	7.50
112	Endangered Flora	7.00
113	Seeing Eye Dogs	6.25
114	Special Olympics	7.50
115	John Paul Jones	7.00
116	15¢ Olympics	8.50
117	Christmas, Madonna	8.50
118	Christmas, Santa Claus	8.50
119	Will Rogers	7.00
120	Vietnam Veterans	9.50
121	10¢, 31¢ Olympics	8.50

1980

No.	Panel	Price
122	W.C. Fields	7.50
123	Winter Olympics	7.50
124	Benjamin Banneker	7.25
125	Frances Perkins	5.50
126	Emily Bissell	6.00
127	Helen Keller/ Anne Sullivan	5.50
128	Veterans Administration	6.00
129	General Bernardo de Galvez	5.25
130	Coral Reefs	8.00
131	Organized Labor	5.50
132	Edith Wharton	5.25
133	Education	5.50
134	Indian Masks	8.00
135	Architecture	6.75
136	Christmas, Epiphany Window	8.00
137	Christmas, Toys	8.00

1981

No.	Panel	Price
138	Everett Dirksen	6.50
139	Whitney Moore Young	7.00
140	Flowers	7.00
141	Red Cross	7.00
142	Savings & Loans	6.75
143	Space Achievements	11.00
144	Professional Management	5.50
145	Wildlife Habitats	8.00
146	Int'l. Year of the Disabled	5.50
147	Edna St. Vincent Millay	6.00
148	Architecture	6.50
149	Babe Zaharias/ Bobby Jones	20.00
150	James Hoban	5.50
151	Frederic Remington	6.75
152	Battle of Yorktown/ Virginia Capes	5.25
153	Christmas, Madonna	7.00
154	Christmas, Bear and Sleigh	8.00
155	John Hanson	5.50
156	U.S. Desert Plants	8.00

1982

No.	Panel	Price
157	Roosevelt	8.25
158	Love	10.00
159	George Washington	9.50
160	State Birds & Flowers	27.50
161	U.S./Netherlands	10.00
162	Library of Congress	10.00
163	Knoxville World's Fair	8.50
164	Horatio Alger	8.75
165	Aging Together	9.50
166	The Barrymores	10.50
167	Dr. Mary Walker	9.00
168	Peace Garden	9.50
169	America's Libraries	8.00
170	Jackie Robinson	30.00
171	Touro Synagogue	9.50
172	Architecture	10.50
173	Wolf Trap Farm Park	10.00
174	Francis of Assisi	10.50
175	Ponce de Leon	10.50
176	Christmas, Madonna	13.50
177	Christmas, Season's Greetings	13.50
178	Kitten & Puppy	14.00

1983

No.	Panel	Price
179	Science and Industry	5.25
180	Sweden/USA Treaty	5.25
181	Balloons	6.00
182	Civilian Conservation Corps	5.25
183	40¢ Olympics	6.50
184	Joseph Priestley	5.25
185	Voluntarism	5.25
186	Concord/German Immigration	5.25
187	Physical Fitness	5.25
188	Brooklyn Bridge	6.00
189	TVA	5.25
190	Medal of Honor	8.00
191	Scott Joplin	7.25
192	28¢ Olympics	6.50
193	Babe Ruth	22.50
194	Nathaniel Hawthorne	5.25
195	13¢ Olympics	7.50
196	Treaty of Paris	5.50
197	Civil Service	5.50
198	Metropolitan Opera	6.50
199	Inventors	6.75
200	Streetcars	7.50
201	Christmas, Madonna	8.00
202	Christmas, Santa Claus	8.00
203	35¢ Olympics	8.00
204	Martin Luther	7.00

1984

205 Alaska 4.50
206 Winter Olympics 5.00
207 FDIC 4.75
208 Love 4.00
209 Carter G. Woodson 4.75
210 Soil and Water Conservation 4.75
211 Credit Union Act 4.75
212 Orchids 5.50
213 Hawaii 6.25
214 National Archives 4.50
215 20¢ Olympics 5.25
216 Louisiana World Exposition 5.00
217 Health Research 4.75
218 Douglas Fairbanks 4.75
219 Jim Thorpe 8.25
220 John McCormack 4.75
221 St. Lawrence Seaway 6.25
222 Preserving Waterfowl 9.00
223 Roanoke Voyages 4.75
224 Herman Melville 4.75
225 Horace Moses 4.75
226 Smokey Bear 15.00
227 Roberto Clemente 25.00
228 Dogs 6.25
229 Crime Prevention 5.25
230 Family Unity 4.75
231 Christmas, Madonna 6.75
232 Christmas, Santa Claus 6.75
233 Eleanor Roosevelt 8.50
234 Nation of Readers 4.75
235 Hispanic Americans 4.50
236 Vietnam Veterans Memorial 8.25

1985

237 Jerome Kern 5.75
238 Mary McLeod Bethune 5.75
239 Duck Decoys 10.50
240 Winter Special Olympics 5.00
241 Love 5.00
242 Rural Electrification Administration 5.00
243 AMERIPEX '86 6.75
244 Abigail Adams 5.00
245 Frederic Auguste Bartholdi 6.50
246 Korean War Veterans 6.00
247 Social Security Act 5.00
248 World War I Veterans 5.00
249 Horses 9.00
250 Public Education 5.00
251 Youth 8.25
252 Help End Hunger 5.00
253 Christmas, Madonna 7.00
254 Christmas, Poinsettias 7.00

1986

255 Arkansas 5.25
256 Stamp Collecting Booklet 6.75
257 Love 6.00
258 Sojourner Truth 7.50
259 Republic of Texas 7.50
260 Fish Booklet 6.75
261 Public Hospitals 4.75
262 Duke Ellington 7.50
263 U.S. Presidents' Sheet #1 6.25
264 U.S. Presidents' Sheet #2 6.25
265 U.S. Presidents' Sheet #3 6.25
266 U.S. Presidents' Sheet #4 6.25
267 Polar Explorers 6.75
268 Statue of Liberty 7.50
269 Navajo Blankets 8.00
270 T.S. Eliot 6.25
271 Wood-Carved Figurines 6.75
272 Christmas, Madonna 5.75
273 Christmas, Village Scene 5.75

1987

274 Michigan 5.75
275 Pan American Games 3.50
276 Love 5.75
277 Jean Baptiste Pointe Du Sable 5.75
278 Enrico Caruso 5.50
279 Girl Scouts 7.50
280 Special Occasions Booklet 5.50
281 United Way 4.75
282 #1 American Wildlife 6.50
283 #2 American Wildlife 6.50
284 #3 American Wildlife 6.50
285 #4 American Wildlife 6.50
286 #5 American Wildlife 6.50
287 Delaware 5.75
288 Morocco/U.S. Diplomatic Relations 4.75
289 William Faulkner 4.75
290 Lacemaking 5.50
291 Pennsylvania 5.25
292 Constitution Booklet 5.00
293 New Jersey 5.25
294 Signing of the Constitution 5.00
295 Certified Public Accountants 20.00
296 Locomotives Booklet 7.50
297 Christmas, Madonna 6.25
298 Christmas, Ornaments 5.50

1988

299 Georgia 5.25
300 Connecticut 5.25
301 Winter Olympics 6.25
302 Australia 5.75
303 James Weldon Johnson 5.00
304 Cats 6.50
305 Massachusetts 5.25
306 Maryland 5.25
307 Knute Rockne 9.00
308 New Sweden 5.75
309 South Carolina 5.25
310 Francis Ouimet 14.00
311 New Hampshire 5.25
312 Virginia 5.25
313 Love 6.50
314 New York 5.25
315 Summer Olympics 6.25
316 Classic Cars Booklet 7.00
317 Antarctic Explorers 6.25
318 Carousel Animals 7.00
319 Christmas, Madonna, Sleigh 6.50
320 Special Occasions Booklet 6.50

1989

321 Montana 6.25
322 A. Philip Randolph 8.00
323 North Dakota 6.25
324 Washington 6.25
325 Steamboats Booklet 7.50
326 World Stamp Expo '89 5.50
327 Arturo Toscanini 6.25
328 U.S. House of Representatives 6.25
329 U.S. Senate 6.25
330 Executive Branch 6.25
331 South Dakota 6.25
332 Lou Gehrig 25.00
333 French Revolution 6.50
334 Ernest Hemingway 8.75
335 North Carolina 5.25
336 Letter Carriers 6.50
337 Drafting of the Bill of Rights 6.50
338 Prehistoric Animals 13.50
339 Southwest Carved Figure, Southeast Carved Wood Figure America/PUAS 7.25
340 Christmas, Madonna and Child, Sleigh Full of Presents 8.50
341 Classic Mail Transportation 6.50
342 Future Mail Transportation 8.00

1990

343 Idaho 5.50
344 Love 7.25
345 Ida B. Wells 12.50
346 U.S. Supreme Court 6.00
347 Wyoming 6.25
348 Classic Films 13.00
349 Marianne Moore 5.50
350 Lighthouses Booklet 10.00
351 Rhode Island 5.25
352 Olympians 8.50
353 Indian Headdresses Booklet 10.00
354 Micronesia/ Marshall Islands 7.00
355 Grand Canyon Tropical Coastline America/PUAS 7.50
356 Eisenhower 8.25
357 Creatures of the Sea 11.50
358 Christmas, Traditional and Contemporary 8.00

1991

359 Switzerland 8.00
360 Vermont 6.00
361 Savings Bonds 6.25
362 29¢ and 52¢ Love 8.00
363 Saroyan 8.50
364 Fishing Flies Booklet 10.00
365 Cole Porter 6.00
366 Antarctic Treaty 5.50
367 Desert Shield/ Desert Storm 25.00
368 Summer Olympics 7.50
369 Numismatics 6.50
370 Basketball 12.50
371 World War II Miniature Sheet 12.00
372 Comedians Booklet 9.50
373 District of Columbia 7.00
374 Jan Matzeliger 7.50
375 Space Exploration Booklet 11.50
376 America/PUAS 6.50
377 Christmas, Traditional and Contemporary 9.50

1992

378 Winter Olympics 8.50
379 World Columbian Stamp Expo '92 8.75
380 W.E.B. Du Bois 10.00
381 Love 8.75
382 Olympic Baseball 30.00
383 Columbus' First Voyage 10.00
384 Space Adventures 10.00
385 New York Stock Exchange 11.00
386 Alaska Highway 7.50
387 Kentucky Statehood 6.50
388 Summer Olympics 8.00
389 Hummingbirds Booklet 10.00
390 World War II Miniature Sheet 10.00
391 Dorothy Parker 6.50
392 Theodore von Karman 10.00
393 Minerals 9.50
394 Juan Rodriguez Cabrillo 10.50
395 Wild Animals Booklet 10.00
396 Christmas, Traditional and Contemporary 10.50
397 Columbus Souvenir Sheets 40.00
398 Columbus Souvenir Sheets 40.00
399 Columbus Souvenir Sheets 40.00
400 Wildflowers #1 27.50
401 Wildflowers #2 27.50
402 Wildflowers #3 27.50
403 Wildflowers #4 27.50
404 Wildflowers #5 27.50
405 Happy New Year 15.00

1993

406 Elvis 20.00
407 Space Fantasy 11.00
408 Percy Julian 10.00
409 Oregon Trail 9.00
410 World Univ.Games 9.00
411 Grace Kelly 17.50
412 Oklahoma! 8.50
413 Circus 9.00
414 Cherokee Strip 8.50
415 Dean Acheson 10.50
416 Sport Horses 10.00
417 Garden Flowers 8.50
418 World War II 12.00
419 Hank Williams 15.00
420 Rock & Roll/R&B 20.00
421 Joe Louis 27.50
422 Broadway Musicals 11.00
423 National Postal Museum 9.00
424 Deaf Communication 9.00
425 Country Western 17.50
426 Christmas, Traditional 10.00
427 Youth Classics 10.00
428 Mariana Islands 8.75
429 Columbus Landing In Puerto Rico 10.50
430 AIDS Awareness 10.00

	1994	
431	Winter Olympics	15.00
432	Edward R. Murrow	9.00
433	Dr. Allison Davis	10.00
434	Year of the Dog	14.00
435	Love	9.50
436	Buffalo Soldiers	13.00
437	Silent ScreenStars	14.00
438	Garden Flowers	11.00
439	World Cup Soccer	12.00
440	World War II	15.00
441	Norman Rockwell	19.00
442	Moon Landing	16.00
443	Locomotives	12.00
444	George Meany	8.00
445	Popular Singers	12.50
446	James Thurber	8.00
447	Jazz/Blues	12.50
448	Wonders of the Sea	11.00
449	Birds (Cranes)	11.00
450	Christmas, Madonna	8.00
451	Christmas, Stocking	8.00
452	Year of the Boar	13.00

	1995	
453	Florida	10.00
454	Bessie Coleman	14.00
455	Kids Care!	10.00
456	Richard Nixon	15.00
457	Love	14.00
458	Recreational Sports	14.00
459	POW & MIA	12.50
460	Marilyn Monroe	22.50
461	Texas	12.50
462	Great Lakes Lighthouses	14.00
463	United Nations	11.00
464	Carousel Horses	14.00
465	Jazz Musicians	17.50
466	Women's Suffrage	11.00
467	Louis Armstrong	16.00
468	World War II	15.00
469	Fall Garden Flowers	11.00
470	Republic of Palau	11.00
471	Christmas, Contemporary	14.00
472	Naval Academy	14.00
473	Tennessee Williams	12.50
474	Christmas, Traditional	14.00
475	James K. Polk	10.00
476	Antique Automobiles	17.50

	1996	
477	Utah	10.00
478	Garden Flowers	10.00
479	Ernest E. Just	12.50
480	Smithsonian Institution	10.00
481	Year of the Rat	17.50
482	Pioneers of Communication	14.00
483	Fulbright Scholarships	10.00
484	Summer Olympics	30.00
485	Marathon	13.50
486	Georgia O'Keefe	10.00
487	Tennessee	10.00
488	James Dean	17.50
489	Prehistoric Animals	17.50
490	Breast Cancer Awareness	11.00
491	American Indian Dances	17.50
492	Folk Heroes	17.50
493	Centennial Games (Discus)	11.50
494	Iowa Statehood	10.00
495	Rural Free Delivery	10.00
496	Riverboats	17.50
497	Big Band Leaders	17.50
498	Songwriters	17.50
499	Endangered Species	27.50
500	Family Scenes (4 designs)	14.00
501	Hanukkah	15.00
502	Madonna and Child	13.50
503	Cycling	15.00
503A	F. Scott Fitzgerald	19.00
503B	Computer Technology	19.00

	1997	
504	Year of the Ox	19.00
505	Benjamin O. Davis	14.00
506	Love	12.00
507	Helping Children Learn	10.50
508	Pacific '97 Triangle Stamps	14.00
509	Thornton Wilder	12.00
510	Raoul Wallenberg	12.00
511	Dinosaurs	20.00
512	Bugs Bunny	16.00
513	Pacific '97 Franklin	40.00
514	Pacific '97 Washington	40.00
515	The Marshall Plan	10.00
516	Classic Aircraft	27.50
517	Football Coaches	17.50
518	Dolls	25.00
519	Humphrey Bogart	14.00
520	Stars and Stripes	13.00
521	Opera Singers	14.00
522	Composers and Conductors	14.00
523	Padre Varela	13.00
524	Air Force	13.50
525	Movie Monsters	16.00
526	Supersonic Flight	16.00
527	Women in the Military	13.00
528	Holiday Kwanzaa	14.00
529	Holiday, Traditional	18.00
530	Holiday, Holly	18.00

	1998	
531	Year of the Tiger	13.00
532	Winter Sports	13.00
533	Madam C.J. Walker	13.00
533A	Celebrate The Century® 1900s	20.00
533B	Celebrate The Century® 1910s	20.00
534	Remember The Maine	13.00
535	Flowering Trees	16.00
536	Alexander Calder	16.00
537	Cinco de Mayo	13.00
538	Sylvester & Tweety	17.00
538A	Celebrate The Century® 1920s	20.00
539	Wisconsin	13.00
540	Trans-Mississippi	20.00
541	Folk Singers	14.00
542	Berlin Airlift	13.00
543	Spanish Settlement of the Southwest	14.00
544	Gospel Singers	13.00
545	Stephen Vincent Benét	13.00
546	Tropical Birds	13.00
546A	Breast Cancer Research	17.50
547	Alfred Hitchcock	13.00
548	Organ Donations	13.00
549	Bright Eyes	13.50
550	Klondike Gold Rush	13.00
551	American Art	20.00
551A	Celebrate The Century® 1930s	20.00
552	Ballet	13.00
553	Space Discovery	13.50
554	Philanthropy	13.00
555	Holiday, Traditional	18.00
556	Holiday, Contemporary	13.00

	1999	
557	Year of the Hare	15.00
558	Malcolm X	15.00
559	33¢ Victorian - Love	20.00
560	55¢ Victorian - Love	15.00
561	Hospice Care	15.00
562	Celebrate The Century® 1940s	20.00
563	Irish Immigration	15.00
564	Alfred Lunt and Lynn Fontanne	15.00
565	Arctic Animals	15.00
566	Nature of America Sonoran Desert	22.50
567	Daffy Duck	22.50
568	Ayn Rand	15.00
569	Cinco de Mayo	15.00
570	John and William Bartram	15.00
571	Celebrate The Century® 1950s	20.00
572	Prostate Cancer	15.00
573	California Gold Rush	15.00
574	Aquarium Fish	15.00
575	Xtreme Sports	15.00
576	American Glass	15.00
577	James Cagney	15.00
578	Honoring Those Who Served	15.00
579	All Aboard!	16.00
580	Frederick Law Olmsted	15.00
581	Hollywood Composers	16.00
582	Celebrate The Century® 1960s	20.00
583	Broadway Songwriters	16.00
584	Insects and Spiders	22.50
585	Hanukkah	15.00
586	Nato	15.00
587	Holiday Traditional, Bartolomeo Vivarini	15.00
588	Holiday Celebrations, Deer	15.00
589	Kwanzaa	15.00
590	Celebrate The Century® 1970s	20.00
591	Year 2000	16.00

	2000	
592	Year of the Dragon	15.00
593	Celebrate The Century® 1980s	20.00
594	Patricia Roberts Harris	15.00
595	U.S. Navy Submarines – *Los Angeles* Class	10.00
596	Pacific Coast Rain Forest	25.00
597	Louise Nevelson	10.00
598	Edwin Powell Hubble	10.00
599	American Samoa	10.00
600	Library of Congress	10.00
601	Wile E. Coyote/ Road Runner	10.00
602	Celebrate The Century® 1990s	20.00
603	Summer Sports	10.00
604	Adoption	10.00
605	Youth Team Sports	10.00
606	Distinguished Soldiers	10.00
607	The Stars and Stripes	25.00
608	Legends of Baseball	25.00
609	Stampin' The Future™	10.00
610	Edward G. Robinson	10.00
611	California Statehood	10.00
612	Deep Sea Creatures	10.00
613	Thomas Wolfe	10.00
614	The White House	10.00

	2001	
615	Love Letters	12.00
616	Lunar New Year - Year of the Snake	12.00
617	Roy Wilkins	12.00
618	American Illustrators	30.00
619	Love Letters (1 oz)	12.00
620	Love Letters (2 oz)	12.00
621	Nine-Mile Prairie	12.00
622	Diabetes Awareness	16.00
623	The Nobel Prize	12.00
624	Mt. McKinley	12.00
625	The Pan-American Inverts	30.00
626	Great Plains Prairie	30.00
627	Peanuts	12.00
628	Honoring Veterans	12.00
629	Frida Kahlo	12.00
630	Baseball's Legendary Playing Fields	30.00
631	Leonard Bernstein	12.00
632	Lucille Ball	12.00
633	The Amish Quilts	12.00
634	Carnivorous Plants	12.00
635	Holiday Celebrations: Eid	12.00
636	Dr. Enrico Fermi	12.00
637	That's All Folks!	12.00
638	Holiday Celebrations: Lorenzo Costa's Virgin and Child	12.00
639	Holiday Celebrations: Santas	12.00
640	James Madison	12.00
641	Holiday Celebrations: Thanksgiving	12.00
642	Kwanzas	12.00
643	Hanukkah	12.00
644	Love Letters	12.00

2002		
645	Winter Sports	12.00
646	Mentoring a Child	12.00
647	Langston Hughes	12.00
648	Happy Birthday	12.00
649	Year of the Horse	12.00
650	U.S. Military Academy	12.00
651	Greetings From America	40.00
652	Longleaf Pine Forest	30.00
653	Heroes 2001	12.00
654	Masters of American Photography	30.00
655	John James Audubon	12.00
656	Harry Houdini	12.00
657	Andy Warhol	12.00
658	Teddy Bears	12.00
659	Love (1 oz.)	12.00
660	Love (2 oz.)	12.00
661	Ogden Nash	12.00
662	Duke Kahanamoku	12.00
663	American Bats	12.00
664	Women in Journalism	12.00
665	Irving Berlin	12.00
666	Neuter or Spay	
667	Christmas: Gossaert	12.00
668	Hanukkah	12.00
669	Eid	12.00
670	Kwanzaa	12.00
671	Cary Grant	12.00
672	Hawaiian Missionaries	12.00
673	Happy Birthday	12.00
674	Greetings From America	42.50
675	Holiday Celebrations: Snowmen	12.00

2003		
676	Thurgood Marshall	12.00
677	Year of the Ram	12.00
678	Zora Neale Hurston	12.00
679	Special Oylmpics	12.00
680	American Filmmaking: Behind the Scenes	30.00
681	Ohio Statehood	12.00
682	Pelican Island National Wildlife Refuge	12.00
683	Old Glory	12.00
684	Cesar E. Chavez	12.00
685	Louisiana Purchase	12.00
686	First Flight	12.00
687	Audrey Hepburn	12.00
688	Southeastern Lighthouses	12.00
689	Arctic Tundra	30.00
690	Korean War Veterans Memorial	12.00
691	Mary Cassatt	12.00
692	Early Football Heroes	12.00
693	Roy Acuff	12.00
694	District of Columbia	12.00
695	Reptiles and Amphibians	12.00
696	Stop Family Violence	12.00
697	Holiday Celebrations: Music Makers	12.00
698	Holiday Celebrations: Gossaert	12.00
699	Year of the Monkey	12.00
700	Paul Robeson	12.00
701	Candy Hearts	12.00
702	Ted "Dr. Seuss" Giesel	12.00
703	Weddings (1oz.)	12.00
704	Weddings (2oz.)	12.00
705	US Air Force Academy	12.00

2004		
699	Pacific Coral Reef	30.00
700	Lunar New Year: Year of the Monkey	12.00
701	Love: Candy Hearts	12.00
702	Paul Robeson	12.00
703	Ted "Dr. Seuss" Geisel	12.00
704	Garden Bouquet: Weddings	12.00
705	Garden Botanical: Weddings	12.00
706	US Air Force Academy	12.00
707	Henry Mancini	12.00
708	American Choreographers	12.00
709	Lewis & Clark Prestige Booklet	12.00
710	Lewis & Clark Pane	12.00
711	Isamu Noguchi	12.00
712	National World War II Memorial	12.00
713	2004 Olympic Games	12.00
714	Art of Disney: Friendship	12.00
715	USS *Constellation*	12.00
716	R. Buckminster Fuller	12.00
717	James Baldwin	12.00
718	Martin Johnson Heade	12.00
719	Art of the American Indian	30.00
720	John Wayne	12.00
721	Sickle Cell Disease	12.00
722	Cloudscapes	30.00
723	Madonna & Child	12.00
724	Hanukkah	12.00
725	Kwanzaa	12.00
726	Moss Hart	12.00
727	Holiday Celebrations: Holiday Ornaments	12.00

2005		
728	Lunar New Year	30.00
729	Marian Anderson	12.00
730	Ronald Reagan	12.00
731	Love: Bouquet	12.00
732	Northeast Deciduous Forest	30.00
733	Spring Flowers	12.00
734	Robert Penn Warren	12.00
735	Yip Harburg	12.00
736	American Scientists	12.00
737	Modern American Architecture	30.00
738	Henry Fonda	12.00
739	Art of Disney: Celebration	12.00
740	American Advances in Aviation	30.00
741	New Mexico Rio Grande Blankets	12.00
742	Presidential Libraries	12.00
743	American on the Move: 50s Sporty Cars	12.00
744	Arthur Ashe	12.00
745	To Form a More Perfect Union	30.00
746	Child Health	12.00
747	Let's Dance/Bailemos	12.00
748	Greta Garbo	12.00
749	Jim Henson & Muppets	30.00
750	Constellations	12.00
751	Holiday Celebrations: Holiday Cookies	12.00
752	Distinguished Marines	12.00

AMERICAN ★ COMMEMORATIVE ★ COLLECTIBLES

Standing Order Program

Get your collection tailored to your own specific taste. Mix and match Stamps, First Day Covers, Stationery, Uncut Press Sheets all in whatever quantities you'd like.

Item #26122. Deposit varies based on selections and quantities orderd.

For information call **1 800 STAMP-24**

Organizations, Publications and Resources

Please enclose a stamped, self-addressed envelope when writing to these organizations.

American Air Mail Society
Rudy Roy
PO Box 5367
Virginia Beach, VA 23471-0367
(p) 757/499-5234
AAMSinformation@aol.com
http://www.americanairmailsociety.org

Specializes in all phases of aerophilately. Membership services include Advance Bulletin Service, Auction Service, free want ads, Sales Department, monthly journal, discounts on Society publications, translation service.

American First Day Cover Society
PO Box 16277
Tucson, AZ 85732-6277
(p) 520/321-0880
afdcs@aol.com
http://www.afdcs.org
Contact Doug Kelsey, Executive Director

A full-service, not-for-profit, noncommercial society devoted exclusively to First Day Covers and First Day Cover collecting. Publishes 90-page magazine, First Day, eight times a year. Offers information on 300 current cachet producers, expertizing, foreign covers, translation service, color slide programs and archives covering First Day Covers.

American Ceremony Program Society
John E. Peterson
ACPS Secretary/Treasurer
6987 Coleshill Drive
San Diego, CA 92119-1953
jkpete@pacbell.net
www.webacps.org

The American Ceremony Program Society is a place to learn about First Day and Supplemental (Second Day or later) stamp Ceremonies and Ceremony Programs. The Society publishes a journal, The Ceremonial, can be sent to members in a hard copy format at $2.50 per issue. The Society dues are $7 a year.

American Philatelic Society
Peter Mastrangelo
Department PG
100 Match Factory Place
Bellefonte, PA 16823-1367
(p) 814/933-3803
(f) 814/933-6128
apsinfo@stamps.org
http://www.stamps.org

America's national stamp society. Membership benefits include various publications, services, and more. Sponsors national stamp exhibitions annually in partnership with the ASDA and USPS. 45,000+ members worldwide.

American Society for Philatelic Pages and Panels
Gerald Blankenship
PO Box 475
Crosby, TX 77532-0475
(p) 281/324-2709
genericmembership@asppp.org
www.asppp.org

The only society with a focus on commemorative cancellations (formerly souvenir pages) and commemorative panels. Free ads, member auction, quarterly publication sent to all members with reports on new issues, varieties, errors, oddities and discoveries. Active web site.

American Stamp Dealers Association
Joseph B. Savarese
3 School St., Suite 205
Glen Cove, NY 11542-2548
(p) 516/759-7000
(f) 516/759-7014
asda@erols.com
http://www.asdaonline.com

Association of dealers engaged in every facet of philately, with 6 regional chapters nationwide. Sponsors national and local shows. Will send you a complete listing of dealers in your area or collecting specialty. A #10 SASE must accompany your request.

American Topical Association
Ray Cartier
Executive Director
PO Box 57
Arlington, TX 76004-0057
(p) 817/274-1181
(f) 817/274-1184
americantopical@msn.com
www.americantopicalassn.org

A service organization concentrating on the specialty of topical stamp collecting. Offers handbooks and checklists on specific topics; exhibition awards; Topical Time, a bimonthly publication dealing with topical interest areas; a slide loan service, and information, translation and sales services.

Ebony Society of Philatelic Events and Reflections
Manuel Gilyard, President
PO Box 1757
Lincolnton Station
New York, NY 10037-1757
(p) 212-928-5165
(f) 212-928-1477
gilyardmani@aol.com
http://www.esperstamps.org

Mailer's Postmark Permit Club
Charles F. Myers
Central Office
PO Box 3
Portland, TN 37148-0003
(p) 615/325-9478
(f) 615/451-7930
cfmyers@mindspring.com
www.mppclub.org

Publishes bimonthly newsletter, Permit Patter, which covers all aspects of mailer's postmark permits. Also available, an 8-page step by step brochure "How to obtain a Mailer's Postmark Permit... a basic guide."

Plate Number Coil Collectors Club
Ronald E. Maifeld
President
PO Box 54622
Cincinnati, OH 45254-0622
Rmaifeld@fuse.net
www.pnc3.org

The Plate Number Coil Collectors Club (PNC^3) is an organization that studies the plate numbers and plate varieties of United States coil stamps issued since 1981. The PNC^3 publishes a monthly newsletter, Coil Line. The website includes a membership application and discusses plate number coils and PNC^3 at length.

Postal History Society
Kalman V. Illyefalvi
8207 Daren Court
Pikesville, MD 21208-2211
(p) 410/653-0665
kalphyl@juno.com

Devoted to the study of various aspects of the development of the mails and local, national and international postal systems; UPU treaties; and means of transporting mail.

The Souvenir Card Collectors Society, Inc.
Dana M. Marr
PO Box 4155
Tulsa, OK 74159-0155
(p) 918/664-6724
DMARR5569@aol.com

Provides member auctions, a quarterly journal and access to limited-edition souvenir cards.

Spring-Ford Philatelic Society
First United Church of Christ
145 Chestnut St.
Spring City, PA 19475-1804
(p) 610/970-5408
DickRoslie@aol.com

Meeting the last Thursday of the month at 7:00 p.m.

Compilation of U.S. Souvenir Cards
United Postal Stationery Society
UPSS Central Office
Cora Collins
Executive Director
PO Box 3982
Chester, VA 23831-8473
upss@comcast.net
www.upss.org

Postal stationary is made up of the post office-issued postal cards, envelopes, letter sheets and other postal products having the stamp already printed. The UPSS is the largest society devoted to the collecting and study of postal stationery of the world with members throughout the U.S. and many foreign countries.

19th Century Envelopes Catalog

20th Century Envelopes Catalog

U.S. Postal Card Catalog

U.S. Commemorative Stamped Envelopes, 1867-1965

U.S. Envelope Essays and Proofs
Canal Zone Postal Stationery

Universal Ship Cancellation Society
Steve Shay
747 Shard Court
Fremont, CA 94539-7419
e-mail: Shaymur@flash.net
http://www.uscs.org

Specializes in naval ship postmarks and cachets.

U.S. Postal Service Stamp Services
1735 N. Lynn St, 5th Floor, Room 5018
Arlington, VA 22209-6432

U.S. Stamp Society
Executive Secretary
PO Box 6634
Katy, TX 77491-6634
http://www.usstamps.org

An association of collectors to promote the study of all postage and revenue stamps and stamped paper of the United States and U.S.-administered areas produced by the Bureau of Engraving and Printing and other contract printers.

Durland Plate Number Catalog

Expertisers

American Philatelic Expertizing Service (APEX)
Mercer Bristow
Director of Expertizing
100 Match Factory Place
Bellefonte, PA 16823-1367
(p) 814/933-3803
(f) 814/933-6128
Ambristo@stamps.org

Krystal Harter
Expertizing Coordinator
Krharter@stamps.org
(p) 814/933-3803
(f) 814/933-6128
http://www.stamps.org

A service of the American Philatelic Society since 1903, APEX utilizes the outstanding reference collections at APS headquarters in conjunction with the nation's best philatelic scholars to pass judgement on the identification, authenticity and condition of stamps from around the world.

Philatelic Foundation
Attention: Chairman
George J. Kramer
70 W 40th Street 15th Floor
New York, NY 10018-2615
(p) 212/221-6555
(f) 212/221-6208
www.philatelicfoundation.org

A nonprofit organization known for its excellent expertization service. The Foundation's broad resources, including extensive reference collections, 5,000-volume library and Expert Committee, provide collectors with comprehensive consumer protection. Book series include expertizing case histories in Opinions, *Foundation seminar subjects in "textbooks" and specialized U.S. subjects in monographs.*

Professional Stamp Experts
PO Box 6170
Newport Beach, CA 92658-6170
(p) 877/782-6788
http://www.psestamp.com
pse@collectors.com

Organization specializing in identification, expertization and grading of U.S. Postage Stamps, Covers, Revenues etc.... PSE issues a Certificate of Authenticity accepted by all auction firms, dealers and collectors. PSE publishes a Guide to the Grading of U.S. Stamps and The Stamp Market Quarterly Price Guide. Either is free upon request.

Periodicals

The following publications will send you a free copy of their magazine or newspaper upon request.

Global Stamp News
PO Box 97
Sidney, OH 45365-0097
(p) 937/492-3183
jbrandewie@woh.rr.com

America's largest-circulation monthly stamp magazine featuring U.S. and foreign issues.

Linn's Stamp News
PO Box 29
Sidney, OH 45365-0029
(p) 937/498-0801
(f) 937/498-0876
(f) 888/340-8388 (toll free)
linns@linns.com
www.linns.com

Linn's Stamp News, the world's largest weekly stamp newspaper, contains breaking news stories of major importance to stamp collectors, features on a variety of stamp-collecting topics, the monthly U.S. Stamp Market Index, Stamp Market Tips and much more. A sample copy of the weekly news-paper is available upon request.

Linn's U.S. Stamp Yearbook
(p) 937/498-0802
(f) 800/572-6885 (US only)
(f) 937/498-0807 (outside US)
linns@linns.com
www.linns.com

Linn's World Stamp Almanac

Stamp Collecting Made Easy

Mekeel's & Stamps Magazine-fa
John Dunn
42 Sentry Way
Merrimack, NH 03054-4407
stampnews@aol.com
http://www.stampnewsnow.com

Weekly magazine for collectors of U.S. & worldwide stamps & covers.

U.S. Stamp News-fb
42 Sentry Way
Merrimack, NH 03054-4407
stampnews@aol.com
http://www.stampnews.com

Monthly magazine for all collectors of U.S. stamps, covers and postal history.

Stamp Fulfillment Services
U.S. Postal Service
8300 NE Underground Dr
Pillar 210
Kansas City, MO 64144-0001
(p) 1-800-STAMP-24

Scott Specialized Catalogue of United States Stamps and Covers
PO Box 828
Sidney, OH 45365-0828
(p) 937/498-0831
(p) 800/572-6885
(f) 937/498-0807
cuserv@amosadvantage.com
www.amosadvantage.com

Scott Standard Postage Stamp Catalogue

Scott Classic Specialized Catalogue: Stamps and Covers of the World including U.S., 1840-1940 (British Commonwealth to 1952)

Scott Stamp Monthly

Museums, Libraries and Displays

Please contact the institutions before visiting to confirm hours and any entry fees.

American Philatelic Research Library
100 Match Factory Place
Bellefonte, PA 16823-1367
(p) 814/933-3803
(f) 814/933-6128
aprl@stamps.org
www.stamplibrary.org

The largest philatelic library in the US, the APRL receives more than 400 periodicals, and houses extensive collections of philatelic literature.

The Collectors Club
Irene Bromberg
Executive Secretary
22 E. 35th Street
New York, NY 10016-3806
(p) 212/683-0559
(f) 212/481-1269
collectorsclub@nac.net
http://www.collectorsclub.org

Bimonthly journal, publication of various reference works, one of the most extensive reference libraries in the world, reading and study rooms. Regular meetings on the first and third Wednesdays of each month at 6:30 p.m., except July and August.

National Postal Museum
Office of the Director
Smithsonian National Postal Museum
2 Massachusetts Ave, NE
Washington, D.C. 20013-0570
(p) 202/633-5502
burmeisterc2si.edu

Located in the Old City Post Office building at 2 Massachusetts Avenue, NE National Postal Museum houses more than 16 million items for exhibition and study purposes. Collections research may be conducted separately or jointly with library materials. Call the museum and its library (202/633-9370) separately to schedule an appointment.

The Postal History Foundation
Betsy Towle
PO Box 40725
Tucson, AZ 85717-0725
(p) 520/623-6652
(f) 520/623-6652
www.postalhistoryfoundation.org
Hours: M-F 8 a.m.-3 p.m.

The Postal History Foundation is located in Tucson, Arizona. Established in 1960, the Foundation has a world class collection of postal history information and artifacts and is a pioneer in its provision of youth philatelic education programs. It offers museum tours, research library, USPS contract post office, philatelic sales, archives and stamp collections.

San Diego County Philatelic Library
Al Kish, Library Manager
7403C Princess View Drive
San Diego, CA 92120-1345
(p) 619/229-8813
Hours: Mon. 1 p.m.–4 p.m. and 6:30 p.m.–9 p.m., Tues. 5 p.m.–8 p.m., Wed. 1 p.m.–9 p.m., Thurs. 6 p.m.– 9 p.m., Sat. 9 p.m.–3 p.m. Closed Fri. and Sun.

Spellman Museum of Stamps and Postal History
Executive Director
235 Wellesley Street
Weston, MA 02493-1538
(p) 781/768-8367
(f) 781/768-7332
info@spellman.org
www.spellman.org

America's first fully accredited museum devoted to the display, collection and preservation of stamps and postal history. Exhibitions feature rarities, U.S., and worldwide collections. Philatelic library and family activity center open with admission. School and scout programs by appointment. Museum store and post office carries gifts, collecting supplies, and stamps.

Western Philatelic Library
PO Box 2219
Sunnyvale, CA 94087-2219
(p) 408/733-0336
stulev@ix.netcom.com
http://www.pbbooks.com/wpl.htm
http://www.fwpl.org

Friends of the Western Philatelic Library

Wineburgh Philatelic Research Library
Erik D. Carlson, Ph.D.
McDermott Library
The University of Texas at Dallas
PO Box 830643
Mailstation: MC33
Richardson, TX 75083-0643
(p) 972/883-2570
http://www.utdallas.edu/library/special/wprl.html
Hours: M-Th 9 a.m.–6 p.m.;
Fri 9 a.m.-5 p.m.

Exchange Service

Stamp Master
Charles Bergeron
PO Box 17
Putnam Hall, FL 32185-0017
Cbergero@bellsouth.net

An "electronic connection" for philatelists via modem and computer to display/review members' stamp inventories for trading purposes, etc.

Literature

ArtCraft First Day Cover Price List
Washington Press
2 Vreeland Road
Florham Park, NJ 07932-1501
(p) 877/966-0001 (toll free)
info@washpress.com
http://www.washpress.com

Includes Presidential Inaugural covers.

Legends of the West
Washington Press

How some collectors struck it rich!

The Inverted Jenny

A Dream Come True

Operation HUSH – HUSH

How the Project Mercury Stamp was Planned and Issued

The Hammarskjold Invert

Tells the story of the Dag Hammarskjold error/invert

The U.S. Transportation Coils

How some collectors struck it rich!

The White Ace Album Format Guide

A Listing of Stamps Required for The 2003 United States White Ace Album Supplements

ANY ABOVE FREE for #10 SASE

Brookman's 1st Edition Black Heritage First Day Cachet Cover Catalog
Arlene Dunn
Brookman/Barrett & Worthen
10 Chestnut Drive
Bedford, NH 03110-5566
(p) 603/472-5575
(f) 603/472-8795

Illustrated 176-page perfect bound book.

Brookman's 2nd Edition Price Guide for Disney Stamps

Illustrated 256-page perfect bound book.

2005 Brookman Price Guide of U.S., and Canada Stamps and Postal Collectibles

Illustrated 384-page perfect and spiral bound catalog.

Postmark Advisory
Paul Brenner
General Image, Inc.
PO Box 335
Maplewood, NJ 07040-0335
Postmark1@earthlink.net
There is also a web site announcing these postmarks. The address is:
http://home.earthlink.net/~postmark1
This site is updated twice a month.
(How-to-do-it is excellent for beginners)

A weekly newsletter is available which provides descriptive information on U.S. pictorial postmarks that you can send away for. A free sample newsletter is available if you send a SASE and ask for a copy. If you are interested in postmarks, you might like to visit the web site.

Fleetwood's Standard First Day Cover Catalog
Fleetwood
Unicover Corporation
1 Unicover Center
Cheyenne, WY 82008-0001
(p) 307/771-3238
(p) 800/443-3232 (toll free)
(f) 307/771-3134
http://www.unicover.com

Precancel Stamp Society Catalogs
Dick Laetsch
3 Shady Creek Lane
Scarborough, ME 04070-8480
(p) 207/883-2505
precancel@aol.com
www.precanceledstamps.com

Precancel approvals available.

Stamp Collecting Made Easy
Amos Hobby Publishing Co.
PO Box 828
Sidney, OH 045365-0097
(p) 937/498-0807
(p) 800/572-6885
(f) 937/498-0807

An illustrated, easy-to-read, 96-page booklet for beginning collectors.

The United States Postal Service: An American History, Pub. 100
Historian
United States Postal Service
475 L'Enfant Plaza SW
Washington, DC 20260-0012
(p) 202/268-2507
mausman@usps.gov
www.usps.com

Tells the history of the U.S. Postal Service from 1775 to the present. Includes bibliography, First-Class rate history. One free copy.

Sources of Historical Information on Post Offices, Postal Employees, Mail Routes and Mail Contractors, Pub. 119

Lists all known federal sources of information on topics covered in the title. Includes a bibliography of books on state postal histories. One free copy.

www.usps.com/postmasterfinder

Provides complete lists of Postmasters for more than 14,000 Post Offices and partial lists for all current Post Offices. Can be researched by Postmaster name, Post Office, state and establishment and discontinuance dates. Post Offices are researched upon request.

International

AUSTRALIA
Max Stern
234 Flinders Street
Box 997 H
GPO Melbourne 3001

CANADA
Canada Post
2701 Riverside Dr.
Suite N0420
Ottawa ON K1A 0B1

CHINA
China National Philatelic Corporation
14, Taipinghu Dongli, Xicheng District
Beijing, 100031

DENMARK
Nordfrim
DK 5450 Otterup

GERMANY
Georg Roll Stamps LTD
Hafenstrasse 8
D-26931 Elsfleth

Hermann Sieger GMBH
Venusberg 32-34
D73545 Lorch Wurttemberg

HONG KONG
Hongkong Post
1706-7, ING Tower
308-320 Des Voeux Road Central
Sheung Wan

ITALY
Alberto Bolaffi
Via Cavour 17
10123 Torino

JAPAN
Japan Philatelic Agency
PO Box 96 Toshima
Tokyo 170-8668

NETHERLANDS
TPG Post
Prinses Beatrixlann 23
P O Box 30250
2500 GC The Hague

SPAIN
Philagroup, S. L.
Manuel Tovar, 1, 4 izda
28034 Madrid

THAILAND
International House of Stamps
98/2 Soi Tonson
Langsuan Rd
Lumpinee, Pathumwan
Bangkok 10330

UNITED KINGDOM
Harry Allen
PO Box 5
Watford Herts WD2 5SW

We always welcome orders from international customers at http://www.usps.com/shop

Philatelic Centers

In addition to the more than 20,000 postal facilities authorized to sell philatelic products, the Postal Service also maintains Philatelic Centers located in major population centers. These Philatelic Centers have been established to serve stamp collectors and make it convenient for them to acquire an extensive range of current postage stamps, postal stationery and philatelic products issued by the Postal Service.

For questions, location and hours of operation about a Philatelic Center near you, please call 800-275-8777 or visit us online at www.usps.com.

U.S. Postal Service Listing of Stamp Series

Listed with Scott Numbers

First Pictorial Series 1869

113 2¢ Post Horse and Rider
114 3¢ Locomotive
116 10¢ Shield and Eagle
117 12¢ S.S. *Adriatic*
118 15¢ Landing of Columbus
120 24¢ Declaration of Independence
121 30¢ Shield, Eagle, and Flags

Columbia Exposition Series 1893

230 1¢ Columbus in Sight of Land
231 2¢ Landing of Columbus
232 3¢ *Santa Maria,* Flagship
233 4¢ Fleet of Columbus
234 5¢ Columbus Soliciting Aid from Queen Isabella
235 6¢ Columbus Welcomed at Barcelona
236 8¢ Columbus Restored to Favor
237 10¢ Columbus Presenting Natives
238 15¢ Columbus Announcing His Discovery
239 30¢ Columbus at La Rábida
240 50¢ Recall of Columbus
241 $1 Queen Isabella Pledging Her Jewels
242 $2 Columbus in Chains
243 $3 Columbus Describing His Third Voyage
244 $4 Queen Isabella and Columbus
245 $5 Portrait of Columbus

America Series 1922-1925

551 1/2¢ Nathan Hale
552 1¢ Franklin
553 1-1/2¢ Warren G. Harding
554 2¢ Washington
555 3¢ Lincoln
556 4¢ Martha Washington
557 5¢ Theodore Roosevelt
558 6¢ Garfield
559 7¢ McKinley
560 8¢ Grant
561 9¢ Jefferson
562 10¢ Monroe
563 11¢ Rutherford B. Hayes
564 12¢ Grover Cleveland
565 14¢ American Indian
566 15¢ Statue of Liberty
567 20¢ Golden Gate
568 25¢ Niagara Falls
569 30¢ Buffalo
570 50¢ Arlington Amphitheater
571 $1 Lincoln Memorial
572 $2 U.S. Capitol
573 $5 Head of *Freedom*, Capitol Dome

American Revolution Sesquicentennial Series 1925-1933

617 1¢ Washington at Cambridge
618 2¢ "The Birth of Liberty"
619 5¢ "The Minute Man"
627 2¢ Independence Sesquicentennial Exposition
629 2¢ Alexander Hamilton's Battery
630 2¢ Battle of White Plains
644 2¢ Burgoyne at Saratoga
645 2¢ Valley Forge
646 2¢ Battle of Monmouth/ Molly Pitcher
651 2¢ George Rogers Clark
657 2¢ Sullivan Expedition
680 2¢ Battle of Fallen Timbers
688 2¢ Battle of Braddock's Field
689 2¢ General von Steuben
690 2¢ General Pulaski
703 2¢ Yorktown
727 3¢ Peace of 1783
734 5¢ General Tadeusz Kosciuszko
752 3¢ violet Peace of 1783 (#727)

National Parks Series 1934-1935

740 1¢ El Capitan, Yosemite (CA)
741 2¢ Grand Canyon (AZ)
742 3¢ Mt. Rainier and Mirror Lake (WA)
743 4¢ Cliff Palace, Mesa Verde (CO)
744 5¢ Old Faithful, Yellowstone (WY)
745 6¢ Crater Lake (OR)
746 7¢ Great Head, Acadia Park (ME)
747 8¢ Great White Throne, Zion Park (UT)
748 9¢ Glacier National Park (MT)
749 10¢ Great Smoky Mountains (NC)
750 3¢ Souvenir Sheet, American Philatelic Society (#742)
751 1¢ Souvenir Sheet, Trans-Mississippi Philatelic Exposition (#740)
756 1¢ green Yosemite (#740)
757 2¢ red Grand Canyon (#741)
758 3¢ deep violet Mt. Rainier (#742)
759 4¢ brown Mesa Verde (#743)
760 5¢ blue Yellowstone (#744)
761 6¢ dark blue Crater Lake (#745)
762 7¢ black Acadia (#746)
763 8¢ sage green Zion (#747)
764 9¢ red orange Glacier (#748)
765 10¢ gray black Great Smoky Mountains (#749)

Army Navy Series 1936-1937

785 1¢ George Washington, Nathanael Greene and Mount Vernon
786 2¢ Andrew Jackson, Winfield Scott and The Hermitage
787 3¢ Generals Sherman, Grant and Sheridan
788 4¢ Generals Robert E. Lee and "Stonewall" Jackson and Stratford Hall
789 5¢ U.S. Military Academy at West Point
790 1¢ John Paul Jones, John Barry, *Bon Homme Richard* and *Lexington*
791 2¢ Stephen Decatur, Thomas MacDonough and *Saratoga*
792 3¢ David G. Farragut and David D. Porter, *Hartford* and *Powhatan*
793 4¢ Admirals William T. Sampson, George Dewey and Winfield S. Schley
794 5¢ Seal of U.S. Naval Academy and Naval Cadets

Territorial Series 1937

799 3¢ Hawaii
800 3¢ Alaska
801 3¢ Puerto Rico
802 3¢ Virgin Islands

Presidential Series 1938-1939

803 1/2¢ Benjamin Franklin
804 1¢ George Washington
805 1-1/2¢ Martha Washington
806 2¢ John Adams
807 3¢ Thomas Jefferson
808 4¢ James Madison
809 4-1/2¢ The White House
810 5¢ James Monroe
811 6¢ John Quincy Adams
812 7¢ Andrew Jackson
813 8¢ Martin Van Buren
814 9¢ William H. Harrison
815 10¢ John Tyler
816 11¢ James K. Polk
817 12¢ Zachary Taylor
818 13¢ Millard Fillmore
819 14¢ Franklin Pierce
820 15¢ James Buchanan
821 16¢ Abraham Lincoln
822 17¢ Andrew Johnson
823 18¢ Ulysses S. Grant
824 19¢ Rutherford B. Hayes
825 20¢ James A. Garfield
826 21¢ Chester A. Arthur
827 22¢ Grover Cleveland
828 24¢ Benjamin Harrison
829 25¢ William McKinley
830 30¢ Theodore Roosevelt
831 50¢ William Howard Taft
832 $1 Woodrow Wilson
833 $2 Warren G. Harding
834 $5 Calvin Coolidge

Famous Americans Series 1940

859 1¢ Washington Irving
860 2¢ James Fenimore Cooper
861 3¢ Ralph Waldo Emerson
862 5¢ Louisa May Alcott
863 10¢ Samuel L. Clemens (Mark Twain)
864 1¢ Henry W. Longfellow
865 2¢ John Greenleaf Whittier
866 3¢ James Russell Lowell
867 5¢ Walt Whitman
868 10¢ James Whitcomb Riley
869 1¢ Horace Mann
870 2¢ Mark Hopkins
871 3¢ Charles W. Eliot
872 5¢ Frances E. Willard
873 10¢ Booker T. Washington
874 1¢ John James Audubon
875 2¢ Dr. Crawford W. Long
876 3¢ Luther Burbank
877 5¢ Dr. Walter Reed
878 10¢ Jane Addams
879 1¢ Stephen Collins Foster
880 2¢ John Philip Sousa
881 3¢ Victor Herbert
882 5¢ Edward A. MacDowell
883 10¢ Ethelbert Nevin
884 1¢ Gilbert Charles Stuart
885 2¢ James A. McNeill Whistler
886 3¢ Augustus Saint-Gaudens
887 5¢ Daniel Chester French
888 10¢ Frederic Remington
889 1¢ Eli Whitney
890 2¢ Samuel F.B. Morse
891 3¢ Cyrus Hall McCormick
892 5¢ Elias Howe
893 10¢ Alexander Graham Bell

Win the War Series 1940-1946

899 1¢ Statue of Liberty
900 2¢ 90mm Antiaircraft Gun
901 3¢ Torch of Enlightenment
905 3¢ Win the War
906 5¢ Chinese Resistance
907 2¢ Allied Nations
908 1¢ Four Freedoms
925 3¢ Philippine
928 5¢ United Nations Conference
929 3¢ Iwo Jima (Marines)
930 1¢ Roosevelt and Hyde Park Residence
931 2¢ Roosevelt and "The Little White House" at Warm Springs, GA
932 3¢ Roosevelt and White House
933 5¢ Roosevelt, Map of Western Hemisphere and Four Freedoms
934 3¢ Army
935 3¢ Navy
936 3¢ Coast Guard
939 3¢ Merchant Marine
940 3¢ Veterans of World War II

Overrun Countries Series 1943-1944

909 5¢ Poland
910 5¢ Czechoslovakia
911 5¢ Norway
912 5¢ Luxembourg
913 5¢ Netherlands
914 5¢ Belgium
915 5¢ France
916 5¢ Greece
917 5¢ Yugoslavia
918 5¢ Albania
919 5¢ Austria
920 5¢ Denmark
921 5¢ Korea

National Capital Sesquicentennial Series 1950

989 3¢ Statue of *Freedom* on Capitol Dome
990 3¢ Executive Mansion
991 3¢ Supreme Court
992 3¢ U.S. Capitol

Liberty Series 1954-1961

1030 1/2¢ Benjamin Franklin
1031 1¢ George Washington
1031A 1-1/4¢ Palace of the Governors
1032 1-1/2¢ Mount Vernon
1033 2¢ Thomas Jefferson
1034 2-1/2¢ Bunker Hill Monument and Massachusetts Flag
1035 3¢ Statue of Liberty
1036 4¢ Abraham Lincoln
1037 4-1/2¢ The Hermitage
1038 5¢ James Monroe
1039 6¢ Theodore Roosevelt
1040 7¢ Woodrow Wilson
1041 8¢ Statue of Liberty
1042 8¢ Statue of Liberty, redrawn
1042A 8¢ General John J. Pershing
1043 9¢ The Alamo
1044 10¢ Independence Hall
1044A 11¢ Statue of Liberty
1045 12¢ Benjamin Harrison
1046 15¢ John Jay
1047 20¢ Monticello
1048 25¢ Paul Revere
1049 30¢ Robert E. Lee
1050 40¢ John Marshall
1051 50¢ Susan B. Anthony
1052 $1 Patrick Henry
1053 $5 Alexander Hamilton

Wildlife Conservation Series 1956-1978

1077 3¢ Wild Turkey
1078 3¢ Pronghorn Antelope
1079 3¢ King Salmon
1098 3¢ Wildlife Conservation
1427 8¢ Trout
1428 8¢ Alligator
1429 8¢ Polar Bear and Cubs
1430 8¢ California Condor
1464 8¢ Fur Seals
1465 8¢ Cardinal
1466 8¢ Brown Pelican
1467 8¢ Bighorn Sheep
1760 15¢ Great Gray Owl
1761 15¢ Saw-Whet Owl
1762 15¢ Barred Owl
1763 15¢ Great Horned Owl
1764 15¢ Giant Sequoia
1765 15¢ White Pine
1766 15¢ White Oak
1767 15¢ Gray Birch

Champion of Liberty Series 1957-1961

1096 8¢ Ramon Magsaysay
1110 4¢ Simon Bolivar
1111 8¢ Simon Bolivar
1117 4¢ Lajos Kossuth
1118 8¢ Lajos Kossuth
1125 4¢ José de San Martin
1126 8¢ José de San Martin
1136 4¢ Ernst Reuter
1137 8¢ Ernst Reuter
1147 4¢ Thomas Masaryk
1148 8¢ Thomas Masaryk
1159 4¢ Ignacy Jan Paderewski
1160 8¢ Ignacy Jan Paderewski
1165 4¢ Gustaf Mannerheim
1166 8¢ Gustaf Mannerheim
1168 4¢ Giuseppe Garibaldi
1169 8¢ Giuseppe Garibaldi
1174 4¢ Mahatma Gandhi
1175 8¢ Mahatma Gandhi

American Credo Series 1960-1961

1139 4¢ Quotation from Washington's Farewell Address
1140 4¢ Benjamin Franklin Quotation
1141 4¢ Thomas Jefferson Quotation
1142 4¢ Francis Scott Key Quotation
1143 4¢ Abraham Lincoln Quotation
1144 4¢ Patrick Henry Quotation

Civil War Centennial Series 1961-1965

1178 4¢ Fort Sumter
1179 4¢ Shiloh
1180 5¢ Gettysburg
1181 5¢ The Wilderness
1182 5¢ Appomattox

Prominent Americans Series 1968-1974

1278 1¢ Thomas Jefferson
1279 1-1/4¢ Albert Gallatin
1280 2¢ Frank Lloyd Wright
1281 3¢ Francis Parkman
1282 4¢ Abraham Lincoln
1283 5¢ George Washington
1283B 5¢ George Washington redrawn
1284 6¢ Franklin D. Roosevelt
1285 8¢ Albert Einstein
1286 10¢ Andrew Jackson
1286A 12¢ Henry Ford
1287 13¢ John F. Kennedy
1288 15¢ Oliver Wendell Holmes
1289 20¢ George C. Marshall
1290 25¢ Frederick Douglass
1291 30¢ John Dewey
1292 40¢ Thomas Paine
1293 50¢ Lucy Stone
1294 $1 Eugene O'Neill
1295 $5 John Bassett Moore
1297 3¢ violet Parkman (#1281)
1298 6¢ Franklin D. Roosevelt (1284)
1299 1¢ green Jefferson
1303 4¢ black Lincoln (#1282)
1304 5¢ blue Washington (#1283)
1304C 5¢ Washington redrawn (#1283B)
1305 6¢ gray brown Roosevelt
1305C $1 dull purple Eugene O'Neill
1305E 15¢ magenta Oliver Wendell Holmes, Type I (#1288)
1393 6¢ Dwight D. Eisenhower
1393D 7¢ Benjamin Franklin
1394 8¢ Dwight D. Eisenhower
1397 14¢ Fiorello H. LaGuardia
1398 16¢ Ernie Pyle
1399 18¢ Dr. Elizabeth Blackwell
1400 21¢ Amadeo P. Giannini

American Folklore Series 1966-1974

1317 5¢ Johnny Appleseed
1330 5¢ Davy Crockett
1357 6¢ Daniel Boone
1370 6¢ Grandma Moses
1470 8¢ Tom Sawyer
1548 10¢ The Legend of Sleepy Hollow

Space Series 1962-2000

1193 4¢ Project Mercury
1331 5¢ Space-Walking Astronaut
1332 5¢ Gemini Capsule
1371 6¢ Apollo 8
1434 8¢ Earth, Sun and Landing Craft on Moon
1435 8¢ Lunar Rover and Astronauts
1529 10¢ Skylab
1556 10¢ Pioneer 10 Passing Jupiter
1557 10¢ Mariner 10, Venus and Mercury
1569 10¢ Apollo and Soyuz after Link-up and Earth
1570 10¢ Spacecraft before Link-up, Earth and Project Emblem
1759 15¢ Viking Missions to Mars
1912 18¢ Exploring the Moon—Moon Walk
1913 18¢ Benefiting Mankind, Columbia Space Shuttle
1914 18¢ Benefiting Mankind, Space Shuttle Deploying Satellite
1915 18¢ Understanding the Sun—Skylab
1916 18¢ Probing the Planets—Pioneer 11
1917 18¢ Benefiting Mankind, Space Shuttle Lifting Off
1918 18¢ Benefiting Mankind, Space Shuttle Preparing to Lane
1919 18¢ Comprehending the Universe—Telescope
2419 $2.40 Moon Landing
2543 $2.90 Space Vehicle
2444 $3.00 Space Shuttle *Challenger*
2544A $10.75 Space Shuttle *Endeavour*
2568 29¢ Mercury, Mariner 10
2569 29¢ Venus, Mariner 2
2570 29¢ Earth, Landsat
2571 29¢ Moon, Lunar Orbiter
2572 29¢ Mars, Viking Orbiter
2573 29¢ Jupiter, Pioneer 11
2574 29¢ Saturn, Voyager 2
2575 29¢ Uranus, Voyager 2
2576 29¢ Neptune, Voyager 2
2577 29¢ Pluto
2631 29¢ Cosmonaut, U.S. Space Shuttle
2632 29¢ Astronaut, Russian Space Station
2633 29¢ Sputnik, Vostok, Apollo Command and Lunar Modules
2634 29¢ Soyuz, Mercury and Gemini Spacecraft
2741 29¢ Space Fantasy
2742 29¢ Space Fantasy
2743 29¢ Space Fantasy
2744 29¢ Space Fantasy
2745 29¢ Space Fantasy
2841A 29¢ First Moon Landing 1969
2842 $9.95 First Moon Landing, 25th Anniversary
3178 $3.00 Mars Rover Sojourner
3238 32¢ Space Discovery
3239 32¢ Space Discovery
3240 32¢ Space Discovery
3241 32¢ Space Discovery
3242 32¢ Space Discovery
3261 $3.20 Space Shuttle Landing
3262 $11.75 Piggyback Space Shuttle
3384 33¢ Eagle Nebula
3385 33¢ Ring Nebula
3386 33¢ Lagoon Nebula
3387 33¢ Egg Nebula
3388 33¢ Galaxy NGC1316
3409 Probing the Vastness of Space
3409A 60¢ Hubble Space Telescope

Space Series 1962-2000 continued

3409B 60¢ Radio Interferometer, NM
3409C 60¢ Telescopes, Keck Observatory, HI
3409D 60¢ Telescopes, Cerro Tololo Observatory, Chile
3409E 60¢ Telescope, Mount Wilson Observatory, CA
3409F 60¢ Telescope, Arecibo Observatory, Puerto Rico
3410 Exploring the Solar System
3410A $1 Sun and Corona
3410B $1 Cross-section of Sun
3410C $1 Sun and Earth
3410D $1 Sun and solar flare
3410E $1 Sun and clouds
3411 Escaping the Gravity of Earth
3411A $3.20 Space Shuttle and Space Station
3411B $3.20 Astronauts working in space
3412 $11.75 Space Achievement and Exploration
3413 $11.75 Landing on the Moon

American Bicentennial Series 1971-1983

1432 8¢ Bicentennial Commission Emblem
1456 8¢ Glass Blower
1457 8¢ Silversmith
1458 8¢ Wigmaker
1459 8¢ Hatter
1476 8¢ Printer and Patriots Examining Pamphlet
1477 8¢ Posting a Broadside
1478 8¢ Postrider
1479 8¢ Drummer
1480 8¢ British Merchantman
1481 8¢ British Three-Master
1482 8¢ Boats and Ship's Hull
1483 8¢ Boat and Dock
1543 10¢ Carpenters' Hall
1544 10¢ "We Ask but for Peace, Liberty and Safety"
1545 10¢ "Deriving Their Just Powers from the Consent of the Governed"
1546 10¢ Independence Hall
1559 8¢ Sybil Ludington
1560 8¢ Salem Poor
1561 10¢ Haym Salomon
1562 18¢ Peter Francisco
1563 10¢ Lexington-Concord 1775
1564 10¢ Bunker Hill 1775
1565 10¢ Continental Army
1566 10¢ Continental Navy
1567 10¢ Continental Marines
1568 10¢ American Militia
1629 13¢ Drummer Boy
1630 13¢ Old Drummer
1631 13¢ Fifer
1633 13¢ Delaware State Flag
1634 13¢ Pennsylvania State Flag
1635 13¢ New Jersey
1636 13¢ Georgia
1637 13¢ Connecticut
1638 13¢ Massachusetts
1639 13¢ Maryland
1640 13¢ South Carolina
1641 13¢ New Hampshire
1642 13¢ Virginia
1643 13¢ New York
1644 13¢ North Carolina
1645 13¢ Rhode Island
1646 13¢ Vermont
1647 13¢ Kentucky
1648 13¢ Tennessee
1649 13¢ Ohio
1650 13¢ Louisiana
1651 13¢ Indiana
1652 13¢ Mississippi
1653 13¢ Illinois
1654 13¢ Alabama
1655 13¢ Maine
1656 13¢ Missouri
1657 13¢ Arkansas
1658 13¢ Michigan
1659 13¢ Florida
1660 13¢ Texas
1661 13¢ Iowa
1662 13¢ Wisconsin
1663 13¢ California
1664 13¢ Minnesota
1665 13¢ Oregon
1666 13¢ Kansas
1667 13¢ West Virginia
1668 13¢ Nevada
1669 13¢ Nebraska
1670 13¢ Colorado
1671 13¢ North Dakota
1672 13¢ South Dakota
1673 13¢ Montana
1674 13¢ Washington
1675 13¢ Idaho
1676 13¢ Wyoming
1677 13¢ Utah
1678 13¢ Oklahoma
1679 13¢ New Mexico
1680 13¢ Arizona
1681 13¢ Alaska
1682 13¢ Hawaii
1686 13¢ *Surrender of Lord Cornwallis at Yorktown*
1687 18¢ *Declaration of Independence, 4 July 1776 at Philadelphia*
1688 23¢ *Washington Crossing the Delaware*
1689 31¢ *Washington Reviewing His Ragged Army at Valley Forge*
1690 13¢ Bust of Benjamin Franklin, Map of North America, 1776

Declaration of Independence #1691-1694

1691 13¢ Delegates
1692 13¢ Delegates and John Adams
1693 13¢ Roger Sherman, Robert R. Livingston, Thomas Jefferson and Benjamin Franklin
1694 13¢ John Hancock, Charles Thomson, George Read, John Dickinson and Edward Rutledge
1704 13¢ *Washington at Princeton*
1716 13¢ Marquis de Lafayette
1717 13¢ Seamstress
1718 13¢ Blacksmith
1719 13¢ Wheelwright
1720 13¢ Leatherworker
1722 13¢ *Herkimer at Oriskany*
1726 13¢ Members of Continental Congress in Conference
1728 13¢ *Surrender at Saratoga*
1753 13¢ *King Louis XVI and Benjamin Franklin*
1789 15¢ *John Paul Jones*
1826 15¢ General Bernardo de Gálvez, Battle of Mobile 1780
1937 18¢ Battle of Yorktown 1781
1938 18¢ Battle of the Virginia Capes 1781
1941 20¢ John Hanson
1952 20¢ George Washington
2052 20¢ Treaty of Paris

National Parks Centennial Series 1972

1448 2¢ Ship at Sea
1449 2¢ Cape Hatteras
1450 2¢ Laughing Gulls on Driftwood
1451 2¢ Laughing Gulls and Dune
1452 6¢ Wolf Trap Farm, Virginia
1453 8¢ Old Faithful, Yellowstone
1454 15¢ Mount McKinley, Alaska
C84 11¢ City of Refuge, Hawaii

Black Heritage Series 1978-Present

1744 13¢ Harriet Tubman
1771 15¢ Dr. Martin Luther King, Jr.
1804 15¢ Benjamin Banneker
1875 15¢ Whitney Moore Young
2016 20¢ Jackie Robinson
2044 20¢ Scott Joplin
2073 20¢ Carter G. Woodson
2137 22¢ Mary McLeod Bethune
2203 22¢ Sojourner Truth
2249 22¢ Jean Baptiste Point Du Sable
2371 22¢ James Weldon Johnson
2402 25¢ A. Philip Randolph
2442 25¢ Ida B. Wells
2567 29¢ Jan E. Matzeliger
2617 29¢ W.E.B. DuBois
2746 29¢ Percy Lavon Julian
2816 29¢ Dr. Allison Davis
2956 32¢ Bessie Coleman
3058 32¢ Ernest E. Just
3121 32¢ Brig. Gen. Benjamin O. Davis, Sr.
3181 32¢ Madam C.J. Walker
3273 33¢ Malcolm X
3371 33¢ Patricia Roberts Harris
3501 34¢ Roy Wilkins
3557 34¢ Langston Hughes
3746 37¢ Thurgood Marshall
3834 37¢ Paul Robeson
3896 37¢ Marian Anderson
3996 39¢ Hattie McDaniel

American Arts Series 1973-1975

1484 8¢ George Gershwin, Composer
1485 8¢ Robinson Jeffers, Poet
1486 8¢ Henry Ossawa Tanner, Artist
1487 8¢ Willa Cather, Novelist
1553 10¢ Benjamin West, Artist
1554 10¢ Paul Laurence Dunbar, Poet
1555 10¢ D. W. Griffith, Moviemaker

Rural America Series 1973

1504 8¢ Angus and Longhorn
1505 10¢ Chautauqua Tent & Buggies
1506 10¢ Wheat Fields & Train

Americana Series 1977-1981

1581 1¢ Inkwell and Quill
1582 2¢ Speaker's Stand
1584 3¢ Early Ballot Box
1585 4¢ Books, Bookmark, Eyeglasses
1590 9¢ Capitol Dome
1591 9¢ Capitol Dome
1592 10¢ Contemplation of Justice
1593 11¢ Printing Press
1594 12¢ Torch, Statue of Liberty
1595 13¢ Liberty Bell
1596 13¢ Eagle and Shield
1597 15¢ Fort McHenry Flag
1598 15¢ Fort McHenry Flag
1599 16¢ Head, Statue of Liberty
1603 24¢ Old North Church
1604 28¢ Fort Nisqually
1605 29¢ Sandy Hook Lighthouse
1606 30¢ Morris Township School # 2
1608 50¢ Iron "Betty" Lamp
1610 $1 Rush Lamp and Candle
1611 $2 Kerosene Table Lamp
1612 $5 Railroad Conductor's Lantern
1613 3.1¢ String Guitar
1614 7.7¢ Saxhorns
1615 7.9¢ Drum
1615C 8.4¢ Steinway Grand Piano
1616 9¢ slate green Capitol Dome
1617 10¢ purple Contemplation of Justice
1618 13¢ brown Liberty Bell
1618C 15¢ Fort McHenry Flag
1619 16¢ blue Head of Liberty
1622 13¢ Flag over Independence Hall
1622C 13¢ Star Flag over Independence Hall
1623 13¢ Flag over Capitol
1811 1¢ dark blue Inkwell and Quill
1813 3.5¢ Weaver Violins
1816 12¢ red brown, beige Torch from Statue of Liberty

American Folk Art Series 1977-1995

1706 13¢ Zia Pot
1707 13¢ San Ildefonso Pot
1708 13¢ Hopi Pot
1709 13¢ Acoma Pot
1745 13¢ Basket Design, Quilts
1746 13¢ Basket Design, Quilts
1747 13¢ Basket Design, Quilts
1748 13¢ Basket Design, Quilts
1775 15¢ Straight-Spout Coffeepot
1776 15¢ Tea Caddy
1777 15¢ Sugar Bowl
1778 15¢ Curved-Spout Coffeepot
1834 15¢ Heiltsuk, Bella Tribe
1835 15¢ Chilkat Tlingit Tribe
1836 15¢ Tlingit Tribe
1837 15¢ Bella Coola Tribe
2138 22¢ Broadbill Decoy
2139 22¢ Mallard Decoy
2140 22¢ Canvasback Decoy
2141 22¢ Redhead Decoy
2235 22¢ Navajo Art
2236 22¢ Navajo Art
2237 22¢ Navajo Art
2238 22¢ Navajo Art
2240 22¢ Highlander Figure
2241 22¢ Ship Figurehead
2242 22¢ Nautical Figure
2243 22¢ Cigar Store Figure
2351 22¢ Squash Blossoms, Lacemaking
2352 22¢ Floral Piece, Lacemaking
2353 22¢ Floral Piece, Lacemaking
2354 22¢ Dogwood Blossoms, Lacemaking

Carousel Animals #2390-2393, 2976-2979

2390 25¢ Deer
2391 25¢ Horse
2392 25¢ Camel
2393 25¢ Goat
2976 32¢ Golden Horse with Roses
2977 32¢ Black Horse with Gold Bridle
2978 32¢ Horse with Armor
2979 32¢ Brown Horse with Green Bridle

Performing Arts Series 1978-1991

1755 13¢ Jimmie Rodgers
1756 15¢ George M. Cohan
1801 15¢ Will Rogers
1803 15¢ W. C. Fields
2012 20¢ John, Ethel, & Lionel Barrymore
2088 20¢ Douglas Fairbanks
2090 20¢ John McCormack
2110 22¢ Jerome Kern
2211 22¢ Duke Ellington
2250 22¢ Enrico Caruso
2411 25¢ Arturo Toscanini
2550 29¢ Cole Porter

Literary Arts Series 1979-Present

1773 15¢ John Steinbeck
1832 15¢ Edith Wharton
2047 20¢ Nathaniel Hawthorne
2094 20¢ Herman Melville
2239 22¢ T. S. Eliot
2350 22¢ William Faulkner
2418 25¢ Ernest Hemingway
2449 25¢ Marianne Moore
2538 29¢ William Saroyan
2698 29¢ Dorothy Parker
2862 29¢ James Thurber
3002 32¢ Tennessee Williams
3104 23¢ F. Scott Fitzgerald
3134 32¢ Thornton Wilder
3221 32¢ Stephen Vincent Benét
3308 33¢ Ayn Rand
3444 33¢ Thomas Wolfe
3659 37¢ Ogden Nash
3748 37¢ Zora Neale Hurston
3871 37¢ James Baldwin
3904 37¢ Robert Penn Warren
— 39¢ Katherine Anne Porter (2006)

Architecture Series 1979-1982

1779 15¢ Virginia Rotunda
1780 15¢ Baltimore Cathedral
1781 15¢ Boston State House
1782 15¢ Philadelphia Exchange
1838 15¢ Smithsonian Institution
1839 15¢ Trinity Church
1840 15¢ Pennsylvania Academy of Fine Arts
1841 15¢ Lyndhurst
1928 18¢ NYU Library, New York
1929 18¢ Biltmore House
1930 18¢ Palace of the Arts
1931 18¢ National Farmer's Bank
2019 20¢ Fallingwater
2020 20¢ Illinois Institute of Technology
2021 20¢ Gropius House
2022 20¢ Dulles Airport

Lighthouses Series 1990-2003

2470 25¢ Admiralty Head, WA
2471 25¢ Cape Hatteras, NC
2472 25¢ West Quoddy Head, ME
2473 25¢ American Shoals, FL
2474 25¢ Sandy Hook, NJ
2969 32¢ Split Rock, Lake Superior
2970 32¢ St. Joseph, Lake Michigan
2971 32¢ Spectacle Reef, Lake Huron
2972 32¢ Marblehead, Lake Erie
2973 32¢ Thirty Mile Point, Lake Ontario
3787 37¢ Old Cape Henry, VA
3788 37¢ Cape Lookout, NC
3789 37¢ Morris Island, SC
3790 37¢ Tybee Island, GA
3791 37¢ Hillsboro Inlet, FL

Love Series 1973-Present

1475 8¢ Love
1951 20¢ Love
2072 20¢ Love
2143 22¢ Love
2202 22¢ Love
2248 22¢ Love
2378 25¢ Love
2379 45¢ Love
2440 25¢ Love
2535 29¢ Love
2537 52¢ Love
2618 29¢ Love
2813 29¢ Love Sunrise
2814 29¢ Love

Cherub from Sistine Madonna by Raphael #2948-3030

2948 32¢ Love, Cherub from Sistine
2949 32¢ Love, Cherub from Sistine
2957 32¢ Love, Cherub from Sistine
2958 55¢ Love, Cherub from Sistine
2959 32¢ Love, Cherub from Sistine (Booklet)
2960 55¢ Love, Cherub from Sistine (Booklet)
3030 32¢ Love, Cherub from Sistine
3123 32¢ Love Swans
3124 55¢ Love Swans
3274 33¢ Love
3275 55¢ Love
3496 34¢ Rose and Love Letter
3497 34¢ Rose and Love Letter
3498 34¢ Rose and Love Letter
3499 55¢ Rose and Love Letter
3657 37¢ Love
3658 60¢ Love
3833 37¢ Love: Candy Hearts
3898 37¢ Love Bouquet
3976 39¢ True Blue

Love Stamped Envelopes Series 1989-2003

U616 25¢ Love
U621 29¢ Love
U637 32¢ Spiral Heart
U644 33¢ Victorian Love
U647 34¢ Lovebirds
U651 37¢ Nurturing Love

Nature of America Series 1999-Present

3293 33¢ Sonoran Desert
3378 33¢ Pacific Coast Rain Forest
3506 34¢ Great Plains Prairie
3611 34¢ Longleaf Pine Forest
3802 37¢ Arctic Tundra
3831 37¢ Pacific Coral Reef
3899 37¢ Northeast Deciduous Fores
— 39¢ Southern Florida Wetland (2006)

Legends of Hollywood Series 1995-Present

2967 32¢ Marilyn Monroe
3082 32¢ James Dean
3152 32¢ Humphrey Bogart
3226 32¢ Alfred Hitchcock
3329 33¢ James Cagney
3446 33¢ Edward G. Robinson
3523 34¢ Lucille Ball
3692 37¢ Cary Grant
3786 37¢ Audrey Hepburn
3876 37¢ John Wayne
3911 37¢ Henry Fonda
— 39¢ Judy Garland (2006)

Lunar New Year Series 1992-Present

2720 29¢ Year of the Rooster
2817 29¢ Year of the Dog
2876 29¢ Year of the Boar
3060 32¢ Year of the Rat
3120 32¢ Year of the Ox
3179 32¢ Year of the Tiger
3272 33¢ Year of the Rabbit
3370 33¢ Year of the Dragon
3500 34¢ Year of the Snake
3559 34¢ Year of the Horse
3747 37¢ Year of the Ram
3832 37¢ Year of the Monkey
3895 37¢ Lunar New Year Souvenir Sheet
3997 39¢ Lunar New Year Souvenir Sheet

Transportation Series 1981-1995

1897 1¢ Omnibus 1880s
1897A 2¢ Locomotive 1870s
1898 3¢ Handcar 1880s
1898A 4¢ Stagecoach 1890s
1899 5¢ Motorcycle 1913
1900 5.2¢ Sleigh 1880s
1901 5.9¢ Bicycle 1870s
1902 7.4¢ Baby Buggy 1880s
1903 9.3¢ Mail Wagon 1880s
1904 10.9¢ Hansom Cab 1890s
1905 11¢ RR Caboose 1890s
1906 17¢ Electric Auto 1917
1907 18¢ Surrey 1890s
1908 20¢ Fire Pumper 1860s
2123 3.4¢ School Bus 1920s
2124 4.9¢ Buckboard 1880s
2125 5.5¢ Star Route Truck 1910s
2126 6¢ Tricycle 1880s
2127 7.1¢ Tractor 1920s
2128 8.3¢ Ambulance 1860s
2129 8.5¢ Tow Truck 1920s
2130 10.1¢ Oil Wagon 1890s
2131 11¢ Stutz Bearcat 1933
2132 12¢ Stanley Steamer 1909
2133 12.5¢ Pushcart 1880s

Transportation Series continued
1981-1995
2134 14¢ Iceboat 1880s
2135 17¢ Dog Sled 1920s
2136 25¢ Bread Wagon 1880s
2252 3¢ Conestoga Wagon 1800s
2253 5¢ Milk Wagon 1900s
2254 5.3¢ Elevator 1900s
2255 7.6¢ Carreta 1770s
2256 8.4¢ Wheel Chair 1920s
2257 10¢ Canal Boat 1880s
2258 13¢ Patrol Wagon 1880s
2259 13.2¢ Coal Car 1870s
2260 15¢ Tugboat 1900s
2261 16.7¢ Popcorn Wagon 1902
2262 17.5¢ Racing Car 1911
2263 20¢ Cable Car 1880s
2264 20.5¢ Fire Engine 1900s
2265 21¢ Railroad Mail Car 1920s
2266 24.1¢ Tandem Bicycle 1890s
2451 4¢ Steam Carriage 1866
2452 5¢ Circus Wagon 1900s
2452D 5¢ Circus Wagon gravure printing
2453 5¢ Canoe 1800s intaglio printing
2454 5¢ Canoe 1800s gravure printing
2457 10¢ Tractor Trailer 1930s
2463 20¢ Cog Railway 1870s
2464 23¢ Lunch Wagon 1890s
2466 32¢ Ferryboat 1900s
2468 $1 Seaplane 1914

Great Americans Series 1980-1995
1844 1¢ Dorothea Dix
1845 2¢ Igor Stravinsky
1846 3¢ Henry Clay
1847 4¢ Carl Schurz
1848 5¢ Pearl Buck
1849 6¢ Walter Lippmann
1850 7¢ Abraham Baldwin
1851 8¢ Henry Knox
1852 9¢ Sylvanus Thayer
1853 10¢ Richard Russell
1854 11¢ Alden Partridge
1855 13¢ Crazy Horse
1856 14¢ Sinclair Lewis
1857 17¢ Rachel Carson
1858 18¢ George Mason
1859 19¢ Sequoyah
1860 20¢ Ralph Bunche
1861 20¢ Thomas H. Gallaudet
1862 20¢ Harry S. Truman
1863 22¢ John J. Audubon
1864 30¢ Frank C. Laubach
1865 35¢ Charles R. Drew M.D.
1866 37¢ Robert Millikan
1867 39¢ Grenville Clark
1868 40¢ Lillian M. Gilbreth
1869 50¢ Chester W. Nimitz
2182 25¢ Jack London
2172 5¢ Hugo L. Black
2195 $2 William Jennings Bryan
2178 17¢ Belva Ann Lockwood
2168 1¢ Margaret Mitchell
2171 4¢ Father Flanagan
2180 56¢ John Harvard
2170 3¢ Paul Dudley White MD
2193 $1 Bernard Revel
2176 14¢ Julia Ward Howe
2169 2¢ Mary Lyon
2175 10¢ Red Cloud
2196 $5 Bret Harte
2177 15¢ Buffalo Bill Cody
2188 45¢ Harvey Cushing MD
2180 21¢ Chester Carlson
2181 23¢ Mary Cassatt
2191 65¢ H.H. 'Hap" Arnold
2194 $1 Johns Hopkins
2183 28¢ Sitting Bull
2173 5¢ Luis Muñoz Marin
2187 40¢ Claire Chennault
2186 35¢ Dennis Chavez
2189 52¢ Hubert H. Humphrey
2192 75¢ Wendell Willkie
2184 29¢ Earl Warren
2185 29¢ Thomas Jefferson
2179 20¢ Virginia Apgar
2940 55¢ Alice Hamilton, MD
2934 32¢ Cal Farley
2933 32¢ Milton S. Hershey
2943 78¢ Alice Paul
2938 46¢ Ruth Benedict
2936 32¢ Lila and DeWitt Wallace
2935 32¢ Henry R. Luce, Editor
2942 77¢ Mary Breckinridge
2941 55¢ Justin S. Morrill

American Culture Series 1995-2003
2908-2910 (15¢) Auto Tail Fin
2911 (25¢) Juke Box
2912 (25¢) Juke Box
3132 (25¢) Juke Box
3208 25¢ Diner
3208A 25¢ Diner
3447 (10¢) New York Public Library Lion
3520 10¢ Atlas Statue
3522 15¢ Woody Wagon
3766 $1 Wisdom

American Design Series 2002-Present
3612 5¢ American Toleware
3751 10¢ American Clock
3757 1¢ Tiffany Lamp
3749 2¢ Navajo Jewelry
3750 4¢ Chippendale Chair
3759 3¢ Silver Coffeepot

American Treasures Series 2001-Present
3524 34¢ Amish Quilts, Diamond in the Square
3525 34¢ Amish Quilts, Lone Star
3526 34¢ Amish Quilts, Sunshine and Shadow
3527 34¢ Amish Quilts, Double Ninepatch
3650 37¢ John James Audubon
Mary Cassatt #3804-3807
3804 37¢ Young Mother
3805 37¢ Children Playing on the Beach
3806 37¢ On a Balcony
3807 37¢ Child in a Straw Hat
3872 37¢ Martin Johnson Heade "Magnolias"
3926-3929 37¢ New Mexico Rio Grande Blankets (4 designs)
— 39¢ Quilts of Gee's Bend (10 designs) (2006)

American Sports Personalities Series 1981-Present
1932 18¢ Babe Zaharias
1933 18¢ Bobby Jones
2046 20¢ Babe Ruth
2089 20¢ Jim Thorpe
2097 20¢ Roberto Clemente
2376 22¢ Knute Rockne
2377 25¢ Francis Ouimet
2417 25¢ Lou Gehrig
2766 29¢ Joe Louis
3936 37¢ Arthur Ashe
— 39¢ Sugar Ray Robinson (2006)

Distinguished Americans Series 2000-Present
3420 10¢ Joseph W. Stilwell
3426 33¢ Claude Pepper
3431 76¢ Hattie Caraway
3432 76¢ Hattie Caraway
3433 83¢ Edna Ferber
3434 83¢ Edna Ferber
3422 23¢ Wilma Rudolph
3436 23¢ Wilma Rudolph
— 87¢ Albert Sabin (2006)
— 63¢ Jonas Salk (2006)

Celebrate The Century® Series 1998-2000
3182 32¢ 1900-1909 Pane of 15
3183 32¢ 1910-1919 Pane of 15
3184 32¢ 1920-1929 Pane of 15
3185 32¢ 1930-1939 Pane of 15
3186 33¢ 1940-1949 Pane of 15
3187 33¢ 1950-1959 Pane of 15
3188 33¢ 1960-1969 Pane of 15
3189 33¢ 1970-1979 Pane of 15
3190 33¢ 1980-1989 Pane of 15
3191 33¢ 1990-1999 Pane of 15

World War II Series 1991-1995
2559 29¢ WWII, 1941: A World at War
2697 29¢ WWII, 1942: Into the Battle
2765 29¢ WWII, 1943: Turning the Tide
2838 29¢ WWII, 1944: Road to Victory
2981 32¢ WWII, 1945: Victory at Last

Ratification of the Constitution Series 1987-1990
2336 22¢ Delaware
2337 22¢ Pennsylvania
2338 22¢ New Jersey
2339 22¢ Georgia
2340 22¢ Connecticut
2341 22¢ Massachusetts
2342 22¢ Maryland
2343 22¢ South Carolina
2344 22¢ New Hampshire
2345 22¢ Virginia
2346 22¢ New York
2347 22¢ North Carolina
2348 22¢ Rhode Island

Pioneers of Aviation Series 1978-1999
C91 31¢ Wright Brothers
C92 31¢ Wright Brothers
C93 21¢ Octave Chanute
C94 21¢ Octave Chanute
C95 25¢ Wiley Post
C96 25¢ Wiley Post
C99 28¢ Blanche Stuart Scott
C100 35¢ Glenn Curtiss
C113 33¢ Alfred Verville
C114 39¢ Lawrence and Elmer Sperry
C115 44¢ Transpacific Airmail
C118 45¢ Samuel Langley
C119 36¢ Igor Sikorsky
C128 50¢ Harriet Quimby
C129 40¢ William T. Piper
2998 60¢ Eddie Rickenbacker
3066 50¢ Jacqueline Cochran
3330 55¢ Billy Mitchell

Garden Flowers Series 1993-1996
2760 29¢ Hyacinth
2761 29¢ Daffodil
2762 29¢ Tulip
2763 29¢ Iris
2764 29¢ Lilac
2829 29¢ Lilly
2830 29¢ Zinnia
2831 29¢ Gladiola
2832 29¢ Marigold
2833 29¢ Rose
2993 32¢ Aster
2994 32¢ Chrysanthemum
2995 32¢ Dahlia
2996 32¢ Hydrangea
2997 32¢ Rudbeckia
3025 32¢ Crocus
3026 32¢ Winter Aconite
3027 32¢ Pansy
3028 32¢ Snowdrop
3029 32¢ Anemone

Looney Tunes Series 1997-2001

3137 32¢ Bugs Bunny
3204 32¢ Sylvester & Tweety
3306 33¢ Daffy Duck
3391 33¢ Road Runner & Wile E. Coyote
3534 34¢ Porky Pig "That's All Folks!"

American Scenes Series 1995-2002

2902 (5¢) Butte
2903 (5¢) Mountain
2904 (5¢) Mountain
3207 (5¢) Wetlands
3693 (5¢) Sea Coast

American Transportation Series 1995-1998

2905 (10¢) Automobile
2906 (10¢) Automobile
3228 (10¢) Green Bicycle
3229 (10¢) Green Bicycle

Classic Collections Series 1994-2001

2869 29¢ Legends of the West
2975 32¢ Civil War
3000 32¢ Comic Strip Classics
3068 32¢ Atlanta Centennial Olympic Games
3142 32¢ Classic American Aircraft
3236 32¢ Four Centuries of American Art
3351 33¢ Insects & Spiders
3403 33¢ The Stars and Stripes
3408 33¢ Legends of Baseball
3502 34¢ American Illustrators

America/PUAS Series 1989-1992

2426 25¢ Southwest Carved Figure
C121 45¢ Southeast Carved Wood Figure
C127 45¢ Tropical Coast
2512 25¢ Grand Canyon
C131 50¢ Eskimo and Bering Land Bridge

Artists Series 1996-Present

3069 32¢ Georgia O'Keeffe
3202a 32¢ Alexander Calder
3383a 33¢ Louise Nevelson
3509 34¢ Frida Kahlo
3652 37¢ Andy Warhol
3861a 37¢ Isamu Noguchi

Scenic American Landscapes, International Rate Series 1999-Present

C133 48¢ Niagara Falls
C134 40¢ Rio Grande
C135 60¢ Grand Canyon
C136 70¢ Nine-Mile Prairie
C137 80¢ Mount McKinley
C138 60¢ Acadia National Park
C139 63¢ Bryce Canyon
C140 75¢ Great Smoky Mountains
C141 84¢ Yosemite National Park
UXC27 55¢ Mt. Rainier Stamped Card
UXC28 70¢ Badlands

Scenic America Stamped Cards Series 1994-Present

UX198 20¢ Red Barn
UY41 20¢ + 20¢ Red Barn
UX241 20¢ Winter Scene
UX306 20¢ Block Island Lighthouse
UX375 21¢ White Barn
UY43 21¢ + 21¢ White Barn
UY44 23¢ + 23¢ Carlsbad Caverns

Historic Preservation Stamped Cards Series 1977-Present

UX71 9¢ Federal Court House
UX73 10¢ Cincinnati Music Hall
UX81 10¢ Iolani Palace
UX83 10¢ Salt Lake Temple
UX96 13¢ Academy of Music
UX97 13¢ Old Post Office, St. Louis, MO
UX119 14¢ Timberline Lodge
UX121 15¢ Blair House
UX125 15¢ Hearst Castle
UX128 15¢ Healy Hall
UX134 15¢ Hull House, Chicago
UX135 15¢ Independence Hall, Philadelphia
UX148 15¢ Isaac Royall House
UX150 15¢ Stanford University
UX151 15¢ Constitution Hall
UX152 15¢ Chicago Orchestral Hall
UX154 19¢ Carnegie Hall
UX155 19¢ Old Red, UT-Galveston
UX157 19¢ Notre Dame
UX159 19¢ The Old Mill
UX160 19¢ Wadsworth Atheneum
UX161 19¢ Cobb Hall
UX162 19¢ Waller Hall
UX165 19¢ Ellis Island
UX166 19¢ National Cathedral
UX167 19¢ Wren Building
UX168 19¢ Holocaust Memorial
UX169 19¢ Fort Recovery
UX170 19¢ Playmakers Theater
UX171 19¢ Massachusetts Hall
UX172 19¢ Lincoln's Home
UX175 19¢ Wittenberg University
UX177 19¢ St. Louis Union Station
UX262 20¢ St. John's College
UX263 20¢ Princeton University
UX280 20¢ City College of New York
UX284 20¢ Fort McHenry
UX290 20¢ University of Mississippi
UX292 20¢ Girard College
UX298 20¢ Northeastern University
UX299 20¢ Brandeis University
UX301 20¢ University of Wisconsin—Madison
UX302 20¢ Washington and Lee University
UX303 20¢ Redwood Library and Athenaeum
UX305 20¢ Mount Vernon
UX312 20¢ University of Utah
UX313 20¢ Ryman Auditorium
UX316 20¢ Middlebury College
UX361 20¢ Yale University
UX362 20¢ University of South Carolina
UX363 20¢ Northwestern University
UX364 20¢ University of Portland
UX400 23¢ Ohio University
UX405 23¢ Columbia University
UX406 23¢ Harriton House

Legends of American Music Series 1993-1999

2721 29¢ Elvis Presley
2722 29¢ Oklahoma!
2723 29¢ Hank Williams

Rock & Roll/Rhythm & Blues #2724-2730

2724 29¢ Elvis Presley
2725 29¢ Bill Haley
2726 29¢ Clyde McPhatter
2727 29¢ Ritchie Valens
2728 29¢ Otis Redding
2729 29¢ Buddy Holly
2730 29¢ Dinah Washington

Broadway Musicals #2767-2770

2767 29¢ Show Boat
2768 29¢ Porgy & Bess
2769 29¢ Oklahoma
2770 29¢ My Fair Lady

Country & Western #2771-2774

2771 29¢ Hank Williams
2772 29¢ Patsy Cline
2773 29¢ The Carter Family
2774 29¢ Bob Wills

Popular Singers #2849-2853

2849 29¢ Al Jolson
2850 29¢ Bing Crosby
2851 29¢ Ethel Waters
2852 29¢ Nat "King" Cole
2853 29¢ Ethel Merman

Jazz & Blues Singers #2854-2861

2854 29¢ Bessie Smith
2855 29¢ Muddy Waters
2856 29¢ Billie Holiday
2857 29¢ Robert Johnson
2858 29¢ Jimmy Rushing
2859 29¢ "Ma" Rainey
2860 29¢ Mildred Bailey
2861 29¢ Howlin' Wolf

Jazz Musicians #2982-2992

2982 32¢ Louis Armstrong
2983 32¢ Coleman Hawkins
2984 32¢ Louis Armstrong
2985 32¢ James P. Johnson
2986 32¢ Jelly Roll Morton
2987 32¢ Charlie Parker
2988 32¢ Eubie Blake
2989 32¢ Charles Mingus
2990 32¢ Thelonious Monk
2991 32¢ John Coltrane
2992 32¢ Erroll Garner

Big Band Leaders #3096-3099

3096 32¢ Count Basie
3097 32¢ Tommy and Jimmy Dorsey
3098 32¢ Glenn Miller
3099 32¢ Benny Goodman

Songwriters #3100-3103

3100 32¢ Harold Arlen
3101 32¢ Johnny Mercer
3102 32¢ Dorothy Fields
3103 32¢ Hoagy Carmichael

Opera Singers #3154-3157

3154 32¢ Lily Pons
3155 32¢ Richard Tucker
3156 32¢ Lawrence Tibbett
3157 32¢ Rosa Ponselle

Classical Composers & Conductors #3158-3165

3158 32¢ Leopold Stokowski
3159 32¢ Arthur Fiedler
3160 32¢ George Szell
3161 32¢ Eugene Ormandy
3162 32¢ Samuel Barber
3163 32¢ Ferde Grofé
3164 32¢ Charles Ives
3165 32¢ Louis Moreau Gottschalk

Folk Musicians #3212-3215

3212 32¢ Huddie "Leadbelly" Ledbetter
3213 32¢ Woody Guthrie
3214 32¢ Sonny Terry
3215 32¢ Josh White

Gospel Singers #3216-3219

3216 32¢ Mahalia Jackson
3217 32¢ Roberta Martin
3218 32¢ Clara Ward
3219 32¢ Sister Rosetta Tharpe

Hollywood Composers #3339-3344

3339 33¢ Max Steiner
3340 33¢ Dimitri Tiomkin
3341 33¢ Bernard Herrmann
3342 33¢ Franz Waxman
3343 33¢ Alfred Newman
3344 33¢ Erich Wolfgang Korngold

Broadway Songwriters #3345-3350

3345 33¢ Ira & George Gershwin
3346 33¢ Lerner & Loewe
3347 33¢ Lorenz Hart
3348 33¢ Rodgers & Hammerstein
3349 33¢ Meredith Willson
3350 33¢ Frank Loesser

Art of Disney Series 2004-Present

3865-3868 37¢ The Art of Disney: Friendship
3912-3915 37¢ The Art of Disney: Celebration
— 39¢ The Art of Disney: Romance (2006)

fficial Mail Series 1983-Present

121 2¢ Postal Savings
122 50¢ dark green
123 $1 ultramarine
124 1¢ dark violet
125 2¢ Postal Savings (0121)
126 10¢ carmine
127 1¢ January 12, 1983
128 4¢ January 12, 1983
129 13¢ January 12, 1983
129A 14¢ May 15, 1985
130 17¢ January 12, 1983
132 $1 January 12, 1983
133 $5 January 12, 1983
135 0¢ January 12, 1983
136 22¢ May 15, 1985
138 "D" Postcard rate (14¢) February 4,1985
138A 15¢ June 11, 1988
138B 20¢ May 19, 1988
139 "D" (22¢) February 4, 1985
140 "E" (25¢) March 22, 1988
141 25¢ June 11, 1988
143 1¢ July 5, 1989
144 "F" (29¢) January 22, 1991
145 29¢ May 24, 1991
146 4¢ April 6, 1991
146A 10¢ October 19, 1993
147 19¢ May 24, 1991
148 23¢ May 24, 1991
151 $1 September 1993
152 (32¢) December 13, 1994
153 32¢ May 9, 1995
154 1¢ May 9, 1995
155 20¢ May 9, 1995
156 23¢ May 9, 1995
157 33¢ October 8, 1999
158 34¢ February 27, 2001
159 37¢ August 2, 2002

fficial Envelopes Series

JO73 20¢ blue Great Seal
JO74 22¢ blue Great Seal, embossed
JO75 22¢ blue Great Seal
JO76 (25¢) "E" Great Seal
JO77 25¢ black, blue Great Seal, embossed
JO78 25¢ black, blue Great Seal
JO79 45¢ black, blue Great Seal (stars illegible)
JO80 65¢ black, blue Great Seal (stars illegible)
JO81 45¢ black, blue Great Seal (stars clear)
JO82 65¢ black, blue Great Seal (stars clear)
JO83 (29¢) "F" Great Seal
UO84 29¢ black, blue, Great Seal
UO88 32¢ Great Seal
UO89 33¢ Great Seal
UO90 34¢ Great Seal
UO91 37¢ Great Seal

Official Mail Postal Cards

UZ6 20¢ Great Seal

Statehood Series 1936-Present

782 3¢ Arkansas
858 3¢ 50th Anniversary of Statehood—Montana, North Dakota, South Dakota, Washington
896 3¢ Idaho
897 3¢ Wyoming
903 3¢ Vermont
904 3¢ Kentucky
927 3¢ Florida
938 3¢ Texas
941 3¢ Tennessee
942 3¢ Iowa
957 3¢ Wisconsin
997 3¢ California
1001 3¢ Colorado
1018 3¢ Ohio
1106 3¢ Minnesota
1124 4¢ Oregon
1191 4¢ New Mexico
1192 4¢ Arizona
1197 4¢ Louisiana
1232 5¢ West Virginia
1248 5¢ Nevada
1308 5¢ Indiana
1328 5¢ Nebraska
1339 6¢ Illinois
1375 6¢ Alabama
1391 6¢ Maine
1426 8¢ Missouri
1711 13¢ Colorado
2066 20¢ Alaska
2167 22¢ Arkansas
2246 22¢ Michigan
2336 22¢ Delaware
2337 22¢ Pennsylvania
2338 22¢ New Jersey
2339 22¢ Georgia
2340 22¢ Connecticut
2341 22¢ Massachusetts
2342 22¢ Maryland
2343 22¢ South Carolina
2344 22¢ New Hampshire
2345 22¢ Virginia
2346 22¢ New York
2347 22¢ North Carolina
2348 22¢ Rhode Island
2401 25¢ Montana
2403 25¢ North Dakota
2405 25¢ Washington
2416 25¢ South Dakota
2439 25¢ Idaho
2444 25¢ Wyoming
2533 29¢ Vermont
2561 29¢ District of Columbia Bicentennial
2636 29¢ Kentucky
2950 32¢ Florida
2968 32¢ Texas
3024 32¢ Utah
3070 32¢ Tennessee
3088 32¢ Iowa
3206 32¢ Wisconsin
3438 33¢ California
3773 37¢ Ohio

Olympic Games Series 1932-Present

716 2¢ Ski Jumper
718 3¢ Runner at Starting Mark
719 5¢ Myron's Discobolus
1146 4¢ Olympic Rings and Snowflake (1960)
1460 6¢ Bicycling and Olympic Rings
1461 8¢ Bobsledding and Olympic Rings
1462 15¢ Running and Olympic Rings
C85 11¢ Skiers and Olympic Rings
1695 13¢ Diver and Olympic Rings
1696 13¢ Skier and Olympic Rings
1697 13¢ Runner and Olympic Rings
1698 13¢ Skater and Olympic Rings
1790 10¢ Javelin Thrower
1791 15¢ Runner
1792 15¢ Swimmer
1793 15¢ Rowers
1794 15¢ Equestrian Contestant
C97 31¢ High Jumper
1795 15¢ Speed Skater
1796 15¢ Downhill Skier
1797 15¢ Ski Jumper
1798 15¢ Ice Hockey
2048 13¢ Discus Thrower
2049 13¢ High Jumper
2050 13¢ Archer
2051 13¢ Boxers
C101 28¢ Gymnast
C102 28¢ Hurdler
C103 28¢ Basketball Player
C104 28¢ Soccer Player
C105 40¢ Shotputter
C106 40¢ Gymnast
C107 40¢ Swimmer
C108 40¢ Weightlifter
C109 35¢ Fencer
C110 35¢ Bicyclist
C111 35¢ Volleyball Players
C112 35¢ Pole Vaulter
2067 20¢ Ice Dancing (1984)
2068 20¢ Downhill Skiing
2069 20¢ Cross-Country Skiing
2070 20¢ Ice Hockey
2082 20¢ Diving
2083 20¢ Long Jump
2084 20¢ Wrestling
2085 20¢ Kayak
2369 22¢ Skier and Olympic Rings
2380 25¢ Gymnast on Ring
2528 29¢ U.S. Flag, Olympic Rings
2539 $1 USPS Logo/ Olympic Rings
2553 29¢ Pole Vaulter
2554 29¢ Discus Thrower
2555 29¢ Women Sprinters
2556 29¢ Javelin Thrower
2557 29¢ Women Hurdlers
2611 29¢ Hockey (1992)
2612 29¢ Figure Skating
2613 29¢ Speed Skating
2614 29¢ Skiing
2615 29¢ Bobsledding
263729¢ Soccer
2638 29¢ Gymnastics
2639 29¢ Volleyball
2640 29¢ Boxing
2641 29¢ Swimming
2807 29¢ Slalom (1994)
2808 29¢ Luge
2809 29¢ Ice Dancing
2810 29¢ Cross-Country Skiing
2811 29¢ Ice Hockey
3863 37¢ 2004 Olympic Games Athens
UC52 22¢ Summer Olympic Games
UC57 30¢ Olympic Games
3996 39¢ Olympic Winter Games Torino

Holiday Celebration: Christmas Series 1966-Present

1321 5¢ Madonna and Child by Hans Memling
1336 5¢ Madonna and Child by Hans Memling
1363 6¢ Angel Gabriel from The Annunciation by Jan Van Eyck
1414 6¢ Nativity by Lorenzo Lotto
1444 8¢ Adoration of the Shepherds by Giorgione
1471 8¢ Angels from Mary, Queen of Heaven by the Master of the St. Lucy Legend
1507 8¢ Small Cowper Madonna by Raphael
1550 10¢ Angel from Pérussis Altarpiece
1579 (10¢) Madonna and Child by Domenico Ghirlandaio
1701 13¢ Nativity by John Singleton Copley
1729 13¢ Washington at Valley Forge by J.C. Leyendecker
1768 15¢ Madonna and Child with Cherubim by Andrea della Robbia
1799 15¢ Virgin and Child with Cherubim by Gerard David

Holiday Celebration: Christmas Series continued **1966-Present**

1842 15¢ Madonna and Child from Epiphany Window, Washington Cathedral
1939 20¢ Madonna and Child by Botticelli
2026 20¢ Madonna and Child by Tiepolo
2063 20¢ Niccolini-Cowper Madonna by Raphael
2107 20¢ Madonna and Child by Fra Filippo Lippi
2165 22¢ Genoa Madonna by Luca Della Robbia
2244 22¢ Madonna and Child by Perugino
2367 22¢ Madonna and Child by Moroni
2399 25¢ Madonna and Child by Botticelli
2427 25¢ Madonna and Child by Caracci
2514 25¢ Madonna and Child by Antonello
2578 29¢ Madonna and Child by Antoniazzo Romano
2710 29¢ Madonna and Child by Giovanni Bellini
2789 29¢ Madonna and Child by Giovanni Battista Cima
2871 29¢ Madonna and Child by Elisabetta Sira
3003 32¢ Madonna and Child by Giotto de Bondone
3107 32¢ Madonna and Child by Paolo de Matteis
3176 32¢ Madonna and Child by Sano di Pietro
3244 32¢ The Madonna and Child by Hans Memling
3355 33¢ Madonna and Child by Bartolomeo Vivarini
3536 34¢ Madonna and Child by Lorenzo Costa
3675 37¢ Madonna and Child by Gossaert
3820 37¢ Madonna and Child by Gossaert
3879 37¢ Madonna and Child by Lorenzo Monaco
— 39¢ Madonna and Child with Bird by I. Chacón (2006)

Holiday Celebration: Holiday Series 1962-Present

1205 4¢ Wreath and Candles
1240 5¢ National Christmas Tree and White House
1254 5¢ Holly
1255 5¢ Mistletoe
1256 5¢ Poinsettia
1257 5¢ Sprig of Conifer
1276 5¢ Angel with Trumpet (1840 Weather Vane)
1384 6¢ Winter Sunday in Norway, ME
1415 6¢ Tin and Cast-Iron Locomotive
1416 6¢ Toy Horse on Wheels
1417 6¢ Mechanical Tricycle
1418 6¢ Doll Carriage
1445 8¢ Partridge in a Pear Tree
1472 8¢ Santa Claus
1508 8¢ Christmas Tree in needlepoint
1551 10¢ *The Road—Winter* by Currier and Ives
1552 10¢ Dove Weather Vane atop Mount Vernon
1580 (10¢) Early Christmas Card by Louis Prang, 1878
1702 13¢ *Winter Pastime* by Nathaniel Currier
1730 13¢ Rural Mailbox
1769 15¢ Child on Hobby Horse
1800 15¢ Santa Claus, Christmas Tree Ornament
1843 15¢ Wreath and Toys
1940 20¢ Felt Bear on Sleigh
2025 13¢ Puppy and Kitten
2027 20¢ Children Sledding
2028 20¢ Children Building a Snowman
2029 20¢ Children Skating
2030 20¢ Children Trimming a Tree
2064 20¢ Santa Claus
2108 20¢ Santa Claus
2166 22¢ Poinsettia Plants
2245 22¢ Village Scene
2368 22¢ Christmas Ornaments
2400 25¢ One-Horse Open Sleigh and Village Scene
2428 25¢ Sleigh Full of Presents
2515 25¢ Christmas Tree
2579 29¢ Santa Claus in Chimney
2582 29¢ Santa Claus Checking List
2583 29¢ Santa Claus with Present Under Tree
2584 29¢ Santa Claus at Fireplace
2585 29¢ Santa Claus and Sleigh
2711 29¢ Horse and Rider
2712 29¢ Toy Train
2713 29¢ Toy Steamer
2714 29¢ Toy Ship
2715 29¢ Horse and Rider
2716 29¢ Toy Train
2717 29¢ Toy Steamer
2718 29¢ Toy Ship
2719 29¢ Toy Train (self-adhesive)
2791 29¢ Jack-in-the-Box
2792 29¢ Red-Nosed Reindeer
2793 29¢ Snowman
2794 29¢ Toy Soldier
2795 29¢ Toy Soldier (2794)
2796 29¢ Snowman (2793)
2797 29¢ Red-Nosed Reindeer (2792)
2798 29¢ Jack-in-the-Box (2791)
2799 29¢ Snowman
2800 29¢ Toy Soldier
2801 29¢ Jack-in-the-Box
2802 29¢ Red-Nosed Reindeer
2803 29¢ Snowman
2872 29¢ Stocking
2873 29¢ Santa Claus
2874 29¢ Cardinal in Snow
3004 32¢ Santa Claus Entering Chimney
3005 32¢ Child Holding Jumping Jack
3006 32¢ Child Holding Tree
3007 32¢ Santa Claus Working on Sled
3008 32¢ Santa Claus Working on Sled
3009 32¢ Child Holding Jumping Jack
3010 32¢ Santa Claus Entering Chimney
3011 32¢ Child Holding Tree
3012 32¢ Midnight Angel
3013 32¢ Children Sledding
3108 32¢ Family at Fireplace
3109 32¢ Decorating Tree
3110 32¢ Dreaming of Santa Claus
3111 32¢ Holiday Shopping
3113 32¢ Family at Fireplace
3114 32¢ Decorating Tree
3115 32¢ Dreaming of Santa Claus
3116 32¢ Holiday Shopping
3117 32¢ Skaters
3177 32¢ American Holly
3245 32¢ Evergreen Wreath
3246 32¢ Victorian Wreath
3247 32¢ Chili Pepper Wreath
3248 32¢ Tropical Wreath
3249 32¢ Evergreen Wreath
3250 32¢ Victorian Wreath
3251 32¢ Chili Pepper Wreath
3252 32¢ Tropical Wreath
3356 33¢ Red Deer
3357 33¢ Blue Deer
3358 33¢ Purple Deer
3359 33¢ Green Deer
3360 33¢ Red Deer
3361 33¢ Blue Deer
3362 33¢ Purple Deer
3363 33¢ Green Deer
3364 33¢ Red Deer
3365 33¢ Blue Deer
3366 33¢ Purple Deer
3367 33¢ Green Deer
3537 34¢ Santa wearing Tan Hood
3538 34¢ Santa wearing Blue Hat
3539 34¢ Santa wearing Red Hat
3540 34¢ Santa wearing Gold Hood
3676 37¢ Snowman w/red & green plaid scarf
3677 37¢ Snowman w/blue plaid scarf
3678 37¢ Snowman w/pipe
3679 37¢ Snowman w/top hat
3680 37¢ Snowman w/blue plaid scarf
3681 37¢ Snowman w/pipe
3682 37¢ Snowman w/top hat
3683 37¢ Snowman w/red & green plaid scarf
3684 37¢ Snowman w/red & green plaid scarf
3685 37¢ Snowman w/blue plaid scarf
3686 37¢ Snowman w/pipe
3687 37¢ Snowman w/top hat
3688 37¢ Snowman w/red & green plaid scarf
3689 37¢ Snowman w/blue plaid scarf
3690 37¢ Snowman w/pipe
3691 37¢ Snowman w/top hat
3821 37¢ Reindeer with Pan Pipes
3822 37¢ Santa Claus with Drum
3823 37¢ Santa Claus with Trumpet
3824 37¢ Reindeer with Horn
3825 37¢ Reindeer with Pan Pipes
3826 37¢ Santa Claus with Drum
3827 37¢ Santa Claus with Trumpet
3828 37¢ Reindeer with Horn
3883 37¢ Santa Ornament, purple
3884 37¢ Santa Ornament, green
3885 37¢ Santa Ornament, blue
3886 37¢ Santa Ornament, red
3949-3952 37¢ Holiday Cookies (4 designs)
— 39¢ Snowflakes (4 designs) (2006)

Hoilday Celebrations Series 1996-Present

3118 32¢ Hanukkah (reissued as #3352, 3547, 3672)
3175 32¢ Kwanzaa (reissued as #3368, 3548, 3673)
3203 32¢ Cinco de Mayo (reissued as #3309)
3532 34¢ Eid (reissued as #3674, and in 2006)
3546 34¢ We Give Thanks
3880 37¢ Hanukkah (reissued in 2006)
3881 37¢ Kwanzaa (reissued in 2006)

Weddings Series 2004-Present

3836 37¢ Garden Bouquet
3837 60¢ Garden Botanical
3998 39¢ Our Wedding
3999 63¢ Our Wedding

Standing Order Program

Get your collection tailored to your own specific taste. Mix and match Stamps, First Day Covers, Stationery, Uncut Press Sheets all in whatever quantities you'd like. Deposit varies based on selections and quantities orderd.

Item #26122

American Commemorative Collection

An easy and uniform way to collect and learn about issues that commemorate people, anniversaries, places and events. You'll find detailed stories on the issue and the subject and included are protective acetate mounts for your stamps. Just $3.25* each, depending on the value of the stamps. An advance deposit of $50 is required.

Item #26123

First Day of Issue Ceremony Programs

Receive detailed information about each first day of issue ceremony held for all new stamps and stationery issuances. Just $4.95* each. An advance deposit of $65 is required. *Unless the stamp value exceeds $4.95 then the price is determined by the actual value of the stamps.

Item #26124

American Commemorative Panels

Obtain photo or steel engravings, mint condition stamps in acetate mounts and subject related text presented on a beautifully designed page. Only $6.00* each.

Item #26125. An advance deposit of $75 is required.

American Commemorative Cancellations

Get official first day of issue cancellations and stamp(s) that have been affixed to colorful sheets featuring technical and historical information about the stamps. Just $2.50* each, depending on the value of the stamps.

Item #25126. An advance deposit of $50 is required.

For information on these items and other philatelic products call **1 800 STAMP-24** **Prices subject to change without notice.*

Accessories
The tools used by stamp collectors, such as tongs, hinges, etc.

Aerogrammes
Air letters designed to be letters and envelopes all in one. They are specially stamped and ready for folding.

Aerophilately
Stamp collecting that focuses on airmail stamps or postage.

Album
A book designed to hold stamps and covers.

Approvals
Stamps sent by a dealer to a collector for examination. Approvals must either be bought or returned to the dealer within a specified time.

Block
A group of unseparated stamps, at least two stamps high and two stamps wide.

Bogus
A completely fictitious, worthless "stamp," created only for sale to collectors. Bogus stamps include labels for nonexistent values added to regularly issued sets, issues for nations without postal systems, etc.

Booklet Pane
A small sheet of stamps specially cut to be sold in booklets.

Bourse
A marketplace, such as a stamp exhibition, where stamps are bought, sold, or exchanged.

Cachet (ka-shay')
A stamp related design on an envelope.

Cancellation
A mark placed on a stamp by a postal authority to show that the stamp has been used.

Centering
The position of the design on a postage stamp. On perfectly centered stamps the design is exactly in the middle.

Cinderella
Any stamp-like label without an official postal value.

Classic
An early stamp issue.

Coils
Stamps issued in rolls (one stamp wide) for use in dispensers or vending machines.

Coil Stamps
Stamps that are produced in a long vertical or horizontal strip

Commemoratives
Stamps that honor anniversaries, important people, special events, or aspects of national culture.

Compound Perforations
Different gauge perforations on different sides (normally adjacent) of a single stamp.

Condition
Condition is the most important characteristic in determining the value of a stamp. It refers to the state of a stamp regarding such details as centering, color and gum.

Cover
An envelope that has been sent through the mail.

Cracked Plate
A term used to describe stamps which show evidence that the plate from which they were printed was cracked.

Definitives
Regular issues of postage stamps, usually sold over long periods of time. They tend to be fairly small and printed in large quantities often more than once.

Denomination
The postage value appearing on a stamp.

Die Cut
Scoring of self-adhesive stamps that allows a stamp to be separated from the liner.

Directory Markings
Postal markings that indicate a failed delivery attempt, stating reasons such as "No Such Number" or "Address Unknown."

Double Transfer
The condition on a printing plate that shows evidence of a duplication of all or part of the design.

Duplicates
Extra copies of stamps that can be sold or traded. Duplicates should be examined carefully for color and perforation variations.

Entire
An intact piece of postal stationery, in contrast to a cut-out of the printed design.

Error
A stamp with something incorrect in its design or manufacture.

Face Value
The monetary value, or denomination, of a stamp.

Fake
A genuine stamp that has been altered in some way to make it more attractive to collectors. It may be repaired, reperfed, or regummed to resemble a more valuable variety.

First Day Cover (FDC)
An envelope or card bearing a stamp cancelled to show its issuance date and place.

First Day Ceremony Program
A program given to those who attend first day of issue stamp ceremonies. It contains the actual stamp affixed and postmarked, a list of participants and information on the stamp subject.

Foreign Entry
When original transfers are erased incompletely from a plate, they can appear with new transfers of a different design which are subsequently entered on the plate.

Franks
Written, hand-stamped, or imprinted markings on the face of a cover indicating that it is carried free of postage. Franking is usually limited to official government correspondence.

Freak
An abnormal variety of a stamp occurring because of paper fold, over-inking, perforation shift, etc., as opposed to a continually appearing variety or an error.

Grill
A pattern of small, square pyramids in parallel rows impressed or embossed on the stamp to break paper fibers, allowing cancellation ink to soak in and preventing washing and reuse.

Gum
The coating of glue on the back of a stamp.

Hinges
Small strips of gummed material used by some collectors to affix stamps to album pages.

Hologram
An image that appears to be three-dimensional when viewed from an angle. Holograms have appeared on some modern stamps and stationery.

Imperforate
Indicates stamps without perforations.

Laid Paper
When held to the light, the paper shows alternate light and dark crossed lines.

Line Pairs (LP)
Most coil stamp rolls prior to 1981 feature a line of ink (known as a "joint line") printed between two stamps at various intervals, caused by the joining of two or more curved plates around the printing cylinder.

Liner
The backing paper for self-adhesive stamps.

Loupe
A magnifying glass used to examine details of stamps more closely.

On Paper
Stamps "on paper" are those that still have portions of the original envelope or wrapper attached.

Overprint
Additional printing on a stamp that was not part of the original design.

Packet
A presorted group of different stamps, a common and economical way to begin a stamp collection.

ane
. full "sheet" of stamps as sold y a Post Office.

ar Avion
rench for mail transported by air."

ictorials
tamps with a picture of some ort, other than portraits or static esigns such as coats of arms.

erforations
ines of small holes or cuts etween stamps that make them asy to separate.

erforation Gauge
. tool used to measure perfora-ons along the edges of stamps r the distance between peaks or dges.

hilately
he collection and study of ostage stamps and other postal naterials.

late Block (PB) or Plate Number Block)
. block of stamps with the mar-in attached that bears the plate umber used in printing that heet.

late Number Coils (PNC)
or most coil stamp rolls begin-ing with #1891, a small plate umber appears at varying inter-als in the roll in the design of he stamp.

ostal Stationery
nvelopes, aerogrammes, tamped postal cards, and letter heets with printed or embossed tamp designs.

ostal Cards
ee "stamped postal cards."

ostcards
ommercially-produced mail-ble cards without imprinted ostage.

ostmark
. mark put on envelopes or ther mailing pieces showing the ate and location of mailing.

recancels
tamps cancelled by a proper uthority prior to their use on nail.

resort Stamp
. discounted stamp used by usiness mailers who presort heir mail.

Prestige Booklet
A booklet commemorating a special topic and containing stamps, narrative, and images.

Reissue
An official reprinting of a stamp that was no longer being printed.

Reprint
A stamp printed from the original plate after the issue is no longer valid for postage. Official reprints are sometimes made for presentation purposes, official collections, etc., and are often distinguished in some way from the "real" ones.

Revenue Stamps
Stamps issued as proof of payment of certain taxes but not valid for postage.

Rouletting
The piercing of the paper between stamps to facilitate their separation, often giving the appearance of a series of dashes.

Scrambled Indicia®
A patented process that conceals encoded text or graphics within the visible design. These hidden images can only be viewed through a special lens, the Stamp Decoder™, available from the U.S. Postal Service.

Se-tenant
An attached pair, strip or block of stamps that differ in design, value or surcharge.

Self-Adhesive Stamp
A stamp with pressure sensitive adhesive.

Selvage
The paper around panes of stamps, sometimes called the margin.

Semipostal Stamp
A First-Class Mail stamp priced to include an additional charge earmarked for a specific purpose, e.g., breast cancer research.

Series
A number of individual stamps or sets of stamps having a common purpose or theme, issued over an extended period of time (generally a year or more), including all variations of design and/or denomination.

Set
A group of stamps with a common design or theme issued at one time for a common purpose or over a limited perid of time (generally less than a year).

Souvenir Sheet
A small sheet of stamps with a commemorative inscription.

Special Issues
Stamps with a commemorative appearance that supplement definitives and meet specific needs. These include Christmas, Love, Holiday Celebrations, airmail, Express Mail, and Priority Mail stamps.

Speculative
A stamp or issue released primarily for sale to collectors, rather than to meet any legitimate postal need.

Stamp Decoder™
A device with a special lens that reveals hidden images on stamps. It is available from the U.S. Postal Service.

Stamped Postal Card
The current term for a mailable card with postage imprinted on it.

Stamped Envelope
A mailable envelope with postage embossed or imprinted on it.

Star Route
A mail route serviced by an outside contractor rather than a postal employee.

Strip
Three or more unseparated stamps in a row.

Surcharge
An overprint that changes the denomination of a stamp.

Sweatbox
A closed box with a grill over which stuck-together unused stamps are placed. A wet, sponge-like material under the grill creates humidity so the stamps can be separated without removing the gum.

Tagging
The marking of stamps with a phosphor or similar coating (which may be in lines, bars, letters, overall design area or entire stamp surface), done by many countries for use with automatic mail-handling equipment. When a stamp is issued both with and without this marking, catalogs will often note varieties as "tagged" or "untagged."

Tied On
Describes a stamp whose postmark touches the envelope.

Tongs
A tweezer-like tool with rounded or flattened tips used to handle stamps.

Topicals
A group of stamps with the same theme—space travel, for example.

Unhinged
A stamp without hinge marks.

Unused
The condition of a stamp that has no cancellation or other sign of use.

Used
The condition of a stamp that has been canceled.

Variety
A stamp that varies in some way from its standard or original form. Varieties can include missing colors or perforations, constant plate flaws, changes in ink or paper, differences in printing method or in format.

Watermark
A design sometimes pressed into stamp paper during its manufacture.

Water-Activated Gum
Water-soluble adhesives such as sugar-based starches on the back of an unused stamp.

Wove Paper
A uniform paper which, when held to the light, shows no light or dark figures.

Index

The numbers listed next to the stamp description are the Scott numbers and the numbers in parentheses are numbers of the pages on which the stamps are listed.

Postmasters General of the United States

Appointed by the Continental Congress

1775 Benjamin Franklin, PA
1776 Richard Bache, PA
1782 Ebenezer Hazard, NY

Appointed by the President with the advice and consent of the Senate

1789 Samuel Osgood, MA
1791 Timothy Pickering, PA
1795 Joseph Habersham, GA
1801 Gideon Granger, CT
1814 Return J. Meigs, Jr., OH
1823 John McLean, OH
1829 William T. Barry, KY
1835 Amos Kendall, KY
1840 John M. Niles, CT
1841 Francis Granger, NY
1841 Charles A. Wickliffe, KY
1845 Cave Johnson, TN
1849 Jacob Collamer, VT
1850 Nathan K. Hall, NY
1852 Samuel D. Hubbard, CT
1853 James Campbell, PA
1857 Aaron V. Brown, TN
1859 Joseph Holt, KY
1861 Horatio King, ME
1861 Montgomery Blair, DC
1864 William Dennison, OH
1866 Alexander W. Randall, WI
1869 John A.J. Creswell, MD
1874 James W. Marshall, NJ
1874 Marshall Jewell, CT
1876 James N. Tyner, IN
1877 David McK. Key, TN
1880 Horace Maynard, TN
1881 Thomas L. James, NY
1882 Timothy O. Howe, WI
1883 Walter Q. Gresham, IN
1884 Frank Hatton, IA
1885 William F. Vilas, WI
1888 Don M. Dickinson, MI
1889 John Wanamaker, PA
1893 Wilson S. Bissell, NY
1895 William L. Wilson, WV
1897 James A. Gary, MD
1898 Charles Emory Smith, PA
1902 Henry C. Payne, WI
1904 Robert J. Wynne, PA
1905 George B. Cortelyou, NY
1907 George von L. Meyer, MA
1909 Frank H. Hitchcock, MA
1913 Albert S. Burleson, TX
1921 Will H. Hays, IN
1922 Hubert Work, CO
1923 Harry S. New, IN
1929 Walter F. Brown, OH
1933 James A. Farley, NY
1940 Frank C. Walker, PA
1945 Robert E. Hannegan, MO
1947 Jesse M. Donaldson, IL
1953 Arthur E. Summerfield
1961 J. Edward Day, CA
1963 John A. Gronouski, W
1965 Lawrence F. O'Brien, M
1968 W. Marvin Watson, TX
1969 Winton M. Blount, AL

Selected by the Presidentially appointed U.S. Postal Service Board of Governors

1971 Elmer T. Klassen, MA
1975 Benjamin Franklin Bail MD
1978 William F. Bolger, CT
1985 Paul N. Carlin, WY
1986 Albert V. Casey, MA
1986 Preston R. Tisch, NY
1988 Anthony M. Frank, CA
1992 Marvin Runyon, TN
1998 William J. Henderson, N
2001 John E. Potter, NY

Acknowledgments

This stamp collecting catalog was produced by Government Relations and Public Policy, Stamp Services, United States Postal Service.

UNITED STATES POSTAL SERVICE

John E. Potter
Postmaster General and Chief Executive Officer

Thomas G. Day
Senior Vice President, Government Relations

David E. Failor
Executive Director, Stamp Services

Terrence W. McCaffrey
Manager, Stamp Development

Cindy Tackett
Manager, Stamp Exhibitions and Products

Sonja D. Edison
Project Manager and Editor

Sharon E. Thomas
Project Assistant

Robert E. Reyes
Project Assistant

HARPERCOLLINS PUBLISHERS

Knox Huston
Assistant Editor, Collins

Lucy Albanese
Design Director, General Books Group

Helen Song
Senior Production Editor, General Books Group

Susan Kosko
Director of Production, General Books Group

DESIGN SERVICES

Design, Layout and Production
Roberta Wojtkowski Design
10992 Thrush Ridge Road
Reston, VA 20191

Cover Design
Night & Day Design
41 River Terrace #2104
New York, NY 10282

RESEARCH AND WRITING

PhotoAssist, Inc.
Regina Swygert-Smith
7735 Old Georgetown Rd
Bethesda, MD 20814

SCANNING AND DIGITAL PREPRESS SERVICES

Dodge Color, Inc.
11941-L Bournefield Drive
Silver Spring, MD 20904

PRINTING AND BINDING

C.J. Krehbiel Company
3962 Virginia Ave
Cincinnati, OH 45227